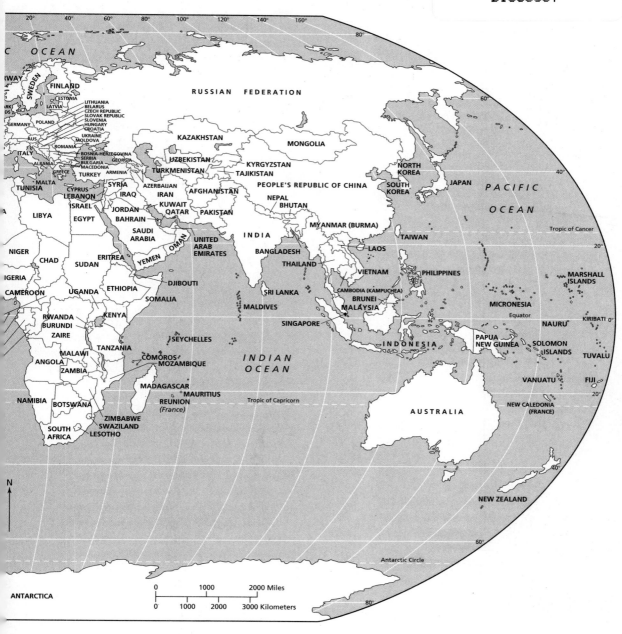

C OCEAN

NORWAY
SWEDEN
FINLAND
ESTONIA
LATVIA
LITHUANIA
BELARUS
GERMANY POLAND
CZECH REPUBLIC
SLOVAK REPUBLIC
SLOVENIA
HUNGARY
CROATIA
AUS.
ITALY
ROMANIA
MOLDOVA
UKRAINE
BOSNIA-HERZEGOVINA
SERBIA
ALBANIA
GREECE
MALTA
BULGARIA
MACEDONIA
TURKEY
GEORGIA
ARMENIA
TUNISIA
CYPRUS
LEBANON
ISRAEL
SYRIA
AZERBAIJAN
IRAQ
IRAN
LIBYA
EGYPT
JORDAN
BAHRAIN
KUWAIT
QATAR
NIGER
CHAD
SAUDI
ARABIA
OMAN
UNITED
ARAB
EMIRATES
NIGERIA
SUDAN
ERITREA
YEMEN
CAMEROON
UGANDA
ETHIOPIA
DJIBOUTI
SOMALIA
RWANDA
BURUNDI
ZAIRE
KENYA
TANZANIA
ANGOLA
MALAWI
ZAMBIA
NAMIBIA
BOTSWANA
ZIMBABWE
SWAZILAND
SOUTH
AFRICA
LESOTHO

RUSSIAN FEDERATION

KAZAKHSTAN
UZBEKISTAN
TURKMENISTAN
KYRGYZSTAN
TAJIKISTAN
AFGHANISTAN
PAKISTAN
MONGOLIA
PEOPLE'S REPUBLIC OF CHINA
NEPAL
BHUTAN
INDIA
BANGLADESH
MYANMAR (BURMA)
THAILAND
SRI LANKA
MALDIVES

NORTH
KOREA
SOUTH
KOREA
JAPAN

PACIFIC
OCEAN

TAIWAN
LAOS
VIETNAM
PHILIPPINES
CAMBODIA (KAMPUCHEA)
BRUNEI
MALAYSIA
SINGAPORE
MICRONESIA

MARSHALL
ISLANDS

NAURU
KIRIBATI

Equator

INDONESIA

PAPUA
NEW GUINEA
SOLOMON
ISLANDS
TUVALU

VANUATU
FIJI

NEW CALEDONIA
(FRANCE)

SEYCHELLES

COMOROS
MOZAMBIQUE
MADAGASCAR
MAURITIUS
REUNION
(France)

INDIAN
OCEAN

Tropic of Capricorn

AUSTRALIA

NEW ZEALAND

Tropic of Cancer

N

ANTARCTICA

Antarctic Circle

0   1000   2000 Miles
0 1000 2000 3000 Kilometers

International Politics

THEORY AND PRACTICE

··

International Politics

THEORY AND PRACTICE

Howard H. Lentner
*Baruch College and the
Graduate School
The City University of New York*

WEST PUBLISHING COMPANY
Minneapolis/St. Paul   New York   Los Angeles   San Francisco

- **PRODUCTION CREDITS**

Copyediting:	Marilynn Taylor
Index:	Catalyst Communication Arts
Composition:	Parkwood Composition Services, Inc.
Interior Design:	Adapted from a design by Roslyn M. Stendahl, Dapper Design.
Cover Image:	© Steven Hunt/The Image Bank

Maps and text as specified from *Strategic Atlas: A Comparative Geopolitics of the World's Powers* 3rd Edition by Gerard Chaliand and Jean-Pierre Rageau. Copyright © 1993 by Gerard Chaliand and Jean-Pierre Rageau. Reprinted by permission of HarperCollins Publishers, Inc.

- **WEST'S COMMITMENT TO THE ENVIRONMENT**

In 1906, West Publishing Company began recycling materials left over from the production of books. This began a tradition of efficient and responsible use of resources. Today, 100% of our legal bound volumes are printed on acid-free, recycled paper consisting of 50% new fibers. West recycles nearly 27,700,000 pounds of scrap paper annually—the equivalent of 229,300 trees. Since the 1960s, West has devised ways to capture and recycle waste inks, solvents, oils, and vapors created in the printing process. We also recycle plastics of all kinds, wood, glass, corrugated cardboard, and batteries, and have eliminated the use of polystyrene book packaging. We at West are proud of the longevity and the scope of our commitment to the environment.

West pocket parts and advance sheets are printed on recyclable paper and can be collected and recycled with newspapers. Staples do not have to be removed. Bound volumes can be recycled after removing the covers.

 TEXT IS PRINTED ON 10% POST CONSUMER RECYCLED PAPER

British Library Cataloguing-in-Publication Data

A catalogue record for this book is available from the British Library.

Library of Congress Cataloging-in-Publication Data

Lentner, Howard H.
    International politics: theory and practice/Howard H. Lentner
        p. cm.
    Includes index.
    ISBN 0-314-20203-X (alk. paper)
        1. International relations.   I. Title.
JX1395.L44   1997
    327—dc20   96-9253
                                                                      CIP

To Samantha and Christopher

Brief Contents

Contents

PART 5 *Fundamental Processes in International Politics* 241

Preface

As the author of an introductory textbook in international politics, I faced two challenges. First, the end of the Cold War introduced more than the usual ferment in academic debates over theories and interpretations of international politics. This circumstance presented the challenge to consider and think through all of the ideas and approaches to the subject that I learned and had been teaching for many years. Such a challenge made writing a particularly engaging but also vexing task. I hope that readers will find the results helpful to their own consideration of the issues and problems involved in analyzing international politics.

The two main schools of thought which contribute to academic discourse in this field, realism and liberalism, form the primary skeleton upon which I have constructed the body of analysis, but at appropriate places I have also brought into the discussion more radical approaches and critical theories. I have presented the views of these theoretical convictions on the main problems and issues of international politics, posing the differences between them. Furthermore, I have indicated my own positions and offered reasons for my interpretations.

A textbook also affords the opportunity to devise analyses to fill gaps in the literature. Thus, the reader familiar with the field will find in this book certain features that depart from conventional analysis. First, a comprehensive problematic—the subject matter, fundamental questions, and methods of study—organizes the argument of the book and provides a tool for locating the contemporary discipline of international politics in the context of its origins and evolution as well as its relation to other disciplines. Furthermore, the problematic, which is centered on the fundamental political questions of power and justice, offers criteria for assessing continuity and change in international politics. International political economy suffuses the entire text even as a separate chapter remains devoted to systematic treatment of IPE, including Marxist analysis and dependency theory. A chapter that gives extended consideration to the many values in contention in international politics provides an unusual feature. Moreover, this is the only text that includes a chapter on the state, which develops a thorough comparative analysis of states and gives insight into contemporary world problems. The concept of state

formation provides a means of treating the relations of states and markets, competition among states, and the interventions of states and international organizations, all within a unified framework. In recent years, attention in the field has tended to shift emphasis more and more to the international system to the neglect of foreign policy and state interactions, but this book devotes three chapters to these topics, at the same time relating them to the context of the international system. New problems such as peacekeeping, environmental protection, and human rights are incorporated in an early chapter on international system management and appear at various points in the text.

The second challenge that I faced had to do with writing style and the level of presentation. To write comprehensively and thoughtfully was not enough. I also wanted to write in a way that was interesting and comprehensible to college sophomores who would be taking the course for which this book is intended. Students will find that the book is written at a demanding level that helps to build vocabulary with both general and specialized terms. I also intend that the material will engage students, prompting thinking about their own values and preferences as well as about analytical matters. To assist readers in mastering the theoretical concepts, I have studded the book with illustrations and short case studies drawn from many countries and regions throughout the world. Each example illustrates a conceptual or theoretical point. In addition, I have provided a number of tools to assist in mastering the material. Among the most important, and one that I hope students will refer to regularly, is an extensive historical glossary. Important terms are emphasized in the text and listed at the end of each chapter. Case studies have sub-headings, and briefer anecdotal examples are noted with references in small capital letters in the text itself. Study questions appear at the end of each chapter. Answers to many of these questions may be found in the chapter, but many are designed to be thought provoking, requiring independent thinking to respond. Maps germane to many of the cases appear throughout. I have summarized main points from the text, and these appear in boxes. Short introductions signal what is to come in each chapter. I appeal to students to use all of these devices as well as the detailed table of contents and the index. International politics is a complicated field with a variety of interesting ideas and theoretical approaches for analysis and understanding, so learning requires dedication and hard work. The tools are there to assist, so, by all means, take advantage of them.

In bringing this work to fruition, a number of people have generously given me help. Patrice M. Donohue read many chapters and offered useful criticisms and encouragement. Weizhi Xie read several chapters with a professional's eye and helped me to see matters from the point of view of a country other than the United States. W. Ofuatey-Kodjoe read the introductory chapter, giving me the benefit of his teaching experience by criticizing in a way that saved me from some errors. Lida Ahmady, Sonja Chapman, and Alan M. Davis each read one chapter, providing me with the valuable perspective that can only come from undergraduates. Effie MacLachlan served as my research assistant in helping to prepare the historical glossary, but she also read several chapters with a critical and helpful eye. Richard Oliver Collin and many anonymous reviewers read a prospectus, preliminary chapter drafts, or revised drafts and made many helpful suggestions that have led to improvements in the organization, presentation, and writing.

Thanks to Joyce Gelb for information regarding prices in Japan appearing in Chapter 8.

I am very grateful for the assistance of several competent production people at West Publishing. Holly Henjum, the production editor, has overseen the process with efficiency and has, at the same time, remained a friendly correspondent and interlocutor on the telephone. Marilynn Taylor did the copyediting, improving my prose and the clarity of presentation. Linda Poirier, assistant to the editor, handled a variety of tasks in a seamless way. Ellen Stanton, promotion editor, has the responsibility of bringing the book to the attention of potential readers, something that she does effectively.

My editor, Clark Baxter, has proven to be not just invaluable but essential to the creation of this book. Some years ago, he invited me to submit a proposal and he has cajoled, criticized, suggested, bolstered, and encouraged the enterprise ever since. At a time when I held the most serious doubts about my ability to meet the challenges noted above, Clark dealt with me in a serious and mature manner that enabled me to confront the difficulties and address the problems. This book would not exist had it not been for his perseverance and patience, his support and encouragement. My gratitude is profound.

International Politics

THEORY AND PRACTICE

· ·

PART *1*

The Study of International Politics: Discipline, Values, Approaches

CHAPTER 1

The Discipline of International Politics

At first glance, international politics may seem bewildering. Not only does it entail wars in places like Bosnia and Chechnya, but it also includes starvation in Africa and trade and loans between Mexico and the United States. Human rights in China, peace negotiations in the Middle East, and friction over trade between Japan and the United States are stories in the news. In short, activities around the world may appear as a swamp teeming with foreign events and dark swirling waters that contain strong pressures and compulsions.

To find dry land on which to stand—that is, to make sense of the jumble of activities that cross international borders every day and the deeper forces that affect our lives over the longer term—scholars have developed systematic and orderly ways of understanding the many phenomena comprising international politics. This chapter sets forth, in broad outline, how academic analysts have approached the subject, and it gives a statement of the problematic—the subject matter, the fundamental questions, and the methods of study—that guide the analysis in the remainder of the book.

Introduction

The world is vast, fascinating, horrible, dangerous, and complicated. Over 5 billion people live in some 185 countries. An abundance of cultures and languages contributes to the treasure of human existence. But such horrors as mass starvation, wanton slaughter, and forced migration also form a part of our complex world. Dangers arise from violence and war as well as from lesser causes of injury such as betrayal and cheating.

Facing this complexity, the student of international politics carves out a portion for examination: those activities that cross international borders or that have implications for people living in other countries. These include instantaneous transactions such as television transmissions and money transfers. Not only the actions of governments but also those of corporations and other private associations contribute. In addition, many intergovernmental organizations, such as the United Nations and the Arab League, are vehicles for interational cooperation. War and military intervention and clandestine subversion comprise important international activities.

Constant **change** generated by economic growth, war, political ideas, leadership, and technology adds to this complexity. Technologies like the computer are applied within a decade after their invention to such diverse activities as writing term papers and preparing personal income tax returns, conducting stock transactions between Paris and Tokyo, and fighting wars with weapons based in space. Although the modern epoch is one in which change occurs with lightning-like rapidity, change has been a constant of human history. Deforestation, an issue of increasing contemporary interest, has occurred throughout the ages as human settlements have spread across the globe. The human population has multiplied over the centuries, but it is now growing faster than ever. Even the modern state that we take for granted can be dated only from 1648, some 350 years ago.

In the context of complexity and change, humans struggle for wealth and power. Individual workers, labor unions, firms, and countries compete for wealth in the form of jobs, sales, and investments. On a global scale, negotiated agreements have led to increased international trade and its orderly management. Meanwhile, Europeans work toward the structuring and improvement of a larger cooperative community that is to include political as well as economic dimensions. Simultaneously in North America, Canada and the United States, building on their 1988 Trade Agreement, joined with Mexico in a broader North American Free Trade Agreement that took effect at the beginning of 1995.

As one looks at particular countries, including very wealthy ones like the United States and Germany, inequalities of economic condition stare the viewer in the face. In poorer countries, like Guatemala and India, the even greater disparities of wealth that abound can be observed firsthand and are reflected in statistical evidence compiled by such institutions as the World Bank. Economic inequality is not a condition limited to particular societies; it is a characteristic of the world as a whole. It is especially apparent when one contrasts a rich area such as Western Europe with a poor area such as sub-Saharan Africa.

In certain places in the world, grinding poverty is only one evil among many. The Iranian government, for example, suppresses its citizens who profess the Baha'i religion. From 1991 to 1994, a government of thugs in Haiti brutalized the population to the degree that thousands of people risked death as they tried to escape aboard small and overcrowded boats headed for the United States. Certain regimes—Saddam Hussein's of Iraq provides a notorious example—maintain themselves in power by arresting and killing opponents, not by gaining the uncoerced consent of their country's people. In other places, political leaders are unable to resolve their conflicts, and political order deteriorates into civil war, as happened in the early 1990s in Yugoslavia.

Great transformations occur. Between World War I and World War II, Germany passed from a liberal democracy to a dictatorship based upon the principle that the will of one man should rule. After World War II, the country was divided into two states, one embodying a democratic polity and a market economy, the other organized according to the authoritarian political principle of one-party rule directing a centrally planned economy. More recently, with the collapse of Communism in what had been East Germany, the country has been united on the basis of liberal principles.

Understanding the many dimensions and the vast complexity of our world seems to call for encyclopedic knowledge. Geography, politics, philosophy, history, economics, sociology, geography, strategy, military science, and psychology are only the most obvious disciplines that might contribute insights into the multifarious phenomena referred to in the examples above.

Great numbers of issues seem germane to international affairs, including the diffusion of manufacturing processes, capital investments, transfers of technology, trade in illegal drugs, environmental deterioration, protection of human rights, and so on. These are but recent additions to traditional concerns about war and peace, diplomacy and trade, the power of nation states, patterns of conflict and cooperation such as balances of power and alliances, as well as foreign policy decision making and the ensuing relations of countries with one another.

As an academic field, international politics is a synthetic discipline, one that draws together contributions from many other fields of study.[1] Because of disagreements about what should be included and excluded, it has been called "the dividing discipline."[2] Despite a rich theoretical tradition, the ideas and emphases of the discipline have been greatly affected by events in the world and by intellectual currents. For example, with the end of the Cold War and the erosion of many of the assumptions underpinning it, there is an unusual ferment and openness to new ideas. Not only have the conceptions of statesmen and scholars been questioned, but some scholars have turned to such sources of analysis as literary deconstruction, the search for meaning in words, and away from traditional kinds of analysis that seek understanding in people and events. When viewed in its aggregate, the discipline appears to be confused and to lack a solid core of theoretical and practical interest.

The fascination of events tends to drive the interested observer in two opposite directions. On the one hand, she hankers to know more, to add more facts and a greater diversity of experience to her knowledge. On the other hand, she yearns to organize those facts in an understandable, theoretical form. Although there is no best solution to this dilemma, some alternatives are quite clear.

One option is to follow the path of adding information and remaining both eclectic and open to pursuing whatever is fascinating. A flood in Bangladesh, a famine in Somalia, an agreement to preserve a Stone-Age Indian tribe in Brazil and Venezuela, a Middle East peace conference, illegal migration into the United States, unification of Germany, loss of a rain forest, comments by a Japanese prime minister concerning the absence of a work ethic among American workers, ending apartheid and making a transition to democracy in South Africa, the breakup of the Soviet Union, and the building of a new luxury hotel on a Caribbean island are stories fed into the information mill. Anyone who watches the news on television or reads a daily newspaper or a weekly news magazine can observe the endless flow of information that is available about international affairs. Unless she wants to be nothing more than a dilettante in this field, however, she will want to formulate some kind of a mental screening device to rank the relative importance of events and facts and to draw out some meaning from them.

As people develop such devices, some are drawn very far in the direction of simplification. Some believe that eternal truths are available to understand today's world, while others think that our world has changed so drastically that we need to invent altogether new ways of understanding.

In the midst of disputes over information and theory, what is called for is some device for weighing and assessing alternative interpretations, for gaining understanding without oversimplification, and for finding a core to the field of knowledge we are pursuing. Several years ago, K. J. Holsti, a Canadian political scientist, addressed this problem for teachers of international politics and presented them with the idea of a **problematic**—the subject area, a basic question, and methods of study.[3]

This book is going to employ a similar device, a problematic, as a guide through a variety of challenging ideas that help us to explain international politics. A problematic aims to develop analytical tools that students can employ not just immediately but also many years in the future. Such tools can be applied in examining contemporary world events as well as those that we cannot now imagine. Furthermore, the analytical tools can be used to assess concepts and theories that may be offered to explain the causes and development of those events.

The Problematic of International Politics

Politics concerns **power** and **justice.** Power is the capacity to preserve one's autonomy, maintain the strength of one's position in relation to others, and exercise influence over others. Justice means that which is proper, morally right, or deserved.

Through politics, people aspire to achieve their values. They want many different things: wealth, power, prestige, respect, serenity, leisure, transcendent meaning, knowledge, salvation, and so on. Sometimes, they achieve their ends simply by dominating others, exercising power and imposing their own values on other people. At other times, they find a way of either compromising or encompassing the aspirations of others. They may be able to achieve justice, which in its political nature implies an agreed set of values that embody a common or public good. However, institutionalizing and enforcing conceptions of justice requires linking them with power.

Although certain values—solitude, insight, and creative accomplishment are examples—can be acquired by individuals acting alone, most aspirations are fulfilled through cooperation with others in groups. Certainly, some goals can be reached by the efforts of groups that form on the basis of coercion. For example, the pyramids of ancient Egypt were built by slave labor. However, even groups employing such systems of domination are ruled by an elite that itself is organized on some, however limited, conception of justice that allows it to forge and achieve goals through cooperation. While one may regret the brutal exploitation of Egyptian slaves, she simultaneously might admire the creative imagination that designed the pyramids and the vast engineering and organizational skills involved in their construction. Further, she might respect the governing and managerial abilities of the elites that arranged for these monuments and brought the enterprise to completion. Whether she takes such a balanced view or emphasizes, for example, her outrage at the treatment of the workers depends to a large extent on her own values and particular circumstances. It is not always easy to separate political analysis from the values and power position of the analyst. Thus, it is important in doing political analysis to maintain an acute consciousness about one's own political situation, for it often shapes the questions that one asks and sometimes affects the answers that one finds.

Nevertheless, all political analysis, however wide-ranging or sophisticated, focuses on the fundamental elements of power and justice. Political analysis seeks to understand which groups seek what values from whom. It also tries to fathom the means by which a struggle of groups is conducted, and it endeavors to determine the rightness and legitimacy of groups that contend over issues and the propriety or justice of the ends that are sought and the means that are used. Because political analysts are themselves political beings located somewhere in a power matrix and possess their own values, analysis may involve not simply learning to satisfy curiosity and to gain control over nature, as chemistry is applied to medicine to treat diseases. It may also involve a quest for power and the use of arguments surrounding justice as instruments of battle.

Politics, or group conflict over values, can occur at many different levels and in varied arenas. In communities, developers sponsoring economic growth commonly are challenged by preservationists who defend traditional land uses and by environmentalists who value protection of natural resources and such public goods as drainage and clean air. Within countries, competing political parties contend to gain control of government as the means to put into effect their respective programs. Groups fight over all manner of things ranging from taxes and monetary policy to transfer payments from one jurisdiction to another, as in deciding where to locate an industrial plant or military base. Groups struggle over giving priority to one function over another, for example, supporting a space program as opposed to medical research. And groups contend over transfers from one group to another, such as a tax deduction for interest payments that acts as a transfer from savers to debtors.

International politics shares some features with all other politics, for it is basically about conflict over values and may be analyzed by asking the same questions: Who is contending? What are their goals? What means do they have? What is the moral and legal standing of the ends and means? On the other hand, international politics possesses certain characteristics that distinguish it from local and national politics. Primarily, activities either involve sovereign states directly or they cross boundaries in such a way as to affect the relations or relative standing of those states in relationship to one another. Secondly, the principle by which the relations of states are ordered is that of **anarchy,** the absence of any authority higher than the states themselves. Although such a principle from time to time may temporarily characterize other political situations, it is the usual and

continuing situation in international politics. Implied in the principle of anarchy is the idea that when other means are exhausted for determining the outcome of a conflict, the parties to the conflict can resort to force.

The close relationship of anarchy and violence can be illustrated in several ways. One vivid, popular image of anarchists is that they are "bombthrowers," an image fomented by the Haymarket riot in Chicago in 1886 and the 1901 assassination of President William McKinley by a violent anarchist. Put another way, it is common to call anarchical those situations in which governments have lost their ability to maintain a monopoly of force. Armed groups rebelling against their governments stand in an anarchical relationship with those governments. Such situations are unusual in domestic politics.

Despite a close relationship between anarchy and violence, they are not the same thing. Anarchism is a philosophy that rejects the state and prefers to have voluntary associations among people rather than groupings that are coerced. Some of the adherents of this philosophy, such as the great Russian novelist Leo Tolstoy, have been pacifists, rejecting violence altogether. From this perspective, violence is not only not associated with anarchy but is embedded in the state, for the state has a monopoly of legitimate violence. In the nature of the state, violence is used to coerce the citizenry to abide by the laws of the regime. Where such laws are unjust, the state that imposes them on people is itself unjust. Pacific anarchists, then, would do away with the state, with its injustice, and with the violent means that it employs to rule. Anarchy means that there is an absence of authority. Such a condition, of course, is ripe for the use of force by groups that try either to impose their views in a conflict or to resist such an imposition.

In international politics, no established authority stands above states. This is not to say that there are no attempts, including successful ones, to create some kind of order either through cooperative practices, the establishment of institutions, some amount of coercion short of violence, or some combination of these. It is to say that in a clash of values, among states they reserve the ability and the authority to use force. Value clashes tend to vary in both content and intensity, so some periods of time include more violence than others. Whether one is attending to a relatively peaceful period such as the decade of the 1920s or to exceptionally violent decades such as that between 1801 and 1810 or the periods of the

First or Second World Wars, the organizing principle of anarchy in international politics has remained constant and continuous.

This condition of anarchy and the many complex relations that take place within it comprise the subject matter of international politics, and the problematic has as one of its primary components the search for the **causes of war** and **conditions of peace.** States bring together such large groups, usually nations but sometimes multinational aggregates, and such immense accumulations of power that wars among them are among the most destructive and evil of human activities. Closely related in the problematic that we use in our analysis are the conduct and consequences of war as well as the maintenance and operation of mechanisms and practices of peace. In examining international politics, the basic considerations of power and justice guide the analysis.

States sometimes strive to cooperate to put conceptions of justice into place. For example, states have signed treaties and passed resolutions in international organizations to establish standards of human rights. Given the claim of each state to decide matters for itself, it remains very difficult to make such standards effective.

In an anarchical order, aggregates of power and embodiments of justice tend to lie in the state rather than in the international realm. Thus, another important component of the problematic of this field is the state, its diffusion, its formation, and the maintenance of its position in the international system. A **state** is a territorially based political unit, recognized by other states, that has the capacity to make choices with respect to its security and economy and provides order and justice for its citizens. Over the centuries, state diffusion has occurred, first as the spread of recognition of independent territorial units and then as the empirical fleshing out of capacities. Formation is the initial and ongoing process of the building and decaying of states and their constant struggle with internal and external forces that help or hinder, compete with or reinforce the striving _for_ completion of the process. Maintenance of position is the task that leaders of states undertake in competing with other states; it is measured by the relative capacities of a state in relationship to other states.

Within any state but especially prominent in those with market economies and democratic polities, individuals and associations maintain an existence that includes an autonomous realm, separate from government. In much of the literature, this realm carries the label of **civil society.** At the same time that civil society preserves its own realm free of government control, it also competes with government by making claims on it for policy preferences and benefits and by resisting others' claims and costs. When projected into the international arena, such activities by civil society create a **market** that acts somewhat outside governmental control and competes with governments for allocation of resources and profits. Thus, a problematic that attends to states must also attend to civil society and markets, for these are important forces affecting state formation and maintenance of position in the international system. Nonetheless, the same questions from politics—who is using what power to achieve what commodities or goods or other values from whom and with what justificatory claims—are available to guide the analysis.

■──────────────────────────────

• • • • • • **The Problematic of International Politics**

Subject matter
• Politics: power and justice
• Anarchy
• War: causes of war, conduct, and consequences
• Peace: conditions; mechanisms and practices
• State: diffusion, formation, maintenance of position
  · civil society and markets
Basic question
• Who is using what power to achieve what values from whom and with what justificatory claims?
Methods
• Historical, scientific, and philosophical

──────────────────────────────

Put in that way, the formula would apply only to descriptive analysis, to the examination of historical and policy materials. But by including considerations of justice, the problematic can just as well be applied to a consideration of alternatives. Canadian political scientist Robert Cox has drawn a distinction between **"problem-solving theory"** and **"critical theory."**[4] For him, the purpose underlying the second is that of "creating an alternative world." The first of these perspectives emphasizes that which is given and continuity, whereas the second stresses that which might be created and change. Our problematic accommodates both of these perspectives.

In addition, political actions often have consequences unintended by those who seek their goals. While potentially present in all circumstances, **unintended consequences** are almost always bound to occur in conflict situations in which powerful contenders struggle on behalf of their respective aims. One of the most outstanding examples of unintended outcomes was the effect of World War II that transformed the overall pattern of power distribution in the world from one in which there were six or seven major powers to a bipolar arrangement in which only the United States and the Soviet Union remained as superpowers. No one had striven for that effect, surely not Germany, which had aspired to be the ruler of all of Europe but was instead reduced to a divided and shrunken country. Neither had the victors in the war fought for the goal of dividing the world between democratic/capitalist states led by the United States and authoritarian/communist states headed by the Soviet Union. Surely, neither of the leaders of these countries had sought to share dominant status with the other: they had been mighty adversaries before the war.

As we proceed, the complexity of the subject matter will become apparent. Moreover, the considerable appeal to include many nontraditional factors in the field will also become obvious. Both in finding our way through the complexities and in deciding which factors should be included and which excluded, the problematic will prove useful for establishing disciplinary boundaries and providing analytical tools.

To summarize, the problematic of this book strives to understand international politics in both a scientific and a philosophical sense, and it includes these concepts and questions: power, justice, causes of war, conditions of peace, anarchy, states—their diffusion, formation, and maintenance of position in the international system, and civil society and markets. In the first instance, the problematic helps to locate the contemporary discipline of international politics in the context of its origins and evolution as well as its relation to other disciplines.

Origins and Development of Discipline

As a course of study in colleges with a cadre of scholars who make their living by researching and teaching, international politics is a modern discipline, originating around the time of World War I. Nevertheless, it draws on a legacy that reaches back to ancient Greece and India. Thucydides, the Greek historian of the Peloponnesian War in the fifth century B.C., is a touchstone for some analysts, and his writings continue to be cited by contemporary scholars.

Additionally, political philosophy has concerned itself over the centuries with issues of war and peace and power and justice.[5] Diplomatic and military history, strategic analysis and military science, colonial administration, and memoirs are also traditional antecedent disciplines. From the time that autonomous political entities first engaged in such relations as diplomacy, trade, and war, attempts have been made to construct rules and law to govern those relations. With all its riches to draw on, nevertheless, this legacy did not determine either the timing or the shape of the new discipline.

Instead, two historical developments came together early in the twentieth century that provided a logic for the creation of a new discipline. First, the Industrial Revolution that began in Britain in the eighteenth century spread to the European continent, the United States, and other parts of the world. Along with the industrial development that produced such consumer amenities as telephones, automobiles, electricity, indoor plumbing, and so forth came more efficient weapons. The rifle, the ironclad ship, machine guns, and the railroad had made the American Civil War the most terrible conflict in the century between the Napoleonic Wars that ended in 1815 and the beginning of World War I in 1914. These inventions were rapidly followed by the development of the steamship and the submarine, more powerful explosives, and more destructive bullets and artillery shells. Then, tanks appeared on the battlefields of Europe in the Great War of 1914–1918, and airplanes were used for the first time to fight. While these weapons were efficient in killing, more than that, the overall evolution of war led to what became known as **total war.**

War was total in the sense that the traditional distinction between combatants and noncombatants was erased. **Industrialization** had led to warfare in which lost weapons could be replaced by the manufacture of others and fresh recruits could take over the positions of killed or wounded soldiers. Thus, in a long war, the outcome depended almost as much on the belligerents' workers and industrial capacity as on the fighting abilities of their armies. With aerial bombing, moreover, belligerents gained the capacity to attack directly civilian production facilities.

These characteristics were added to the conscription of mass armies that had originated in the Napoleonic Wars, with the result that war in the twentieth century became a struggle among entire state populations using efficient and replaceable industrial instruments in battle. Both the character and direction of these developments were apparent in the early twentieth century, and the force of their logic increased in World War II with deliberate mass bombing of civilians, the invention of long-range rockets, and the explosion of the atomic bomb.

The second historical development was **democracy.** A democratic movement was launched with the American and French revolutions at the end of the eighteenth century and grew with the introduction of democracy to Britain in the 1830s and the expressed aspirations of many Europeans in uprisings in 1848. At the core of democracy is the idea that the people should exercise control over their own lives, that governments should be accountable and responsive to their citizens. Of all of the decisions that governments make, none is more important or has greater implications for the lives of its citizens than the choice of war. In earlier historical periods when wars were fought mostly by small professional armies, the implications of decisions on behalf of war were less apparent. However, in the context of industrialization, the importance and impact of war on a citizenry stood out as clearly as flashes of lightning on a dark night.

Thus, in the late nineteenth century, some citizens in democratic countries organized themselves into peace education societies. Another movement at the end of the nineteenth and beginning of the twentieth centuries sought to strengthen international law, in particular to conceptualize war as illegal in place of regarding war as a natural activity of states.

The idea of having citizens participate in the making of decisions with respect to war and international affairs generates a logic that those citizens should be educated. They should understand how international affairs are conducted, and they should be aware of visions for making the world a better place. Thus, primarily in the United States but to some extent in Britain, courses on international affairs began to be offered at about the time of World War I. Following World War II, other countries have introduced such courses in their university curriculums.

Evolution of the Discipline

Events and historical developments have helped to shape the concerns and emphases of the field of study, though intellectual life finds sustenance in ideas as well. In the discipline's early days after World War I, idealist scholars worked from a liberal vision that stressed international law and organization, cooperation, and the power of public opinion.

Unfortunately, darker events began to take place at the beginning of the 1930s. Japan invaded Manchuria in 1931, Adolph Hitler came to power in Germany in 1933, and the deep economic depression that had begun in 1929 led many countries to turn to authoritarian rulers. These events affected the study of international politics as an older tradition of **realism** was revitalized in response to **idealism.** Rather than stressing harmony, realists emphasized conflicts of interests. They gave more attention to experience of the past and assigned great weight to power. More attention was devoted to states as aggregates of power and less to the force of public opinion.

Although realism became the dominant approach after World War II, it never completely displaced idealism. The two traditions continue in tension in the field of study. In Chapter 3, these two approaches will be described and analyzed in detail.

Both realism and idealism are strands in a tradition rooted in history, philosophy, political theory and practice, and law. That traditional approach was attacked in the post-World War II period by a different intellectual tradition growing out of nineteenth-century positivism and twentieth-century logical positivism. In logical positivism, philosophy and metaphysics are set aside as important activities but not subject to empirical proof. The logical positivists attempted to render the social sciences in the mold of natural sciences. These **behavioralists,** as they were frequently called, thus insisted on a strict distinction between facts and values.

The scientific approach continues to affect the discipline by having raised consciousness about grounding knowledge in careful research, giving precise definitions of terms, and pursuing a research agenda. Nevertheless, the Vietnam War impressed itself on American political scientists by calling into question the dominant assumption of the logical positivists that morality could be set aside, completely separated from factual information. Thus, a postbehavioral concern with political philosophy and ethics has joined the discipline's discourse.

Another important development in the world reintroduced economics to the study of international relations. In the post-World War II era, the dominance of the United States in the world economy and the prominence of security issues on the national agenda led analysts to make a clear separation between politics and economics. Political scientist Hans Morgenthau asserted the utility of the "defense of the autonomy of the political sphere against its subversion by other modes of thought."[6] Thus, a generation of political scientists specializing in international politics learned nothing of economics.

However, as the economies of other countries recovered from the devastation of World War II and the United States lost its economically dominant position, it became apparent that economics required attention. Five important long-term economic processes had occurred. First, the other industrial countries became trading competitors, which made it necessary for the United States to enlarge its markets and adjust to the competition. The United States, for example, had produced nearly 50 percent of world output in 1945, and this share had fallen to just over 20 percent in 1970. Second, the United States' guarantee of a gold-backed dollar, which had supported international trade, was slowly eroded; and in 1971, President Richard Nixon ended the arrangement, giving rise to a currency market that replaced the gold standard. Third, the industrialized world had converted the energy base of its modern economy from coal to petroleum after World War II, eventually making the industrial powers vulnerable to disruptions in supply and sensitive to pricing of petroleum. The price of oil has since been reduced to its 1972 level and supply has been rendered more secure, but crises in 1973–74 and again in 1979 pointed to the importance of oil in the economic base of the industrialized countries and their reliance on a stable supply system. Fourth, certain domestic trends in the United States were exhausted. These included the mechanization of agriculture, with its attendant movement of population to cities and then to the suburbs. In addition, heavy industrial development in steel and automobiles had been completed, and these industries proved to be relatively inflexible in adjusting to foreign competitors. Last, American corporations moved many of their operations abroad, giving great prominence to the activities of these multinational firms. Some observers questioned whether these undertakings in the private domain served the national interest of the United States.

Events had other effects on scholarship. The Vietnam War defeat and the period of detente with the Soviet Union in the 1970s resulted in renewed respect for Marxist analysis among American scholars. Rather than separating economics and politics, Marxism offered a broad theoretical analysis that

related the two. Marxist analysis was one of several coherent ways of describing and explaining the intersection of economics and politics that answered the need for incorporating political economy into the curriculum.

The rising focus on international political economy renewed interest in such liberal concerns as firms and markets. In addition, liberals noted that cooperation had been neglected, and they increasingly emphasized international institutions and the concept of interdependence.

■
●●●●●● **Evolution and Components of the Discipline**

Tradition: realism and idealism
- rooted in history, philosophy, political theory and practice, and law

Behavioralism: scientific approach
- sharp distinction between facts and values
- rooted in positivism and logical positivism
- added sociology and psychology

Post-behavioralism
- political philosophy and ethics

Political economy
- liberal and Marxist analysis
- firms and markets

Neorealism: structure of international system

Neoliberalism: processes
- cooperation through international institutions
- peace among liberal democracies

Critical theory: radical alternatives

With the publication in 1979 of a seminal book,[7] realism was restored as the outstanding mode of thought in the field. Since then, a dialogue has been continuing between **neorealists,** who emphasize the structure of the international system, and **neoliberals,** who stress processes of cooperation. Furthermore, in the mid-1980s, democracy gained increasing interest not only as a form of government but as a means of establishing peace, for many accepted the view that liberal democracies do not go to war with one another.

With the end of the Cold War, the field was dominated by this discourse, but critical theorists also challenged the commanding emphasis on positivist thought. They called attention to alternatives and to political philosophy that provoked people to imagine more just and more peaceful worlds than the one that we live in.

The collapse of Communism in Eastern Europe in 1989, the demise of the Soviet Union in 1991, and the end of the Cold War brought to the fore a fundamental question that had nagged at international politics theory. Neorealism emphasized structure and regularity in international politics. One of the most telling criticisms of it points out that neorealist theory possesses neither a conception nor an explanation of change.[8] In a world so full of discontinuities as existed in the early 1990s, this conceptual and theoretical gap was glaring, and it represents a very striking challenge to scholars of international politics to understand change.

Science and Its Limits in the Study of International Politics

Science is the activity aimed at describing, explaining, predicting, and controlling the physical world. It includes the body of accumulated knowledge established through earlier discovery, theorizing, investigation, and empirical demonstration, but it also entails a set of attitudes and practices involved in doing science. Science involves careful observations of phenomena to be studied. Scientists note patterns of regularity, and they formulate hypotheses by a process of **induction.** They construct theoretical explanations of patterns or laws, and from theory they generate further hypotheses by a process of **deduction.** Finally scientists test their hypotheses by experiments or carefully controlled observations. Sometimes, established laws and theories are overturned by new observations and knowledge. Thus, the scientific attitude requires maintaining an openness to new findings that compel giving up adherence to established knowledge or at least modifying old understandings.

A number of problems concerning the use of science present themselves to social scientists. First, considerable doubt exists about whether human beings in their social relations follow behavioral patterns like units in the physical world. Whereas a chemical reaction occurs in conformity with observable laws, political activities are much harder to predict. Even political actors who themselves are at the center of events, as was the Shah of Iran in 1978 and early 1979 just prior to his overthrow, do not understand the pattern and direction of the activity swirling around them. It is possible to observe certain regularities, particularly in established social circumstances, but many observers would argue that the social world fundamentally differs from the physical world.

In addition to the irregularity of human patterns of behavior, human beings may change in response to knowledge. Motions of the planets persist regardless of human ability to observe and predict those motions. In contrast, new insight that is obtained into, say, the operations of bureaucratic organizations may affect the behavior of those holding governmental positions.

A third problem is that physical laws operate without any consideration of justice or morality. But human activities incorporate both behavioral and ethical dimensions. As we saw above, logical positivists claim that facts and values can be analytically separated. However, value conflicts are sometimes hidden by dominant groups, and values are shaped by one's position in life and history. If social science is at all valuable, its contribution must be to an understanding of the human condition and of social reality. Because this reality—or, more properly, these realities—is composed of both behavioral and ethical considerations, they need to be studied together, and the logical positivists' position of setting philosophy aside from empirical science must be rejected.

This is not to say that certain of the attitudes and practices of science should not be adopted. It is very worthwhile to be as conscious as one can of one's own values and to suspend these when trying to make careful observations of behavior. Moreover, the use of precise and clear definitions of terms and concepts is essential to systematic study. Hypotheses need to be carefully formulated and as rigorously tested as the material and subject matter allow.

As used in this book, a **hypothesis** is a statement of a causal relationship between at least two variables. In formulating a hypothesis, a person identifies that which she wants to explain, and that dependent variable needs to be cast in conceptual terms. For example, if she is curious about why some countries engage in more foreign policy activities than others, she might conceive the dependent variable as foreign policy activity and give it a precise definition, possibly by defining activity as membership in alliances, maintenance of diplomatic relations with other countries, and attendance at conferences of international organizations. Then, the investigator hopes to be able to explain activity by the level of economic development. After giving definition to economic development, she then needs to express a causal logic that links the independent and dependent variables.

In this example, the logic that links the variables might proceed along the following lines.

Economic development leads to increased activity for two reasons: it creates greater capacity to participate in international affairs because it is composed of a larger contingent of trained personnel and greater wealth to support activities. Furthermore, it makes the country more valuable as an ally and as a contributor to the implementation of cooperative decisions reached in the international forums. Thus, hypothesis formulation includes the conceptualization and definition of dependent and independent variables and the construction of a causal logic that connects the variables.

Conceptualization of the hypothesis linking economic development to foreign policy activity might have resulted from observation, thus embodying an inductive process, which is a procedure of generalizing on the basis of observing regular patterns through careful examination. Induction often leads to classification of the observed behavior and to the formulation of lawlike statements of the patterns.

The induction process is supplemented by deduction, or the making of logical inferences from elementary assumptions, definitions, and axioms. Often, such theoretical statements contain assumptions that are not true. An example from physics illustrates the utility of such assumptions. The law of the pendulum assumes that there is no friction and that there is no mass. These assumptions are obviously contrary to fact, for no real pendulum does not have mass and friction. Thus, if one wished to develop a theory about pendulums, an inductive approach would not be so useful, for statements drawn from such an empirical approach would not result in elegant theory like the law of the pendulum. On the other hand, one can deduce hypotheses from the law of the pendulum that can be tested empirically. It remains that the theory itself cannot be tested, for it contains statements that can be demonstrated to be false.

In international politics, few theories either generate interesting and elegant hypotheses or contain false assumptions, but a few do. A structural theory of balance of power, for example, assumes that all states are the same except that they vary in capabilities or power. However, it is plain that France and China, say, or Canada and Somalia are very different from each other. Nevertheless, by making the false assumption that they are like units, it is possible to generate some quite interesting hypotheses that can be tested, as we will see.

Thus, the standard that scientists apply to *hypotheses* that are arrived at by either induction or deduction is that they are true, that they can be verified empirically through experiments or by careful observation. *Theories*, in contrast, are, and must be, assessed by a different standard: whether they are useful. Usefulness means that they can be used to explain patterns of behavior and that they are fruitful in generating new, testable hypotheses that lead to new research.

Even though the analysis undertaken in this book is very limited in its science, for politics as conceived here does not divorce science and philosophy, certain elements of science are considered very valuable. First, there is a respect for evidence and logic in making arguments. Second, we will be conscientious in defining terms and concepts carefully and in making logical connections when we claim that variables are causally linked. Third, it is important to recognize that both deduction and induction are valid methods of generating hypotheses. Fourth, we will apply appropriate tests to empirical hypotheses. Finally, we will try to remain open to new knowledge and to the potential for growth. At the same time, we expect to apply the same standards to new materials as to old and do not assume that what is new is therefore better.

It is important to recognize when we are considering scientific questions and when we engage in philosophical thought. Both require care, consideration, imagination, and logic. But just as certain tests are inappropriate for particular scientific questions, so such criteria of science as empirical verification are not appropriately brought to bear on considerations of justice. Frequently, the issues can be considered together, but we neither want to allow questions of philosophy to get in the way of our search for scientific knowledge nor let the power of scientific truth interfere with careful, contemplative thought about justice.

Considerations of Rationality

Evidence of irrationality in political life can be found everywhere. American taxpayers simultaneously demand more services but are unwilling to pay the higher taxes necessary to provide them. Emotional appeals by leaders are an essential part of the politics of mobilizing followers, but passions are antithetical to rational deliberation. Struggles in international politics often engender unintended consequences, which implies that something other than rational calculation is at work. The very central belief lying at the root of action based upon idealism is that one needs to strive to achieve some end without any careful calculation of means, an irrational belief. If a small revolutionary group were rationally to assess the entrenched power of a regime, they would very likely have to conclude that achieving victory for their cause would be impossible. Even though their dedication to the struggle might involve the rational thesis from Marxist theory that an inevitable historical process favors them, they nevertheless have to possess a profound faith in the theory.

In the face of overwhelming evidence that politics involves both rational calculation and great emotional and other irrational forces, it seems necessary to make the assumption that our explanations need to incorporate irrational factors. Such an assumption would make our analysis very complicated, for the range of misperceptions, strong emotions, miscalculations, gaps in information, and so forth is virtually endless. To strive for understanding and explanation requires simplifying assumptions, and one that will prove useful is the **assumption of rationality.**

By making that assumption, we will be able to make sense in our analysis of why states or groups or leaders act. Our first attempt will be to grasp the rational goals sought and the calculations of the means to achieve those goals. Sometimes, we may find that irrational considerations are present, but our own analysis will use reason for understanding them and taking them into account. In other cases, when unintended consequences present themselves, we will attempt to find the logic of the unfolding of events and try to account for the consequences on the basis of the logic of the situation or, in other words, on the basis of a rationality not taken into account by the participants.

By making this assumption of rationality, the analysis of events and situations can proceed by asking and answering a few, fairly simple questions. Who was involved? What objectives did they have and how did they go about seeking them? What happened? What were the results and consequences? How justifiable were the intentions and the consequences? What alternatives were available?

Relation to Other Disciplines

At its core, international relations deals with politics, the struggle for power and justice. As often as not, politics revolves around government, for government is the means for achieving authority, for setting at least temporarily issues surrounding the allocation of values. Governments themselves in international politics are required to behave in the absence of authority, thus needing to engage in negotiations through diplomacy to settle disputes or to determine the outcome of conflicts through force. Governments also engage in activities that fall somewhere between diplomacy and war, such as espionage, clandestine operations, subversion, and paramilitary campaigns. Moreover, nongovernmental activities such as trade, migration, finance, communications, travel, and so forth also occur across international boundaries. Some of these have obvious effects on governmental affairs, while others make a more subtle impact on the long-term evolution of relative strengths of different countries, and still others have a negligible effect on politics.

This inquiry is most closely tied to political science, for the study of international politics is a field within that discipline. The principal questions comprising our guiding problematic are power and justice, considerations that international studies share with other fields in political science. What distinguishes international from other aspects of political science is the anarchical character of the realm that it studies and a number of implications that flow from that character.

Nevertheless, the study of international politics requires exploration of activities occurring within the units that have no authority above them. Within states, the activities to be studied are not very different from those studied by political scientists specializing in the study of government or some other aspect of domestic politics. Often the issues are different, for example, in the areas of diplomacy and war as opposed to elections and judicial behavior. Nevertheless, some issues overlap, as do governmental regulation and support of business, whether operating entirely within the country's boundaries or transnationally. With respect to certain issues—tariffs and trade are clear examples—it is virtually impossible to distinguish international and domestic politics, for the debates and the processes involved are identical. An additional phenomenon has grown in recent years in which issues that were once regarded as entirely within one country's jurisdiction—human rights, for instance—have become the object of attention and influence of other countries and nongovernmental groups operating across international boundaries.

Whatever form such issues take or however the conflicts are channeled, they all involve politics in which different groups contend to achieve their values. The problem for the political analyst is to become clear about what is at stake, who is contending or cooperating on behalf of which values and by what means, the justice of the matters involved, and the outcomes and their implications.

Because political analysis is often applied to historical materials, the relationship with history is strong. Particularly, studies that examine long-term trends and the unfolding of conditions over time rely very much on history. Despite some overlap and affinity, however, political science and history differ in the way in which their practitioners shape their questions and arrange the materials. Historians use time as their basic organizing device, while political scientists employ an analytical focus.

Those political scientists who stress the scientific side of their work identify themselves with social sciences, in contrast to the humanities with which historians mostly affiliate. On the other hand, political scientists stressing their philosophical side also fit easily into an identification as humanists.

Some disciplines such as geography and military science are drawn on in the analysis of international politics to supply background and supplementary knowledge. For example, in studying the relations of North America and Europe, it aids understanding of alliance relations and trade matters to have a firm grasp of topographical features, natural resources, population distribution, industrial base, and other components of geography. Also, knowledge of strategic concepts, military planning, and tactical maneuvers assists any political scientist studying the military activities of states and threatening situations.

Still other disciplines offer thicker connections to political analysis. Perhaps the most important of these is economics. Although some scholars separate power, the central concept of politics, and wealth, the principal focus of economics, wealth and power are so essential to each other that it is not always easy to disentangle their relations. The basic factors of production—land, labor, and capital—are essential components of state power. International trade and finance—the movement of goods and money among countries—comprise an important portion of transactions moving across international boundaries. Government policies are critical to the shaping of wealth-producing activities within any particular country's borders, and states compete economically with one another to maintain their positions in the international system. These are only examples of the myriad ways in which politics and economics intersect. In the ensuing analysis, there will be many places at which the problematic of international politics will find relevance for concepts, theories, transactions, and phenomena from economics. The simultaneous existence and interactions, as well as relevance for each other, of states and markets will be made apparent as we investigate international relations.

Two other disciplines have had a considerable impact on thinking about state decision making, an important aspect of foreign policy analysis. They are organizational behavior and psychology. Because governments are complex organizations, insights can be gained into the operations of particular areas such as foreign policy making from general organizational behavior. In addition, foreign policies are formulated and carried out by individuals. Thus, the discipline devoted to the analysis of the individual—psychology—offers insight into the many components of behavior, ranging from cognition and complex thinking to misperceptions and the operation of irrational impulses. Additionally, relations of human beings with one another have a psychological base inasmuch as the exercise of influence is more often than not done through the shaping and manipulation of others' minds and wills.

Finally, mathematics has contributed in several ways to the analysis of international politics. Some political questions can be treated statistically, so statistics forms part of the repertoire of quantitatively oriented behavioral analysts. More important, game theory has helped to clarify and express certain important international relationships. Nuclear deterrence theory, which has shaped both academic and policy analysis, draws its fundamental logic from the mathematics of game theory. In addition, the theory of cooperation has developed out of game theory to provide an analytical scheme for examining incentive structures and other components of cooperative behavior.

In the spirit of the scientific attitude, we need to remain open to the ideas and methods that may contribute to understanding that which we choose to study. Therefore, arbitrary disciplinary boundaries should not be allowed to prevent our progress in learning. At the same time, the relevance and bearing that various other disciplines have upon our own can be determined by the conscientious application of the problematic of international politics.

• STUDY QUESTIONS

1. What is a problematic, and why is it useful?

2. In considering a problematic for international politics, what should be the criteria for inclusion and exclusion?

3. How can one explain why the systematic study of international politics arose at the time and in the place that it did?

4. What secular trends in history have helped to shape the modes of thought, methods of analysis, and normative concerns of international politics analysts?

5. To what extent can the study of international politics be conducted using the principles of science? What elements impose limits on the use of scientific analysis in the study, and what are those limits?

6. Why is it useful to make an assumption of rationality in the political behavior that we wish to study? What arguments can you think of that could be used to make the case against the employment of that assumption?

7. In what sense is the study of international politics a synthetic discipline?

8. What related disciplines do you believe bear most importantly on the study of relations among states? Why do you think so?

• IMPORTANT TERMS

anarchy	market
behavioralists	neoliberals
causes of war	neorealists
change	power
civil society	problem-solving theory
conditions of peace	problematic
critical theory	realism
deduction	science
democracy	scientific approach
hypothesis	state
idealism	total war
induction	trading state
industrialization	unintended
international political	consequences
economy	rationality assumption
justice	

• ENDNOTES

1. The author of one textbook noted that the field was built on twenty two antecedent disciplines: see Quincy Wright, *The Study of International Relations* (New York: Appleton-Century-Crofts, 1955).

2. This is the title of a book that seeks to cut through the disagreements by defining a core. K. J. Holsti, *The Dividing Discipline: Hegemony and Diversity in International Theory* (Boston: Allen & Unwin, 1985).

3. Holsti, *The Dividing Discipline*, p. 2 and fn. 1, p. 13.

4. Robert W. Cox, "Social Forces, States and World Orders: Beyond International Relations Theory," in *Neorealism and Its Critics*, edited by Robert O. Keohane (New York: Columbia University Press, 1986), p. 208.

5. An excellent review of the philosophical literature concerned with the causes of war is Kenneth N. Waltz, *Man, the State and War: A Theoretical Analysis* (New York: Columbia University Press, 1959).

6. Hans J. Morgenthau, *Politics among Nations: The Struggle for Power and Peace*, 5th ed. (New York: Alfred A. Knopf, 1973).

7. Kenneth N. Waltz, *Theory of International Politics* (Reading, Mass. Addison-Wesley, 1979).

8. See John Gerard Ruggie, "Continuity and Transformation in the World Polity: Toward a Neorealist Synthesis," and Kenneth N. Waltz, "Reflections on *Theory of International Politics*: A Response to My Critics," in *Neorealism and Its Critics*, edited by Robert O. Keohane (New York: Columbia University Press, 1986).

CHAPTER 2

Values in Contention in International Politics

No one has easy access to the motives and goals of others. What we do know is that people have values that they try to satisfy. These fall into both the public and the private realms, conceptually distinct spheres that cannot always be untangled in practice. For clarification, one of the most helpful things that we can do is to examine directly our own values and articulate them.

This chapter treats the problem of making values explicit, and it examines the most prominent common values that people seek through politics—power, justice, wealth, security, order, peace, community—as well as others. At its conclusion, the chapter places the values over which people contend in the context of the problematic of international politics.

Introduction

Values are embedded both in the activities of people who act in politics and in the analytical and theoretical schemes of those who study politics. Everyone's values are shaped by his respective time and place in history. Political leaders strive for such values as increasing the power and prestige of their countries, while ordinary citizens give their support to those aspirations or rally on behalf of different values, such as protection of their economic privileges. Analysts, too, use frameworks and theories that contain values. These may range from a commitment to a political value such as free trade to the embrace of a particular conceptualization of a problem such as interdependence. Some espouse a disinterested search for truth. Thus, in the quest for understanding, it is important to try to sort out and clarify the main values at stake in international politics. This chapter aims to elucidate the values that are in contention in politics and to describe some of the analytical controversies that engage analysts who study that field.

Three things need to be said at the outset. First, individuals and groups most often pursue different

values simultaneously, and there is in reality considerable motivational overlap. Nevertheless, actors are sometimes forced to choose one value over another, and their choice reveals the order of their preferences: it tells us which is their dominant value. Second, it is not necessary to force analysis into an either-or formula. Political life is filled with trade-offs and dialectical processes as well as a great complexity that mocks as simpleminded any assertion that one must choose between two sharply defined alternatives such as politics and economics or security and order. Third, it is useful for analytical purposes to treat a unit such as a state as an entity pursuing values. An underlying consensus or mind-set usually exists among decision makers that gives reality to that analytical assumption. Nevertheless, it is also important to keep in mind that a state is a complex organization in which those who act on its behalf may differ sharply in their views of an international situation and how it should be addressed. Moreover, they contend in a political process to produce a decision that may or may not clearly reflect adherence to certain values. That is to say, values can become quite muddled when they are put into practice.

The values over which groups contend in the political process are not always obvious. Indeed, a fairly common political tactic is to veil preferences or even to use duplicity to mislead opponents. When Adolph Hitler declared in 1938 at the Munich Conference that he wanted to absorb the Sudentenland, the German-speaking area of Czechoslovakia, he argued that his purpose was simply to bring the territory's German-speaking residents into the German nation. In view of the fact that this objective necessarily involved German territorial expansion, it left Prime Minister Neville Chamberlain of Great Britain and Prime Minister Edouard Daladier of France, who were asked to endorse Hitler's demand, in the position of either accepting or rejecting both goals. They had hoped to avoid war by believing that Chancellor Hitler's primary value was national integration. As it turned out a year later when the German army attacked Poland, however, his primary values were shown to be the acquisition of territory and assets, the domination of other peoples, and the enhancement of Germany's power.

Authoritarian and evil leaders are not the only ones who hide their values. Democratic politicians sometimes resolve conflict through compromises that obscure what is at stake. For example, a tax increase may be partly offset by spending part of it on projects favored by those who oppose the added tax burden; or a currency devaluation in a developing country may be partly offset by a wage increase.

Neither is it easy to unravel the values of analysts who often conceal or are unaware of their own preferences. Nevertheless, values are embedded in the subjects that all social scientists deal with, and personal values affect the selection of problems to be examined and the tools of analysis used to study them. In making his distinction between critical and problem-solving theory, Robert Cox noted that "critical theory can be a guide to strategic action for bringing about an alternative order, whereas problem-solving theory is a guide to tactical actions, which, intended or unintended, sustain the existing order."[1] That is to say, the posture that analysts take may have practical effects on the politics that they are writing about, either supporting current policy or favoring an alternative.

Human beings hold and pursue many different values, most often more than one simultaneously, but this discussion can be narrowed to consider only the main values that are in contention in international politics.

Power

The most frequently used concept in political science, power has been given many meanings. Commonly it is defined as control of others, as the ability to gain others' compliance with one's own wishes. For example, political scientist Robert Dahl in a well-known essay has written, "A has power over B to the extent that he can get B to do something that B would not otherwise do."[2] This behavioral and strictly relational definition can lead, however, to the false conclusion that a failure to gain compliance means that one does not have power. Thus, in the aftermath of the Vietnam war, many American analysts reached the judgment that the United States no longer possessed great power. Others concluded that force had lost its utility.

If one considers the matter from the perspective of Vietnam, however, he notes that the military forces of the country during the war were divided between those allied with the United States and those aiming to drive out the United States. In addition, by using force to resist the American invasion, Vietnam was able to retain its autonomy, and those Vietnamese who wished to unite their country were successful. The outcome was not determined solely by force, for the United States commanded more force than Vietnam did, but the military instrument was a critical ingredient in the unfolding of events and the outcome of the war. Then, if one compares the United States and Vietnam, the United States has continued to be a major participant in many parts of the world, in greatly diverse agenda matters, and has been able to exercise a good deal of influence—more than any other country—on the outcomes of controversial issues. In contrast, VIETNAM has remained mired in poverty and backwardness, many of its citizens fleeing to other countries as "boat people" refugees to escape the harshness of life in Vietnam, and the country has enjoyed political influence outside its borders only in neighboring Cambodia, which it invaded in 1978 and where its army remained until 1991.

As a value, power is the capacity to act with **autonomy.** Since actions almost always involve interactions with others, such a capacity is relative and implies that one is able to bring his own capabilities to bear on a situation. The concept of relative capacities means that some are more powerful than others, which is to say that they can more effectively resist attempts at intrusion on their autonomy and more greatly shape their environments than can less powerful actors. For example, Mexico holds more control over its own national life than does Honduras, and it exercises more influence over matters outside its borders.

Unlike some other values, power may be an end in itself, or it may be instrumental to achieving other values. The ability to act autonomously, to resist intrusions on that autonomy, and to shape the environment and influence others are all components of the value of power as an end. It is difficult for a country's leaders to know what demands or challenges might emanate from other states, but they can be assumed to strive to meet challenges and to take advantage of opportunities whenever and wherever they occur.

On the other hand, power forms the means for achieving other values such as justice or security. For example, the maintenance of a secure border when faced with a hostile neighbor can be achieved only with military force, and the settlement of a border dispute may be attained through diplomacy and economic compensation. In more narrowly focused issues, power may be the means to resist a demand for compliance from a neighboring state. Whether such means bring about a successful outcome depends not simply on the power but on its use, the response of others, and the structure of the situation.

Power capacity can be composed of many different instruments and capabilities, the most important of which are military and economic. To these **hard power** components, Joseph Nye adds **soft power** resources, or "co-optive power," which is "the ability of a country to structure a situation so that other countries develop preferences or define their interests consistent with its own. This power tends to arise from such resources as cultural or ideological attractions as well as rules and institutions of international regimes."[3] For example, the United States remains attractive to many as a liberal democracy, and international institutions such as the World Trade Organization (formerly the General Agreement on Tariffs and Trade, or GATT) embody those market values that it espouses. Nevertheless, states with economic capabilities and military forces are most able to act autonomously, and soft power resources tend to belong more to those who also possess hard power resources than to those possessing only intangible assets.

Powerful states with vast economic capacities not only can underpin and support their own autonomy but also can enter into realms of international activity that poorer, weaker states are unable to contemplate. Thus, a wealthy JAPAN has entered into such activities as the G-7, the group of the seven leading industrial countries that confer from time to time on global economic management. Japan has also become a major investor not only in Asia but in Latin America and North America, and it achieved a position in 1990 as the world's greatest contributor of economic assistance to developing countries. As part of the package of bringing an end to the Cold War in Europe, Germany agreed to finance housing in Russia and other successor republics to the Soviet Union for troops returning from their stations in what had been East Germany. Such activities as these cannot even be contemplated by poorer countries.

With enormous military resources, the UNITED STATES is in a position that cannot seriously be threatened by any other country. Moreover, its military strength also allows it to extend its protection to many allies. Even during the Cold War, when the Soviet Union had comparable military resources, the two superpowers stood in a privileged position, for only the one could threaten the other. Their military capabilities also undergirded their diplomacy throughout the globe and gave them leverage in moments of crisis, not just in their own occasional confrontations but in third-party disputes as well.

Power is never fixed, for change occurs constantly in the technological and economic components that go into it, and political choices often affect capabilities. Thus, it would be an error to believe that any country's power has a permanent character. A century ago, BRITAIN was the most formidable power in the world, but today it belongs to the second rank. Note also the present weakened condition of the successor states to the Soviet Union, which only twenty years ago laid claim to the status of superpower. Power is always relative, and it would be a mistake to assess one country's power without comparing it to that of others. Taking just one component into account, we note that the French army stood as the most powerful one in Europe in 1918 and was no less potent in 1937, but meanwhile, the German military had risen from defeat to rebuild and surpass the French forces to such an extent that Germany easily defeated France in 1940.

On the impermanence and relativity of power, there is little disagreement. Nevertheless, three conceptual differences divide analysts on matters concerning power: its definition, its **aggregation** or **disaggregation,** and its **fungibility.**

Most contemporary political scientists define power exclusively as a relational phenomenon in which one person or group influences the actions of another in the direction of his or its own will. Cast in terms of international politics, this definition is rendered as "the ability to control other actors and/or the international environment."[4] Such a definition may mislead observers. Some might think that the inability of a major country to control the behavior of a small one on an issue that is tenaciously held by the latter is evidence of powerlessness.

Alternatively, power is defined as the capacity to act autonomously, to shape the agendas of relationships, and generally to achieve goals and acquire values.[5] This definition clearly makes power a quality of a person or group rather than a relational characteristic. Surely, in the exercise of influence it is always relational, but the capacity itself does not depend on interactions with others. Great powers often are unable to manipulate their clients. For example, when Israel decided to invade Lebanon in 1982, the United States was not able to dissuade it from doing so. While this episode illustrates the ability of an independent state to act with autonomy, it surely does not suggest that the United States is deficient in power. The United States' power relies on the country's own capabilities and capacities to act across a wide range of endeavors.

■
● ● ● ● ● ● **Dimensions of Power and Conceptual Differences Concerning Power**

Dimensions of power:
• Hard and soft power resources
Conceptual differences:
• Definitional stress on autonomy versus relational character
• Aggregation versus disaggregation
• Fungibility

But this discussion leads to the second controversy over power: whether it is more useful to treat it in the aggregate. In recent years, various writers have pointed to Japan as a major economic but not political or military power. Such an observation is based upon the disaggregation of power, the separation of its political, economic, and military dimensions. Obviously, for certain purposes a focus on economics alone is quite useful, for example, in a treatment of

international trade negotiations. On the other hand, if one is interested in identifying the major powers in an international system, one would want to use a single, aggregate standard of power that would include all of the dimensions. Thus, there are occasions for treating power in either an aggregated or a disaggregated fashion, depending on one's purposes. In general, though, treating power in the aggregate is more useful because the capacity to act autonomously and to shape one's relationships is determined by many different factors.

Part of the academic argument over disaggregating power stems from the third controversy about the fungibility of power. Fungibility means that a commodity is interchangeable, that it can be used for many different functions. Money is fungible, for one can use it to buy many things: an ice cream cone, a house, a vacation, a bodyguard, an education, and so on. An argument mounted by liberal analysts in recent years avers that power is not fungible because power resources, such as military force, often cannot be brought to bear in specific issue areas usually affected by other resources. For example, in a trade dispute between the UNITED STATES AND CANADA, the former's military superiority ordinarily cannot be brought to bear on the dispute. Moreover, neither can its overall superior capabilities necessarily determine the outcome of, say, a conflict over how much American beer can be sold in Canada or how much Canadian lumber can be exported to the United States. Even military force, of course, shares the character of fungibility. Armies can conduct war, build roads, suppress riots, educate a citizenry, provide a powerful symbol and source of pride for a state, and even run governments. It is true that the military force in the hands of an army cannot be brought effectively to bear on trade negotiations. On the other hand, it is also true that a banking system cannot conquer territory. When defined as the capacity to make autonomous choices and to exercise influence, power obviously is fungible even though certain instruments are not always applicable to every circumstance. Those instruments are many, including not just military and economic resources but also intelligence and training, morale, technology, population, confidence and leadership.

An inventory can only be suggestive rather than exhaustive or definitive. For the conduct of war, existing military forces and the potential of a country to mobilize provide reasonably good indicators of its power. Nevertheless, such indicators do not predict the outcome of a particular war, for that will also be determined by three other factors: the response of the other conflicting parties, the structural constraints of the international system, and the domestic politics of support for and opposition to the war. Similarly, the wealth and productive capacity of a country provide the basis for rough estimates of a state's position in international trade but do not indicate how a particular multinational trade negotiation will turn out.

What we are trying to capture in the concept of power is a great diversity of components. Some of those components change over time as technology and circumstances change. Since the invention of the computer, the guidance components of explosive projectiles have leapt to levels of sophistication far surpassing previous generations of weaponry, resulting in "smart bombs." Other factors such as the bravery and cowardice of those who use weapons remain very much the same, although rigorous training often compensates for individual weaknesses and bolsters personal strengths.

In the following analysis, then, power will be treated as a capacity that attaches to individuals, groups, and states—most often as an aggregate, though occasionally in a disaggregated fashion, and as fungible insofar as that quality has meaning. Power is the capacity to act autonomously and to exercise influence over others. While certainly not a supreme value, power remains the essential instrumental value. Other values require power for their achievement or acquisition. Since humans are not prescient, they strive to achieve, at a minimum, sufficient power to protect their autonomy, security, and well-being. This often requires affecting the outlooks and actions of others. In highly organized politics like that practiced by states, specific insecurities and perceived dangers lead policy makers to devise particular instruments to meet threats and take advantage of opportunities as they present themselves. They raise armies, establish diplomatic relations with other countries, and join alliances and international organizations.

As established in Chapter 1, politics involves not simply power but also justice.

Justice

The modern emphasis on the value of power grew out of a new economic and political order that emerged in Europe at the time of the Renaissance. Its new attitude was articulated effectively by Niccolò Machiavelli. Placing power politics at the core of political values represented not simply a departure from the medieval way of thinking that stressed other values such as piety and charity, but the new political analysis also differentiated itself from an older concern with justice. At least since the time of Plato's *Republic* in which Socrates poses and pursues the simple question: "What is justice?" those devoted to analyzing politics had sought to understand the place of justice in political processes and arrangements.

Among those involved in politics, justice tends to be regarded as a value in different ways depending upon one's position in current political arrangements. Dominant groups construct systems of justice based upon law as a means to retain their power that is cheaper than reliance exclusively on force. Subordinate groups, on the other hand, seek to improve their situations by appealing to justice and related concepts such as fairness, equality, respect for basic rights, and so forth. Frequently, justice is invoked as an ideological appeal by all manner of political actors who set out claims to receive their just due. For example, in the name of "fair trade" and simple justice, President George Bush demanded that Japan open its economy to American products.

Justice basically means that each person receives his "just due." Nevertheless, the term is abstract, and calculating what everyone deserves turns out to be complex. This leads to a dialectical process of considering justice. That is to say, people compete to define the meaning of justice.

Traditionally, the concrete problem of pursuing justice for individuals and groups occurred within the confines of political units. In both theory and practice, international politics traditionally drew a clear boundary between what went on inside countries and the interactions that governments conducted among units. Questions of justice arose in international relations primarily as means of regulating the interactions of states.

In the medieval period, the Christian doctrine of **just war** was devised, and in the recent past, this matter has formed a renewed topic for consideration under contemporary circumstances. The doctrine holds that wars must be fought only for just causes, that the means used must be proportionate to the ends pursued, and that a distinction must be maintained between combatants and noncombatants.[6] Part of the debate in the United States during the late 1960s and early 1970s about the WAR IN VIETNAM turned on the issues of just war. Critics held that American intervention in a civil war being fought for national independence did not constitute a just cause. They also argued that the use of devastating aerial bombing against an agricultural country constituted disproportionate means. Moreover, certain policies such as free-fire zones and carpet bombing, in addition to the very nature of guerrilla warfare, contributed to the erasure of the distinction between soldiers and civilians.[7]

■
•••••• **Dimensions of Justice in International Politics**

- Different states have distinctive conceptions of justice.
- Clashes over justice in international politics in international organizations may result in:
  - No resolution, such as demands for new international economic order in the 1970s and the Earth Summit in 1992
  - Successful outcomes, such as the Helsinki Final Act in 1975
- Just war doctrine:
  - Fought for just purpose, usually defense
  - Proportionality
  - Distinction between combatants and noncombatants
- Intervention in other countries, particularly in revolutionary situations

---

More recently, in 1983, the Catholic bishops of the United States issued a document that declared as immoral not only initiating and fighting a nuclear war but also the policy of NUCLEAR DETERRENCE.[8] Responding to that position, a group of analysts stressed that a distinction should be drawn between intentions and consequences. Their argument was that the consequence of nuclear deterrence was the maintenance of peace, an eminently moral outcome, despite the obviously immoral intention of nuclear deterrence that might include the promise deliberately to kill civilians.[9]

Inasmuch as domestic law tends to be the vehicle for embodying justice, it would seem that international law would serve the same function in international relations. However, the decentralized character of legislating, enforcing, and judging international law has rendered it a frail reed in the quest for justice. Moreover, international law, except where it embodies convenience or common interests that emanate from customs, tends to reflect the interests of the more powerful states. In the contemporary world of some 185 states, an absence of consensus and a great diversity of values have weakened international law even more.

Some have sought to achieve justice through international organizations, which provide mechanisms for all states to make their claims for their respective due. However, wide chasms of what justice may mean separate the different claimants, particularly along lines of wealth and power. In the 1970s, the states of the Third World, the poorer countries, demanded through the United Nations General Assembly and other forums the establishment of a NEW INTERNATIONAL ECONOMIC ORDER, but this was rejected by the leading industrial countries that were the objects of the demand. As pointed out by an astute observer, that demand was not simply a call for more aid within an existing international order but rather an insistence on a complete restructuring of the international political economy, replacing the liberal order with one based upon statist principles.[10] In 1992, at the Earth Summit in Rio de Janeiro, a similar lineup of opposed forces clashed over environmental and economic development concerns. In both of these cases, a discord occurred between opposing conceptions of justice that grew out of different economic circumstances and philosophies. Rich and satisfied states that had constructed and benefited from a liberal trading order defended that order. They were opposed by poor and dissatisfied states that sought a different set of arrangements that promised to be more beneficial to them. A standoff was the result in both of these contests.

Sometimes, clashes over opposed conceptions of justice have more salubrious outcomes. One example is the HELSINKI AGREEMENT of 1975 among the thirty-five countries in the Conference on Security and Cooperation in Europe (CSCE). The main parties—the countries of Eastern Europe, Western Europe, and North America—sought very different goals. Led by the Soviet Union, the Eastern European countries had long sought recognition of existing international boundaries, something that the West German government, backed by its allies, had denied in the early Cold War years. Western Europe, led by West Germany, wanted to have greater economic exchange with Eastern Europe. Meanwhile, the United States, promoting human rights, pressed for commitments by the Eastern European governments not to abuse their own citizens and to concede to those citizens such democratic rights as freedom of speech and of association. The Helsinki Final Act included all of these goals, and it helped to lay the basis for the deep changes that occurred in Eastern Europe in 1989. In addition to governmental pressure on behalf of human rights, a number of nongovernmental organizations, such as Helsinki Watch and Americas Watch, regularly report on and agitate against human rights abuses, at least sometimes with effect.

These international activities seeking justice are very limited, compared with the concern for justice in the state. As we will see in Chapter 6, justice is a crucial component of the state. Thus, it is mostly within domestic politics that justice is pursued and embodied. However, the implication of this embodiment of a conception of justice linked with the power of the state is that each state brings to its dealings with other states its peculiar conceptions of justice, and these produce very substantial value clashes in international politics.

Particularly at times of revolution, when new regimes acquire the power to implement their conceptions of justice, immense fears are generated that lead to the **intervention** of one state in the affairs of others, frequently with military force.[11] To protect the new regime from the threat of reversal by the intervention of other countries, the new government itself may attempt to spread the revolution to other countries to avoid isolation. Other countries, faced with such destabilizing threats, may themselves intrude to reverse the revolution. In anticipation of these dynamics, large countries sometimes intervene to preempt revolutions, as the Reagan administration did in El Salvador during the 1980s, when it gave massive assistance to the beleaguered government in the face of a broad insurgency.

Often, as during the Cold War, deeply held conceptions of justice are disparaged as evil or as mere ideologies masking base motives. However, groups do have very deep convictions, often developed over centuries of national histories, about what it means for everyone to receive his due. These different answers to Socrates's question help to shape the deepest values for which men and women fight. Thus, insight into what different groups and their states consider to be justice helps in understanding **conflict** and **cooperation** in international relations.

In addition to power and justice, people and states seek to acquire many other values. One of the most important of these is wealth.

Wealth

The pursuit of wealth in modern life is such a pervasive activity that one might think that wealth is the primary value, if not the only one, that drives human behavior. Whereas justice has been neglected in modern political analysis, wealth as the determining factor of political outcomes has been exaggerated. Economics has been employed as the basic dynamic to explain, among other phenomena, imperialism, the dependency of poorer countries on richer ones, the process of integration taking place in the European Union, and the transformation of the international system from one in which the units seek territorial control to one characterized by a quest for market shares. Some writers have posed corporate and market forces as superseding and displacing states and politics. Full treatment of the relations between economics and politics will be taken up in Chapter 8 on international political economy, but it is necessary here to gain perspective on the place of wealth as a value that helps in understanding international relations.

Wealth in the form of real and movable property and material possessions can be enjoyed for its own sake. In addition, land, labor, and capital can be employed to generate additional wealth. Aside from using it as savings and investment, wealth in the form of money is largely instrumental, to be exchanged for commodities and services. To accumulate possessions and other forms of wealth is a common human aspiration and fundamental value that most people strive for. Groups, too, aspire to accumulate wealth for use in the achievement of their purposes. National wealth is the bedrock of a country's power, although noneconomic assets and intangible considerations also enter into power equations.

The universal quest for wealth implies competition with others in a process of accumulation. Moreover, when particularly scarce goods are at stake, conflict arises as two or more economic competitors desire to possess the same goods. Thus, the value of wealth is a source of competition and conflict in human affairs, both at the individual and private organizational level as well as in international affairs.

Producers of wealth tend to specialize in a **division of labor** and wish to exchange their production for the goods and services offered by others. This condition gives rise to the formation of a market in which producers offer their goods and services to consumers who strive to accumulate wealth. Such trade is facilitated by the use of money, which is fungible and can be exchanged for any goods or services. The market generates greater wealth than would have been produced by self-sufficient workers or groups relying only on their own production. Thus, the value of wealth is transformed into a source of cooperation in human affairs, within both domestic and international economies.

■ ———————————————————————

●●●●●● **Wealth as a Value in International Politics**

- Wealth is a universal motivation, both as an end and a means.
- Accumulation of wealth is the bedrock of power.
- Quest for wealth is a source of competition and conflict.
- Division of labor leads to formation of a market, which engenders cooperation.
- A country's international trade is shaped by its comparative advantage.
- Realists stress competition among states.
- Liberals stress cooperation among states and other actors.

———————————————————————

Thus, both conflict and cooperation are inherent in the pursuit of wealth. **Realists** tend to stress the conflictful aspects involving this value, whereas **liberals** are inclined to emphasize cooperation. Therefore, the ensuing analysis will draw on both liberal and realist views, as appropriate, for gaining insight into international politics and political economy. What is clear is that wealth is a prominent value in human affairs, though not the only one. At places in the analysis, it will become necessary to consider the view that economics provides the fundamental dynamic for politics, a more radical view than the one that shapes this book's analysis and a perspective that lies outside both the realist and liberal approaches. Wealth will be treated as both an end in itself and as instrumental to the achievement of other values.

Security

Another important value in international politics is security, the sense of feeling safe. As a very dangerous place, the world presents us with many threats. A farmer in Bangladesh who ekes out a bare existence on a piece of land without an enforceable legal claim to the property is threatened by other hungry peasants who may covet his land to grow crops to feed their families. Through hard work and vigilance, this farmer may hold on to the patch of soil that he works, only to be driven from it, perhaps even drowned, by a vicious monsoon. In such circumstances, it is difficult to feel safe.

A Brazilian mother living in a *favela* or slum neighborhood in Rio de Janeiro not only has to worry about feeding her children and eluding the criminals who rule the neighborhood and who keep out the police. She also must fear that her children may become either victims or victimizers in drug dealing, robbery, and other criminal activities. Her wealthy compatriot, a prosperous businessman in Sao Paolo, enjoys the security of his home and office, both protected by bodyguards, but he makes every attempt not to stop his car at traffic lights for fear of being robbed.

An American urban teenager, living in one of the most prosperous countries in the world, faces a high risk of being killed by a gun or hooked on drugs in the highest drug-consuming nation in the world. He and his fellow citizens face threats of poverty, disease, lack of health care, AIDS, and so forth. His contemporary in early 1990s Yugoslavia faced the potential of death in a civil war, as did his older brother or sister in El Salvador in the 1980s.

With the exception of those living in the midst of civil wars, people like those mentioned live in political units governed by authorities who rule over orderly and legal arrangements. Governments act to protect their citizens from one another, and they claim a legitimate monopoly on the use of force to uphold their authority. In orderly societies based on systems of justice, with enough wealth to maintain adequate standards of living for their populations, individuals and groups are able to feel reasonably secure, for security rests upon peace, wealth, justice, order, and authority. Underlying and ensuring the existence of all of these components is government, which maintains military **control** over a territory.

In places where these are missing or incomplete, insecurity reigns. The absence of property rights for the Bangladeshi peasant and the failure of the Brazilian police to ensure control over the *favela* translate into fear and insecurity for those who dwell in those places. It is part of the struggle of life to achieve arrangements in which there is security, and that condition of safety has been and is realized in many times and places. Although difficult enough to achieve within established states, security is much harder to reach in international politics, for the components are either weak or missing.

In addition, a security problem arises in international politics as a result of the anarchy that characterizes the relations of states. Anarchy fosters insecurity in two ways, the first of which is called the **security dilemma.**[12] In the absence of any international authority to which it can appeal, each state arms to defend itself. Another state observes this activity, and, suspecting that the first state may harbor aggressive intentions, it decides to build up its arms against a potential threat. In response, the first state increases its buildup, and a spiral of competing arms buildups begins. The second way in which insecurity arises as a result of anarchy is from the deliberate announcement of intentions or the taking of provocative acts that indicate that a state means to expand or to seek some value that is opposed by other states. Such activity is most likely to occur in a situation in which the first state has a grievance or is nursing a sense of injustice, but it might also occur in the context of revolutionary exuberance or overweening leadership ambitions. A country following the second course of trying to change an established situation is called a **revisionist power,** and one defending it is labelled a **status quo power.**

■
• • • • • • Conditions of and Threats to Security

- Security rests on peace, wealth, justice, order, and authority, backed by a government that maintains military control over a territory.
- Two effects of anarchy in international politics, both involving threats of the use of force, are a security dilemma and revisionist foreign policies.

Acute insecurities arise in such situations because they involve force, at first only implicit threats but then the potential for war. Depending on historical circumstances, then, countries may make gigantic preparations for war either to deter it through the implicit threats of their war potential or to be ready to fight it. In the post-World War II period, great amounts of armaments were built in response to the insecurities that arose from the dynamics of both the security dilemma and revisionist foreign policies. The SOVIET UNION followed revisionist policies based on its view of history. Regarding itself as the leader of the forces of historical progress against the capitalist countries headed by the United States, the Soviet Union supported those who aimed for an overturn of the capitalist system in the world. Although not exactly parallel, the United States also practiced a revisionism that aimed to moderate the Soviets' view of themselves and the world. As the Soviet Union consolidated by drawing back from the rest of the world in the second half of the 1980s, insecurities diminished. When in 1989, Soviet President Mikhail Gorbachev made it eminently clear that his country would not use force to keep Communist regimes in power in Eastern Europe, an even greater step to easing insecurities was taken. Following the failed August 1991 coup

against Gorbachev and the final dismantling of the Soviet Union in December of that year, the way was paved for the significant arms reductions agreed to in the June 1992 summit meeting in Washington between Russian President Boris Yeltsin and American President George Bush. Plans had been made for drastic reductions in strategic nuclear weapons earlier, but the 1992 agreement provided for halving the limits of the earlier agreement. Thus, full implementation promised to reduce the total number of strategic nuclear warheads held by the two powers from roughly 22,500 to about 7,000.

It is an interesting irony that the improved security situation in the world in the early 1990s has resulted from the economic weakness and disintegration of the former Soviet Union and a reduction in weaponry, for this period follows a long span of time in which readiness and hostility, arms buildups and deadly strategic planning were the hallmarks of policies aimed at achieving security. As with the other values at stake in international relations, then, security remains importantly in play, but the means of achieving it are not unilinear, and the causal relationships between security and policy are not straightforward and unidirectional.

Although threats to security arise in many circumstances, within families and societies as well as in international politics, the scope of threats widens considerably when large-scale war becomes a possibility. Particularly in the context of the means available for destruction in the modern age, war puts at stake large numbers of human lives and can be devastating to economic assets such as factories, houses, infrastructure, and so forth. The most destructive war in history, World War II, took approximately 50 million lives and destroyed economic assets of some of the belligerents on the order of one-quarter to one-third or more of their productive capacities and housing stocks. Another way of putting the point is that large-scale war is the most destructive and evil of human activities, incurring higher costs than any other.

Because of the destructive potential and scale of suffering that organized, major-power war threatens and the fear that the threat engenders, security often rises to first priority in the scale of values that foreign policy leaders pursue. Moreover, security often is the main impetus for the pursuit of other values, such as the accumulation of wealth and the search for international order, which in turn become instrumental to the quest for security. To illustrate, the Preamble of the Charter of the United Nations has as its first determination, "To save succeeding generations from the scourge of war . . . ," and the first-stated purpose of the organization is, "To maintain international peace and security. . . ."

As the discussion has tried to make clear, many values are involved in international politics, each having its independent existence. On the other hand, certain values sometimes become so compelling that they are given precedence, and others then become at least temporarily instrumental to the achievement of the dominant values. Probably no value other than security so frequently takes on such a primary character. Among those that maintain their own merit but that also can serve as instrumental values is order.

Order

One of the most intriguing book titles in the field is *The Anarchical Society*.[13] Despite the absence of authority, the author claimed, a society functions in international politics, using a range of instruments from diplomacy and balance of power to war to maintain order. Conducting ordinary, predictable relations internationally would be impossible without a modicum of order, for transactions such as trade and travel require safety and predictability. So, too, do diplomatic negotiations and other ongoing interactions—such as managing alliances and coordinating policies on the environment—need some kind of order to be fruitful.

At times, those who challenge an order promote disorder as the antecedent to change. Nevertheless, when they are successful, such proponents of disorder are transformed into upholders of the new order that they put into place. So, order is a universal value in human affairs, including international relations. In addition to contending over which order or whose order is to prevail, political thinkers disagree over the appropriate conceptual place for order in the analysis of international politics. Three identifiable positions on this issue are derived from the views of the writers Thomas Hobbes, Hugo Grotius, and Immanuel Kant.

English philosopher Thomas Hobbes conceived a state of nature that existed before the establishment of government in which life was "nasty, brutish, and short" and characterized by "a war of all against all." Although he devised this view in his explanation of the origins of government, Hobbes extended his analysis to characterize the relations of

states as a similar state of nature. In the Hobbesian view, every state exists in a state of war with every other state. To the extent that international agreements are reached or institutions are created, they are mere conveniences that states use only so long as it is in their respective national interests to do so. When these are inconvenient or objectionable, a state may simply choose to withdraw from an agreement or refuse to support an institution. For example, when NICARAGUA brought a case in the International Court of Justice against the United States for mining its harbors in 1983, the United States opposed both the Nicaraguan claim and the court's assertion of jurisdiction. Following the court's rejection of the American contention that it did not have the right to hear the case and its finding for Nicaragua, the United States simply refused to recognize the jurisdiction of the court in this matter. Later, when the court ruled against it, the United States did not acknowledge any obligation to pay the money that the court awarded to Nicaragua. This occurred despite the fact that the United States had long been an advocate of the court and of international law. Moreover, in combating the taking of AMERICAN HOSTAGES IN IRAN in 1979, the United States rallied international support by emphasizing Iran's violation of international law. In the Hobbesian, or realist, perspective, order is a value that is contended over rather than a condition that can be assumed. Furthermore, realists point out that whatever order does exist is put into place and upheld by the powerful, and they particularly note that this is the case when dominant political actors claim that the interests represented in their order are everyone's. A realist would note that in the contest between Nicaragua and the United States, it was convenient for and in the national interest of Nicaragua to embrace the order offered by the International Court of Justice, even though it had not signed an agreement to do so. On the other hand, our realist would note, this case proved inconvenient and not in the **national interest** of the United States, even though that country had long assured the world of its respect for **international law** and the court.

An alternative perspective derived from Dutch jurist Hugo Grotius emphasizes not the imperfections but the existence and functioning of an international order. In his memoirs, George Kennan related his experience as an American diplomat in Germany when that country declared war on his in 1941. Despite the declaration, Germany adhered to the conventional diplomatic practice of providing safe conduct out of the country for him and other diplomats. Similarly, the United States extended protection to Japanese diplomats after their country attacked Pearl Harbor on December 7, 1941. Such an orderly procedure under established international law demonstrates the workings of an order as claimed by Grotian analysis. Like other orders built by human ingenuity, international order does not work automatically but requires formal and informal institutional arrangements and sometimes enforcement. Thus, in this view, a mechanism such as a balance of power contributes to world order through the opposition of many countries to any other that aspires to dominance. Furthermore, should the power that seeks to dominate not be dissuaded by an array against it, it may go to war, and the opposing alliance needs to fight to restore order.

■
• • • • • • Three Perspectives on Order in International Politics

Realism, derived from Hobbes:
- Order reflects the wishes of the powerful, who adhere to it when it is in their interest and ignore it if inconvenient; anarchy prevails.

Anarchical society, derived from Grotius:
- Agreed-upon order is maintained through diplomacy, balance of power, institutions, and war.

Idealism, derived from Kant:
- Order will be achieved by transformation and maintained by a parliament of republics.

In the third perspective on order, derived from German philosopher Immanuel Kant, the anarchical character of international relations needs to be transformed, with order based upon a principle different from anarchy. Kant believed that a world parliament of republican countries could be constructed. As a function of their democratic political systems, they would not go to war with one another, and this would be the basis for appropriating the authority that would allow a world legislature to pass laws. Those laws would then be followed voluntarily by the nations of the world. Kant's modern-day disciple, Michael Doyle, stresses the basic point that liberal democratic countries do not go to war against one another.[14]

Others have pushed the idea of transforming the international order even further. Clarence Streit promoted the idea of an Atlantic union of North American and European states.[15] Unfortunately, his

idea lost credence when World War I broke out shortly after his book came out. As World War II was coming to an end, Emery Reves published a book calling for the **transformation** of international politics, for the end of anarchy.[16] As the Cold War developed, another project advocated transformation through world law.[17] In recent years, a broad literature that is the successor to the transformational tradition has accumulated. Holsti brings much of this literature together for criticism under the rubric of "World Order Modeling Project."[18]

This view explicitly rejects the realist premise that the essential units in the international system are states. Additionally, many modern transformation writers argue that already there are processes at work that are forming a new global order. As such, they hold that the appropriate unit of analysis is the earth as a whole, and they challenge the traditional problematic of international politics as too narrow. In this view, all of the broad social concerns across the globe need to be treated as the problematic: war, social justice, protection of the environment, and so forth. The problem of the world is not simply that of recognizing or creating an order that would smooth and pacify the relations among people organized into separate political units called states but rather the formation and perfection of a global unit. It is a conception from the age of astronauts: we live on "spaceship earth."

These deep divisions on the question of order imply that other profound values are at work. Everyone values order, but orders are based upon fundamental principles and values. For example, many of those who adopt a global perspective and favor a world unit in preference to a multiplicity of state units assume that the world would be organized on principles that they consider to be just. However, a single global political unit might very well be dominated by the democratic principle that majorities rule. Since the majority of the world's population is poor and downtrodden, the global rulers might conceivably adopt legislation ruinous to the economies and well-being of the rich countries. It is not inconceivable that repression and domination would be the lot of the formerly strong and rich.

In contrast, realists believe that such values as social justice, freedom, equality, prosperity, and so forth are more likely to be realized within the context of state units. For states that have achieved prosperity through their efforts, however, the resulting privileges are something to be protected and cherished, even fought for. Furthermore, realists fear that a global system would be a totalitarian one, a gigantic government with massive powers for repression.

It is not clear that there is analytical utility in treating order separately from other values. Any consideration of order needs to be placed in the context of understanding what other values may be embodied in particular orders. On the other hand, the diverse literature and profound disagreements testify to the importance of the value of order. Unlike power and wealth, though, order is not an instrumental value, one that provides a means for the achievement of other values. Instead, it embraces other values in institutions and processes. Moreover, existing orders primarily reflect the values of the powerful and dominant groups in a particular time and place. In defending and justifying an order, the powerful most frequently claim that the order embodies universal values and the preferences of everyone. To the extent that the interests of those living within the order are not in harmony—and they seldom are—there will be conflicts between those cherishing the values embodied in the extant order and those championing competing values.

Peace

The scourge of war throughout human history has made peace an important value. As modern technology has changed the face of war, this value has gained particular prominence in the twentieth century. In the most renowned textbook on international politics in the post-World War II period, Morgenthau devoted fully half of it to the problem of peace.[19] It was not uncommon following the most devastating of history's wars to claim that peace was *the* problem of the twentieth century.

Whereas in most earlier times war was regarded as an almost natural and inevitable evil, a good deal of thinking in the past hundred years or so has sought to abolish or control it. An exception was the fascist extolling of war because it provided the occasion for the display of heroic virtues. Many of the attempts to build international organizations grow out of theories of war and the construction of solutions. A belief has grown about the **indivisibility of peace,** a conviction that war anywhere threatens everyone in the world. Central to the League of Nations and the United Nations is the doctrine of **collective security,** an arrangement to maintain international peace.

Thinking about peace is rooted in understanding the causes of war. For millennia, writers have offered a great many ideas, many of which are contradictory. Kenneth Waltz has arranged the literature of Western political philosophy that comments on war by placing the alleged causes of war in three categories, or **images.**[20] First, many writers assign the causes of war to human nature. That is, humans are greedy or aggressive or evil, and these characteristics lead to war. Others tend to emphasize social and political arrangements. Woodrow Wilson thought that despotic leaders caused wars and that, if only they could live in democratic political systems, people would not choose war but rather would opt for peace. To the contrary, but falling into the same image, Lenin believed that wars are caused by capitalist systems. Bring on the socialist revolution, and wars would not occur. To the third image belong those writers who think that the system of states, based as it is on the principle of anarchy, is the fundamental cause of war.

■ •••••• Causes of War and Conditions of Peace

- Three "images" of causes of war:
  - Nature of humans (wars caused by greed, aggressiveness, etc.)
  - Character of state (wars caused by authoritarian states, capitalist states, nondemocratic states)
  - International system (wars caused by anarchy)
- Indivisibility of peace
- Collective security
- Peace as a condition for the achievement of other values, such as accumulation of wealth, order, etc.

The concern with and analysis of war extend back centuries. But a conception that is new to our era is that of the indivisibility of peace. This notion means that a war that breaks out anywhere in the world threatens everyone, and it implies that one cannot remain isolated. On this premise, collective security embodies an arrangement whereby the states of the world would come to the aid of a victim in case of aggression against it by another state by bringing overwhelming force to bear against the aggressor state. War would be controlled under this scheme, first, by deterrence. If a country is contemplating an attack against another, it must first calculate the consequences of the rest of the world opposing its action. Should the potential aggressor miscalculate, then the overwhelming force of the world community could be brought to bear in a police action that would quickly end the aggression. Note that collective security carries several interesting implications. First, war is illegal in that it is an offense against the world community; it is not simply an action against another state. Second, aggressors and victims can easily be identified and distinguished. Third, other countries are dedicated to peace as a first priority, standing above the value of alliances, particular national interests, and so on. Finally, in order to array overwhelming force against one state, no state can be a superpower, for a forceful action against a superpower would be a war, not the imposition of the world community's will on an outlaw state.

All of these premises and implications are readily challenged. Although it is true that the two world wars of the twentieth century involved or threatened the entire world, many other wars have proved to be quite easily cordoned off, thus providing evidence that peace is not indivisible. Even quite large wars like the French and American wars in Vietnam pitted particular enemies against each other without threatening to draw in others. Smaller wars like those in the former Soviet Union in the early 1990s and the ones associated with the breakup of Yugoslavia have little impact on the rest of the world. At the same time, diplomats work very hard to find solutions and to ameliorate the hardship and suffering associated with such wars. They do so partly moved by a belief in the indivisibility of peace and partly to alleviate suffering. In the latter endeavors, they are often joined by private relief agencies and monitoring groups dedicated to liberal principles of human rights.

Not only is peace a value in its own right, but it is also instrumental to other values. Little else can be achieved during a war, so order and justice, for example, require conditions of peace for their accomplishment. More than others, the production of wealth in the long run relies on peace. As a matter of fact, the growth of international trade and commerce has contributed strength to the emphasis on peace in the twentieth century.

Disinterested parties are more likely to give peace priority in their systems of values, for committed parties show their willingness to fight for other values. Belligerents, too, value peace but not above other things they hold dear, such as autonomy or domination or wealth. People often feel very intensely about certain values, whereas the value of peace is not one that engenders strong emotions.

Community

Human beings are political and social creatures who live in groups and gain their identities and their values from those groups. As members, they look out for others in the group, and they cherish the group for what it gives to them. Thus, groups and communities become values that are contended over. People fight for the autonomy of their communities and against the domination of their communities by others.

One of the difficulties of including **community** as a value in the analysis is that there is no set boundary to a community. It may consist of a small linguistic and cultural group in the mountains of Guatemala that preserves its traditions in the context of a larger state. On the other hand, it may be coterminous with a state, such as Poland. To take yet another example, some may aspire to create a larger community than any now in existence, such as a European Union or an African community.

A community may want no more than to participate in a larger political system while retaining its cultural autonomy. Thus, a tiny country like Singapore retains its customs and political system while it participates in a global economy. On the other hand, Iran since 1979 has sought to put in place a very different culture based upon religious principles that rejects the market economy and secular culture.

In struggling over the value of community, issues of boundaries and the relations of any particular community with larger and smaller communities enter the arena. There is no real theory that helps us to analyze the problem, but we see evidence of contention over the value of community all around us. As Europe, particularly Southeastern Europe, goes through the throes of community definition, economic restructuring, ethnic conflict, and so forth, much empirical material is provided for trying to understand the ways in which conflicts over this value proceed.

Very often, the problem may be framed as a tension between **pluralism** and **centralization**.[21] Centralized government offers efficiency, whereas consent often relies on local autonomy. Certain countries have continued to wrestle with this problem with mixed success. For example, Spain has not yet thoroughly achieved a definition of Spanish nationalism that would integrate the entire society, and the difficulty of doing this is compounded by local autonomy movements, for example in the Basque region. Neither have Canadians been able completely to resolve the challenge to central authority and the concept of a Canadian nation posed by Quebec separatists. In some cases, demands for local autonomy within a state are transformed into quests for secession and complete independence. From 1967 to 1970, Nigeria suffered a devastating civil war as Biafra fought for its independence as a separate state.

■
• • • • • • Community: A Value with Many Principles

- People live in groups from which they derive their identities and values.
- The principles on which communities are founded vary, and relations of any particular community with larger and smaller communities always form part of its definition.
- Nationalism has been the predominant vehicle of community identification for over two hundred years.
- With the lifting of the suppression that was characteristic during the Cold War, increasing demands for ethnic and linguistic identity along with other principles of community have become prominent.

During the Cold War, the international structure had the effect of suppressing ethnic identification within the European countries. Since 1989, however, **ethnicity** has become a rallying point for community formation, in contrast to nationalist and ideological associations. In the breakup of Yugoslavia into ethnically based states and the Bosnian Serb policy of "ethnic cleansing"—the killing and removal of non-Serbs from territories sought or conquered by Serbs—is a horrifying example of the great human cost of shaping politics on the principle of ethnicity. Nevertheless, ethnicity remains a powerful magnet for community identification. Its major limitations are its implicit intolerance for others and its lack of conception of how to conduct relations with other communities.

Nationalism was the predominant vehicle of community identification over the course of nearly two centuries, from the end of the eighteenth century to near the end of the twentieth century. A **nation,** in Ernest Renan's still valid conception, is a group of people who share a sense of common heritage and the will to shape a common destiny. Although language, religion, race, geographical propinquity, and other shared characteristics may contribute to the sense of nationhood, none is essential. Because the working out of a common destiny is achieved most effectively through the mechanism of the state, the nation-state became the ideal, or frequently the reality, during these centuries. With the dissipation of the Cold War, however, more and more people are rethinking their community identities.

This rethinking is apparent in Eastern Europe, but more subtle forms are taking place in more set-tled locales. For example, in the context of such new circumstances as a large Islamic immigrant population, the French people are agonizing about what it means to be French. That meaning, for example, has traditionally included Catholicism. Is it possible, in a new world, that a French nation can encompass both Catholicism and Islam?[22] Within the United States, a wave of **multiculturalism** sentiment has washed against a traditional conception of Americanism, and some observers believe that this wave has the capacity to erode the rock of American unity.[23] In Germany, where identification as a member of the national community has traditionally been determined by blood and strengthened by language, many wish to admit to the community immigrants of other races and traditions, and in some places, a resurgence of local dialects challenges the domination of the German language.

These complexities associated with the value of community suggest that, despite its universal quality, a great amount of contention takes place in particular circumstances over just how to shape specific communities. Not only does conflict occur among the parties fighting over nation versus ethnic group, centralized efficiency versus consent through autonomy, and so forth, but also disinterested parties are often drawn into such conflicts. External intervention is most likely to occur when such disputes threaten to spill over state boundaries or when they give rise to such effects as massive migration of suffering refugees. In addition, the brutality of such **human rights abuses** as those inflicted by Serbs against Muslims in Bosnia-Herzegovina and by Croatians against Serbs in Croatia draws the attention of groups in democratic countries who call for intervention to bring an end to murderous and other cruel behaviors.

These values that have been surveyed comprise the most visible and significant values that continue to be at stake in international politics. Nevertheless, other values also enter into contention and need to be considered in the analysis.

Other Values

Among other important values that statesmen pursue, **prestige** and **respect** rank high. Prestige is the reputation that one has among others, and respect is the esteem in which others hold one. For large, powerful countries, prestige and respect enable them to exercise influence at a cost lower than they would need to pay without these components of soft power.

A power with a reputation for fulfilling its commitments and keeping its word will be listened to by others without having to persuade, bribe, or bludgeon them. During the Cold War, for example, the United States often was able to gain the support of allies simply by virtue of the esteem in which it was held.

Weaker countries also strive to preserve their prestige to acquire other values. For example, despite a very high economic cost to its workers, Mexico strove mightily during the 1980s to service its huge debt, which was owed to foreign banks and other governments. By maintaining its reputation as a country that took its international financial obligations seriously, Mexico was able to maintain an adequate flow of foreign funds to allow its economy to endure the severe depression that it passed through in what was known in Latin America as "the lost decade."

Personal ambition is a value in international affairs that was more apparent in an age of kings when struggles were more the extension of a monarch's aspirations than the result of national interests. Nevertheless, even in the age of democracies in which we live, personal ambition can serve as a value that shapes foreign policy, although it less frequently is a predominant value. For instance, in the 1992 U.S. presidential election campaign, President Bush authorized arms sales to Saudi Arabia and Taiwan in order to win votes. In this case, a democratic leader put his personal ambition above such other values as a national interest in slowing down the spread of modern arms and of honoring an American promise to China not to sell the most modern equipment to Taiwan.[24]

From time to time, considerations of domestic politics become compelling values that drive important foreign policy activities. For example, history offers many illustrations of elites, unable to manage problems at home, turning the attention of their people to conflict abroad. In 1982, the military rulers of Argentina, faced with rising opposition and severe economic problems, decided to resolve the country's dispute with Great Britain over the Falklands Islands by military action, expecting that a military triumph would distract the nation from its internal woes. However, their adversary was led by a determined prime minister, Margaret Thatcher, who—in the face of her own declining political fortunes at home—led Britain's armed forces to a victory over the Argentineans.

Sometimes governments, especially revolutionary ones, derive their legitimacy from a broadly based **ideology,** and they regard the triumph of that ideology in their countries as a vindication of its truthfulness, which provides an impetus to spread it to other countries. This was the case following the November 1917 revolution in Russia, in which the promotion of communism abroad became the policy of successive governments of the Soviet Union. More recently, the Cuban government, under its leader Fidel Castro, promoted revolution in a number of Latin American countries in the 1960s.

Another way in which domestic values can drive foreign policy activities is through the operation of **liberal democracies** that aspire to promote the liberal values of equality, freedom, human rights, and democracy. Such values become foreign policy considerations in two distinct ways. First, groups within democratic polities may petition their own government to extend protection to foreign groups with which they sympathize. Certain ethnic groups in the United States, the Greeks and the Poles for example, have on occasion sought to have the U.S. government respond to a crisis in Poland or Greece, for instance, to defend liberal values.

A second way in which such liberal values have become important considerations in international affairs is through a **hegemonic** mechanism, when liberal democracies are the most powerful states in the international system. Such states promote an international order that is based on the values embedded in their polities.

Another value that in the late twentieth century has increasingly become prominent in international politics is **health.** Many people's consciousness of health considerations in foreign affairs was raised in the 1950s as atmospheric nuclear testing was shown to carry with it severe dangers through contamination of the food chain. In following years, the health hazards of air and water pollution became important considerations in public policy, both in many countries and as an issue on the agenda of world politics. In Western Europe, "green" parties came on the political scene, and in North America, a significant environmental movement became increasingly prominent. The United Nations held conferences on the environment and development in Stockholm in 1972 and in Rio de Janeiro in 1992. Growing out of the first conference was a new international organization charged with concern for the issues of environment and development.

Knowledge has always been an important value in international relations. Intelligence about other countries, especially adversaries, forms the basis on which officials assess intentions and capabilities as a prelude to deciding on their own actions. As technology has become increasingly complex and determinative in modern economies, the quest for knowledge has gained in importance as a value that is instrumental to the central values of power and wealth.

●●●●● **Other Values**

- Prestige and respect
- Personal ambition
- Domestic politics:
  - deflection of attention from domestic problems
  - spread of ideology
  - liberal politics of interest groups and of hegemony
- Health and environment
- Knowledge
- Clash of cultures

Sometimes, clashes over entire systems of values arise in international politics. Historically, the Islamic attack on Europe and the counterattack in the Crusades provide clear examples of this kind of conflict. Other encounters of vastly different civilizations—the European conquest of the Western Hemisphere and the opening of Japan are examples—illustrate that, however uncommon such cultural clashes are, they are recurrent. In the contemporary world, the most apparent manifestation of this sort of deep and wide divergence of values is that between devout and fundamentalist Islamic culture and the Western secularism that it rejects.[25]

This survey of values germane to international politics may not be complete, for states and those who act on the international stage may quest for other values as well. Nevertheless, the list includes the most important values in play in the game of international politics, and it is long enough to make the point that many different values are at stake in international relations. On limited occasions, a single value may come to dominate an issue or conflict among states, but in this analysis, the values over which people contend in international politics will not be reduced to a single value consideration as an analytical device. Some writers do posit that security or power always is the dominating value that drives foreign policy and international politics, but this approach overlooks very important realities that need to be accounted for in a general explanation of international politics.

Values and the Problematic of International Politics

None of the values surveyed in this chapter is exclusive to international relations. Human beings seek power, justice, wealth, security, order, peace, community, and other values in their lives as individuals, as members of families and private organizations, and as citizens of states. Moreover, they strive for values in many different avenues and through many processes and institutions. However many ways these values remain in contention, they are at play in international politics, which embodies concrete actions, structures, and processes in which values provide the goals.

Some of these values, like equality and freedom, apply to both individuals and groups. Even though they more commonly enter into political conflict within states, they also sometimes are germane to international politics. For example, smaller and weaker states struggle at least for recognition as legal equals with larger, stronger states.

Other values such as human rights logically are applicable only to individuals, though even these values are subject to international negotiation, as in the Universal Declaration of Human Rights, a resolution passed by the United Nations General Assembly in 1948. Additionally, both states and nongovernmental groups advocate the protection of human rights, and they monitor governments' violations of the rights of their own citizens.

The values that are most germane to international politics have been discussed in this chapter. Each of them is brought into our problematic insofar as it bears on these concepts and questions: power, justice, causes of war, conditions of peace, anarchy, states, state diffusion, state formation, and maintenance of position in the international system.

The kind of analysis that this book has undertaken has sometimes been challenged. For example, the transformational view of order claims that a global unit is now in the process of forming. This view, however, substitutes the value held by the analyst for the empirical reality.

It is surely true that analysts hold their own values, being in part political actors. At the same time, understanding and commitment to a search for truth are also values that many analysts hold. Nevertheless, every analyst lives in a particular era and specific place in which he forms his value preferences. Both he and his readers should make every effort to be clear about the values at work in his analysis.

• IMPORTANT TERMS

aggregation	international law
autonomy	intervention
centralization	just war
collective security	knowledge
community	liberal democracy
conflict	liberals
control	multiculturalism
cooperation	nation
disaggregation	national interest
division of labor	nationalism
ethnicity	personal ambition
fungibility	pluralism
hard power	prestige
health	realists
hegemony	respect
human rights abuses	revisionist power
ideology	security dilemma
images	soft power
indivisibility of	status quo
peace	transformation

• STUDY QUESTIONS

1. Why do leaders sometimes obscure their values? Is there ever a positive justification for doing so?

2. Which values are solely ends in themselves, and which also may be instrumental to the achievement of others? Do these two characteristics make it easier or more difficult to understand the values at stake in international politics?

3. What are the major components of power? Is it more useful to aggregate or disaggregate power?

4. Is power less fungible than wealth? What difference does your answer make for the analysis of international politics?

5. What difference does one's position in political arrangements make in one's conception of justice?

6. What are the three main criteria of a just war?

7. In what ways do conceptions of justice within states differ from those in international politics?

8. To what extent does the universal quest for wealth engender conflict, and in what ways does it lead to cooperation?

9. How does the condition of anarchy in international politics promote insecurity?

10. In what ways do views about order derived from Hobbes, Grotius, and Kant vary? Which view is more nearly correct?

11. Do you believe that peace is divisible? What difference does your answer imply for foreign policy?

12. Does it seem to you that international politics might better be understood by treating a single value, such as power or security, as dominant over other values? Why or why not?

• ENDNOTES

1. Cox, "Social Forces, States and World Orders," p. 210.
2. Robert A. Dahl, "The Concept of Power," *Behavioral Science* 2 (July 1957): 202–3.
3. Joseph S. Nye, Jr., "Soft Power," *Foreign Policy* 80 (Fall 1990): 168.
4. John M. Rothbeg, Jr., *Defining Power: Influence and Force in the Contemporary International System* (New York: St. Martin's Press, 1993), p. 44.
5. Waltz, *Theory of International Politics*, pp. 194–95.
6. See Michael Walzer, *Just and Unjust Wars: A Moral Argument with Historical Illustrations* (New York: Basic Books, 1977).
7. The literature on American policy in Vietnam is broad. For examples, see David Halberstam, *The Making of a Quagmire* (New York: Random House, 1965); Frances Fitzgerald, *Fire in the Lake* (Boston: Atlantic-Little, Brown, 1972); and Norman Podhoretz, *Why We Were in Vietnam* (New York: Simon & Schuster, 1982).
8. United States Catholic Bishops' pastoral letter, *The Challenge of Peace: God's Promise and Our Response* (Catholic Church: National Conference of Catholic Bishops, 1983). See also *Catholics and Nuclear War: A Commentary on the Challenge of Peace, the U.S. Catholic Bishops' Pastoral Letter on War and Peace*, ed. by Philip J. Murnion (New York: Crossroad, 1983).
9. The Harvard Nuclear Study Group: Albert Carnesale, Paul Doty, Stanley Hoffmann, Samuel P. Huntington, Joseph S. Nye, Jr., and Scott D. Sagan, *Living with Nuclear Weapons* (Toronto: Bantam Books, 1983).
10. Stephen D. Krasner, *Structural Conflict: The Third World against Global Liberalism* (Berkeley: University of California Press, 1985).
11. Stephen M. Walt, "Revolution and War," *World Politics* 44 (April 1992): 321–68.
12. The security dilemma was first described by John Herz, "Idealist Internationalism and the Security Dilemma," *World Politics* 2 (January 1950): 157–80, and has been elaborated more fully by Robert Jervis, *Perception and Misperception in International Relations* (Princeton, N.J.: Princeton University Press, 1976), and "Cooperation under the Security Dilemma," *World Politics* 30 (January 1978): 186–214.
13. Hedley Bull, *The Anarchical Society* (London: Macmillan, 1977).
14. See Michael Doyle, "Kant, Liberal Legacies and Foreign Affairs," *Philosophy and Public Affairs* (Summer/Fall 1983): 205–35, 323–35; and "Liberalism and World Politics,"

American Political Science Review 80 (December 1986): 1151–69.

15. Clarence K. Streit, *Union Now: A Proposal for a Federal Union of the Democracies of the North Atlantic* (New York: Harper & Brothers, 1939).

16. Emery Reves, *The Anatomy of Peace* (New York: Harper & Brothers, 1945).

17. Grenville Clark and Louis B. Sohn, *World Peace through World Law,* 3d ed. (Cambridge, Mass.: Harvard University Press, 1966).

18. This point of view and much of the literature is criticized by K. J. Holsti in Chapter 3 of his *The Dividing Discipline* (London: Allen & Unwin, 1985).

19. Morgenthau, *Politics among Nations,* 5th ed.

20. Kenneth N. Waltz, *Man, the State, and War: A Theoretical Analysis* (New York: Columbia University Press, 1959).

21. See *International Political Science Review* 10 (July 1989), which is devoted to the theme of pluralism, regionalism, and nationalism, especially Philip Mawhood, "State Formation in Tropical Africa," 239–50.

22. See William Safran, "State, Nation, National Identity, and Citizenship: France As a Test Case," *International Political Science Review* 12 (July 1991): 219–38.

23. Arthur M. Schlesinger, Jr., *The Disuniting of America: Reflections on a Multicultural Society* (New York: W. W. Norton & Company, 1992).

24. During the 1992 campaign, Bush announced that Taiwan would pay $4 billion for 150 F-16 fighters built by General Dynamics Corporation and that Saudi Arabia would spend $5 billion for 72 F-15 jets built by McDonnell-Douglas Aircraft Company. In justifying the sales, the president stressed jobs.

25. Samuel P. Huntington has extended this argument to project civilization as the most important fault line in international politics. See his, "The Clash of Civilizations?" *Foreign Affairs* 72 (Summer 1993): 22–49.

CHAPTER 3

Approaches to Analysis of International Politics

Certain crude metaphors echo distinctive approaches to the analysis of international politics. To conceive the world as a set of billiard balls suggests the ways of thinking of realists. Conceptualizing the world as a set of webs moves more toward the approach used by liberals.

Billiard balls bump into one another, and their interactions cause them to move in different directions. But one never has any impact on the nature or internal composition of another. Unit boundaries are never penetrated. Contacts between units tend to be exclusively official. There is a clear distinction between the internal construction of the units and the arrangement of their relations.

In contrast, webs consist of strands that tie components together across boundaries. Tension on one strand reverberates throughout and causes changes not just in relationships but in the internal composition of the connected parts. Strands running from one state to another may be official or unofficial. No evident distinction can be drawn between the arrangements of internal and external relations.

This chapter describes the two dominant approaches to the study of international politics—realism and liberalism—as well as other approaches, and it assesses their advantages and weaknesses.

Introduction

The complexity of international relations has ensured that different people approach the subject matter in diverse ways. The endless problems and myriad twists and turns of politics offer open-ended opportunities for definition and analysis. Nevertheless, a limited set of approaches has commanded the following of those who work in the field. In the sense that communities of scholars work within the context of specific theories and approaches to the subject matter, there is a science. At the same time, continuing differences of opinion over how to approach the same basic questions means that no consensus unites an entire community of scholars.

Actors and Observers

One source of different viewpoints stems from the difference between **actors** and **observers.** An actor is a person who participates in international politics. For example, prime ministers, foreign ministers, diplomats, and other officials who make and carry out foreign policy decisions are actors. So, too, are officials in international organizations such as the Commission of the European Union, the United Nations, or the International Monetary Fund. Other actors might include activists in groups that try to influence foreign policy in their respective countries, as well as those who participate in groups such as Amnesty International that operate in many countries. Revolutionaries who try to overturn their government are also actors, particularly as they make contacts with and receive advice and material assistance from other countries. These are the people who actually "do" foreign policy and international politics.

Many of these actors, though not all, are also observers. Faced with concrete problems, challenges, and opportunities, they are compelled to figure out policies and actions to cope with those occasions for decision. Sometimes they disseminate their analyses through speeches, memoranda, and more formal writings such as memoirs. Some of them go beyond the relating of events and concrete decisions to conceptualize on a broader basis. At that point, such actors become analysts as well.

However, many writers and analysts are nothing but observers, never becoming actors. Rather than "doing" international politics, they simply "watch" the behavior of actors. Observers are more inclined to conceptualize, compare, generalize, and try to develop theoretical approaches to the subject. Just as some actors become also observers, so do some observers become actors, if not permanently, then at least on occasion. For example, a professor from, say, Harvard University who is also a Republican may work on the staff of the National Security Council in the White House for two years during the term of a Republican president and then return to his teaching duties.

Although actors may employ certain concepts and theories in their work, they are more inclined to think in categories other than those used by analytic observers. Their work requires them to look out for the interests of their country, their organization, or their cause. Actors are much less concerned with explaining political behavior in general. Thus, most of the approaches that are described in this chapter are those used by observers whose main work is to explain the actions of actors.

An observer and an actor each has advantages and disadvantages that she brings to understanding international relations. Actors deal with concrete situations and facts. They face tough decisions and bear important responsibilities, often for the fate of many people. For them, politics is not abstraction or theory; it involves dollars and cents, sometimes life or death, independence or submission to others. Such harsh realities in the experience of actors give them a grasp of foreign affairs that is extraordinarily difficult for an inexperienced observer to understand in a practical way. On the other hand, actors suffer disabilities, for their focus on concrete problems may

interfere with their gaining insight into larger questions and patterns of behavior. Especially, it is difficult for a decision maker responsible for her country to grasp the objective merits of her own and her opponent's aspirations. Generally, actors are hard-pressed to perceive a longer-term view that may offer deeper understanding than they are able to gain when they are immersed in events. In addition, pressures of time and other responsibilities interfere with gathering complete information about events as they are occurring.

Observers, in contrast, enjoy the luxury of time and distance from their subject matter. Particularly as documentation becomes available, they can gain a virtually omniscient view of events that enables them to understand an episode in its entirety. More important, comparative analysis of many events helps observers to generalize about patterns of behavior rather than simply describing discrete episodes. Above all, observers can develop theoretical explanations for patterns of behavior.

These advantages for observers are matched by disadvantages. In their wish to generalize, observers may lose touch with practical affairs and do analysis that does not provide insight into or explanation for events. Just as the actor's analysis may be driven by her national or group preferences, so may the observer's personal, national, or group biases or value preferences skew her analysis.

For both actors and observers, there are tests of their analyses. An actor's ability to size up a situation gets tested in the application of policies that emerge from the analysis. Observers present their work to colleagues and publish it. When many other workers in the field are persuaded of the soundness of the analysis, they teach it in their classes and build their own research upon it. In both kinds of tests, ineffectiveness and nonsense tend to get weeded out.

Strategies of Analysis: Theory and Policy

Both actors and observers carry out **policy analysis** as they investigate the concrete problems and issues germane to the conduct of affairs. In this kind of analysis, the problems to be examined are defined by governments and other actors as well as by the circumstances and events that occur at particular times and in certain situations. To confront a challenge, seize an opportunity, or pursue an aspiration, actors need to devise policies designed to cope with the situation at hand, and they turn to policy analysts for assistance. Often, too, policy analysts proffer their ideas without being asked.

For policy analysts, whether in governments and other organizations actively involved in international affairs or in university or research centers, a prime criterion applied to their work is its **policy relevance.** Moreover, policy research tends to be committed to an institutional or partisan position, for policies are designed to be implemented by governments or other entities. This does not mean that a policy analyst necessarily follows the predispositions of a current government: her intention may be to bring about a change in her government's policy. Thus, an American or a Japanese analyst in a research institute may advocate a shift in policy away from the hostility that sometimes characterizes official policy. At the same time, it is unlikely that a conservative viewpoint will emerge from a liberal institution or that an American policy initiative will be produced by a Brazilian university professor.

In contrast, some analysts maintain a certain distance from policy questions and seek, instead, to build **theoretical, scientific knowledge.** While certain actors might aspire to theory building, such analysts are more likely found in universities. Not only do those analysts with a theoretical bent seek to describe general patterns of behavior, but they also try to find explanations for why those patterns occur. Instead of policy relevance, their criteria for judging their work are **elegance, parsimony, generalizability,** and **heuristic value.**

Elegance refers to scientific precision and simplicity and involves an aesthetic, for an elegant theory possesses beauty. Parsimony is the employment of the fewest explanatory factors that the subject matter allows. It is, for example, parsimonious to explain imperialism as a stage of capitalism with the single differentiating characteristic of the export of capital. In contrast, a nonparsimonious analyst might invoke a variety of factors such as a will to dominate, the search for raw materials and markets, adventurism, security, religious drive, and so on. Generalizability is the quality of making statements that cover many different events, circumstances, and episodes. A declaration that states tend to balance rather than to bandwagon—that is, that they oppose any state that aspires to domination rather than joining with it—is a general statement. It applies across centuries and continents, different political leaders and arrangements, and different economic and technological stages. The last criterion applied by theorists to their

work is its heuristic value, the quality that generates new questions and opens new lines of inquiry, that leads to the enrichment of knowledge.

Levels of Analysis

In their quest for theory in international politics, many analysts take care to draw distinctions among **levels of analysis.** Most important for clear analysis is that a distinction be drawn between the levels of **system** and **unit,** or wholes and parts. One reason for separating these levels is that purely descriptive statements that apply at one level do not apply at another.[1] For example, in describing the international system, one can refer to a balance of power among leading states. However, such a reference would be nonsensical in discussing the states themselves, for a balance of power is a positional relationship of states with one another; altogether different descriptive statements would be made about specific states.

An analogy is the distinction between forests and trees. One can describe a forest as a mixture of coniferous and deciduous trees, but it would be nonsensical to refer to a single tree in the same way, for most trees fall into one or the other category. Just as it is possible, as the old saying goes, not to see the forest for the trees, it is possible not to perceive the international system for the actors in it.

A second reason for making the distinction between levels of analysis is to clarify **causal relationships.**[2] In international politics, outcomes are often different from what anyone intended. For example, in the aftermath of World War II there emerged an international system with only two superpowers, the United States and the Soviet Union, replacing a system that had included eight major powers—Britain, France, Germany, Italy, China, and Japan, plus the two already mentioned. None of the powers intended such an outcome, certainly not Germany, which had sought to dominate all of Europe, and certainly not Britain, which did not intend to lose its rank as a leading power. Neither the United States nor the Soviet Union had sought the war, and neither aspired to lead the major alliances of the postwar period. Thus, one cannot find a cause for the arrangements in the world at the state level. That cause or those causes lie at the system level, making it crucial to conceptualize the system in such a way as to understand what was at work, a task taken up in the next chapter.

A third reason for insisting on a levels-of-analysis distinction is that the development of a theory often requires making simplifying, sometimes false, **assumptions** about other levels. For example, a theory of balance of power, which helps to explain the operation of international politics at the system level, provides a very useful explanation of behavior in that isolated domain. To achieve such a theory, however, requires the simplifying and false assumption that the units in the system are similar in every way except their power. It is patently obvious that countries are very dissimilar. They vary in their linguistic and ethnic makeup, their cultures, their political and economic systems and histories, to name just a few of the components of variation. These variations are obvious in such examples as Canada, Argentina, Kenya, Pakistan, Hungary, Belgium, and Philippines. By assuming that they are similar, an analyst flies in the face of empirical reality, but doing so is useful in constructing a theoretical explanation.

At the same time, an analyst would set aside the false assumption about states if she wished to study foreign policy rather than the operation of the international system. At the state level, she would examine the differences as well as the similarities, doing a comparative analysis with the aim of achieving generalizations about state behavior.

In addition to this primary distinction between the system and state levels of analysis, some analysts make further distinctions between the state, the group, and the individual. Some of the same considerations apply with these distinctions as were pertinent in the case of the primary distinction. For example, there is a condition in psychology called schizophrenia in which an individual mentally separates herself from her surroundings in such a way as to appear to have a personality not connected with her environment. Having diagnosed schizophrenia, a psychiatrist can prescribe a course of treatment that may alleviate the symptoms and allow the individual to function in the world, sharing the same understandings of reality as others have. It would be quite inappropriate to apply such a category to a state, for example, which has an entirely different composition from a person. It would make no sense to designate a state as schizophrenic and try to prescribe treatment as the psychiatrist does to her patient.

The most rigorous separation of levels of analysis is employed by those using the approach called structural realism, of whom Kenneth Waltz is the outstanding spokesman.[3] Waltz isolated a structure that constrains the behavior of states. He did so by setting aside everything that pertains to the unit level of analysis and identifying that which characterizes the system structure. The structure includes just two components: the ordering principle of anarchy and a distribution of capabilities across the units. This spare theory will be elaborated in the next chapter.

With these three distinctions in mind—actor/observer, theory/policy, and state/system—we can delve into the major approaches to the analysis of international politics. Already alluded to in the preceding chapters, realism and liberalism comprise the two main traditional approaches to analysis of international politics. The tension between them arises from their distinctive philosophical postures toward several fundamental questions bearing on international politics.

Realism and Liberalism

Until recently, the two parts of the tradition of international politics were referred to as realism and idealism, or, in the words of E. H. Carr, realism and utopianism, but the modern rendering of the latter is liberalism. Liberals tend to promote a vision that emanates from a British and American tradition of belief in a harmony of interest, as expounded by Adam Smith.[4] In this view, the common good and morality are served by each individual's pursuit of her own interests. At the international level, peace and stability are served by the self-determination of nations. That is, there is a fundamental assumption that no genuine clash of interests can occur, except between tyrants and ordinary people. Idealists emphasize international organization and law, cooperation, and the construction of a more perfect world. Liberals also hold a deep belief in democracy and the power of public opinion supporting a harmony of interests internationally.

Realists approach the world rather differently. Instead of stressing harmony, realists emphasize conflicts of interests. They give more attention to experience of the past and assign great weight to the importance of power. More attention is devoted to states as aggregates of power and less to the force of public opinion. As put by the leading textbook writer of the post-World War II period, realism takes profound issue with a "legalistic-moralistic approach" to international politics.[5]

Drawing on Carr, one can outline the basic differences between these two traditional approaches.

Realism emphasizes power. In observing the world, realists see that social groupings, laws, and order are determined by power arrangements. Rules are not written by the weak and downtrodden; they are shaped by dominant groups that have the power to work their will. Those who desire to change a status quo would need to recognize the obstacles to be overcome and to accumulate sufficient power to surmount them. As moral human beings, realists find morality rooted in the facts of particular circumstances, not in universal principles.

In contrast, idealism emphasizes theory and ideas instead of power, and it is devoted to free will rather than **determinism.** For the idealist, human choice plays a crucially important role in affairs. By looking to the future, idealists tend to be radical compared to realists' more conservative outlook. They also are more likely to be intellectual, with a tendency to try to fit facts to theory, whereas realists focus on practical affairs and incline to fit theory to facts. Finally, the idealist or utopian position is rooted in ethics and maintains universal moral standards that do not depend on context.

■ •••••• **Realism and Liberalism**

Associated Concepts

Concepts associated with realism:
- Power
- Conflict
- Action
- Groups
- Determinism
- Conservative
- Contextual ethics
- Prudence

Concepts associated with liberalism:
- Ideas
- Harmony
- Theory
- Individuals
- Free will
- Radical
- Universal ethics
- Justice

Each of these traditions has advantages and disadvantages. For realism, the advantage is clarity about the limits to human will, but its disadvantage is sterility. In the end, realism fails to rise above the status quo. Idealism, on the other hand, brings the advantage of imagination, and it gives full rein to the role

of human ideas and will. Nevertheless, a great disadvantage of idealism is its naivete, its lack of recognition of the limits imposed by power. Additionally, idealists tend to fail to perceive that standards are not really universal but rather are rooted in one's own existence. Beliefs and norms emerge from particular cultures at given periods of history.

Carr comes to the conclusion that

any sound political thought must be based on elements of both utopia and reality. Where utopianism has become a hollow and intolerable sham, which serves merely as a disguise for the interests of the privileged, the realist performs an indispensable service in unmasking it. But pure realism can offer nothing but a naked struggle for power which makes any kind of international society impossible. . . . The human will will continue to seek an escape from the logical consequences of realism in the vision of an international order which, as soon as it crystallizes itself into concrete political form, becomes tainted with self-interest and hypocrisy, and must once more be attacked with the instruments of realism.[6]

Despite a variety of approaches to the analysis of international politics, realism remains the center of a tradition of long duration, and liberalism plays off that tradition in a continuing dialogue. In recent years, that dialogue has enriched our understanding of international politics by encouraging thinking anew about the subject and inventing some new ideas in the attempt to explain how the world works.

• REALISM

A tradition of realism means that all realists share three assumptions: 1) human affairs are essentially conflictual; 2) the group, not the individual or the class, is the basic social unit; and 3) power and security are the primary human motivations.[7] Nevertheless, the structural or neorealist approach is a distinctive departure from more traditional realist considerations. Structural realism emphasizes the constraints of the international system, which are always operating and need to be taken into account. On the other hand, these constraints fail to explain a good deal of activity.[8]

Unlike structural realism, the traditional realist approach does not make a rigorous distinction between levels of analysis. Additionally, realists adopt a posture that is much closer to actors. In contrast, structural realists mark themselves off clearly as observers with a scientific demeanor. Morgenthau asserted that the realist, as it were, looked over the shoulder of the statesman, viewing the world through her eyes, though also criticizing her when her actions departed from realist norms. Waltz's approach of abstracting out a structure that bends and shapes the actions of statesmen in unintended directions marks a clear difference in approach.

• • • • • • Realism

All realists agree that:

- Human affairs are essentially conflictful.
- The group is the basic social unit.
- Power and security are the primary human motivations.

Structural realists stress:

- Rigorous distinction between levels of analysis
- System structure
- Scientific demeanor
- Theoretical utility

Traditional realists emphasize:

- Power
- Prudence
- National interest
- Practical demeanor
- Success

Traditional realists emphasize the centrality of power. Whatever interests a group has, they can only be accomplished by the accumulation and employment of sufficient power to achieve them, for history moves in a sequence of cause and effect. In that sense, a determinism is at work, for purposes can only be accomplished with power. However, realists also point out that interests develop out of power and that ethics are a function of power. Politics has primacy over other realms, such as economics and ethics. Theories of social ethics are formulated by powerful groups. Thus, thought is a function of power arrangements.[9] Implicit in the placement of power at the center of rational analysis are "the moral precept of prudence and the political requirement of success."[10] As the supreme virtue of realism, prudence is not a heroic one. It requires a calculation of what the consequences of one's actions will be, to take into account how others will react and with what means. Such a calculation precludes fanaticism and holds no intrinsic values of its own. Critics often point to the vacuity of purpose, but realism can also be defended for its moderation. Anyone who takes into account the interests of all parties to a conflict seeks to find a ground agreeable to all. Thus, diplomacy is the chosen instrument of the realist.

Without any external criterion of justice or other benchmark for assessing what occurs, realism measures politics by its **success.** If one is going to take action, the only rational course to follow is one that ensures success. Because success relies on having sufficient power to achieve goals, the realist emphasizes power. In doing so, of course, the realist approach opens itself to the criticisms that it tends to defend the status quo and fails to make any sharp distinctions based upon morality.

Thus, realism contains no universal moral precepts. Neither does it include that essential ingredient of politics: passion. No intrinsic purposes form part of the realist approach. For these other dimensions of politics, it is necessary to search in other approaches that incorporate them. As we have stressed in giving form to a problematic to guide study in the field of international politics, politics includes both power and justice. Realism makes an important contribution to understanding power, but to examine justice, other approaches are necessary. For many, particularly Americans whose society is the home of so many analysts, basic values and the purposes of politics come from liberalism, the political philosophy that most Americans embrace.

• LIBERALISM

Liberals value freedom and equality for individuals, limits on government, and democracy as a form of government. In both economics and politics, the liberal belief embraces **harmony of interests.** In contrast to realism's view that the group is the basic unit of social life, liberalism holds that the individual is the fundamental unit. Rather than accepting whatever status quo that extant power arrangements have determined, liberals strive to expand human freedom, protect human rights against violation by governments, widen the ranks of those participating in democratic political systems, and seek ways to achieve harmony. Whereas a realist assumes conflict to be the central characteristic of human affairs, a liberal stresses and strives for cooperation, and she gives more credit to institutions that promote cooperation. Although liberals concede that power and security are components of human interactions, they argue that human affairs are not always dominated by these considerations, for other issues such as economics or preservation of the environment may dominate an agenda at certain times and under particular circumstances.

● ● ● ● ● ● **Liberalism**

Liberals agree that:

- The individual is the basic unit.
- Individual freedom and equality should be expanded.
- Government should be limited.
- Democratic government is better.
- Cooperation should be stressed.
- International actors other than states are important.
- Security is not always the dominant motivation.

Neoliberal institutionalists include process as well as structure at the system level of analysis.

In recent years in the field of international politics, liberals have drawn on economics to center attention on an increasing interdependence across the globe. In this view of international political economy, issues such as trade, investment, and banking have become just as important as—some would argue more important than—security issues. Moreover, because economic activities are conducted by firms, the importance of multinational corporations has risen to equal or surpass that of states in international political economy. In addition, the complexity of governments in this context has generated links, called intergovernmental coalitions, among bureaucratic agencies that conduct business across international boundaries without central control.

In its neoliberal institutionalist variant, liberalism stresses that cooperation in international relations is supported by international organizations

---

● ● ● ● ● ● **Reflective Theory**

All of the approaches discussed in this chapter are well established and widely recognized in the field of international politics. Students vigorously contest which is more useful or provides the best intellectual foundation for a research program. Each is driven by different values and generates different questions. Many of the differences in view can be traced to the assumptions about the fundamental nature of social existence—conflict or harmony—and the elementary unit of human existence—group, individual, or class. From the basic assumptions and definitions that they offer, these different approaches emphasize different aspects of reality, but each addresses and contributes insight into some aspect of the problematic of international politics.

Another approach that has been articulated only in the last several years finds its unit not in the constructs of social reality but rather in words. This so-called "third-wave"[1] is discursive and somewhat unfocused, but much of its methodology is derived from a form of literary analysis called deconstructionism. Entirely an observer phenomenon, deconstructionism carefully examines texts and the historical and social milieu in which they were written with the view to discovering all of the assumptions and beliefs with which the words of the text are freighted. For example, if a writer employs a concept such as power in her analysis, a reflective theorist might explore all of the meanings of power, the historical context in which the concept was first formulated, the social circumstances of, say, Machiavelli, who promulgated the concept as a tool of analysis, and so on. That analysis, then, might be criticized on the basis not of how the author used the concept but of the meaning with which Machiavelli freighted it in fifteenth-century Florence.

In addition to deconstructionist methodology, writers using this approach also call attention to problems and actors that have not drawn the interest of conventional analysts. In part, the argument is that in forging the boundaries and assumptions of a discipline, some issues and interests are inevitably set aside or "marginalized." These neglected problems and people, then, are worth studying and ought to be included as legitimate topics in the discipline.

As in other attempts to incorporate new subject matters into the discipline, this sort of analysis aims to expand the problematic beyond international politics with its central concerns of power and justice, war and peace, state formation and anarchy, and the related questions that we defined in Chapter 1. This concern is to define the problematic of study so as to include saving isolated individuals from a feeling of alienation. The unit of analysis, then, is the individual, but not as a person in a social context but rather standing aside and suffering from a modern condition of isolation from the social context. Some of the issues raised are not uninteresting, but, as Robert Keohane has written, those caught up in this new approach have not formulated a research program, and that is the crucial test for an approach to command the attention of a discipline.[2]

---

1. "Third wave" refers to a debate between positivists and critical theorists, which follows two other great debates in the field: between realists and idealists, and then between traditionalists and behavioralists. See, for example, Richard K. Ashley and R. B. J. Walker, "Speaking the Language of Exile: Dissident Thought in International Studies, Introduction," Special Issue of International Studies Quarterly 34 (September 1990): 259–68; Friedrich Kratochwil, "Errors Have Their Advantages" in Neorealism and Its Critics, ed. by Robert O. Keohane (New York: Columbia University Press, 1986); and John Gerard Ruggie, "Territoriality and Beyond: Problematizing Modernity in International Relations," International Organization 47 (Winter 1993): 139–74.

2. Robert O. Keohane, "International Institutions: Two Approaches," in International Institutions and State Power: Essays in International Relations Theory, ed. by Robert O. Keohane (Boulder, Colo.: Westview Press, 1989).

that provide services and information to governments. Moreover, the existence of such agencies gives governments confidence to cooperate by making more predictable the actions of other governments that have pledged through the organizations to cooperate.

In addition to these considerations, the liberal position takes issue with the structural realist view by asserting that the interactions of states take place at the system level. They argue that it is misleading to place everything other than structure at the unit level. For a neorealist, the formation and maintenance of an alliance occur at the unit level, but for a liberal, those are system-level activities.

These academic disputes make a difference to the formulation of research programs, development of theoretical explanations, and understanding of international relations. To that extent, such disputes are of no more than marginal interest to the world of affairs. But such disputes carry implications for policy as well. For example, a liberal analyst who places interactions at the system level will tend to advocate a policy of maintaining a nonproliferation regime for nuclear weapons. She regards an international agreement with an institutional implementing mechanism as critical to slowing down or arresting the further spread of nuclear weapons. Thus, she stresses international cooperation to avoid the dangers arising from nuclear proliferation.[11]

In contrast, a structural realist who believes that nuclear weapons are a unit-level phenomenon does not regard proliferation as much of a problem at all. If many governments acquire a nuclear capability, the unintended result for the international system will be increased stability, a diminished chance for war because of the deterrent effects of nuclear weapons.[12] As this example illustrates, ideas have practical consequences. It is thus not idle or merely academic to be concerned about these theoretical debates.

By turning their attention to **low politics** involving nongovernmental activities, liberals contributed to restoring economics to the agenda in the study of international relations. This interest was also taken up by realists. Meanwhile, other strands of thought that had treated political and economic matters together entered the mainstream discourse of international relations. Several distinct modes of thought came together to form a **political economy approach** to the study of international relations.

Political Economy Approach

For the most part, a political economy approach comes at international relations from an inside-out perspective. That is to say, analysts are concerned mainly with affairs occurring within states. They nevertheless tend to be driven to treat international relations because of a realization that economic developments within states are affected importantly by arrangements and events at the international system level. Similarly, they also draw attention to the fact that international system arrangements result from domestic developments. Three contributing schools of thought to a political economy approach are **Marxism, dependency,** and **mercantilism.**

• MARXISM

In an age that has widely rejected communism as a guide to practical life and dismissed governments based on Marxist principles, one might ask: Why bother with Marxist analysis? The answer is that Marxism offers a coherent and serious analysis of capitalism, the dominant mode of arranging economics in the modern world. Not only does it help us to gain insight into how modern life works, but it also provides an alternative conception of justice. For the most part, Marxism offers an analysis of domestic arrangements and does not include a theory of international relations. Nevertheless, for an important recent period of history, one of the world's two superpowers, and other states as well, were ruled by people who thought in Marxist categories. If we are to understand that period, it is important to grasp how they thought. In addition, the mode of analysis continues to be useful for some analysts, and the values embodied in the system of thought continue to be germane to contemporary life. Moreover, from Marxism have been derived certain ideas about international relations, particularly concerning relations among unequal states and the processes of change.

Unlike realism, whose basic unit of human existence is the group, and in contrast to liberalism, which treats the individual as fundamental, Marxism regards **class** as the elemental category of human existence. A person's essential social condition is determined not by her individual character, nor by her group affiliation—her language, religion, or nation—but by the economic class to which she belongs. In the capitalist system that followed feudalism, there are just two classes: the owners and the workers, or the **bourgeoisie** and the **proletariat.** If a person owns tools and the means of production, she is an owner. If she possesses no production factor other than her labor, she is a worker who must sell her labor for wages.

In the preceding feudal period, artisans who labored also owned their tools. But, through a historical process, the new factory system of the Industrial Revolution led to a concentration of ownership in the hands of fewer and fewer owners. Writing in the mid-nineteenth century, Karl Marx believed that as this process went forward, more and more people who owned small businesses would be driven into the working class and that ownership would be concentrated in fewer and fewer hands. Over time, the result would be increasing misery for the workers and the concentration of wealth in monopolies.

Life was shaped by the **means of production** and the **relations of production.** When production was done by artisanal hand labor, the fashioning of pots and pans, say, by a single worker and perhaps an apprentice using hand tools, the artisan found meaning and dignity in her craft and work and autonomy in her ownership of her tools.

In the industrial age, however, pots and pans began to be produced by large machines staffed by workers who did not have sufficient accumulated capital to own them. Therefore, meaning and dignity could not be found in the work itself, for the repetitive actions performed on a factory production line produced standardized goods over which the worker had no control. Her only contribution to the process was her manual labor. Meaning, dignity, and autonomy were reserved for the owner, or entrepreneur, who could take pride in her inventive and organizational accomplishments and who gained increasing autonomy through the amassing of wealth.

Underlying these developments was an inevitable historical process called **dialectical materialism.** Marx drew on German philosopher Georg Hegel's concept of a dialectic in which history moved through the clash of ideas. According to Hegel's concept, from one idea, called a thesis, arises its opposite, called an antithesis. They then clash to form a synthesis. Marx rejected the belief that ideas formed the basic dynamics of history. Instead, he argued, although history moves in a dialectical process, it is driven by **material forces.** Thus, out of the economic arrangements of feudalism arose the bourgeois, or owner, class, which gave birth to the **capitalist sys-**

tem. The factory system that the bourgeoisie owned required workers to perform labor, and the workers formed a new class, the proletariat. As the processes of monopolization of ownership, increasing impoverishment, and enlargement of the working class moved forward, the stage would be set for a **revolution** by the proletariat. In this view of the world, government is merely a **superstructure** in the hands of the exploiting class. Thus, a state is not a unit in an international political system, as realists would argue. It is specific to the underlying economic order of the moment. That is, in a capitalist economic order, capitalist states serve as the instruments of the bourgeoisie.

The revolution that would overturn the capitalist order would create a new economic arrangement called **socialism** in which the workers would own the means of production. Because this material order would eliminate the exploitation of one class by another, there would be no need for a state, and it would wither away.

Things did not work out this way when an actual socialist revolution occurred in Russia in 1917. Not only did the revolution occur in the most backward rather than the most advanced of capitalist countries, it also required leadership in the form of the Bolshevik Party led by Vladimir I. Lenin, who articulated the historical need for what he called a **revolutionary vanguard.** Following the revolution, it was necessary to establish a government, and Lenin did so. His explanation was that the vanguard that had led the revolution should rule in the name of the proletariat, and he called this government the **dictatorship of the proletariat.** Not only did the proletariat not rule, but the dictatorship that ruled in its name operated on the principle of **democratic centralism.** This doctrine allowed debate within the restricted confines of the small ruling group until decisions were made. Once made, however, those decisions became binding, and full compliance without dissent was required. In this way, orders once issued could not be questioned, and "democratic" debate ended. By such means and by such logic, therefore, the Communist Party of the Soviet Union (CPSU) ruled by authoritarian means from November 1917 until August 1991, and the state called the Soviet Union persisted for a few more months until it disintegrated and was formally abolished in December 1991.

Once the Soviet Union was established, it became the vanguard for the revolution in the rest of the world. A creature of the Soviet state, the CPSU maintained relations with other Communist parties throughout the world, at times requiring that they submit to the discipline of the vanguard and at other times providing them with advice while the Soviet government furnished them material assistance. This put the Soviet Union at odds with many other governments, for the socialist leader often assisted those who aimed to overthrow their political orders.

Although Marx himself did not have a theory of international politics, the practical implications of Marxist thought have provoked others to analyze international relations. As an aspiration, class solidarity across national lines establishes links that are not channeled through foreign offices or other official connections among governments. Moreover, analysis proceeds from asking what is the class interest, quite different from the realist approach, which inquires about the national interest. In common with realists, though, Marxists do assume the essentially conflictual nature of social life, which is in contrast to liberals, who adhere to belief in the harmony of interest. With this approach's emphasis on the economic basis for politics, Marxist writers contribute to the analysis of international political economy. Basic to this analysis is the notion of domination of one class by another, with inherently unequal relations between the exploiting and the exploited class. This conception adds an interesting approach to the study of international relations.

• DEPENDENCY

So-called **dependency theory** did not originally emerge from Marxist analysis. It emerged from the thinking of some Latin American capitalist economists, particularly Raul Prebisch of Argentina, who sought an answer to the question of why Latin American countries were not developing in the post-World War II period. The existing liberal theory of **modernization** had held that all capitalist countries went through **stages of growth.**[13] In time, every country would accumulate savings and investments, adopt manufacturing through the factory system, become urban and bureaucratized, reach a stage of self-sustaining economic development, and eventually become a high-consumption society. Despite some economic advances, development did not proceed as modernization had it, and the highly developed countries in North America and Western Europe continued their extraordinary economic growth in the 1950s and 1960s, while the underde-

veloped countries grew more slowly, many languishing in their poverty and lack of progress to new stages of development.

To explain the condition of the **less developed countries,** Prebisch and his associates invented the concepts of **core** and **periphery.**[14] Discarding the notion that every country passed through similar stages at different times, these analysts argued that all countries developed simultaneously. However, the more advanced countries—the core—held advantages in technology, capital, and so forth. The less developed countries—the periphery—existed in a state of dependency on the core. Important decisions concerning investment and production remained the province of the core, whereas the peripheral countries lagged because they were not autonomous, and they depended on the wealthy.

Prebisch and his associates noted that the poorer countries depended on the wealthier countries for imports. Producing mostly primary products, the underdeveloped countries had to buy most of their consumer products from the United States and other highly industrialized countries. Furthermore, they had to sell the products produced by their agricultural and mining industries at prices determined in markets dominated by the rich countries. To overcome this dependent relationship, these economists contended, the poor countries needed to adopt an **import substitution industrialization strategy,** manufacturing the consumer goods that their populations had been buying from suppliers in the advanced countries. By adopting such a strategy, the dependent countries would be able to modernize and achieve the self-sustaining growth that had eluded them.

However, when the disadvantages of the new strategy became clear, Marxist analysts stepped in to provide a different explanation of dependency.[15] First of all, they conceived of the relations of developed and underdeveloped countries as existing in the same **world capitalist system.** In this worldwide system, the core, advanced industrial states exploited the peripheral poorer states. Marxists held that the core states were able to develop only by extracting resources and wealth from the periphery. That is to say, the periphery was locked into a position of dependency with a world capitalist system, and their only escape lay in revolutionary change. It would not be possible for them to lift themselves from poverty and backwardness through economic development. The analysis is slightly more complicated, for, within each state, there is also a core and a periphery, that is, a ruling class and an exploited class. Relations

● ● ● ● ● ● **Problem-Solving versus Critical Theory**

One kind of theory—problem-solving theory—operates within a given political arrangement, seeking to understand how the arrangement works. For example, during the Cold War, theorists noted patterns of interaction between the superpowers and between them and other countries, and they sought to understand why those patterns persisted—indeed, why the pattern of the bipolar distribution of power with only two superpowers persisted. This kind of theory is modeled by many of its exponents on the natural sciences. Assuming that a stable order of things is in place, the analyst seeks to gain insight into that order, understand how it works, and devise laws and explanations for the laws. So long as the assumptions hold, it is possible to do this kind of theory, but the edifice is considerably weakened by the collapse of one of its pillars, as happened with the consolidation and then the disintegration of the Soviet Union. Problem-solving theory is best done during periods of stability, but the social and political world is constantly changing, making it difficult indeed to develop theories of international politics.

A second kind of theoretical analysis is critical theory. Analysts writing in this genre seek to identify and create alternative arrangements in the world. Thus, they can work in both stable and unstable periods of history, for their imaginations are not limited to any particular circumstances. Nevertheless, periods of stability produce less receptive audiences than times of change and uncertainty in which people are looking for alternatives when an old order is crumbling or has passed into history. Critical theorists are related to policy analysts in the sense that they have goals that would change current arrangements. On the other hand, their more immediate aim is to create an understanding of current arrangements that envisions these arrangements' being undermined, pointing out their flaws and weaknesses. In addition, critical theorists want to understand the nature and the outlines of arrangements that would replace what we have now. In short, they are utopians.

Problem-solving and critical theorists may agree completely on their understanding of an extant system of politics. They depart only in their acceptance of it, for the critical theorist seeks to replace it, whereas the problem-solving theorist attempts to make it work.

---

among states, then, are conducted between the core class in the core states and the core class in the peripheral states, both exploiting the peripheral class in the periphery. Within the core, the peripheral class supports the arrangement because of its benefits, such as cheap products, to the members of even the working class in the rich countries.[16]

Dependency extends to many dimensions. For example, as import substitution industrialization strategies were adopted, investments were made in developing countries by firms from the developed countries. They provided both the capital and the technology for manufacturing, and the decisions to invest were made largely in the developed rather than the underdeveloped countries. Moreover, top-level management and research and development facilities remained located in the advanced countries. In addition, less developed countries were required to import the machinery and often the raw materials and intermediate products for their import-substituting industries. These imports turned out to use up such a large portion of export earnings that the poor countries could not accumulate the savings that would enable them to embark on self-sustaining growth. Thus, the dependent condition of the poorer countries was perpetuated. In addition, divisions within the less developed countries often widened as modernized sectors of the economy prospered while traditional sectors fell behind.

A vital component of maintaining the condition of dependency was the strength of the dominant class in the dependent countries, which provided access and cooperation to the firms from the developed countries that accumulated profits from their operations abroad. For many dependency analysts, there was no escape from this condition. For others, though, the Marxist prescription of a socialist revolution showed the way out of dependency. However, because the capitalist system had come to characterize not just discrete countries but a worldwide arrangement, only an extensive worldwide revolution would lead to the end of dependency.

Of course, with the end of the Cold War, the retreat from Marxist beliefs among those in power, and the ascendancy of liberalism, dependency theory's predictive powers are no longer looked to by those who aspire to a different world order. Nevertheless, as a technique for understanding the relations of rich and poor countries and the part played in those relations by the interplay of markets and states, the dependency approach raises important questions and offers certain insights into these unequal relations. Particularly as we explore the state and civil society in Chapter 6, a number of lines of inquiry suggested by dependency writings will open up interesting insights into the dynamics of international politics.

Dependency theory contributed to the writing on the world capitalist system by Wallerstein and other Marxist systems theorists.[17] These writers describe the creation of capitalism in Europe in the sixteenth century and its evolution and spread throughout the world since then. The ideas of the relations of production determining the relations of states are derived from this approach.

• MERCANTILISM

Another approach to the analysis of international political economy is mercantilism, which gives the state the central place in analysis and regards the accumulation of wealth to be the primary means to achieve power. In the era preceding the formation of the liberal state at the time of the American and French revolutions, major powers like Spain and Portugal were mercantilist, their rulers believing that the accumulation of wealth in the form of gold and other precious commodities gave them a power advantage over their competitors. In today's world, mercantilism emphasizes the strengthening of the state through economic production, accumulation of savings and their investment in productive enterprises, maintaining leads in technological innovation, maintaining trade balances, and otherwise ensuring that a country is competitive. Mercantilists advocate industrial policies, coercion against trading partners to resist unfair trade practices, and home investments in such things as education and infrastructure to maintain a country's competitive position in the international political economy.

A liberal expounds the virtues of free trade, with tariffs used for nothing other than revenue enhancement, all other trade restrictions removed, full opportunity for foreign investment, a minimal role for government in the economy, and reliance on comparative advantage. In contrast, a mercantilist advocates an important role for the government in the economy, the use of protective measures to ensure that her state maintains its advantages, and governmental policies that create new advantages for the country in the international economy. Additionally, a mercantilist is quite wary of foreign investment out of fear that it holds the potential of loss of control of her state's wealth to the nationals of another country. Even though mercantilists emphasize wealth as a component of state power, they do not adhere to the Leninist thesis of economic imperialism and the search for wealth as the fundamental cause of war.[18]

Decision-Making Approaches

For those analysts interested in explaining policy making at the state level of analysis, **decision-making approaches** have dominated their endeavors. For the most part, these approaches try to replicate the perspectives of authorities who make foreign policy decisions. In doing so, analysts stress the subjective aspects of reality and draw heavily on concepts from psychology, such as perception, misperception, and cognition. They also emphasize the organizational settings in which foreign policy is made, thus drawing on such notions as conformity in small groups and the pressures exerted on decision makers by their bureaucratic affiliations.

Because the unit of analysis is the decision, this approach tends to employ descriptive analysis using various analytical tools, but it does not result in theoretical explanation. With the exception of Alexander George, who uses a method that he calls focused comparison,[19] theoretical work in the decision-making approach has tended to concentrate on analytical methodology rather than on the discovery of explanations for patterns of behavior. On the whole, decision-making analysis is derived from traditional realism and is policy-oriented. While analysts are observers, their closeness with actors is apparent. At the same time, a number of interesting insights from this approach enrich our understanding of foreign policy.

Two important sets of distinctions can be made regarding decisional analysis. First, a foreign policy decision-making unit can be treated as a coherent group, faced with an occasion for decision, searching for a rational solution to the problem it confronts, and making a clear choice from among several alternatives. In the most studied decision of the Cold War period, the CUBAN MISSILE CRISIS, for example, a small group brought together by United States President John Kennedy deliberated over the course of several days. Faced with the building of Soviet missile sites in Cuba and the imminence of their becoming operational, its members dismissed the alternative of doing nothing and then considered three responses: 1) try to resolve the crisis through diplomacy; 2) exert pressure on the Soviets to remove their missiles by imposing a limited blockade around Cuba and threatening military action; or 3) use an air strike to bomb the missile sites. Following careful deliberations that weighed the chances for success and the probable consequences of each alternative and calculated the probable responses of the Soviet Union, the group recommended the second option, and Kennedy ordered it implemented.[20]

As an alternative to this rational calculation model of decision making, a **bureaucratic politics** model is sometimes employed. Whereas the rational model assumes that a group acts together, with the same set of incentives, to pursue the national interest, the bureaucratic politics model conceives of a more complicated political process that produces outcomes. No individual has either the time or the knowledge to make foreign policy, a condition that leads to compromises on the basis of varied incentives. Often the compromises are not rational, coherent responses to clear problems. To illustrate, let us examine a decision made in 1968 by the United States to deploy a "light" antiballistic missile (ABM) system.[21]

• DECISION TO DEPLOY AN ABM SYSTEM

The decision was announced by Secretary of Defense Robert McNamara, who stated that the ABM system would protect the United States against an attack from an adversary like China. However, in 1968, China did not possess the capability to attack the United States with long-range missiles, and it still did not have that capacity in 1995. In that context, the decision appears altogether irrational, for it was designed to protect the United States against a nonexistent threat while doing nothing to defend against the real, formidable threat from the Soviet Union. Thus, using a rational decision-making model the decision is inexplicable, and the challenge is to explain it.

According to the bureaucratic politics model, there were two opposed forces in American politics—primarily in the executive branch and among those in Congress concerned with defense matters—on this issue. On the one side were those who feared the growth of Soviet capacity in its long-range missile force to attack the United States. They advocated developing and deploying a broad-based ABM system to defend against a comprehensive Soviet attack. On the other side were opponents of ABM systems. They believed that an ABM system would not work, simply because the cost for the Soviet Union of increasing the number of its long-range missiles would be so low relative to the cost of the ABM system that the Soviets could easily build up their long-range missile

capacity and simply overwhelm whatever defenses the United States might build. In addition to these two clear alternatives, other interests were involved in the bargaining over this matter. Scientists and engineers who had invented the weapons had an investment. Congressional representatives from districts where production would occur maintained an interest in deployment on behalf of the businesses that would gain contracts and workers who would be employed building missiles. Within the military were those who would gain an important new mission in defending the country against the most formidable weapons in the world. At the same time, other participants could only look aghast at costs involved, for the design of the 1968 model ABM system included three separate components, each of which was to have been more expensive than any previous weapon system. Included too were participants who disagreed over nuclear strategy. Thus, rather than having a small group carefully and rationally deliberating a few clear alternatives, there were many actors in this drama, with clearly separate interests and incentives. They may have shared, at some level of abstraction, a conception of the national interest, but that common view was supplemented by other, diverse considerations. Through an extended and fragmented process of bargaining, an outcome was finally reached that represented a compromise of the variety of forces at work. Whereas the ABM decision makes no sense within a rational framework, it can be explained as the outcome of an understandable political process.

* * *

As a supplement to the bureaucratic process model, an **organizational process** model gives some insight into the **implementation** of foreign policy decisions.[22] Sometimes the effects of decisions can be changed from those intended by central decision makers because of the actions of those charged with carrying out policies. For example, blunders as well as acts of deliberate disobedience occur sometimes among soldiers, diplomats, and others charged with implementing policies, and sometimes subordinates pursue a policy with more zeal than was intended by a central authority.

Another useful distinction within the decision-making approach is that drawn between **analytical** and **cybernetic decision making.**[23] Analytical foreign policy making involves that rational model referred to above. However, officials have to deal often with an environment that is characterized by

complex uncertainty. Not only are they unsure of the objectives and plans of others, but they are unable to calculate with certainty the effects of their own actions. As a means of coping with complex uncertainty, officials screen out information by adopting simplified definitions of the situations they face. Whereas the analytical mode of decision searches for additional information and alternative choices, the cybernetic rejects complicated information and bolsters choices already made. The policy implications are nicely captured in an anecdote related by Steinbruner. At the edges of a meeting in the White House, political scientist Richard Neustadt remarked to former Secretary of State Dean Acheson that the president needs options. "No," replied Acheson, "The president needs reassurance."

Whether rational or bureaucratic, analytical or cybernetic, decision-making analysis focuses on a relatively small core of officials. Sometimes members of the legislature specializing in foreign affairs are included, but decision-making analysis tends to limit itself to the executive branch of government. A few studies have been done of interest groups and of public opinion, but, for the most part, decision-making analysis does not encompass the wider political system in which authoritative choices are made. In addition, by emphasizing the subjective elements of decisions, this approach has little connection with the broader systemic considerations that neorealists analyze. More often than not, reality for a decision-making analyst is that which is perceived by authorities and has no independent existence.

In one sense, then, many of the approaches that have been described have no coherent connection among them. Instead of meshing approaches and building comprehensive theory in the field, scholars using the different approaches talk past each other or criticize the inadequacies of others. A writer may, for example, criticize structural realists for ignoring the state level of analysis but then go on to do a decision-making study that is based upon different assumptions, deals with different units of analysis, and examines altogether different questions than structural realists do, thereby avoiding any link between the different approaches and making it impossible to develop any theory that might link the two.

This is a very difficult problem in the field, but it is not impossible to address. The problematic adopted in this book defines the field in a way that enables us to explore all of these approaches. It will also be possible to make connections between the

levels of analysis. To do so, however, we need to introduce a concept that provides the link.

The State

Although there are other actors in international politics, every approach that falls within the problematic that we have adopted includes the state. In exploring some dimension, it may be very useful to carve out a domain and develop a theoretical explanation that sets the state aside, but it is impossible to imagine any broad theoretical analysis that does not include the state. Even a utopian analysis that aims to create an alternative to our present world needs to take into account the way in which power and justice are organized and institutionalized in reality. Modern states have not existed forever, and they may not last in the long run, but they are the main form of political organization in today's world. Consequently, the state cannot be ignored.

It goes without saying that traditional realist analysis, which takes the group as its elemental social unit, includes the state, for the state is the mechanism by which the group is able to organize to protect itself, make its common decisions, and pursue its future. Moreover, traditional realists emphasize the stark reality of balance of power politics in an anarchical world of states that do not recognize any outside authority. Structural realists make the false assumption that states are identical in every way except their capabilities, but they use states as the fundamental units comprising the system structure, which is the main component of their theory. Although liberals employ the individual as the basic unit of social existence, they conceive of the individual in a social and political setting. For liberals, the values are individualistic, but the means of achieving those values are institutional, the state being foremost though not the exclusive institution. Marxists regard the state as superstructure but do fix much of their analysis on the capitalist state. While decision-making analysts tend to reduce the state to authoritative decision makers, they, like other realists, use the state as the focus of inquiry. From whatever perspective of international political economy, writers in this tradition treat states and markets as the two basic units driving events.

Despite the intersection of concerns with the state, none of these approaches has given extended treatment to the state, its formation, evolution, and sometimes disintegration. By incorporating such an analysis, we will be able to provide a coherent and consistent view of the field of international politics.

As the review of differing approaches implies, not everyone will accept the approach pursued here, for there are some important assumptions and values over which people differ. In keeping with the advice to make one's assumptions and values as clear as possible, I note here that I believe that the basis of social life is the group, that evidence and logic are the essential components for a rational analysis, that it is useful to employ the concept of a system structure that constrains human activity, that force continues to play a fundamental and important role in human affairs, that prudence is a valuable guideline for political action, but that intelligence is equally as important as power in the attainment of success. For the most part, this places me in the realist camp, but I go beyond that honorable tribe by insisting that the state needs to be explored much more fully than has been the realist wont, and that implies that political life—domestic and international—is unitary, that the fissures and cleavages of domestic life are often matters for international relations, that civil society and individuals comprise important components of the state, and that states come and go, rise and deteriorate.

• IMPORTANT TERMS

actors
analytical decision
 making
assumptions
bourgeoisie
bureaucratic politics
capitalist system
causal relationships
class
complex uncertainty
core
cybernetic decision
 making
decision making
democratic centralism
dependency
dependency theory
determinism
dialectical materialism
dictatorship of the
 proletariat
elegance
generalizability

harmony of interests
heuristic value
implementation
import substitution
 industrialization
less developed countries
levels of analysis
low politics
Marxism
material forces
means of production
mercantilism
modernization theory
observers
organizational process
parsimony
periphery
policy analysis
policy relevance
political economy
 approach
proletariat
relations of production

revolution
revolutionary vanguard
socialism
stages of growth
success
superstructure

system
theoretical, scientific
 knowledge
unit
world capitalist system

• STUDY QUESTIONS

1. What are the advantages and disadvantages of each of the differing perspectives of actors and observers?

2. Which makes a greater contribution to practical affairs: an analyst concerned primarily with theory, or one who focuses on policy? Does the answer depend on a long- versus a short-term perspective?

3. What utility accrues from maintaining a rigorous distinction between levels of analysis?

4. Would you expect to be able to explain real world events by attending to a single level of analysis, or would you anticipate better explanations by examining more than one level of analysis?

5. Compare and contrast the philosophical differences between realism and idealism or liberalism.

6. Do you believe that human affairs are basically conflictful or cooperative? What is the basis for your belief?

7. Would you prefer to negotiate with a person who holds strong, universal ethical principles or with a person whose foremost concern is with power and who thinks that ethics are situational?

8. In what ways are neorealists similar to and different from traditional realists?

9. List and define the essential concepts in Marx's analysis of capitalism. Also explain how his underlying philosophy and understanding of history contributed to his views. Assess the continuing relevance of Marxist analysis in the post-Cold-War period.

10. Separate the sense from the nonsense in dependency theory.

11. Why is it important to examine decision making within states? How successful have international relations scholars been in developing an autonomous theory of decision making that concerns international affairs? Give some reasons for theoretical advances or their absence.

12. Why does it seem useful for an international politics analyst to give serious consideration to the state?

• ENDNOTES

1. J. David Singer, "The Level-of-Analysis Problem in International Relations," in *The International System: Theoretical Essays*, ed. by Klaus Knorr and Sidney Verba (Princeton, N.J.: Princeton University Press, 1961).

2. The arguments of this and the following paragraph are drawn from two books by Kenneth N. Waltz: *Man, the State, and War: A Theoretical Analysis* and *Theory of International Politics*.

3. Also see the work of John J. Mearsheimer, especially "Back to the Future: Instability in Europe after the Cold War," *International Security* 15 (Summer 1990): 5–56.

4. Adam Smith, *The Wealth of Nations*, Books I–III (Harmondsworth: Penguin, 1970).

5. Hans J. Morgenthau, *Politics among Nations: The Struggle for Power and Peace*, 6th ed., rev. by Kenneth W. Thompson (New York: Alfred A. Knopf, 1985), p. 14.

6. E. H. Carr, *The Twenty Years' Crisis, 1919–1939: An Introduction to the Study of International Relations* (New York: Harper & Row, 1964; originally, New York: St. Martin's Press, 1939), p. 93.

7. Robert Gilpin, "Political Realism's Richness," in *Neorealism and Its Critics*, ed. by Robert O. Keohane (New York: Columbia University Press, 1986), pp. 304–5.

8. For a strong case making this point, see Miriam Fendius Elman, "The Foreign Policies of Small States: Challenging Neorealism in Its Own Backyard," *British Journal of Political Science* 25 (April 1995): 171–217.

9. Carr, *The Twenty Years' Crisis*, chapter 5.

10. Morgenthau, *Politics among Nations*, 6th ed., p. 10.

11. See Joseph S. Nye, Jr., *Understanding International Conflicts: An Introduction to Theory and Practice* (New York: HarperCollins College Publishers, 1993: pp. 188–89.

12. See Kenneth N. Waltz, "The Spread of Nuclear Weapons: More May Be Better," *Adelphi Papers*, no. 171 (London: International Institute of Strategic Studies, 1982).

13. See W. W. Rostow, *The Stages of Economic Growth* (London: Cambridge University Press, 1960).

14. For a good overview of Prebisch's thinking, see *International Economics and Development: Essays in Honor of Raul Prebisch*, ed. by Luis Eugenio DiMarco (New York: Academic Press, 1972), especially Luis Eugenio DiMarco, "The Evolution of Prebisch's Economic Thought," and

Aldo Antonio Dadona and Luis Eugenio DiMarco, "The Impact of Prebisch's Ideas on Modern Economic Analysis."

15. For a sample of the literature of dependency, see Part III of *Perspectives on World Politics*, 2d ed., ed. by Richard Little and Michael Smith (London: Routledge, 1991).

16. See, for example, Andre Gunder Frank, "The Development of Underdevelopment," *Monthly Review* (September 1966): 17–30.

17. Immanuel Wallerstein, *The Modern World System* (New York: Academic Press, 1974).

18. See, for example, Jacob Viner, "Peace as an Economic Problem," in *International Politics: Anarchy, Force, Political Economy, and Decision Making*, 2d ed., edited by Robert J. Art and Robert Jervis (Boston: Little, Brown, 1985), pp. 291–302, reprinted from *New Perspectives on Peace* (Chicago: University of Chicago Press, 1944). See also Lester Thurow, *Head to Head: The Coming Economic Battle among Japan, Europe, and America* (New York: Warner Books, 1992).

19. See Gordon A. Craig and Alexander L. George, *Force and Statecraft: Diplomatic Problems of Our Time*, 2d ed. (New York: Oxford University Press, 1990), and Alexander L. George, *Forceful Persuasion: Coercive Diplomacy as an Alternative to War* (Washington, D.C.: U.S. Institute of Peace, 1991).

20. Graham T. Allison, *Essence of Decision: Explaining the Cuban Missile Crisis* (Boston: Little, Brown, 1971).

21. The following narrative is based on Morton Halperin, with the assistance of Priscilla Clapp and Arnold Kanter, *Bureaucratic Politics and Foreign Policy* (Washington, D.C.: Brookings Institution, 1974).

22. See Allison, *Essence of Decision*, and Graham T. Allison and Morton H. Halperin, "Bureaucratic Politics: A Paradigm and Some Policy Implications," *World Politics* 24 (Spring 1972 Supplement): 40–79.

23. John Steinbruner, *The Cybernetic Theory of Decision: New Dimensions of Political Analysis* (Princeton, N.J.: Princeton University Press, 1974).

PART 2

The International System and Participating Units

CHAPTER FOUR
International System Structure and System Management

CHAPTER FIVE
Units of Analysis/Participants in International Politics

CHAPTER 4

International System Structure and System Management

Just as a family has a structure—that invisible way in which the relations of its members are arranged and lines of authority and specific roles are assigned to affect the behaviors of each member—international politics has a structure that constrains state behaviors. Although it possesses neither visibility nor will, structure rewards those states conforming to abstract constraints and punishes those failing to abide by them. Moreover, when the policies of statesmen fall short of achieving their goals, the place to look for an explanation may not lie in their personalities and imaginations or in the character of their states. It may lie, rather, in the structure of the system.

Despite the fundamental ordering principle of anarchy that characterizes the relations of states, their complex interactions require management at many levels. Recognition, dispute settlement, and long-term agreements to cooperate exemplify the many sorts of collective matters that states engage in to manage their varied international relations.

This chapter treats these two aspects of the international system: the abstract structure, not subject to human will, that shapes and constrains behavior; and the concrete problems and practices that leaders address and employ to sustain joint endeavors and to facilitate cooperative interactions.

System Structure

"A **system** is composed of a structure and of interacting parts."[1] A structure is the "arrangement . . . of parts as dominated by the general character of the whole."[2] In the case of international politics, structure refers to the positional arrangement of states in an anarchical relationship with one another. Although abstract, structure describes an overall pattern of international politics.

• BALANCE OF POWER

The traditional way of describing an overall pattern of international politics is the **balance of power.** This idea holds that any state that tries to achieve a position of dominance will be opposed and defeated by a coalition of other states. Despite its apparent simplicity, the concept balance of power is shot

through with ambiguities. Thus, balance of power has long been an object of controversy among analysts.[3]

One ambiguity that crops up immediately concerns the issue of whether its central metaphor of balance or equilibrium even makes sense. On the one hand, a balance connotes an even distribution of capabilities and implies stability in the system. However, to defeat a state that seeks dominance, the opposing coalition has to have a preponderance of power, for it is impossible to win in a situation in which the sides are evenly balanced. For example, had Germany and Japan possessed capabilities equal to those of the Grand Alliance in World War II, it would have been impossible to defeat them.

Analysts also divide on the question of whether balance of power operates as an automatic mechanism or as the result of deliberate policy decisions.

Implied in the metaphor is the idea that all of those threatened would automatically oppose a state or coalition seeking dominance. Thus, employing a logic like that of the market's **invisible hand,** some analysts argue that merely by competing to secure their respective national interests, states bring about a balance without anyone's having sought it. On the other hand, some conclude that it is effective only if states pursue a balance as a policy objective.

Additionally, disagreements abound regarding the components of a balance of power system: Is it necessary to have five states to make it operate, or do balances recur in arrangements with only two powers? What about three powers? Some analysts argue strongly that only if there is a **balancer** or **holder of the balance,** will a balance of power operate.

Moreover, we observe that the concept of a balance of power and the mode of thinking that it involves belong firmly in the ambit of realism. Even realists acknowledge that the balance of power is an imperfect description of the international system and mechanism for preserving peace.[4] Liberal and radical critics seek to reform or transform the balance of power, which they perceive as, at best, a very flawed mechanism. At worst, critics think of the balance of power itself as a cause of war.

To a large extent, the evolution of the concept of balance of power and debates about it have followed historical events. In the wake of the French Revolution, the dictator Napoleon Bonaparte came to power through a *coup d'etat* in 1799 and launched a campaign to make himself master of all Europe. Over the course of time other countries joined together in several coalitions to defeat him and his mass armies. The allied victory followed Napoleon's retreat from Russia in 1812, his abdication following his enemies' penetration into France in 1814, and his final defeat at Waterloo in 1815.

The Napoleonic Wars appear to vindicate balance of power analysis, and the victors sought to restore a balance in Europe at the Congress of Vienna in 1814–1815. However, the powers also acknowledged the inadequacy of the balance by creating a system of cooperation referred to as the Concert of Europe that operated throughout much of the nineteenth century. When problems arose that threatened war, the powers held conferences in which they sought common solutions to those problems. Among the most famous was the Conference of Berlin in 1884, which set down guidelines to regulate the behavior of the major powers in their conquest of Africa. In contrast to a balance of power that oper-

ates on the principle of one alliance holding another in check, a concert brings all the major powers together to work out a common solution to systemic problems.

By the end of the century, however, the concert arrangement was no longer functioning, and the powers formed themselves into opposing coalitions that ended up facing each other in the Great War that broke out in 1914. On the one side were Germany, Austria-Hungary, and Italy, forming the Triple Alliance. Opposing were Britain, France, and Russia, comprising the Triple Entente. So long as peace was maintained, the two coalitions seemed to balance each other, and they continued to do so in the war (although Italy remained neutral), which rapidly became a fight from the unmoving positions of trench warfare. The stalemate was broken only after the entry of the United States in 1917, the addition of the new ally providing the winning coalition with a preponderance of power.

Under the leadership of President Woodrow Wilson, the United States opposed restoration of a balance of power in Europe. In its place, Wilson advocated **self-determination** for the constituent parts of the Austro-Hungarian Empire and the establishment of a global international organization that would keep the peace through the mechanism of collective security, in which a grand, worldwide coalition would decisively resist the attempt of any country that committed **aggression.** This organization, the League of Nations, represented an attempt at system reform, to replace the balance of power with a distinctive set of alternative ways of maintaining peace.

Unfortunately, the reforms did not prevent Germany and Japan and their Axis allies from seeking dominance. To Japan's conquest of Manchuria in 1931 and Italy's of Ethiopia in 1936, the League of Nations was unable to mount an effective response. Germany's attack on Poland in 1939 opened the SECOND WORLD WAR. After conquering most of Europe but failing to defeat Britain, Germany invaded the Soviet Union in 1941. Japan then opened hostilities with the United States at the end of 1941, and Germany declared war on the United States. The Axis powers were countered by the Grand Alliance composed of Britain, the United States, and the Soviet Union, as well as their allies, which included China and the free French forces under Charles DeGaulle. This coalition brought its superior power to bear and defeated the Axis allies. Once again, the balance of power seemed to be operating, especially as the Second World War demonstrated that a common enemy seeking dominance brings together countries that otherwise would have opposed one another: democratic Britain and United States with authoritarian Soviet Union.

In recognition of the inadequacy of the balance of power, however, the victorious allies established the United Nations as a mechanism through which the victors could confer on common problems in the postwar world. To the conference mechanism of the United Nations were added a number of other arrangements to address common problems. For example, international financial institutions—the International Monetary Fund and the World Bank—were created to assist in recovery from the war and in promoting international trade.

As the **Cold War** arose in the late 1940s following World War II, however, the United Nations fell victim to the confrontation between the communist and noncommunist parts of the world. Both leaders of these two camps sought, in traditional balance of power fashion, to build security alliances. Although centered in Europe, their competition extended throughout the world.

In one sense, then, it seemed that a balance of power was continuing in operation. However, some observers thought that because the history of the balance of power had always involved five or more powers, the postwar order with only two **superpowers** expressed something entirely new. These writers claimed that the balance of power system had been superseded by a **bipolar system** with completely different characteristics.[5] Even for those who continued to think that a balance of power system was at work, the essential balancing mechanism was the alliance system. Thus, they believed that the coalitions were the basic units in postwar international politics and that the state had been superseded or was on its way to being replaced as the fundamental unit of social action in international politics. For example, John Herz wrote that the territorial principle of defense had moved in the postwar period from state boundaries to coalition boundaries.[6] That is to say, he argued that the defensible border lay in the middle of Europe between **East** and **West** rather than at the frontiers of each state.

As both critics and supporters note, balance of power thinking concentrates only on the great powers. It is an approach to thinking about relations of equality, that is, interactions among states that belong to the class of great powers. In the post-1945 world, there were only two great powers, the United States and the Soviet Union. To take but one measure, between them they possessed well over 90 percent of the world's arsenals. While these massive stores of weaponry were deployed on behalf of the countries these two powers were pledged to protect, those other states did not share fully in controlling the weapons. In the vivid Cold War metaphor, the fingers that would have pushed the nuclear buttons remained in Moscow and Washington. Members of the North Atlantic Treaty Organization (NATO) and the Warsaw Pact were protected; those states were not equal partners in the security arrangements that the alliances represented. Thus, the claim that coalitions had displaced great powers as the units of social action in international politics could not be supported. These and other considerations led many analysts to believe that balance of power thinking belonged solely to the past, that it was no longer useful for gaining any understanding of modern international politics.

• STRUCTURAL REALISM

It was at this point, in the late 1970s, that Kenneth Waltz published his important analysis that introduced the concept of political **structure,** an idea that reformulated balance of power thinking and advanced a theory of international politics called structural realism, or neorealism.[7] Noting that many writers had included causes of the balance of power at both the system and the state levels of analysis, Waltz sought to make a rigorous distinction between levels of analysis. He pointed out that the absence of such a distinction had led to considerable confusion. In particular, it is virtually impossible to specify what the effects of the system are if decisions at the level of the state are included in the analysis, for it appears that everything is controlled by the decision makers. Nevertheless, one can observe that international politics is filled with unintended consequences that do not result from the decisions of statesmen.

If one wants to develop a theoretical explanation of those unintended consequences, then one needs to isolate a limited domain to which the theory applies. In the case of an international system, one needs to specify what the structure is, separating it conceptually from everything else. It was for this reason that Waltz so rigorously distinguished the system from the units and offered a simple, theoretically useful definition of the international structure.

Given the absence of any authority above states to provide a constitutional framework for the international system, it is apparent that international politics is a **self-help system** of self-regarding units. That is to say, each unit must look after its own interests. For example, only France can determine its interests and take responsibility for them. There are no guidebooks or laws to determine how each state should choose to cope with the opportunities and challenges presented to it. Nevertheless, to construct a system theory, it is necessary to assume that at least two such units exist and that, at a minimum, they wish to survive. From those two assumptions grows the theory of system structure.

To distinguish the units from the system, it is important to identify what belongs at which level. Most obviously attaching to the unit level are the characteristics, or attributes, of the units. Such attributes include territorial size, natural resources, population size, and other characteristics such as age distribution and education, form of government, languages, societal traits, and so on. To construct a theory of the system, these attributes are set aside. Thus, for purposes of system-level theory, the analyst ignores such phenomena as the federal structures of states like Nigeria and India or the authoritarian character of China and Vietnam.

Also excluded from the system level are the actions of states as they conduct relations with one another. Diplomatic notes, foreign ministers' visits to other countries, threats, spying, wars, trade, alliances, and other state conduct—these actions occur at the state level. While it is easy enough to assign attributes to the state level, the allocation of the interactions of states to the unit level is far from obvious. It seems to put everything at the unit level, leaving nothing to the system.

However, as Waltz explains, international relations consist of two distinct things. First, there are interactions among states. Regardless of the language employed, interactions are in reality successions of discrete actions of particular states. The formation of an alliance, for example, includes the individual decisions of two or more states to cooperate for their security. It is clear that, standing alone, each decision is a unit-level activity and not something that occurs at the system level. For example, when Britain, the United States, and their allies founded NATO in 1949, each country signed the treaty and agreed to cooperate. To consider the discrete decisions of two countries to join an alliance as an interaction is an analytical formulation, not something that actually occurred in a system. This can be clarified further by noting that two such decisions, even when recipro-

cal, demonstrate absolutely no systemic actions. Thus, the interactions of states fall exclusively into the state level of analysis.

However, relations among states are not simply the interactions that they conduct. There is a second dimension of the relations among states, which is the positions they occupy in relationship to one another. This positional relationship is the system's structure.

A political system's structure consists of three components: an **ordering principle,** the **specification of functions,** and a **distribution of capabilities** across the units.

An ordering principle is the basis upon which the relations of the units are arranged. Essentially, two ordering principles are available for arranging political relations: **hierarchical** and **anarchical.** Domestic political systems are ordered hierarchically, with a set of superordinate and subordinate relations prevailing. In the absence of any authority higher than the state in the international system, the relations of states are based upon the ordering principle of anarchy. This is a more formal way of specifying that the international system is one of self-help, with each unit looking out for its own interests.

In a domestic political system, specialized functions are specified. For example, in the United States, the Constitution specifies that Congress is required to do certain things, that some powers are reserved to the states while others are assigned to the national government, that the president must perform certain duties, and so on. Unlike a domestic system, however, this component of a structure drops out of a definition of an international structure, for states do not have specialized functions. Instead, they duplicate one another's tasks. In a self-help system, each unit needs to provide for its own interests, basically doing what every other state does.

• • • • • • **International Political System**

Structure and Interacting Units

SYSTEM LEVEL	UNIT LEVEL
Political Structure:	States:
• Anarchy as ordering principal	• Attributes.
• Distribution of capabilities across the units	• Interactions

---

The last component of structure is the distribution of capabilities across the units. Because capabilities are included in attributes of units, it would seem that neorealist theory is flawed by breaching its clear distinction between levels of analysis. A false assumption had been made that all units are the same. However, it is necessary to assume that the units have one characteristic by which they vary, and that is their capabilities. Still, the levels of analysis distinction remains intact, for attention is not paid to the discrete power of the respective units. The theory does not dwell on the capabilities of Russia or the United States. Instead, this theory concentrates on the distribution of capabilities across the units, particularly on whether it is **bipolar** or **multipolar,** and that distribution is a system-level characteristic.

Thus, this spare theory of system structure includes but two components: the ordering principle, which is anarchy, and the distribution of capabilities across the units. Because of the inequalities present in international politics, balance of power theory—of which structural theory is a variant—focuses its attention only on the great powers. Thus, the distribution of capabilities across the units can be described by concentrating on the fairly small numbers of major powers. **Major powers** are those that belong, using their aggregate capabilities, to a distinctly separate class from other states. Such powers do not need to be equal in power to one another. They only need to be distinguishable together as a class, different from the remaining states.

For example, in the period after World War II, only two superpowers were clearly distinguishable from other states. Each had certain attributes that placed them in this special category: continental size, rich natural resources, large and well-educated populations, modern industrial bases, coherent social systems, strong military capabilities, and dedicated leaderships. No other state approached them in these aggregate terms. Nevertheless, at no time in the postwar era did the Soviet Union's economy surpass 50 percent of the economy of the United States. In other words, the United States remained over the course of the forty-five years of their competition at least twice as wealthy as the Soviet Union. Nevertheless, these two states stood together in a separate class; unequal in relationship to all other states.

• BIPOLARITY AND MULTIPOLARITY

This situation is called **bipolarity,** a distribution of capabilities across the units in a pattern in which only two superpowers compete against each other. When there are more than two major powers, the distribution of capabilities occurs in a pattern called **multipolarity.** As the term implies, then, structure is

very stable. So long as the principle of anarchy prevails and there are at least two autonomous units wishing to survive, an international system will be perpetuated. The only significant change that occurs is in the distribution of capabilities from multipolarity to bipolarity or to some other pattern.

For patterns other than multipolarity and bipolarity, such as the unnamed one that resulted from the end of the Cold War and the collapse of the Soviet Union, the theory is incomplete, for no one has yet worked out deductively the ways in which the system structure constrains behavior.[8] But the theory does describe and explain the ways in which the system operates in the two identified patterns of distribution of capabilities across the units. In addition to constraining—though not determining—the behavior of the units, the theory also helps to account for the **unintended consequences** of state behavior.

Although system constraints in the two patterns are different, essentially two mechanisms are at work in both: **imitation** and **socialization.** States imitate the activities of their successful competitors in order to maintain their positions. If one major power develops a weapons system based upon technological innovation, other competing powers will strive to develop similar weapons systems and will seek to improve on them. Moreover, as states compete they will tend to learn from their interactions patterns of behavior that enable them to achieve their goals. For example, during the Cold War, the adversaries learned to manage crises as a means of resolving some of their disputes short of war.[9]

Most basically, balance of power theory holds that, when challenged, states will act so as to balance or oppose the actions of the state or coalition that strives for dominance. Inasmuch as each state looks after its own security, its interests lie in balancing rather than in joining the challenger, for it is the challenger that threatens its security. However, the steps taken to oppose adversaries vary with the structure of the system.

In multipolar systems with many powers belonging to the class of great powers, there is a tendency to form alliances to build up the strength to oppose any power or coalition that might strive for dominance. The situation is quite different in a bipolar system, where the superpowers compete more by building their domestic economies and military forces than in seeking allies. In the post-World War II period, the increases in strength of the Soviet Union and the United States resulted more from their respective arsenals than from the alliances that they headed. Note also that they sought new allies only in the first decade after the end of the war, during the time that the bipolar structure was increasingly recognized but when initial behaviors followed old patterns remaining from the multipolar period. After that time, the United States and the Soviet Union accelerated their military buildups. Using their immense capabilities, the two superpowers extended their protection to other countries.

In large part this phenomenon resulted from a dynamic engendered by bipolarity. Because the other superpower is the only threat, each is constrained to view every event in the world through the lens of superpower relations. Thus, a civil war in Angola in southern Africa engaged both the Soviet Union and the United States in the 1970s and 1980s. There was nothing in Angola that could threaten either superpower, but each overreacted to the other, fearing the possibility that its adversary would make some gain. This tendency to interpret all manner of events in terms of superpower relations results from facing only one genuine threat in the world. The danger implicit in the bipolar system is that of **overreaction.**

A different pattern of behavior occurs in multipolar systems, and the danger is **miscalculation,** which results from the uncertainty that characterizes such a structure. With many great powers, any one of them needs to be concerned about the relations of the others, out of fear that a coalition might be formed that could seek dominance in the system. It is impossible to know whether the relations of, say, Italy and Germany might portend dire consequences for, say, France. However, the uncertainty might very well induce France to form an alliance with, say, Russia. But, in that case, Germany may be moved to strengthen its alliances because of the uncertainty of the effects on it deriving from the French and Russian alliance.

Such uncertainties can have devastating consequences. For example, in one interpretation of the origins of World War I, Germany's decision to go to war was based upon its projection that England would not join France and Russia against it and Austria-Hungary. In the end, Germany's entry into war proved to be a terrible miscalculation that stemmed from the uncertainty that characterized the multipolar system existing in 1914.

Uncertainty of this magnitude simply did not exist during the bipolar period that lasted from the late 1940s to 1991. Both the Soviet Union and the United States were very clear that in a high-stakes situation, the other would respond. For that reason, a stalemate stood in place in Central Europe for forty-five years. Germany became during the Cold War the location of the greatest array of armaments outside the territories of the superpowers themselves. No ambiguity whatsoever existed over the question of whether the other would join the fray, should one of them begin a war in Central Europe.

This structural arrangement had important consequences for the European countries, many of them former great powers. In the absence of uncertainty, they did not need to be concerned about the relations of the others. Because their security was guaranteed by the superpowers, no space for miscalculation was provided. If West Germany and Italy conferred on some diplomatic matter, France had no reason to be concerned about the impact of the relations on its own security. Only the Soviet Union offered a threat to France's security; and the United States stood solidly as France's defender against that threat. As a consequence, the Western Europeans have been able to make great progress in constructing and developing arrangements for economic cooperation. By removing security as the predominant concern, the bipolar structure allowed the European states to bring economics to the top of their agenda. By diminishing uncertainty, the bipolar structure removed the severe dangers attached to miscalculation and thus freed the Western European states to engage in very complex relations unencumbered by fears of injury to their security. In these circumstances, the European Union has flourished and has become a magnet for the northern countries such as Sweden that had earlier stood aloof, the poorer southern countries such as Greece, and the Eastern European lands such as Poland that threw off the constraints of communism in 1989 and following years.

• HOLDER OF THE BALANCE

Another difference between multipolar and bipolar structures is the presence in the former of a holder of the balance and its absence in the latter. Although the role of a holder of the balance is recognized in history, there is no conceptualization of it in the international relations literature. To aid in our theoretical examination, we will briefly note historical examples of this player in international politics and then derive the abstract characteristics of the balancer that will make it a useful concept in our subsequent analysis.

The country that has played this role, par excellence, on the world stage is Great Britain. During the eighteenth and nineteenth centuries, Britain formed temporary alliances with different European partners and spent its money to subsidize forces fighting for issues that coincided with British interests. Britain took these actions to maintain a balance of power on the European continent. In the first half of the twentieth century, the United States played a similar role in the two world wars, joining one coalition against the powers striving for domination and helping to restore a balance.

If we ask what the characteristics of these countries that have played the balancer role are, it is fairly easy to reply that there are two essential characteristics. First, the country playing such a role must be powerful enough to make a difference in the outcome of a struggle between adversaries. With its great wealth generated by the Industrial Revolution, Britain laid claim to being one of the powers, and its resources could be placed on one side of a struggle to determine the outcome. By the early twentieth century, the United States had surpassed Britain in wealth and, to some extent, inherited the role.

■
● ● ● ● ● ● Balance of Power

Under bipolarity:
- Two major powers
- Balance by increasing capabilities
- Events viewed through lens of superpower relations
- Danger of overreaction

Under multipolarity:
- Three or more major powers
- Balance by forming alliances
- Uncertainty
- Danger of miscalculation

Holder of the balance characteristics:
- Great power
- Disinterest in others' disputes

Why would these two, rather than other great powers like France or Russia, say, exercise the functions of a holder of the balance? To answer that question, one has to consider the second characteristic. It is a fundamental disinterest in the substance of the disputes in an antagonistic relationship. Britain's interests lay in its empire, not in European continental politics. England's only concern on the European continent in the eighteenth and nineteenth centuries and most of the twentieth was to ensure that no power became strong enough to

threaten the British Isles. Practically, that meant that no powerful country should dominate the Low Countries, from which an invasion could be launched. In the case of the United States, its very founding was based on the principle of separating itself from Europe. For the United States, the only European threat would emerge from the domination of the continent by a hostile power. Whether France or Germany should control Alsace and Lorraine was of no interest to Americans. When Germany did dominate virtually the entire continent in the early 1940s, the United States acted to reverse that position. When it seemed that the Soviet Union had the ambition, after World War II, to seek domination of Europe, the United States established a position on the continent to preclude the fulfillment of that ambition.

From this discussion of balance of power theory, we can derive a few conceptual tools to help us to analyze overall patterns of international politics in the contemporary world. For at least twenty years, there have been much discussion and much controversy about the shape and direction of the world. For example, in his State of the World message to Congress in 1970, President Richard Nixon articulated a conception of a **pentagonal system,** suggesting that there either existed or would soon emerge a pattern of world politics in which five great powers would be active. Other writers claimed or projected the development of a multipolar system in the 1970s. As the Soviet Union collapsed, Charles Krauthammer wrote about a "unipolar moment."[10] In the mid-1990s, there seems to be only one superpower, but there is also a great diffusion of power in the world. Joseph Nye has suggested that the United States is "bound to lead" the various holders of this diffused power, thus implying that there may be something like a concert of power emerging in the contemporary world.[11] Let us use the concepts from the discussion of balance of power theory to guide our way through this thicket of claims.

● BALANCE OF POWER IN THE POST-1970 WORLD

By 1970, so many changes had occurred in the postwar world that it seemed plausible that a broad new pattern of international politics was either already established or in the process of being built. One of these was the strategic parity of the Soviet Union with the United States. Although the United States had pioneered nuclear and thermonuclear weapons and had maintained a lead over its main adversary in military prowess, the Soviet Union had built up its navy and its nuclear rocket forces, especially following the 1962 Cuban missile crisis. By the beginning of the 1970s, for all intents and purposes, the Soviet Union was the equal of the United States in strategic weaponry, that is, those weapons that could be used directly against the territory of the other. From the Soviet perspective, a shift in the world balance of forces had occurred, leading Foreign Minister Andrei Gromyko to claim that no world problem could be solved without the participation of his country.[12] As events have demonstrated, this analysis was flawed, for the Soviet Union did not have the array of capabilities needed to address many problems. For example, its deficiency in wealth as compared with the United States did not allow it to provide significant economic benefits to other countries in exchange for political cooperation. Meanwhile, the United States was able to exercise greater influence by using its economic assets. Nevertheless, the strategic parity did lead to some arms control agreements between the superpowers and other agreements that comprised a joint endeavor at **detente,** or the relaxing of tensions between them. Strategic parity also consolidated bipolarity, as the superpowers strengthened their military arsenals, setting them even further apart from the remainder of the countries of the world.

Nevertheless, additional changes had been occurring that brought new prominence to other countries and strengthened claims that bipolarity was being replaced by a multipolar distribution of power. Central to this argument was the long-term recovery of Japan and the Western European countries. Emerging from the devastation of World War II, these countries enjoyed remarkable economic growth. By the late 1950s, they had already become important trade competitors to the United States, and by the late 1960s, the world monetary system based on the dollar's convertibility to gold had been so seriously weakened that the International Monetary Fund created a new form of money called Special Drawing Rights to support international trade. So successful had the European Economic Community (EC) become that some people began to think of it as a new entity in international politics. Thus, Japan and the EC were put forward as new great powers taking their places in a multipolar system.

In addition to these two candidates, some analysts also named China as a candidate for great power status. After the successful Communist revolution in China in 1949, that country had aligned itself with the Soviet Union, but over the course of years, the two leading communist states quarreled over a range of issues and eventually made a public break. Instead of remaining as allies, they became adversaries. Feuding over leadership of the Communist movement worldwide, they disagreed on such matters as economic development policy, the appropriate role of nuclear weapons, and foreign policy issues. One of the most serious issues between them concerned border territories that Russia had acquired from China in the nineteenth century. This dispute deepened until, in 1969, Soviet and Chinese troops clashed on an island in the Ussuri River. With the obvious cleavage in what had previously been conceived as a unified Communist bloc, the United States government, which had not established diplomatic relations with the Communist regime in China during the twenty years it had been in power, began thinking about treating China as an important independent country in international politics.

Thus, the pentagonal system to which Nixon referred was composed of, in addition to the United States and the Soviet Union, the European Community, Japan, and China. To evaluate how sound this analysis was, we need, first, to determine whether each of these candidates had gained sufficient capabilities to be ranked in the class of superpower. That is to ask: Had these entities become more like the United States and the Soviet Union, or did they remain outside the class to which these two belonged? If the distribution of capabilities across the units had changed so that any one was a superpower, then we would have to conclude that the international system had changed from bipolar to multipolar. Let us consider each in turn.

The European Community, then and now, does have certain attributes that resemble those of the superpowers. In addition to its continental size with attendant natural resources, the EC is a wealthy advanced industrial area with a well-educated population and impressive military resources. Two of its members possessed then and still have nuclear weapons. However, the EC clearly was not in 1970 a unified entity with a determined leadership. Rather, it was and continues to be a group of countries that collaborates on a limited set of issues, primarily economic. Although more promise for the evolution of a single entity appears to be present in the mid-1990s than in the early 1970s, a new state has not yet been formed. In the basic function of providing security against external enemies, the Western European countries in the 1970s and 1980s remained dependent

Balance of Power in the 1970s

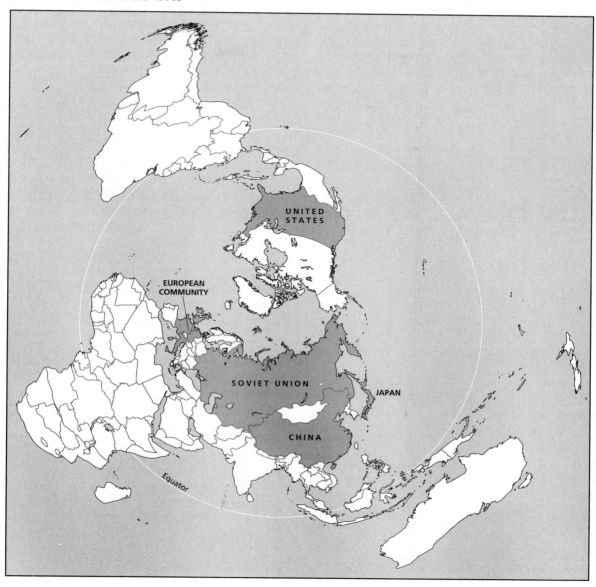

on the United States for their protection. Without a unitary state, Western Europe could not act in the same way that the United States and the Soviet Union could. For these reasons, we must dismiss the EC as an entity that would demonstrate the presence of another superpower in the international system.

Turning to Japan, we find different but altogether substantial reasons for rejecting it as a superpower. Japan had shown remarkable economic growth by 1970, and that increase in productive

wealth has zoomed since then. By the end of the 1980s decade, Japan had become the world's largest donor of foreign economic assistance, and it was home to the world's nine largest financial institutions. Nevertheless, the Asian economic leader lacked other attributes of a superpower in the contemporary era: continental size and natural resources, a politically determined leadership, and military capabilities. Given the circumstances that had emerged in the aftermath of World War II, the

Japanese were very reluctant to take on a military role. Their remarkable economic growth was aided greatly by their reliance on American protection. It seemed that, unless the United States were to decide to withdraw its security guarantee, Japan was and is unlikely to build up its military capabilities and acquire nuclear weapons for its own protection. Thus, Japan did not then and does not now qualify as a superpower with the aggregate capabilities attributable to such an entity.

Finally, let us consider China. With continental size and the world's largest population, together with a large army, China has some of the characteristics of a great power. However, China in the 1970s was a very poor country: its annual per capita income in 1980 was $566, compared with $8,612 in the United States.[13] Despite the size of its armed forces, China's military equipment was old and outdated. In the contemporary world, the evolution of military technology was producing a new generation of weapons roughly every four years. In the 1970s, China's army was equipped with weapons dating from the mid-1950s. On the basis of its aggregate capabilities, then, China did not belong in the same class as the United States and the Soviet Union.

However, recalling that the Soviet Union always possessed a much smaller capability than the United States, it is worthwhile to carry the examination of China and the international system farther. If we compare the security situation of the EC and Japan, on the one hand, and China, on the other, it is clear that China was not dependent on another power for its security, whereas the American allies banked on superpower protection. Thus, although China did not rank in aggregate capabilities with the others, it did have the characteristic of an independently determined foreign and security policy. With such ambiguity arising out of the assessment of China's attributes, the analysis needs to be taken a step further.

We noted above that a multipolar system often has present a balancer or holder of the balance whose characteristics are (1) sufficient power to make a difference in outcomes and (2) disinterest in the substance of disputes among other states. If we can observe these characteristics and also balancing behavior, we would have to give more serious consideration to the proposition that the system had changed to a multipolar one. Let us begin with an examination of disinterest.

All three of these countries—China, Soviet Union, and United States—have demonstrated their

lack of interest in the disputes of the others. For example, in 1958 in a dispute between the United States and China over Quemoy and Matsu, two islands lying off the China coast, the Chinese government sought the assistance of the Soviet Union, but the Soviet Union refused. The clear separation of national interests between the two Communist powers was further demonstrated in 1962 when China and India went to war while the Soviet Union continued to send military supplies to India. As the differences between China and the Soviet Union opened, China encouraged NATO to continue its vigilance against a Soviet threat. To the Chinese, the confrontation between the Soviet Union and its Eastern European allies with the Western European states and their protector ally, the United States, was of no moment, except that pressure from NATO might require the Soviets to attend more to their western flank than to their border with China. In other words, the Chinese sought to balance the Americans against the Soviets. Finally, it is quite clear that the United States was fundamentally disinterested in the feud between the two Communist giants who disputed the best strategy and tactics for conducting the revolution that would sweep the United States and other imperialist powers before it. To take advantage of the split and to balance the two against each other, the United States government in the 1970s first established quasi-diplomatic relations with China under Nixon and then full diplomatic relations under President Jimmy Carter.

With disinterest established, it is now necessary to inquire whether these balancers possessed sufficient power to determine the outcomes of the various substantive disputes between the others. The answer seems clear: none of the three possessed such power. Each was autonomous. Each was disinterested. But the United States could not determine the outcome of the Sino-Soviet dispute; the Soviet Union could not determine the outcome of the differences between China and the United States; and China was pretty much irrelevant to the rivalry between the superpowers except in the most marginal way.

When we extend the analysis to the wider world in which the United States and the Soviet Union competed, China was at times active, but the rivalry had more of the characteristics of a two-sided rivalry than a three-sided one. For example, even though China was for a time involved in the politics of the Angolan civil war, the conflict carried with it more of the characteristics of a Soviet-American dispute.

A few communists in Latin America were affiliated with the Chinese, but to the extent that there was a communist-noncommunist competition in Latin America, it involved U.S.-Soviet competition, as was the case in Nicaragua in the 1980s.

From this analysis emerges the conclusion that China was not quite a great power that belonged to the same class as the United States and the Soviet Union, but it and the superpowers exhibited a certain amount of balancing behavior. Even though each of them had one of the characteristics of a balancer—disinterest in the substantive disputes of the others—clear evidence was lacking that any of them possessed the other characteristic of a holder of the balance—sufficient power to determine the outcome of those disputes. While there was evidence of change in the world in the 1970s, the conclusion is inescapable that the international system continued to be characterized by bipolarity. It is necessary, therefore, to reject the hypothesis that the structure of the international system had changed to a multipolar one. Nixon's conception of a pentagonal system represented a flawed analysis of system structure, even though it did refer accurately to the increased wealth of the EC and Japan and the growing political importance of China.

• BALANCE OF POWER IN THE 1990s

Following the withdrawal of the Soviet Union from confrontation with the capitalist world after 1985 and its collapse in 1991, the international system structure was no longer clearly bipolar. In place of the Soviet Union were fifteen republics, the largest of which was Russia, which held approximately three-quarters of the land, 60 percent of the population, and much of the wealth of the former Soviet Union. In addition, Russia controlled most of the former superpower's nuclear arsenal, though it negotiated the dismantling of approximately two-thirds of it. Instead of adopting a posture of conflict toward the United States and Western Europe, the successor states looked for tutelage and financial assistance in transforming their economies from centrally planned ones to market-driven systems.

With only one remaining superpower in the world, a few observers applied the label "unipolar" to the post-Cold War international system. Others referred to a diffusion of power not just among other states but also to other entities such as corporations and banks. In addition, the air was filled with dialogue about new opportunities for an enhanced role for the United Nations and other international organizations. At the same time, the European Community—now the European Union (EU)—expanded economically and admitted new members. It also took steps in 1985 and 1991 to consolidate its gains and deepen the links that bound its members together by combining its central banking functions and creating a new currency. The Europeans also pledged themselves to strive for advanced political coordination. On the other side of the globe, Japan had so impressively grown economically that some projected that it would have the world's richest economy by the turn of the century. In addition, China's leaders had instituted economic reforms that resulted in extraordinarily high rates of economic growth in Guandong Province, the area adjacent to Hong Kong, and impressive growth in the country as a whole. An exceptionally broad-based coalition of states had gone to war in 1991 to achieve the ouster of Iraq's army from Kuwait, but the international community's attempts to intervene in the war surrounding Yugoslavia's disintegration were fumbling. The superpowers negotiated very deep cuts in their nuclear armaments, and President George Bush announced in 1992 that all American nuclear weapons that had been stationed in other countries had been returned to United States soil. In short, the evidence of flux in the world in the early 1990s was overwhelming.

With bipolarity at an end and change more prominent than continuity, it is not clear that balance of power theory can be brought to bear in the descriptive analysis of the world's international political arrangements in the early 1990s. In certain ways, a pattern of concert is apparent, for there is a widespread agreement on the principles of democratic governance and market economics. Even former Communist countries have embraced these principles, and they strive to put them into practice. Instead of a balance, there is a spirit of collaboration.

Nevertheless, that spirit masks a number of tensions, animosities, and uncertainties. Tensions arise out of the deep rift between rich and poor, the powerful and the weak. Notwithstanding an optimism generated by the expansion of freedom in the world, hundreds of millions of people continue to live in poverty. At the moment there is no inspiring idea linked to power, as was **socialism** when the Soviet Union was strong, but the economic and social conditions that socialism tried to address remain. Unless they change, resentments and aspirations of the poor are likely to continue as sources of instability, ready to be harnessed by a political leadership at some time in the future. Moreover, the Gulf War of 1991, in achieving its immediate goal of securing Kuwait's independence, engendered profound animosities among the poor masses in the region's weak countries that had supported Iraq's defiance of the powers. Such animosities have been further inflamed by the suppression of democratic elections in Algeria in 1992 that would have brought an Islamic party to power. Overall, Western hostility to Islam and its reciprocation by many devout Islamic people hold a potential for further clashes in the future. As we noted in discussing the multipolar distribution of power, uncertainty and its implicit space for miscalculation mark such an international arrangement. While it cannot be said that a multipolar distribution characterizes the international system in the mid-1990s, the presence of uncertainty is too prominent to be missed.

One of the crucial areas of uncertainty lies in the realm of international political economy, where a central question turns on which of two potential directions the future will take us. One is that of a **world market** in which international trade will flourish to everyone's benefit and in which disputes may be amicably, if tensely, settled. In contrast, the other direction would take the world to **regional trading blocs** that would compete viciously against one another and contain the seeds for animosity and conflict.

Neither structural nor traditional balance of power thinking gives us the tools fully to describe the world in the mid-1990s, when this book is being written. On the other hand, balance of power theory does provide a partial description of the contemporary world and does allow us to predict with confidence the circumstances under which the concert-like behavior is likely to be displaced by balancing behavior. As the Cold War wound down, the United States as the remaining superpower held the potential for aspiring to dominate the international system but chose not to do so. Instead, it negotiated with its former adversaries and its allies a peaceful resolution of such outstanding issues as political and economic transitions in Eastern Europe, the unification of Germany, and the management and control of nuclear weapons. Continuing to provide leadership in trade negotiations and in the Gulf War, the United States chose to work together with other states rather than assume a position of dominance. Together with others, the United States pressed hard for direct negotiations between Israel and the Arab states plus the Palestinians to find a solution to one of the foremost problems of the Middle East. In some cases, such as the question of intervention in the Yugoslav wars, it deferred to its European allies. Flexibility was retained in facing questions of institutional adjustments in Europe. In assuming this collaborative and leadership role rather than seeking domination, the United States did not induce others to balance against it.

However, should the United States over time choose to approach the rest of the world in a different way, aspiring to gain a position of dominance, balance of power theory tells us that other countries would form a coalition against it. In addition, it is quite likely that in the long run, other states will grow into positions that will place them in the rank of great powers and the international system will take on a multipolar character. Should one of those new great powers, or a coalition of them, go after the conquest and domination of others, those others would combine to oppose such an attempt.

Thus, balance of power theory explains something quite important. It describes the circumstances under which balances are likely to be formed. On the other hand, there is a great deal that the theory does not go into. It remains an important component of theoretical analysis in international politics, but it is far from sufficient, by itself, to explain all of the things that fall within our problematic.

For its defenders, the balance of power is one of many mechanisms that help to preserve order in the international society of states. Others are international law and organizations, diplomacy, conferences at all levels, and other means. Clearly, these are the tools of the powerful, for it is they who manage the international order.

System Management

Although international politics is a self-help system in which each state determines its own interests and acts on them, problems clearly arise that affect the stability and well-being of the order as a whole as well as the individual units, and these require management of some kind. For example, even though the war in Yugoslavia in the early 1990s took place within that country's borders, it generated a significant migration of refugees to other European countries. Moreover, recalling the history of earlier times in which Balkan wars drew in all of the European powers, Chancellor Helmut Kohl of Germany and other leaders coordinated the efforts of the European

Union in adopting policies designed to contain and bring an end to the hostilities.

Similarly, in the discussion above concerning the balance of power, a coalition under threat acts to oppose a country that seeks to gain a position of domination. That, too, is a mechanism of managing the international system by preserving an arrangement in which states retain their autonomy only through collaboration with others. This is not to say that the balance of power always defends the autonomy of states. In the most notorious example in history, Poland was partitioned three times at the end of the eighteenth century until it ceased to exist as an independent country. Every one of the partitions was done in the name of the balance of power.

The coordination necessary to manage an international system is easier to achieve in a bipolar structure than in a multipolar arrangement, for two reasons. First, fewer parties to management activities need to be satisfied. Second, the greater inequality in the bipolar system makes the superpowers more willing to pay the costs of managing the system.[14] As superpowers grow to take an interest in activities throughout the world, they are more inclined to identify world order interests as their own and to act accordingly. In the period after World War II, for example, the United States promoted an international trading order based on market principles. In doing so, it recognized the competitive weaknesses of its European and Asian allies and allowed them to engage in restrictive trade practices to strengthen their economies. This amounted to a sacrifice by the United States on behalf of the world order that it was promoting, for its own industries suffered in competition with those of its allies. Nevertheless, the international order as a whole was rendered more stable and the United States and its allies were made more secure by such economic sacrifices.

In multipolar systems, in contrast, it is less likely that any single country or even small group of countries would identify its or their own interests with those of the system as a whole. More likely is their dividing into opposing coalitions, because the aspirations of one to take on a global management role would appear to be a quest for a position of domination. Given the uncertainty implicit in the multipolar system, others are likely to organize to oppose that quest as the balance of power goes into operation.

After the Cold War, in the situation with a single superpower, management seems quite feasible so long as the United States does not seek to impose its own unique vision as a world order and continues to lead in a cooperative endeavor. In the first years of this new structural arrangement, the acceptance of democratic and market principles—the principles of American society—by so many states smoothed the way to such management. However, should a cleavage open up over time as the result, say, of a worldwide economic depression, the United States might then try to impose its order on reluctant states. It is worth recalling that in the 1960s, the United States made tremendous expenditures and suffered extensive casualties in bringing its vision of world order to Vietnam even in the face of the political and moral opposition of its allies and others throughout the world. In the Gulf War, many others joined in the coalition to bring a certain order by means of military force to the problems of that region. Both because of the widespread support and the formidable efficiency of the force, the action appeared to be done in the name of global management. However, another challenge in the same region might not command a broad consensus. Nevertheless, the force remains available—indeed, the United States' military presence in the Gulf region has been enhanced—for the imposition of a particular conception of order. Whether other states would join or oppose or, alternatively, stand aside from such a managerial task would depend on their own respective definitions of their interests. If those interests coincided with American management, they would either join or, at a minimum, remain on the sidelines. However, if they were to perceive an attempt by the United States to dominate the region, they would forge a coalition to oppose that attempt.

Problems of management of the international system vary with the structural arrangements determined by the distribution of power across the units, but the tasks of management remain similar. These fall into the categories of political recognition and legitimation; disputes, war, and related concerns; economic conditions and interactions, including development, trade, and debt; weapons transfers; environmental concerns; and issues centering on human rights, humanitarian issues, and equality.

• POLITICAL RECOGNITION AND LEGITIMATION

Even though in a self-help system the units decide on their own interests and the means for pursuing them, their effectiveness depends in part on their **recognition** as actors by other units in the international system. For the most part, such recognition is extended when a government has control of a territory and is able effectively to control it and to carry out its international obligations. Nevertheless, there remains considerable discretion in the area of international system management.

Disintegration of Soviet Union and Yugoslavia

For example, in the process of the Soviet Union's disintegration, the Baltic republics of Lithuania, Estonia, and Latvia asserted their independence in advance of President Mikhail Gorbachev's willingness to let them secede from the Soviet Union. Part of the politics of secession occurred in Washington, for Lithuania sought recognition by the Bush administration of its independence from Moscow. A basis for anticipating that Washington would be receptive to an overture from Lithuania lay in the long history of America's withholding recognition of Soviet sovereignty over the Baltic republics. Those countries had been absorbed by the Soviet Union in 1940 as part of the Soviet Union's expansion prior to its entry into World War II, and the United States had never officially conceded the legitimacy of this incorporation of previously independent states into the Soviet Union.

With the complete breakup of the former Soviet Union, the establishment of independent republics has been mostly determined by a peaceful process of negotiation and acceptance by the leaders of the former constituent republics themselves. For example, Russia, Belarus, Ukraine, Kazakhstan, and the other members of the Commonwealth of Independent States (CIS) accept one other's existence in an act of management. However, some parts of these republics attempted by force of arms to establish their own independence. For instance, Nagorno-Karabakh, which had been an autonomous region within the Soviet Union, fought to retain its autonomy against the claims of Azerbaijan. If these units succeed in gaining military control over their own territory, their legitimacy will be partly determined not simply by recognition by the governments of the territories out of which they are carved but also by acknowledgement of their legal existence by the remainder of the international community.

To cite another recent example, the United States and the Western European governments in early 1992 dickered over whether to continue to work for the unity of Yugoslavia or to recognize as new states Croatia and Slovenia—and later, Bosnia-Herzegovina—which had declared their independence. In the end, German wishes prevailed in the European Union, with the United States following the European lead, when diplomatic recognition was extended to the newly independent states.

Decolonization

This elementary management task is not reserved for such unusual circumstances as the breakup of states in Eastern Europe. It extends back in time over the centuries and has been exercised regularly in the modern period. Most prominently, political recognition and legitimation formed a crucial part of the **decolonization** process that established over one hundred new states in the post-World War II era. Despite the prominence in the news of a few violent cases such as French Indochina, Indonesia, and Algeria, decolonization was on the whole managed peacefully. For the most part, the **territorial boundaries** established by the colonial powers were accepted. Even though some of the new governments did not fully exercise control over their populations, the international community, primarily through the United Nations, conferred status and recognition on them.[15] With the inclusion of very small states as members, the United Nations offered some countries their only opportunity to act in the international arena, for they are too small and too poor to have a capacity to conduct an ordinary foreign policy that entails sending representatives to other countries' capitals.

In certain cases, the management of decolonization shaped not just the foreign policy dimensions of the new states but also their internal political arrangements. For example, when the minority white regime under Ian Smith in Rhodesia unilaterally declared its independence in 1965, the international community followed the leadership of the colonial power, Great Britain, in imposing sanctions against the breakaway state. After a number of years, Britain with the assistance of the United States under President Carter negotiated independence for the newly named state of Zimbabwe under conditions of majority rule. At the end of the 1980s and early 1990s, a massive United Nations presence in South-West Africa brought to power under a supervised, democratic election a new government in now-independent Namibia.

Recognition of Nongovernmental Political Organizations

For the most part, the management task is limited to extending political recognition to and conferring legitimacy on states. Nevertheless, there are dimensions of the task involving other entities. For example, in 1981, France and Mexico extended recognition to the FMLN, the Farabundo Marti National Liberation Front in El Salvador and called on other governments to treat the coalition of guerrilla organizations as a negotiating partner. Another way in which this task sometimes involves nongovernmental organizations is the extension of participatory rights by United Nations organs to private organizations. Many private associations are granted access to the UN Economic and Social Council. Although very controversial, the United Nations General Assembly in 1973 even allowed Yasir Arafat, the leader of the Palestine Liberation Organization, to address it. Additionally, through subcontracting, governments confer legitimacy on private relief organizations and private firms that are active in humanitarian and economic development assistance activities.

Withholding Recognition

Just as the conferral of legitimacy and recognition helps to shape the effectiveness by which entities participate in international politics, so too does the withholding of recognition and the denial of legitimacy form part of this management task. From the triumph of Mao Tse Tung and his communist cohorts in China in 1949, the United States was able to persuade the United Nations and many countries to withhold recognition of the regime that ruled China from Bejing. Instead, the Chinese seat at the United Nations was held by the former Nationalist government that had fled to the island of Taiwan following its defeat on the mainland. Not until 1971 did the United States and its followers bend to the will of the majority in New York and accede to the formal seating of the Bejing government in the United Nations.

During civil wars, one of the formidable tasks of ruling governments is to persuade other governments not to recognize the rebellions. The outcome of the American Civil War was shaped to some extent by Washington's ability to dissuade European governments from extending recognition to the Confederacy. Nearer to our own time, the secessionist movement of Biafra, the province that fought to establish its independence from Nigeria from 1968 to 1971, was substantially hindered because the Organization of African Unity withheld recognition, and governments from other parts of the world followed the African lead.

While this management function is the most fundamental one, for it helps to determine which are the acceptable partners in the international system, the tasks of management extend much farther. Among the most central of management tasks are those associated with war and peace.

• DISPUTES, WARS, AND RELATED CONCERNS

Fighting wars to restore a balance is only one way in which the powers do system management related to war and peace. War avoidance and dispute settlement comprise extremely important management activities. Bringing an end to a war and handling its aftermath also form part of management tasks in the international system. Finally, peacekeeping and international assistance with transitions of governing arrangements within states that are ending civil wars constitute other management tasks that the international community sometimes takes on.

The Middle East Since 1945

A survey of the history of the Middle East since the end of World War II emphasizes strife and wars. One of the central conflicts of the region—that between Israel and the Arabs—has produced five wars that give dramatic emphasis to the continuing strife. With Israel's assertion of its independence in 1948 came the first war with its Arab neighbors. In 1956, Israel together with France and Britain attacked Egypt to initiate a second major war. In 1967, Israel achieved a brilliant military victory against Syria, Jordan, and Egypt, following the last country's opening attack. To recover its losses and prestige, Egypt then attacked Israel to begin the fourth war in 1973. After having signed a peace treaty with Egypt, Israel then invaded Lebanon in 1982 in the fifth Arab-Israeli war of the era.

Other wars have also marked this history. Disputes and armed border clashes have occurred between Yemen and Southern Yemen and their neighbors. In the bloodiest war in the region, Iraq and Iran fought for eight years, between 1980 and 1988. Then, following Iraq's invasion of Kuwait in 1990, an Arab and out-of-region coalition fought an extremely violent though brief war to remove Iraq's forces from the neighboring kingdom.

The horrors of war and the thrill of victories provided drama and commanded headlines throughout this history, but the quieter management tasks of dispute settlement, arrangements of truces, peacekeeping, and dealing with the aftermath of war formed an equally important part of the history. It is true that many of these arrangements failed to prevent the wars and solve all of the problems at issue, but it is equally apparent that the wars did not settle matters either. In some cases, such as the liberation of Kuwait from occupying forces, war was successful. In other cases, such as the settlement of the Israeli-Egyptian dispute, peaceful management succeeded equally well.

Prior to the first Israeli-Arab war in 1948, many efforts had been made to deal with the Palestine issues. One aspect was bringing to a conclusion the British mandate, undertaken after World War I, to guide Palestine to independence. This entailed withdrawal of British control of the territory and handing over sovereignty to a successor regime. Complicating the management of this withdrawal were contradictory British pledges to assist Jews in securing a homeland, on the one hand, and to ensure that Arab Palestinians were not injured in doing so, on the other. Unable to accomplish this task, Britain brought the issue to the United Nations, where the General Assembly approved two different versions of a plan for partition of Palestine between Jews and Arabs. It was in that context that Israel declared its independence as a sovereign state and from which emanated the modern Palestinian "problem."

Prior to the second Arab-Israel war in 1956, Secretary General of the United Nations Dag Hammarskjöld under the direction of the powers in the Security Council sought to avoid a war that appeared imminent throughout the summer. In addition, the United States sought during the same time to restrain its allies, Britain and France, and certain other countries like Canada made attempts to find a peaceful solution to the crisis that had emerged in the wake of Egypt's assuming control from a British and French company of the Suez Canal. Following Israel's armed thrust toward the Suez Canal at the end of October and France and Britain's subsequent invasion of Egypt, the United States compelled them to desist by refusing Britain's needy request for foreign exchange credits. A diplomacy that involved the mounting of the first United Nations peacekeeping force was employed to bring about the withdrawal of the invading forces. In addition, the secretary general arranged for clearing the Suez Canal of ships that had been sunk during the hostilities.

The United Nations Emergency Force (UNEF), which was created in the midst of the crisis and then stationed on Egyptian territory along the Israeli border, provided an effective instrument standing between the hostile parties to the dispute. Being a diplomatic instrument rather than a fighting force, however, UNEF was withdrawn in 1967 when Egypt requested its removal, and a new war broke out in which Israel was victorious.

Conquered in that war were territories that had been controlled by three states: the Sinai Peninsula and Gaza Strip from Egypt, the West Bank and East Jerusalem from Jordan, and the Golan Heights from Syria. To regain its territory, Egypt again went to war in 1973, with an initial success but then an ultimate defeat.

Over the course of three administrations, however, the United States negotiated a series of agreements that led to Israel's withdrawing from Egyptian territory. The process was an intricate one that began with a very active step-by-step diplomacy by U.S. National Security Advisor Henry Kissinger following the 1973 war. Then, in 1977, Egyptian President Anwar Sadat made a dramatic trip to Jerusalem to meet with Israeli Prime Minister Menachem Begin to start face-to-face negotiations. Continuing the process, in 1979, Begin and Sadat concluded the Camp David Agreement, which was negotiated personally by U.S. President Carter. Finally, the disputants signed a peace treaty, and Israel returned all Egyptian territory that it had occupied. All of these steps, but particularly the Camp David Agreement, were assisted by American wealth being expended on Israel and Egypt as an inducement to their historic diplomatic and political agreement.

Inasmuch as the other territorial issues remain unresolved, as does the issue of a homeland for Arab Palestinians and the acceptance of Israel as a legitimate state in the eyes of some of the neighboring Arabs, very substantial efforts over the years have been made to bring about diplomatic agreements to settle the disputes and to avoid war. In the aftermath of the Gulf War of 1991—under pressure of the powers—the Arab states, representatives of the Palestinians, and Israel held a series of face-to-face meetings, continuing the attempt to find resolutions of their differences in order to avoid further wars. Results of these negotiations include the establishment of full diplomatic relations between Israel and Jordan and the creation and implementation of a Palestinian Authority on parts of the West Bank. In late 1995, representatives of Israel and Syria met in the United States together with Americans to discuss terms for restoring the Golan Heights to Syria and establishing normal relations between the two Middle East antagonists.

Canada in the Korean War

Management tasks associated with peacefully settling disputes, avoiding and controlling war, and dealing with the aftermath of war tend to accrue more to the major powers than to smaller ones. Nevertheless, subordinate allies and regional states sometimes act to restrain the belligerent behavior of the great powers. Unable to employ such tools as forceful coercion and economic assistance, they have to rely on intelligent diplomacy and patience in their system management efforts.

One example of such an undertaking was Canada's diplomacy during the Korean War, in which the United States acted in what appeared to others to be dangerous and provocative ways. First undertaken as a world order management task itself, the American intervention in the Korean War passed in the fall of 1950 from a defense of South Korea against a North Korean invasion to an attempt to unify the Korean peninsula by force. Canadian and others' fears that the American army's thrust north would provoke China proved to be well founded when several million Chinese forces entered Korea to drive the Americans back from the Chinese border. Furthermore, allied countries had reason to fear that the United States might employ nuclear weapons in Korea, and they sought to restrain American policy makers.[16]

Central America in the 1980s

A less fearsome but nevertheless threatening situation occurred in Central America in the 1980s, when the United States government under President Ronald Reagan undertook a belligerent policy toward Nicaragua. Fearful of a larger war with dreadful consequences, neighboring Latin American countries sought through diplomacy to find solutions short of war to Central American disputes and to wrest initiative from the threatening United States. One of these efforts, called the Esquipulas process, succeeded in moving Nicaragua's Sandinista government in early 1988 to reach a cease-fire agreement with the Nicaraguan contras. Eventually, with the support of the United States and other countries as well, Nicaragua held elections in 1990 that brought an opposition coalition to power, displacing the Sandinista government.

In the aftermath of this war, both the United Nations and the Organization of American States provided assistance in disarming and relocating the armed opposition. Moreover, donor countries extended some economic assistance to help Nicaragua to rebuild its economy, which had been devastated both by the war and by policy errors of the Sandinista government. Reconstruction and development in the aftermath of destructive wars is one of the tasks undertaken by the international community, and it forms one part of the management falling under the rubric of economics.

• ECONOMIC CONDITIONS AND INTERACTION

Restoration of Defeated Powers

Traditional balance of power tenets inform us of the need to restore defeated countries after wars in order to rebuild an equilibrium of power. A certain logic underlies this guideline. Any country that had aspired to dominance is not only a great power but also a major prize as measured by the resources it would offer to another would-be conqueror. Rebuilding its economy and legitimizing its government occupies what otherwise would be a vacuum waiting to be filled by others aspiring to increase their power. Thus, rehabilitation and economic strengthening become international system management functions.

Embedded in the logic is a management alternative: the defeated country can be thoroughly repressed or obliterated. When Rome conquered Carthage, the Romans killed all of the adult males, made slaves of all of the females and children, and sowed the entire land of Carthage with salt, rendering it completely unproductive. Thus, Carthage neither remained a great power nor persisted as a prize that might be coveted by others. Given such a choice in the modern world, most observers would adopt the balance of power alternative response to the logic as a moral and just solution, but the logic does impel one course of action or another.

Such stark choices were avoided in the aftermath of World War I. Instead, the victorious allies required defeated Germany to pay onerous reparations to them for the costs of the war. Being neither repressed nor restored, Germany went on to provide a breeding ground for deep resentments that led, eventually, to broad support for the vicious Nazi regime under Hitler and his policy of conquest that became World War II. Seeking to avoid a replay of those devastating consequences of a misguided policy, the democratic victors in World War II took a different approach in handling the aftermath of the war. After rejecting the Carthage option, formulated in the so-called Morgenthau Plan to reduce Germany to a pastoral country, the United States wanted to restore German power, though without a strong military capacity. However, the Soviet partner in the Grand Alliance, whose homeland had been devastated by the German onslaught, sought such extensive reparations from Germany that Americans would have been required to subsidize German living standards in their zone of occupation while Germans made transfer payments to the Soviets. This conundrum proved unsolvable and disagreements over reparations policy comprised one of the issues that divided East and West and led to the Cold War.

As the rivalry between the superpowers evolved, the United States turned to the balance of power option and followed policies that led to the full recovery of Western Europe, including what became the Federal Republic Germany in 1949. Employing the mechanisms of the Marshall Plan, which transferred large capital resources to Western Europe, and the North Atlantic Treaty Organization that eventually incorporated West Germany, the United States led the way to building a mighty bastion in Europe. Seeking to restore an unarmed Japan to economic health and political democracy, the United States established an economic program parallel with the Marshall Plan to strengthen that country, and efforts toward achieving both economic development and a peace treaty that returned self-government to the Japanese were accelerated after the Korean War began in 1950.

Because of its enormous power and wealth, the United States had been in a position to manage the aftermath of the war pretty much according to its own interests and to restore a balance against the revisionist power of the Soviet Union and its allies. Although not without certain weaknesses and chinks in its armor, the broad alliance system put into place over the years under American leadership went substantially beyond balance to a preponderance of power.[17]

Post-World War II Liberal Economic Order

In its overall system management, the United States dealt not just with the aftermath of the war but also constructed a liberal order in the international political economy. Together with British, Canadian, and French planners, Americans developed the conceptual framework and the institutional arrangements for this order at a meeting in Bretton Woods, New Hampshire, in 1944, a year before World War II ended. Agreed to at the Bretton Woods Conference were two important institutions, the International Monetary Fund (IMF) and the International Bank for Reconstruction and Development (IBRD), the latter more popularly known as the World Bank.

Designed to support the flow of international trade through support to its members in times of balance of payments difficulties, the International Monetary Fund has also become deeply involved in domestic macroeconomic policies as a means of assisting countries in difficulty to restore their balanced relationship with the international political economy. This role has become controversial in recent years; both the functioning of the IMF and the debate over its actions in the contemporary world will be treated in Chapter 8. Central to the maintenance of a stable international monetary system was pegging the U.S. dollar to the gold standard. Over time, other countries that were dependent on the United States for their security and other matters began accumulating dollars in amounts that exceeded the ability of the American government to redeem them for gold. Eventually, in 1971, President Nixon took action to correct American international economic difficulties that included the severing of the fixed relationship between the dollar and gold. Although attempts were made over the next couple of years to structure a new system of fixed exchange rates, this proved in 1973 to be unsuccessful, and the world has lived since then with floating exchange rates. Instead of a state-managed international monetary system, then, a market in currencies determines the relative values, although states intervene in the currency market when they decide that some action in their interests is necessary. Thus, even though the institutions created at Bretton Woods continue intact, some observers comment that the **Bretton Woods system** was ended in the early 1970s.[18]

Unlike the IMF, which was designed to assist governments in temporary difficulties, the World Bank promotes long-term economic development. It lends investment funds and provides technical assistance to countries for capital and infrastructure projects. Capital projects are those that create new productive wealth, such as a manufacturing or an agricultural facility. Infrastructure projects are governmental undertakings that provide support facilities for production and commerce, such as electrical power grids, roads and other transport facilities, warehouses, and so forth. In addition to commercial loans, the IBRD extends concessionary loans to poorer countries. Concessionary terms include significant periods of grace in which no repayments are required, periods of up to fifty years for repayment, and very low interest rates.

Although consideration had been given at the Bretton Woods Conference to the creation of an International Trade Organization, it was rejected. In its place, the powers created in 1948 the General Agreement on Tariffs and Trade. Dedicated to the promotion of liberalized international trade, the GATT established norms for trade and offered a forum for the negotiation of additional agreements that would expand free trade by reducing national restrictions on it. A number of rounds of multilateral negotiations have succeeded in this task, although the so-called Uruguay Round was stalled in the early 1990s by a disagreement over ending agricultural subsidies and did not successfully conclude until April 1994, taking effect on January 1, 1995.

Following the monetary difficulties in the early 1970s arising from floating exchange rates and the financial troubles caused by the fourfold increase in oil prices in 1973–1974, consultations among the leading industrial states have increased. One of the prominent mechanisms used to try to manage the international political economy are the annual summit meetings—that is, encounters of the heads of government—of the leading industrial countries, referred to as the Group of Seven, or G-7. The G-7 countries are Britain, Canada, France, Germany, Italy, Japan, and United States. In recent years, Russia has been invited to attend these meetings though not to participate in the main discussions.

Debt Crisis

A new problem in the international political economy crying out for management in the late 1970s and early 1980s was the debt crisis. Originating in the 1973–1974 oil price increases, the accumulation of debt by less developed countries grew to proportions that seemed for a time to threaten the entire world financial system. Quadrupling the price of petroleum entailed an extensive transfer of payments from the oil-importing countries to the members of the Organization of Petroleum Exporting Countries (OPEC). However, those countries were insufficiently large and economically developed to be able effectively to use the massive funds available to them, and a way had to be found to "recycle" the funds. Without putting the monies available to effective use, they simply would have been withdrawn from the world economy, causing a deep economic depression. Governments left the recycling task to private banks, and the banks promoted extensive lending without the ordinary caution that conservative bankers ordinarily exercise. Many less developed countries borrowed money not only to cover their costs of importing oil but also to pay for other forms of consumption. In other words, the funds available were not plowed into productive enterprises that would secure the earnings necessary to pay back the debt; they were used to pay current expenses.

First indications of inability to pay even the interest charges on the debt emanated from Poland in 1980. Although that problem was to some extent managed by the banks' complete withholding of any further credit to any Eastern European country, a crisis nevertheless occurred in 1982, when the Mexican government informed the American government that it would not be able to meet the interest payment on its international debt. This caused the Reagan administration to extend a temporary loan to Mexico and make arrangements for a longer-term solution. In addition, the United States government pressured private banks to accommodate by participating in a series of measures that restructured and, in some cases, reduced the debts of the developing countries. After more than a decade of managing the international debt problem, no one any longer fears a general worldwide financial crisis arising from it. On the other hand, many less developed countries in Latin America and Africa continue to suffer from the need to use some of their precious export earnings to pay back debts that were contracted under circumstances very different from those prevailing more recently.

Although there are monetary, trade, and financial aspects to the transfer of weapons and related technology, the subject of weaponry, particularly that part concerned with the spread of nuclear weapons, is a topic with its own characteristics, deserving of separate treatment as a problem of system management.

• WEAPONS AND NUCLEAR TECHNOLOGY TRANSFERS

Because military force is so closely associated with securing and challenging the state and the production of arms is unevenly distributed among nations, a substantial international traffic in arms tends to occur. Part of this traffic flows from major allies to dependent allies as grants that enable the dependent allies to employ the weapons on behalf of mutual interests. For example, during the Cold War, both the

United States and the Soviet Union transferred large amounts of military hardware to smaller allies both in peacetime and during wars. In the Indian subcontinent, for example, the United States was a major arms supplier to Pakistan, and the Soviets contributed many arms to India. During the Vietnam War, not only did the United States engage in combat with its own weapons, but also it contributed massive amounts of weaponry and training to the South Vietnamese army. North Vietnam, meanwhile, was greatly aided in carrying on its fight by military assistance flowing from the Soviet Union.

Some weapons transfers among allies, rather than being granted, are commercial sales in which an ally sells hardware to other countries or to opposition movements. Saudi Arabia, a wealthy oil producer, buys military equipment from the United States. Although the examples here are drawn from the Cold War era in which the arms trade was dominated by the superpowers, other countries that are arms manufacturers also engage in the transfer of arms. Czechoslovakia, Britain, France, and Brazil are some examples of such participants in what one author called "the arms bazaar."[19]

As the Iran-Contra affair unraveled and came to public notice in 1986 and subsequent years, it provided a rare glimpse into the world of private arms dealers. Inasmuch as the intricate and often illegal activities of transferring weapons both to governments and to opposition groups retain a clandestine character, not very much public information is available. Nevertheless, the regularity with which armaments show up in both internal and international disputes indicates the existence of a market. That market is partly shaped by the governments that retain oligopolistic control over production. But it also partly conforms to market forces of supply and demand and is affected by the activities of merchants and brokers.

Proliferation of Nuclear Weapons

Since the beginning of the nuclear era, political leaders and ordinary, thoughtful people have been concerned about the proliferation of nuclear weapons. Continuing efforts have been made by the international community to slow the spread of nuclear weapons technology. Starting in 1945 with a single nuclear power, the United States, the world has witnessed the open acquisition of nuclear weapons by four other powers: the Soviet Union in 1949, Britain in 1952, France in 1960, and China in 1964. Although India exploded a nuclear device in 1974, the government denied that it was developing a nuclear weapons program. Most attentive observers believe that Israel has a nuclear weapons capability, but there is no direct evidence that Israel possesses a nuclear arsenal. Pakistan has worked on a nuclear weapons program, as has North Korea. For a while, Brazil and Argentina had nuclear weapons development programs, but both have abjured them. Iraq had begun a nuclear weapons development program, but Israel attacked the Iraqi facility in 1981 and destroyed it. Subsequently, Iraq renewed its quest for nuclear weapons through a deceptive program of acquiring pieces of technology from many different Western countries. Part of the Gulf War settlement imposed on Iraq was the requirement that the defeated country grant access to international inspectors who would ensure that all of Iraq's facilities associated with nuclear weapons development were destroyed.

From early in the nuclear era, efforts have proceeded to find a means of system management of nuclear weapons. A more systematic analysis of these efforts will occur in Chapter 13, but we note here that a comprehensive plan to have the United Nations Security Council supervise nuclear weapons, offered in 1946, was an early casualty of the emerging Cold War. Most notable as a multilateral effort to manage this problem is the Nonproliferation Treaty, which came into effect in 1970. This treaty provides that the nuclear signatories will not transfer nuclear weapons technology and that the nonnuclear signatories will neither develop nuclear weapons nor accept their transfer from suppliers.

Although a war that employed nuclear weapons would be a catastrophe for very large numbers of people, it is a remote possibility. Other remote but potentially devastating catastrophes are threatened by environmental degradation flowing from relentless industrialization that ignores its environmental consequences.

• ENVIRONMENTAL CONCERNS

Certain environmental concerns have been present and obvious for some time, while others have come into consciousness only in recent years, and still others are based upon speculation and indefinite data. Poisoning of the environment by chemicals, acid rain, and deforestation are well-recognized phenomena. More recently, the world has become increasingly aware of the extinction of many animal and plant species, with the consequent reduction in diversity of biological life. Concerns that pollution in the upper atmosphere results in **depletion of the ozone layer** and carries the potential threat of **global warming** are partly speculative and not wholly established. What all of the problems of environmental degradation have in common is that more than one country is involved, with the sources of pollution in any country crossing borders indiscriminately. Some of the problems have global repercussions and even potentially catastrophic consequences for the entire planet and all its inhabitants. Many, if not most, environmental problems are by-products of a common type of industrialization that occurs without consideration of its environmental costs.

In her book published in 1962, Rachel Carson heavily documented and persuasively argued that the widespread use of chemical insecticides was slowly killing animal life. One day, she contended, there would be a "silent spring," a world devoid of animal and insect noises.[20] Her book alerted ordinary people, scientists, business people, and government officials to the devastating effects that were being wrought by the heavy employment of the widely used insecticide DDT. With this new awareness, people not only adopted new policies and new techniques but also new attitudes that grew into an environmental movement. Groups like Greenpeace were formed to actively advocate for preserving the environment. In Europe, "green" political parties were formed that elected representatives to legislatures. By 1972, the United Nations sponsored a conference on the environment in Stockholm, and an International Agency on the Environment was formed, with its headquarters in Nairobi, Kenya. Twenty years later, in 1992, an Earth Summit was held in Rio de Janeiro, Brazil, which expanded the agenda to include agreements on the ozone layer, global warming, and the protection of **biodiversity.**

Another environmental problem that has impressed itself on political consciousness is that of **acid rain.** From the smokestacks of heavy industry flow particles and gases that combine with precipitation to form acid rain. This precipitant corrodes beautiful, classic monuments like the Parthenon in Athens, and it falls on forests and lakes, defoliating the former and killing fish and other marine life in the latter. Although such deleterious effects burden mainly the countries from which the pollution emanates, the contamination also is carried by winds across international borders. As serious as these problems are in the highly industrialized, democratic countries, they are acute in the former communist countries in Eastern Europe. In addition to the contaminants generated at industrial sites, the burning of fuel in automobiles adds to the pollution of the air in localities.

Both of these activities as well as burning trees and other combustibles produce carbon dioxide in great quantities, and the effects extend far beyond the originating sites. Carbon dioxide is the main source of global warming: as the gas collects in the atmosphere, it creates in essence a greenhouse effect around the earth. Although this effect is still the subject of heated controversy in the scientific community, the potential consequences of a warmer world are chilling to contemplate. Given the potential global implications, this matter seems destined for management on an international system basis, not something that can be handled individually by separate countries.

Similarly, depletion of the ozone layer, which blocks the sun's harmful ultraviolet rays, would affect the entire world. Holes in the ozone layer have been observed, particularly in Antarctica, where none of the chlorofluorocarbons that cause depletion of the layer is released. Given the potential for broad devastation around the world, this problem seems naturally to belong on the agenda of the international community for consideration and management. In 1992, the industrial countries signed a treaty providing for the phasing out of the use of chlorofluorocarbons.

These and other concerns such as preserving the diversity of plant and animal life are long-term problems. Some of them remain remote. More immediate are smaller catastrophes resulting from natural disasters, civil wars, and governments' repression of their own citizens. These offer another challenge for international system management.

• HUMANITARIAN ISSUES AND HUMAN RIGHTS

Crop failures resulting from drought or disease, earthquakes, volcano eruptions, floods, desertification, and similar events comprise part of the human condition, but their impact is uneven, striking particular populations in specific places. In modern times with good communications, such temporary conditions are brought to the attention of governments and people throughout the world. Wealthy countries tend to respond through both governmental and private agencies by providing relief to the victims of natural disasters. International networks of nongovernmental associations such as the International Red Cross and Red Crescent Societies, as well as international organizations such as the United Nations, carry food, medicine, temporary shelter, clothing, bedding, and so forth to the sites of suffering.

The international community also helps in managing such problems by making advances in scientific knowledge available. For example, in 1991 in the Philippines, the Mount Pinatubo volcano erupted, spewing its rocks and lava so extensively that tens of thousands of people were deprived of their homes and the lava destroyed Clark Field, the huge American air base nearby. Despite the enormous physical destruction, no lives were lost because of the application of scientific knowledge: American experts in volcanic activity gave such timely warning of the impending disaster that people had time to flee the path of destruction.

Other catastrophes are caused by humanmade events. Wars and economic policies create victims. Following the overthrow of Mohammed Siad Barre in Somalia in 1991, for example, warring factions brought about not just death and devastation for the people of that country but also destruction of the agricultural base. Both the fighting and the inability to produce food contributed to the disaster. Generalized violence in Mogadishu, the capital, prevented international relief agencies from bringing supplies to starving people. Small children acquired weapons and joined in the fighting because it gave them a better chance of obtaining food to avoid starvation. To cope with such tragedies, the international community works to arrange cease-fires so relief workers can bring in supplies, while diplomats labor on behalf of longer-term settlements.

In addition to these large-scale catastrophes, governments commit substantial human rights abuses in which individuals, one by one, are tortured and killed by police and military agencies; clandestine groups that act for governments intent upon repressing their dissident citizens also commit such abuses. Some of these incidents, like the killing of over a half million communists in Indonesia in 1965, pass almost without notice and completely without outcry. Others, like the expulsion of the entire population of Phnom Penh, Cambodia, by the Khmer Rouge in 1976, are remarked upon but without any effect on the victims. In some cases, foreign governments and private groups draw considerable attention to systematic killing by governments of their citizens, as hap-

pened in the Guatemalan army's extensive repression of citizens between 1978 and 1983. In this case, the United States government suspended military assistance to Guatemala in the late 1970s. Some testimony maintains that foreign intervention can save the lives of the tortured and the repressed, as occurred in Argentina during its "dirty war" in the 1970s.[21]

Humanitarian assistance to victims of natural disasters often helps a weak government cope with a problem that it lacks the material and organizational resources to handle. Thus, the impulses that have moved others to help victims may give political support to the government that exercises control over a territory and people. On the other hand, efforts to alleviate suffering that is caused by governments is more likely to be met by resistance, for it may obstruct political goals. In some cases, the withholding of food and shelter may be a deliberate policy to induce compliance. In other cases, relief efforts may interfere with military objectives. As in the case of Guatemala, any foreign assistance to the victims of "death squads" would be regarded by the government as subversive and subject to the same kind of repression that was being meted out to the government's opponents. From 1992 to 1995, the world witnessed the difficulties of bringing relief supplies to Sarajevo, the capital of Bosnia, because the city lay under siege by Bosnian Serb forces.

In the crosscurrents of international politics in the 1990s, a very practical as well as academic debate pits a tenuous but tough consensus on the protection for human rights against a deeper and longer-lived principle that foreigners do not have the right to interfere in matters that fall within the **domestic jurisdiction** of states. No clear resolution of these contradictory guidelines is in sight, and the extent to which the international community does attend to human rights violations is determined by practice, exigent circumstances, and political interests.

Some observers argue that the broad problems of system management can only be addressed by a transformation of the international system. Those arguments will be examined and assessed in Chapter 14. Meanwhile, we will continue to assume that the international system essentially as we know it will continue to exist. To get a firmer grasp on why the international system persists, it is necessary to examine carefully the basic units that comprise the system and the other units that participate in international affairs.

• IMPORTANT TERMS

acid rain
aggression
anarchical
balance of power
balancer: see *holder*
biodiversity
bipolar
bipolar system
Bretton Woods system
Cold War
decolonization
depletion of the ozone
    layer
detente
distribution of
    capabilities
domestic jurisdiction
East
global warming
hierarchical
holder of the balance
imitation
invisible hand

major powers
miscalculation
multipolar
ordering principle
overreaction
pentagonal system
recognition
regional trading blocs
self-determination
self-help system
socialism
socialization
specification of
    functions
structure
superpowers
system
territorial boundaries
unintended
    consequences
West
world market

• STUDY QUESTIONS

1. What is a balance of power in international politics? Does balancing occur automatically? Or must states pursue deliberate policies of balance to achieve an equilibrium?

2. What are the relationships between balance of power and war, on the one hand, and the preservation of order, on the other?

3. How have structural realists carved out a domain for scientific examination, and how successful have they been in isolating the international system's structure?

4. Explain the main points in the structural realist argument.

5. Compare and contrast the most important differences in the effects, respectively, of bipolar and multipolar structures.

6. What are the essential characteristics of a holder of the balance?

7. What is the evidence supporting the argument that a balance of power has continued to operate throughout the post-World War II era and persists in doing so? What is the evidence supporting the claim that the balance of power is a thing of the past?

8. Discuss the varied tasks of international system management that are carried on by states. Do you think that some of these jobs are more important or more basic

than the others? Which ones? Why are they more significant?

9. Why are major powers more concerned with system management than smaller countries? How would a realist assess this role of the great powers? How would a liberal regard great power domination?

• ENDNOTES

1. Waltz, *Theory of International Politics*, p. 79.
2. *Webster's New Collegiate Dictionary* (Springfield, Mass.: G. & C. Merriam Company, 1973).
3. For broad analyses of the many meanings of balance of power, see Frederick H. Gareau, ed., *The Balance of Power and Nuclear Deterrence* (Boston: Houghton Mifflin, 1962); Ernst B. Haas, "The Balance of Power as a Guide to Policy Making," *Journal of Politics* 3 (August 1953): 370–98; and Inis L. Claude, *Power and International Relations* (New York: Random House, 1962).
4. See, for example, Morgenthau, *Politics among Nations*, 5th ed., chapter 14.
5. A leading exponent of this view was Morton A. Kaplan. See his *System and Process in International Politics* (New York: Wiley, 1957) and *Towards Professionalism in International Theory: Macrosystem Analysis* (New York: Free Press, 1979).
6. John H. Herz, "The Rise and Demise of the Territorial State," *World Politics* 9 (July 1957): 473–93, which condensed portions of his book, *International Politics in the Atomic Age* (New York: Columbia University Press, 1959). Herz later retracted his position and acknowledged that the state continued to be the basic unit. See his "The Territorial State Revisited—Reflections on the Future of the Nation-State," *Polity* 1 (Fall 1968): 11–34.
7. Waltz, *Theory of International Politics*.
8. But see Kenneth N. Waltz, "The Emerging Structure of International Politics," *International Security* 18 (Fall 1993): 44–79.
9. See Charles McClelland, "The Beginning, Duration, and Abatement of International Crises: Comparisons in Two Conflict Arenas," in *International Crises: Insights from Behavioral Research*, ed. by Charles F. Hermann (New York: Free Press, 1972), and Alexander L. George, Philip J. Farley, and Alexander Dallin, eds., *U.S.-Soviet Security Cooperation: Achievements, Failures, Lessons* (New York: Oxford University Press, 1988).
10. Charles Krauthammer, "The Unipolar Moment," *Foreign Affairs* 70 (Special Issue 1991): 23–33.
11. Joseph S. Nye, Jr., *Bound to Lead: The Changing Nature of American Power* (New York: Basic Books, 1990).
12. To the Twenty-Fourth CPSU Congress in 1971, Gromyko declared, "There is no question of any significance which can be decided without the Soviet Union or in opposition to her." Cited in Coit D. Blacker, "The Kremlin and Detente: Soviet Conceptions, Hopes, and Expectations," in *Managing U.S.-Soviet Rivalry: Problems of Crisis Prevention*, ed. by Alexander L. George (Boulder, Colo.: Westview Press, 1983), p. 125.
13. Figures are taken from *The World Almanac and Book of Facts 1983* (New York: Newspaper Enterprise Association, 1982).

14. This is Kenneth N. Waltz's point, made in Chapter 9 of *Theory of International Politics*.

15. See Robert Jackson and Carl Rosberg, "Why the New African States Persist: The Juridical and Empirical in Statehood," *World Politics* 35 (October 1982): 1–24.

16. This story is clearly and brilliantly told by Denis Stairs, *The Diplomacy of Constraint: Canada, the Korean War, and the United States* (Toronto: University of Toronto Press, 1974).

17. See Melvyn P. Leffler, *A Preponderance of Power: National Security, the Truman Administration, and the Cold War* (Stanford, Calif.: Stanford University Press, 1992). Also see George F. Kennan, *Memoirs, 1925–1950* (Boston: Little, Brown, 1967), for the views of a diplomat who disagreed with President Harry Truman's policy of preponderance.

18. For a full treatment of this topic, see Leland B. Yeager, *International Monetary Relations: Theory, History, and Policy*, 2d ed. (New York: Harper & Row, 1976).

19. Anthony Sampson, *The Arms Bazaar: From Lebanon to Lockheed* (New York: Viking, 1977).

20. Rachel Carson, *Silent Spring* (Boston: Houghton Mifflin, 1962).

21. See Jacobo Timerman, *Prisoner Without Name, Cell Without Number*, trans. by Toby Talbot (New York: Alfred A. Knopf, 1981), a testament of a noted journalist's torture at the hands of the military regime in his country, Argentina.

CHAPTER 5

Units of Analysis/Participants in International Politics

One may think of the international system as a chessboard and its pieces, with the system structure as the rules and arrangements of the pieces in the game of chess. The kings, queens, knights, bishops, castles, and pawns may be thought of as the participating units. As in chess, international politics involves different sorts of actors, but some are much more important than others. International politics involves many "chessboards"; and, unlike chess, the "pieces" can often manipulate the "games," the "rules," and even the shapes of the "chessboards."

For the analyst, moreover, certain units of analysis do not constitute actors or participants but nevertheless remain very useful for explaining aspects of international politics. The international system—dealt with in the last chapter—forms one such unit of analysis; the market—discussed in this chapter—is another.

This chapter describes and explains the main units comprising actors in international politics. It also employs other units of analysis that shape and influence those actors and their behaviors. Among the most crucial of the effects of these unlike units is that between states and markets. Even though a state is an actor and the market is an effect of actions, the utility of treating them together will become apparent.

Introduction

In the last chapter, we saw that the structure of the international system results from the existence of states seeking to survive in the context of the organizing principle of anarchy. This chapter begins by addressing the origin and character of states and the way in which the organizing principle comes into existence. We also noted that a variety of other units were at work in the interactions of international affairs, so it is important to define and describe such other units as nations, groups, and so on, along with their standing in relation to states and the roles that they play in international politics. Recall also that plans for reform of the international system involve the assignment of enhanced roles to units, such as international organizations, other than the state. Visions of transformation generally aim at replacing the state altogether, either by eroding it, transcending it, or dominating it. A careful look at the various units will enable us to evaluate the prospects for maintaining or doing away with the state.

State

The modern state is founded on the principle of sovereignty, which was formulated conceptually in 1576 by Jean Bodin and first recognized in the 1648 Treaty of Westphalia, which ended the Thirty Years' War in Europe.[1] That war had been a particularly vicious one of religion, between Protestants and Catholics, and the agreement that ended it removed religion from the realm of political conflict by making the religion of the "sovereign," that is the ruler, the mode of worship of her country. A new **principle of internal order** was born, replacing that which had prevailed in the medieval period.

People living in Europe in the Middle Ages were subject to several different authorities. The pope and his church assumed **authority** over their spiritual lives, and territorial princes held reign over their secular status and activities. This system was somewhat more complicated by the existence of the Holy Roman Emperor, who was neither holy nor Roman nor emperor but who held at least symbolic authority. The principle by which people and territory were governed in this arrangement was that of **overlapping jurisdictions.**

With the Treaty of Westphalia, the authority of the pope and of the emperor were ended. Meanwhile, certain territorial princes had consolidated their rule over larger areas and became sufficiently strong to hold exclusive sway over their domains. Thus, instead of being the subject of overlapping jurisdictions of several rulers, people were now subject only to their own sovereign.

Although its origins assigned the authority to a single ruler, sovereignty has been extended since then to the state itself, whether ruled by a monarch, a small elite group, or a democratic system. Fundamentally, sovereignty is the principle of internal order in which there is only one source of authority over a territory and its people, and that authority is internal to the state. No entity outside the state has any jurisdiction within the territory of the state. Instead of the overlapping jurisdictions of the medieval period, the modern principle of internal order is that of **exclusive jurisdiction.**

This legal principle means that legislation and enforcement of laws may only proceed from within the state, that no authority outside the jurisdiction of a given state may extend its rule to the territory of a state. In our discussion above of the state in the international system, we stressed the autonomy of the state, that only the state itself had authority to decide how it should act. To make authority within the state effective, the government must maintain **military control** of the state's **territory.** Max Weber tied this political implication to legal jurisdiction by saying that the state has a **monopoly on legitimate violence.**[2]

First and foremost, then, sovereignty embodies exclusive jurisdiction as its principle of internal order. However, consider the situation in which there are at least two states, both of which are sovereign, that is, each is ruled by the principle of exclusive jurisdiction. In this situation, there is no author-

ity; no one has jurisdiction in the relations between the sovereign states. Thus, the principle ordering their relations is that of **anarchy.**

As we have tried to show, anarchy is not an invention or the result of anyone's determination. Instead, it is simply the logical outcome of sovereignty as a principle of internal order. External anarchy is a secondary characteristic of sovereignty. Thus, sovereignty has these two characteristics: 1) exclusive jurisdiction as the principle of internal order within states; and 2) anarchy as the ordering principle of the relations among states.

■
• • • • • • Characteristics of Sovereignty

- Exclusive jurisdiction as the principle of internal order
- Anarchy as the ordering principle in relations among sovereign units

Even though each state is autonomous and there exists no authority governing their relations, states nevertheless are able to cooperate and construct arrangements to facilitate that cooperation. In the absence of authority, however, there is a problem of **obligation.** Within states, obligations emerge from systems of morality and are created by law that emanates from authority. In an anarchical system, obligations cannot be handed down but only undertaken by the units that accept them. The obvious weakness of relying only on this—what is called **positive** or human-made **law**—is that obligations undertaken can also be renounced. Without authority in the international realm, however, there is no escape from anarchy. States can undertake obligations in international affairs, but there is no authority to enforce those obligations.

We have noted that states have the characteristics of sovereignty, territory, population, authority, and ability to undertake obligations to other states. With a legal system and military control of the territory, it is also clear that states possess a coercive apparatus to maintain authority within their jurisdiction. Existing in a world of other states, a state also protects itself against other states by expanding its military power to be able to fight. This definition will be elaborated and expanded on in the following chapter, but here let us put the matter in a nutshell. A **state** is an apparatus or a mechanism for governing and getting things done, for achieving what is just for its citizens and their common or public well being. Associated with the state are authority and power.

Comprising the state's power are a military and coercive apparatus.

In common discourse, states are often referred to as nations. For example, the name of the international organization that was founded in 1945 by the victors in World War II and other states is called the United Nations. However, it is important to draw a clear distinction between states and nations, as the discussion in the next section will make clear. But one immediate point is that, whereas the modern state can be dated from 1648, the modern nation originated only in 1789, with the French Revolution. With the rise of nationalism in the nineteenth century, the **nation-state** came to be the predominant form of political organization, for the nation was the basic group around which politics was organized. As the breakup of the Soviet Union has dramatized, however, a state may contain many nations; for many of the successor republics form new states based upon distinct nations. A relationship clearly exists between these two distinct entities, but before exploring that relationship, it is necessary to establish the meaning of nation.

Nation

As suggested by the confused usage that treats state and nation interchangeably, different meanings have been attached to the concept of **nation.** While using a vocabulary not attuned to our sensibilities, the nineteenth-century French writer Ernest Renan captured its essence when he wrote that "a nation is a soul, a spiritual principle."[3] It is based, Renan proclaimed, on a "heritage of memories" and "the will to continue to make the most of the common heritage." Having the advantage of living after Freud and Nietzsche, we substitute psychological for spiritual and identity for soul. A nation, then, is a group of people who identify themselves as belonging together, believe that they share a common past, and wish to share a common destiny.

In the literature on nations and **nationalism,** claims are made that a nation is formed on the basis of race, language, religion, a community of interest, or geography. However, there are many multiracial nations such as the United States, Malaysia, most Latin American nations, and others. Moreover, single races are divided into many different nations. If we take yellow people as a race, for example, some belong to a Japanese nation, while others are Korean, Chinese, Laotian, Mongolian, and so forth. Physical

resemblance does often coincide with a common past and facilitates a sense of belonging to the same group, so it can contribute to the sense of nationhood. On the other hand, historical developments have brought some people together in ways that do not coincide with racial characteristics.

Language is a stronger contributor to nationhood, although complexities abound in the associations of language and nation. Many nations are multilingual. Canada and Belgium each has two languages, while Switzerland has four and India, fourteen. In Nigeria, there are hundreds of languages, and nearly a hundred are spoken in Guatemala. England, Australia, and the United States are all predominantly English-speaking but obviously separate nations, and people in France and Cameroon use the same tongue in widely dissimilar nations. Nevertheless, language makes a direct contribution to the formation of nations. Language provides the vehicle for storing and passing on the heritage of memories upon which the nation is based. For groups with a written language, the literature not only contributes a source of pride but also serves to bind together those who have read and vicariously experienced the conflicts and triumphs of the characters that people the stories and dramas and poems. Historical and biographical writings are repositories of the nation's memory. In both oral and written traditions, myths and heroes bind the members of the nation with shared emotional ties.

In certain cases, religion, too, bonds people together, though many nations include people of varied religions as well as those with no religion. Given that three world religions—Judaism, Christianity, and Islam—are spread across many nations and that two of these, Christianity and Islam, have given rise to terrible strife within themselves, it is clear that religion is not a necessary ingredient for a nation. Indeed, it can often be antithetical to a nation.

Finally, geographical propinquity may contribute to a nation, for those living together are more likely to have had similar historical experiences and to gain a sense of belonging together. However, in situations where one group dominates another, the experience of the dominant group is so different from that of the repressed group that they divide rather than unite. Indigenous peoples in North America, for example, have not tended to develop a sense of inclusion in the nations of the United States and Canada. Indians in Mexico present a somewhat different situation in that a great nineteenth-century president, Benito Juárez, was Indian, and the Mexican Revolution of 1910 included Indians, although Indians continue to form the least privileged stratum of Mexican society. In some cases, a repressed group may form an identity as a separate nation. Even in the absence of overt repression, certain groups retain an identity as a nation or develop such an identity over time, as has been the case with Quebecers in Canada and Scots in Britain. Moreover, the case of Jews who for ages had been scattered across the globe but developed an identity as a nation in this century indicates that geographical proximity is not critical for the formation of nationhood.

For the most part, nationalism is exclusionary, providing a sense of pride or "we-ness" to a group of people. To the extent that it affords unity and contributes to a common purpose for the group itself, nationalism gives strength to a group without injury to others. However, the sense that "we" are different occasionally leads to what some call **hypernationalism,** or an attitude that "we" are better than "they" are. Going further, nationalism then sometimes tends to become expansionist, for a people who believe themselves to be better may become convinced that they have the right to rule others, and such attitudes may lead to conquest.

■
• • • • • • **States and Nations**

Characteristics of a state (originated in 1648):

- Based on power and law
- Territory
- Authority
- Coercive apparatus
- Military power

Characteristics of a nation (originated in 1789):

- Based on sentiment
- Group identity
- Heritage of memories
- Wish to share a common destiny

States are mechanisms for working out the future that nations yearn to achieve. Nation-states are aggregations of power united to political purpose.

Nations are related to states because the latter are mechanisms for working out the common future that nations yearn to achieve. Thus, as national identity rises, the nation aspires to have its own state. Italian nationalists in the nineteenth century who yearned to unite the peninsula did so through the creation of an Italian state. When the separatist

Parti Quebecois arrived in power in Quebec City in 1976, its leaders sought to carve out of Canada a separate, sovereign state of Quebec. In these cases, the nation preceded the state.

In other cases, however, the state precedes the nation. As decolonization swept across Asia and Africa in the post-World War II era, states were put into the places where the colonial powers had ruled without regard to indigenous peoples' identities. Thus, the new state elites sought to create new nations out of the disparate groups that peopled their territories. In some cases, such as Ghana and Indonesia, those elite efforts have met with success. By way of contrast, though, others such as Nigeria and Pakistan have been more problematical. Pakistan broke into two states in 1971, and Nigeria suffered a civil war that ended with a Nigerian victory over secessionist Biafra, but the nation-building process in Africa's largest state is far from complete. Although the situation in which the state precedes the nation is common in the contemporary period, it is not unique to our time. Long before there was a French nation, there was a French state; and the 1861 secession of the states of the Confederacy attests to existence of an American state for three-quarters of a century before the American nation was fully formed.

Apart from the disjuncture in time of state and nation, there often is a lack of coincidence in territorial boundaries between the two, and that imbalance is a source of conflict. In cases in which many nations exist within a single state, pressures sometimes build for separation. The Soviet Union is only a very recent and particularly dramatic example. In some cases, a single nation's people live within the confines of more than one state. For example, the Kurdish people live in Turkey, Iraq, Iran, and the former Soviet Union, and some of them have aspired at one time and another to found their own state. During the 1970s, the Ogaden war between Ethiopia and Somalia occurred as the Somali government sought to bring the Somali people who lived in Ethiopia's Ogaden region within the confines of its state.

Even when there is a coincidence between the nation and the state, no certainty exists that such a happy status quo will continue indefinitely. It is always possible that a group may over time discover or rediscover its identity as a nation and seek to have its own state. Autonomy movements among the Welsh in England, the Bretons in France, and the Flemish in Belgium attest to the potential, and the

■ **States and Nations**

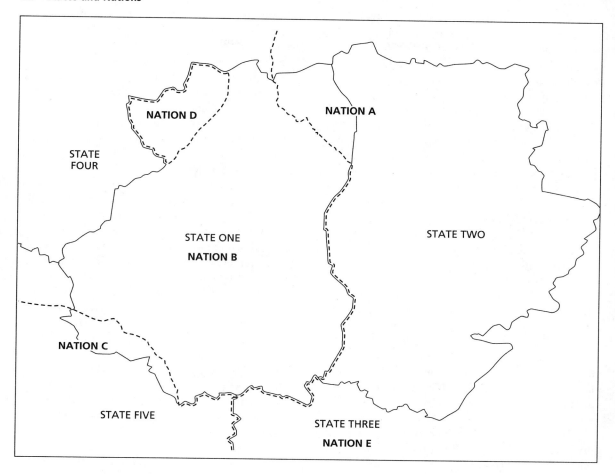

breakup of Czechoslovakia in 1992 into two states—Czech Republic and Slovakia—evidences the reality. While a state may remain stable, the members of its nation may agonize over and debate the meaning of their nation in the face of new challenges. For example, transnational developments in Europe and the addition of large numbers of new Moslem residents who came to France from North Africa have provoked the French people to rethink the meaning of the nation, which has long been thought of as based on voluntary adherence to the ideals of the French Revolution as well as on a common ancestry and a common, Catholic religion.[4] Demographic trends in Japan leading to a labor shortage and the potential of admitting large numbers of foreigners into what has traditionally been a very closed society portend a Japanese debate of similar dimensions.

These complexities should make clear that the sentimental, identity-based nation that achieves group coherence is quite distinct from the legal and power-based, territorial state that provides the vehicle for achieving the aspirations of the nation and that gives structure to the international system.

When these units are merged into a nation-state, however, it is a formidable aggregation of power united to political purpose. As such, only the reckless would predict its imminent demise. History gives strong illustrations of the strength of the nation-state, for a number of explicit challenges have been raised to it. Shortly before the First World War, the Second Socialist International, an association of socialist parties from all across Europe, beseeched workers not to fight capitalists' wars. That is to say, the organization appealed to class interests to override nationalism. But the response of German workers was to go to war against French workers, and Russian and British workers fought and died on behalf of their respective nation-states against German and Austro-Hungarian workers.

Western European integration in the post-World War II period raised a different challenge to the nation-state. Indeed, over the course of forty-some years, the European Union (formerly the European Community) has made great strides in overcoming national rivalries and developing common economic policies. Still, it is not clear that nation-states have been eroded or that national sentiments have disappeared. In the area of concrete policies, we note that France and Britain both have independently controlled nuclear weapons capabilities in their arsenals and that in 1990 Germany united what had been claimed during the Cold War to have been two separate nations in two distinctive capitalist and socialist states.

Current discourse about international politics includes discussion about other challenges that we will give consideration to below. For an institution that we can clearly identify as having originated only some 350 years ago, the state may indeed pass from the scene at some time in the future. Some even claim its demise is already in process. While remaining open to evidence that the state is on its way out, we have to keep in mind that it has not only survived but has also spread and grown in the face of earlier challenges. Given this record, it is appropriate to accompany our openness with a measure of skepticism.

State and nation are two of the fundamental units in international politics, but they are not the only units that need to be considered. Another very important one is the market.

Market

Whereas state and nation are political entities that embody group interests and are characterized by power and identity as a basis for group action, **market** is an economic mechanism that embodies individual and firm interests and is characterized by the quest for wealth. Whereas states duplicate one another's tasks, markets are driven by a division of labor based upon a principle of comparative advantage. States allocate values on the basis of political goals and conceptions of justice, whereas markets make their allocations through a **price mechanism.** States are distinctive and protective of national cultures, but markets would overcome political and cultural barriers in the name of **economic efficiency.**

State and market both emerged out of the Middle Ages. While remaining distinct from each other, they interact in a number of ways. **Production** in a market may be contrasted with **subsistence** production in which the producer consumes her own products and with that in a **command economy** in which a government allocates production. In a market, **producers** and **consumers** are separated, their exchanges determined by price. However, markets work only in the context of political protection of **property rights, enforcement of contracts,** and **regulation** on behalf of public safety, health, and other standards such as maintaining competition. Although wealth is generated through markets, it is the basis for power and, thus, is of the utmost concern to states. Markets affect the positions of states in the international system, and the state of the market often influences elections in democratic states. Those who benefit most from markets—that is, the rich—are able to use their wealth as well as the dependency of the state on their production to affect state decisions. Corporations receive, in the words of Charles Lindblom, a "privileged position" in democratic capitalist societies.[5]

Writing about capitalism in the era following the collapse of socialism, Robert Heilbroner noted "the presence of the market as the principal means of coordinating economic activity," but he also pointed to ' the existence of two realms of authority in capitalism . . . the state . . . [and] the world of business." Importantly, Heilbroner observed that "the two realms create a social space from which state coercion is largely excluded. Second, the relationship of the two realms, at once mutually dependent and mutually rivalrous, sets the stage for a political tension. . . ."[6] Much of politics within states concerns this tension in which economic groups skirmish over policies, and the state not only provides arenas for the contenders but also brings its own agenda to the fray. But the politics of economics and the basic tension between the differently conceived realms of the state and the market are not confined to domestic politics. They also infuse international politics in ways that display the tensions sharply.

By the demonstration of their effectiveness, market principles have been accepted as the basis of economic organization across virtually the entire globe. Following the decline and collapse of socialism as an alternative and the acceptance of market principles by both the former communist states and remaining communist regimes like the one in China, some observers perceive the emergence of an **international business civilization.**[7] As governments have opened up their countries to business activities, including not just sales of products but also investments by foreign firms along with banking and other service activities, private economic exchanges take place increasingly across international borders based upon worldwide rather than national standards of competition. Implicit in this increasingly international market, antithetical to the state, is the logic of comparative advantage, the idea that each country should produce those goods and services that it does most efficiently and that earn it the largest amount of foreign exchange. For example, a country may be able to produce widgets at a cost of ten units of investment and ten units of labor. The same country produces its own rice with fifteen units of investment and fifteen units of labor. Instead of producing its own rice, it should specialize in widgets, selling its product in the world market and buying its rice in that same market at a world price that is lower than its domestic production costs. Another country that needs to expend fifteen units of investment and fifteen units of labor to produce its widgets but only ten units on each of investment and labor to produce rice should sell its rice to the first country and buy its widgets from it. In this way, both countries prosper and gain more wealth than if each produced its own widgets and rice for domestic consumption.

This logic of the concept of comparative advantage runs into two difficulties, one economic and the other political. Political economists make a distinction between absolute and relative gains. Absolute gains are those made by an entire universe, while relative gains refer to the uneven distribution of those gains. In the example of the two countries that produce widgets and rice, at the international level there is an overall gain in wealth, but the country producing widgets may gain more than its rice-producing trade partner. A similar pattern occurs at the domestic level, for the investors and labor force who were previously rice producers in the widget-producing country may suffer a loss of income even while the country as a whole enjoys an increase as a result of its sales of widgets abroad. Of course, such economic effects also carry political consequences, for displaced rice producers who are now unemployed may generate political instability as they seek food and income. In addition, a separate political problem stems from the tension between the market and the state.

Governed by a price mechanism, the market allocates production, goods, and services on the basis of efficiency. For many reasons including inherited wealth, technological change, chance, and other fac-

tors, the market tends to create **inequalities.** Without accepting Karl Marx's analysis in its entirety, one sees the great insight that he had into how capitalism works as some people accumulate wealth while others suffer impoverishment. Modern governments have done much to overcome the natural tendency of the market to allocate rewards in a deeply unequal manner, but such a redress by the state should not be allowed to obscure the fundamental dynamic of the market.

■
● ● ● ● ● ● **State and Market**

State:
- Duplication of tasks
- Allocation of values by politics and justice
- Protects position and culture
- Citizens
- Protects property rights, enforces contracts, and regulates to allow markets to operate

Market:
- Division of labor
- Allocation of values by price mechanism
- Economic efficiency overcomes political and cultural barriers
- Producers and consumers
- Affects positions of states in international system and influences politics in capitalist states

---

The modern liberal **welfare state** deliberately acts to offset the negative effects of the market precisely because it is founded on a conception of justice that includes **equality.** Socialists built their states to go at the same problem in a different way. Instead of relying on the market to generate wealth and on the state to moderate it on behalf of its citizens, the socialist state attempts to achieve justice through the direct control of the economy. In doing so, it gives up the efficiency of the market. Nevertheless, in both cases, the tension between the state and the market is apparent, for they are conceived upon different principles and different values.

With the spread of the international business civilization, this fundamental tension can be expected to continue. Governments acting for states need to be concerned about the broad well-being of their citizens at the same time that they recognize the benefits of competing on a global basis. States need to duplicate the tasks of other states, but markets pressure them to specialize in a global division of labor. Thus, political leaders face very difficult choices as they steer their countries through the turbulent waters of international affairs in the contemporary world.

Multinational corporations (MNCs) are prominent among the vehicles that carry market principles across state frontiers. In spreading capital and technology through foreign investments and other transactions, MNCs hold very different significance for different interpreters. Although they are not the only sort of transnational, nongovernmental actor in international relations, no others seem to have presented a challenge to the state.

Transnational Organizations

A transnational organization is a nongovernmental, hierarchically organized entity that has headquarters in one country and operates in other countries. Apart from multinational business enterprises, there are few others. One of the oldest and most prominent is the Roman Catholic Church. Another unusual one that has operated from the mid-1960s is the Palestine Liberation Organization. Some observers believe that certain clandestine organizations—such as the Red Army Faction, a terrorist group—also qualify under this rubric. However, the most apparent and clear examples are such corporations as General Motors Corporation of the United States, Toyota of Japan, Nestlé of Switzerland, British Petroleum of Britain, and other companies that make investments in, hire workers from, and sell products in many different countries.

The sweep and growth of the activities of these enterprises have made them the object of quite serious consideration. Apart from the dependency relationships that are sometimes created and questions as to whether they are the instruments of their governments, a number of observers have regarded them as threats to the existence of the state. One reason such an issue gets raised is the comparative sizes and wealth of corporations and states. Each of some 400 companies has annual sales that are greater than the gross national products of any of 120 countries. In addition, the capital, technological, and managerial resources of such companies are clearly formidable, even when compared with the governments of small countries. These companies operate in many different countries, often under advantageous conditions. Thus, even though the purposes and activities of states and companies are substantially different, some observers have speculated that corporate activities do or will undermine the state.[8] We can identify three alternative interpretations with respect to this ques-

tion: neoimperialist, neofunctionalist, and interdependentist. After surveying them, we will present our own position.

In the neoimperialist perspective, the multinational corporation is an instrument of domination by such large, rich countries as the United States that will, in the long run, deprive smaller, poorer countries of their ability to make their own choices. From this point of view, multinational corporations dictate the terms of their investments in weak countries and exploit them, taking profits back to their home countries and paying low wages to native workers. Rather than helping the poor countries, the MNCs impoverish them by drawing out more resources and dollars than they invest. With little experience and in great need of investment, the poor countries are forced into bargains by the superior strength of the companies that command such grand resources. Projected as the end result of this process is the decline and eventual complete domination of the poor countries by these instruments of imperial exploitation.

Coming from a deeply different intellectual tradition, the neofunctionalist view also foresees the decline of states at the hands of multinational companies, but as a benign rather than a pernicious process. According to this view, the MNC is a very efficient way of spreading wealth and knowledge across the globe. States, in contrast, are obstacles to technological progress and economic growth. In place of an image of domination, neofunctionalists present a portrait in which companies are efficient mechanisms for making investments and spreading technology. They train workers and pay them wages that are not exploitative but rather exceed the average in their countries, thus making these workers the highest paid. A consequence of the relatively high wages paid by MNCs is the raising of the country's average level of compensation. Moreover, companies effectively spread the best elements of the culture of advanced industrial societies—work habits, skills training, teamwork, and so forth. In this view, the end result will be erosion of the state because it is an obstacle to progress and the spread of wealth and knowledge.

The third interpretation embodies very different convictions.[9] Although it is true that many companies are powerful in bargaining with small countries, the countries control access to their own territories, and this is a crucial tool in their bargaining with MNCs. As transnational economic activity grows, that access will become increasingly valuable, for different companies will vie for it. This competition, in turn, will increase the bargaining position of states, which will become stronger as more activities occur. In this interpretation, then, states and corporations are dependent on each other—states for capital and technology, and firms for access to territory. Rather than one replacing or dominating the other, they both retain different functions and will continue to bargain. The tension that we referred to above, in this view, will persist in the interactions between states and companies.

Each of these three interpretations was based upon theoretical projections into the future, and the authors could not help but express their hopes and fears. As we offer a different interpretation, it will be based more upon history. Rather than projecting into an unforeseeable future, let us survey a clearly patterned past. Although it is possible to find illustrations of every one of the facts that were cited in the discussion of the three interpretations, it will be more useful to treat a case study over time. Oil provides a case that illustrates many of the observations of our interpreters, but the conclusion emerges at a different place from any of them.[10]

The first encounters of multinational oil companies and states that possessed petroleum reserves were clearly dominated by the companies. Oil was discovered in the Middle East only in this century. Oil companies paid large initial fees to governments for exclusive exploration and production rights and then agreed on the allocation of income between royalties and taxes. A private firm, such as Standard Oil Company, or a conglomerate of firms helped to set the level of a tax for, as an example, the Saudi government. Over time, Saudi Arabia accumulated revenues and made investments that resulted in additional accumulation. Saudi princes sent their sons to Harvard and Princeton to learn business, engineering, diplomacy, and economics, and to gain knowledge and increase the skills of those who ran the country and dealt with the transnational oil giants. In 1960, the Organization of Petroleum Exporting Countries (OPEC) was founded by Saudi Arabia and other countries that wished to strengthen their bargaining power in the international political economy. By 1970, Saudi Arabia announced that it would take over the physical facilities built by the oil companies within its territory and that it would change the formulas for sharing income with the companies. By 1973, OPEC was in a position to increase the price of oil fourfold, and in early 1974, the price was pushed up further, to five times what it had been in 1972. By the end of the 1970s, the oil

companies were left in the position of being marketers of Saudi and other countries' petroleum. Exxon—Standard Oil's successor—and other companies purchased the oil at a price determined by OPEC, transported it to the consuming countries, and refined it into consumer products that they sold through their retail outlets.[11]

What occurred in this case was that the bargaining position of the multinational firms and the states shifted over time. Oil production had garnered for the producing states great wealth, which their elites used to enrich themselves, build the wealth of their countries, and develop their skills. Then, they used their organizational skills as well as the vulnerabilities of the consuming countries to gain the upper hand in their bargaining with the oil firms.

Our different conclusion drawn from this case is that even weak states may grow in strength over time in their relationship with multinational corporations. It would, of course, be possible for governments to be stupid, to fail to use the wealth and skill that they get from their bargains with companies. However, this case does demonstrate that governments do control the territories of their countries. They may provide access at a sacrifice in a bargain when they are weak, but the long-term benefits gained put them in a stronger position as time goes on, leaving them able to bargain extremely effectively if they do so intelligently.

Not all commodities lend themselves to the paradigm of the oil case. Moreover, some governments have nationalized foreign investments prematurely, before they had the skill to operate them and without the research and development base to compete with new technology. But these are problems of power, intelligence, and judgment. In no way do they provide evidence that the state will be overwhelmed by the firm.

It does seem clear that the tensions between broad market forces and state imperatives, as noted above, will continue. But there is little reason to believe that either the state or the market, both of which made their appearance on the world stage as the curtain fell on the Middle Ages, will overwhelm the other. So long as both operate, they will be in tension, and very complicated repercussions flow from that tension. These will be taken up in Chapter 8, which is devoted to the subject of political economy.

In addition to multinational firms that command vast economic resources, many other nongovernmental organizations with lesser resources operate across borders. Many of these are organized on an associative rather than a hierarchical principle, which is to say that components originate and maintain a relationship on the basis of free association, without taking orders from an authority in a single country. Most such associations—like the International Political Science Association, which is made up of individuals from countries around the world and managed by national professional associations—promote the limited, nonpolitical purposes of their members, coming together on an occasional basis—in this case, every three years—and maintaining communications through journals and other publications. Some of them, like the human rights organization Americas Watch, address an important political agenda and maintain activities that have a more immediate impact on individuals' lives by drawing attention to the abuses of governments and engaging in lobbying activities designed to influence governmental and intergovernmental organizational behavior.

As some of the above discussion has made clear, private organizations are quite active in international affairs, and some of them contribute importantly to the activities that occur across international boundaries. To coordinate and manage international problems, however, governments seldom turn to nongovernmental organizations. Instead, they have constructed intergovernmental organizations (IGOs) to address an extremely broad range of issues and problems that fill the international agenda.

Intergovernmental Organizations

For centuries, states have associated in order to address problems affecting them, but an explosion of such organizations occurred after the end of World War II.[12] The United States government, for example, belongs to many IGOs and dispatches its representatives to hundreds of meetings per year of these organizations. **Intergovernmental organizations** come into being through the negotiation of a treaty, often called a charter, among its member states. These so-called international organizations may be classified along two dimensions: general-purpose and limited-purpose, and global and regional.

Foremost among general-purpose organizations is the United Nations, which deals with security, political, economic, cultural, and other concerns that its members bring before it. Other organizations, such as the Organization of American States (OAS) and the Organization of African Unity (OAU), also devote themselves to broad-based purposes that encompass many aspects of political life. As their names make clear, the OAS and the OAU are regional organizations that deal only with particular parts of the world. In contrast, the United Nations is a global organization, with universal membership that includes virtually every state in the world.

Limited-purpose organizations most frequently are functional ones, such as the Food and Agricultural Organization and the International Civil Aviation Organization, that deal with a circumscribed area of concern. These two organizations are global, dealing with their functional problems almost everywhere on earth. Other limited-purpose organizations focus on regional problems of specialized concern. Dedicated to providing security for its region, the North Atlantic Treaty Organization exemplifies a limited-purpose entity, and the Latin American Development Bank provides another illustration.

Intergovernmental organizations provide mechanisms for the coordination of policies, resolution of differences of view, and implementation of agreed-upon courses of action. They include deliberative bodies, such as the United Nations General Assembly, to which governments send representatives to plan, debate, and make decisions together. Complementing such intergovernmental coordinating mechanisms, these organizations also include bureaucracies that bring international civil servants to work for the organization itself, rather than for the individual governments.

As in the case of multinational corporations, interpreters have disagreed on the significance and meaning of intergovernmental organizations in relation to states. Realists regard intergovernmental organizations as arenas for the interplay of state interests. When those interests coincide or are parallel, IGOs reflect the governmental policies by passing resolutions and carrying out activities. Using the UNEF case after the Middle East war of 1956 that was outlined in the last chapter, we can see that this interpretation does not dismiss international organizational activity as unimportant. On the other hand, realists also note the many vetoes—the negative vote cast by any of the five permanent members that prohibits action—that were cast in the UN Security Council during the Cold War, making it impossible for the organization to act. Whether paralyzed or effective, however, IGOs in this interpretation lack any autonomy from the member states.

Employing a very different interpretation, liberal analysts believe that intergovernmental organizations perform certain functions independent of governments that make them invaluable to governments. For example, international bureaucracies become **centers of communication** with which all governments correspond. This function has two important effects. Governments can trust a neutral agency with information more than they can trust one another, thus conveying to the international civil service more information than would otherwise be available. Because of its obligation to disseminate such information on an impartial basis, the international organization contributes independently to the negotiations that are otherwise conducted among governments alone. Secondly, the possession of information gives to the bureaucracy the ability to employ its own intelligence in formulating compromises of or creative alternatives to the initiatives of governments. This effect has been especially important in the European Union where the head of the administrative institution in Brussels has been able to persuade governmental representatives in the Council of Ministers to adopt proposals that have come not from them but from his bureaucracy. Simply from its position as the center of a communications network, then, the international organization achieves autonomous influence.

Additionally, the provision of more complete information as well as the commitment of governments to work within an organization facilitate cooperation. Both the promises of other governments to cooperate and the **transparency** in transactions provided by an impartial flow of information create functions for intergovernmental organizations that do not exist in their absence, thus making them at least partly independent actors in international relations.

In the area of security, organizations not only provide forums for coordination among governments and act as facilitators of their cooperation but also add on diplomatic, economic, and military coercive instruments to work their will against challenging states. Such capabilities were clearly on display for many years in Europe as NATO and the Warsaw Pact faced each other across the divide of Eastern and Western Europe that ran through the middle of Germany. Coercive instruments also were mobilized by the United Nations in the Korean War, in opposition to South Africa's *apartheid* policies, and against Iraq in the Gulf War and its aftermath. Short of such coercive activity, international organizations have also created **peacekeeping forces** to stand between belligerents or assist in domestic transitions from civil war to unified, peaceful regimes.

The economic area also gives us examples of intergovernmental organizations that have coercive instruments that allow them to act autonomously in relationship to states. The International Monetary Fund, an intergovernmental organization designed to assist its members with balance of payments problems, provides an illustration. Every member state makes a financial contribution to the IMF and thereby gains the right to draw upon its portion of the fund to ease it through temporary difficulties in its balance of payments. However, some countries have suffered deeper and longer-term difficulties, requiring them to apply for more extensive assistance from the IMF. A large number of less developed countries have mired themselves in this predicament as a result of the immense increase in their oil import bills and their resorting to borrowing to pay those bills. From that borrowing ensued an international debt crisis, as many countries found it impossible to service their debts. In response, the International Monetary Fund has imposed conditions for its assistance. These have involved such sensitive domestic governmental matters as determining fiscal and monetary policy, setting exchange rates, paying subsidies, fixing rates of taxation and tariffs, and establishing the size of the government's budget and civil service. The ostensible and declared purpose is to strengthen the long-term competence and efficacy of governments in order to bring about a permanent solution to the problems that caused the balance of payments difficulties in the first place. Nevertheless, these **structural adjustment programs** represent a mighty instrument in the hands of an international organization's civil service. Although the organization could not exist without the consent and continued cooperation of its state members, its instruments are operated without the direct supervision of those members.

Although intergovernmental organizations play important roles in international politics and economics and even constrain the behavior and indeed affect the structures of states, their overall and long-term effect is to strengthen rather than to diminish states. Such organizations cannot function in the absence of states, for they are governments' creatures. As with any institution that is put into place by political power, the organizations are primarily the instruments of the powerful, although they also serve the interests of order in the international community.

In treating the units of analysis in international politics, our attention has been drawn to those that are most obviously active in affairs that cross borders. Nevertheless, some units do not act so directly. Instead, they form part of the politics that occur within states. Inasmuch as they are crucial to the analysis of the politics that shape and are affected by states, it is important to think about these other units. First to be considered is the **group,** the basis of all politics.

Group

One of the most significant of human groups for purposes of the analysis of politics, the nation, has already been discussed, but the quest for power and justice is conducted by groups that take many different forms. Humans are born into and nurtured by families or other units that substitute for families. Study of social formation and the strengthening of personality within the **family** belongs to different disciplines than international politics, although we note that these processes may or may not contribute to state formation. Families pertain in other ways to politics in that groups seeking power not infrequently use their families as bases for political support and recruitment to political positions. Some political systems, such as the British constitutional monarchy, employ family membership as the criterion for specific offices. Political regimes regulate families by promoting or discouraging, for example, the propagation of more children. Sometimes family background, wealth, and advantage give to certain individuals a competitive edge in their striving for their goals within the larger society. And families provide refuge from politics and the hurly-burly of economic and social struggles. Primarily, families are not political groups. They are inward-looking, seeking to satisfy the needs of their members, rather than conglomerates that quest for power and justice in the larger world. They do pursue autonomy, insulating themselves against the demands and buffeting of the political world, but, in general, they do not represent units that can provide a basis for political analysis.

Larger kinship groups like tribes or even small nations do sometimes make up the stuff of politics. With sufficient power to pose a threat to others and with enough heritage to aspire to command a large voice in national politics, autonomy within a nation, or, still greater, a state of their own, such groups engage in political struggles that are acutely germane to international politics. As South Africa has been going through the throes of painful state formation in the transformation from minority rule to democracy, the struggle to a large extent is conducted among such kinship groups as the white Afrikaaners, the Zulu nation, whose political organization is the Inkatha Freedom Party, and the Xhosa and other tribes, whose strength is channeled through the Africa National Congress. The attempt to found a new state, Biafra, by seceding from Nigeria in 1968 grew largely from the Ibo tribe.

Apart from their importance in domestic politics, such groups also participate in international politics by seeking support from groups abroad as well as from states, corporate actors, and international organizations. For example, before it came to power, the African National Congress was very effective in generating support for sanctions against South Africa by governments who coordinated their actions through the United Nations and by corporations that withdrew investments from that country.

Groups are also formed on the basis of **religion.** As we observed in the discussion early in this chapter about the origin of the modern state, divisions between Protestants and Catholics in Europe had constituted the basis upon which extremely bloody wars were fought. Moreover, a long history of political struggle including many wars has been and continues to be written between Christianity and Islam. Shortly after the founding of Islam, Mohammed's followers conquered important outposts of Christianity that included holy places associated with the latter's founding. In a centuries-long counterattack, the Crusades sought to wrest those lands back from their conquerors. By the end of the First World War, the Ottoman Empire, which had ruled the lands in question, collapsed and France and Britain gained control of them. But new issues have arisen in the wake of the independence of those territories from European rule, as Israel was founded by European refugees, not entirely on the basis of religion but in part. In 1947, Pakistan was founded as an Islamic state. With the Iranian revolution of 1979 came a new wave of religiously oriented politics in the Middle East that contributed importantly to the turmoil of that area for at least a decade. With strategy and economics shaping so much of the politics of the Middle East, it would be going too far to argue that religion and religious groups dominated the agenda, but it would not go far enough if religion were altogether set aside.

Groups also form on the basis of the shared interests of their members. Strongest are the economic interests of business associations and labor unions. Scientific and cultural interests also bring people together in groups. In recent years, groups concerned with environmental degradation and ecology have become prominent. Private human rights groups have been established in both the West and the Eastern European countries before the demise of the communist regimes. Interest groups primarily act within the domestic political arena as they attempt to shape government policy, but many carry on such activities across frontiers. Some—human rights groups exemplify these—gather information in one or more countries and then disseminate it in others. Groups such as Oxfam and the International Rescue Committee carry on relief activities where people are suffering from dislocation, hunger, and famine, drawing on resources from both private and governmental contributors.

Some groups are formed by the citizens of one country at the behest of or with the support of another country basically for the purpose of promoting the foreign policy aims of the country that is not their own. During the 1980s, for example, when many American citizens strongly disagreed with their government's policy toward Nicaragua, support groups were formed throughout the United States. These groups disseminated information provided by the Nicaraguan government, and some engaged in low-level activities, such as importing and selling small quantities of Nicaraguan coffee, that defied the United States government's embargo of Nicaraguan goods.

More significant, more widespread, and longer lasting were the activities of **Communist parties** throughout the world that accepted the discipline of the Communist Party of the Soviet Union. Because the head of the government of the Soviet Union was also the leader of the CPSU, the implication was that such parties were agents of the Soviet government. The clarity of this relationship was rendered brilliant in the position of long-time leader of the French Communist Party Maurice Thorez, who held that if NATO, including France, should go to war against the Soviet Union, he and his fellow French communists would fight on the side of the Soviet Union. Thus, Communist parties in most countries of the world were tools of Soviet foreign policy, ready to subvert the governments of the Soviet Union's adversaries.

In 1948, the Communist Party of Czechoslovakia overthrew the democratically elected government and, in submitting to Soviet discipline, made that country into what was called during the Cold War a satellite of the Soviet Union. Such discipline broke down partly at the time of the Sino-Soviet conflict in the 1960s. With the replacement of the Communist Party as the government and the disintegration in 1991 of the Soviet Union itself, communists in other countries have no international discipline to which to submit and have lost their function as a tool of Soviet foreign policy.

Before World War II, similar activity by parties associated with the Nazis in Germany paved the way for Germany's takeover of Austria and the Sudetenland portion of Czechoslovakia. In the contemporary world, indigenous groups acting under the discipline of foreign governments are not so many. Neither are they the open tools of major powers. Most prominent in the 1980s were groups such as Hezbollah—the Party of God—in Lebanon, which operated under the discipline of the Iranian government. Such units appear less crucial to an analysis of international affairs in the contemporary period. On the other hand, they are critical to an understanding of international politics at certain moments in history, and they offer a potential force in the future.

Somewhat different are groups that, while not submitting to the discipline of a foreign government, are nevertheless sympathetic to the aims of a foreign government and are supported by it. During the Reagan administration, the United States created the National Endowment for Democracy as a mechanism for channeling funds and nonpartisan advice to other countries to promote democracy. In Nicaragua, for example, the National Endowment provided funds for voter registration, printing of ballots, and other such activities to the opposition coalition that elected President Violeta Barrios de Chamorro as president in the 1990 election against Sandinista Daniel Ortega. Furthermore, as part of its promotion of a program of neoliberal economic restructuring, the United States Agency for International Development (USAID) extends financial and advisory support to groups of business people in Third World countries who work to strengthen the free enterprise system. In Costa Rica, where such a group did not already exist, USAID created one—it is called CINDE, its Spanish acronym—and supported it for about a decade before it was in a position to operate without United States government funds.

As this discussion suggests, one must include many types of groups for a full descriptive analysis of international affairs. On the other hand, the effectiveness of such groups almost entirely depends on their relationship to and impact on governments. For theoretical purposes in analyzing international politics, then, they can be treated within the context of the state, as we will do in the next chapter.

Meanwhile, there is another unit—the **individual**—that is also important for a descriptive analysis of international affairs.

Individual

With such abstract structures and impersonal units as states and markets held clearly in mind, it is nevertheless difficult to imagine human events occurring without the participation of individuals. In the industrial culture in which we live, individuals often appear to be interchangeable. For example, while discussing the development of total war, we noted that fresh troops are sent to the front lines of battle to replace those fallen, in virtually the same way that replacement bullets substitute for those fired in battle. Nonetheless, it seems unlikely that twentieth-century history would have unfolded precisely as it did in absence of such outstanding personalities as Woodrow Wilson, Vladimir Lenin, Josef Stalin, Adolph Hitler, Winston Churchill, Franklin D. Roosevelt, Mao Tse Tung, Dag Hammarskjöld, John F. Kennedy, Margaret Thatcher, or Mikhail Gorbachev, to mention only some of the more prominent political leaders. Each put the stamp of his or her personality on the policies of his or her country and the time in which he or she lived.

In the midst of the Battle of Britain in World War II, when England stood alone in Europe against a German onslaught that had already reached domination of the continent and German planes incessantly bombed British cities, Prime Minister Winston Churchill spoke in his stentorian tones on BBC radio, rallying his countrymen to defend their homeland. He promised "toil, tears, blood and sweat," but he instilled hope and promised victory. His confident voice steeled British citizens in what might have been a moment of despair. Eventually, Hitler called off his *Luftwaffe*—his air force—and his projected invasion of the British Isles. The steel, bullets, skills, and courage of England's air corps proved critical to that happy outcome, but who could deny that Churchill's will and oratory were important in moving history the way that it did? He paid tribute to the pilots defending their homeland when he said, "Never have so many owed so much to so few." The tribute fit the occasion, but the words that memorialized the event so fittingly themselves contributed to the cause.

An obvious quality attaches to the imprint that visible leaders make on historical events, but individuals can have less obtrusive while not less important impacts on political outcomes. In his novel of Russia in the Napoleonic Wars, *War and Peace*, Leo Tolstoy made the argument that, despite the most brilliant conceptions of strategy and the most carefully laid battle plans of the generals, the outcome of a great battle depends on the individual courage and decision of the soldier on the front line of attack. If she is brave and goes forward against enemy fire, her army is more likely to succeed and her leaders given adulation for their battle plans. On the other hand, if she decides to turn and run, shouting to her comrades that the battle is worthless or lost, the enemy is more likely to overwhelm her and her compatriots, and her general will be humiliated in defeat. Despite certain appearances of being nothing but a cog in a machine, to use a dehumanizing metaphor, each particular individual makes a difference in the politics of her group.

Added to these roles of leaders and players in politics, the **citizen** forms a most important component of the state. States take on meaning and strength as citizens accept obligations and responsibilities, and citizens combine their power into effective public units as they develop regard for one another and act together for common purposes. Citizens mobilized in political support of their governments provide immense strength to their state's actions, as did Americans who fought and supported the immense war effort from 1942 to 1945. On the contrary, when citizens withhold their support or actively oppose their government's policies, their state loses effectiveness. During the war in Vietnam, the choice made by many citizens of the United States not to support or to oppose their government's policy helped to render that policy less impressive. In the Soviet Union, absenteeism from work as well as drunkenness and surliness among citizens contributed to the economic weakening and political ineffectiveness that eventually led to Communism's downfall and the disintegration of that country. Disaffected citizens may go farther by taking up arms against what they decide is an unjust government, as did a number of guerrilla groups in Afghanistan before and after the Soviet intervention on behalf of a client government in 1979.

Individuals also frequently become the objects of other political actors who aim to eliminate them because of their opposition or to convince them to defect from their political group. Often, too, individuals have not made commitments in a conflict situation, and the contending political groups vie for their support. Those who have been targets for elimination range from the dictator Fidel Castro of Cuba to obscure labor union organizers in Guatemala who were "disappeared," tortured, and killed. The United States government during the Cold War used the technique of attempted political assassination against various leaders. At roughly the same time during the Kennedy administration that Cuba's Castro was targeted by the United States government in a program called "Operation Mongoose,"[13] the Central Intelligence Agency (CIA) collaborated in a successful assassination plot against Prime Minister Patrice Lumumba in Congo, now called Zaire. More recently, President Reagan ordered an attempt on the life of Muammar Khaddafi by air attacks against his homes. Although the Libyan leader escaped, his adopted two-year-old daughter was a victim of the United States bombing.

Individuals can become targets of arrest rather than assassination. In December 1989, the United States under President Bush invaded Panama for the express purpose of arresting the dictator Manuel Noriega and bringing him to the United States for trial on drug charges, and in 1990, the same administration promoted the kidnapping and delivery to its agents of a Mexican doctor who had been an accessory to the torture and killing in 1988 of a U.S. Drug Enforcement Agency employee in Mexico.

Other groups also target individuals as objects against whom they use assassination, kidnapping, intimidation, and other violent acts. For the families of the victims in particular, the practice of taking hostages in Lebanon during the 1980s by shadowy groups closely or distantly connected with the Iranian government was a nightmare of international affairs crossing state boundaries. The plight of the hostages also became an issue in the relations between the Western countries and Iran. During the 1972 Olympics in Munich, a group affiliated with the Palestine Liberation Organization entered an athletes' compound and murdered twelve Israelis.

Whether as leader, player, citizen, or object, the individual is an important unit in politics, including international politics. In descriptive analysis, attention needs to be directed to individuals in all of these roles. For the most part, the political significance of individuals can be understood in their impact upon and relationship to groups. Aside from the "great man" school of historical analysis, which holds that individuals shape the destiny of nations, theoretical treatment of individuals in politics is largely absent. The individual is a unit of analysis in the discipline of psychology, where the construction of personality and individual behavior are the important dependent variables of analysis. For the political analyst, the difficulty of relating individuals to political outcomes presents a challenge. We will return to this theme in the ensuing analysis of foreign policy in Chapter 9. Until then, however, let us keep in mind that individuals remain important units in international politics in all of the ways that we have seen above.

These are the main units for analysis in international politics. While acknowledging that many different units contribute to international relations, the most important one remains the state. As we have seen, many people, coming from quite diverse points of view, foresee the demise of the state or wish to bring about its end. We have also seen that the state persists, that it remains strong and continues as the predominant form of political organization in the world. Such a controversial yet persistent entity deserves a closer look and further analysis. So, we now turn to devote a chapter to this concept and phenomenon as well as its crucial roles in international politics.

• IMPORTANT TERMS

access	market
anarchy	military control
authority	monopoly of legitimate
center of	violence
communication	multinational
citizen	corporations
command economy	nation
Communist parties	nation-state
consumers	nationalism
economic efficiency	neofunctionalist
enforcement of contracts	neoimperialist
equality	obligation
exclusive jurisdiction	overlapping jurisdictions
family	peacekeeping forces
group	positive law
hypernationalism	price mechanism
individual	principle of internal
inequalities	order
interdependentist	producers
intergovernmental	production
organization	property rights
international business	regulation
civilization	religion

state

structural adjustment
　programs

subsistence

territory

transparency

welfare state

• STUDY QUESTIONS

1. Describe the basic characteristics of a state.

2. Lay out the essential characteristics of a nation.

3. What is the relationship between a state and a nation?

4. Describe the fundamental elements of a market.

5. How are states and markets related?

6. Define and evaluate transnational organizations, and describe and assess their roles in international relations?

7. Define and categorize intergovernmental organizations, and discuss their roles in international relations.

8. Which are the important groups that participate in international politics? What are the methods and means that they use to participate?

9. Are individuals important in international politics? If you think that they are, name one or two, and explain their importance. If you think that individuals are subsumed in groups or classes, give your reasons for treating them so.

10. Do you believe that it is likely that some other entity will surpass or replace the state in international and political life? Explain your views.

• ENDNOTES

1. Jean Bodin, *De Republica*. For a good discussion of the evolution of the concept of sovereignty and its place in international law, see J. L. Brierly, *The Law of Nations: An Introduction to the International Law of Peace*, 6th ed. (New York: Oxford University Press, 1963), especially Parts I and II.

2. Max Weber, "Politics as a Vocation," in *From Max Weber: Essays in Sociology*, trans. and ed. by H. H. Gerth and C. Wright Mills (New York: Oxford University Press, 1946). Also see Charles Tilly, ed., *The Formation of National States in Western Europe* (Princeton, N.J.: Princeton University Press, 1975).

3. Ernest Renan, "What Is a Nation?" reprinted in *World Politics: The Writings of Theorists and Practitioners, Classical and Modern*, 2d ed., ed. by Arend Lijphart (Boston: Allyn and Bacon, 1971).

4. See Safran, "State, Nation, National Identity, and Citizenship."

5. Charles E. Lindblom, *Politics and Markets: The World's Political-Economic Systems* (New York: Basic Books, 1977).

6. Robert L. Heilbroner, "The Future of Capitalism," in *Sea-Changes: American Foreign Policy in a World Transformed*, ed. by Nicholas X. Rizopoulos (New York: Council on Foreign Relations Press, 1990), pp. 111–12.

7. See, for example, Susan Strange, "The Name of the Game," in *Sea-Changes: American Foreign Policy in a World Transformed*, ed. by Nicholas X. Rizopoulos (New York: Council on Foreign Relations Press, 1990), pp. 238–73. Also see, Susan Strange, *States and Markets*, 2d ed. (London: Pinter, 1994).

8. This argument was first made in the 1960s by Jean Jacques Servan-Schreiber, a French journalist, in his book, *The American Challenge*, trans. by Ronald Steel (New York: Atheneum, 1968). Another strong statement of the thesis was Kari Levitt, *Silent Surrender: The Multinational Corporation in Canada* (New York: St. Martin's Press, 1970). Both of these authors thought that activities of U.S. corporations would reduce the scope for autonomous decision making by their respective states, France and Canada. A different, more positive view is Raymond Vernon, *Sovereignty at Bay: The Multinational Spread of U.S. Enterprises* (New York: Basic Books, 1971).

9. A good and interesting presentation of this view is Samuel P. Huntington, "Transnational Organizations in World Politics," *World Politics* 25 (April 1973): 333–68, although he somewhat confuses the issue by treating together both governmental and private multinational entities.

10. For a fine, detailed analysis of the politics and economics of oil, which addresses the theme of this section, see Howard L. Lax, *States and Companies: Political Risks in the International Oil Industry* (New York: Praeger, 1988).

11. A good narrative that presents these developments in all their complexity is Dankwart A. Rustow, *Oil and Turmoil: America Faces OPEC and the Middle East* (New York: W. W. Norton, 1982).

12. Since the beginning of the 1980s, however, the number of intergovernmental organizations has declined, with the greatest decreases occurring in Africa. Personal communication from Harold Karan Jacobson, June 20, 1995.

13. For an account of this assassination program in the context of overall American foreign policy, see Lloyd S. Etheredge, *Can Governments Learn? American Foreign Policy and Central American Revolutions* (New York: Pergamon Press, 1985).

PART 3

Long-Term Patterns and Policy Concerns

CHAPTER SIX

State Diffusion, State Formation, and Maintenance of Position in the International System

Among other things, a state is an instrument of coercion and, sometimes, of repression. To create the institutions that make the state an effective instrument to achieve the things that citizens want, elites use force and other means at their disposal to champion their cause against recalcitrant groups. Yet the suffering entailed in the forging of states is sometimes matched by the horror and anguish of failed states, which lose whatever ability they once had to protect their people from one another and provide for their needs. In the post-Cold War period, such failed states have gained prominence. The people in one of them, Somalia, suffered extraordinary levels of malnutrition in the early 1990s, when internal clan warfare seriously disrupted agricultural production. Only in well-formed states do people find order, security, wealth, basic needs, and justice.

This chapter examines the complex processes by which states have spread throughout the world, how they are formed, of what they are constituted, and how they decay. The analysis also considers the fundamental issue, widely debated in the post-Cold War period, of whether sovereignty is being eroded. In addition, we examine various types of states embodying different conceptions of justice that have been built in the twentieth century.

Introduction

Human beings have always lived in groups that afford them security and the means for cooperating to achieve things that individuals cannot accomplish by themselves. Such groups have ranged from very small bands of hunters and gatherers to vast empires encompassing great stretches of land and extremely large populations. Even today, examples abound of small groups such as Eskimo settlements in northern Canada and isolated population units in Papua New Guinea. Very large groups, such as the more than 1 billion Chinese, are also present in our time.

To accomplish the purposes for which groups coalesce, they form political units. So many purposes may be involved in group activity that it is impossible to name them all. Nevertheless, among the most important are those of maintaining the autonomy and identity of the group, affording it security from both other group members and outsiders, and accomplishing the economic endeavors that sustain the group. All groups develop institutions for performing the tasks that groups decide they want done. In some groups, the institutional arrangements are undifferentiated, with, for example, religious and political and economic tasks being carried on by the same institutions. On the other hand, more complex arrangements often involve some division of functions among different institutions. Thus, governments in most modern industrial societies are clearly separate from religious and other institutions that are regarded as private. In capitalist societies, the two realms of private business activity and public governmental action are maintained separately but in tension with each other. With all this diversity, it is obvious that no blueprint exists for determining how groups organize themselves and structure their political, economic, and other arrangements. Nevertheless, the overall trend in the world since the end of the Middle Ages in Europe has been the diffusion of the modern state, with its characteristic of sovereignty.

The state is a territorial-based political unit providing security, order and justice, and welfare for its citizens' common good. Sovereignty is the principle of exclusive jurisdiction within the territory and has the implication of anarchy in the relations of two or more states.

Importance of State Formation for International Politics

Conventionally, writers on international politics assume the existence of the state and do not attend to the matters that this chapter treats. After all, the very term *international politics* means the political relations among states. Contention arises among scholars over issues of whether the internal politics of a state can effectively be separated from the international system. Another quarrel arises over the future of the state: Is the state being undermined by transnational forces, interdependence, and international organizations, or is it likely to persist for the indefinite future?

To the extent that **state formation** is dealt with in political science, it is bracketed in the field of comparative politics, with a wholly different literature and set of concerns than those pertaining to the study of international politics. Foreign policy is conventionally thought to be concerned primarily with the short-term problems that arise in the relations among countries and less with maintaining the long-term positions of countries in the international system. Despite some attention given in recent years to the merging of international and domestic policy issues, particularly in matters of trade, theoretical concerns in this area merely perpetuate an old debate over whether the domestic and international realms are really different. To the extent that foreign policy analysts do treat the state as a unit,[1] they mostly separate the top-level decision makers from the larger polity on behalf of which they presumably act.

This chapter shows the critical importance of the state in several ways. Although it is very useful analytically to draw a sharp distinction between the structure of the international system and the units that comprise that system, state formation nevertheless provides an essential connection between the structure and the units. As Waltz notes, structural theory tells us a few important things.[2] However, it leaves out most states, and it does not even address the issue of change.[3] State formation theory does both of these things. By drawing attention to the fundamental, long-term activity of every state, the theory gets at what states do, helps to account for their different positions in the structure, and addresses the question of change. State formation theory also overcomes the separation of top-level leaders from the larger polities in which they exist. In doing so, it addresses the domestic purposes and processes that themselves often become issues in international politics. The concept of state formation provides a means of treating the relations of states and markets, competition among states, and the interventions of states and international organizations within a unified framework.

States have not always existed in their modern form, and they are constructed over time rather than created instantaneously. They have spread from one place to another, and they have taken different forms. These activities comprise a process of diffusion.

State Diffusion

The history of the modern state from its origins in Europe to its nearly complete diffusion throughout the world at the end of the twentieth century did not follow a straight path. Forged in the fires of war, the state faced the giant of balance of power that helped to strengthen it. Then, it was mired in the swamp of imperialism before emerging clearly as the political organization of choice as a majority of the world's people shifted after World War II from being dominated by others to being independent.

In addition to following a twisted path in being diffused, the state has taken on different forms. With sovereignty originally a characteristic of the ruler of a territory, that fundamental attribute was, over time, attached to the state itself. When the Treaty of Westphalia endorsed sovereignty as the principle of internal order, large states were smaller and at a very different stage of technological development than now. Kings fielded small professional armies. With the coming of nationalism, mass armies and total war became the normal methods of combat. Modern Spain was formed by the marriage of Isabel of Castile and Ferdinand II of Aragon and their conquest of Granada from the Moors, but Spain's colonies in Latin America fought wars to liberate their already well-defined territories. England as a small island won and lost two empires, and now the pieces of those realms are states ranging from superpower United States to tiny Bahrain. Requirements for meeting the needs of states' peoples and protecting their autonomy have shifted drastically over these centuries. It was not until the twentieth century, for example, that the state took on the function of providing for the welfare of its citizens as a response to conditions generated by industrial society. Technological changes over the centuries have redefined the requirements for economic competition among states. Providing security against the musket-bearing armies of the eighteenth century was a much more manageable task for states than providing security at the end of the twentieth century, equipped as armed forces are with nuclear weapons and missiles, accurate artillery, supersonic aircraft, poison gas, and other horrible weapons.

Any discussion of the state, then, needs to consider not just the essential characteristics shared by all states and to compare the differences that help to shape their foreign policy activities. It must also take account of the shifting characteristics that states take on as they strive to maintain position in the international system.

Thus, there are two aspects of **state diffusion.** The first is the formal spread of the state, beginning with the state formation process in Europe that emerged out of the medieval period. England, France, Spain, Prussia, Sweden, Netherlands, and others were formed in this period. New states were formed in the Western Hemisphere from the late eighteenth century to about 1820, when the Spanish and Portuguese colonies achieved their independence. The United States, Chile, Mexico, Brazil, Argentina, and Bolivia were among these. During the nineteenth century, the process turned back to Europe, where Germany and Italy were formed as new states. Then, after World War I, the breakup of the Ottoman and Austro-Hungarian empires resulted in the creation of a number of new states in Eastern Europe and the Middle East. Poland was restored as a sovereign state, and Austria and Hungary were separated. Czechoslovakia and Yugoslavia were created. Modern Turkey began a drive toward Westernization and modernization. Following World War II, which had severely weakened the European imperial powers, large numbers of new countries in Asia and Africa achieved their independence. India, Indonesia, Egypt, Nigeria, and Kenya are but a few examples of the more than one hundred new states created in the post-World War II period. More recently, a number of very small states in the South Pacific and the Caribbean were formed on the territories of former colonies. Nauru and Vanuatu in the Pacific and St. Lucia and Barbados in the Caribbean exemplify these tiny new states. In the 1990s, the breakup of the Soviet Union, Yugoslavia, and Czechoslovakia brings to 185 the number of sovereign states whose existence is recognized by the international community. This aspect of state diffusion includes just those characteristics of states recognized in international law: a territory, a people, a government, and the capacity to enter into relations with other states.[4] Such states are formally characterized by sovereignty as a principle of internal order, and they are formally recognized by other states as legitimate partners in the international order. They are **juridical states.**

The second aspect of state diffusion is the empirical fleshing out of states. To phrase it somewhat differently, the second aspect refers to state formation as a process of achieving the reality of **autonomy** and **capacity.** States duplicate one another's tasks: providing security for their citizens, developing their economies, strengthening themselves, and maintaining position in the international system. Over time, the most successful and innovative states are imitated by others that strive to keep up. For example, if a leading state creates a particularly effective taxation system that provides the government with a flow of revenue while maintaining high morale among its citizens, others are likely to adopt similar systems. Acquisition of new weapons systems by one state leads to the invention or purchase of similar systems by other states. As implied in this discussion, the requirements of empirical statehood shift over time, so the process of diffusing this aspect of the state is never-ending. Moreover, it is quite distinct from the first dimension of state diffusion, which is merely the spreading of states to additional territories.

In addition to the juridical and **empirical states** encompassed in the state diffusion and state formation processes, there is a normative state. As an idea, the state means certain things, such as being a vehicle for the achievement of a **common good.** While some states may have approached some of the norms of statehood, most have not. For the laggards, the most advanced states give evidence that some of the norms are achievable. To the leaders, certain norms such as **citizen participation** may be held out in the realm of ideas as something yet to be achieved. As with most normative considerations, there is not a single standard, for thinkers may conceive many different ideas about what is a desirable state of affairs. Just so, there are quite conservative conceptions of the state in which the government may require the complete obedience of its citizens. On the other hand, the **liberal state** is founded on principles of respect for **individual rights** and **limited government**. Still another normative conception is the Soviet **socialist state,** which acts on behalf of the proletariat to protect itself against the opposing class interests championed by capitalist states. These well-formulated normative conceptions do not exhaust the principles upon which the state might be based.

■
• • • • • • Components of State Diffusion and State Formation

Characteristics of juridical states recognized in international law:

- Territory
- Population
- Effective government
- Capacity to enter into relations with other states

Empirical states achieve autonomy and strength through duplication of tasks:

- Provide security
- Maintain order and advance justice
- Develop economy
- Maintain position in international system
- Promote citizenship and political participation

Alternative conceptions of normative states' achievement of common good:

- Conservative
- Liberal
- Fascist
- Socialist
- Moslem
- Hegelian

Another normative model of the state that has commanded some attention in recent years is the **Moslem state.** The holy Koran, the basis of the Moslem system of ethics and religion, merges the realms of public life and religion, thus providing comprehensive guidance to its devout followers. In the state established by the Iranian revolution of 1979, a theocracy headed by the Ayatollah Khomeini ruled both religious and secular life. The example of Iran has not found many admirers in the Moslem world because of the major division between Shi'ite and Sunni Moslems. Nevertheless, the turn to a normative state to be ruled by *shari`a*—principles from the Koran—has become a widespread movement. In the 1990s, the prospect of establishing other states that are guided by Koranic principles rather than liberal ones appears increasingly likely as more and more people are attracted to this model.

Apart from all of these considerations about juridical, empirical, and normative aspects of statehood, state diffusion also provides over time an empirical testing process. It appears, for example, that the command economy of the Soviet Union, which embodied a model of extensive production,[5] failed to make a transition to an information-based, postindustrial, intensive-production economy. The Soviet Union, consequently, did not meet the requirements for empirical statehood in the contemporary period and was, thus, unable to meet the needs of its people or maintain its position in the international system in competition with the United States and the other leading industrial countries. In adapting to these circumstances, the successor states to the collapsed Soviet Union have chosen as their normative state the politically democratic and economically capitalist liberal model. Whether Russia, for example, will succeed in forming a stronger, more autonomous, and leading state on the basis of such a model will be seen as that country works out its future.

The discussion of normative states has noted that states are formed on the basis of various principles of organization of political life, and this acknowledges that the state is not the simple conception that is assumed for theoretical reasons in neorealist theory. In addition, states vary considerably more than the normative models we have discussed suggest, for the normative states may be imitated by others with variations.

In contrast, states also serve to protect the peculiarities of culture of their populations, and, in this way, they do not imitate one another. The **duplication of tasks** includes the responsibility of preserving autonomy in order to protect that which is unique to a particular state. Such cultural peculiarities, however, sometimes come under extraordinary pressures resulting from the operations of the market, the policies of other states, and the competition involved in maintaining position in the international system. Recent history provides many examples.

• STATE DIFFUSION IN RECENT HISTORY

To compete in the international market for agricultural products, for example, Mexico has found it necessary to privatize its *ejidos*, the lands held by farmers as communal property, because they are very inefficient as production units. Not just markets but also state policies bring pressures, such as the United States' drive to try to get the Japanese to restructure their retailing system. Traditionally, Japanese commerce operates through very small stores owned by families and serviced through an intricate distribution network. This system is difficult for foreign competitors to penetrate because of the personal relations involved and the complexity of the established patterns of doing business. Led and supported by both the Bush and Clinton administrations, Americans pressed the Japanese to do their marketing through department stores and other large units that would be more accessible to foreign competitors. In Europe, the members of the EU have determined that their positions in the international system can be more effectively maintained through the perfection of their common market. But this choice sometimes involves adjustments, such as Germany's giving up its quality controls on beer that had prevailed since the Middle Ages and made German beer the world's standard for quality.

Beer and Sovereignty

Such pressures on states are sometimes regarded by certain analysts as representing an erosion of autonomy. If the Germans cannot uphold their beer standards, it means that something other than the German state is shaping the decisions that, under the principle of sovereignty, belong to Germany alone. A different interpretation consistent with state formation theory is available. In this view, the Germans made the decision, thus vindicating their sovereignty. Sovereignty means only that the German state has exclusive jurisdiction within its territory. It does not mean that there is some objective standard that the Germans must meet in making their own decisions. Neither does it mean that Germany is not subject to the pressures to compete in the international political economy, as well as extraordinary pressures from its allies and its own citizens. If one focuses only on the disaggregated issue of beer standards, then he can conclude that the Germans caved in to outside market and political forces. However, from a perspective that treats the state in the aggregate, Germany acquires more power and an enhanced position in the international political and economic system by changing its beer policy. Had it clung to its admirable but noncompetitive medieval standards, its autonomy with respect to a single

industry would have been preserved. But that accomplishment would have been made at the expense of its overall power and international position. By adjusting to the requirements of new conditions in the international political economy, Germany remains in a better international position than it would have been by clinging to its beer standard peculiarities. On the other hand, the transaction involved a trade-off of something that was culturally unique for the benefit of overall state power. So long as that trade-off was decided by the Germans alone, however, the principle of sovereignty remained intact.

Substantial room for interpretation exists in such instances. Some observers think that policy actions like modification of German beer standards and acceptance of European Union standards is evidence of an erosion of sovereignty because it illustrates the substitution of supranational authority for nation-state authority. Scope for interpretation increases as consideration is given to the community-building process that is occurring within the European Union. What may be occurring is the formation of a new state of Europe.

If, indeed, the Europeans are building a continental-size, populous, industrialized, wealthy state, that would further indicate the second aspect of state diffusion that was treated above. Formation of a new superpower would culminate from the imitation of the other superpower, not particularly in its social arrangements but in the main attributes that characterize leading states in this era of history.

International Organizations and Sovereignty

Within the interpretation that the state is being superseded and eroded, an argument is made that international organizations have become much more important actors in international politics. Some, like the European Union, are held to be displacing states. Others, like the United Nations, are regarded as being added to states as important actors. In considering international organizations within the context of state diffusion, it is possible to arrive at a very different interpretation, for international organizations may serve state diffusion.

The state being the fundamental unit of the international order, member states have constructed international organizations designed in part to preserve and strengthen states. Throughout its entire history, the United Nations has promoted the first aspect of state diffusion, which is the formation of juridical states. More recently, its members have directed it to take on the second aspect of state diffusion, which is the formation of empirical states. In both kinds of undertakings, the global organization has been an effective instrument of state diffusion.

Actually, the fundamental idea of employing a global organization as an instrument of state diffusion was embodied in the League of Nations Covenant, which included a provision for bringing certain colonies to independence. This provision, termed a **mandate system,** was modified and updated in the United Nations Charter, where it was referred to as a **trusteeship system.** Territories that had been taken from the losers in World War I and World War II were not given to the victors as rewards for winning the wars, as had been the earlier tradition. Instead, countries belonging to the victorious coalitions were given the responsibility for preparing the territories for independence, and this responsibility was to be exercised under the supervision of the international community through a United Nations organ, the Trusteeship Council. For example, Great Britain was awarded the former German colony Kenya at the end of World War I. On the basis of its mandate—later, trust—Britain prepared Kenya for independence, which it achieved in 1963. Although few territories achieved independence under this arrangement, it established the principle that state diffusion was to be supported by the international community.

That principle gained considerable strength in another chapter of the United Nations Charter called "Declaration Regarding Non-Self-Governing Territories." Included in this provision were two matters significant for state diffusion. First, the principle of promoting statehood by the international community was extended to the colonial territories of the victors in the war, making the principle a universal rather than a restricted one. Perhaps even more significantly, the declaration made explicit that the international community's state diffusion responsibilities included the building of institutions and related practices of self-government. With this, the United Nations became committed to making a contribution to the second aspect of state diffusion, that of building empirical states.

Much greater strength was lent to this undertaking with the passage in the United Nations General Assembly in the late 1950s of a resolution on decolonization that included the establishment of a special committee of the General Assembly. Member states from Africa and Asia pressed for more rapid implementation of the declaration on non-self-governing territories, and this pressure was instrumental in speeding the process that swelled the ranks of member states in the United Nations. Founded in 1945 with only 51 members, the United Nations had nearly 150 by 1970. Interim events and then the splintering of the Soviet Union brought total membership to 185 states in September 1995.

In addition to promoting the independence of dependent territories, the United Nations conferred juridical statehood on the newly independent states by admitting them as members of the organization. Such status was reinforced by the implicit, and often explicit, recognition of their statehood in the independent acts of other states. On top of that, membership in the international organization gave to many of these new states, especially the smaller ones, a vehicle for exercising a foreign policy. Most of the new states were too poor and short of the requisite resources to establish embassies around the world. Thus, their membership in the United Nations gave them a forum and a process in which they could evolve and exercise a foreign policy.

Additionally, the institutions of the international community assisted the new states with the enormous tasks of building empirical states through economic and technical assistance, scientific and educational aid, and other means aimed at forming modern states. Implicit in this international commitment to state diffusion was a liberal model of the state. Nevertheless, states that adopted a socialist model or embodied a conservative one were also able to take advantage of the support provided by international organizations. In keeping with the liberal state model, the international assistance tended to be limited to the private realm and to those limited governmental tasks, such as economic planning to support the private economic sector, that are compatible with a liberal philosophy.

In more recent years, however, the United Nations has been given new tasks of state formation that address the public realm in the liberal state. Some of the prominent examples are Nicaragua, Namibia, El Salvador, and Cambodia. As a means of bringing an end to the civil war in NICARAGUA, the United Nations provided an international supervisory operation for the 1990 elections and a ballot-counting capacity. In addition, a joint undertaking of the United Nations and the Organization of American States supported a mechanism for disarming the Nicaraguan contras, the armed opposition that had fought the Sandinista army during the 1980s. As cease-fire and peace agreements were reached by the government and its guerrilla opposi-

■ **Central America**

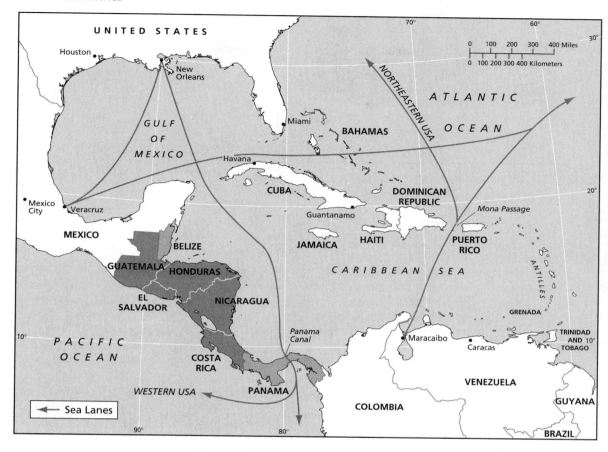

tion in EL SALVADOR, the United Nations provided both supervisory capacity for implementing the agreements and joint participation with the government in restructuring state institutions. These activities included disarming the guerrillas and resettling them and their families as well as restructuring the army and police forces, including recruiting some former guerrilla soldiers into the new police force. The activities of international organizations in both of these cases included matters pertaining to the structuring of public and governmental state practices and institutions. Even more far-reaching in this regard were the operations of the United Nations in Namibia and Cambodia.

NAMIBIA provided one of the world's most difficult cases of bringing a non-self-governing territory to independence. At the end of World War I, South-West Africa was taken from Germany, and South Africa was given responsibility under the League of Nations mandates system to administer South-West

Africa and to prepare the way for it to become independent. Following World War II, South Africa refused to submit to the greater constraints of supervision under the United Nations trusteeship system, a decision that placed it in conflict with the international community. Part of South Africa's strategy of preserving its internal arrangements of *apartheid*, or separate development for different racial and ethnic groups, was to maintain friendly governments in bordering countries. This strategy required diplomacy in certain areas, but domination of its dependent territory of South-West Africa served the purpose as well. However, a guerrilla movement known as SWAPO, the South-West African Peoples' Organization, began fighting for the independence of the territory, which it called Namibia. Following the outbreak of civil war in neighboring Angola in the mid-1970s, South Africa decided to intervene there on the grounds that SWAPO was using Angolan territory as a sanctuary from which to launch attacks against South African forces in Namibia. After many years of bitter warfare that mixed the issues of self-government with international war and the conflict among the superpowers, South Africa was finally persuaded to accede to the independence of Namibia, and the United Nations mounted an exceptionally large operation to supervise elections that took place in the context of an uncertain cease fire arrangement and flammable racial politics. In the end, the personnel sent by the United Nations acquitted themselves admirably, and Namibia at last achieved its independence in 1991. Thus, the task of state diffusion that had been assigned to a mandatory power at end of World War I was taken over and carried out by an international operation

■ Namibia

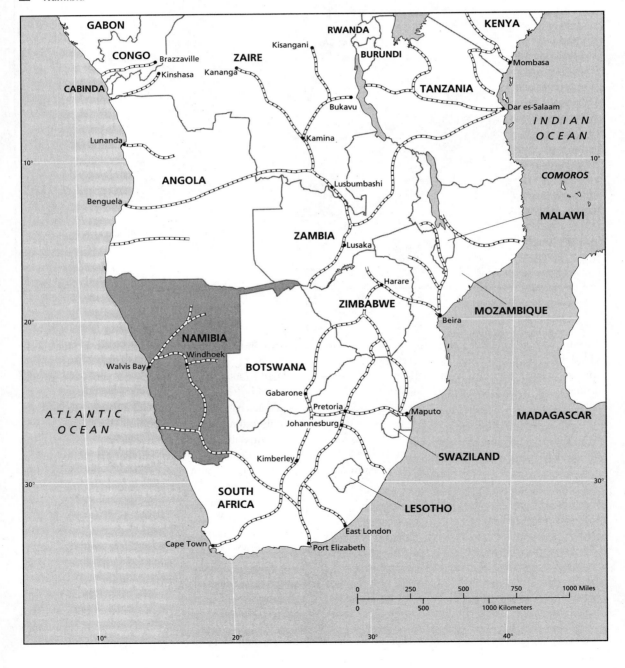

that did its work under authority of the United Nations.

CAMBODIA offers another exceptionally difficult example of state diffusion but in quite different circumstances from those in the Namibia case. One of the successor states of French Indochina, Cambodia recovered its independence in 1954. Although aligned indirectly through the Southeast Asia Treaty Organization with the United States, Cambodia sought to keep its neutrality during the American war in neighboring Vietnam throughout the 1960s. Its ruler, Prince Norodom Sihanouk, skillfully maneuvered among the factions that supported, respectively, the Americans and the North Vietnamese. However, in 1970, he was overthrown in a coup by his right-wing premier Lon Nol, whose troops then engaged North Vietnamese forces on Cambodian soil, and the United States supported Cambodian government fighting first by extensive aerial bombing and then by a land incursion. Among the effects of this fighting was the rapid growth of support for the Communists known as the Khmer Rouge. By 1975, when the Americans withdrew completely from the region, the Khmer Rouge tri-

umphed in the civil war and took over the government, initiating one of the bloodiest reigns in history, and killing over 1 million of the estimated population of 7 million. Prince Sihanouk had established a government in exile, and right-wing forces fought the Khmer Rouge until 1979, when Vietnam intervened and installed a new government headed by Heng Samrin. After several years of negotiations among the various groups, an arrangement was made in 1991 to install a coalition government, disarm the belligerents, and attempt to restore order and the economy; agreement was also reached that a very large United Nations contingent would be the instrument to accomplish this state restoration exercise. The agreement included a provision for elections in 1993, to be carried out under the auspices of the United Nations.

In the Cambodian situation as in those in Nicaragua and El Salvador, civil wars had disrupted the normal functioning of the state, and international organizations were used to facilitate the repair of state processes or to reassemble state institutions. Rather than being antithetical to the state, then, international organizations in these cases have

■ **Cambodia**

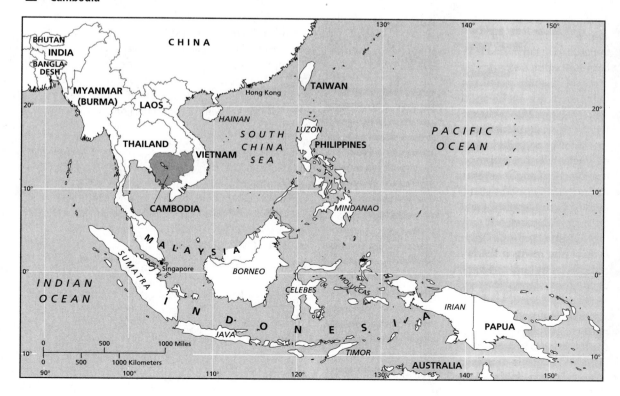

repaired and strengthened states. They have done so, moreover, by assisting states to perform domestic political functions or, as in the Cambodian case, by performing some of those functions temporarily on behalf of states.

State Formation

Brief allusions to juridical, empirical, and normative states in the discussion of diffusion did not flesh out these concepts. They need to be elaborated further, and consideration must also be given to the state as an idea.

• STATE AS IDEA

First and foremost, the state is an idea. During its civil war that lasted from 1975 to 1991, LEBANON was torn apart, a substantial number of armed factions controlling small bits of territory and fighting against others. Several other countries intervened—first Syria in 1976, then Israel in 1982, and the United States in 1983, not to mention the nongovernmental entity, the Palestine Liberation Organization (PLO), that fought there between 1975 and 1983. Of these, only the PLO and the United States have retreated. For much of the time, Lebanon's government held only a few square blocks in Beirut. Throughout the turmoil and the fighting that wholly suspended the empirical reality of statehood in Lebanon, the idea of Lebanon persisted. None of the factions aspired to separation and autonomy, and none of the foreign interveners sought to annex Lebanese territory. Given the deep cleavages in the society between Christians and Moslems, among local warlords and families, and across an ideological spectrum of political beliefs, there was no nation to be identified. Yet everyone remained committed to the idea of Lebanon, even though no empirical reality intruded. The strength of this idea may be attributed to both the minds and wills of the fighters and citizens of Lebanon and to the legitimacy conferred on the state by the international community. In the face of the animosities and hatreds, differences of religion, and the lack of a national consciousness, all of the combatants clung to the idea of Lebanon as an independent state.

The state also exists as an idea carried by nations. Following Poland's disappearance after its third partition in 1795, the Polish nation was maintained. When self-determination of peoples was included in the settlement of World War I, a state of POLAND was put in place in 1918. It was then carved up by the Germans and the Soviets in 1939 and had its boundaries redrawn at the end of World War II. Throughout, the Polish people by their language, culture, and church retained the idea of Poland as a state.

In another case, Jewish nationalism arose in the last decade of the nineteenth century at a time when the Jewish people were scattered across the globe. Nevertheless, the idea of a Jewish state—ISRAEL—that would provide the means for this nation to work out its common future took hold and then assumed empirical reality after World War II. Despite the horrendous suffering and human toll wrought by the Nazis' attempted extermination of European Jewry, the idea of a Jewish state remained in the minds of those who sought its actualization as a refuge and a protector of their security.

More recently, Palestinians form a nation that aspires to have its own state. Through negotiations with Israel following the 1991 Gulf War, a state of PALESTINE approaches reality through the Palestinian Authority, which exercises governmental functions in limited areas of the West Bank. Even during the period when the PLO subsisted as a wretched expatriate organization without a land of its own, the idea continued to present itself and to exist, not just in the minds of those who lived in the Middle East where the state would be located but also in the visions of Palestinians in a diaspora that resided all over the world.

From the idea, states form and reform. As such examples as Lebanon, Poland, Soviet Union, and Yugoslavia indicate, states also decline and disintegrate, sometimes even disappear. State formation, then, is not a straightforward progress to some predetermined ideal. Neither is it a simple process in which states are suddenly created, full-blown and equal to all other states. Never thoroughly divorced from a certain empirical reality, state formation has several dimensions. One of these is the juridical state.

• JURIDICAL STATE

Clear examples of juridical states are many of the former colonies in AFRICA that gained their independence from the European imperial powers after World War II.[6] States such as Sudan and Ivory Coast, Zaire and Nigeria, Cameroon and Mozambique embodied a minimal empirical base. Formal requirements for statehood under international law were fulfilled. They had territory, although the territorial boundaries were those inherited from the colonial era and

■ **Africa**

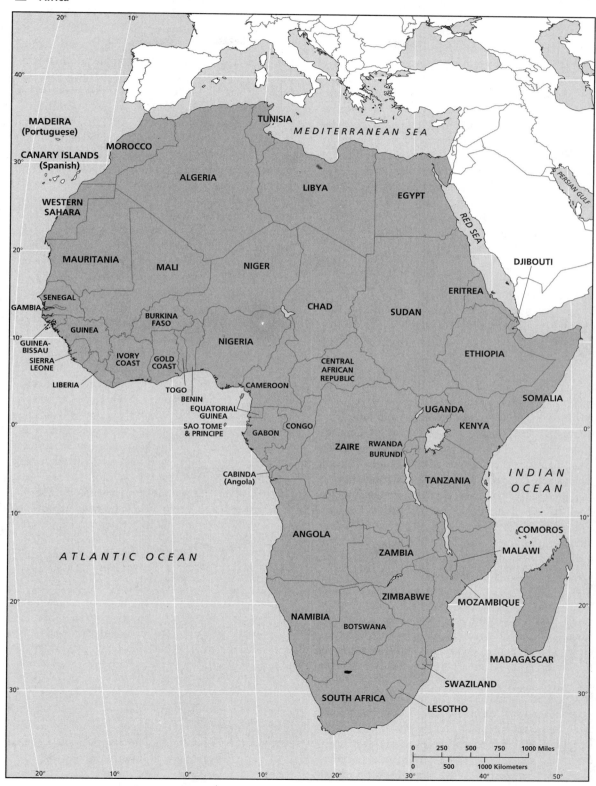

had been arbitrarily determined by the European powers without regard to African traditions or ethnic or linguistic groups. Each state possessed a population, mixed and hostile as different elements might be to one another. Governments were in place, but either they were those selected by the imperial powers to succeed European rule or they represented factions that gained through military means the levers of governmental power without the ability to exercise jurisdiction throughout the entire territory.

These governments also had the capacity to enter into agreements with other governments, although much of that capacity flowed from other states and international organizations that conferred recognition and **legitimacy** on them. Sovereignty prevailed in the sense that other states had given up their claims to jurisdiction within the new states, but the ability of the states to exercise their exclusive jurisdiction within their own respective boundaries remained very limited.

Africa gives some obvious contemporary examples, but the juridical state is hardly limited to one time period and one continent. In the early part of the twentieth century, the quintessential "banana republic" HONDURAS was a juridical state with minimal empirical substance. Its public finances remained under the control of the British from the 1870s to the 1920s, and American businesses effectively exercised control over the government through a system of bribes and other corrupt practices. American social customs of the time, such as racial segregation and discrimination, prevailed on the banana plantations, where the working language was English. Even as a pawn of the United States during the 1980s in its surrogate war against Nicaragua, Honduras possessed greater autonomy—there was more empirical reality to its statehood—than had been the case, say, in the decade preceding World War I.

In addition to these weak or "soft" states,[7] other states are affected by their juridical status. Following wars, occupied countries are denied this status, allowing victors to exercise jurisdiction within their territories. After a time, however, usually upon signing a peace treaty, they return to being juridical states. After World War II, though, the absence of a peace treaty with Germany did not stand in the way of creating two successor states, each of which had a good measure of juridical statehood. Nevertheless, for many years, it was the policy of the Federal Republic Germany—West Germany—to withhold recognition of other countries, with the exception of

the Soviet Union, that had normal diplomatic relations with the People's Democratic Republic of Germany—East Germany.

Sometimes, revolutionary states are denied juridical status, and this may have the effect of denying them such benefits as normal trade relations, access to capital for economic development, and so forth. An example of this is Russia following the Bolshevik takeover of October 1917 and withdrawal from the allied coalition that was fighting Germany in World War I. Not until 1933 did the United States extend diplomatic recognition to the Soviet Union.

Is Sovereignty Breaking Down?

Some observers think that sovereignty, the fundamental legal principle of exclusive jurisdiction, is breaking down under the weight of several developments in the contemporary world.[8] Taking on responsibility for protecting the human rights of individuals against their own governments, international organizations represent one such development. In Western Europe, an international court has direct jurisdiction over individuals who wish to bring community law to bear against their governments. In 1988, the Inter-American Court of Human Rights, an organ of the Organization of American States, ruled that the government of Honduras was guilty in the disappearance in 1981 of one of its citizens and ordered Honduras to pay damages to the man's family. In this case, the government of Honduras accepted the verdict.

Another kind of overlapping jurisdiction occurs, it is argued, when international financial institutions such as the International Monetary Fund apply **conditionality** to the loans extended to governments. Often, the conditions attached to such loans include such domestic matters as deciding how many employees the government should have. Finally, liberals claim that the broad growth of interdependence in which private firms and intergovernmental coalitions participate in international affairs reveals a further erosion of sovereignty, or, to put it another way, it indicates the growth of overlapping jurisdictions.

Each of these considerations is a serious interpretation of events that may be assessed in the context of the juridical state. Concerning the commitment of states through such agreements as the United Nations Charter and the Helsinki Agreement of 1975 to uphold an international standard of human rights, even international advocacy and enforcement of such standards makes a contribution to the formation of empirical states. Anticipating an argument to be made later, one of the intrinsic and logical components of state formation is the promotion of **citizenship,** and citizens cannot be formed without fundamental respect for individuals.

Direct jurisdiction by international courts of justice makes a better case for overlapping jurisdiction. When an individual is subject to the authority of both his own country's courts and the international court and neither his state nor that individual has any choice in the matter, then, indeed, there is overlapping jurisdiction. Whether the authority of the regional international court is autonomously derived remains the essential question.

In the medieval period, when the Pope exercised authority over subjects within territories that were ruled by princes, the source of his authority was divine law, an independent source that was not subject to the will of the prince. The case of the authority of a regional international court contrasts with this, for the source of authority is that conceded by the states that created the court by a treaty. For a variety of reasons, member states may be willing to be bound by the agreement that they made, but they reserve the right to withdraw from such courts and to reject their jurisdictions. Thus, the reality of overlapping jurisdiction in this case rests upon the autonomous decisions of states, not upon any independent source of authority.

Similarly, the same question can be used for assessing international financial institution activities. The IMF, for example, becomes involved, through the conditions it attaches to the assistance that it provides to states, in such internal affairs as taxation and employment policies of governments. Its authority, too, derives from that conceded by states through their adherence to the IMF treaty. States have two opportunities for not accepting IMF conditionality: they can withdraw from the treaty, and they can reject IMF assistance in particular applications. Many states do not do so because they determine that it is in their interest to accept the conditions, with the implication that the international institution has some jurisdiction over the same matters as the state. Nevertheless, the basis of the IMF's authority is not autonomous: it derives from the agreement of states.

It is possible that, over time, these matters of empirical overlapping of jurisdictions would become so accepted as law that they would be held to be inviolate. However, such an outcome seems very unlikely, for any state that decides that its security interests are negatively affected by such institutional activities would fairly readily be able to renounce its obligations. Should others oppose its renunciation, their only recourse would be to war or other forms of coercion. Actions such as these would demonstrate the realist premises of state autonomy, the absence of overlapping jurisdictions, and an anarchical ordering principle as an implication of the exclusive jurisdiction of states.

• EMPIRICAL STATES

The last chapter presented a succinct definition of state to which it is useful to return. A state is an apparatus or a mechanism for governing and for getting things done, for achieving what is just for its citizens and their common or public well being. Associated with the state are authority and power. Comprising the state's power are a military and coercive apparatus.

Some writers reduce the empirical state to a coercive apparatus,[9] leaving aside the functions that it performs and the purposes for which it exists. Although an empirical state includes military control over a territory and its people, that dimension, by itself, does not comprise a state. For example, in the aftermath of a war, an occupying army exercises military control over a territory and people, but the coercive apparatus of that army is not a state. It is the instrument of the occupying state. The occupation under General Douglas MacArthur in Japan after World War II held authority and controlled the coercive apparatus, but it obviously did not constitute the Japanese state. Although the coercive apparatus is a crucial component of a state, the state cannot be divorced from the achievement of the public purposes for which it is constructed. These purposes include autonomy, security, order, justice, and welfare for the state and its citizens.

Stressing that states embody public or common purposes acknowledges a basic distinction that is drawn by many observers between state and civil society. This distinction contrasts the aggregate good for the state as a whole and specific interests of individuals and groups. Jean Jacques Rousseau, the French philosopher, formulated a difference between the **general will** and the **will of all,** and the German philosopher George Hegel sharply differentiated the **universal** and the **particular.**[10] For any individual in a state, there are public aspects of his existence that he shares with other citizens, and alongside these exist group interests that combine his and others' concerns. **Civil society** refers to particular and group considerations, whereas *state* designates common or universal matters.

In ordinary times, it is sometimes difficult to draw such a distinction, for every individual and each organization strives to achieve its selfish, or particular, purposes. Even in a public situation in which a law is under consideration, all of those, in a democratic state at least, who might be affected by the law attempt to influence it. The representative of a company that might gain a contract under the new law may be found stalking the corridors of a congress or a parliament attempting to have included provisions that favor his company. Taxpayer associations try to shape the revenue-raising aspects of legislation. Even those charged with the duty to seek the public good—the legislators and political leaders themselves—never allow considerations of their own reelection to wander far from their attention in calculating votes on legislation.

On the other hand, **war** tends to bring the common good to the fore. Although particular considerations are never absent, the threat to an entire state—to its way of life and its vision of how political life ought to be organized—makes the common good, the universal interest, more apparent. It is in such circumstances that many individuals more readily are prepared to sacrifice not only their selfish interests in such things as salaries, homes, and the company of loved ones but even their lives for the good of the whole.

In **totalitarian states,** very little space is allowed conceptually for civil society. On the other hand, liberal states are based on a conception of a vast space for **private** individual activities as well as private economic enterprise. Regardless of such conceptual differences, empirical states always include both civil society and a **public** arena. Despite its dedication to the principle that no division existed between class interests and group interests on the one hand and state interests on the other, the Soviet Union sustained elite privileges, acknowledged nationalities, and allowed a minimum of market activity. Moreover, it was believed before and has become clear since the fall of communism that individuals within the Soviet state found refuge in drunkenness and other forms of escapism that allowed them to maintain some distance from the state. On the other side, sometimes the **public space** is almost entirely taken over by civil society, and an **elite group** dominates the coercive instruments to serve private rather than public concerns. In both

Latin America and Africa in the modern period, government has commonly been in the hands of small, corrupt elites who rule in their interests in the face of vast reservoirs of poverty and disadvantage. The ability of dominant groups to seize power and turn it to their own ends lends weight to the political importance of civil society, for the strength of groups that is not dependent on government provides a basis for bringing public matters to the political agenda. Sometimes, it requires the activities of civil society to form states.

The formation of empirical states includes, first of all, the development of the **capacity to govern.** Governing includes, in the first instance, the provision of justice: a police function to afford personal security to citizens; the enactment and putting into practice of constitutional arrangements and laws; the providing of economic well-being that aims at equality; and the education of citizens. Secondly, the development of governing capacity requires the creation of **institutions,** especially for deliberation but also for implementing the decisions that arise from deliberation. **Financing** is critical for the achievement of state goals, so this capacity encompasses the ability to extract taxes from the citizenry and the management of public finance. Through a political process, the empirical state also builds its capacity to govern by working toward **unity** within the state, bridging the cleavages that separate groups and classes, and strengthening the identity of the state. Capacity to govern also grows as there is consistency between the state's foreign and domestic affairs.

Along with the capacity to govern, empirical states develop the capacity to provide for their **security** and to maintain their **freedom of action** in their dealing with other states. An additional activity that an empirical state undertakes is the formulation and putting into effect of an **economic development strategy** that acts, in the long run, to maintain the state's position in the international system. Finally, the empirical state promotes **citizenship** and **political participation.** These last activities of empirical states are logically required by the conception of the state as the deliberative and implementing instrument for the achievement of the common good of the citizenry. Only when the maximum involvement of an informed and critical citizenry can be relied on can it be said that a state empirically approximates the idea of the state. Otherwise, the deliberations of small groups are more likely to lead to actions on behalf of the interests of those groups.

■
_____

●●●●●● **Empirical State Formation Components**

- Capacity to govern
  - Justice: personal security, constitution and laws, economic well-being
  - Institutions: deliberation and implementation
  - Financing: taxes, public finance
  - Unity: identity, consistency between domestic and foreign affairs
- Security and freedom of action in dealing with other states
- Economic development strategy
  - To maintain position in international system
- Citizenship and participation

_____

The formation, maintenance, and protection of the empirical state are formidable undertakings, neither easily achieved nor readily defended. Fundamental as this process is, it is constantly faced with challenges from several fronts: civil society and the market, the competition and advancement of other states, and intervention by other states.

● CHALLENGES TO THE EMPIRICAL STATE

El Salvador

From 1932 until 1984, the small Central American country of El Salvador was ruled directly by the armed forces on behalf of a small oligarchy, while the greater part of the population was denied participation in the political process and an equitable share in the distribution of the national wealth. In the 1970s, when the rulers resorted to blatant electoral fraud and then violently suppressed demonstrations against that abuse, many Salvadorans turned to organized arms to fight the government. For twelve years, the Farabundo Marti National Liberation Front (FMLN) fought a guerrilla war against the government, which was backed by the United States with large economic resources and military training and advice. A government headed by the Christian Democrat José Napoleón Duarte ruled from 1984 until 1989 in a project that aimed militarily to defeat the FMLN, a goal identical to that of the United States. Duarte was succeeded in 1989 by National Republican Alliance (ARENA) President Alfredo Cristiani, who, with the assistance of the United Nations, negotiated a peace agreement with the FMLN that was signed at the beginning of 1992. The ARENA government, too, enjoyed the support of the United States, although the end of the Cold War had contributed to some reduction in the level of American assistance.

In this case, what features embodied the empirical state, and which were the challenges to state formation? Clearly, the territory and the institutions of government comprise part of the empirical state. Beyond those, however, the issues are less clear. For example, insofar as the armed forces ruled on behalf of a landowning oligarchy, they served particular or civil society interests. They surely also did so by committing electoral fraud and then by repressing protestors against their crimes. On the other hand, this state institution served state purposes in fighting against an armed insurrection, for it protected citizens from illegitimate violence. During the course of that fight, on the other hand, the armed forces engaged in death squad activity, putting to death citizens who dared to speak out and organize against the government, an activity clearly incompatible with state purposes. Finally, when the armed forces supported the government in its negotiations with the FMLN and in the implementation of the agreements reached, it acted as part of the state. In those instances in which high-level army officers opposed carrying out certain provisions of the peace agreement in order to protect their individual interests or the privileges their positions gave them, they acted on behalf of civil society considerations against the state.

Just as these institutions of the state embodied both state and civil society dimensions, so also did civil organizations and even the FMLN encompass both particular and universal interests. Those citizens who voted in elections and who protested against fraud and injustice, although having no official capacities, exercised their functions as citizen participants in state processes. Even those leaders and soldiers who took up arms against the corrupted institutions of the state served the common good insofar as they strived for inclusion in a more just state. That is not to say that all of their activities were free of civil society considerations. Some of them committed atrocities against their fellow citizens, and many fought for personal ambition or on behalf of limited class interests, all such activities fitting into the jacket of civil society matters. Nevertheless, evolving out of the thoughts and experiences of the warriors came conceptions of a just society and the willingness to come to agreements with the adversarial government to construct arrangements that would allow every Salvadoran to strive for the common good. Such activities belong properly to the state, for they are expressions of the universal side of individuals and civil society, which themselves comprise constituent elements of the state. A more complete and careful analysis of the situation in El Salvador would reveal more subtle and extensive variations on the theme of state and civil society actions by Salvadoran individuals, organizations, and officials, for every Salvadoran embodies both the particular and the universal.

For the other actor in the situation—the United States—however, there are neither gross nor subtle discriminations to be made. Americans in El Salvador can never act in a Salvadoran state capacity, for they are agents of a foreign state. The relations of El Salvador and the United States consist wholly of civil society interactions, each acting in its particular interest, for no shared universal interest exists in their relationship. The United States and El Salvador are each states; they do not comprise constituent elements in another state. Even though on occasion American actions might have the effect of contributing to Salvadoran state activities—in lending support to free and honest elections, for example—the overall effect of intervention in this case, as in others, is to weaken the autonomy of the smaller state.

When Duarte joined a military junta in 1980 that determined to defeat rather than to negotiate with leftist opponents, his project was identical to the American project, and both were civil society undertakings. In addition, as American officials became so involved in the internal politics of El Salvador that the superpower was essentially another component of Salvadoran civil society, the autonomy of the Salvadoran state was diminished.

Civil Society

This example of El Salvador should not be allowed to detract from the larger point that civil society and the state are always present, even in large, well-established, and autonomous states. In point of fact, the great industrial democracies—such as France, Germany, Canada, and the United States—are founded on a liberal principle that concedes a privileged position to the market and private enterprises. Because of both its crucial role in conducting economic activities and the resources it commands as a result of its productive endeavors, the business world in the liberal state comprises, ordinarily, the most important segment of civil society. No other part of civil society enjoys such access to government on such an array of subjects as does the economically productive sectors of society.

On the other hand, civil society is broader and more encompassing than business, for it includes all associations that strive for their particular ends as well as the nonstate dimensions of citizens. In some circumstances, an array of people and organizations from civil society can play a role in state activity that surpasses that of business. For example, in the late 1960s in the United States, opponents of government policy in Vietnam had an extraordinary effect in changing that policy in 1968 from one of the escalation of military force to deescalation and the opening of negotiations with the adversary.

States and Markets

Even more important than the specific political activities conducted by elements of civil society, the market presents specific as well as continuing challenges to the state. Unlike the state, which is a deliberative organ and control mechanism based on collaborative decision making, the market embodies antithetical characteristics. Premised on the conception that each producer and consumer acts in his own selfish interests, the market should produce a common good through the operation of a price mechanism that is not under anyone's control. This view that a public good is produced by the operation of an "invisible hand" implies that there is harmony of interests among all economic actors. Such a conviction runs exactly counter to the conception that state and civil society are in tension.

Many counterpoints exist between states and markets. Through the operation of a price mechanism the market rewards efficiency, and this process tends to promote differential rates of accumulation among producers, with inequality as a result. In contrast, the state promotes justice, which includes equality. Equality often requires the redistribution of wealth, but such redistribution is inconsistent with efficiency, for it implies that rewards are given to the inefficient. Thus arise debates over welfare programs, housing and transportation subsidies, and many other government activities that involve income redistribution.

In addition, the rationalization of production on the basis of efficiency ignores territorial boundaries, one of the fundamental attributes of the state. Corporations find scattered around the globe the materials, labor, facilities, and other components of production that they need to produce efficiently. States, on the other hand, are dedicated to accumulating wealth to maintain their relative positions and are devoted to maintaining their security. These very different concerns lead not to use of efficiency but rather to safety and well-being as the relevant standards. For those in private enterprise, the state's defense of culture and identity is an impediment to cooperation, whereas the market's indifference to the requirements of statehood is a problem to be contended with. Thus, governments regulate markets and impose restrictions on businesses to ensure that state purposes are served. Many observers have noted the difficulty that governments sometimes have in capturing taxes from multinational corporations or imposing detailed regulation on transactions by computer. Such observations lead to a profounder consideration about states and markets.

In a primitive environment, markets may arise spontaneously as producers, seeing the advantages arising under a division of labor, enter exchange relations. Very rapidly, however, as exchanges become more complex, involving money, credit, a large variety of products, and so forth, property rights and contracts become increasingly important. Money is issued by states, property rights are created by states, and contracts are enforced by states. Moreover, transactions are richer and economies become more prosperous under conditions of security, which is provided by states. While it may be true that states are unable or find it not worthwhile to monitor millions of transactions by computer, either within single states or across boundaries, those transactions occur only within the context of security and property rights established by states. Rather than being undermined or rendered irrelevant by sophisticated technology, then, states become more important to ensure that transactions can continue to occur.

As Robert Gilpin has explained,[11] the market operates through a process of uneven development to shift the accumulation of relative gains from one country to another and from region to region, but this phenomenon poses the challenge to the state to maintain its position in the international system. The long-term test is not that of gaining control over small transactions, which occur at the rate of millions every day. It is rather that of attending to its own economic base and its economic relations with other states in such a way as to enhance its chances of maintaining its standing in the international system as a whole. Fundamentally, this problem is one of determining an economic development strategy that enables a country to compete effectively against other states that also are striving to maintain their positions in the international system.

Thus, the market, while existing in tension with and presenting some limited challenge to the state, does not present the profound challenge that other states do. It is the competition and advancement of other states that present such great challenges that they might even turn into threats. Such important challenges do not arise in daily headlines, for they occur over longer periods of time. Their seriousness may have acute consequences, but the basic processes at work are structural.

Challenges from Other States

In 1850, the leading powers were Britain, France, Prussia, Russia, and Austria-Hungary. Although the United States was an important regional power, it did not involve itself in European politics. Japan was a closed, feudal country that did not engage in commerce or other transactions with the outside world. Europeans, particularly the British, and others pressed a weak China for concessions and extraterritorial privileges. Neither Germany nor Italy had yet been formed as modern nation-states. Since that time, Germany was created and fought three wars with France and its allies, its defeat in the two world wars only slowing down its march to stand as Europe's leading economic power at the end of the twentieth century. Following its forced opening in 1854, Japan restructured its politics and launched a modern economy, achieving great power, only to be defeated in World War II, then to recover to become the world's second economy. Austria-Hungary disintegrated as a result of World War I, with none of its successor states belonging to the first rank. Italy's unification in the nineteenth century formed the basis for the creation of substantial power that has placed it among the leading industrial countries of the late twentieth century. Russia went though a revolution to be succeeded by the Soviet Union, which underwent an industrialization process that brought it to the first rank, then, only since the early 1970s, to decline economically and in 1991 to disintegrate. At the end of the century, Russia remains as the state with the largest land mass of any but with an economy in shambles and without the empire that it once controlled. Britain and France both lost their empires and are reduced to second-rank powers dependent during the Cold War on the United States to ensure their security against the Soviet Union. Following its devastating civil war, the United States developed the world's greatest economy and became the world's strongest military power in the post-World War II period. As the twentieth century comes to an end, the United States, while beset by many apparent weaknesses, remains the leading power in the world. At the same time, other countries strive to improve their positions in the international system, and the memory of the shifting fortunes of the powers over the past century and a half leads to the expectation that change will continue to occur.

Although the challenges of competition and advancement of other states are most visible in the case of the powers, similar competition throughout the world affects smaller states. Saudi Arabia assumed its present form only in 1932 as a state whose economy was based on nomadic herding of animals. Following the discovery of oil in 1936, the country so increased its wealth and development that by the late 1970s, it became only the sixth country whose executive director at the World Bank casts a vote for only one country (the other five are United States, Japan, Germany, France, and United Kingdom). South Korea offers another example of a country that has risen in position through its economic development. Devastated by a war that ended in 1953 and with its economy in shambles, the country has become known variously as one of the "tigers" or "little dragons" of Asia because of its impressive economic advance that brought its 1988 gross national product to $171 billion and its population in 1990 to nearly 44 million. Other countries, notably many in Africa and some in Latin America and Eastern Europe, have failed to maintain their positions in the international system over the course of forty or fifty years.

Maintenance and improvement of position primarily contribute to the autonomy of the state and to the welfare of citizens. On occasion, however, they are important for security. An increase in capabilities for a state may provide it with the instruments for making claims on neighbors or for fulfilling ambitions for conquest. Iraq's development was an ingredient in its initiation of a war with Iran that became the longest and bloodiest of the 1980s. With the end of that war, Iraq made claims to Kuwaiti territory and demands for oil-pricing policy, followed by an invasion of Kuwait. Regarded as a security threat by many other countries, Iraq was then forced out of Kuwait by a coalition of forces that included most of the major powers. This example is only one in a long line of experiences—Germany and Japan providing the main examples during the last hundred years—in which growing powers present security challenges to other states. Moreover, for small states, their relative positions make them extraordinarily vulnerable to the whims or ambitions of large states, as Grenada found in 1983 and Panama at the end of 1989 when the United States chose to use its power to intervene in those countries.

■

• • • • • Sources of Challenge to the Empirical State

From civil society:

- Fraud
- Repression
- Rule on behalf of an oligarchy
- Death squad activity
- Use of coercive apparatus for private gain and to protect privilege
- Personal ambition
- Promotion of class interests

From market:

- Philosophical: harmony of interests
- Premises: efficiency, price mechanism, rationalization of production
- Results: inequality

From other states:

- Uneven development
- Competition to maintain position

Intervention by other states and international organizations:

- Temporary loss and long-term erosion of autonomy

Intervention

This leads to a discussion of the third major challenge to state formation: intervention by other states, both unilaterally and through international organizations. In El Salvador, the United States reduced that country's autonomy by intervening and joining as a participant in internal affairs. The same country was assisted in its state formation, however, by the United Nations, which helped to arrange and implement a peace agreement between the warring sides in the civil war. In other cases, a major power or an international organization may contribute to state formation by intervention. Because state formation is a continuing process, it can be helped or hindered by intervention, depending on the actions of the intervenor and the effects of those actions. A basic criterion for determining whether intervention contributes to or detracts from state formation is that it supports the whole state or a segment of civil society. Thus, the difference between the American and United Nations interventions in El Salvador turns on the support for the oligarchic government by the United States in contrast to support for conciliation between the government and the FMLN by the United Nations.

Another criterion for making this distinction is the inclusion of purposes pertaining to the object state. In the case of the intervention in Panama by the United States in 1989, for example, the invading force had as its goal the arrest of the dictator Manuel Noriega, not assistance to Panamanians to perfect their state. In contrast, the United States occupied Japan in the aftermath of World War II with the aim of building a state that would function independently, although the limitation on defense decisions written at American insistence into the Japanese constitution restricted Japan's autonomy. It is unclear in the mid-1990s whether the constitutional limitations on Japanese defense prerogatives can be changed autonomously.

Throughout this discussion of state formation—the idea, the juridical state, civil society, the empirical state, and challenges to state formation—a conception of a normative state has underlain the analysis without having been made explicit. It is now time to give explicit meaning to the concept of a normative state.

• NORMATIVE STATES

If a state is never fully formed, the ideal that embraces its full formation is the **normative state.** A common good in the sense that Rousseau or Hegel would have it is an abstraction that can never be attained; it can at best be approximated in unusual circumstances; but that abstraction forms part of the normative state. A state should incorporate justice, but no state has ever been free of injustice. Whereas injustice may represent empirical reality, justice epitomizes the normative state. Moreover, because justice means giving everyone his just due and everyone's life continuously unfolds, the quest for justice must forever exist in a condition of becoming. For an individual living in a state that suppresses his ability to participate as a citizen, his loyalty is not owed to the repressive apparatus; his allegiance goes to the normative state that he is promised as becoming. When empirical states exist in a condition of chaos and turmoil, driven by irrationalities on all sides, unity and rational deliberation remain the alternatives of the normative state. During a foreign intervention when critical decisions are being made by outsiders, autonomy remains as a cornerstone of the normative state. In a secession of a part of the territory of a state that occurs as an empirical reality, two normative states contend, one envisaged by those seceding and the other held in mind by the defenders of the preexisting state.

Contention over normative states forms a significant part of politics, which is not limited to policy matters. The normative state is very often directly the matter in contention. When citizens protest electoral fraud, for example, they are striving to construct a more well-formed state. Bosnians loyal to the government struggling against Bosnian-Serb and Bosnian-Croatian forces are contending for their normative state. At other times, the normative state is an issue intertwined with a public policy dispute. Part of the struggle in the Clinton administration in the early 1990s in the United States over energy taxes was concern about the relative vulnerability of the country resulting from its dependence on both imported petroleum and foreign borrowing, both of which have long-term implications for the country's autonomy.

There is a broader sense in which normative states frame conflict and cooperation in domestic and international politics. Despite the potential for an unending series of alternative conceptions, in the modern world a limited number of normative state concepts frame disputes and create affinities entering international relations. Among them may be listed conservative, liberal, socialist, and Moslem. In addition, a modern cleavage occurs between national and ethnic principles. Finally, although a Hegelian ideal state hardly contributes to the practical dialogue of international politics, it does offer a benchmark for assessing the normative states under consideration.

Conservative states encompass a variety of forms, including monarchy and military rulers. Their unifying principle is defense of a culture or way of life against outside forces of change that is guarded by an authoritarian ruler or political system. The Hashemite Kingdom of Jordan provides one example of a poor country with a conservative state. At the other end of a scale of wealth is Saudi Arabia, which defends Islam's holiest cities, Medina and Mecca, as well as a Wahabi—a conservative Islamic sect—way of life. In Myanmar (formerly Burma), a military regime resists the intrusion of the global forces of change at the expense of development. As defenders of particular cultures, conservative states tend not to develop ambitions to have their normative states duplicated elsewhere. Instead, they tend to wish merely to retain their autonomy by limiting the access of disruptive ideas and institutions. Saudi Arabia's experience illustrates that such a posture need not restrict economic modernization, for the kingdom has given access to many foreign firms to assist in the development of the country. During the Gulf war, foreign troops with such strange customs as the drinking of alcoholic beverages and allowing women to participate in fighting forces served on Saudi territory. Even while giving access to such foreign institutions, the Saudi government restricts their activities so as to defend its conservative normative state. In general, opponents of such a state who themselves envisage an alternative normative state are more likely to arise from within the polity rather than from outside it. Legitimacy in such a state derives from the tradition that is being defended or from a traditional principle of rulership such as monarchy.

The liberal state is quite distinct from the conservative state. Its legitimacy rests in the consent of its citizens, and it extends a broad scope to individuals and to civil society for activities free of governmental interference. Moreover, governments are elected through processes in which citizens are free to speak and organize on behalf of a wide range of candidates as well as to criticize their public officials. The state is limited to those activities assigned to it, in a constitution and in practice, and these do not include economic functions. Performing these is the realm of business that operates with only minimal restrictions by the state.

Unlike the conservative state, the liberal state enters into international relations in two ways. First, the basis of legitimacy holds an appeal to oppressed citizens everywhere, for the normative liberal state promises them dignity and the opportunity to pursue justice together with their fellow citizens as well as wealth on their own. Secondly, the private economic activities allocated to civil society are not bounded by the polity that grants them. In capitalism, efficiency of production and the price mechanism are universal norms that have no intrinsic respect for state and cultural boundaries. Thus, the liberal capitalist state is an expansionary one, not in the sense of territorial conquest but in the logic of its principles. As Michael Doyle has written, the characteristics of the liberal state foment cooperation and dampen the prospects of war among liberal states.[12]

On the other hand, the activities of large corporations in the short run extract value from small countries that appear to make them dependent on the countries in which the headquarters of the firms are located. Over time, smaller countries tend to acquire increasing advantage from their relationships with firms so that the distribution of power between them is reversed.[13] Nevertheless, the firms continue to act in the uneven development process, being the carriers of capital and technology that are the instruments of the rationalization of production.

Despite its loss of attraction through defeat in World War II, another normative state is the **fascist state,** as exemplified by Nazi Germany and Fascist Italy. Founded on a principle of building state power from which the citizenry may benefit, the fascist state finds its basis of legitimacy in the leader whom citizens obey in order to achieve greater state power. Such a state enters international politics as a result of its ambition to increase power by adding the territory and resources of others to its own. Moreover, as Benito Mussolini wrote in the Italian encyclopedia, war is regarded as a great human activity, for it affords an opportunity for the expression of the noblest of human virtues—bravery, courage, self-sacrifice, and so forth.

Another type of normative state that has become significant in international relations is the **authoritarian socialist state.**[14] Deriving its legitimacy from a Marxist theory of history that makes it the inevitable successor to the capitalist state, the principles of the socialist state are public ownership of the means of production and equality of distribution. In place of the two realms of the liberal state, responsibility for economic matters belongs to the government, which also wields the coercive apparatus of the socialist state. From the socialist conception, economic rights of citizens have a standing equivalent to the political rights of the liberal state. The normative socialist state enters international politics by holding out the promise to the exploited and the oppressed that a successor vision will follow liberal capitalism. Classes that have been dominated by private owners of the means of production will themselves come to dominate.

Even though empirically authoritarian socialist states have, for the most part, faded from the world scene, such norms as equitable distribution of product and the provision of equal welfare to all citizens remain. Following the Cold War, the liberal state has triumphed as the world standard, but it is far from clear that considerations of economic equality have vanished. Neither does it appear that the economic role of states has lessened insofar as the state seeks to maintain position in the international system. Should a deep world recession occur, it is altogether possible that some states would choose to adopt a socialist state as a means of coping. Meanwhile, the authoritarian socialist state remains primarily a normative one, as a result of the failure of empirical socialist states to compete effectively with liberal states.

While authoritarian socialist and liberal states coexisted, they competed both directly by opposing the existence in the other of a different type of state and indirectly by offering models to other states to imitate. In the end, the liberal state triumphed in this competition, for the successor states of the Soviet Union and the Eastern European countries have taken the normative liberal state to heart. In the interim, the fortunes of the models faced an ebb and flow, as many poorer countries chose the socialist normative state as their own while others chose the liberal state.

As the authoritarian socialist normative state was diminishing, another normative state—the Moslem one—rose to prominence following the 1979 Iranian revolution. Based upon the Koran, the Moslem state does not distinguish between the public and the private dimensions of life but rather conveys a set of rules that encompasses both. Religion, interpreted by religious leaders, provides the basis for conduct both in an individual's personal life and his relationships with his family and others, on the one hand, and in the political life of the state. Thus, legitimacy proceeds neither from the consent of the governed, as in the liberal state, nor from a historical process, as in the socialist state, but rather from the Koranic text and religious authority.

In the long run, it may be possible to find a basis of reconciliation between the liberal state and the Moslem state, but the history of interactions between the two has been marked by great hostility. When the 1979 Iranian revolution drove the shah from his country and led to the return from exile of Ayatollah Ruhollah Khomeini, the new leader denounced the United States as "the Great Satan." During a struggle for power among a number of factions, one of them took the occasion of the shah's admission to the United States for medical treatment to seize the American embassy in Teheran and take a number of hostages, including sixty-two Americans. Even when an arrangement was finally made for release of the hostages in January 1981, an intense animosity continued to characterize the relations between Iran and Western countries, particularly the United States. The Iranian state provided both inspiration and material assistance to a variety of groups that engaged in two activities that contributed to further hostility.

First, Iran promoted the spread of its normative state to other Islamic countries, thus fomenting the replacement of regimes that cooperated with the West. Secondly, the Iranian regime supported a variety of groups that engaged in terrorism, particularly in Lebanon where they kidnapped and held hostage a number of Westerners.

Adherence to a normative Moslem state spread throughout the Middle East and other areas of major Islamic influence. Hostility to the Moslem state has come not just from liberal states but also from conservative regimes. Perhaps the most dramatic clash came in Algeria, when the regime that had been established by revolution in 1962 opened its political process to elections in which other parties were allowed to participate. However, when a party committed to a normative Moslem state won Algeria's first free parliamentary elections in December 1991 and was expected to win a mid-January 1992 run-off, President Chadli Benjedid resigned under pressure from the army, and the new government called off the second round of elections and arrested hundreds of leaders of the Moslem party.

These experiences of hostility between Moslem states, whether empirical or normative on the one hand and liberal and conservative states on the other, bode ill for peaceful accommodation. They also intimate that the conceptions of liberal and Islamic normative states are as diametrically opposed as are their respective bases of legitimacy.

The illustrations that have been used suggest the ways in which the Moslem normative state pertains to international politics. In principle opposed to both the liberal and socialist states, Iran and other adherents to a normative Moslem state have a fundamental attitude of hostility to secular regimes. Such an attitude has led to a rejection of some of the international norms that are nearly universally shared in the modern world, such as giving protection to diplomats. Although the use of terror as an instrument of foreign policy was neither invented nor monopolized by Iran and its cohorts, they have openly promoted kidnapping as a lever of influence in international politics. Finally, the Islamic normative state is a powerful impetus to groups in Moslem countries that seek to supplant regimes that do not accept their principles. All of these ways of connecting with international politics involve conflict with existing states. Cooperation enters only at the point where Iran extends its assistance to opposition groups. Hostility in state-to-state relations, of course, would be supplemented should other empirical Moslem states be actualized.

Meanwhile, these different normative states provide inspiration and goals for different people. Inasmuch as they involve very different conceptions

Normative States

TYPE OF STATE	PRINCIPLES	BASIS OF LEGITIMACY	HOW GERMANE TO INTERNATIONAL POLITICS
Conservative	Defense of culture	Tradition	Retains autonomy Resists outside pressure
Liberal	Limited government Individual freedom Economic functions assigned to market	Consent of governed	Model for ordinary people Private economic activities Peace with other democracies
Fascist	Build state power	Leader	Glorifies war Seeks expansion
Socialist	Public ownership of means of production Equality of distribution	Historical inevitability	Vision of progress Supports other socialists
Moslem	Ethical guidance for life, without distinction between public and private	Holy Koran Religious authority	Hostile to secular states Rejects international norms Uses terror Aids advocates of other Moslem states
Hegelian	Actualization of ethical idea Common good Rationality	Common good served through rational deliberation	Protects autonomy Provides security Maintains position

and significantly diverse bases of legitimation, they may be expected to continue to contribute to conflict in international politics.

Unlike these, the **Hegelian normative state** does not constitute an ideology for action. Instead, it offers a benchmark, or an ideal, against which other normative states as well as empirical reality can be assessed. Premised on the conception that the state is the actualization of an ethical idea, the state serves the common good. Whereas individuals, communities, associations, firms, and other components of civil society pursue the particular, the state embraces the universal. Because the universal must also be rational, the state gives expression to the rational process in life. Since objective rationality cannot be determined except by those whose public good is served, the state is required to be an organ of deliberation in which rational debate comprises politics. It is necessary to construct institutions, including legislatures and executives, but these merely play their parts in carrying forward the process of making public policy. In the context of an empirical state that can never completely achieve what the normative state embodies, a process of **rational deliberation** requires that there be a citizenry that can participate in that process. Thus, it is a requirement of the normative state that it promote the **education of citizens** who may become better informed and better able to participate in the process. Such a state is one whose diplomacy gives intelligent direction to its foreign

policy in dealing with other states. Because the state seeks autonomy, security, and wealth in those interstate relations, intelligent direction does lead to the advancement of an economic development strategy that will enhance the state's capabilities to **maintain its position** in the international system. However, nothing in this theory of the state promotes aggression and the use of force to compel other states. Legitimacy rests on the fulfillment of the ideal of achieving the common good through the deliberation of educated citizens who participate rationally in the political process.

• IMPORTANT TERMS

authoritarian socialist
   state
autonomy
capacity
capacity to govern
citizen participation
citizenship
civil society
common good
conditionality
conservative states
duplication of tasks
economic development
   strategy
education of citizens

elite group
empirical states
fascist state
financing
freedom of action
general will
Hegelian normative
   state
individual rights
institutions
juridical states
legitimacy
liberal state
limited government
maintain position

mandates system
Moslem state
normative state
particular
political participation
private
public
public space
rational deliberation
security

socialist state
state diffusion
state formation
totalitarian states
trusteeship system
unity
universal
war
will of all

• STUDY QUESTIONS

1. How have states changed since 1648? What forces or conditions induced or required changes in the state?

2. Distinguish the two aspects of state diffusion, and explain how they are related.

3. Why is it useful to distinguish among juridical, empirical, and normative states? How is each related to state formation?

4. What does it mean to say that state diffusion provides an empirical testing process?

5. Is the autonomy of states being eroded by modern pressures of interdependence? What evidence and analysis can be brought to bear in answering this question?

6. Do international organizations contribute to or detract from state diffusion and state formation? What is the significance of the many new activities undertaken by the United Nations in the post-Cold War period?

7. By what means can a state remain intact as an idea when it has no empirical referent?

8. Upon what does a juridical state depend, and in what ways does such a dependency affect international politics and state formation?

9. What is the connection between civil society and the state? Why is it difficult to distinguish them? Do you believe that the distinction is a valid and useful one?

10. Considering all of the counterpoints between states and markets, why does the market not offer a profound challenge to state formation?

11. What are the major normative states in the contemporary world, and how do they differ from the Hegelian state? How do the different normative states vary in their germaneness to international politics?

12. What is the theoretical utility of the concept of the state to the analysis of international politics?

• ENDNOTES

1. See, for example, Stephen D. Krasner, *Defending the National Interest: Raw Materials Investments and U.S. Foreign Policy* (Princeton, N.J.: Princeton University Press, 1978).
2. Waltz, *Theory of International Politics*, p. 70.
3. Ruggie, "Continuity and Transformation in the World Polity."
4. These are the traditional qualifications for statehood in international law, cited by Phillip C. Jessup, "Discussion of Israeli Application for Membership," *Department of State Bulletin*, 12 December 1948, pp 723-24, reprinted in *The State in International Relations*, comp. and ed. by Richard H. Cox (San Francisco: Chandler Publishing, 1965), pp 23–26.
5. See Seweryn Bialer and Michael Mandelbaum, eds., *Gorbachev's Russia and American Foreign Policy* (Boulder, Colo.: Westview Press, 1988).
6. See Robert H. Jackson and Carl G. Rosberg, "Why Africa's Weak States Persist: The Empirical and Juridical in Statehood," *World Politics* 35 (October 1982): 1–24, for a full treatment of the argument here.
7. "Soft" state is a term coined by Gunnar Myrdal in his *Asian Drama: An Inquiry into the Poverty of Nations*, 3 volumes (New York: Pantheon, 1968).
8. I am especially grateful to Professor Lawrence Finkelstein, with whom I have had conversations and correspondence about this matter, for outlining the argument that sovereignty is breaking down and for helping me to think the matter through.
9. See, for example, Theda Skocpol, *States and Social Revolutions: A Comparative Analysis of France, Russia, and China* (Cambridge: Cambridge University Press, 1979).
10. Jean Jacques Rousseau, *On the Social Contract*, ed. by Roger D. Masters, trans. by Judith D. Masters (New York: St. Martin's Press, 1983), and G. W. F. Hegel, *Hegel's Philosophy of Right*, trans. by T. M. Knox (Oxford: Clarendon Press, 1952).
11. Robert Gilpin, *The Political Economy of International Relations* (Princeton, N.J. Princeton University Press, 1987).
12. Doyle, "Kant, Liberal Legacies, and Foreign Affairs."
13. Lax, *States and Companies*.
14. Democratic socialist states, which combine a liberal welfare state with some government ownership, form another type that is not discussed here. A number of Western European countries, including Sweden and France, exemplify such a model. With regard to international politics, these states fit comfortably with other liberal states.

CHAPTER 7

The Role of Force in Contemporary International Politics

The Soviet Union in the late 1980s withdrew from its long-term challenge to the United States, thus bringing the Cold War to an end. With its subsequent collapse, the Soviet Union's main successor state, Russia, no longer represented a sufficient aggregate of power to form a counterbalancing pole in a bipolar system, and that structure came to an end. This extraordinary transformation, occurring without war, led certain writers to conclude that force had lost much of its efficacy in international politics. That is, not only had the structure changed, but also the means and nature of politics had changed.

However, in 1990–91, the United States led a broadly based coalition of states that deployed well over a half million troops in the Persian Gulf area to oust Iraqi forces from their positions in Kuwait. That venture's success seemed to vindicate the position of those who believe that force retains its efficacy in international politics.

This chapter explores the issue of how efficacious force remains in contemporary international politics. Not only does the overt employment of force remain useful in the post-Cold War period, but also force in its latent form underlies those political orders that enable groups and states to go about their ordinary activities.

Introduction

Force is a fundamental element in human affairs. Employed by the greedy, the power-driven, and the acquisitive, force leads to brutality and domination in intimate and person-to-person as well as group relations. When a husband beats or rapes his wife, he intimidates and dominates her, bending her to his will and humiliating her. A street gang member may establish his social rank and political position within the group by beating up on others. To impose a social order and different norms of behavior in the circumstances noted also requires the use of force, not its rejection. Societies become civilized through the enactment of laws and their enforcement. Force's role in society can be reduced by what Antonio Gramsci called hegemony[1]—the putting into place of convincing ideas that lead people to accept societal norms and customs—but force always remains the tool for coercing those individuals who do not accept the norms or who aspire to create different arrangements. Police forces and prisons stand out as the most obvious institutions wielding force to ensure compliance with laws and punishment for violating them. Although courts stand between police and prisons and are not themselves institutions that brandish force, they necessarily operate on a foundation of force that protects them, requires criminal defendants and civil respondents to appear, and carries out the judiciaries' decisions. Thus, force permeates both criminality and politics; it endures in vile activities and in the achievement of justice; it remains pertinent to both civil society and the state.

Force plays an important role in the economic dimension of civil society, for property that has been privately accumulated requires protection. Such protection is provided by both governmental agencies like the police and private security arrangements, including armed guards and mechanical means of defense against the use of force by thieves and burglars. Private guards need to be authorized by the state, which has a special role in the use of force. Moreover, rights to property are ultimately guaranteed by the force that underlies the state, and contracts are enforced by the same mechanism.

In the most widely accepted definition of the state in the twentieth century, the essential characteristic is that the state has a monopoly on the legitimate use of violence.[2] Indeed, the twentieth century has seen the increase of governmental control over force within modern states, with local warlords and vigilantes being supplanted by regular police and constitutional governments. At the same time, state diffusion in the twentieth century has revealed the critical role of force in the formation of states, as groups have struggled for autonomy and groups with alternative ideologies to reigning hegemonic ones have tried to use force to achieve control of states. In the great revolutions in France, Russia, and China, outcomes were determined by force. During the nineteenth century, the decision that the United States should remain a single state rather than divide into two units was made by the bloodiest war of the century, and the unification of Germany was forged by violence. Force upheld the decision of Israeli leaders to proclaim the independence of their new state in 1948, and force is the arbiter of the outcome of the conflict among contending groups in what had been Yugoslavia before 1992, most obviously in Bosnia-Herzegovina.

As the discussion in the last chapter made clear, state formation involves a fairly complex process with several dimensions. Nevertheless, the most primitive, essential meaning of state includes nothing more than military control over a territory. Without that, it is impossible to form the other components that comprise a complete state. Although circumstances do occur in which military control can be gained with little or no fighting, the more usual case manifests armed conflict among groups that aim to control the territory in question. Sometimes such fighting is conclusive, as in the unification of Germany, in the American Civil War, and in the 1949 Communist triumph in China. In different circumstances, the opponents fight to exhaustion, and diplomacy enters to bring the fighting to a conclusion, as occurred in the Thirty Years' War.

In settled circumstances, it is not always apparent that military force provides the foundation of the state. Commerce, industry, and everyday life go forward without the manifestation of force. Order, justice, and welfare prevail without remark or comment. Despite its lack of appearance, nevertheless, **latent force** underlies the visible tranquility. Latent force is that capability that lies at the ready without any obvious display: police truncheons remain in their holsters, and troops stay in their barracks. Those forces contribute no less to public order than they would if unleashed and employed in fighting or suppression.

Military control of territory includes not just domination within the realm but also protection of the territory against other states. The armed forces of a country are seldom called on to defend their country from attack by another, but their function is critical on such occasions. Moreover, their existence sometimes acts as a deterrent to those who harbor ambitions to take some or all of the territory under their control.

When interstate war does occur, force may or may not, as in state formation, determine the outcome. Iran and Iraq fought for eight years, from 1980 to 1988, without a clear resolution of their dispute. On the other hand, World War II was decided by the superior forces of the Grand Alliance, which triumphed unequivocally over those of the Axis powers. Whether or not decisive, force remains at the ready for employment in interstate relations, although there are many circumstances in which it cannot effectively be brought to bear.

During the last quarter of the twentieth century, many observers have concluded that force is losing its efficacy in international politics.[3] This argument was given a boost by the peaceful ending of the Cold War when the Soviet Union chose not to use force to protect Communist governments in the Eastern European countries and then itself collapsed, ending the bipolar structure.[4] It certainly was unusual to experience the collapse of a major state and its empire and the ensuing structural transformation without a war. Soon after that experience, however, the Gulf War of 1990–91 seemed to demonstrate the continuing efficacy of force in international politics. Such contradictory evidence compels us to consider seriously the question of how important and pertinent is force to international politics. It is to that question that this chapter is addressed. The short answer is that force remains fundamental, but the longer response requires a look at many aspects of force. The first of these aspects is an examination of the instruments of force, their origins, and their development.

Instruments of Force

Like other tools that serve other purposes, the instruments of force are in part products of the extant technology at any given period of time. In the battle of Agincourt made famous in William Shakespeare's *Henry V,* the new technology of the crossbow, introduced by the English, set the tide of battle and determined the lopsided outcome. In addition, quantities and quality are determined by modes of production. Twentieth-century wars of attrition, such as the Second World War, have been shaped as much by the industrial production that replaces arms expended on the battlefield as by the actual fighting that occurs there. Finally, the instruments of force are affected by their organization into effective fighting units directed by the commanders who control them. Just as the modern corporation is an efficient organization to produce goods, the modern military force is a professionally directed and efficient organization to fight wars. Just as Rome was effective at administering a far-flung empire and building marvelous public works like aqueducts and roads, its army was a well-organized, well-trained, and well-led organization to triumph over Rome's enemies.

• EXPANSION OF FORCE

Over the last couple of centuries, the Industrial Revolution and the formation of the modern state have combined to produce what Robert Osgood has called "the expansion of force."[5] Unceasing technological innovation has given the world the rifled gun, ammunition with greater explosive power, dynamite, chemical gases that incapacitate or kill, biological agents that spread disease and death, the tank, the machine gun, the submarine, and airplane, radar, radio- and television-controlled guidance systems, the **atomic bomb,** the **thermonuclear bomb,** and guided and **ballistic missiles,** as well as the **multiple independently targeted reentry vehicle (MIRV),** a missile containing several bombs directed at separate targets. In the transition to the postindustrial society that is affected so deeply by information and communications, weaponry has been linked to the computer and other instruments in ways that enhance battlefield direction and promise to extend battle zones into space. This link provides such weapons as the **cruise missile,** a pilotless aircraft that evades enemy radar by flying close to the ground. In the post-World War II period, a new generation of strategic weaponry was introduced about every four years. These technical innovations were developed largely by the superpowers, the United States and the Soviet Union, but weapons that were not very many generations behind were also transferred to other countries.

■──────────────────────────

• • • • • • **Instruments of Force**

Products of:

- Technology
- Mode of production
- Organization

Such transfers, through sales or grants, were rendered feasible because of the tremendous productive capacity of the economies of the industrialized countries, many of which engaged in **arms transfers.** In addition to generating surpluses that spread sophisticated weapons throughout the world, the industrial mode of production had important effects on the producing countries. Sufficient numbers of weapons could be produced to arm millions of soldiers who have been mobilized by modern nation-states. Moreover, any arms lost in battle could easily be replaced in factories that mass-produced those arms. Yet another effect of the industrial mode of production allowed manpower to be replaced as easily as weaponry. Newly trained recruits stepped into the organizational slots of fallen soldiers as readily as guns or ships were inserted into the firing line to replace those lost to enemy action. Such rationalization and organization has also allowed the deployment of massive armies in very short periods of time. For example, in 1968, the Warsaw Pact countries placed over a half million troops in Czechoslovakia within a few days to suppress that country's reformist government. Then, in 1990–91, the American-led coalition that ousted Iraqi forces from Kuwait moved over 500,000 troops as well as an immense arsenal and enormous armada into place within a few months, coordinating the activities of many countries that had not before worked together. While the mode of production and organization were necessary ingredients in the brew, the sufficient contribution was political leadership.

Technology and the industrial mode of production have conspired to make civilians the targets of massive force. Because the industrial worker who produces the weapons to be used by the frontline soldier has become as critical to a war effort as the soldier herself and because strategists came to believe that civilian morale was important to a war effort, massive bombing of cities was conducted in World War II in Europe and Japan. Over time, the technique of creating a firestorm that consumed city centers was perfected.[6]

These massive bombing raids in World War II were impressively destructive and killed more people than did the atomic bombs dropped on Hiroshima and Nagasaki. Undoubtedly, the invention of the atomic bomb and, later, of the hydrogen bomb introduced weapons whose destructive power far surpassed that of any previous ones. Commonly used measures of destructive capability convey a sense of the dramatic increases that occurred with nuclear and thermonuclear weapons. Using the high explosive trinitoluene (TNT) as the standard, the explosive power of nuclear weapons is measured in thousands of tons (kilotons) of TNT, and that of thermonuclear weapons is calculated in millions of tons (megatons) of the explosive.

Clearly, such weapons are efficient killers. In the context of the numbers cited above, it was possible for some observers to argue that efficiency marked the only difference between nuclear and what have come to be called conventional weapons. Because more people were killed in Tokyo than in Hiroshima, the differences were obscured. The atomic bomb used on Hiroshima was cheaper and more efficient than the many weapons dropped on Tokyo, but the question remained whether there were other differences.

One way to differentiate nuclear and conventional weapons, even of the 1945 variety, is to note that nuclear weapons operate with greater speed. The time frame within which destruction occurs is reduced from days to minutes. With the addition of long-range missiles to nuclear arsenals, civilians and economic assets immediately become the targets of attack, with no need for an attacker to conquer the target country's defenses. Such **vulnerability** leads to the conclusion that nuclear weapons are useful only for deterrence. The overwhelming devastation that would occur as a result of a nuclear attack would leave the attacked country with such few remaining assets that it would not be worth conquest. Thus, no political purposes can be achieved through the use of nuclear weapons. Threatening their use, however, can deter a major country from attacking.

Nuclear **deterrence** is the threat to retaliate with one's own weapons if an opponent should attack with its. With a minimal arsenal, this threat can easily be made credible because of the speed and destructiveness of nuclear warheads and the inability to defend against them.[7] So long as a country has a **second-strike capability**—weapons that can survive an initial nuclear strike and then be ready for retaliation—it can plausibly pledge to inflict such severe consequences on the striking adversary that the potential initiator will not attack in the first place. After the end of World War II, the United States possessed such second-strike capability against the Soviet Union, and by the early 1960s, the Soviet Union, too, held such a capability against the United States. There then existed a condition in which each held a second-strike capability vis-à-vis the other, a situation often designated as **mutual assured destruction,** or MAD, capability. Conventional weapons had never in history achieved such a deterrent effect.

• NUCLEAR ARMS RACE IN THE COLD WAR

Despite the logical ease of maintaining nuclear deterrence, the United States and the Soviet Union engaged in an extraordinary arms race in which they piled up a total of some 21,000 strategic nuclear warheads—those that could reach the homeland of the other superpower—and another 45,000 or so weapons of more limited range. These immense arsenals were built out of a sense of insecurity in both countries but also because of the attempt of each to protect allies as well as themselves and in response to the inertia of technological innovation and bureaucratic and political pressures from within their own polities.

Insecurities that fed the arms race between the United States and the Soviet Union in the post-World War II period stemmed more from ideological differences than from material interests. Even though under Josef Stalin the Soviet Union had built "socialism in one country" against what was perceived as a hostile capitalist world, its army occupied most of Eastern Europe at the end of the war. Persuaded by a universal ideology of communism, the Soviets put into place in the Eastern European countries governments that were subservient to Moscow's direction rather than autonomous governments that would serve national interests. Furthermore, in the one case in which a democratic election had occurred—Czechoslovakia—a Soviet-directed coup led to a Communist takeover of that government in 1948. Finally, despite a series of conferences dealing with Germany, the wartime allies were able neither to conclude a peace treaty with the defeated enemy nor to coordinate policies in their respective zones of occupation. In the context of this impasse, Germany was effectively divided between East and West, and the superpowers faced off in the crisis of the Berlin blockade and airlift in 1948–49 that eventually reached a negotiated resolution. In addition, Communist parties whose leaders were loyal to the Soviet Union rather than their own nations were active in such Western European countries as France and Italy. These activities frightened many in the West who thought that the Soviet Union was an expansionist power that needed to be defended against. In that context, the North Atlantic Treaty Organization was formed to defend Western Europe against the Soviet Union and its Eastern European allies.

Meanwhile, Stalin and his colleagues were convinced of the intrinsic hostility of the United States and other capitalist countries. The commitment of capitalist countries to private entrepreneurial activity and relatively free access across international borders contained a threat to Stalin's total control of the political and economic life of his own and the Eastern European countries. Moreover, some voices in the United States were eloquent in their hostility to the Soviet Union and communism. Added to these sources of insecurity for the Soviet Union was the fact that the United States possessed the atomic bomb, the most advanced weapon in the world and one that gave it an advantage. Stalin, therefore, sought to acquire the bomb, by both committing resources to research and attempting to obtain American secrets by spying.

To counter what it saw as Soviet expansionism, the United States adopted a strategy of containment. This strategy sought to prevent the Soviet Union from extending its realm and influence beyond the sphere it had acquired as a result of World War II. Containment had the long-term objective that internal strains would lead the Soviet Union to mellow from within and give up its worldwide ambitions. Over the years, events such as the triumph of the Communists in China, the Korean War, arms sales to Egypt, suppression of the Hungarian revolution, an extended crisis over Berlin, the Cuban revolution, the Cuban missiles crisis, and competition in the Middle East, Africa, and Asia continued to feed the insecurities of the two opponents. Through nuclear weapons programs, both sought to gain security but also to avoid open warfare. They also both offered protection to their respective allies, and this extended deterrence greatly complicated the thinking that went into military planning and led to an expansion in the numbers of weapons.

To insure against an attack against one's own country required only **minimum deterrence.** A superpower would need only enough weapons that could survive an initial attack to retaliate and inflict unacceptable damage on the adversary. Given the extraordinary destructiveness of nuclear weapons, it would take only a few to destroy several cities and much of the economic capacity of the targeted country. Assuming errors and building in significant redundancy to ensure a survivable capacity to retaliate, perhaps three hundred warheads would be adequate to achieve minimum deterrence. An arsenal of that size could inflict enough damage to dissuade any rational leader from initiating hostilities. In the negotiations between the United States and Russia in 1992, it was agreed to reduce arsenals to a level ten times that figure. Implementation proceeded slowly, however, for in 1994, Russia still possessed approximately 29,000 weapons, and the United States retained nearly 15,000.[8]

By guaranteeing the security of allies through **extended deterrence,** the Soviet Union and the United States entered a realm of complicated calculations. First, it became possible to imagine a great number of contingencies, at many levels of force, that would need to be met by adding weapons. For example, speculation about a possible Soviet and Warsaw Pact invasion of West Germany induced the United States to develop nuclear land mines, nuclear artillery shells, and short-range and intermediate-range missiles to fight a limited war in Central Europe. It was thought that deterrence was very complicated and that the only way to make it effective would be to meet every conceivable contingency. Possessing the means to fight a war, it was thought, made the threat to retaliate more plausible. Secondly, such an array of weapons became mechanisms for reassuring allies. In the 1980s, for example, the United States agreed to deploy Pershing II short-range missiles and cruise missiles in Europe largely as a way to bolster the confidence of the West Germans in America's commitment to defend them.

Another factor promoting the superpowers' arms race was the momentum of technological innovation. In modern industrial society, the quest for knowledge

◼ Divided Europe During the Cold War

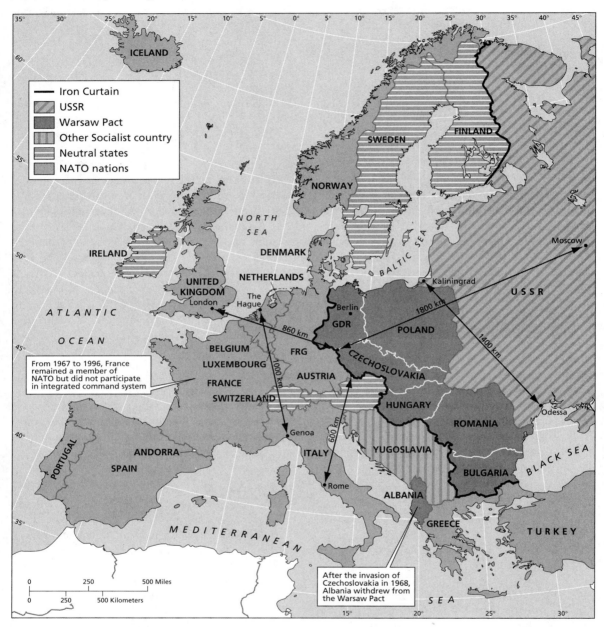

Iron Curtain
USSR
Warsaw Pact
Other Socialist country
Neutral states
NATO nations

From 1967 to 1996, France remained a member of NATO but did not participate in integrated command system

After the invasion of Czechoslovakia in 1968, Albania withdrew from the Warsaw Pact

and its application in new products create an important dynamic. During the Cold War, much of the investment in research and development was made in the military sector of the economy because the dangers to security seemed so apparent. Moreover, it was thought that some advantage might accrue to the adversary from technological innovation. Thus, some intensity was added to the normal quest for new weapons. Some of the major new weapons and related innovations were thermonuclear weapons, ballistic missiles, **antiballistic missile (ABM) systems,** miniaturization, guidance systems, and multiple independently targeted reentry vehicles. Of all of the myriad technologies, it was the last that contributed to the largest numerical increase in strategic nuclear weapons.

After agreeing in 1972 to limit the number of strategic missiles, both land- and submarine-based, the two countries began deploying multiple warheads on each of the missiles. Thus, from an arsenal of some 2,500 strategic missiles each was allowed under the agreement, the superpowers deployed MIRVs on the same number of missiles until their warheads reached 21,000 in 1991. In that year, the United States deployed a total of 1,640 ballistic missile launchers with 7,890 warheads, and the Soviet Union deployed 2,306 launchers with 10,352 warheads. Additionally, both superpowers' arsenals were enhanced by bombers and cruise missiles that brought their totals of strategic weapons to 9,745 and 11,159, respectively.[9]

The intellectual quest forming part of modern society is not limited to the hardware of weapons and related guidance software. Those responsible for planning defense and deterrence also think through strategy and tactics. Certain ideas emerging from this process also contributed to the superpowers' arms race. For example, contemplating the horrors associated with attacks on civilians and industries, strategists devised a **counterforce** doctrine. A plan to attack nonmilitary targets is referred to as a **countervalue** strategy, whereas a counterforce strategy aims to attack only military targets. From such a seemingly humane doctrine emerges the implication that more, larger, and more precisely guided weapons are needed to attack the less vulnerable targets. In the immense wave of military spending that occurred in the Reagan administration in the early 1980s, another idea drove the race to acquire more and higher quality weapons. **Escalation dominance** is the notion that one can surpass whatever level of destruction the adversary can promise. Thus, in a logic of moving through a series of steps from the introduction of one level of force to another until the utmost force is employed, the United States would be able to introduce the threat of greater force. Such a notion holds that in this way the Soviet Union could always be deterred from an escalation of force, even if it made the mistake of introducing some level of nuclear force. The 1980s arms race was driven by another idea as well. In his annual reports, Secretary of Defense Caspar Weinberger wrote that the United States sought a **war-fighting capability.** This concept acknowledges that deterrence might fail and avers that it is less likely to fail if one possesses the means actually to fight a war with nuclear weapons. All of these ideas added to the pressures to build more and better nuclear weapons and delivery systems.

Added to these influences pushing the nuclear arms race were bureaucratic and political pressures. Two bureaucracies, one public and the other private in the United States but both public in the Soviet Union, held intense interests in the acquisition of arms. They were the military and other government agencies that had responsibility for procuring and employing the weapons and the industries that built them. These bureaucracies were more influential during than after the Cold War, but in some ways, they are more apparent in the post-Cold War period. In the early summer of 1993, governmental bureaucracy brought to bear a good deal of pressure on President Clinton to continue testing nuclear weapons through underground explosions. Moreover, pressure from private interests opposing defense procurement cutbacks and base closings became apparent at the same time. Although these pressures were resisted effectively in a different political climate, they had been very forceful during the Cold War.

• • • • • • Factors Promoting the Cold War Nuclear Arms Race

- Sources of insecurity
  - Ideology
  - Material interests
- Minimum and extended deterrence
- Technological innovation
- Strategic and tactical concepts
  - Escalation dominance
  - War-fighting capability
- Bureaucratic and political pressures

Fluctuation in political pressure has proven to be dramatic from the Cold War to the new era, but shifts in politics are hardly restricted to such dramatic circumstances. The superpowers' arms race was not a smooth progression to ever-higher levels of armaments. Instead, bursts of innovation and acquisition tended to follow on events that shaped the politics of the period. After World War II, the United States drastically reduced its armed forces, only to rebuild them following the onset of the Korean War. New acquisition, particularly in the navy, moved forward in the Soviet Union following the Cuban missiles crisis that had exposed the great inferiority of the Soviet fleet. After its defeat in Vietnam and the demoralizing Watergate scandal that led to President Richard Nixon's resignation in 1974, the United States was reluctant to exhibit belligerency in its relations with the Soviet Union.

Despite the massive increase in nuclear warheads resulting from the deployment of MIRV technology, the political climate that prevailed at the time was that the country should adjust to new circumstances in the world. In response, a conservative argument was mounted, with Ronald Reagan as its most eloquent spokesman, that the problem was not changed circumstances but rather the loss of will by the United States. Eventually, that argument prevailed in the political arena, and the country's leaders were then able to brandish both new weaponry and a more belligerent rhetoric in international affairs.

The superpowers' nuclear arms race was exhausted in the late 1980s and early 1990s, when the Soviet Union accepted most proposals made by American negotiators to bring the weapons under control. With the breakup of the Soviet Union in 1991, the long race came to an end.

No nuclear war had occurred. Despite issuing various threats over the years, neither superpower ever used one of the terrible weapons against the other. In light of this history, we are left with the question: Were nuclear weapons fundamental, or has force lost its efficacy in the modern world?

John Mueller's answer is that nuclear weapons were largely irrelevant to the **stability** of the world in the post-1945 period. His argument is that war was discouraged by the memory of World War II, by the contentment of the major powers, by Soviet ideological emphasis on subversion rather than expansion by military force, and by a belief in escalation based on the potential for the rapid mobilization of American production capacity.[10] Mueller's analysis rests merely on comparing alternative factors that existed simultaneously when a result was produced. In contrast, most analysts compare different situations that have different outcomes. Since the 1945–91 period was the longest interval in history without the occurrence of war between the dominant powers, most analysts would attribute that happy outcome to a bipolar structure and to the existence of nuclear deterrence, which is easy to achieve.

Additionally, Mueller's arguments are refutable. The memory of war in other eras did not lead to stability. For example, the memory of World War I did not promote stability and was a partial cause of, rather than a deterrent to, World War II. Although it is true that the superpowers acted with restraint during the Cold War, that does not show their basic contentment. Indeed, their ideological hostility was so great that neither conceded the ultimate right of the other to exist. Believing themselves to be the

agents of history, the Soviets thought that they would surpass and ultimately triumph over the United States. Even though the American policy of containment was a moderate one, its ultimate aim— eventually achieved—was to bring about radical internal change in the Soviet Union, a clear rejection of the legitimacy of the regime.

Moreover, the Soviet Union relied not only on subversion but also on military force to extend its domain. In 1939, the Soviet Union used its military force to partition Poland, and in 1940, it provoked and fought a war with Finland. As a function of its liberation of Eastern Europe in World War II, the Soviet Union used force to acquire a dominion in the postwar period. That dominion was upheld by the use of military force in East Germany in 1953, in Hungary in 1956, and in Czechoslovakia in 1968. Later, in 1979, a military expedition was sent into Afghanistan to maintain Soviet influence. With respect to Mueller's last argument—that stability was retained simply by the capacity to mobilize the productive power of the United States—that contention is neither verifiable nor falsifiable. During the Cold War, in reality, the United States did mobilize considerable efforts to ensure that it and its allies remained safe.

It is difficult to imagine that the Cold War would have ended as it did without the deterrent effects of nuclear weapons. On many occasions, in the absence of those weapons, it seems likely that there would have been a risk of the two countries coming to blows. It is quite likely that they would have behaved as major powers had done in past eras, with major wars growing out of the tensions and conflicts that divided them. Although the "long peace" can partly be accounted for by the bipolar structure that emerged after World War II, the speed and destructiveness of nuclear weapons can hardly be ignored, for their impact on the thinking of policy makers during the Cold War was immense.

• PROLIFERATION OF NUCLEAR WEAPONS

As crucial in the superpowers' relationship as nuclear weapons were, this destructive weaponry was not confined to the United States and the Soviet Union. British scientists had participated in the development of the first atomic bomb. Thus, Britain acquired its own weapons early in the nuclear era. Then, by the mid-1950s, France also decided to build its own nuclear arsenal. China exploded a nuclear bomb in

■ Nuclear Weapons Proliferation

COUNTRY	DATE OF FIRST NUCLEAR TEST	DATE OF FIRST THERMONUCLEAR TEST	NUMBER OF STRATEGIC WARHEADS		
			(ACTUAL) 1993	(LIMITS) 2000	(LIMITS) 2003
United States	1945	1952	9,970	6,000	3,500
Soviet Union	1949	1954			
Britain	1950		48		
France	1960		100		
China	1964	1967	80		
India	1974				
Israel	n.a.	n.a.	100*		
Pakistan	1987	n.a			
Russia			8,972	6,000	3,500
Ukraine	All controlled by Russia		208		
Belarus			80		
Kazakhstan			1,434		

*Estimate of "up to 100 warheads"

Source: International Institute of Strategic Studies, *The Military Balance 1993–1994* (London: Brassey's, 1993), pp. 42, 62, 73, 91, 118, 140, 230–31, 235.

Under the Strategic Arms Reduction Treaty (START), the United States and the Soviet Union were limited to 6,000 warheads each, including air-launched cruise missiles. Subsequently, in May 1992, the United States and the four successor states possessing nuclear weapons (Russia, Belarus, Ukraine, and Kazakhstan) reached an "agreement that opens the way for ratification of the 1991 [START] treaty." Moreover, "Ukraine, Belarus, and Kazakhstan also agree to destroy or turn over all strategic warheads to . . . Russia, and to adhere 'in the shortest possible time' to the 1968 Nonproliferation Treaty." Barbara Crossette, "4 Ex-Soviet States and U.S. in Accord on 1991 Arms Pact," *New York Times,* 24 May 1992, p. 1.

A further agreement was made by President George Bush of the United States and President Boris Yeltsin of Russia that "requires each nation to reduce its nuclear force to between 3,000 and 3,500 warheads by 2003, and by the year 2000 if the U.S. helps Russia destroy its weapons." ("Bush and Yeltsin Agree to Cut Long-Range Atomic Warheads; Scrap Key Land-Based Missiles," *New York Times,* 17 June 1992, p. A1). The START II agreement was signed by Bush and Yeltsin in January 1993.

1964 and a thermonuclear device in 1967, becoming the fifth nuclear power. Ten years after China's first test, India detonated a nuclear explosion but has not since built a nuclear weapons arsenal. Pakistan conducted its first nuclear test in 1987.[11] Although it has not conducted an overt nuclear test, Israel is thought to possess nuclear weapons. South Africa had a nuclear weapons program. Other countries have evidenced ambitions to develop nuclear weapons. Notable among these have been Iraq, Brazil, Argentina, and North Korea. Iran appears to be interested in acquiring advanced weaponry. Many advanced industrial countries have the capacity to produce nuclear weapons should they choose to do so. This process of spreading nuclear weapons technology to an increasing number of states is usually referred to as **nuclear proliferation.** It has been a slow process, with a ten-year lag between the acquisition of nuclear weapons by the superpowers and Britain and the acquisition by France, the fourth power, and then a roughly equal interval until the fifth, China, acquired the bomb, followed by another ten-years before India exploded its nuclear device. Then, thirteen years elapsed before Pakistan tested its first device. No nuclear weapons tests have been conducted by any other country since 1987, although evidence exists of additional countries' attempts to acquire nuclear weapons. In 1981, Israel bombed Iraq's Osirak nuclear weapons facility, and ten years later, other capacities in Iraq were destroyed in the bombing associated with the Gulf War. The United Nations Security Council established a special monitoring agency to ensure that Iraq did not renew its efforts to build nuclear and other weapons of mass destruction. Argentina, Brazil, and South Africa have all renounced nuclear weapons.

Clearly, some countries wish to acquire nuclear weapons while others wish to slow down and even arrest nuclear proliferation. A **nonproliferation regime** is embodied in the Non-proliferation Treaty (NPT), whose provisions are administered by the International Atomic Energy Agency. Under the terms of the NPT, signatories already possessing nuclear weapons agree not to transfer either the weapons or the knowledge of how to build them to nonnuclear states, and nonnuclear signatories agree not to build nuclear weapons or to accept them from nuclear states. Additionally, the treaty provides that the nuclear weapons states will work for the reduction of nuclear armaments.

What drives the cooperation underlying the nonproliferation regime, and what incentives and ambitions induce some countries to acquire nuclear weapons? Two elements, one negative and the other positive, lie at the base of the nonproliferation regime. Fear shapes the outlook of many who consider the consequences of the spread of nuclear weapons to many countries. One dimension of that fear is rooted in the intrinsic characteristics of the weapons themselves, their terrifying destructiveness and the speed with which they can be employed. Small countries, many with 25 percent of their populations concentrated in a single city, are extraordinarily vulnerable to extinction as organized and productive societies by the explosion of a single nuclear weapon. Larger countries with more diverse and scattered assets are hardly immune, for it would take only a larger number of weapons to have a similar effect. Particularly in a context of believing that deterrence is difficult to achieve and therefore unreliable, immense fear for survival is generated by thinking about the problem.

Another dimension of fear comes from the lack of regard for the rationality of potential adversaries. While in the late 1940s Americans placed a good deal of trust in their own wisdom and ability to behave rationally, they were suspicious of the brutality and fanaticism of Stalin and his Soviet cohorts. After the Soviets demonstrated their prudence in managing nuclear weapons, both superpowers' concerns were raised by Chinese leader Mao Zedong's (Mao Tse-tung) depiction of the atomic bomb as a "paper tiger." Once having acquired the weapons, however, the Chinese, too, demonstrated their prudent approach. More recently, fears have been expressed about the horrors that would follow should nuclear weapons fall into the hands of "irrational" dictators like Muammar Khadaffi of Libya or Saddam Hussein of Iraq. Although it would be foolish to rule out the possibility that a "madman" might someday flaunt or even fire nuclear weapons, experience so far suggests that possession of the weapons imposes its own constraints in favor of prudence.

Added to the negative element that supports the nonproliferation regime is the positive factor of maintaining position in the international system. Nuclear weapons form a component of the capabilities of a state, and those states possessing nuclear weapons have an interest in retaining their privileged positions. Any nuclear weapons-equipped country possesses a second-strike capability against any of its conventionally armed opponents, thus insuring its security against them. Moreover, each of the nuclear powers has a measure of capacity to retaliate against the attack of another nuclear power and, thus, maintains some deterrent effect that needs to be taken into account by any potential adversary.

Even many small, nonnuclear weapons states have a maintenance of position interest in opposing proliferation. Although for advanced industrial states nuclear weapons are relatively cheap means to achieve security, nuclear programs require great investments of resources, and these assets cannot then be used for other, more basic economic development. Because the weapons are used only for deterrence, smaller countries are dissuaded from developing the weapons unless they are faced with a major threat. In some situations, such threats are posed, and threatened states are compelled to shift from support for nonproliferation to acquisition of nuclear weapons to provide their own deterrent capability.

A threat presents a powerful incentive to a state to develop and/or acquire nuclear weapons, but there are other incentives as well. A brief narrative of the spread of nuclear weapons provides illustrations of the varied incentives. World War II furnished the occasion for the invention of the atomic bomb. Because the theoretical knowledge was widely available, several belligerents inaugurated a search for the application of that knowledge lest an enemy arrive at the essential discovery first. Despite great theoretical contributions made by Germans, Germany's program appears to have failed because of "the lack of central organization in the German program, which seemed to have been run like a collection of competing academic physics departments."[12] In contrast, the United States launched the Manhattan Project, which succeeded in producing a chain reaction and then the first atomic explosion, which was set off at Alamogordo, New Mexico, on July 16, 1945. Two bombs were produced and dropped on Japan on August 6 and 9, 1945, hastening the end of World War II as the Japanese were shocked into surrendering. Four years later, the Soviet Union exploded its first nuclear device, duplicating the threat posed to it by the United States' possession of atomic bombs. These early developments occurred under the cloud of serious threats, and they have been duplicated in at least the cases of China and Israel. China's initial attempt to acquire nuclear weapons proceeded under a cooperative transfer of nuclear technology from the Soviet Union. However, as relations between the two large Communist states unfolded, the Soviet

Union in 1959 withdrew its assistance to China's nuclear weapons development program. As the fissure between them grew and the Soviet Union became a threat, China launched an independent program that produced a nuclear explosion in 1964 and a thermonuclear bomb in 1967. Unlike China, Israel never did enjoy a period of cooperation with its neighbors. From its founding in 1948, Israel faced not just hostility but rejection and active war from the surrounding Arab states. Even with a small economy, Israel chose to counter the threat to it by developing nuclear weapons, although it has conducted no tests. Nevertheless, the presumed existence of Israel's capability has entered the consciousness of leaders and their discourse in Middle Eastern international politics.[13]

Other incentives than threats may be found in the cases of Britain, France, and India. Drawing on the experience of its participation in the Manhattan Project, Britain developed a program that produced its first nuclear explosion in 1950. Although it had not been completely evident during the war, it was clear by 1950 that Britain relied for protection on the United States. Moreover, Britain was not faced with any serious threat other than the one shared by its protector. Thus, the explanation for British nuclear developments lies elsewhere. It appears that the primary incentive was to retain autonomy and support Britain's position in the international system. Nuclear weapons conferred not only prestige but also the assurance that essential decisions to provide security still lay in London. In the face of substantial evidence that such is not the case, the British have relied on the possession of nuclear weapons to save some of the position that they once had as the center of the world's most powerful empire. Both the Suez crisis in 1956 and the Skybolt affair in 1962 effectively demonstrated Britain's dependency on the United States in matters of war and weapons.

Similar incentives were at work in France. Driven from its Southeast Asian colonies in 1954, France undertook a nuclear weapons development program that produced an explosion in 1960. Not only did the nuclear capability add to France's prestige, but it also functioned as a valuable tool in domestic politics. The impending loss of Algeria provoked an army revolt, precipitated the fall of the Fourth Republic, and brought about Charles DeGaulle's return to power. As part of his solution to the underlying dissatisfaction in the armed forces, DeGaulle assigned to the armed forces a national—as opposed to an alliance—mission

to defend France's glory, and the independent nuclear deterrent provided a cornerstone of that policy.[14] The nuclear deterrent furnished the underpinning for France's withdrawal from NATO's integrated command system and its insistence that no foreign troops be stationed on French soil in peacetime. It seems not just coincidental that NATO's most recalcitrant ally possessed nuclear weapons of its own, just as China proved to be the most obstreperous of the Soviet Union's allies.

Although India has not obviously developed a nuclear weapons program, its explosion of a nuclear device as a means to prestige and to maintain position in the international system is consistent with other foreign policy behaviors. India was an outspoken proponent of nonalignment when pressed by the superpowers to choose sides in the Cold War, although it later developed a much closer relationship with the Soviet Union than with the United States. Moreover, India has continued to assert its position in South Asia, as it did by its intervention in Sri Lanka from 1987 to 1990, where it unsuccessfully aided the government against an armed rebel movement. In the absence of a nuclear weapons program, it seems clear that India has not been induced to match the threat posed by Chinese nuclear weapons. Thus far, the acquisition of nuclear weapons by Pakistan does not appear to pose a sufficient threat to India to persuade the government to decide in favor of a weapons program.

One or more Arab states likely will develop nuclear weapons in the face of the threat posed to them by Israel's capability. Unclear, however, is whether North Korea has an active weapons development program in response to the hostile situation posed by the threat of American nuclear weapons in Northeast Asia. Given the fundamental divergence between the ambitions of Iran to spread fundamentalist Islam and the secular nature of most powers, the Iranians likely will attempt to develop nuclear weapons. In Latin America, Brazil and Argentina, which had seemingly posed a threat to each other, have abjured nuclear weapons programs.

Two other potential candidates for nuclear weapons acquisition are Germany and Japan. Under the conditions of the Cold War, both were protected by America's extended deterrence, and neither faced a significant threat in the early to mid-1990s. Both are hobbled by constitutional and political constraints that would make the choice to embark on a nuclear weapons development program more difficult than in other states. Contemporaneously,

Germany remains preoccupied with the integration of the two previously autonomous states of West and East Germany. Moreover, weakened Russia offers no serious threat, and traditional enemy France is tied closely to Germany through the European Union and some bilateral institutions. In addition, the United States remains involved in European affairs through the continued existence of NATO. Conditions are conceivable, however, under which the Germans would choose to inaugurate a nuclear weapons program. These would include a more nationalistic proclivity in Europe than prevails under the European Union, as well as a recovered and potentially hostile Russia and a United States that had reverted to its nineteenth-century policy of hands off of Europe. Already possessing the most powerful economy in Europe and the largest army in Central Europe, Germany might find the incentives of facing threats and gaining prestige sufficient to embark on a nuclear weapons program.

Similarly, Japan benefited from America's extended deterrence, and the political obstacle of a populace zealously opposed to nuclear arming of its security forces would make a decision to do so exceptionally difficult. The country has been built to become the world's second largest economy, and it faces no obvious military threats. As in Europe, the United States remains in East Asia as a stabilizing military force. However, economic issues have strained the relationship between the United States and Japan. Should Americans decide to retire from the Pacific and East Asian arena and should some threat arise that the Japanese thought was menacing, they would face immense pressure to choose nuclear weapons.

These conjectures about the proliferation of nuclear weapons to other major powers remain contingent on the withdrawal of American force from Europe and the Western Pacific. In this analysis, then, force endures as fundamental, for the issue turns only on which countries wield latent force and how it is organized, not on whether force will be an important foundation of order in the world.

• CONVENTIONAL WEAPONS

Under the rubric of conventional weapons are gathered all those means of fighting and killing except for nuclear weapons and, sometimes, chemical and biological agents. Like nuclear weapons, they may be classified by generations, in which more recent technologies give advantage over those that preceded them. For example, the standard rifle of the American infantryman in World War II and the Korean War was the semiautomatic M-1, whereas the counterpart weapon used in Vietnam was the automatic M16, matched by the Soviet-made AK-47. Such innovations succeed one another in all categories of weapons, from artillery pieces to tanks to aircraft. What has proven to be perhaps the most significant instrument determining the outcomes of battles is domination of the air over the battlefield on the ground, as demonstrated in the 1967 Middle East (Six Day) and 1991 Gulf wars. As important as weapons innovations are, they are equalled by the advance in the apparatus of command and control. In the case of domination of the air, for instance, computers and radar that provide the means for overall direction of the battle have become as important as the actual aircraft and ordnance by which a campaign is fought.

While the technologically most advanced weapons tend to remain available only to the major powers, a plethora of less and more sophisticated conventional weapons continues to be available to states and groups throughout the world. Such availability is supplied by both political and economic incentives. Demand for the weapons emanates almost exclusively from political imperatives.

In addition to equipping their own armed forces with conventional weapons, the major powers and a small number of other manufacturers supply weapons to other countries and to nongovernmental groups. Political incentives for transferring weapons include cooperation for security purposes between a power with the wealth and technology to supply the weapons and a client or ally whose soldiers use the weapons. Another inducement to supply weapons is to gain either access to or political influence in a smaller state. For example, one means for the United States to gain basing rights in countries with a strategic location—Somalia in the late 1970s, for example—is to supply weapons to the host country. A regime or a cause that advances the power's strategic goals provides another incentive for extending support by means of arms transfers. In the early 1960s, for example, the Castro regime in Cuba announced its support for Communism, and this proclamation provided the grounds for extended Soviet military and economic assistance. Earlier, arms assistance from Czechoslovakia to Egypt in 1955 gave the Soviet Union its first access to a regime outside its adjacent sphere of influence.

In addition to these various political incentives for transferring arms are economic inducements. Arms form an important part of international commerce, both governmental and private. Brazil and Israel are two arms producers that sell weapons to other countries as normal exports rather than because of any political motivation. Powers also participate in purely economic transactions as well as those involving political considerations. During the Cold War, the Soviet Union relied in some measure on hard currency export earnings from its arms manufacturing industries. Following the Cold War, Russia and some of the other successor republics, beset by dire economic circumstances, have been eagerly selling arms to other countries that can pay for them with hard currency. Britain, France, and the United States, as well, have sold arms abroad as a means of economic enrichment, although in these cases, a mixture of economic and political incentives has tended to prevail.

● ● ● ● ● ● **Incentives to Supply Conventional Weapons**

Political incentives:

- Security cooperation with ally
- Access to bases
- Political influence
- Support for regime that advances strategic goals

Economic incentives:

- Export earnings for the country
- Acquisition of hard currencies
- Profits for private traders
- Profits for manufacturers and jobs for workers

Private arms merchants as well as states trade in conventional weapons. To a large extent, the international market in arms is hidden from public view, for many of the consumers are clandestine groups that either do not enjoy the patronage of a major power or need to supplement the weaponry supplied to them through governmental channels. Sometimes an arms embargo has been imposed, as in the war among the successors of Yugoslavia or in the case of South Africa for many years ending in 1994. Then, the private international market may offer virtually the only means of obtaining weapons other than domestic manufacture. Frequently, though, the murkiness of the market allows clandestine governmental agencies to extend assistance to groups they support under the cover of private activity. In extreme cases, government officials can act in capacities outside official channels to deal in the international arms bazaar, as President Ronald Reagan and his National Security Council staff did in the Iran-Contra affairs.[15]

Unlike nuclear weapons that function only as means of deterrence, conventional weapons can be used in many ways and for many purposes. The uses include the establishment of order, defense of territory and institutions, threats against others, intervention in foreign situations, and conquest of territory. Definitive outcomes are not always decided by the force that is applied, but when force is brought to bear on a situation, it always has an effect in shaping the consequences.

One of the themes that has been echoed in the literature is that the world is divided into those regions occupied by advanced democracies, which do not go to war with one another and which comprise "zones of peace," and those areas in which development is still occurring, "zones of turmoil."[16] Such an argument bears on the thesis of this chapter—that force remains fundamental to all international politics—and needs to be examined.

Zones of Peace?

The zones of peace argument is an extension of "the end of history" thesis propounded by Francis Fukuyama, who argued that the collapse of Communism and the triumph of liberalism represented the end of profound ideological conflict in the world.[17] In the future, the only things to be decided were the modalities of the extension of liberalism to the entire world. Although many problems will have to be worked out, the author continued, politics in the future will be essentially dull because no important principles will remain in conflict. By extension, liberalism—defined as democracy and capitalism, which bring peace—has already been solidified in a portion of the world, and it will eventually be extended to the remainder. Meanwhile, turmoil, development, and war will continue in the nonliberal sections of the globe, and the use of military force will persist there.

Although it is true that liberal regimes have gained substantial legitimacy through the wealth that they produce and the individual freedom that they allow, their political orders, like others, continue to rely on force as a foundation and as an active tool to maintain domestic order. In addition, they rely on force to protect their states from outside threats, and they have no compunctions about using their force to intervene in other countries when situations arise that threaten or offend them. The peace that reigned among the liberal countries during the Cold War was largely a function of the world bipolar structure in which all of them cooperated to face the common threat posed by the Soviet Union and its supporters. In the wake of the Cold War, they collaborated once again in the Gulf War against a different threat.

Whether force will be used in the future by democracies against one another depends on whether any of them is faced with a serious threat from another. Given the deep cleavages based on economic inequality or ethnicity in some democratic societies, it is not altogether inconceivable that civil wars might arise from within some of them. For example, the attempted separation of Quebec from the rest of Canada might, under some circumstances, be opposed by force. International war among democratic states seems possible under either of two circumstances. First, a direct claim of one state upon another might lead to armed hostilities. One such claim might be a demand for better treatment of a minority ethnic group that had migrated from the state making the demand to the state in which the minority resided. In addition, economic conflicts, over either resources or trading policies, might arise within the liberal trading system that would come to be regarded as serious enough to be resolved by force. Another plausible circumstance in which liberal states might be drawn into a war would be an armed conflict in a nonliberal area in which the liberal states became involved through their respective support for different parties to the dispute. Moreover, it goes without saying that liberal regimes can be replaced by other types of regimes within states, and those states in turn could become hostile to the interests of certain liberal states.[18]

Overall, the greatest source of friction in a liberal world remains the tension between the liberal promise of political equality and the free market mechanism that, despite the opportunities it offers, results in inequality. Economic and political inequality persist within liberal states, but, for international politics, the most important manifestation of inequality is precisely between the rich and poor parts of the world. Although the world is not inevitably structured that way, as the rise of certain previously poor countries to prosperity evidences, the problem persists. It is smug to suggest that the underdogs will not respond and that the rich portion of the world can be free to use force against "zones of turmoil" while enjoying tranquility itself. In the rich zones, observers can watch the steady flow of both heroic and plodding immigration, as great numbers of people from poor, politically repressive, or wartorn countries flee toward prosperous states. Although nonforceful solutions to such problems may be discovered, force persists as a last resort in coping with them.

Uses of Force

Force is used by the state in international politics to maintain stability; to deter attacks from other states; to fight defensive wars protecting the state's assets; to fight expansionist wars; to provide the strength that underlies diplomacy; to threaten as a means of bargaining, coercion, or signaling; to intervene in other states either unilaterally or as part of a coalition; and to preserve its own order and domestic tranquility. Additionally, force is employed by groups to conduct revolutions and to gain international recognition. In one way or another, these uses occur in the context of international anarchy that produces various unintended effects.

• FORCE AS A CONDITION OF ORDER

In a society, there are many ways of achieving conformity, upholding laws, and persuading individuals and groups to live peaceably together. As a result of taboos, folkways and mores, ideologies, myths, institutional arrangements for resolving conflict, and political processes, the role of force as the foundation stone of political order tends to be obscured. Political order itself often fades into the background as people pursue their activities in a context of various degrees of freedom and different conditions of equality. Civil society functions to produce goods and services as well as cultural satisfactions that promote the well-being and happiness of members of society. Yet civil society relies for its viability on order, and political conditions of freedom and equality are made possible only within an established order. Moreover, the ultimate reliance of order on force is evidenced when order begins to break down in civil disorder and civil war.

Force becomes manifest in circumstances of social disruption, turmoil, and fighting. While not used in its latent state, however, force is no less relevant and effective than it is when openly wielded. Such was made evident in the discussion of nuclear weapons, and the same is true in the case of conventional weapons.

Beyond its latency, though, force has many uses in international politics.

• SECURITY DILEMMA

Unlike the state where a government claims a monopoly on legitimate violence, the international system is a realm of anarchy in which each unit retains the prerogative to use force to protect its existence and its position in the international system. Although anarchic conditions may occur domestically when groups wield force in conflicts to dominate, anarchy is the normal condition in international politics. Such circumstances, in which each state reserves its option to use force, sometimes give rise to a **security dilemma.**

This is a phenomenon in which one country may choose to arm itself simply out of recognition of the predicament of relying for its defense on its own resources and judgments. However, the project of armament may provoke in a second state a concern about why the activity is being undertaken. Fearing that the building of armaments may have offensive overtones mixed with expansionist ambitions, the second state responds with its own arms program.[19] Thus, the origins of armed hostility may lie merely in the relations of adversaries, irrespective of their internal characteristics or their policy orientations. Following on such origins of conflict in the security dilemma, a spiral dynamic may ensue.[20] With each state responding to the other, they enter an arms race in which both build large stockpiles to offset the other's. Although other determinants were also at work, the security dilemma helps to account for the arms race between the Soviet Union and the United States in the post–World War II period.

As Jervis has pointed out,[21] the unintended provocative effects of such action can to some extent be mitigated when defensive weapons and postures can be differentiated from offensive ones, and this effect can be enhanced when **defense** has clear advantages over **offense.** For example, prospects for avoiding a spiral dynamic in a nuclear arms race would be greater should both parties deploy only obviously defensive weapons, such as single-warhead, submarine-based nuclear missiles, which can be used only for retaliation. Because they are less accurate and less formidable than land-based, multiple-warhead intercontinental missiles, such weapons cannot be used in an initial counterforce strike that would threaten to disarm an adversary. Moreover, because of their relative invulnerability to an initial attack, they are also less likely to be launched in circumstances of crisis. Although it is extraordinarily difficult to win the cooperation of adversaries, these distinctions do point the way to mitigating anarchy.

At the same time, there are subtleties and complexities to such issues, and it is important to be conscious of them. For example, the building of blast and fallout shelters designed to save lives as well as the deployment of antiballistic missile systems designed to intercept attacking missiles appear to be defensive measures. Paradoxically, however, their overall effect moves in the direction of creating a first-strike posture, which makes them especially provocative. If a country can intercept incoming missiles from a retaliatory attack and can protect its citizens from the effects of warheads that are able to evade the defenses, then it possesses a **first-strike capability** and is in a position to launch a first strike without fear of retaliation. Such a situation would put a state in a dominant bargaining position in relation to its adversary.

Thus, while the effects of the security dilemma can be overcome, the path is a tortuous and difficult one. This topic will be treated more extensively in Chapter 13 on cooperation. Meanwhile, the security dilemma remains present and often works its effects as forces are used largely for self-regarding purposes by states acting in the international system.

• MAINTENANCE OF INTERNATIONAL ORDER AND STABILITY

World and regional powers deploy their forces, respectively, across the globe and throughout their regions, going beyond providing security for their own countries to maintaining orders that they favor. In doing so, they tend to provide security for other countries, but they may on occasion also use their forces for purposes that offend their protectorates. For example, during the nineteenth century, the British navy provided security for the United States by controlling the Atlantic, but Britain offended the United States on some occasions during wartime by violating neutral shipping rights.

Since World War II, United States forces have been deployed across much of the globe in a **forward defense strategy,** that is, a posture that protects American security by stabilizing a wide environment reaching far from the shores of the country. At the same time, this posture merges with overall system stabilization and the extension of protection to other countries. Since the end of the Cold War, the American presence has remained as a stabilizing influence even as the threats to the country's security have virtually disappeared. In the Pacific, for instance, many countries feel reassured by the presence of American force because it renders unnecessary their deployment of defense forces to cope with the security dilemma.

Such overlaps between the self-regarding interests of a power and the stabilization of a more extensive area are not confined to the largest powers like Britain in the nineteenth century and the United States in the twentieth. India has acted in such a capacity in South Asia, and during the 1970s, Iran played a similar role in the Persian Gulf area. In the years following World War II, the Soviet Union's security interests in Eastern Europe also served to stabilize that region. These cases all involve the deployment of force as the crucial component of stabilization.

United States Power and East Asian Order: China and Taiwan

Given the close connection between the state interest of a power and its larger stabilization function, it should not be surprising that not every country in a region will always prove accepting of such forceful domination. Thus, through diplomacy but also sometimes by the employment of force, challenges may be mounted against the power. For example, part of the American order in the Pacific in the period after the outbreak of the Korean War in 1950 was its reintervention in the Chinese civil war. That war had ended in 1949 with the triumph of the Communists on the mainland and the retreat of their Nationalist enemies to Taiwan. Although American aid had been given during the civil war to the Nationalists, the United States pledged not to intervene further in China. Despite that promise, President Harry Truman ordered the U.S. Navy's Seventh Fleet in the Taiwan Strait to ensure that the mainland and island governments did not resume their fighting. Unsurprisingly, the Communist Chinese government in Beijing strongly opposed this aspect of the American order and at times bombarded offshore islands that were occupied by the Nationalists. Because American force has remained superior, the Chinese have not resorted to large-scale force to bring Taiwan within the state's jurisdiction, and the issue has been handled diplomatically.

Examination of this case fosters an appreciation of the subtleties of realist and idealist analyses. A realist analysis would stress the American national interests that are served by its forward strategy as well as the Chinese interests that oppose the interference in its domestic affairs that is implied by United States actions. In contrast, an idealist analyst would stress the world order functions provided by the actions of the United States because they stabilize a situation and require that change be brought about by peaceful means. What seems clear in the present analysis is that an intertwining of a single country's strategic interests and regional order pursuits has occurred. In addition, one observes that a continuing political process goes forward in which the concerned parties, including Taiwan, which has gained both viability and legitimacy under American protection, participate. A cynical realist would point to the truism that power—whose main component is force—will determine the outcome. An optimistic idealist, on the other hand, would hold out the hope for justice and a peaceful future. Clearly, an interplay of power and justice is at work. Even the alternatives are structured by force, for an independent or autonomous Taiwan would have been inconceivable without the United States' force. With the emergence of prosperity and democracy on that island, it would be difficult for an impartial observer to deny the benefits of the stability achieved by force. At the same time, that imposition of force ensured that China could not be unified, even though both parts of the country justly claimed that it ought to be.

The fundamental impulse behind the exertion of force in East Asia by the United States was one of self-regard and a defensive strategy, but the American claim on behalf of order and stability cannot be reduced to a cynical mask for that self-regard. Powers' interests do extend more broadly to an environmental stability that does bring benefits to other countries and regions. In the event of clashes of interests with other powers or states in the regions affected, considerations of principle and force tend to become entangled on every side, although both considerations may weigh more heavily on one side than another.

• DETERRENCE AND DEFENSE

From the Romans we have received the admonition, "Let him who desires peace prepare for war."[22] In modern parlance, that counsel argues that adequate preparation to fight acts as a deterrent to war. In the case of nuclear weapons, deterrence has proven a valid application of the Roman dictum. On the other hand, the massing of conventional weapons often fails to deter opponents, and those weapons actually have to be used to repel an attack.[23]

Although modern writers sometimes read current conceptions back into history,[24] traditional strategists tended to hold lower expectations about the ability to prevent war by the preparation and display of force. Before the nuclear age, preparations for defense mingled ideas of avoiding war with expectations that the weapons and forces developed would have to be used in combat. For example, as the most injured country in World War I, France adopted a defensive strategy, including the famous Maginot Line, but its interwar military debates concerned questions of how most effectively to fight a defensive war. In its weakened position, France preferred not to have to fight at all, and its preparations implicitly were designed to deter, but there was not a sharp distinction between deterrence and planning to fight a war.[25]

Even in the nuclear age, the mingling of expectations often occurs in all situations except the strategic relationship of nuclear-armed opponents. In the Middle East, for example, the 1967 war began with a preemptive attack by Israel, whose leaders became convinced that their efforts at deterrence had failed. Israel employed the forces that it had relied on for deterrence and was able to go on to a swift victory over the forces of the countries that had not been deterred.[26] Such a close association of expectations of deterrence and defense is not restricted to nonnuclear states, for even the United States has handled many nonstrategic situations with conventional forces. One such case mixing deterrence and defense were United States actions during the Korean War.[27]

More frequently, states do not direct their efforts at deterring specific threats and actions but rather maintain forces that can be used for a variety of purposes, mostly defensive. In the summer of 1990, for example, when Iraq threatened to use force against Kuwait, neither the United States nor Saudi Arabia nor other countries invoked any deterrent to dissuade the Iraqi regime from its intended action. However, those states did bring their forces to bear to reverse the Iraqi action once it had occurred.

Deterrence played no part in the defensive war fought by the Grand Alliance—Britain, Soviet Union, and United States—in World War II. Brought together only after the war was well underway, the three partners that defeated the Axis Powers coordinated their policies but fought essentially for different national interests on different fronts for different purposes.[28] Nevertheless, their efforts subdued the German and Japanese armies and rolled back their advances across Europe and Asia.

It does not always prove feasible to establish clearly whether a use of force is expansionist or defensive. For example, in 1967, EGYPT required the withdrawal of a United Nations peacekeeping force that had been stationed on its territory at the frontier with Israel. Together with the mobilization of its troops, this action was construed by Israeli leaders as a prelude to an attack, and they ordered a preemptive assault against Egypt, Syria, and Jordan. ISRAEL achieved a rapid victory in this Six Day War and occupied parts of all three countries: Egypt's Sinai Peninsula, Syria's Golan Heights, and Jordan's West Bank and East Jerusalem. Thus, what could plausibly be argued to have been a defensive use of force by Israel resulted in that country's territorial expansion. The Sinai was returned to Egypt in 1979. Through prolonged negotiations, Israel has conceded to a Palestinian Authority control of parts of the West Bank. Israel retains control of the Golan Heights and Jerusalem, while negotiations with Syria for return of Golan have proceeded slowly, and the future of Jerusalem remains as the final item on the Israeli-Palestinian agenda.

• EXPANSIONIST USE OF FORCE

Some military actions clearly aim at the conquest of territory either to incorporate it permanently within the boundaries of the state or to dominate it as a colony or empire. Britain acquired its North American empire in the eighteenth century by defeating the French, and it similarly drove other Europeans from India, where it gained another empire that lasted until the mid-twentieth century. In 1846–48, the United States initiated a war with Mexico that resulted in the conquest of roughly 40 percent of Mexico's territory and its incorporation into the United States. In the 1930s and 1940s, both Germany and Japan launched policies of conquest to expand their imperial domains. Iraq's conquest of Kuwait in 1990 and its incorporation as a province marked a clearly expansionist employment of force. History is filled with examples of wars of expansion, of which these are but a few. As the examples illustrate, such expansions may be temporary or long-lasting, only to be reversed, or they may be permanent.

• DIPLOMACY, SIGNALING, AND COERCION

Force provides the underlying strength for diplomacy. Without necessarily wielding or even threatening the use of its force, a country commands attention and respect in its dealings with others as an effect of the latent force that it controls. Such force sets boundaries to what other countries may demand, and it backs up demands that a state's diplomat may present to her counterparts from another state. Effects such as these emerge from the very existence of forces in being, but those forces can also be employed in direct uses that communicate more explicitly in interstate bargaining.

During the nineteenth and twentieth centuries, a common device employed by the great maritime powers was the dispatch of naval vessels to trouble spots to signal the interest of such powers—Britain and the United States were the major but not the only ones—and to support the policy their diplomats were pursuing. In the Caribbean Basin, for example, the U.S. Navy quite frequently steamed to a country where turmoil was occurring that might threaten American commercial interests or the lives of American citizens. Implicit in the presence of such an impressive piece of equipment as a battleship or a cruiser, usually carrying a contingent of Marines, was a threat to employ force to suppress the undesirable activity. Sending American vessels of war to the Persian Gulf area has become quite frequent in the last quarter of the twentieth century. On occasion, port cities are bombarded and troops are put ashore to carry out the actions threatened by the presence of the warships.

Not only do threats get carried out from time to time, but force also can be employed to send a stronger message than that implied by the simple presence of force or the threat of its use. For example, in August 1964, the United States in the Gulf of Tonkin incident launched air bombardment attacks against some North Vietnamese facilities—oil storage depots, a torpedo boat base, and so forth. This action fit neither a pattern of fighting a war nor the execution of a threat. Instead, it provided a strong, tangible signal that threatened the use of even greater force if North Vietnam were not willing to conform to American wishes, in this case, desisting from its campaign to unite North and South Vietnam by the use of force. In this case, the signal did not convince North Vietnam, and the United States then began in early 1965 to apply further force in the form of **coercive diplomacy.**[29]

Coercive diplomacy entails the employment of force to persuade an opponent to change its behavior. Partly, it rests on the ability to threaten the application of even greater force in the expectation that the targeted country will seek to avoid that punishment by accepting the terms of the state wielding the coercive instruments. Where the response is defiance, an additional step of **compellence** may be taken.

Compellence is the application of pain, sometimes to the point of unrestrained use of force, to compel the opponent to give in by desisting from its action or by changing its behavior.[30] It requires that some alternative be given, for example, that the laying down of arms will not lead to the conquest and enslavement of the resisters. Nevertheless, those who have entered into combat usually fight for serious and strongly held convictions, are willing to make great sacrifices, and do not very readily give in to pain and suffering. In the case of the United States' attempt to compel North Vietnam to give up its campaign to unite with South Vietnam, immense casualties, extraordinarily high numbers of deaths, great deprivations, and the suffering of exceptional pain were not sufficient to induce that object state to give in to the will of the United States government.

Given the limits to coercive diplomacy and the use of force to inflict pain and suffering for compellence, the alternatives left to the wielder of force are withdrawal, negotiation of a settlement, or conquest and slaughter. Each of these gives up the purpose of the use of force, which was the imposition of one's will on another by influence rather than by defeat or annihilation of the adversary.

• UNILATERAL INTERVENTION

Another use of force involves the temporary intervention in one country by another. Ordinarily, such action is taken to require the subject government to conform to the norms established by the intervenor or to replace the recalcitrant government with another that promises to capitulate to the directives of the dominant power.

During the early part of the twentieth century, it became common for the UNITED STATES forcefully to intervene in the countries of Central America and the Caribbean as well as in Mexico. In some cases—the Dominican Republic, Haiti, and

Nicaragua are examples—the interventions lasted many years, from 1912 to 1925 and again from 1926 to 1933 in the case of Nicaragua. Other situations resulted in briefer interventions, such as the 1914 intrusion ordered by President Woodrow Wilson into Vera Cruz, Mexico, that resulted in a change of Mexican presidents from Victoriano Huerta to Venustiano Carranza.

Following World War II, the SOVIET UNION maintained its order in Eastern Europe partly by intrusions with force into the affairs of East Germany in 1953 to suppress demonstrations and military interventions in Hungary in 1956 and Czechoslovakia in 1968, both of which resulted in a change of government. To ensure compliance within its sphere of influence, the United States employed its troops to bring about a change of government in the Dominican Republic in 1965, to end a Marxist and murderous regime in Grenada in 1983, and to arrest the head of government and install another government in Panama in 1989.

Not only superpowers but other powers also occasionally use force to intervene in the affairs of smaller neighbors to maintain the powers' norms or to bring about the downfall of an abhorrent government. INDIA was active in East Pakistan, which later became Bangladesh, in 1971–72, both to restore some order in the face of Pakistani army massacres and to stem the flow of refugees into its own territory. In Sri Lanka, after a period of providing sympathy and some material support for ethnic Tamil rebels, India in 1987 played a role in negotiating an agreement to end the ethnic conflict between that minority group and the majority Sinhalese. To enforce the accord, India introduced troops, aligning itself with the government. However, after three years of fighting, the Indian army was unable to defeat the powerful guerrilla army, and India decided to withdraw its forces.

In another case, VIETNAM invaded Cambodia in January 1979 to depose the Khmer Rouge regime of Pol Pot, installing a new government headed by Heng Samrin. Vietnam then signed a Treaty of Peace and Friendship with the new government that allowed Vietnam to keep advisers in Cambodia. It was not until the 1991 agreement negotiated under auspices of the United Nations that Vietnam withdrew all of its forces.

That invasion provided part of the reason for CHINA's invasion of Vietnam in February 1979, although its forces were withdrawn two months later, in April. Designed to demonstrate its power and interest, China's action was also related to a border dispute and to Vietnam's campaign to eliminate private enterprise and relocate population, both of which had an impact on ethnic Chinese in Vietnam. Additionally, Vietnam and the Soviet Union had recently signed an agreement that gave the Soviets access and influence in Vietnam. Thus, the varied events preceding the invasion undoubtedly led the Chinese to conclude that they needed to take some action to impress an awareness of their importance to and presence in the region.

Yet another example illustrates that even quite small countries intervene in their neighbors' affairs. In January 1979, a combined Tanzanian army and Ugandan rebel force intervened in Uganda to topple the brutal dictatorship of Idi Amin, who fell in April. In addition to the repression that he imposed within his own country, Amin had reached some of his enemies who were in TANZANIA. Thus, Tanzanian assistance to Ugandan forces was, in part, designed to protect its own territory.

• MULTILATERAL INTERVENTION

Working through international organizations such as the United Nations, the Organization of American States, and the Organization of African Unity, states have also devised a number of interventions that employ force to achieve a variety of goals. At the beginning of 1993, for example, the United Nations was operating thirteen peacekeeping operations of varying sizes and with distinct missions.

A fairly long tradition has developed in the United Nations that employs soldiers and police in monitoring, supervising, and diplomatic activities in which force largely is not brought to bear. Lightly armed peacekeeping forces operate under rules that allow them to defend themselves but forbid them from using their weapons to coerce or even signal the citizens of the countries in which they operate. One of the norms governing such operations that was formulated after early experience is respect for sovereignty, which includes refraining from interfering in the internal affairs of the country in which a force is stationed. Since the end of the Cold War, some of the operations have involved policing and other administrative tasks, but United Nations operations still must refrain from using their force as a military instrument, and they are not supposed to favor one faction over another.

With antecedents in the observer missions associated with the 1948 Middle East truces between

Israel and each of its Arab neighbors, the tradition was forged in 1956 and 1957 when the UNITED NATIONS EMERGENCY FORCE took up its position in Egypt between Egyptian and Israeli military forces, as the Israeli army withdrew from Egypt following its invasion at the end of October 1956 in collaboration with Britain and France. An even larger operation (ONUC) in the Congo (present-day Zaire) took on responsibilities beyond the restricted ones of UNEF. In a chaotic situation, the civilian operation functioned at least partly as a government, and in 1962–63, the military side of the UN operation undertook offensive military action against the armed forces of the breakaway province of Katanga. Inasmuch as these activities engendered tempestuous strains between the superpowers in the United Nations, they formed the last use of force as a coercive or fighting instrument in the context of peacekeeping operations before the end of the Cold War.

As a legal instrument, the United Nations Charter includes provisions for the use of force against recalcitrant states, but the invocation of the appropriate article of the charter must be done explicitly by the Security Council, whose actions are subject to the veto of any of the five permanent members (Britain, China, France, Russia, and the United States). It was impossible to achieve the necessary consensus until the end of the Cold War; but then, the Security Council did authorize the employment of force against Iraq. In contrast, the powers were unable to agree before 1995 to bring force to bear on the situation in Bosnia-Herzegovina, where Serbians and Croatians used force to gain control of territory in which their respective ethnic groups would prevail, leaving a rump Bosnia-Herzegovina in the hands of Muslims.

However, the powers developed a concept of peace enforcement and protection of "safe havens." Together with NATO bombing, haltingly applied, the United Nations Protection Force (UNPRO-FOR) attempted to use force to bring food and other supplies to a few cities, including Sarajevo, Tuzla, and Srebenica. Unfortunately, the confusion of concepts led to the collapse of this effort in 1995. The dynamics that produced this result will be treated in Chapter 10.

In addition to United Nations-sanctioned forceful interventions, there are multilateral intrusions using force under the auspices of regional organizations. LIBERIA was the site of a particularly brutal civil war that left over 70 percent of the population as displaced persons by 1993. Fighting began in December 1989, and in August of the following year, the sixteen-member Economic Community of West African States (ECOWAS) dispatched a force of some three thousand troops to impose a cease-fire. However, ECOWAS was unable to make much headway in the face of President Samuel K. Doe's unwillingness to give up power. Even later, after Doe was captured and killed by rebel forces and the multilateral force grew to nine thousand troops, the peacemaking effort remained bogged down. Indeed, the ECOWAS force resorted to using food as a weapon, threatening the starvation of some two-hundred thousand refugees as well as tens of thousands of people in rebel-held territory by bombarding relief shipments. Basically, the ECOWAS force was allied with two Liberian groups fighting against a faction led by Charles Taylor. In late 1995, a cease-fire was achieved. However, brutal fighting broke out in the capital city, Monrovia, in spring 1996.

Conceptual consideration of interventions have tended to be discussed under the rubric of world order, but theoretical guidance is not reassuring. As Stanley Hoffmann has pointed out, "Virtually all discussions of world order are based on four principles, all of them flawed and in conflict with one another."[31] They are: state sovereignty, self-determination, democracy, and human rights. In addition to the inability to apply all of the principles simultaneously, the close association of intervention with superior power leads the realist to point out that the phrase "world order" supplies a justification for the use of force on behalf of the interests of the powerful. Moreover, some cases of ineptness and lack of commitment—such as the United Nations effort in Bosnia and the West African intervention in Liberia—reduce any dialogue about world order and principled behavior to the level of farce, while the situation on the ground occurs as deep tragedy.

Former Yugoslavia, 1991–95

The difficulties of applying principles to the use of force as a means of multilateral intervention is illustrated by the case of foreign intrusion in 1991 and following years after the breakup of Yugoslavia. That same case can effectively be analyzed by examining the place of force in state formation and by scrutinizing the interests of the powers.

Following the death of Tito in 1980, the groups whose nationalist aspirations had been suppressed under the Communist regime maneuvered for influence in the Yugoslav state, but their inability to accommodate one another led to the breakup of that state as groups claimed their own new states. In

■ **Former Yugoslavia**

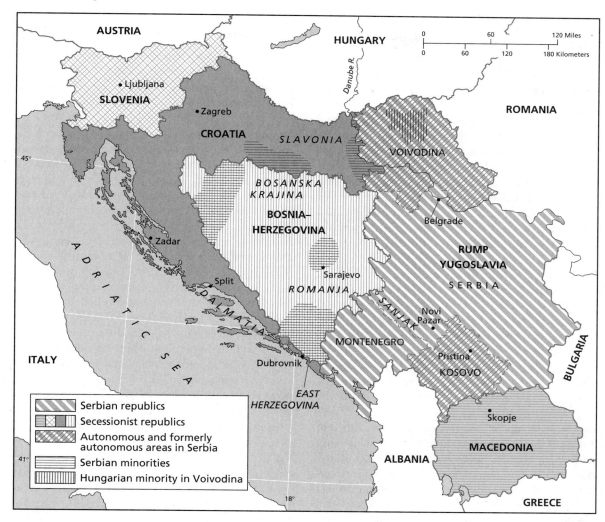

1991, Slovenia and Croatia, respectively, declared their independence as new states, while Serbia dominated a rump Yugoslavia that included Bosnia-Herzegovina and Kosovo as well as Serbia. Although Slovenia was not required to defend its territory, Serbia and Croatia began fighting over the extension of Croatian boundaries into Bosnia. By April 1992, Bosnia-Herzegovina declared its independence, which was founded on a newly discovered Moslem nationalism (in contrast to Slovenia and Croatia, Bosnia-Herzegovina had never before existed as an independent state). At that time, Bosnian Serbs and Bosnian Croats began fighting to establish ethnically pure territories separate from Moslem Bosnia-Herzegovina, and each group was aided by the state whose population resembled its own people. As the fighting proceeded, the respective powers considered how to respond. Although there was a general agreement that the international community should strive to bring the fighting to an end, the powers did not coincide in their views of the best way to accomplish that objective.

Nevertheless, the United States and the other Western European countries, which had been reluctant to extend diplomatic recognition to the states that had declared their independence, followed the lead of Germany, which argued in favor of such recognition. Although the German argument was presented as a means to bring the fighting to an end, Germany's traditional cooperation—particularly during World War II—with Croatia undoubtedly influenced the German government to side with the Croats against the Serbs, who had traditionally been supported by Russia. That support, generated by Russian Orthodox religious leaders, remained sufficiently strong in the crisis to prevent forceful international action against Serbia and the Bosnian Serbs. Although the powers recognized the independence of Bosnia-Herzegovina, they also sanctioned through the United Nations Security Council an embargo on arms shipments that would have given to the Bosnian Moslems the means to defend their state against the campaigns of the Bosnian Serbs and Bosnian Croats to establish control over territory. By their religious affiliation, the Bosnian Moslems had the sympathy of Turkey. Because Turkey was regarded as a critical ally in the Middle East by the United States, some support for the Moslems existed in the United States. Britain and France, meanwhile, provided the forces to send food and medical supplies to besieged Moslem cities, such as Sarajevo and Srebrenica, as a human rights activity. A joint United Nations-European Union diplomatic mission, meanwhile, first sought to bring about an end to the fighting on the basis of a plan to guard Bosnia-Herzegovina's independence by extending to the three groups considerable autonomy over ethnically organized regions within a state headed by a weak central government. Later, the plan was modified to partition the country into three parts: Moslem, Serb, and Croat. Human rights advocates frowned on the plan for partition because it would seemingly extend approval to the Bosnian Serbs' brutal "ethnic cleansing" program in which large numbers of people were forcibly removed from their homes and many of them were killed, tortured, or raped. Similar activities by others, particularly Croats, tended to be overlooked.

Despite many calls for forceful intervention by the international community, the powers proved themselves extremely reluctant to bring their force to bear. One reason for such reluctance was the fact that there was no obvious preferred outcome. The central conflict was over territorial boundaries and ethnic self-determination, neither of which provided any clear principle around which the international community might coalesce. These are issues in state formation that are determined by force and politics, not by principle. Without a new kind of colonialism in which the powers might occupy the country (countries?) and impose a political system of democracy, the conditions for democratic arrangements

were simply not present. Thus, the international community was left to provide some humanitarian assistance in order to relieve the most horrendous—though not all horrendous—suffering.

From the point of view of the powers, was any interest served by their refraining from intervention by force? With each of the powers supporting different factions in the former Yugoslavia, the interests of the three largest powers—Germany, Russia, and United States—appear to have been well served by their inaction. In the post-Cold War period, maintenance of peace among the major powers formed a pillar of world order. Whatever disasters and outrages occurred in the Balkans would pale beside those that would have resulted from the intrusion into the situation on opposing sides of the major powers. Avoidance of war among Germany, Russia, and United States is not an inspiring triumph, but averting such a disaster is in the interests of each of them as well as many other countries that would be affected or drawn into such a conflict. Inaction in the face of the tragedy of former Yugoslavia is reprehensible and lamentable. On the other hand, the intrusion of the powers on opposing sides would be an utter disaster, and the maintenance of their cooperation is valuable for all of Europe. Given their divided interests and the absence of a principle upon which they could unite for forceful intervention, their behavior was prudent and understandable even though not heroic.

Finally, in 1995, NATO bombing of Bosnian Serb positions and an important territorial conquest by Croatian forces led to a peace negotiation in Dayton, Ohio, under auspices of the United States, between a Bosnian-Croatian Federation and the Bosnian Serbs, who were represented by Serbian President Slobodan Milosevic. To implement the agreement, a force of sixty thousand NATO troops was deployed. To help to build a viable federation, NATO also created a large civilian force. United Nations forces withdrew from Bosnia, their mission having failed.

Undoubtedly, the powers will continue to deal pragmatically with situations in which established and well-formed states have not yet developed. Each situation will find some kind of response from the powers acting as an international community, but it is unlikely that a world order solution will be found. Because force is so fundamental to the process and an incomplete state diffusion and state formation process continues to be underway, there will continue to be gaps in the political organization of the world. It is unlikely that the powers have enough force to establish the order, democracy, and wealth necessary for long-term stability. These requirements need to be brought to fruition in well-formed states individually, and that is a very long-term undertaking.

• ORDER AND DOMESTIC TRANQUILITY

Even though military organizations may be formed for the purpose of maintaining the security of a state against external enemies, armed forces are also employed to preserve domestic order. In modern states, such forces offer only backup strength to ordinary police in situations of social disorder, and they take on a more central role when revolutions arise. However, in some states the armed forces act to suppress even peaceful demonstrations in the first instance, as occurred in El Salvador in the late 1970s.

Inasmuch as governments carry the responsibility for maintaining order, they need to invoke the forces at their disposal when social disorder threatens to engulf the police. For example, in late April and early May 1992 in south central Los Angeles, rioting and looting occurred in the wake of the acquittal of four police officers who had beaten a driver when taking him into custody after a high-speed chase. As part of the response, the governor of California called out National Guard troops to suppress the disturbances.

All of the uses of force discussed thus far comprise activities of states. However, groups also employ force in ways that are germane to international politics. These include revolutionary activities and efforts to gain international recognition.

• REVOLUTIONS

Given the monopoly of legitimate violence that governments hold, substantial force has to be brought to bear to overthrow them. It is difficult to do so in any case, but it would prove impossible to mobilize a substantial part of a passive population except in circumstances in which the government exercises serious repression of the state's people. Revolutions tend to be led by small, dedicated cadres, but their success depends upon the support of extensive segments of the population. At their inception, revolutionary movements contain few fighters. Unless those few are quashed or the conditions for revolution are lack-

ing, a movement grows until it incorporates substantial numbers of fighters.

Many types of force figure in patterns of revolution. To acquire weapons and money to conduct their activities, revolutionaries engage in ordinary criminal activities such as robbing banks and stealing from arsenals. To undermine a population's confidence in their government, they may resort to assassination of government officials. Eventually, they use direct force to attack government troops and to destroy their country's infrastructure. Inasmuch as such movements begin in weakness, they tend to use the tactics of the weak, such as hit-and-run attacks, ambushes, and other small-unit activities. Over time, as they grow in strength, revolutionaries may move to **conventional warfare** against the governments they are opposing.

At any point in this sequence revolutionary violence may be defeated by the government against which it is directed, either by effective suppression or by a combination of violence directed against the revolutionaries and reforms addressed to the conditions that feed support for the revolution. Successful opposition to revolutionary activities occurred in the post-World War II period in the Philippines, Malaya, and Venezuela. More recent holding actions against not completely defeated revolutionary groups have been mounted by the governments of Guatemala and Peru. On the other hand, the last half century has also witnessed the success of revolutions in China, Cuba, and Nicaragua.

Infrequently, essentially revolutionary activities spontaneously arise in which populations begin actively to use force against the authorities repressing them. An outstanding example in recent times is provided by the *intifada*, the widespread uprising against Israeli authorities by Palestinian young people on the occupied West Bank. Reaching a bit farther back in history, one notes the powerful effect that Korean university students have had over the years, beginning with the forced resignation of President Syngman Rhee in 1960.

• INTERNATIONAL RECOGNITION

Groups sometimes use force to gain recognition from the international community. Perhaps the most successful of these was the PALESTINE LIBERATION ORGANIZATION, founded in 1964. The PLO used airplane hijacking, guerrilla raids in Israel, and other techniques employing force to shift the world's perception of the Palestinian issue from one of downtrodden refugees languishing in camps in several Middle Eastern Arab countries to one of a nation with a government in exile seeking its own state. So successful was the PLO in its course of action that its leader, Yasir Arafat, was invited to address the United Nations General Assembly in 1974 and many governments extended diplomatic recognition to the PLO as the government in exile of the incipient state of Palestine. Although exceptionally weakened over the years, often by its own tactical mistakes, the PLO nevertheless was accepted in 1993 by Israel as a participant in the Palestinian delegation to the Middle East peace talks that originated in Madrid, and it forms the governing apparatus of the Palestinian Authority on the West Bank.

• TERRORISM

Another use of force germane to international politics entails assaults against civilians and civil targets, such as works of art, monuments, and other public valuables. Both groups and governments conduct such activities. Among the most infamous have been the takings of Western hostages in Lebanon by the Party of God, an Iranian-government-backed organization, and other groups. Anarchist groups target government officials, businesspeople, and civilians to undermine confidence in government. Before its agreement with the British government in 1994, the Irish Republic Army (IRA) exploded bombs in busy stores and other crowded places in London and set off another bomb in 1996. Islamic fundamentalist groups have attacked foreign tourists in Egypt. Small groups of militants recruited from among *mujahidin* fighters in Afghanistan bombed the World Trade Center in New York in February 1993 and prepared to bomb tunnels and other targets in the same city later in the year. Terrorists planted bombs in 1993 near a number of Italian art museums and churches, repositories of immense cultural treasures.

It is not always immediately apparent whether such activities are directed by or have the support of governments, on the one hand, or are independent groups' endeavors. In other cases, though, governments clearly direct assassination attempts and engage in other acts of terror. Stung by the defeat of its clients at the Bay of Pigs in Cuba in 1961, the American government under the direction of President John F. Kennedy sought to assassinate Fidel Castro, the head of the government of Cuba. Bombs from American planes ripped into the home of Muammar Khadaffi of Libya on April 14, 1986, under direct orders of President Ronald Reagan. In July 1993, the Israeli government, in response to rocket attacks from southern Lebanon against its territory, bombarded villages in southern Lebanon with the object of driving out at least 150,000 people. Israel employed a similar tactic in 1996, aiming to drive about 400,000 civilians out of their villages.

The Continuing Efficacy of Force

The immense range of instruments and the extensive uses of force attest to the continuing efficacy of force in politics, international as well as domestic. As the Cold War has come to an end, the frantic searching for new and more devastating weapons has diminished, but the expansion of force continues, though at a less hurried and intense pace. Old uses of force, such as the employment of violence to establish autonomy for groups that insist on having their own states, have become more common as the shackles of the Cold War dropped away.

However much idealists may long for transformation of the world to one in which civility and accommodation would replace brutality and conflict, that utopia appears unrealistic in the face of the unprecedented aerial war against Iraqi troops in Kuwait and of the Bosnian Serbs' and Croats' ethnic cleansing in the former Yugoslavia. In the course of only a few weeks of the early summer 1994 in Rwanda, an estimated half a million people were butchered with primitive weapons and small arms. Surely the world has seen no more intense bombing nor more brutal treatment of human beings by their fellows than these episodes from most recent history. Force remains everywhere, and it remains fundamental to the conduct of human affairs.

• IMPORTANT TERMS

antiballistic missile (ABM) system	escalation dominance
arms transfers	extended deterrence
atomic bomb	first-strike capability
ballistic missile	forward defense strategy
coercive diplomacy	latent force
compellence	minimum deterrence
conventional warfare	multiple independently
counterforce	targeted reentry
countervalue	vehicle (MIRV)
cruise missile	mutual assured
defense	destruction (MAD)
deterrence	nonproliferation regime
	nuclear proliferation

offense

second-strike capability

security dilemma

stability

thermonuclear bomb

vulnerability

war-fighting capability

• STUDY QUESTIONS

1. What are the functions of latent force?

2. What logic and evidence produce a plausible argument that force has lost its efficacy in the late twentieth century in all or part of the world? Do you think that the argument is convincing? Why or why not?

3. In what ways do technological change, modes of production, and organization affect the supply of weapons?

4. How have the Industrial Revolution and the formation of the modern state affected the expansion of force over the last two centuries?

5. To what extent are nuclear weapons similar to and how do they differ from conventional weapons? Do the differences produce different effects and, if so, what are they?

6. Explain the meaning of deterrence and distinguish between nuclear and conventional deterrence. Why is nuclear deterrence easier to achieve, and why is it more effective?

7. What factors generated and sustained the superpowers' arms race during the Cold War? Do any of these factors remain after the end of the Cold War?

• ENDNOTES

1. See Benedetto Fontana, *Hegemony and Power: On the Relation between Gramsci and Machiavelli* (Minneapolis: University of Minnesota Press, 1993), pp. 129–32 and p. 207, fn. 8.
2. Weber, "Politics as a Vocation."
3. See John E. Mueller, *Retreat from Doomsday: The Obsolescence of Major War* (New York: Basic Books, 1989).
4. See Robert C. Tucker, "1989 and All That," in *Sea-Changes: American Foreign Policy in a World Transformed*, ed. by Nicholas X. Rizopoulos (New York: Council on Foreign Relations Press, 1990), pp. 204–37.
5. See Robert E. Osgood, "The Expansion of Force," in *Force, Order and Justice*, by Robert E. Osgood and Robert W. Tucker (Baltimore: Johns Hopkins University Press, 1967).
6. See Donald J. C. Irving, *The Destruction of Dresden*, 2d ed. (London: W. Kimber, 1963). Also see Sir Arthur T. Harris, *Bomber Offensive* (London: Collins, 1947).
7. This argument accepts the view put forth by Kenneth N. Waltz in his "Nuclear Myths and Political Realities," *American Political Science Review* 84 (September 1990): 731–45.
8. Matthew L. Wald, "Today's Drama: Twilight of the Nukes," *New York Times*, 16 July 1995, p. E5, citing Robert S. Norris and William M. Arkin of the Natural Resources Defense Council.
9. International Institute for Strategic Studies, *The Military Balance 1991–1992* (London: Brassey's, 1991), pp. 219–20.
10. Mueller, *Retreat from Doomsday*.
11. Statement by General Mirza Aslam Beg in a story entitled "Pakistani Quoted as Citing Nuclear Test in '87" in the Urdu-language newspaper, *Awaz International*, published in London, reported in *New York Times*, 25 July 1993.
12. Jeremy Bernstein, "The Farm Hall Transcripts: the German Scientists and the Bomb," *New York Review of Books*, 31 August 1992, p. 51.
13. See Jacov Harel, *Regional Nuclearization and the Moderation of Conflict* (Ph.D. diss., City University of New York, 1994).
14. See Edgar S. Furniss, *DeGaulle and the French Army: A Crisis in Civil-Military Relations* (New York: Twentieth Century Fund, 1964).
15. See Theodore Draper, *A Very Thin Line: The Iran-Contra Affairs* (New York: Hill & Wang, 1991).
16. The quotations are taken from the subtitle of *The Real World Order: Zones of Peace/Zones of Turmoil* by Max Singer and Aaron Wildavsky (Chatham, NJ: Chatham House Publishers, 1993). Drawing on Immanuel Kant's views in his *Perpetual Peace*, published in 1795, Michael Doyle has led the way in promoting a contemporary theme that liberal democratic states do not go to war with one another.
17. See Francis Fukuyama, "The End of History," *National Interest* 16 (Summer 1989): 3–18.
18. For a defense and explanation of the so-called democratic peace, see Bruce Russett, with the collaboration of William Antholis, Carol R. Ember, Melvin Ember, and Zeev Maoz, *Grasping the Democratic Peace: Principles for a Post-Cold War World* (Princeton, N.J.: Princeton University Press, 1993).
19. See Herz, "Idealist Internationalism and the Security Dilemma."
20. Jervis, *Perception and Misperception in International Politics*, pp. 62–67.
21. Jervis, "Cooperation under the Security Dilemma."
22. Flavius Vegetius Renatus, *De Rei Militari*, III, "Prologue." The quotation is an English translation of "*Qui desiderat pacem, praeparet bellum.*"
23. For a discussion of deterrence theory and of psychological and empirical case studies that challenge that theory, see "The Rational Deterrence Debate: A Symposium," with contributions by Christopher H. Achen and Duncan Snidal, Alexander L. George and Richard Smoke, Robert Jervis, Richard Ned Lebow and Janice Gross Stein, and George W. Downs, in *World Politics* 41 (January 1989): 143–237.
24. As do George and Smoke when they state, "Theorizing about deterrence seems to be a rather new phenomenon, but its practice in a commonsensical, instinctive way must be as old as the military art." Alexander L. George and Richard Smoke, *Deterrence in American Foreign Policy: Theory and Practice* (New York: Columbia University Press, 1974), p. 12.
25. For an analysis of the French and British interwar defense debates, see Brian Bond and Martin Alexander, "Liddell Hart and DeGaulle: The Doctrines of Limited Liability and Mobile Defense," in *Makers of Modern Strategy from Machiavelli to the Nuclear Age*, ed. by Peter Paret with the collaboration of Gordon A. Craig and Felix Gilbert (Princeton, N.J.: Princeton University Press, 1986).
26. See Janice Gross Stein, "Deterrence and Miscalculated Escalation: The Outbreak of War in 1967." Paper presented at the American Political Science Association meeting, Washington, D.C., September 1988.

27. This case and others are presented in George and Smoke, *Deterrence in American Foreign Policy: Theory and Practice*.

28. See Maurice Matloff, "Allied Strategy in Europe, 1939–1945," in *Makers of Modern Strategy*, ed. by Paret.

29. See Alexander L. George, *Forceful Persuasion: Coercive Diplomacy as an Alternative to War* (Washington, D.C.: United States Institute of Peace, 1991).

30. See Thomas C. Schelling, *Arms and Influence* (New Haven: Yale University Press, 1966).

31. In Stanley Hoffmann, "Delusions of World Order," *New York Review of Books*, 9 April 1992, pp. 37–43.

CHAPTER 8

Political Economy: Power and Wealth in International Relations

What is the relationship between politics and economics? Does economics drive politics, or does politics provide the basic dynamic that drives economics? To what extent is the relationship between wealth and power a reciprocal one? Answers to these questions vary considerably from one school of thought to another, and this chapter explores many of these different views of the matter.

From the last chapter on force, we know that a secure order underlies complex economic activity, and from the preceding chapter on state formation, we know that effective states provide the protection, enforcement, and welfare that enable economic activity to occur. On the other hand, those analyses also demonstrated the weakness and decay of states not sufficiently supported by economic production. Both to retain autonomy and exercise influence with other states, wealth has to be accumulated to maintain and increase power. Moreover, economic forces also bear back on the state.

This chapter examines these complexities and shows the powerful reciprocal relationship between politics and economics.

Introduction

Politics and economics can be analytically separated into the quest for power and the pursuit of wealth, but they are clearly related. Power assists in the acquisition of wealth, and wealth forms an important part of the basis for power. Whereas the state is the fundamental unit of analysis of politics, the firm remains the basic economic unit. An international system structured by a distribution of power provides the pattern within which conflict occurs in world politics. On the other hand, the market arises as an unintended consequence of the activities of producers and consumers who strive for selfish advantage. While these parallels illustrate some of the analytical and conceptual differences between politics and economics, the connections between them should be regarded as crucial.

As will become clear later in this chapter, the relationships between economics and politics are dif-ferently conceived by distinct schools of thought. For example, Marxists consider that economics fundamentally drives politics, whereas realists believe that politics drives economics. Such divergences go to root of causation of social phenomena, but there are also many more divisions of analytical opinion. Within the context of the problematic of this book, the main question is: What concepts and theories does economics contribute to an understanding of politics conceived as power and justice, and what economic phenomena bear on the causes of war and conditions of peace and on state formation and maintenance of position in the international system?

States and Markets

Both states and markets are compelling, modern concepts that have evolved and spread across the world. Although each is based in its essential ideas of sovereignty and capitalism upon the same principle of differentiation—minimal regard for other actors[1]—they are often thought to comprise contrasting ways of organizing human affairs.[2] These contrasts are extensive and may be summarized in two models.[3]

In the first, neorealist model of the international system, strong, independent states occupy various positions in an international arrangement and duplicate one another's tasks.[4] Each state maintains order within its territorial boundaries and provides for its security against other states. In this model, the state is the elemental and lasting unit, and its rational decision making rule is self-preservation through the accumulation and maintenance of power. Prudence is the main virtue in this model, and the most compelling feature of the system is inequality among the units, with power concentrated in a few. Although for prudential and self-serving reasons, states may cooperate,[5] the primary value is self-regard, and this value often entails conflict. This model stresses the distinction between domestic and international politics. In this model, politics is in command of economics. As implied in its decision rule, the state is founded on a preservative ethic, that of protecting the integrity of the community and its values that are encompassed in the unit. Adherents of this view see the world as pluralistic, full of diverse cultures and interests in conflict, and the future they would predict is one in which the state continues to exist to protect those diversities. When confronted with the vision of a future united world, they are repelled by the nightmare of an omnipotent, totalitarian state.

The second model is that of the market. Primarily an entity that has been conceived within the confines of the state, the market when thought of internationally has characteristics much like those of civil society.[6] Thus, advocates of this concept of the international system stress the similarities between domestic and international life. They emphasize growing interdependence, specialization of tasks, and economic integration. Unlike the first model, this one has as its elemental units the individual, the firm, and the national economy, with the price mechanism as the criterion of rationality. In this model, the state is regarded as a facilitator or an intruder but always as instrumental rather than fundamental, something to be used or overcome. Pursuit of profit and efficiency are the foremost virtues, and individual competition is the primary value. Inequality takes the form of concentration of wealth in individuals, firms, classes, and states. Further, a process of change occurs as the result of uneven development. In this model, economics is in command. A neofunctionalist variation projects a spillover effect from economics to politics, with the creation of larger, integrated political units.[7] In its fundamental ethic, the capitalist market is expansive, knowing no political or community bounds, and thus embodies a dynamic that leads to change. Adherents of this perspective see spreading global trends that are creating binding ties among peoples all over the world, and they foresee a future in which all of humankind will share a future together, for better or worse depending upon the world community's ability to find ways of solving common problems. Insofar as it is a protector of distinctive cultures or peculiar ways of doing things, the state is viewed as an obstacle to the achievement of these solutions.

Not only do these two models project contrasting analytical perspectives and dissimilar visions, they also champion divergent development strategies. The touchstone of the liberal, market model is David Ricardo's theory of **comparative advantage,** introduced in Chapter 5. Ricardo treated comparative advantage as composed of fixed factor endowments, such as Portugal's soil and climate. In a more recent rendering called the Heckscher-Ohlin theorem, factor endowments are seen as more flexible and somewhat open to choice. For example, although Japan does not enjoy factor endowments of iron ore and coal, it has nevertheless developed steel, automobile, and shipbuilding industries by making choices to specialize in these products while importing the necessary components. Instead of competing on the basis of its raw materials, Japan's economy forges ahead more on the basis of efficient modes of production. According to Heckscher-Ohlin, a country still enjoys a comparative advantage by deciding to specialize in the production of some goods while importing others.

Liberal economic policy, then, advocates that countries pursue development strategies derived from the theory of comparative advantage. For example, countries in CENTRAL AMERICA that traditionally have produced agricultural products for export employing a low-wage labor force are urged to continue to rely on the factor endowments of land and cheap labor and produce for the export market. Further diversification is sometimes advocated, and some policy analysts stress other factor endowments, such as splendid natural environments and recreational opportunities, that would attract tourism. Whatever the variant, however, the emphasis is always placed on specialization within a free market of relatively unconstrained exports and imports.

In contrast to this liberal view, state formation theory, which draws on realism, offers an alternative development strategy based upon the **duplication of tasks.**[8] Comparative advantage becomes a component of duplication of tasks as states seek to maintain their positions in the international system. Instead of making choices in the context of a fixed international political economy, states are urged to enhance all of the factors of production—land, labor, capital, entrepreneurship, and technology—with emphasis on developing a scientific and knowledge base that will particularly strengthen the skills of the labor force. In the context of building a quality base upon which to construct a modern economy to compete in the world market, the state still needs to make choices of what to emphasize as its comparative advantage. For example, a small country such as COSTA RICA would undoubtedly make a costly error in choosing to build a steel mill and an automobile industry. On the other hand, its tropical forests could be used to advantage if it sought to compete for world market shares in biotechnology, a promising growth industry for the future. Biotechnology, though, is a so-called high-tech industry that requires the allocation of major resources to research and development, which presupposes a cadre of highly trained scientists, engineers, administrators, and supportive personnel. At the same time, such a state formation approach to comparative advantage suggests retaining a flexibility that would allow the state to shift its emphasis to a different industrial sector should technological and world market conditions encourage striking out in a new direction. Thus, this realist model departs considerably from the liberal model. Instead of relying on natural or limited factor endowments for comparative advantage, the realist model recommends addressing all the factors of production so as to change the terms under which the country competes, and it stresses the necessity for choices to be made, not just once but continually over time. The so-called East Asian model of development has demonstrated empirically that technology and education are important components of economic growth.

As this analysis makes clear, the concepts of states and markets are characterized not just by structural differences but embody widely different ways of thinking about long-term and fundamental policy matters. Moreover, the analysis indicates that the liberal separation of states and markets, while valid to an extent, needs to be dealt with cautiously and not carried too far. As their relationship is explored, it will become even clearer how the tensions between these two concepts work.

• PROPERTY RIGHTS AND ORDER

Even though primitive markets arise spontaneously through the division of labor and some economic exchange continues under the most horrendous conditions of turmoil and war, large-scale trade and the accumulation of wealth flourishes only where order has been established and property rights are secure. It is the state that creates such conditions. Markets alone do not possess the capacity to maintain order, for they rely on this state capacity to supply such a common good. Moreover, rights to ownership of property can be guaranteed only by states that exercise legitimate force to back up the legal structures supporting private property.

Large-scale commerce within a single state relies on secure property rights, but so too does international trade. Although no sovereign rules over transactions between countries, each country's government has created those conditions that allow, say, an exporter of automobiles legally to represent ownership to his buyers. Those importers, in turn, are able to make payments to the car exporter as a result of the property rights and ownership of the currency that has the backing of their respective governments. In case of disputes, orderly procedures established by states can be invoked to settle them.

In a conception that extends to the international realm, **hegemonic stability theory,**[9] a global or nearly global **liberal trading system** owes its existence to the creation of a security order by a hegemonic state. Historically, the hegemonic states were Britain in the nineteenth century and the United States in the post-World War II period. This theory argues that a global market, which requires extensive cooperation, is conditioned on the stability provided by the hegemonic power. In addition, that power provides **public goods,** such as a currency exchange regime in which it sacrifices its own national interest for the sake of the cooperation that it is promoting.

According to this theory, the extensive commercial cooperation leading to unprecedented economic growth in the post-World War II world resulted from the security system established by American power and from the international economic arrangements that had been established at the end of the war. These arrangements included the World Bank (officially named the International Bank for Reconstruction and Development, or IBRD), which assisted in recovery from the war and in development projects; the International Monetary Fund, which assisted member states with balance of payments problems; and the United States-guaranteed gold standard, under which the American government promised to exchange dollars for gold at the fixed rate of thirty-five dollars per ounce of gold, a standard that the United States abandoned in 1971. Once cooperation is attained, incentives remain to continue it even in the absence of a hegemonic power, for the regimes established offer information as well as predictability to the members.[10] In the absence of a hegemon, cooperation needs to be explained on other grounds.[11]

Whatever the specific conditions required to promote international economic exchange, it is clear that political arrangements must underlie the economic transactions if they are to be rewarding and grow. Only in the context of secure property rights, contract enforcement, and general political order can economic activity thrive. Simultaneously, prosperity engendered by economic activity gives support to political order. Economists have the luxury of assuming that the antecedent conditions prevail as they construct their theories, whereas political scientists need to figure out and explain what those conditions are and how they are brought about.

In addition to providing the underlying conditions that allow international economic activity to proceed, states also remain involved in facilitating or restricting international trade and commerce.

• MONEY AND REGULATION

One of the most important commodities that states provide is a supply of **money.** In the absence of currency, commerce cannot expand beyond barter, a primitive system of trading. So long as a government issues money in an ample supply to accommodate the needs of the economy, commerce can expand, investment and development can grow, and wages can be paid that can then be used to purchase goods and services. However, should monetary authorities provide too little currency, they can drive an economy into **recession** in which unemployment increases, production contracts, investments are cut back, and economic stagnation sets in. On the other hand, governments sometimes try to address their countries' economic difficulties by issuing more currency than the economy can effectively absorb in useful activities, thereby generating **inflation,** which tends to detract from the governments' ability to address the real problems of production and distribu-

tion. Although it decreases unemployment by reducing the real value of **wages,** inflation erodes the value of the **savings** that are necessary for the **investment** that generates **economic growth,** and it causes many distortions in the **incentive structures** that make an economy operate efficiently. Moreover, savers may export their money to other countries where its value is less likely to be eroded and where they are more likely to earn a return on their savings. Such **capital flight** became a typical situation in many Latin American countries in the 1980s when the **debt crisis** presented itself.

The supply and management of money becomes an even more complicated problem in the context of international trade where one currency is exchanged for another, for the **rate of exchange** affects the **imports** and **exports** of a country, its inflation rate and **standard of living,** and other areas of public policy. For example, in the summer of 1993, the American dollar and 100 Japanese yen reached parity. The dollar continued to fall until it was worth 85 yen in 1995. These values stood in contrast to the situation in 1985 when one dollar could be exchanged for over 250 yen. Such a shift in the exchange rate indicates that Japanese goods were much more expensive in the United States than previously and that American goods could be sold more cheaply in Japan. On the other hand, an American traveling to Japan was often faced with incredibly steep prices, paying in Tokyo in 1995 from about $2.20 in a MacDonald's to about $5 in a hotel for a cup of coffee, as opposed to from 70 cents and up in New York.[12] Governments can also use exchange rates to suppress their own workers' wages by allowing the foreign goods that are purchased by the workers to rise in price in the home currency.

Apart from these issues involved in monetary policy, the effectiveness with which the government maintains the position of the state in the international system can be affected by policies governing access to **foreign exchange reserves.** Sometimes governments give preferential treatment to specific sectors, political decisions that ignore economic efficiency and that undermine the country's efforts to compete internationally. For example, an economy with a mixed agriculture and manufacturing base may gain 75 percent of its export earnings from the agricultural sector and the remaining 25 percent from the manufacturing sector. In this hypothetical case, however, the government may authorize the manufacturing sector to use 60 percent of the available foreign reserves to import machinery, component parts, and so forth, thus starving the agricultural sector by preventing it from buying the imported products that it needs (machinery, fertilizer, etc.). Such a policy leads to what is called an **antiexport bias.** Over time, such a policy undermines the competitiveness of the agricultural sector and supports inefficiencies in the manufacturing sector. Both sectors are then less well positioned to compete in the world market, leaving the country behind in international competition and allowing its position to erode.

Thus, governmental monetary policy and foreign exchange policy contribute importantly to the elementary state maintenance of position function. Such policies operate as navigational devices in a sea of civil society activities in capitalist states, and these government mechanisms are also constrained by the actions of individual firms. In the buffetings of economic complexity and public policy debates, governments are beset by extraordinary pressures that present many different criteria for choice: the demands of other countries and those of their own workers and enterprises as well as such constituencies as elite economic opinion and consumer interests. Sometimes, officials grope for single and simple guidelines, like the gold standard, but there is no uncomplicated choice. Mainly, in the vortex of policy pressures, the state needs to maintain its position, and the policies should be measured against the successful accomplishment of that goal.

Another economic policy activity affecting the relations of states and markets is **regulation of trade.** Regulations range from imposing quality standards on imported products and levying tariffs to protect domestic industries to negotiating quotas of specific products that may be imported into a country from particular trading partners. In wartime, much more severe regulations may be put into effect. These include blacklists of firms and products, purchase of the entire production of a product to deprive an enemy of its supply, and blockade to prevent goods from being exported or imported. In between the normal activities and the severe actions that are taken in war, economic sanctions are sometimes applied as a means of coercion against a state that has in some way offended the international community.

In the post–World War II period, the trend has moved toward **free trade,** in which regulation, particularly tariff and quota barriers, that impedes the free flow of international economic activity is reduced. A series of **multilateral trade negotiations** has succeeded in reducing trade barriers and engendering a substantial amount of economic growth

based on exports. Nevertheless, states retain control over access to their territories in the areas of trade, foreign investment, and so forth.

The difficulty for governments in regulating international activity lies in finding a balance that, while preserving autonomy, encourages economic growth and the accumulation of wealth.

• ACCUMULATION AND EXTRACTION

To maintain position in the international system, a state must accumulate wealth at the average rate of all countries in the world. Other things being equal, **accumulation** at a faster rate will enhance the state's position, whereas slower accumulation allows other countries to gain position. Because there is no precise way to calculate and project such results, prudent leaders are likely to accumulate as fast as they are able to manage.

In precapitalist agricultural societies, accumulating wealth is difficult, for production often reaches a level of subsistence in which the only surpluses that are not consumed are needed for seed for the following year's planting. To the extent that surpluses are produced, political systems attempt to extract those surpluses for public purposes. History is filled with examples of such extraction for the building of military capabilities and the means of domination. Often, agricultural surpluses are siphoned off to support urban communities that generate different kinds of production: commerce, learning, infrastructure, leisure activities, and others. Some international commerce emanated from such urban settlements as Athens, Alexandria, Amsterdam, Venice, Hong Kong, Lagos, and others. Another mode of accumulation engendered administrative and military centers that pursued armed conquest, as was the case with Rome, Moscow, Sweden, Turkey, the German tribes that conquered Rome, and others. Commercial expansion and military conquest came together in the Spanish, British, French, Belgian, German, Italian, Portuguese, American and other builders of empire.

With the development of capitalism in the Industrial Revolution, the production of manufactured goods burgeoned to ever-increasing, unprecedented levels as previously unimagined wealth was generated. Not only did standards of living rise but also greatly enlarged populations participated in enjoyment of the new wealth. That wealth was unevenly distributed as the new class of owners of the means of production accumulated wealth at a

■   **Levels of World Economic Performance, 1500–1992**

	1500	1820	1992
World population (million)	425	1,068	5,441
Gross domestic product per capita (1990 $)	565	651	5,145
World gross domestic product (billion 1990 $)	240	695	27,995
World exports (billion 1990 $)	n.a.	7	3,786

Source: Angus Maddison, *Monitoring the World Economy, 1820–1992* (Paris: Development Centre of the Organisation for Economic Cooperation and Development, 1995). Used with permission.

substantially greater rate than did the new class of workers who used means of production—the machines and factories—that were not their own. In those countries where industrialization took hold, the revolution profoundly overturned previous economic and political arrangements. From a nation of farmers, artisans, and merchants came a nation of factories and cities. New social conditions led to governmental interventions to address the new problems arising from the new modes of production. These ranged from the quite conservative social programs of Bismarck's Germany to the modern welfare states based on socialist principles that prevail throughout Western Europe at the end of the twentieth century.

When the Industrial Revolution got underway late in the eighteenth century, the prevailing public philosophy of political economy had been **mercantilism.**[13] In this conception, which had governed the economic development strategies of the major European powers during the preceding three centuries, states acted to accumulate precious metal wealth in exchange for exports. Control of commerce remained in governmental hands to ensure the maximimization of gold and silver accumulation. This policy was weakened as monetary surpluses produced inflation, but, in addition, the philosophy was challenged by Adam Smith in his book, *The Wealth of Nations*.

Drawing attention to the inefficiencies built into mercantilist policy, he advocated a policy of laissez-faire in which private producers would be allowed to seek their own interests without governmental interference. He argued that through the operation of an "invisible hand," the public good would often be promoted by those who sought no interest but their own. Smith pointed out that real wealth resided in the productive assets of the country, not in money and bullion. Those productive assets, he argued, could most effectively be employed

by members of civil society acting in their own selfish interests, pursuing their private wealth. As the title of his book suggests, Smith concerned himself with state accumulation but thought that it was served best by a policy that minimized direct government action to achieve that end.

A long historical record of extraordinary economic growth in the countries that have operated largely on the capitalist principles advocated by Smith has vindicated his insight. Although there have been deviations and detours, and some complications that are going to be discussed below, the freedom that allows entrepreneurs to innovate, inventors to create, and consumers to make purchasing choices has promoted more extensive markets and greater accumulations of wealth than have other systems. Nevertheless, the dark side of capitalism has been pointed out and criticized, and alternatives have been offered. The profoundest criticism came from Karl Marx and Friedrich Engels in the nineteenth century, and their ideas led to the alternative for the accumulation and extraction of wealth, **socialism.**

Marx's analysis of capitalism was embedded in his conception of history, **dialectical materialism.** Materialism refers to the belief that economic, or material, forces provide the basic dynamics of human existence and historical development. In this, he opposed Hegel, who believed that ideas furnished the fundamental dynamics of historical unfolding. For Hegel, ideas existed before material forces, whereas for Marx, material forces were basic. In contrast to his rejection of the German philosopher's idealism, Marx embraced Hegel's dialectic. Hegel had argued that an idea—a thesis—contained the seed of its opposite—an antithesis. Over time, the antithesis came into conflict with the thesis, and the result of the clash was a new idea, a synthesis. Substituting material for idea, Marx thought that one set of economic arrangements—the forces of production and the relations of production—composed a thesis and that an antithesis contained within those arrangements gave rise to a conflict that would ultimately produce a synthesis of new arrangements. Thus, he analyzed the origins of capitalism out of feudalism, and he projected the future formation of socialism.

Marx explained that under feudal arrangements, artisans owned their own tools of production. As capitalism developed, however, the forces of production changed from small-scale, artisan-owned tools to the factory system in which the large-scale machinery belonged to a class of owners, called the **bourgeoisie,** while the machinery was operated by workers—called the **proletariat**—who owned nothing. Instead, the workers sold their labor for wages. Thus, ownership of the means of production in the hands of one **class** provided a thesis, and the need for labor to operate those means of production—contained within the thesis—provided an antithesis. Membership in a particular class defined an individual, for whether he was an owner or a worker imposed the most fundamental meaning on a person's life.

Marx also explained how conflict arose historically between these opposed classes. Drawing on Ricardo's view that "the natural price of labor"[14] is that necessary for subsistence and reproduction, Marx noted that, under capitalism, owners paid workers wages only sufficient to maintain and reproduce themselves while expropriating the **surplus value.** Furthermore, capital tends to concentrate in the hands of fewer and fewer owners, with small owners—the petit bourgeoisie—falling into the working class. As the working class grows, it becomes increasingly miserable, until, developing a class consciousness, the proletariat rises up in revolt and overthrows the bourgeoisie. Under capitalism, the state had remained merely the **superstructure,** a coercive apparatus used by and on behalf of the ruling class to exploit the workers. With the triumph of the working class through revolution, the means of production are put in its hands. Then, with the means of production owned by the working class, there is no further need for a repressive state, for exploitation has ended, and the state may wither away.

Even though Marx had great insight into social conditions under capitalism in the mid-nineteenth century, he did not foresee that states would act to correct many of the evils of the capitalist economic system or that labor would organize itself along national and industrial lines rather than class lines and become effective in gaining better working conditions, higher wages, and other benefits. These gains by labor avoided the impoverishment that Marx had predicted and, additionally, enabled workers to share in the accumulation that the capitalist system produced. States gained control of monopolies or regulated and taxed them in ways that corrected some of their abuses and turned the corporate activities to public advantage.

In addition to the structural features of capitalism that Marx analyzed, the cyclical nature of boom and bust that alternately produced prosperity and depression characterized capitalism. Another economist, John Maynard Keynes,[15] found the key to correcting, or at least alleviating, the depression cycle through increased government spending that added to demand, thus creating purchasing power, employment, and investment.

None of this is to say that all of the problems of capitalism have been solved or that future prosperity is ensured without difficulty. It is to say, however, that **capitalism** has proved itself to be an enormously productive way of organizing the economy and that politics, government decision making, and the state have been, and can be, used to correct its deficiencies and compensate for its weaknesses. The choice of market principles by failed former socialist states attests mightily to the strength and appeal of the capitalist mode of production. Nevertheless, socialism provided a set of ideas that stirred many people's souls for 150 years and remains a basis for criticism of capitalist arrangements. Additionally, socialism was embodied in real states, with institutional arrangements and important public policies, for seventy-some years following the Bolshevik revolution in Russia in 1917.

Of necessity, socialists have to be concerned with production, and as denizens of the industrial age, they work within the factory system. Under socialism, private property is abolished and the ideal concern aims at equality, at providing for everyone's needs. Although in certain, limited respects authoritarian socialist regimes did provide generally for people's needs on an equitable basis—education and health care, for example—they were mostly very repressive governments that did not hesitate to intimidate, spy on, incarcerate, torture, and kill their citizens. Although achieving a certain success in industrialization, they never had the **flexibility** to adapt to the changing requirements of a **postindustrial society.** They had little respect for nature and the environment and thus have caused the worst environmental pollution in the world. Privileged classes arose in socialist societies while most workers had to make do with low-level consumption of shoddy products. To try to understand how such distortions of intelligent analysis and lofty ideals could have occurred, it is necessary to trace the history of both thought and practice of socialism, particularly in the Soviet Union but in other countries as well.

Marx and Engels had published *The Communist Manifesto* in 1848, but it was left for Lenin to devise a conception of the mechanism that would promote the revolution. In view of the unawareness of most workers of their condition, their lack of class consciousness, Lenin conceived of a revolutionary leadership cadre that he termed the **vanguard of the proletariat.** Not only would this vanguard lead the charge, but it would also serve, following the revolution, as the **dictatorship of the proletariat.** Moreover, rule would be discharged according to the principle of **democratic centralism,** which meant that every party member and every citizen was expected to conform, without dissent or further debate, to the decisions made by the small committee that acted on behalf of the proletariat. These ideas were put into practice by Lenin and his colleagues in the SOVIET UNION. Further shrinking of the leadership group occurred after Lenin's death in 1924, when Stalin eliminated his rivals and became dictator of the Soviet Union. In what has been termed "the war against the nation,"[16] Stalin caused the death of millions under his five-year plans that collectivized agriculture and forced industrialization. This massive brutality was emulated in CHINA under Mao Zedong during the "Great Leap Forward" in the late 1950s and the "Great Proletarian Cultural Revolution" in the late 1960s. More recently, in the CAMBODIA (called Kampuchea during this time) of Pol Pot, who ruled from 1975 to 1979, the Khmer Rouge regime caused the deaths of over 1 million people out of a population of some 6 million in the name of ending corruption and imposing its version of a socialist society.

Central Planning in the Soviet Union

Dedicated to controlling all economic production and distribution, the Soviet and other socialist regimes employed **central planning,** which involved the allocation of all factors and components of production for the entire national economy. Inasmuch as it was impossible to manage the immense complexity of an industrial economy, the system worked only by cheating and through the operation of entrepreneurs who "fixed" things. For example, managers sometimes acted as brokers to ensure that components arrived at factories where they were needed to keep production going, even though those components were not available as determined by central planners. Without these extrasystemic contributions, bottlenecks, shortages, and other inefficiencies tended to occur. Despite the inefficiencies, the economies of the Soviet Union and of the Eastern European countries did advance industrialization, produce wealth, and enhance the position of the Soviet Union in the international system. The Soviets did so by concentrating on heavy industry

and military production. Not until after Stalin's death in 1953 did Soviet leaders attempt to gain legitimacy by satisfying the consumption needs of their population. Under Stalin, ideology under the slogan "Socialism in One Country" provided the foundation for state legitimacy.

Throughout Soviet history, the regime competed with the capitalist states. In 1956, Nikita Khrushchev proclaimed that "we [socialists] will bury you [capitalists]."[17] To Sir William Hayter, he said, "Maybe not you, but at all events your grandson will surely be a Communist." However, Soviet socialist arrangements did not compete very well with capitalist arrangements. There were many weaknesses, although some of these could be attributed to noneconomic factors such as the devastation of World War II and to the absence of conditions that would have attracted foreign capital. Particularly, though, the extensive mode of production that worked for industrialization proved inappropriate for the postindustrial age, based as it was on information, communications, and decentralized control. In the extensive or Stalinist model of development, the Soviets added investments to their economy but did not improve the productivity of those investments.

In the Soviet system, the state controlled not just economic decisions but other parts of its people's lives. There were inefficiencies, to be sure, but people were not allowed to be citizens who participated in a public discussion and trusted to make decisions for themselves. As a consequence, people lied, and they accepted the goods and services that were provided by the regime.

Decline of the Soviet System

Following a long decline in the vitality of the Soviet economy, it became apparent in the 1980s how problematical things were. Then, in 1985, Mikhail Gorbachev took over the leadership and began to address his country's problems. Although tentative at first, he developed important policies summed up in the terms *glasnost'*, *perestroika*, and "new thinking." *Glasnost'* means openness, in which people were encouraged to speak what was on their minds and which led to the rehabilitation of Khrushchev and an emphasis on Lenin's "New Economic Policy," which had allowed a certain amount of free enterprise in the early 1920s. *Perestroika* means restructuring. Gorbachev introduced such political reforms as allowing elections in which more than a single candidate ran. The Soviet leader's "new thinking" primarily referred to a Soviet pulling back from its overseas extensions and, most important in 1989, his announcement that the Soviet Union would not use force to ensure the domination of Communist parties in the Eastern European countries. Pulling back within Soviet borders in an effort to consolidate the country's assets amounted to a profound shift in Soviet orientation. In the domestic realm, there were deep political changes, as people were allowed to speak and to publish, and the Communist Party gave up its claim to a monopoly of power.

On the other hand, in the economic sphere there were important but not vital changes, for Gorbachev aimed to save socialism and, thus, was unwilling to make the fundamental transformation to a market economy. That alteration occurred in the successor states only after the disintegration of the Soviet Union in December 1991. With that disintegration and transformation, socialism no longer remained as a viable alternative economic model for others to aspire to emulate. States wish to maintain their positions in the international system, and the Soviet Union stands as an example of a state that decayed from within, unable to cope with the competition of other states, and finally toppled from the pinnacle of superpower status to that of a group of backward successor states dependent on the outside world for knowledge and financing.

Thus, even though capitalism allocates to civil society the primary responsibility for production, capitalist states have accumulated immense wealth. Moreover, those states have also proved themselves capable of extracting adequate amounts of resources to maintain and improve their positions in the international system. At the same time, they have gained legitimacy both by allowing consumption choices to be made in the market by individuals and firms and by promoting citizen capacities, with capacious scope for meaningful political participation. In this sense, the capitalist division of great matters into those belonging to the state and those belonging to the market has resulted in civil society's performing a role as a component of the state.

• UNEVEN DEVELOPMENT

Just as Marx and Engels noted the inequality of distribution under capitalism within nations, Lenin pointed to the phenomenon of **uneven development** among states. Gilpin has included this in his analysis of the relationship between politics and economics.[18] He stresses that politics creates the conditions for economic growth by providing secu-

rity, order, and the fundamental underpinnings for complex economic activities. At the same time, he draws attention to the fact that the market, once established, tends to function in ways that are not easily controlled by politics. Indeed, the phenomenon of uneven development, in which diverse states grow at very different rates, erodes the international position of some and enhances the position of others.

In the post-World War II period, the broad effects of uneven development have been obvious. Essentially unscathed by the war, the United States in 1945 produced nearly half of the combined gross national products of the world. As other countries recovered from the devastation, their economies grew at a more rapid rate than that of the United States, so that the latter's share of the world's production had declined to about 23 percent by the mid-1970s and remained at about that proportion in the years since.[19]

In the decades of the 1950s and 1960s, the center of the world's wealth lay in the Atlantic region, but it shifted in the 1970s and 1980s to the Pacific. In the early 1990s, the most economically dynamic region of the world was East Asia, where Japan, China, South Korea, Taiwan, Singapore, and Hong Kong—all poor countries forty years earlier—led the world's production. As discussed in broader terms above, the Soviet Union grew in the decades following the war but began such a steep decline after 1970 that its economy was in shambles by 1990. Meanwhile, Latin America grew economically from the end of the war until the late 1970s, then entered a severe downturn in the early 1980s and began to rebuild in the mid-to-late-1980s and the 1990s. At the same time, most of sub-Saharan Africa has suffered a relatively steep decline in its economic fortunes, with countries possessing great resources such as Nigeria with oil having lost position in the international system.

As suggested by the varied fortunes of different countries, there is no fixed pattern to the path that uneven development follows. Each country's circumstances are unique, and each faces the challenge of making decisions that maintain or enhance its position. Moreover, some countries benefit more than others from the assistance of others; such aid is often critical to their coping effectively with their circumstances. Sometimes, chance plays a part, or the unforeseen consequences of others' actions redound to the benefit of a particular state. For example, the origins of Japan's spectacular growth lie partly in

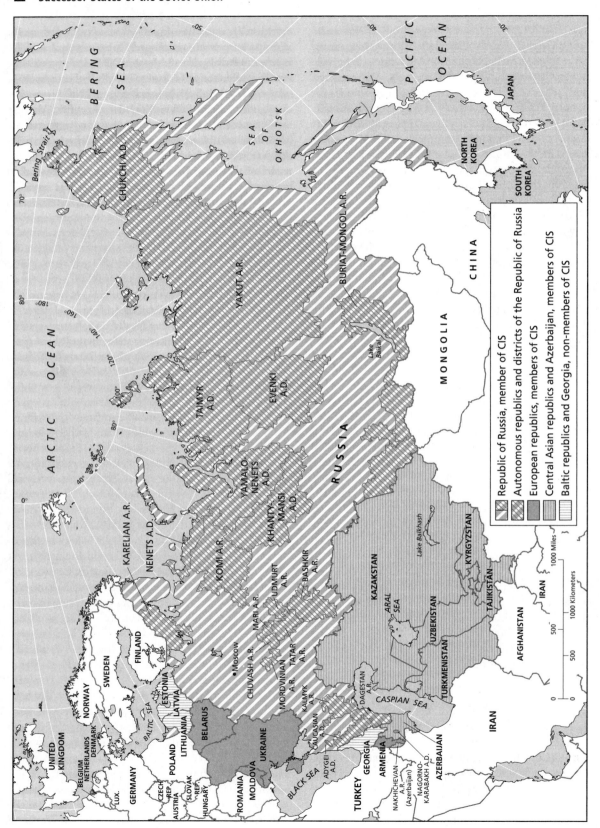

Republic of Russia, member of CIS

Autonomous republics and districts of the Republic of Russia

European republics, members of CIS

Central Asian republics and Azerbaijan, members of CIS

Baltic republics and Georgia, non-members of CIS

■ **A Confrontation of the Growth of GDP Per Capita by Region, 1950–73 and 1973–92**

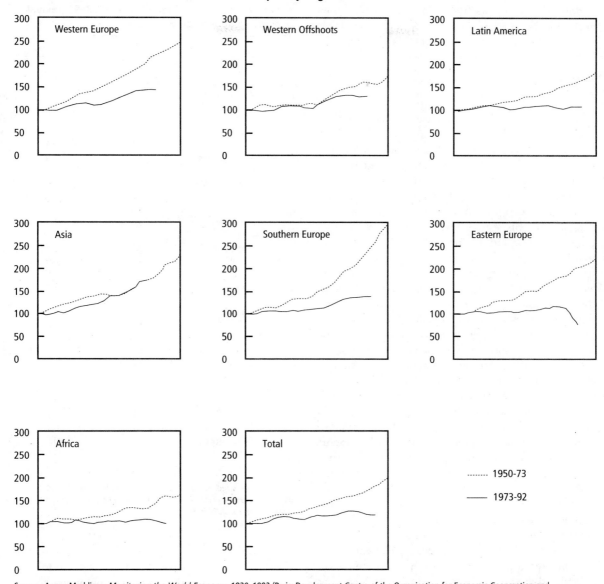

Source: .Angus Maddison, *Monitoring the World Economy, 1820–1992* (Paris: Development Centre of the Organisation for Economic Cooperation and Development, 1995). Reprinted with permission.

North Korea's decision to invade South Korea in 1950, for the United States chose to rely on Japan as a base of supply for its operation in the Korean War. This choice required that emphasis be shifted from democratizing Japan to industrializing it as a bastion of the American forward strategy of defense. South Korea, too, benefited from American support and investment in the years following its terrible suffering in the Korean War. Given the difficulty of extracting savings from poor economies, the impor-

tance of capital investment from abroad and of trade concessions should not be underestimated.

A number of attempts have been made to find broad formulas that can be applied to many or all countries to place them on the road to sustained economic development. One of these is the Marxist analysis and another is the stages of economic growth thesis, both of which hold that every country passes through the same process.[20] Rostow presented a model of development in which a country begins at a subsistence level, then moves to extract savings and make investments and build infrastructure, then accumulates enough production and savings to achieve self-sustained growth, and finally reaches the last stage of mass consumption society.

Structuralist Analysis of Uneven Development

A very different conception arose out of the analysis of Raúl Prebisch, an Argentine economist who headed the United Nations Economic Commission for Latin America (ECLA). Prebisch and his colleagues noted that Latin American countries remained underdeveloped while the advanced industrial countries continued to grow, and they sought to explain why this was so. Their response was a structuralist center and periphery thesis.[21] Instead of treating countries discretely, they conceived that the world was a single capitalist economic system in which the less developed countries played a different role from that of the developed countries. For the most part, they observed, the developed countries produce industrial products which they export to the less developed countries. The latter, in turn, produce mainly the primary products that come from mining and agriculture, and they had to import manufactures from the richer nations. From this analysis, they reasoned that the Latin American countries should no longer rely on industrialized countries for manufactured goods. Instead, they should follow an **import substitution industrialization** strategy in which they would manufacture the products that their internal markets consumed. In this way, the less developed countries would not have to spend their export earnings on manufactured goods that, over the long run, enjoyed a **terms of trade** advantage over primary products. In arguing that the Latin American countries suffered a decline in terms of trade, they were asserting that the amount of primary products that needed to be produced to purchase a given quantity of manufactures increased over time. To use a wholly invented example, if in 1950 a Chilean could buy a new American or French car for the same price that he would pay for, say, forty tons of copper mined in his country, then he would be obliged in 1980 to pay the equivalent of fifty tons of copper. In trading terms, then, the price of copper had declined over those years while the price of cars had increased.

Convinced of the soundness of the ECLA analysis, most Latin American countries embarked on import substitution industrialization strategies, producing for their home markets consumer goods that

■ **Uneven Development Per Capita Real GDP Growth in Selected Countries, 1950–73 and 1973–92 (annual average compound growth rates)**

	1950–73	1973–92
Western Europe		
France	4.0	1.7
Germany	5.0	2.1
Italy	5.0	2.4
Britain	2.5	1.4
North America		
Canada	2.9	1.5
United States	2.4	1.4
Eastern Europe		
Czechoslovakia	3.1	−0.1
Hungary	3.6	0.0
Poland	3.4	−0.6
Soviet Union	3.4	−1.4
Latin America		
Argentina	2.1	−0.2
Brazil	3.8	0.9
Chile	1.2	1.9
Mexico	3.1	1.1
Asia		
China	2.9	5.2
India	1.6	2.4
Indonesia	2.5	3.1
Japan	8.0	3.0
South Korea	5.2	6.9
Thailand	3.2	5.3
Africa		
Egypt	2.7	3.8
Ghana	0.2	−1.2
Nigeria	3.2	0.1
South Africa	2.4	−0.6
Tanzania	1.9	−0.5
Zaire	0.8	−3.9

Source: Angus Maddison, *Monitoring the World Economy, 1820–1992* (Paris: Development Centre of the Organisation for Economic Cooperation and Development, 1995), Table 3–2.

previously they had imported. In some cases, the strategy was strengthened by the cooperation of a number of countries that formed common markets so that the goods produced in any of them could be sold in all without encountering high tariffs and other barriers to trade. The Central American Common Market, founded in 1960, was such a collaboration. Strides were made in this strategy, with many products ranging from Coca-Cola to automobiles being manufactured in Latin America.

Over time, however, it became clear that import substitution industrialization had a very high cost. Although GUATEMALA, for example, no longer had to import Coca-Cola, it did have to import the machinery for bottling the product and the ingredients that were mixed to produce the drink. The identical principle applied to most of the products that were manufactured under the import substitution industrialization strategy: components and the tools of production had to be imported. Resulting from this principle came the recognition that the less developed countries continued to import goods from the developed countries, although they were now intermediate goods rather than finished products. Because the goods were designed for the internal market, moreover, they did not form the basis for export earnings. Those earnings continued to be generated by the export of primary products. However, this situation led to distortions in the use of foreign reserves earned by exports, for the earnings tended to be plowed into import substituting industries rather than into export industries. Thus, export industries were denied the tools, components, and intermediate goods that might have increased their efficiency to allow them to compete more successfully in the world market. By the mid-1970s, more and more analysts and public policy makers recognized the problem and began to think about restructuring their economies to orient them more toward production for export. In the 1980s, as the Latin American countries went into a severe depression and suffered from the debt crisis, those that sought restructuring were strongly backed by the United States and the international financial institutions, which promoted **structural adjustment programs.**

East Asian "Tigers"

In contrast to the Latin American experience, certain East Asian countries followed a different development strategy that proved to be very successful. Japan stood as the leader, but the four Asian "tigers," or "little dragons," posted remarkable economic gains. They are South Korea, Hong Kong, Taiwan, and Singapore. Sometimes, their pattern of development is held up as the correct path that all countries should follow.

Although the East Asian model is sometimes referred to as manufacturing for export, it contains more ingredients than this simplistic rule of thumb. With JAPAN as the leading example, each of the countries employs strict government monitoring and intervention. Governments make strategic economic decisions, such as the choice of which industries to concentrate on. Favored industrialists collaborate closely with the government, both the political and the bureaucratic sides. Each country chose at first to emphasize industries standing at a secondary stage in the product cycle, such as steel, shipbuilding, and

automobiles. That is to say, these industrial products were first generated in the advanced industrial countries such as Britain, France, and Germany, but their production was adopted by other countries that chose to make rather than import them. Eventually in the cycle, these countries were then able to export the products back to countries in which their production had been initiated. For example, the Japanese Toyota Motor Company successfully exported cars to the United States and the Western European countries. Another component of the successful development model of East Asia was very serious investment in education to produce a labor force with the skills not only for working on assembly lines but also for the more advanced tasks of organizing large-scale planning and production, developing industrial designs, creating new products, and so forth. Finally, the model included effective and efficient government to provide the political underpinnings for economic development. In many cases—South Korea, Taiwan, and Singapore being the main examples—strong, efficient governments exhibited authoritarian characteristics, remaining repressive for many years. Democracy and its associated freedoms were long in coming to South Korea and Taiwan and in the mid-1990s had not yet made their appearance in Singapore.

Looking at the success of the Asian countries, some advocates encourage other countries to adopt the **East Asian model.** Sometimes, they characterize it simply as manufacturing for export, but the several parts comprise more than this. It is unlikely that other countries can simply acquire a model of development that has succeeded elsewhere without both a great deal of insight concerning what made the model successful and the requisite cultural characteristics to make the model work in their own states.

In general, uneven development results from a combination of favorable international environment, factor endowments, and the choices made by the elites of countries. As in other kinds of competition, incorrect as well as correct choices can be made. In interstate economic and political rivalry, the game holds substantial uncertainties, including unstable rules that can sometimes be shaped creatively by the players. Thus, no simple rule can be applied, and no model offers a magic solution to economic development for less developed states.

One certainty does present itself: the market does produce uneven development and, thus, inequality. As a result of the operation of the market, a state's position may be eroded, maintained, or enhanced.

Thus, those responsible for the direction of state policy face the immense challenge of making correct decisions that will avoid the first alternative, preserve the second, and, with luck, promote the last.

Rise and Fall of Great Powers

A special case of uneven development arises with the leading powers of the world.[22] The immense capabilities of the great powers lead them to take an interest in many parts of the world, and these interests may induce them to expend resources in the promotion of those interests. They even have a tendency to identify their interests with a common good for the entire world, or at least for a region. Kennedy argues that, typically, great powers face the dilemma of husbanding and promoting growth in their base economies at the expense of those foreign interests on the one hand or protecting the foreign interests while neglecting their base on the other. Those powers that adopt the second choice face overall decline in their positions. As an American, Kennedy's concern has tended to focus on the United States, but Britain provided an exemplar in the late nineteenth and early twentieth centuries, and the Soviet Union furnished a particularly dramatic instance of great power decline in the last quarter of the twentieth century.

In the last quarter of the nineteenth century, three countries—GERMANY, JAPAN, and UNITED STATES—grew rapidly as industrial powers, challenging the preeminent position of Britain. Their more rapid economic growth alone would have proved sufficient to bring about the relative deterioration in Britain's position, but other considerations contributed to that decline. Part of Germany's strategy consisted of a naval arms race with Britain. Taking up the challenge, Britain expended large resources in trying to maintain the dominance of its navy. Secondly, Britain found it necessary to sell off many of its assets to finance its war effort during 1914 to 1918. Finally, because so much of the British economic position relied on its empire, the country chose to spend large sums to ensure its control of that empire. By the 1930s, the British economy had deteriorated to the extent that governments considered themselves unable to provide the military preparations that would have been necessary to back up a strong diplomacy in opposing Germany's revisionist demands made by Hitler at Munich in 1938. Following the devastation of World War II, Britain's economic base had so decayed that the country was obliged to withdraw from its overseas empire, beginning with recognizing

■ Rise and Fall of Great Powers: The Ten Leading Economies/Powers

1820 (Gross domestic product/billion 1990 $)

1. China	199
2. India	111
3. France	37
4. Britain	36
5. Russia	34
6. Japan	22
7. Austria	13
8. Spain	13
9. United States	12
10. Prussia	12

1914 (National income/billion current $)

1. United States	37
2. Germany	12
3. Britain	11
4. Russia	7
5. France	6
6. Italy	4
7. Austria-Hungary	3
8. Japan	2

1937 (National income/billion current $)

1. United States	68
2. British Empire	22
3. Soviet Union	19
4. Germany	17
5. France	10
6. Italy	6
7. Japan	4

1978 (Gross national product/billion current $)

1. United States	2,135
2. Soviet Union	968
3. Japan	885
4. West Germany	632
5. France	473
6. Britain	319
7. Italy	261
8. China	219
9. Canada	204
10. Brazil	180

1992 (Gross domestic product/billion 1990 $)

1. United States	5,676
2. China	3,616
3. Japan	2,417
4. Germany	1,360
5. India	1,188
6. France	1,030
7. Italy	940
8. Britain	928
9. Russia	802
10. Brazil	756

Sources: 1820 and 1992 data from Angus Maddison, *Monitoring the World Economy, 1820–1991* (Paris: Development Centre of the Organisation for Economic Cooperation and Development, 1995), Table 1–8; 1914 and 1937 data from Paul Kennedy, *The Rise and Fall of the Great Powers: Economic Change and Military Conflict from 1500 to 2000* (New York: Random House, 1987), Tables 21 and 31 (Kennedy derived his figures from Quincy Wright, *A Study of War.* Chicago, 1942); 1978 data from Charles Lewis Taylor and David A. Jodice, *World Handbook of Political and Social Indicators, Vol. 1: Cross-National Attributes and Rates of Change,* 3d ed. (New Haven and London: Yale University Press, 1983). All figures rounded from original.

India's independence in 1947 and continuing until its withdrawal from east of Suez in 1971.

A similar but more rapidly evolving pattern characterized the trajectory of the SOVIET UNION's position. Although Russia had embarked on industrialization in the early part of the twentieth century, its progress was set back by the damages of World War I and by the Russian revolution of 1917 and the ensuing civil war. During the Stalin years, the country pursued industrialization through central planning that extracted savings from the agricultural sector of the economy and invested in large-scale heavy industries and military goods. Despite the devastation wrought by World War II, the Soviet Union emerged from the war as a major industrial and military power, one of the world's two superpowers. With the exception of its innovations in missile technology, the Soviet Union tended to lag behind the Western industrial countries, and it continued to rely on the centrally planned, extensive model of industrialization. By the early 1970s, the country's economy became strained for a number of reasons. Although the regime had acceded a bit to the needs of consumers, its economic system did not satisfy demands for quality and diversity in consumer goods. Perhaps the most fundamental problem, however, was that the regime did not possess sufficient flexibility to adapt to the contemporary conditions of postindustrial society. Such an adaptation was undertaken only in the last half of the 1980s in the political sphere and only following the breakup of the Soviet Union in the economic realm. A flawed calculus became apparent in 1971 when Foreign Minister Andrei Gromyko averred that no problem in the world could be settled without consultation with the Soviet Union as a result of the shift in the world **correlation of forces** stemming from his country's nuclear buildup to equivalency with the United States.

Correlation of forces is a concept employed by Soviet analysts to calculate the array of political power in a given situation. Despite its utility as a general concept, Gromyko's application of it to the world situation of the early 1970s remained seriously defective, for it contained one of the classic mistakes of power calculations, that of using military power as the equivalent of overall power. Surely, the Soviet's military capabilities did give them some basis for influence. For example, by supplying arms to Third World countries, the Soviets gained political access. In addition, at that time socialism held ideological appeal for many. On the other hand, the Soviet Union did not possess the economic base to offer sig-

nificant economic benefits to client states to gain leverage. Neither did the Soviet Union command influence with other major powers that conferred prestige on its diplomatic campaigns. As the analysis of power in Chapter 2 made clear, power rests on a broad capabilities base. In the early 1970s, then, it was true that the two superpowers had a rough parity with each other in armaments, but it was patently mistaken to believe that their power was equivalent. Never in history had the Soviet economy achieved more than one-half the production of the American economy. Over time, the abyss between the power of the two opened so wide that even the most avid supporters of the Soviet Union had to acknowledge its economic weaknesses. In the successor states, market principles have been adopted as the radical departure that is needed for economic recovery and rebuilding. Only in the future will it become possible to determine whether the fundamental restructuring of the economies will prove successful.

These cases of Britain and the Soviet Union as well as the anxieties concerning the position of the United States involve only the decline side of the uneven development process. While some countries may decline, others improve their positions in the international system. Germany, Japan, and the United States offer the most prominent examples of the rise of powers to new heights as a result of uneven economic development. In recent years, though, all of the countries of the European Union as well as the East Asian "tigers" and China offer other prominent examples of the growth process.

Germany and Japan provide particularly interesting examples, for they not only illustrate the enhancement of position through economic growth but also offer evidence that economics may be a more important and more profound source of change than war. This theme is treated in Chapter 14.

Although the market plays a role in uneven development, the examples also make clear that state decision making contributes mightily to the process. Moreover, states do compete with one another in a relationship resembling civil society, but their competition does not entirely conform to the conception of civil society. Civil society comprises a component of the state, and the state remains crucial for creating the conditions in which economic activity can thrive. In the competition among states, on the other hand, the units do not comprise a component of a state, for international politics is anarchical. Sometimes, a great power may perform a hegemonic function that facilitates market activity, and international institutions have demonstrated their utility in promoting economic cooperation. Nevertheless, states remain the guarantors of property rights and enforcers of contracts as well as issuers of money and regulators of commerce.

Furthermore, in carrying out these essential tasks, states serve purposes larger than economic ones, and they reserve the right to use military force in those cases they deem appropriate. Specifically, states always in their normative conception and often in their empirical expression promote the equal rights and benefits of their citizens. As a corollary of their commitment to equality, they must offset the deleterious effects of the unequal distribution of production, a principle that contrasts sharply with the indifference of the market to equality. Redistribution of wealth in favor of the dispossessed, the poor, the ill, the elderly, and other inefficient members of society is thoroughly antithetical to the market principles of efficiency and price. Not only do these purposes contradict those of the market, they are enforced by the coercive apparatus of the state. Moreover, the retention of the right to settle matters with other states by the use of force includes a coercive principle that is also antithetical to market principles.

States and markets, thus, are quite distinct, even as they coexist and interact. While the elements that go into the distinction are many, the vital one is **security.** States seek security for themselves, and they provide it for their civil societies. Only irresponsible state authorities could ignore the security implications of economic exchange.

Economics and Security

On a day-to-day basis and in an analytical sense, economics and security occur as separate activities. Ministries of trade and commerce within governments handle exchanges of goods and services; ministries of finance deal with money and foreign reserves; and ministries of war and defense, along with foreign affairs departments, dedicate themselves to carrying out security functions. For the most part, civil society remains involved in economic activities, whereas governments allocate to themselves responsibility for defining and executing the security function.

Looked at in a longer-term and more profound sense, however, economics and security are intimately related. Economic activity prospers only under secure conditions, and the prosperity generated strengthens the capabilities base of a state from which the means are derived to protect its security. From a civil society perspective, the object of economic activity remains exclusively the acquisition of wealth. Drawing on Adam Smith's conception of a free market and harmony of interests, this viewpoint includes indifference to whether other states also acquire wealth. Indeed, this point of view promotes international cooperation, for collaborative broadening of markets raises the prosperity of all. What concern this civil society aspiration are the **absolute gains** derived from economic activity by the world as a whole. For example, if over the course of years the United States economy grows at the average rate of 4 percent per year, the American standard of living will increase to such an extent that, other things being equal, the population will be more prosperous at the end of the period than it was at the beginning. It does not matter that, say, the Chinese economy grows at the rate of 7 percent per year over the same time period or that, say, the Japanese economy increases at the rate of 6 percent per annum. In this scenario, the **relative gains** of China and Japan have significantly outstripped those of the United States, but the important point is that everyone has prospered.

Although from a civil society perspective absolute gains hold the more significant meaning, from a state point of view a concern looms for the meaning of relative gains for security. Recalling that uneven development remains constant, greater relative gains by a competitor state need not inevitably affect the security of a given state. On the other hand, authorities in the given state cannot assume that its competitor's enhanced position in the international system will not affect its security. Much depends on international conditions and how decision makers in the competitor state respond to those conditions. An additional factor that might affect the security implications of relative economic gains arises from the internal politics of the competitor state. These various considerations can most effectively be treated by speculating about specific countries. For illustrative reflection, the following discussion will deal with the United States, Japan, and China as cases that exemplify the analytical problem of the security implications of relative economic gains.

• UNITED STATES, JAPAN, AND CHINA

During the Cold War, the relations among these three countries were mostly dominated by security

■ **Relative Gains: Comparative Growth Performance of United States, Britain, and Japan, 1820–1992 (annual average compound growth rates)**

	1820–70	1870–1913	1913–50	1950–73	1973–92	1820–1992
Gross Domestic Product						
United States	4.22	3.94	2.84	3.92	2.39	3.61
Britain	2.04	1.90	1.19	3.00	1.59	1.89
Japan	0.31	2.34	2.24	9.25	3.76	2.77
Total Factor Productivity						
United States	−0.15	0.33	1.59	1.72	0.18	0.63
Britain	0.15	0.31	0.81	1.48	0.69	0.57
Japan	n.a.	−0.31	0.36	5.08	1.04	1.38*

Notes: *"1890–1992, for the corresponding period, the rate was 1.18 for the USA, 0.78 for the UK" (note in original).
"In calculating total factor productivity, crude labour input (hours) was given a weight of 0.7, education was given a weight of 0.42, nonresidential capital 0.27, and natural resources 0.03. Surface area was taken as a proxy for natural resources."

Source: Angus Maddison, *Monitoring the World Economy, 1820–1992* (Paris: Development Centre of the Organization for Economic Cooperation and Development, 1995), Table K–2.

considerations. Japan's economy prospered under the security protection of the United States, and the two remained allied against the Soviet Union and China. As the Cold War diminished and Japan's relative gains mounted until it possessed the world's second largest economy, that country served in a broader economic partnership with the United States. Japan willingly participated as the subordinate partner. Japan built its defense forces to comply with American requirements and paid subsidies to the United States that supported the latter's military presence in Japan. Furthermore, the Asian state clearly did not develop an independent military and did abjure the acquisition of nuclear weapons. In its subordinate status, Japan neither nurtured a political outlook on the world nor created a strategy of its own for orienting itself to global politics.

As Japan prospered, it became a competitor of the United States. Japanese automobile manufacturers, for example, provided the fuel-efficient cars needed to adjust to the 1973–74 increase in petroleum prices. Additionally, they led the way in the industry in innovative production techniques that were paragons of efficiency. Even while incorporating Japanese production as part of its energy conservation strategy by buying Japanese cars, the United States used its economic muscle to secure "voluntary" restraints on Japanese automobile exports to its market. During the profligate 1980s, Japanese savers supplied the funds to cover the United States government's budget deficits and much of the private debt that Americans undertook during that decade of leveraged buyouts and consumer indulgence. Yet, the Japanese trade deficit approximately equaled the flow of capital to the United States, and it became the object of American efforts to pressure Japan to reori-

ent its economy in a way that would absorb more American imports. During the Gulf War in 1990–91, strategy was made in Washington, but the American president and others demanded that Japan contribute both personnel and money to the allied coalition effort. These demands disregarded American-imposed constitutional constraints on the use of Japanese military forces and the absence of consultation with the Japanese about the political strategy that their yen would support. Although opinion in Japan remained predominantly favorable to continuation of the partnership with the United States, some voices were heard that demanded consultation, enhanced status, and a willingness to make independent decisions.[23] Some American voices engaged in "Japan bashing"; Congress passed vindictive legislation, such as the 1988 Trade Act with its "Super 301" provisions; and Presidents Bush and Clinton formulated specific demands for Japanese compliance with American demands on trade.

It is, of course, impossible to know how this relationship, with its mixture of consistent alliance and persistent tensions, will unfold in the future. Nevertheless, one can speculate about the conditions that might affect the security considerations arising out of differential relative gains. First considering the international situation, the end of the Cold War has dissolved the primary security bond between the two countries, which had been aligned against the common threat of the Soviet Union and its allies. Even as that threat vanished, the United States kept its military presence in Asia partly to reassure all the actors who retained memories of Japanese behavior in World War II. In the early and mid-1990s, there appeared to be no imminent threat to Japan, although relations with Russia had not yet been normalized because of the Russian occupation of four small islands at the end of World War II. One shadow that fell on the Northeast Asian region was cast by North Korea, whose nuclear weapons ambitions remained in doubt. The general uncertainty in East Asia did result in significant new arms acquisition by most of the states in the region, including the very large powers, Indonesia and China.

Continuing trading tensions between the United States and Japan seemed to be eased with the fall of the Liberal Democratic Party's government and its replacement in 1993 by a coalition of small parties composed largely of disaffected Liberals. Nevertheless, in 1995 the severe threat issued by the United States to impose 100 percent tariffs on imported Japanese luxury cars increased tensions for a short period. Prospects for an improvement in Japan's status seemed presaged by American support for reform of the United Nations Security Council to include Japan and Germany as members. Over time, it seems likely that the Japanese will debate and agree on an external political role to supplement their global economic importance. Part of their successful conclusion of that debate will undoubtedly rest on United States policies regarding its own position in Asia and its acceptance of Japan as an equal partner in joint undertakings. So long as the United States remains committed to Japan's defense and the Japanese tolerate the American presence on their soil, the security partnership may work indefinitely. However, it is unlikely in the long run that the Japanese will be ready to continue their subordination in that partnership, and a transformation to a more equal relationship will depend on the realism and sensitivity of each to the other.

Should the United States be incapable of accepting equality or should the country revert to its historic tradition of withdrawal from world affairs, Japanese thought would seem inevitably headed toward providing for Japan's security. In the end, that line of thinking leads to the acquisition of nuclear weapons and the development of a strategy for the armed forces, implying a more important role for the military in the national debate. Neighboring countries would necessarily come to their own conclusions in that case, and Japan would have to take into account in its own planning the policies that emanated from its neighbors' conclusions. The United States is far from omnipotent in Asia, but what comes out of this analysis is the importance that American choice has for determining the regional security conditions of East Asia. Furthermore, all of these questions arise because of the rapid economic growth that enables the East Asian countries to have the option of arming for security.

As China prospers and grows stronger, it will undoubtedly acquire additional arsenals to achieve a number of foreign policy goals. As a purely defensive measure, the Chinese need to be concerned about an overall regional balance of power and the potential of threat. With the United States so distant and Russia so weak, Japan is, for the Chinese, the country to watch. In addition to these broad security considerations, the Chinese have territorial interests in East Asia. Hong Kong will become part of China in 1997, but the future of Taiwan remains to be resolved. Additionally, China has claims to the Spratly Islands in the South China Sea, which are also claimed by Vietnam, Philippines, and others. These territories contain economic assets that, if gained, would further enhance China's wealth. On the other hand, a certain danger lurks behind the simple addition in this equation, for the maintenance of Hong Kong's wealth, for example, may rest upon assurances by the Chinese government that capitalist economic freedoms will be maintained in that colony after its accession to China. Should the Bejing government decide, for political reasons, to restrict freewheeling economic activities in its new territory, it might prove impossible to continue generating the wealth that Hong Kong has been noted for over the last several decades. Furthermore, should the economic attraction of Taiwan appear to warrant the employment of military force to reunite the island with China, an invasion could very well provoke an armed response by the United States, and the pursuit of wealth could then prove to be an occasion for war.

Although economics and security have these links, they need to be treated separately to get at a number of problems. One of these is the tension between accumulation and exchange.

Accumulation and Exchange

In attempting to maintain position in the international system, each state strives to accumulate as much wealth as it can, for no calculus exists that can determine the exact level of accumulation necessary to maintain position. At the same time, Ricardo's theory of comparative advantage makes it clear that a country can accumulate more by exporting those

■ East Asia in the Post-Cold War Period

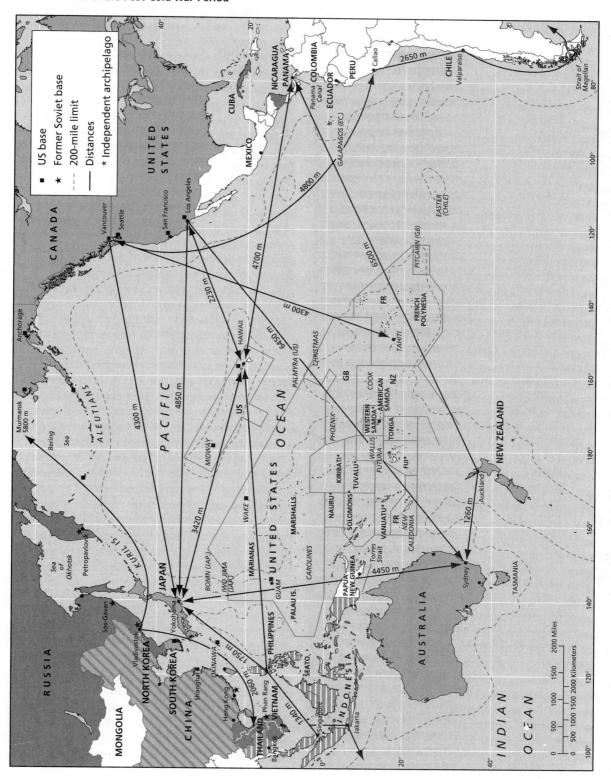

Legend:
- ■ US base
- ★ Former Soviet base
- --- 200-mile limit
- --- Distances
- * Independent archipelago

items it produces most efficiently and by importing other products. In the vernacular of economists, specialization and exchange in a system of free trade produce absolute gains with **Pareto optimality** in which no one is worse off as a result of the transactions that occur. Nevertheless, uneven development can leave some countries in a situation in which they are not accumulating wealth or are accumulating at such a slow rate as to cause them to lose position in the international system. Moreover, slow growth may also give rise to political demands for national policies that protect the facilities and jobs that have previously been accumulated. In such cases, observers often stress national policies that will erect barriers to promote accumulation without free trade. Even without the context of security concerns that give emphasis to relative gains, domestic economic and political conditions may lead some to embrace accumulation over **exchange.**

International trade extends the ever-changing process of competition for profits and jobs from the domestic arena to the international one. In the domestic sphere, firms rely on their own management resources, and workers organize into unions to protect their positions in the national market. Additionally, both firms and unions engage in domestic politics to affect the political and legal constraints within which they operate, and they less often rely on courts for protection under bankruptcy and other laws. For example, laws protect copyrights on inventions created in corporate laboratories, and they lay down the rules under which workers may organize. When firms fail, they are protected from their creditors by bankruptcy laws. Laid-off workers are protected by unemployment compensation laws.

Moreover, firms and workers respond to governmental initiatives in order to maintain their positions. For example, in the broad health care debate that occurred in the United States in late 1993 and early 1994, small businesses visibly fought to ensure that the new legislation would not add significantly to their costs, and labor unions lobbied effectively to prevent the treatment of health care benefits as taxable income. Thus, economic associations struggle not only through economic competition but also through politics as a normal activity.

Similarly, when such economic associations are constrained in international competition by the laws and practices of countries, they try to enlist the aid of their own governments to protect their market shares, in the case of firms, or their jobs, in the case

of workers. For example, American automobile manufacturers and the auto workers union successfully petitioned their government during the Reagan administration to press the Japanese to restrain "voluntarily" imports of cars to the North American market. Even though the restrictions added some two thousand dollars to the cost of every car sold in the United States, the positions of both firms and workers were protected, although the costs were borne by American consumers.

Sometimes, economic associations respond to governmental initiatives in the realm of international trade just as they do domestically. For example, during the Uruguay Round of multilateral trade negotiations that lasted from 1986 to 1994, the French government agreed with its trading partners to reduce agricultural subsidies as an impediment to free trade. In response, French farmers mounted massive protests to protect those subsidies.

In cases such as these, proponents of protectionism cast their arguments in terms of relative gains. When the American automobile industry is extended protection, it is clear that that industry profits in comparison with its foreign competitors. However, it is less clear that the country's relative gains have been protected, for the added marginal cost that consumers bear represents **foregone opportunities** for alternative investments and job creation. Each dollar added to the cost of automobiles might have been spent on widgets manufactured by American workers, with a multiplier effect that would contribute more to the growth of the national economy than was the historical case.

With such clashes between civil society and state interests, outcomes affect the respective positions of the states in the international system. Should civil society interests, on balance, prevail, the state's position will more likely than not decline.[24] In contrast, states that find the leadership and the will to choose on behalf of the common good—in this case, the state's as opposed to portions of civil society's relative gains—are more likely to preserve or enhance their international positions. These issues become quite complicated, for, in some instances, the relative position of the state can best be protected by extending privileges to a particular industry. Thus, choices are not simply between government and private interests but rather concern the deeper but also more abstract conception of the public good. Nevertheless, such debates tend to be conducted in the ideological terms of free trade, protectionism, and managed trade.

Free Trade, Protectionism, and Managed Trade

Although liberal economists have mostly accepted Adam Smith's and David Ricardo's arguments on behalf of free trade, mercantilist ways of thinking have remained formidable. Historically, the secular trend shows the advance of free trade over the last two centuries. Nevertheless, tensions between free trade and **protectionism** have resulted in a continuing struggle that has preserved elements of protection of sectors of economies almost everywhere and periods in which governments erected effective barriers to international commerce to protect their own industries and jobs.

As Winham has argued, the regulation of trade follows closely upon the trade itself, but in the contemporary period, international trade agreements seek to reduce both protectionism and the need for protectionism.[25] Thus, the promotion of a liberal trading order has entailed the development of institutions that foster cooperation among trading partners by promulgating and enforcing rules, supplying information, and affording procedures for negotiating. The most effective of these institutions are the General Agreement on Tariffs and Trade and the European Union. In addition to these, a significant number of regional associations have been established to promote economic cooperation among members. Included among them are the Association of Southeast Asian Nations, the Economic Community of West African States, the European Free Trade Association, the North American Free Trade Association, and Asia and Pacific Economic Cooperation.

Central to the maintenance of an open trading system since the Second World War, the GATT embodies the principles of **reciprocity** and **nondiscrimination.** These are incorporated in the **most favored nation (MFN) principle,** which holds that every trading partner must be offered the same terms as those applied to the most favored nation with which one country trades. In a series of multilateral negotiations in the more than forty years since World War II, the members of the GATT have extended the MFN principle to more sectors of commerce and have negotiated reduced tariffs and other barriers to trade. Most recently, the Uruguay Round negotiations, successfully concluded at the end of 1993, extended liberal trading principles to agriculture, services, and intellectual property. The long-term, successful main-

tenance of a liberal trading order through GATT mechanisms contributed to the sustenance of unprecedented world economic growth. At the same time, protectionism has been maintained and, in some cases, increased. Three specific sources of protectionism nourish opposition to free trade.

One of these is the development of regional associations for cooperation, which tends to favor the countries belonging to them. For example, the European Community devised a common agricultural policy in the 1960s under which governments subsidized production and protected their markets from external competition. Additionally, the EC concluded the Lomé Convention, which extended preference to agricultural products from African countries over those from other regions.

The second source countering free trade stemmed from the poor countries in the 1970s when the Group of 77 passed a resolution in the United Nations General Assembly in 1974 that called for a New International Economic Order. As Krasner effectively argued, as a result of the internal weakness of governing regimes and external weakness of the poor countries in competition with the rich, the Third World sought to organize international trade on statist rather than market principles.[26]

Finally, opposition to free trade emanates from individual countries where powerful economic interests achieve governmental assistance in protecting firms' profits and workers' jobs. The "voluntary export restraints" that the United States has negotiated with Japan provide illustrations. Such arrangements, which fall outside GATT rules, are referred to as **managed trade.** According to one estimate, 25 percent of world trade falls into this category.[27]

In the United States, a debate proceeds among both economists and politicians over the relative merits of protectionism and free trade. For the most part, arguments are cast in terms of ensuring the continued prosperity of specific industries. However, a different perspective arises from political scientists concerned with maintenance of state position in the international system. Basically, the argument of liberal economists is that free trade promotes increasing prosperity for all countries, with global gains. In contrast, realist political scientists note that individual states must worry about their relative gains, for the relative increase in wealth of others may be turned to a security advantage and become a threat to a given state.

Some politically conscious economists have also joined the debate by drawing on the work of

Friedrich List, an early nineteenth-century economist who stood in opposition to Adam Smith, J. B. Say, and the predominant liberal school of economics.[28] List criticized the dominant school for treating the individual, the family, and the firm as the equivalent of the state or nation and for failing to draw a distinction between the good of a country and the good of all nations. List drew sharp distinctions between the state and such components as firms and individuals, and he argued effectively that what was good for a single country did not necessarily result in prosperity for others. He counterposed "productive power" to "division of labor." Although both concepts appeared in Smith, the author of *The Wealth of Nations* stressed the latter, emphasizing the values emanating from exchange or free trade.

In contrast, List accentuated the need for any given country to develop all of its resources and to build a system of the cooperation of labor to develop more productive power. In policy terms, he advocated the use of tariffs to protect infant industries and any other industries that might have the chance of matching or surpassing the efficiency of the most competitive exemplars in the world. On the other hand, he stood in favor of free trade in agricultural products. Most basically, the argument turns on treating the state as distinctive, rigorously differentiating the various levels of analysis, and focusing on the accumulation of productive power rather than on mere trade.

Contemporary Political Economy

As one century draws to a close and a new one begins, the importance of both states and markets remains evident. Disagreements abound with respect to their relationships, the processes of their interactions, and the consequences of their operations. Moreover, analysts have distinct preferences for the future. Nevertheless, no school of thought engaging international political economy can disregard the impact of states and the effects of markets.

A global rationalization of production is occurring in the international market as multinational firms engage in a restructuring of their operations and states adopt policies that open their economies to foreign investments. To the extent that states can derive economic benefits to themselves from this process, they will be able to maintain their positions or enhance them. In contrast, a failure to extract payoffs from the operations of the market more likely will lead to a loss of position. An important point in the consensus that prevails among different schools of thought in the 1990s holds that working with the market rather than in opposition to it leads to a greater chance of success for economic development and for maintaining a state's position in the international political economy.

While the market may operate in largely uncontrollable ways, states are organizations that make choices through deliberative mechanisms. Thus, states formulate and implement policies. Analysis of foreign policy forms a distinct subfield of international politics studies, and to that topic we now turn.

● IMPORTANT TERMS

absolute gains	liberal trading system
accumulation	managed trade
antiexport bias	mercantilism
bourgeoisie	money
capital flight	most favored nation
capitalism	(MFN) principle
central planning	multilateral trade
class	negotiations
comparative advantage	nondiscrimination
correlation of forces	Pareto optimality
debt crisis	postindustrial society
democratic centralism	proletariat
dialectical materialism	protectionism
dictatorship of the	public goods
proletariat	rate of exchange
duplication of tasks	recession
East Asian model	reciprocity
economic growth	regulation of trade
exchange	relative gains
exports	savings
flexibility	security
foregone opportunities	socialism
foreign exchange	standard of living
reserves	structural adjustment
free trade	programs
hegemonic stability	superstructure
theory	surplus value
import substitution	terms of trade
industrialization	uneven development
imports	vanguard of the
incentive structures	proletariat
inflation	wages
investment	

● STUDY QUESTIONS

1. Why is there a necessary tension between states and markets?

2. What do states do for markets?

3. What do markets do for states?

4. Define uneven development, and explain how it bears on the life of states.

5. Do you believe that economic matters and security matters can be separated, or do you think that one affects the other? Explain how you arrive at your viewpoint.

6. Is it better for a country to engage in the maximum possible amount of international trade or to be more concerned with its own productive capacity? What are the implications of the respective alternatives?

7. What are the sources of pressures on behalf of protectionism and managed trade?

8. Where is the contemporary world political economy going? What are the forces driving it that way?

9. Discuss interdependence in the contemporary world, and assess its importance for the world as a whole and for particular states.

• ENDNOTES

1. Ruggie, "Continuity and Transformation in the World Polity."
2. Gilpin, *The Political Economy of International Relations*.
3. The following two paragraphs, in English version, are taken from the author's article, "*Los Estados Unidos y Sus Vecinos: La Política Internacional en América del Norte a Fines del Siglo XX*," *Foro Internacional* 30 (octubre–diciembre 1989): 246–72.
4. Waltz, *Theory of International Politics*.
5. Robert O. Keohane, *After Hegemony: Cooperation and Discord in the World Political Economy* (Princeton, N.J.: Princeton University Press, 1984).
6. Robert O. Keohane and Joseph S. Nye, Jr., "International Interdependence and Integration," in *Handbook of Political Science, Vol. 8: International Politics*, ed. by Fred I. Greenstein and Nelson W. Polsby (Reading, Mass.: Addison-Wesley, 1976).
7. See Ernst B. Haas, *The Uniting of Europe: Political, Social, and Economic Forces, 1950–1957* (London: Stevens, 1959).
8. See Howard H. Lentner, *State Formation in Central America: The Struggle for Autonomy, Development, and Democracy* (Westport, Conn.: Greenwood Press, 1993).
9. See Gilpin, *The Political Economy of International Relations*, and Keohane, *After Hegemony*.
10. Keohane, *After Hegemony*.
11. For an example of a different treatment of incentives to cooperate, see Donald Crone, "Does Hegemony Matter? The Reorganization of the Pacific Political Economy," *World Politics* 45 (July 1993): 501–25.
12. Although journalists sometimes cite prices of particular items to stress the differences, prices in Japan have a range just as they do in the United States. Nevertheless, the exchange rate makes a substantial difference for travelers whose purchases, in effect, are exports of the country in which they buy them.
13. See E. F. Heckscher, *Mercantilism*, 2 volumes, rev. 2d ed, ed. by E. F. Söderlund and trans. by Mendel Shapiro (London: George Allen and Unwin Ltd., 1955).
14. Quoted from George H. Sabine, *A History of Political Theory*, 3d ed. (New York: Holt, Rinehart and Winston, 1961), p. 692.
15. See John Maynard Keynes, *The General Theory of Employment, Interest, and Money* (New York: Harcourt Brace Jovanovich, 1936).
16. See Adam Ulam, *Stalin: The Man and His Era* (New York: Viking Press, 1973).
17. Daniel B. Baker, ed., *Political Quotations: A Collection of Notable Sayings on Politics from Antiquity through 1989* (Detroit: Gale Research, 1990), p. 11.
18. See Gilpin, *The Political Economy of International Relations*, p. 39 and passim.
19. Joseph S. Nye, Jr., *Bound to Lead: The Changing Nature of American Power* (New York: Basic Books, 1990), p. 74. Nye draws on several sources to calculate his approximations. Herbert Block, *The Planetary Product in 1980: A Creative Pause* (Washington, D.C.: U.S. Department of State, Bureau of Public Affairs, 1981); Simon Kuznets, *Economic Growth and Structure* (New York: W. W. Norton, 1965); Council on Competitiveness, *Competitiveness Index* (Washington, D.C.: 1988); and Central Intelligence Agency, *Handbook of Economic Indicators, 1988* (Washington, D.C.: U.S. Government Printing Office, 1988).
20. See Rostow, *The Stages of Economic Growth*.
21. See Raúl Prebisch, *The Economic Development of Latin America and Its Principal Problems* (Lake Success, N.Y.: United Nations Economic Commission for Latin America, 1949); *Towards a Dynamic Development Policy for Latin America* (New York: United Nations, 1963); and *Change and Development—Latin America's Great Task* (New York: Praeger Publishers in cooperation with the Inter-American Development Bank, 1971).
22. See Paul Kennedy, *The Rise and Fall of the Great Powers: Economic Change and Military Conflict from 1500 to 2000* (New York: Random House, 1987).
23. See Shintaro Ishihara, *The Japan That Can Say No*, trans. by Frank Baldwin (New York: Simon & Schuster, 1991).
24. For an extended analysis of this problem, see Mancur Olson, *The Rise and Decline of Nations: Economic Growth, Stagflation, and Social Rigidities* (New Haven: Yale University Press, 1982).
25. Gilbert R. Winham, *The Evolution of International Trade Agreements* (Toronto: University of Toronto Press, 1992), p. 21.
26. Krasner, *Structural Conflict*.
27. Winfried Ruigrok, "Paradigm Crisis in International Trade Theory," *Journal of World Trade* 25 (February 1991): 77–89, cited by Winham, *The Evolution of International Trade Agreements*.
28. List's most well-known work is *The National System of Political Economy* (New York: Augustus M. Kelley, 1966; reprint of London: Longmans, Green, and Co., 1885, trans. Sampson S. Lloyd). A contemporary presentation of the argument is made by James Fallows in three articles in the *Atlantic Monthly*: "Looking at the Sun," November 1993; "How the World Works," December 1993; and "What Is an Economy For?" January 1994. Also see Fallows, *Looking at the Sun: The Rise of the New East Asian Economic and Political System* (New York: Pantheon Books, 1994).

PART 4

Foreign Policy and State Interactions

Foreign Policy: Striving to Maintain Position, Protect Autonomy, and Exert Influence

"Politics stops at the water's edge." That phrase was a cliché in the United States during the early Cold War years when Republicans and Democrats worked to forge a bipartisan foreign policy. When the effort worked, leaders of both parties consulted together and gave enough support to agreed-upon policies to prevent the issues involved from becoming matters of public partisan debate. In other cases, by contrast, foreign policy became a matter of sharp friction, particularly in presidential election campaigns. Because the stakes in international politics are important and the prize in a presidential election so rich, it cannot be surprising that issues become contentious. Additionally, people hold very different views on foreign policy issues.

Foreign policy lies at the intersection of international and domestic politics, where the constraints and interactions of the international system are faced by authorities and groups in the state. Within systemic structural constraints and the capabilities that shape a particular state's position, a country's elite selects its objectives and mobilizes the resources to accomplish them, and then pursues fulfillment of those objectives.

This chapter examines the nature of the problems faced by a country in determining and carrying out its course in foreign policy. In addition, the analysis describes the process through which foreign policy is shaped; and it presents the main approaches—decision making and bureaucratic politics—employed by political scientists to treat topics falling within the foreign policy rubric.

Introduction

Each state strives to **maintain its position** in the international system, to **protect its autonomy** from the incursions of others, and to **exert influence** in order to shape its environment according to its own preferences. These endeavors occur within the context of the international system's structure and institutions, the world market, and the exertions of other states to achieve similar ambitions. Although clear and straightforward enough in the abstract, such aspirations require policies involving specific goals and objectives, together with the means and support to achieve them. Foreign policies are devised and carried out by governments acting in a broad context shaped by international **constraints,** the **capabilities** of their own states, and the complexities of the **political systems** that they govern. Foreign policy analysis emphasizes **choices,** but it is also necessary to describe the context in which choices are made, to identify which individuals, groups, and institutions participate in the decision making process, and to examine the **formulation** and **implementation** of policies as well as to trace their **consequences.**

■————————————————————

•••••• **Values Pursued in Foreign Policy**

• Maintain state's position in the international system
• Protect state's autonomy
• Exercise influence in international environment

————————————————————

The term *foreign policy* may be applied to many different circumstances and may take on many different meanings. In the broadest sense, it applies to a general orientation of a country toward the outside world. For example, many states during the Cold War adopted a posture of nonalignment, that is, a refusal to join either of the two grand military alliances headed, respectively, by the United States and the Soviet Union. Similarly, the members of the two alliances maintained a formal posture of hostility toward their adversaries. Some countries—Canada is an example—are generally oriented toward cooperation with their dominant ally but also seek latitude to moderate alliance policy and to act independently on behalf of such activities as United Nations peacekeeping, which Canadian Lester Pearson helped to invent.

■————————————————————

•••••• **Constraints on Foreign Policy**

• International system
• Market
• Actions of other states
• Capabilities
• Political systems

————————————————————

Still other countries adopt a distinctive posture that orients them definitively. Revolutionary Iran after 1979, which stood foursquare against modern secularism as embodied in both Western culture and communism, provides a clear example.

In contrast to a broad orientation, the term *foreign policy* is also used to characterize such a quite specific policy endeavor as Russia's quest in the early 1990s to gain access to forums like the Group of Seven summit conferences. During the 1980s, the United States extended major economic support and some military advice to the government of El Salvador in its civil war against the Farabundo Marti National Liberation Front. It was not unusual at the time to speak of American policy toward El Salvador. In 1994, the United States pursued a focused policy toward North Korea that centered on bringing that Asian country's nuclear energy program into conformity with the commitments it had made under the Nuclear Non-proliferation Treaty.

Thus, foreign policy encompasses a range of activities and different time frames. What it always includes, however, is a choice to achieve some goal or objective in relationship to other states. Foreign policy may be as short-term as French President Charles DeGaulle's veto in 1963 of Britain's application to join the European Common Market. On the other hand, a foreign policy may last as long as the United States' containment policy that endured from about 1947 until the end of the Cold War in 1989. Moreover, foreign policy may be directed at a single country, as the examples illustrate, or at an array of states, such as has occurred in the multilateral trade negotiating rounds held under auspices of the GATT since the 1950s.

■————————————————————

•••••• **Foreign Policy Analysis Choices**

• Formulation
• Implementation
• Consequences

————————————————————

Because foreign policy concerns maintenance of position, protection of autonomy, and exercise of influence abroad, it cannot be restricted to any limited subject matter. Instead, foreign policy addresses whatever challenges and opportunities arise in international politics and promotes whatever goals and objectives state authorities choose. Those goals and objectives may be quite modest and limited, or they may include such ambitious aims as shaping global arrangements and territorial conquest. They may fall within the compass of high politics—matters dealing with diplomacy and security—or of low politics—economic, cultural, and other matters that more emphatically bring into play civil society.

Constraints, Choices, Chance, Error

Foreign policy is always subject to constraints in the international system and to the activities of other states. Perhaps the primary challenge in formulating policy lies in correctly calculating those constraints. The difficulty of such calculations may be illustrated by the cases of miscalculations of United States intentions by North Korea in 1950 and Iraq in 1990. In both of these cases, the United States modified its declared policy, thus presenting its adversaries with the challenge of grasping unarticulated, underlying principles rather than official statements.

• KOREAN WAR

Korea had been divided by the victors at the end of World War II, and the occupiers—the United States and the Soviet Union—had withdrawn in 1949, with separate governments ruling North Korea and South Korea. Following the victory in late 1949 by the Communists in the Chinese civil war, both President Harry Truman and Secretary of State Dean Acheson made statements designed to clarify American policy in the Western Pacific area. Acheson declared that the United States would take responsibility for the security of Japan, Okinawa, and the Philippines, implicitly excluding South Korea and Formosa (Taiwan), the latter of which was held by the losing side in the Chinese civil war. Security for those areas, Acheson stated, would fall under the jurisdiction of the United Nations. Furthermore, Truman had promised that the United States, which had assisted the Chinese Nationalists during their struggle with the Communists, would no longer interfere in the civil war in China. When North Korea launched its attack against South Korea in June 1950, however, Truman took two decisions. He determined that the United States would repel the North Korean attack, and he ordered the U.S. Seventh Fleet to be stationed in the Taiwan Strait, effectively intervening to keep the Chinese civil war adversaries from attacking each other.

To emphasize the point that the calculation of constraints poses a formidable challenge to decision makers, two other aspects of the Korean War give clear illustrations. Although the American decision had been made in June to defend South Korea, United States officials decided in October to push on to North Korea to unite the Korean peninsula by force, thus shifting from a defensive undertaking to an offensive one. Then, approaching what the Americans thought was the end of that operation, China intervened to push the Americans back to the 38th parallel, close to what had been the dividing line between the two parts of Korea.

• GULF WAR

Forty years later, a similar sequence unfolded in the Persian Gulf region. Faced with a decline of oil revenues in the wake of the long and devastating war with Iran during the 1980s, Iraq sought to negotiate its territorial dispute with Kuwait, which refused, and to press its partners in the Organization of Petroleum Exporting Countries to increase oil prices, which some of its partners opposed. In the last week of July

1990, Iraq placed its army on its border with Kuwait and, on August 2, invaded. United States policy prior to the invasion had been to encourage the Kuwaitis to resist Iraqi demands in the two countries' negotiations and to inform the Iraqis that Washington had "no opinion on Arab-Arab conflicts, like your border disagreement with Kuwait."[1] However, President Bush chose to reverse the Iraqi invasion of Kuwait and, to that end, formed a very broad coalition of countries that dispatched an exceptionally large army to Saudi Arabia, issued an ultimatum, and launched a war that drove Iraq out of Kuwait.

* * *

These two cases illustrate vividly the challenge of calculating the international constraints at work and of reckoning the response that other states will take in reaction to a situation newly created by one's own initiative. Other cases demonstrate that miscalculations need not turn out to be so extreme, and still others show the correct insight that officials can bring to bear in their assessments of the forces at work. Nevertheless, it remains a primary challenge for authorities to calculate the intentions of the leaders of other states.[2]

In addition to the difficulties of calculating intentions, another problem lies implicit in the very nature of international politics. That problem is that **unintended consequences** inevitably flow from foreign policy actions. There are two structural sources of unintended consequences in international politics. One of them emerges from the distribution of power across the units, with (as was seen in Chapter 4) quite different effects being exerted, depending on whether the structure is multipolar or bipolar. Regardless of the bipolar or multipolar distributions, however, ambitions by particular states to dominate the system will elicit balancing responses.[3] The other source of unintended consequences stems from the structure of conflict. In the very nature of conflict, opponents struggle not only to promote their own aims but also to hinder other's objectives: the clash itself produces consequences that neither of them anticipated or aimed for.

In addition to these structural sources that make it difficult to calculate the outcomes of undertakings, a phenomenon that the German strategist Karl von Clausewitz designated the "fog of battle" can also obscure the unfolding of conflicts.[4] In addition, intensity of feeling and commitment to a cause also affect outcomes, and different political structures produce varied levels of willingness to sacrifice among citizens and can result in unfore-seen effects. For example, in the war of Vietnam against United States intervention from 1961 to 1973, nationalism and attachment to their own land caused the Vietnamese to fight with an inten-sity surprising to Americans. Furthermore, the totalitarian character of the North Vietnamese gov-ernment enabled that country to accept casualties at a phenomenal rate.

■
• • • • • • **Sources of Unintended Consequences**

- Structure of the international system and the tendency to balance against threats
- Nature of conflict: opponents interfere with the achieve-ment of objectives
- "Fog of battle": difficulty perceiving the consequences of one's own actions as well as those of the adversary in the context of the struggle
- Intensity of feeling
- Character of the political system

In contrast, American anticommunist ideology had a considerably less intense character, and the demo-cratic character of the American polity produced outrage and protest against—in comparison with the millions of casualties suffered by the Vietnamese—a relatively moderate casualty rate.

As a result of these and other factors, the diffi-culties of correctly perceiving the constraints at work pose formidable obstacles to making appropriate choices. Some analysts present this problem as a dis-tinction between the "psychological environment" and the "operational environment."[5] In constructing their analytical frameworks, they stress that decision makers often are unable correctly to perceive reality as it objectively exists. Brecher goes so far as to argue that the ability accurately to perceive the opera-tional environment is the main criterion for success in foreign policy decision making.[6] Not only does such an argument ignore the internal political dynamics that may impel a state to seek goals in its environment but it also overlooks the potential for changing some of the international constraints in the course of a conflict. Although choices may be constrained by structural and other contextual fea-tures, they are not determined by those constraints. Authorities within countries develop their own objectives, capable of accomplishment while still subject to existing and unmodifiable constraints. These objectives may be driven by such causes as ide-ology, a quest for glory or revenge, a redress of a pre-viously inflicted grievance, internal political pres-sures, or other circumstances, needs, reasons, and emotions.

• MANIPULATING CONSTRAINTS IN EGYPTIAN-ISRAELI RELATIONS

When President Anwar Sadat of Egypt determined in the early 1970s to seek an end to the impasse between his country and Israel, he acted in such a way as to create new realities, that is, to modify the constraints. Egypt had been badly beaten in its 1967 war with Israel and sought to regain the territories that it had lost. Following an inherited policy, Sadat's Egypt was relying on the Soviet Union for military and economic assistance, but it became clear that the communist superpower did not possess the wealth to address Egypt's economic needs. Sadat, therefore, determined to reverse alliances: to expel Soviet advisors from Egypt and to seek economic and other assistance from the United States. Addi-tionally, he chose to go to war with Israel to over-come the humiliation of the 1967 defeat and to strengthen Egyptian morale enough to enter into ne-gotiations with Israel. Following early successes in 1973, the Egyptian army was driven back to the Suez Canal.

Nevertheless, the situation provided an oppor-tunity for the beginning of negotiations with the assistance of American National Security Council Advisor Henry Kissinger and for the beginning of American economic assistance. After several years of relatively small negotiating successes that led to the Israeli withdrawal from some of the Sinai Peninsula, Sadat made the dramatic gesture of traveling in November 1977 to Jerusalem, the Israeli capital, where he addressed the Knesset, or parliament. He thereby initiated the direct negotiations that led to the Camp David agreements of September 1978 and to the signing of a peace treaty in March 1979 and establishment of full diplomatic relations between the two countries that had been in a state of war since 1948. As this case so eloquently testifies, con-straints operate powerfully, but choices can modify constraints as well.

Nevertheless, not all constraints can be adjusted. Not only was there no way for Egypt to change the capabilities of the Soviet Union, neither could the Soviets themselves alter their economy to make it the equal of that of the United States. Some constraints always operate on choice, and decision makers are thus faced with the challenge of grasping the limits on their choices. They then engage in **decision making.**

* * *

Making decisions requires a definition or conceptualization of the problem or circumstance in which choices are made. Furthermore, **objectives** need to be formulated and selected, the **means** to accomplish those objectives have to be mobilized or supplied, and, within the context of the situation, **political support** has to be generated. Implicit in a decision making process are a **leadership** and a politics of both inspiration and management. These activities included in making choices do not occur in any particular sequence. In the 1990–1991 GULF WAR, for example, President Saddam Hussein and the Revolutionary Command Council of Iraq acted in the sequence outlined in this paragraph when they determined to invade Kuwait, for they analyzed their needs for oil revenues and domestic political support, sent an already mobilized army into Kuwait, and sought political support in the Arab world.[7] In contrast, Winston Churchill in his first statement as prime minister of BRITAIN in 1940 told his beleaguered nation, "I have nothing to offer but blood, toil, tears and sweat"[8] in alone facing Hitler who had to that time worked his will in Europe. Churchill's inspirational leadership showed determination; but more specific analyses, selection of discrete objectives, and the mobilization of the means to achieve victory required different tasks that had to be done later.

Regardless of the sequence, decision making remains fundamentally a rational process. Both constraints and a number of other considerations that will be addressed below militate against rationality. Nevertheless, in examining the choices that states make, one must always remember that authorities calculate and strive to achieve objectives that may be understood in the rational terms that characterize foreign policy and state formation analysis.

In addition to constraints and choices, two other elements affect foreign policy: **chance** and **error.** It is impossible to control all the details in the unfolding of events, so unforeseen circumstances crop up and opportunities present themselves that could not have been foreseen. Similarly, the participants in a conflict may—most often do—make mistakes, again presenting unexpected situations that can be capitalized on. Neither of these factors is present at the outset of a sequence of events, but rather each occurs within an unfolding succession of activities. This characteristic emphasizes that choice selection possesses a dynamic nature in which calculations remain open to turns of events and that authorities retain sufficient flexibility to respond. On the other hand, leadership often embraces rigidity in the determination to pursue fixed goals despite the temptations to compromise them.

Homer made this point in relating Odysseus's journey, when to sail between the islands of the sirens and resist the temptation to go aground, he tied his men to the mast. Closer to our subject, President Franklin D. Roosevelt insisted on the unconditional surrender of Germany despite various proposals to seek a compromise peace. Both he and Prime Minister Churchill knew Hitler to be a human embodiment of evil, whose regime had to be extirpated. Moreover, they also remembered that Germany had not been completely defeated in World War I, a fact that provided fertile ground for the growth of the myth that the country's surrender had occurred because of "a stab in the back" by unpatriotic German leaders. This myth, in turn, gave sustenance to Hitler and his hateful regime, which professed to be reclaiming German honor.[9]

One of the tests of leadership, then, presents the need to distinguish, on the one hand, flexibility in the face of chance and error in order to capitalize on unsuspected opportunity and, on the other, rigidity of purpose in the face of temptations to compromise and back away from the achievement of final goals. In the midst of political controversies and pressures, this analytical distinction may not always be clear, so leaders may err in either direction.

As this discussion makes clear, foreign policy decision making presents formidable and complicated challenges. Among its more interesting aspects are politics and policy making, to which we now turn.

Politics and Policy Making

The politics of foreign policy mostly involves contention over the values, goals, and means that a particular country should pursue in its relations with other countries.[10] These politics tend to vary over time, by circumstances, by specific states, and among the individuals and groups that participate, in one way or another, in formulating and carrying out policies. In periods of fairly stable policies, such as the American policy of containment of the Soviet Union in the 1950s and 1960s, a country's elites and people may possess a mind-set that provides overall guidance to thinking about specific policies. At other times, division over the country's proper course may be more likely to characterize the politics of foreign policy, as occurred in the United States in the late 1960s and early 1970s, when a deep cleavage opened up in both the government and most social groups over American policy in Vietnam.[11]

International circumstances also cause great variation in foreign policy. An example that attests to the depth of change that can occur is the shift of the United States from a determined neutrality in 1937 that was based in a near-universal consensus to an equally determined and virtually universal willingness to wage a two-front war in 1942. That conversion happened almost entirely in response to the ominous events in Europe and the Far East that transpired in the intervening period. Germany and Japan had launched wars of conquest that were increasingly recognized by Americans as threatening. The United States itself was finally drawn into hostilities when the Japanese attacked Pearl Harbor and Germany declared war in December 1941.[12]

Foreign policy tends also to be shaped by the constitutional and other arrangements of particular states. Democracies, for example, tend to provide a more important role in debates for their legislatures and their general publics, media, interest groups, and elections than do authoritarian political systems. For example, elections in democratic systems provide an important incentive for leaders to explain their policies and listen to their constituents. Moreover, foreign policy debates may be shaped by an electoral calendar. Ronald Reagan's election in 1980 against incumbent President Jimmy Carter, for example, was partly but importantly determined by the debate over America's standing in the world. Under Carter, many voters had felt humiliated by the Iranian taking of hostages in the American embassy in Teheran; Reagan promised a more active and tougher foreign policy in which citizens could take pride. On the other hand, dictators have a freer hand in both timing and electoral constraints, for they do not need to stand for reelection and thus need not be responsive to an electorate. Variations in political systems and their effects on foreign policy are wide-ranging and go far beyond the simplicities of these illustrations. Some variables concern the homogeneity or diversity of countries, their laws and traditions, and their recent experiences, among others.

Other variables that affect foreign policy are group arrangements and individuals. Apart from the diversity of group interests and power distributions within different countries, often groups focus on single regions or issues. For example, a very small country like Barbados may have only a small and coherent business elite, whereas Canada contains an array of economic groups divided along lines of importers and exporters, manufacturers in different industries, agricultural interests, labor unions organized by industry (some international and others exclusively domestic), organized consumer groups, a fishing industry, and so on. Groups in countries with command economies tend to be structured by professional affiliation, such as factory managers, government bureaucrats, military officers, and so forth, in such a way that they do not parallel the civil society of a state that has a market economy. In some countries, religious, ethnic, and linguistic groups may be attentive to issues that concern them, whereas other countries may be religiously and linguistically homogeneous and not include any immigrant groups that maintain an interest in their countries of origin.

Finally, particular individuals make a difference in foreign policy. It would be difficult to imagine the reversal of Mexico's foreign policy from an orientation that was independent and, in some ways, anti-American to one that has sought economic integration with the United States and Canada without the personalities of presidents Miguel de la Madrid (1982–1988) and Carlos Salinas de Gortari (1988–1994). To cite another example, there is a school of thought about the origins of the Cold War that attributes a major cause to the transition from President Franklin D. Roosevelt to Harry S Truman in the United States.[13] Undoubtedly, the impact of such men as Josef Stalin and Mikhail Gorbachev on the foreign policy of the Soviet Union is difficult to overestimate, for they had profound influences.

All of these variables bear on processes of foreign policy formulation and implementation. At the center of those processes stands a chief executive, for established states normally assign primary responsibility for foreign policy to a single person or, occasionally, a small leadership group. In very small, less developed states, such as St. Lucia, and in authoritarian police states, such as Zaire under Mobutu Sese Seko, a single person can usually make decisions in foreign policy without conferring with others. Moreover, in relatively simple matters that do not require others to carry out the decision, such executives need not rely on bureaucratic organizations to implement the decisions.[14] Larger, more developed states that undertake major initiatives in foreign policy or face strong pressures from others, however, usually require complex consideration and planning as well as deliberation and debate that cannot be done by a single person. Such processes are sometimes referred to as **bureaucratic politics.** In the words of I. M. Destler, "[B]ureaucratic politics arises from two inescapable conditions: no one has the power, wisdom, or time to decide everything and officials differ on how issues should be resolved."[15] Despite this insight and other contributions to understanding certain aspects of foreign policy, a good deal of the literature belonging to the bureaucratic politics school of thought blurs some important distinctions.[16]

• POLITICIANS AND BUREAUCRATS

To avoid confusion between a larger political process that bears responsibility for decisions and the institutional processes that go on within governments that are mainly concerned with implementing those decisions, it is important to draw a clear distinction between **politicians** and **bureaucrats.** Politicians are generalists and amateurs, while bureaucrats are specialists and experts. Politicians have independent political bases, either powerful groups or electoral constituencies, that give them standing in the decision making process. As opposed to such foundations for their authority, bureaucrats derive their influence from their positions in hierarchical organizations and from their expertise. Bureaucrats do have an effect on policy making, for political officials rely on their specialized knowledge and careful analysis, but they do not bear responsibility for those policies. Politicians are valued for their judgment, not for their expertise. In the context of political struggle among opposed groups, politicians often seek and find compromises, either by fudging issues, making value trade-offs, or creating a solution that transcends the differences among interested parties.

Bureaucrats may demonstrate sensitivity to broader politics, but they remain insulated from any responsibility to the general public. On the other hand, politicians in democratic societies maintain electoral contact with broader constituencies, and those in authoritarian systems, with powerful groups upon which their leadership depends. Thus, both politicians and bureaucrats remain involved in the politics of making foreign policy, but they have distinct roles to play and bear significantly different responsibilities. In carrying out their political roles, politicians are brought into contact with **interest groups** and **public opinion.**

• • • • • • **Politicians and Bureaucrats**

Politicians:

- Amateurs and generalists
- Authority grounded in political base
- Bear responsibility for policies
- Valued for judgment
- Find compromises by:
  - Fudging issues
  - Making value trade-offs
  - Creating solutions that transcend differences
- Connected to broader politics:
  - Electoral contact in democracies
  - Ties to powerful groups in authoritarian systems

Bureaucrats:

- Experts and specialists
- Influence derived from positions in organizations
- Provide specialized knowledge and careful analysis
- Valued for expertise
- Find technical or substantive solutions to problems
- Insulated from broader politics, though may show sensitivity to it

Polities differ in terms of the size of the group that possesses authority to affect decisions and the width of the circle of those before whom issues are debated. For example, in a kingdom, the sovereign might seek the advice only of a few trusted advisors and would not be required to gain political or financial support from a legislature or to explain her decisions to any broader public. In a democracy, on the other hand, a circle of advisors in the executive branch or in a cabinet might confer and come to conclusions about a course of policy, but reference to a legislature and to elections would also have to be made from time to time. Such a political system can be thought to conduct a public debate about foreign policy that includes authorities, opinion elites, an attentive public, and a mass public.[17] With constitutional and legal authority, political leaders and bureaucrats discuss and debate foreign policies on an ongoing basis as well as consider and devise policies to meet specific challenges and opportunities. Much of this discussion occurs in confidential settings, but an important dimension is also public: in speeches, testimony in legislative hearings, news conferences, budgetary and other governmental documents, and official publications. Debate is joined by opinion elites, including opposition politicians and their supporters, important journalists, newspapers and other media, scholars and research centers, spokespersons for organizations, television commentators, and writers. To some extent, such a debate occurs directly among those engaged, but there also exists an attentive audience that listens to that debate: the readers of elite journals and newspapers, watchers of television programs carrying the debate, academic specialists, and others whose roles require them to be informed about foreign affairs.

▪▪▪▪▪▪ Public Opinion and Interest Groups in Democracies

- Public debate by authorities (politicians and bureaucrats) and opinion elites
- Listened to by attentive public, which has structured opinions
- Affected by:
  - Mass public, responding to events and debate by moods of support and withdrawal of support, and through elections
  - Interest groups, receiving information from government and passing it on to their members and providing support to government policy as well as recommending policies that affect their interests (more effective in low politics)

When government is unresponsive, organized groups and broader public can try to influence policy by street demonstrations, strikes, civil disobedience, and other direct actions.

Analysts vary in their estimates of what portion of the population in a democracy can reasonably be included in the attentive public, but it falls most likely within a range of over 5 percent to perhaps 20 percent in the United States.[18] Members of all of these components tend to have specific knowledge of at least some aspects of foreign policy and to possess structured opinions on important questions. Governmental elites provide information to organized groups in an attempt to engender support for their policies, and organized groups, in turn, attempt to influence policy by bringing their concerns to government. Organizations also pass on information to their members, and the members respond by giving or withholding their support. The larger, mass public operates more according to moods of supporting or withholding support for government policies in general terms. While in a democracy, the debates themselves bring influence to bear on official policy, the most important constraints are presented by the broad **electorate** that votes. In cases in which the government responds insufficiently to broad constituencies, opposition

groups may bring their concerns to the attention of the public by such direct means as demonstrations, and, sometimes, large segments of the public may join in supporting them.

▪▪▪▪▪▪ High Politics versus Low Politics

- HIGH POLITICS concerns political, diplomatic, and security issues
- LOW POLITICS concerns economic, cultural, and other issues.

Civil society tends to be more active and influential in low politics.

Involvement of nongovernmental groups tends to vary along two dimensions: issue area and level of development of civil society. In the areas of high politics, governments, if not monopolizing authority, take decisions on behalf of the polities that they head with minimal impact of civil society. On the other hand, low politics tends to hold implications and consequences for constituent groups in civil society. Thus, economic and other groups become more active in societies in which civil society forms an important component of the state. Where civil society has been repressed or has never fully developed, of course, governments are free to act without the influence of private groups. On the other hand, it needs to be pointed out that such states in which this phenomenon occurs are poorly formed, for they tend to be dominated by a single group, such as a class of landlords or an ideologically driven political party that itself has come to dominate a state apparatus on behalf of that group that can be no more than a part of civil society. In conducting arms control negotiations in the 1970s, a matter of high politics, both the Soviet and American governments made decisions with little constraint emanating from civil society. In contrast, both countries simultaneously negotiated trade and cultural agreements, concerns of low politics. On the Soviet side, without a highly developed civil society, these negotiations paralleled those dealing with arms control. With a full civil society, on the other hand, in the United States, the government was importantly affected by agricultural and consumer groups, business groups, presidential politics, and ethnic groups.[19]

Activities in opposition to unresponsive governments also occur in nondemocratic political systems. Street demonstrations, labor strikes, and even guerrilla wars provide outlets for dissatisfied citizens and groups. Although such activities more often than not are directed against internal political arrangements and practices, they also sometimes involve foreign policy issues or include demands for autonomy, which entails such international dimensions as intervention or recognition by other states.

Whatever political arrangements prevail in a country, the effective conduct of foreign policy requires leadership to achieve three things: making decisions, mobilizing resources and political support, and implementation. Except in the most terror-based polities, leadership occurs primarily through persuasion and "building support among those who have power to affect the outcome."[20] A president or prime minister, for example, needs to convince others to support her decision, and often this entails some compromise on details or at the margins. Occasionally, other powerful politicians can extract greater compromises. In an electoral process, political leaders need to remain sensitive to the electorate, but they also need to generate support by articulating their goals and inspiring their followers to support them. Mobilizing labor and material resources and implementation also require leadership, though of a more managerial than inspirational kind.

These functions of leadership are exercised by individuals who have the intelligence and skills to decide, command, persuade, inspire, compromise, judge, and manage. Shrewdness, cunning, ruthlessness, calculation, determination, energy, and perseverance are other qualities of leaders that have an impact on their effectiveness. Aside from the international and domestic political constraints that operate on individual leaders, the constraints of value complexity and uncertainty also affect rational decision making.[21] Value complexity means that competing values and interests are involved in a single issue. For example, in facing a disastrous human rights situation in HAITI and an exodus by boat of Haitian refugees in the early 1990s, the United States government wanted to protect human rights and restore an elected president who had been overthrown in a coup in September 1991 on the one hand and to avoid taking refugees in the face of substantial internal political pressures to slow down immigration on the other. In the face of the value complexity, the Clinton administration, in particular, floundered by shifting its policy from one position to another. Uncertainty means that either information about a specific situation or the availability of general knowledge is inadequate. One of the aspects of the end of the Cold War was the choice made in Russia and other Eastern European countries to transform their command economies to economies based on market principles. Inasmuch as such transformations had never before been done, there was no general knowledge available. Nevertheless, the United States and other capitalist countries were placed in a position of providing assistance to facilitate the transitions, making the best guesses they could in pursuing that course of action.

In addition to these constraints, individual leaders are also affected by their conscious beliefs and by biological and psychological variables.[22] Strong commitments to such beliefs as capitalism or socialism or Islam affect the way that leaders respond to events. In addition, certain physical disabilities or even medications affect behaviors, and psychological phenomena such as stress may affect behavior.[23] Personality characteristics, such as propensity to take risks and chronic suspiciousness, very likely also make a difference in the way individual leaders behave.[24] There is an extensive literature that brings psychological knowledge to bear on foreign policy decision making, but such knowledge has never been placed in the context of explaining state behavior in foreign policy as part of a general analysis that examines the array of constraints and variables that bear on the topic.[25]

Many writers have accepted de Tocqueville's famous formulation that democracies do not fare so well as authoritarian governments in the conduct of foreign policy. The astute French observer of American democracy wrote:

Foreign policies demand scarcely any of those qualities which are peculiar to a democracy . . . [A] democracy can only with great difficulty regulate the details of an important undertaking, persevere in a fixed design, and work out its execution in spite of serious obstacles. It cannot combine its measures with secrecy or await their consequences with patience.[26]

Standing in stark contrast to this view, Waltz concluded his study of the foreign policies of two leading democracies with an observation highly favorable to popular governments as compared to authoritarian ones. He wrote:

Disagreement about ends openly expressed in democratic states may cause some opportunities for gaining national advantage to be missed. But the running of risks foolishly is then also impeded. Democracies less often enjoy the brilliant success that bold acts secretly prepared and ruthlessly executed may bring. With the ground of action more thoroughly prepared and the content of policy more widely debated, they may, however, suffer fewer resounding failures. Coherent policy, executed with a nice combination of verve, is difficult to achieve in any political system, but no more so for democratic states than for others.[27]

So far, the discussion has examined the elements of domestic arrangements and politics as they affect the formulation and carrying out of foreign policy, but foreign policy also has a reverse effect on domestic politics. Particularly, foreign policy activities have the effect of bolstering the authority, standing, and popularity of chief executives. In part, the authority of a chief executive is bolstered at home because she symbolizes the state in her conferences with other leaders and in representations to other states. When their leader is adulated by foreigners, citizens bask in the reflected glory. Additionally, ordinary citizens place their hopes and fears in the hands of the chief executive in times of crisis, rallying to her support because they realize that she holds their fate in her hands. The BAY OF PIGS invasion in 1961 involved a force of United States-backed Cuban exiles that was utterly defeated by the Cuban armed forces. Despite this episode's constituting one of the few examples of utter failure in the history of American foreign policy, President John F. Kennedy's approval rating in public opinion polls rose substantially. Finally, chief executives can use foreign policy to bolster their popularity at home or to deflect the attention of their people from unsatisfactory conditions. These two motivations appear to have characterized, respectively, the leaders of Britain and Argentina in the MALVINAS/FALKLANDS WAR in 1982. Faced with deteriorating political and economic conditions in Argentina, the generals heading the government mounted an invasion of the British territory to enforce their country's longstanding claim to the islands. Prime Minister Margaret Thatcher's popularity rose during the war, her personal gains in public opinion polling showing greater strength than her Conservative Party's increase.[28]

Although the politics of foreign policy making and implementation shape the directions of a state's action in the international arena, the underlying strength of the state has greater determinative effect on available choices and the probability for success of a country's external undertakings.

Capacity

The most fundamental limit on foreign policy choice is the **capacity** of the state, which means its ability to achieve its goals. Underlying capacity are the material and human resources that can be mobilized into means of implementation. From the point of view of systemic analysis, the distribution of capabilities across the units forms a crucial component of the definition of the system's structure. In examining that distribution, the most germane analysis treated aggregate capabilities. When looked at from the perspective of foreign policy analysis, however, it makes more sense to disaggregate capabilities, for the primary concern aims at understanding choice in the context of constraints and opportunities. Thus, specific capabilities need to be understood in relationship to particular objectives and goals.

For example, important components of capabilities are size and topographical features of territory. A state with an expansive territory generally enjoys an advantage in relationship to one possessing only a small geographical area. When RUSSIA (later the Soviet Union) was invaded by France in 1812 and Germany in 1941, the expanse of territory combined with a severe climate proved an important asset in repelling the invasions and protecting autonomy. On the other hand, maintaining an integrated state in such a vast territory, with diverse ethnic and national groups inhabiting it, may prove more difficult than conserving cohesion in a smaller state. A state with a sophisticated banking system may aspire to exert its influence outside its boundaries, whereas as small state that falls into dependency on the banks of another country may find it difficult simply to achieve autonomy, and its decision makers cannot even consider reaching outside by financial means to influence other countries.

Capabilities do tend to go together, so it becomes possible to make some broad comparisons in some circumstances, but the exceptions are so common that the prudent analyst always exhibits caution in relating capabilities to objectives. Consider two illustrations: as a small island, Britain climbed to become the world's leading power for well over a century, and Israel's tiny territory and population of 3 million survived in a sea of 80 million hostile Arab neighbors for several decades.

Standard lists of capabilities include territorial size and topography, natural resources, size and training of population, industrial base, size and quality of military personnel and equipment, political cohesion, and quality of leadership.[29] States that have accumulated great capabilities do not ordinarily need to concern themselves with preserving their autonomy and they can choose to extend their influence abroad, whereas small and weak states constantly struggle to preserve their autonomy and to work toward its achievement in the first place.

Sometimes small states in particular circumstances can be effective in influencing their international environments, but they cannot do so in general. When in the CYPRUS crisis of 1964 the United States sought to have the issue handled within NATO and the government of Cyprus preferred the arena of the United Nations, the small state prevailed on this issue. However, in July 1974, it was invaded by its larger neighbor, Turkey, in response to a coup led by Greek officers. Unusual circumstances did allow Cyprus external influence on a limited issue, but the more profound truth in the situation remains Cyprus' loss of and inability to regain its autonomy.[30]

States strive to increase their capabilities by both their own economic development efforts and the acquisition of components from other countries. Successful endeavors along these lines lead to the achievement of such goals as maintaining position and preserving autonomy. In some circumstances—wartime or other stressful situations are examples—governments extract resources to mobilize more capabilities than is normal for state purposes. Drawing down a fund of capabilities and expending them in a war or other emergency leads to loss of position, although it may preserve autonomy. In both world wars in the twentieth century, Britain reduced its capabilities while preserving its autonomy.

Sometimes, states buy technology, equipment, and manpower from other states to build up their capabilities. As proved to be the case in Iraq's resort to this strategy, it is inferior to the development of one's own state and to those states that developed the capabilities in the first place. On occasion, a country conquers territory to add resources to its own. If successful, as in the case of the United States' conquest of two-fifths of Mexico in 1848, the state's international position may be enhanced. On the other hand, repulsion through the operation of a balance of power, as in the case of Japan in 1945, may result in a loss of position and autonomy. Because every state seeks to maintain and enhance its position, however, successful states need to strive to increase their capabilities in order to preserve and enhance their possibilities for choice.

Interactions and Consequences

Chapter 11 will treat interactions at length and systematically, but here it needs to be mentioned that,

by its nature, foreign policy deals with interactions with other states. Even when the value sought is preservation of autonomy and the actions required lie for the most part within the realm of the state itself, the value and the actions exist in relationship to other states. Actions may come in the choice to resist others' demands, but seldom, if ever, can a state simply remain alone. Closing its borders and cutting off commerce with other states does not necessarily lead to isolation, for even domestic events invite foreign pressures. MYANMAR, formerly Burma, for example, chose isolation for a long period beginning in 1962. Nevertheless, opposition groups within the country resisted the military government's policy and sought outside assistance. Communist guerrilla groups received arms from China for several years, although China switched its policy to support for the government and began military deliveries to the ruling regime in 1990. The political opposition that was repressed found support from groups in the United States and other countries acting on behalf of human rights. For example, Aung San Suu Kyi, a leading dissident, won a Nobel Prize in 1991 for her efforts on behalf of democracy in Myanmar, even while under house arrest by the military government. Aung was released from her confinement in 1995.[31]

Interactions become even more apparent when states seek to increase their autonomy against states that have penetrated them, as PANAMA did under General Omar Torrijos in his campaign to gain control over the Panama Canal and its adjacent territory that were controlled by the United States. Successful conclusion of the Panama Canal Treaties in the late 1970s came only after considerable political struggle with members of the United States Senate and groups devoted to retaining the canal.

●●●●●● **Foreign Policy Is Always Interactional**

- To preserve autonomy against other states
- To acquire autonomy from other states
- To seek influence with other states

The interactional quality necessarily involved in foreign policy becomes obvious in those cases in which a state tries to affect the international system or the behaviors of other states, for the exercise of influence entails action by others. Moreover, those actions in response to one state's demands present new information and/or conditions requiring further choices and responses on the part of the initiating state. America's frequent pressures against China because of its human rights violations provoke responses that vary from diplomatic reprisals to the arrest of Chinese dissidents.

Following the implementation of policies and the interactions of others, foreign policy actions have consequences. Those may be direct in the sense that a goal may have been achieved or, at least, a compromise may have been reached. Panama demanded control of the canal, and it will have achieved that goal at the end of 1999. Consequences may also be indirect as costs or externalities of the policy action. For example, the British-French-Israeli invasion of Egypt in 1956 during the Suez crisis involved many casualties of combatants, ancillary deaths of civilians, and physical destruction of shipping in the Suez Canal. In addition to direct and indirect consequences of foreign policy actions, there may be unintended consequences. For example, the Suez crisis produced a new capacity of the United Nations to mount peacekeeping operations on a scale that had not before been imagined: for the first time, the UN placed lightly armed peacekeepers between antagonistic states to facilitate the withdrawal of invading Israeli troops from Egypt and to supervise a separation of armed forces.

The founding of the state of ISRAEL provides a particularly dazzling example of an unintended consequence. None of the major powers that fought in World War II intended that a Jewish state should be formed. The Nazi regime in Germany aspired completely to wipe out the Jews and went quite far toward achieving that aspiration by putting to death some 6 million Jews in the Holocaust. Germany's enemies—the United States, the Soviet Union, and Britain—fought to oppose its domination of Europe and to bring down the Nazi regime, not to determine the future either of the Jews or of the Middle East. Despite the absence of intentions, Israel began as a state in 1948, caused in part by the Nazi policy of extermination and supported by states whose sympathy was aroused by that policy as well as by determined Jews who believed that a Jewish homeland would provide the means of avoiding the possibility of another Holocaust.

Unintended consequences are also demonstrated in the 1948–1949 BERLIN BLOCKADE and airlift. In response to a currency reform that the Western countries effected in their zones of occupation, the Soviet Union imposed a blockade of all surface routes between the western zones and the city of Berlin, located about 110 miles inside the Soviet

occupation zone. To combat that obstruction, the United States mounted an airlift that brought supplies of food, medicine, and coal to Berlin. When the dispute was finally settled through negotiations in 1949, not only had the Western plans advanced to the point of creating the state of West Germany (Federal Republic Germany), but also the hatred remaining from World War II between the defeated Germans and their Western conquerors had dissipated. It was replaced by admiration that eventually included both friendship and alliance. Neither the Soviets nor the Americans had intended such consequences.

As this discussion has emphasized, many variables affect foreign policy. These have been grouped in a limited number of categories, but it has proven impossible, despite substantial efforts by many scholars, to find any relatively simple and scientific means of explaining foreign policy. Insight into the ways in which the diverse elements discussed operate in foreign policy can perhaps best be achieved through case studies that illustrate some of the general points that have been made.

United States and Central America in the 1980s

For a number of years prior to the end of the 1970s, the Soviet Union and the United States had made attempts to reduce tensions in their relationship. Despite those efforts, the United States remained adamantly opposed to the extension of Soviet influence, by either direct intervention or offering advice to Communist movements and governments. From the mid-1970s onward, the Soviet Union had become unusually active in Africa. It supplied military equipment and advice to Ethiopia during its war with Somalia, and it helped the Marxist MPLA (Popular Movement for the Liberation of Angola) government of Angola in its civil war against a group called UNITA (National Union for the Total Independence of Angola). Additionally, Moscow's ally Cuba had also dispatched its troops to these areas.

Then, two other events in 1979 provided other critical ingredients in the international context that greatly affected the views of American officials. In one of these, the Soviet Union sent troops into Afghanistan to prop up a Marxist government that was under attack by guerrilla forces. This action represented a departure for Soviet foreign policy by deploying its own troops in large numbers in an area

■ **Soviet Union in Africa, Afghanistan, and Nicaragua**

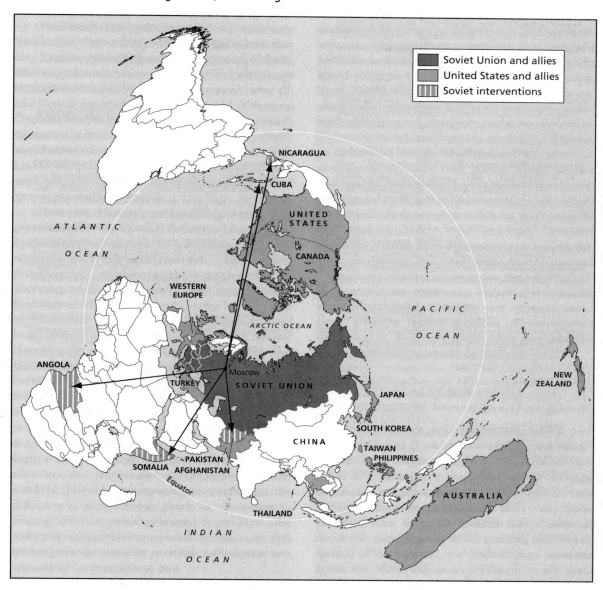

in which they had not previously operated, and it frightened and angered many Americans who regarded the Soviet invasion as a challenge that needed to be countered. The second event in 1979 was the triumph of the Sandinista National Liberation Front (FSLN) and its allies in Nicaragua that included the overthrow of dictator Anastasio Somoza and his government. Shortly before that triumph and immediately afterward, the United States attempted to prevent the FSLN from coming to power by negotiating to substitute a non-Marxist coalition as the

rulers of Nicaragua. Nonetheless, President Jimmy Carter did extend economic assistance to the new government to help in rebuilding the war-torn country. At the same time, agitation for reform and restructuring in nearby El Salvador had been met with repression by the military government, and an armed opposition under the umbrella organization Farabundo Marti Front for National Liberation (FMLN) began a guerrilla war. Other events, too, made many Americans sense that they lived in a hostile world that could no longer be bent to the will of the United

States. A second oil crisis that led to a doubling of prices occurred in 1979 with the triumph of Ayatollah Ruhollah Khomeini in Iran; and a number of Americans were taken hostage when crowds stormed the American embassy in Teheran. Less traumatic but nonetheless contributing to the sense that the United States did not win every conflict was a bruising battle in the U.S. Senate over the controversial Panama Canal treaties, although in the end that body did give its consent to them.

The 1980 presidential election brought to a conclusion a broad debate that had been going on in the United States for a decade. That debate pitted those who believed that the world had changed, requiring the United States to adapt to the changes, against those who believed that the country had simply lost its will to shape the international system according to its own desires. With the election of Ronald Reagan, the latter side not only triumphed in the debate but formed the government that was determined to put its beliefs into practice. One who chose the first field of battle was Secretary of State Alexander Haig.

He believed that the place to take a stand was El Salvador, where the FMLN presented an important armed challenge to the government of the country. Throughout the 1980s, the United States extended to El Salvador exceptionally large amounts of financial assistance to keep its economy going in the face of the destruction caused by the war. In addition, the United States provided military equipment and training to the Salvadoran army, and Washington lent its support to José Napoleón Duarte and Alfredo Cristiani, the presidents during the war years. Within a short time, however, the focus of American policy shifted from El Salvador to Nicaragua and, thereby, to all of Central America. That policy was driven by the "Reagan doctrine," which strove not simply to contain the Soviet Union and communism but to defeat and oust any government with a Marxist bent that was friendly with the Soviet Union. In addition to a complex strategy that involved military, diplomatic, and economic activities that drew in several countries, the policy also included a clandestine component and illegal activities. It also engendered a tumultuous politics at home that included significant deception by the White House and others in the executive branch.

Although El Salvador and Nicaragua are not contiguous, the thread that linked them was the American claim that the newly installed Nicaraguan government was supplying arms to the Salvadoran guerrillas. This claim provided the rationale for the United States to impose economic sanctions against Nicaragua and to withdraw its Agency for International Development mission—the agency that administered financial assistance—from that country. In addition, the United States found a tool to use in actually conducting a war against Nicaragua, although it never broke diplomatic relations with the Managua government. That implement was a counterrevolutionary force called the contras.

This military force—supplied, guided, and assisted by the United States—grew out of two sources of manpower and leadership. During the dictatorship, one of the family Somoza's bases of power was the National Guard, and this combined army and police force earned a reputation for brutality during the civil war in 1978 and 1979 by bombing civilian population centers. With the triumph of the revolution, many Guard officers and men escaped to neighboring Honduras, where they were organized by the United States to reenter Nicaragua and conduct hostile actions in the northern part of the country. A second source of recruitment for the contras was the young men of the peasantry in northern Nicaragua. Many of them joined the contras because they resented arrogant Sandinista officials and government policies that favored city dwellers against rural people, both of which coerced individual farmers into government-sponsored cooperatives. The United States gained the toleration of the Honduran government for the counterrevolutionary force's presence in its territory through large-scale economic and military assistance to Tegucigalpa. Although the contras fought only on Nicaraguan soil, they trained and encamped, with their families, in Honduras.

The war that the United States conducted against Nicaragua did not rely solely on the contras, for the Americans themselves actively employed a number of techniques of "low intensity warfare." In conjunction with the Honduran armed forces, United States military forces conducted for several years almost continuous training exercises that were designed to intimidate Nicaragua and required the government to prepare for an invasion. Naval maneuvers in the waters near Nicaragua applied additional pressure. Furthermore, radio broadcasts to Nicaragua carried a propaganda campaign aimed at turning the people of the country against their government. This strategy of intimidation formed the open part of policy that included, as well, a covert dimension. Using the Central Intelligence Agency as the operating instrument, the United States con-

United States in Central America

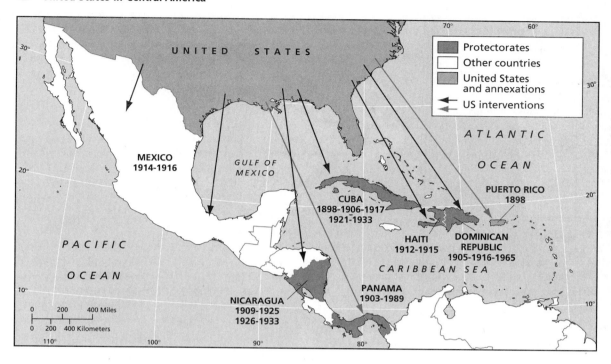

tracted to fly supplies into Nicaragua for the contra forces until a supply plane was shot down in 1986. Moreover, the CIA directly entered the fighting by mining Nicaraguan harbors in January 1984. Discovery of this action led to Nicaragua's taking its case to the International Court of Justice and eventually finding vindication there in the court's verdict that the United States had violated international law. The CIA had also operated clandestinely on Costa Rican territory, building an airfield for contra forces operating there. Although the United States had attempted to draw Guatemala into its Central American policy, that country resisted on the grounds that, despite a common opposition to communism, Guatemala did not share the United States' interest in intimidating Nicaragua and had no reason to be drawn into the conflict as a pawn of American foreign policy. Nevertheless, the United States pursued a comprehensive policy of intimidation of Nicaragua and support to the government of El Salvador against the FMLN that involved in one way or another two other countries, Honduras and Costa Rica.

However, the policy was strongly opposed by important segments of American society, and Congress passed legislation to inhibit the Reagan administration's determination to conduct its war in

Central America. The Boland amendment forbade the use of any funds available to American intelligence agencies to support any military or paramilitary activities in Nicaragua. Despite that prohibition, a Marine colonel, Oliver North, on temporary assignment to the staff of the National Security Council in the White House, ran a covert operation termed "the Enterprise" that channeled funds to the contras. He had the support of National Security Council Advisors Robert McFarlane and John Poindexter as well as of President Reagan. One source of funds was voluntary contributions from wealthy individuals who met with Reagan and from whom afterwards North solicited money. Another source came from other governments that were asked to contribute to this American foreign policy undertaking. Yet another source came from an equally covert operation in which arms were clandestinely sold by the United States to Iran in exchange for Iranian government assistance in securing the release of some American hostages being held by terrorist organizations in Lebanon. The sales violated a declared policy of Reagan that his administration would never bargain for the release of the hostages. To compound that hypocrisy, North diverted some of the "profits" from these arms sales to the contras, thus linking the two illegal, covert undertakings. When knowledge of these activities became public in November 1986, covert funding of the contras came to an end. By that time, Congress relented and approved funds to pay for nonlethal assistance to the contras to be administered under careful supervision. American politics continued in a turmoil over Central American policy and came to a head in 1987 when, following a scene in which Speaker of the House of Representatives Jim Wright and President Reagan publicly struggled to define the terms of United States policy toward Central America, the two men came to an agreement. They gave their support to an initiative of the presidents of the Central American countries that had been introduced by President Oscar Arias of Costa Rica and presented at a meeting called by President Marco Vinicio Cerezo of Guatemala in the city of Esquipulas.

The war of the United States in the 1980s against Nicaragua affected all of the Central American countries and threatened to engulf them. Other countries had tried to affect the situation but without overall success. In August 1981, France and Mexico declared their recognition of the FMLN as a legitimate party to negotiations in hopes of finding a peaceful end to the Salvadoran conflict. Nicaragua itself had engaged in a quite creative diplomacy, turning to the United Nations and to many other countries for support. In the context of divided American society, Nicaragua was able to amplify its voice in Congress through close contacts with sympathetic congressional representatives and "support groups" throughout the country. The Sandinistas also encouraged Americans to travel to Nicaragua to see the situation for themselves, rather than learning about it only through the filter of hostile United States government officials. To try to bring peace to the troubled region, a group of neighboring countries—Colombia, Mexico, Panama, and Venezuela—organized under the name "Contadora group," sought to find a diplomatic solution. However, the "Contadora process" proved fruitless, and it was succeeded by the "Esquipulas process," in which the Central Americans themselves acted to wrest control of the destiny of their region from United States control.

Although in its preliminary formulation, the Esquipulas process aimed to exclude Nicaragua from its deliberations, the formula adopted in August 1987 gave support to existing governments, sought to bring about national reconciliation in each of the five countries, promoted regional cooperation, and institutionalized ongoing consultations among representatives of the participating countries to seek peace in the region. Implicitly, this formula sought to move the region in a different direction from that advocated by the United States. Important steps in the process included the Sapoá agreement between the Nicaraguan government and the contras in March 1988 to a cease-fire and the 1990 elections in Nicaragua that brought an opposition coalition under President Violeta Barrios de Chamorro to power. Negotiations with the contras led to an agreement for the contras to disband and return to Nicaragua for reintegration into the society.

Eventually, at the beginning of 1993, the government of El Salvador and the FMLN reached an agreement that was implemented in the ensuing months and years. In July 1994, a basic though not detailed agreement was reached between the government of Guatemala and the UNRG (National Guatemalan Revolutionary Unity), the coalition of small guerrilla groups that had been operating in that country since the early 1960s. When George Bush took office as president of the United States in 1989, he reoriented American policy toward Latin America to a more traditional balance in which the larger states received more attention and the smaller region of Central America took a place that was proportionate to its size and position.

This case illustrates the behavior of a superpower projecting its influence to shape part of its international environment. It also includes examples of small countries responding to superpower intrusion to protect their autonomy and to gain a measure of influence over the shape of politics within and among themselves. In addition, the case brings in the political process not just of decision making and bureaucratic politics but also of an executive-legislative struggle in a democracy and the shadowy aspect of politics exemplified in the underworld of the Iran and Contra affairs.[32]

The case study covering the longer time period of Germany's gaining of autonomy after its defeat in World War II and its successful quest for unification provides material that illustrates other aspects of foreign policy, including many features of constraints, opportunities, internal politics, and choices.

Germany's Quest for Autonomy and Unification

Following its defeat in 1945, Germany was occupied by the victorious powers—Britain, the Soviet Union, and the United States, with an occupation zone given to France as well. All had expected that, in time, a peace treaty would be signed with a united Germany, as had been customary at the end of previous wars. However, the bipolar structure of the international system produced the unintended consequence of dividing Germany into two separate states, the Federal Republic Germany and the People's Democratic Republic of Germany. The previous capital, Berlin, was located within the territory of East Germany; and it existed in the anomalous condition of being governed by a joint military *commandatura* of the occupying powers. In 1949, West Germany and East Germany were created as separate states, associated, respectively, with the United States and the Soviet Union.

Because of the enormity of the crimes of the Nazi regime, Germany sought to regain its position as a respected member of the society of states. The East German regime denied any responsibility for the actions of the Nazis. In contrast, West Germany worked to regain respect by a clearly Western orientation that involved full cooperation with its Western European partners and the United States. The European Community and the North Atlantic Treaty Organization provided the main institutions to accomplish the West German objective, but they are the result and instruments rather than the cause or process of West German foreign policy. Causes lay in the structure of the international system and the choices of both West Germany and of other states, especially France and the United States.

In the late 1940s, the United States and the Soviet Union disagreed on many issues, ranging from appropriate policies toward Eastern Europe to control of the atomic bomb. A series of negotiations to bring the Second World War to a formal end foundered on Germany. Facing the prospect of a slow economic recovery from the war in Europe and the attendant potential gains for Communist parties in Italy and France, the United States in 1947 offered Marshall Plan aid to the European countries. A condition attached to that assistance required the European countries to decide jointly how the funds were to be spent, and the Soviet Union and the Eastern European countries under its tutelage chose not to participate. In the following year, Canada and Britain approached Washington about the prospect of expanding the Brussels Pact, a defensive alliance of Western European countries, and the United States responded by leading in the formation in 1949 of NATO. These two actions by the United States

committed it to the prosperity and security of Western Europe. Inasmuch as the main security threat to Western Europe was posed by the Soviet Union, the American guarantee effectively solved the security problem for those countries. This condition allowed the Western Europeans to cooperate with one another without any concern for the relative gains accruing to any partner.

In that context, West Germany performed what became known as the "economic miracle," expanding its economy at an incredibly rapid rate that has been sustained over the course of some forty years to make the German economy the largest by far in Europe and third in the world. Given the historical background of German invasions of France in 1870, 1914, and 1940, the ordinary expectation would be that France would have been frightened by Germany's rapid economic growth. France did not become alarmed, however, not only because of the effects of the bipolar structure but also because of French policy itself.

The French produced the Schumann Plan that led to the creation of the European Coal and Steel Community (ECSC) in 1951. ECSC brought all aspects of the production and marketing, including labor law and relations, under the jurisdiction of an international commission with representatives from each of the six member countries—Belgium, France, Germany, Italy, Luxembourg, and Netherlands. At the center of this scheme were Germany and France, whose foreign policies dovetailed to produce the outcome. Recalling their humiliation by Germany, the French determined to gain control of German policy through a system of intergovernmental institutions that would provide scope for France significantly to affect that policy. By taking part in the ECSC, France acquired the means of directly participating in the formulation of policies germane to German coal and steel production. Through its cooperation in the scheme, West Germany demonstrated its cooperation and goodwill, regaining the international respect that had been lost during the Nazi rule. Thus, the fitting of West German and French objectives in the context of the postwar structure of the international system engendered the very successful development of Western European institutions and economic cooperation that has persevered and flourished to the 1990s. The narrative and analysis of the institutional developments will be taken up in Chapter 11.

German cooperation with the West also occurred in the area of security. In the face of Soviet

Germany between East and West

European Union
Commonwealth of Independent States

hostility that seemed more threatening with the Korean War, the Western allies united in NATO sought a means to rearm West Germany. France proposed a European Defense Community (EDC), modeled on ECSC, that would have brought the Germans under direct French influence. However, it was the French Parliament that defeated the EDC. Subsequently, in 1954, West Germany joined NATO. This action, incidentally, led the Soviet Union to form the Warsaw Treaty Organization as a response to German rearmament. Not only did West Germany cooperate as a member of the organization, but its territory also provided the main base for allied troops who were stationed there to deter a Soviet attack. Additionally, it supplied the second largest military force in NATO.

Having secured a fundamental position in Western Europe both as the richest country and as a major contributor to Western European security, West Germany then turned its attention to the East, with the long-term goal of unifying the two parts of Germany into a single country.

Although West Germany followed the Hallstein Doctrine of refusing to recognize any country other than the Soviet Union that also recognized East Germany, Chancellor Konrad Adenauer went to Moscow in 1954 to consolidate diplomatic relations with the Soviet Union. In Timothy Garten Ash's interpretation, this gesture marked the first move in *ostpolitik*,[33] although that designation came into usage only in 1969. Meanwhile, the West German government claimed to speak for all Germans and continued to build and consolidate Western European institutions, with the European Economic Community and the European Atomic Energy Community being established in 1957. Furthermore, after Charles DeGaulle became president of France, he and Chancellor Adenauer sought to consolidate a special French-German relationship through a series of meetings beginning in 1958 and culminating in the Elysee Treaty in 1963, which provided for collaboration on various matters.

Groundwork for the more dramatic turn toward the East in the detente called *ostpolitik* occurred in West German domestic politics in the 1960s. During the entire postwar period, German politics had been dominated by the Christian Democratic Union/Christian Social Union (CDU/CSU), with the Socialists (Socialist Democratic Workers' Party/SPD) in opposition. After determining to moderate their ideological position in 1959 by moving away from Marxism toward democratic socialism, however, the Socialists began gaining electoral strength. In December 1966, they joined in a "grand coalition" with the Christian Democrats. Taking the portfolio of foreign minister in the grand coalition was the former mayor of West Berlin Willy Brandt. Under his leadership, the West German government inaugurated *ostpolitik*, a sustained policy to develop relations with East Germany and the other countries of Eastern Europe. Finally, in 1969, the Socialists formed the government, with Brandt as chancellor, and they continued the eastern-looking foreign policy by developing relations with East Germany. The two countries signed a Basic Treaty of 1972 that allowed family contacts across the border and established some economic an cultural relations between them. Tensions reached a still lower level when West Germany and the Soviet Union signed a nonaggression treaty in August 1970. West Germany recog-

nized the Oder-Neisse line as the border between East Germany and Poland and abandoned claims to the Sudetenland, that part of Czechoslovakia that had been seized by Germany in 1938. Although the policy of *ostpolitik* emanated from Germany, the detente policy of the United States and the Soviet Union provided a supportive context for it. Moreover, the occupying powers in 1971 made their first formal agreement on managing Berlin, a step that ensured that no further crises such as had arisen in the late 1940s and late 1950s to 1961 would occur again.

Western European, American, and Soviet detente policies culminated in the Helsinki accords of 1975. These agreements embodied the basic objectives of the parties. Germans and other Western Europeans aimed at greater contacts across the divide between East and West, with increased economic, cultural, and personal exchanges. Concerned with stability and the maintenance of existing states, including East Germany, the Soviet Union sought recognition of existing state borders. The United States sought the expansion of human rights in the Eastern European countries. Embracing three "baskets," the Helsinki accords included provisions dealing with each of these areas of concern. From the West German perspective, the long-term goal of unification would be achieved through the accretion of contacts and in the context of an overall East-West detente. In 1975, no one imagined that unification would be achieved as early as 1991, but the deterioration of the Soviet Union and the disintegration of its empire in Eastern Europe proceeded inexorably beneath the surface of the more obvious renewal of the Cold War in the 1980s.

Change came quickly in 1989 and 1990. Soviet President Mikhail Gorbachev in October 1989 abjured the right of the Soviet Union forcibly to interfere in the Eastern European countries, and the police in East Germany did not use force to suppress demonstrators in Leipzig in November. East German citizens had been fleeing their country through Hungary, which opened its border with Austria in September. With this collapse of the old order in East Germany, Erich Honecker was succeeded by Egon Krenz, who was soon supplanted by another temporary leader. In November, the East German government allowed its people to drive to the West German border through Czechoslovakia, and it began to give them passports, enabling them legally to travel abroad and return. On November 9, 1989, the Berlin Wall fell, allowing East Germans to travel back and forth freely between East and West Germany. On the first of December, the provision of the East German constitution conferring a monopoly on the Communist Party was amended, and elections were held in March 1990, victory being won by Christian Democrats (a West German party) and allied parties, which amounted to an endorsement of unification. Chancellor Helmut Kohl had initiated talks with his East German counterparts in fall 1989. With Soviet endorsement, Kohl and his Foreign Minister Hans Dieter Genscher moved toward unification. Although it was a complicated negotiation, the two Germanies were effectively united on July 1, 1990, when West German currency was adopted in East Germany in a German economic and monetary union; formal unification was accomplished only later.

Inasmuch as a peace treaty between Germany and its opponents in World War II had never been signed, the victors retained interests in a German settlement. The United States extended its support to the West German drive for unification, but it was not until July 1990 that the Soviets accepted membership in NATO, with certain restrictions, for unified Germany. Despite initial French and British reticence to accept German unification, the powers agreed in Ottawa in February 1990 to a "2 + 4" formula within which to negotiate the terms of German unification. The formula enabled the two Germanies to negotiate the terms for unification, with the four occupying powers endorsing these arrangements. A Treaty on the Final Settlement with Respect to Germany was signed by the parties in Moscow in September 1990, completing all the terms for the unification of the country. Germany agreed with the Soviet Union to supply it with meat on concessional terms and to pay a substantial part of the costs of removing Soviet troops from German soil and providing them with housing when they returned to the Soviet Union. In return, the Soviets agreed to remove their troops from Germany within four years. Germany signed treaties with the Soviet Union and Poland. Finally, the Soviets handed over their ratification document for the 2 + 4 treaty on March 15, 1991.[34] All Soviet troops had left Germany by the end of 1994, and all foreign troops were withdrawn from Berlin by September of that year.

Formal unification marked the achievement of the long and sustained aspiration of West Germany to become one with the part of the country that had been ruled by the Communists in the Cold War. But that achievement only began the internal state forma-tion task of bringing the two parts of the country together, another long-term undertaking, and the external task of defining Germany's roles and orientation in foreign policy. In the mid-1990s, Germany remained embedded in the institutional arrangements of what was now called the European Union and of NATO. Hints of positions to come were shown by German leadership in recognizing Croatia's and Slovenia's independence in 1991 and in the country's first tentative steps in 1994 to deploy German military troops abroad. German military pilots, with an undetermined mission as part of NATO forces dealing with Bosnia, were dispatched to air bases in Italy in the summer 1995. Whatever the future might bring in German foreign policy, however, the country's unification remained grounded in the sustained policy of cooperation, first with the West and then with the East, that West Germany pursued from 1952 to 1991.

This case illustrates the regaining of autonomy by a country defeated in war and divided as a function of the structure of the international system. Despite the severe constraints, Germany had choices to pursue. These were shaped importantly by the internal politics of the country as well as by its remarkable economic growth. Also shown in the case is the sustained working toward an aspiration that no specific policy could be devised to achieve immediately. At the same time, the case provides an example of how the international environment can be shaped by a dedicated orientation of cooperation. Finally, the case notes how, when the international environment changed, the West German government took advantage in pursuing the goal of unification as soon as it proved to be a feasible goal. Lastly, the support of other countries also proved to be an important factor. In the cases of Britain and France, their postures proved malleable under pressure from the United States. Soviet indulgence of German unification became acceptance of German membership in NATO under the influence of the deft exercise of German wealth to induce cooperation. In a final note, it needs to be stated that the masses of East Germans who fled their country and/or gave voice to their opposition to the Communist regime also played an important part in the way this story unfolded.

• IMPORTANT TERMS

bureaucratic politics	chance
bureaucrats	choices
capabilities	consequences
capacity	constraints

decision making
electorate
error
exert influence
formulation
implementation
interest groups
leadership
maintain position

means
objectives
political support
political systems
politicians
protect autonomy
public opinion
unintended
 consequences

STUDY QUESTIONS

1. Discuss various ways of conceiving foreign policy, and then provide a conceptualization of it that you think would be most useful for analysis.

2. In what ways is a state constrained by the international system? What are the appropriate ways for leaders to cope with or try to change those constraints?

3. What is the meaning of unintended consequences? What are their sources?

4. Do you think that statesmen and women always have choices available? Or do you feel that circumstances are sometimes so constraining that officials have no choice? Argue your view, bringing to bear both logic and evidence.

5. Which do you think is a more important attribute for a political leader: determination or willingness to accommodate? Give reasons and evidence for your position.

6. Which attributes of states have the greatest effect on foreign policy? How do those characteristics work to shape decisions and behavior?

7. Define and explain bureaucratic politics.

8. Explicate the role and importance of leadership in the conduct of foreign policy. Are there clear leadership qualities that one could identify in advance that would contribute more effectively than others to success in foreign affairs?

9. Do authoritarian states have great advantages over democratic polities in the formulation and implementation of foreign policy? Which characteristics have what effects?

10. What effects does foreign policy have on domestic politics?

11. How do capabilities affect foreign policy?

12. What systemic constraints and opportunities for choice differentiated the foreign policies of the United States in Central America in the 1980s and Germany's quest for unification in the post-World War II period? Did the leaders and people of the two states cope equally wisely and/or foolishly with their respective constraints and opportunities? If not, how do you account for greater wisdom and/or greater foolishness?

ENDNOTES

1. Iraqi transcript of U.S. Ambassador April Glaspie's interview with President Saddam Hussein, published in the *New York Times*, 23 September 1990, cited by Jean Edward Smith, *George Bush's War* (New York: Henry Holt and Company, 1992), p. 7.

2. This problem is analyzed at length by Robert Jervis in his *Perception and Misperception in International Politics*.

3. See Bull, *The Anarchical Society* and Stephen M. Walt, *The Origins of Alliances* (Ithaca, N.Y.: Cornell University Press, 1987).

4. Carl von Clausewitz, *On War* rev. ed., edited and translated by Michael Howard and Peter Paret (Princeton, N.J.: Princeton University Press, 1984).

5. See, for example, Harold Sprout and Margaret Sprout, *Foundations of International Politics* (Princeton, N.J.: D. Van Nostrand Company, 1962), and Michael Brecher, *The Foreign Policy System of Israel: Setting, Images, Process* (New Haven: Yale University Press, 1972).

6. Brecher, *The Foreign Policy System of Israel*, p. 5.

7. See Mohammad-Mahmoud Mohamedou, *State-Building and Regime Security: A Study of the Iraqi Leadership's Decisionmaking Process during the Second Gulf War* (Ph.D. diss., City University of New York, 1995).

8. Winston S. Churchill, first statement as prime minister to the House of Commons, May 13, 1940, cited in John Bartlett, *Familiar Quotations*, 15th ed. (Boston: Little, Brown, 1980), p. 743.

9. John Lewis Gaddis, *The United States and the Origins of the Cold War 1941–1947* (New York: Columbia University Press, 1972), pp. 8–10.

10. A useful analysis of what is involved in foreign policy making is Alexander L. George, *Bridging the Gap: Theory and Practice in Foreign Policy* (Washington, D.C.: U.S. Institute of Peace Research, 1993). See also Philip Zelikow, "Foreign Policy Engineering: From Theory to Practice and Back Again," *International Security* 18 (Spring 1994): 143–71, for a broad discussion of the components involved in foreign policy, including an extensive bibliography.

11. See Sidney Verba, Richard A. Brody, Edwin B. Parker, Norman H. Nie, Nelson W. Polsby, Paul Ekman, and Gordon S. Black, "Public Opinion and the War in Vietnam," *American Political Science Review* 61 (June 1967): 317–33.

12. See Samuel Flagg Bemis, *A Diplomatic History of the United States*, 4th ed. (New York: Holt, Rinehart and Winston, 1955), chapter 43.

13. See Gar Alperovitz, *Atomic Diplomacy: Hiroshima and Potsdam* (New York: Simon and Schuster, 1965).

14. See Donatus St. Aimee, *The Foreign Policy of Very Small States in the Caribbean* (Ph.D. diss., City University of New York, 1996).

15. I. M. Destler, *Presidents, Bureaucrats, and Foreign Policy: The Politics of Organizational Reform* (Princeton, N.J.: Princeton University Press, 1974), p. 52.

16. For a criticism of this approach that also reviews much of its literature, see Robert Art, "Bureaucratic Politics and American Foreign Policy—A Critique," *Policy Sciences* 4 (1973): 467–90.

17. This scheme and the ensuing discussion draws on the analysis of Gabriel Almond, *The American People and Foreign Policy* (New York: Harcourt, Brace, 1950).

18. See Almond, *The American People and Foreign Policy.* Also see Charles W. Kegley, Jr., and Eugene R. Wittkopf, *American Foreign Policy: Pattern and Process* (New York: St. Martin's Press, 1979), p. 229, and the sources that they cite.

19. For a good treatment of the Jackson-Vanik amendment to the 1974 Trade Act that constituted the main legislative result of the events in question, see Paula Stern, *Water's Edge: Domestic Politics and the Making of American Foreign Policy* (Westport, Conn.: Greenwood Press, 1979).

20. Art, "Bureaucratic Politics—A Critique."

21. See Alexander L. George, "Adapting to Constraints on Rational Decisionmaking," in Robert Art and Robert Jervis, eds., *International Politics: Enduring Concepts and Contemporary Issues*, 3d ed. (New York: HarperCollins Publishers, 1992).

22. Emphasis on conscious beliefs was placed by Alexander L. George in his article, "The 'Operational Code': A Neglected Approach to the Study of Political Leaders and Decision-Making," *International Studies Quarterly* 13 (1969): 190–222, where he distinguished between "philosophical beliefs" and "instrumental beliefs." A similar distinction among "world views," "principled beliefs," and "causal beliefs" is made by Goldstein and Keohane in their introductory essay to *Ideas and Foreign Policy: Beliefs, Institutions, and Political Change*, ed. by Judith Goldstein and Robert O. Keohane (Ithaca, N.Y.: Cornell University Press, 1993).

23. See Jervis, *Perception and Misperception in International Politics.*

24. See Margaret Hermann, "Effects of Personal Characteristics of Political Leaders on Foreign Policy," in *Why Nations Act: Theoretical Perspectives for Comparative Foreign Policy Studies*, ed. by Maurice A. East, Stephen A. Salmore, and Charles F. Hermann (Beverly Hills: Sage Publications, 1978).

25. See Alexander L. George, *Presidential Decisionmaking in Foreign Policy: The Effective Use of Information and Advice* (Boulder, Colo.: Westview Press, 1980). For a review of foreign policy analysis that includes selections discussing psychological approaches, see Laura Neack, Jeanne A. K. Hey, and Patrick J. Haney, *Foreign Policy Analysis: Continuity and Change in Its Second Generation* (Englewood Cliffs, N.J.: Prentice-Hall, 1995).

26. Alexis de Tocqueville, *Democracy in America* (New York: Vintage Books, 1959 [1835, 1840]), p. 243.

27. Kenneth N. Waltz, *Foreign Policy and Democratic Politics: The American and British Experience* (Boston: Little, Brown, 1967), p. 311.

28. See Helmut Norpoth, "The Falklands War and Government Popularity in Britain: Rally without Consequence or Surge without Decline?" *Electoral Studies* 6 (1987): 3–16.

29. For a good quality analysis of capabilities, see Klaus Knorr, *The Power of Nations* (New York: Basic Books, 1975).

30. For a broad review of the Cyprus situation, placed in the context of United States-Turkey relations, see Suha Bolukbasi, "The Johnson Letter Revisited," *Middle Eastern Studies* 29 (July 1993): 505–25.

31. A critical survey may be found in John B. Haseman, "Destruction of Democracy: The Tragic Case of Burma," *Asian Affairs: An American Review* 20 (Spring 1993): 17–26. Offering a balanced analysis of the situation is Robert H. Taylor, "Change in Burma: Political Demands and Military Power," *Asian Affairs: Journal of the Royal Society for Asian Affairs* 22 (June 1991): 131–41.

32. The best overall analysis of these activities is Draper's *A Very Thin Line.*

33. Timothy Garten Ash, *In Europe's Name: Germany and the Divided Continent* (New York: Random House, 1993), p. 50.

34. Many of the facts in this narrative are drawn from Timothy Garten Ash's account in Chapter 7, "German Unification," of his *In Europe's Name.*

CHAPTER 10

Instruments and Techniques of Interaction among States

The practice of any craft or profession requires appropriate tools and skills in their employment. The statesman draws on the capabilities of the state—diplomats and warriors, treasure and blood, his own imagination and the hopes or anger of his compatriots—and makes them serve state goals. This chapter describes the main instruments and techniques of diplomacy, economics, information, and military force. We also analyze the strengths and drawbacks of each, and we illustrate how each may be employed to serve state interests.

Introduction

By its nature foreign policy directs actions at other countries, and they in turn respond. Thus, interactions using a variety of techniques and means occur between and among states in sequences in which one state responds to the actions of another state and vice versa. These interactions range from peaceful and friendly on the one hand to forceful and hostile on the other. Actions may offer assistance and reassurance, or, they may make demands and threats. Reactions may resist, reinforce, comply with, or acquiesce in the components involved in initiatives of other states. Although authorities responsible for foreign policy seek to anticipate how other states are likely to respond to their undertakings, they are frequently mistaken in their calculations, and, therefore, their initiatives evoke reactions that lead to unintended consequences.

To examine the variety of activities involved in the conduct of foreign policy and to illuminate its interactive nature, in this chapter the instruments and techniques of foreign policy activity are descriptively analyzed and illustrated with anecdotal and case study material. This is followed in the next

chapter by the delineation of the patterns of interaction resulting from discrete actions.

The array of means and techniques used in the conduct of foreign policy can hardly be exhausted in any survey, for innovations in both technology and political style occur continuously. Nevertheless, the instruments that states employ in promoting their objectives in dealing with other states are treated below in four categories: 1) diplomacy, 2) economics, 3) information, and 4) military force.[1] Various types of instruments will be surveyed in each category, and each will be treated in the context of interactions—the play of initiative and response between countries. Illustrative case materials will be employed to demonstrate how the instruments of foreign policy are used in practice.

Diplomacy

Traditionally, **diplomacy** meant the conduct of relations between states through representatives using communication and negotiation on a bilateral basis.[2] With an ancient tradition dating to practice in India, China, and Egypt, diplomacy achieved a formalized method developed by the Greeks, who also created the concept of immunity for diplomatic personnel. After a decline in the Middle Ages and a resurgence in the Renaissance, diplomacy reached its highest period of development in the nation-state system, and rules of precedent and procedure were formalized at the Congress of Vienna in 1815. As the world changed, effects were felt in diplomacy.

Settled tasks of the diplomat within the tradition included **representation** of his sovereign or state in the capital of the country to which he was accredited. A diplomat's participation in ceremonies and his presence in the capital symbolized his government's interest in international affairs. As an instructed agent, the traditional diplomat communicated his government's views to the host government, and he engaged in **negotiations** with that government's representatives on matters of mutual concern. This second diplomatic task always involved the promotion of his own country's interests and viewpoint, and sometimes it culminated in the conclusion of agreements. A third traditional task was **intelligence gathering** and **reporting.** As he worked in a capital, the diplomat observed all that he could about the personalities, affairs, intentions, and policies of the host state impinging on matters of concern to his own government and conveyed that information back home, where it helped to influence the formulation of policy.

At the conclusion of World War I, President Woodrow Wilson of the United States launched an attack on traditional diplomacy, claiming that its duplicity and secrecy had contributed to the outbreak of the war and urging that the old system be replaced by a new one that would embody openness, multilateral contacts, and international institutions. As a result of that initiative as well as of other developments, new techniques, institutions, and styles were introduced. Not only was America's crusading, moralistic style inserted into diplomatic practice, but also Russia's crude, histrionic style entered the diplomatic repertoire. The latter hit its low point in 1960 when Premier Nikita Khrushchev, in a United Nations General Assembly meeting, disrupted British Prime Minister Harold Macmillan's address with shouts and then pounded his table with his shoe during the applause.

The primary institutional change occurred with the introduction of **multilateral conferences.** Although ambassadors are still posted to state capitals, with increasing frequency in the twentieth century diplomats have gathered at various places in the world

to address a variety of topics and issues. Some of these conferences occur in a permanent setting, such as the variety of United Nations organs and committees that meet in New York, Geneva, Nairobi, and other centers where international agencies are permanently housed. Other multilateral encounters take place on an ad hoc basis. Recent examples include the International Conference on Development and the Environment in Rio de Janeiro in June 1992, the Population Conference in Cairo in September 1994, and the Conference on Women in Beijing in September 1995.

A variety of new methods of diplomacy have been introduced into international relations in response to three developments. Improvements in communications have not just increased the speed with which talk and other forms of communication can be carried on but also have made it much easier for high-level officials to travel and take personal charge of selected diplomatic affairs. Furthermore, the number of states has increased tremendously. In 1945, there were 51 original members of the United Nations, whereas in 1995, a total of 185 states sent delegates to that organization. The proliferation of states has also brought into the circle of diplomatic communications a range of different values that supplement those growing out of the European and North American traditions. A third development that has greatly expanded the diplomatic agenda is the increase in the substance of affairs that states now treat in their relations. Such matters as economic development, trade, human rights, population policy, and environmental protection have been added to the concerns that states take up as matters of interest. These low politics issues supplement the traditional matters included in the high politics of political, security and prestige considerations.

Because low politics matters are often addressed in multilateral conferences in discrete issue areas, as in the environmental, population, and women's conferences mentioned above, some analysts perceive a shift in the way that international politics processes occur.[3] They argue that under conditions of complex interdependence, military force has little efficacy; issues are not hierarchically organized and dominated by high politics; and multiple channels exist for handling international affairs. These conceptual and theoretical arguments were designed to help understand the increased complexity and the new techniques of international politics in the late twentieth century; to some extent, they do help to organize thinking about new methods and new agenda items. On the other hand, two aspects of diplomacy and the new methods draw attention to some underlying continuities in diplomacy and international interactions.

■────────────────────────────
•••••• Traditional and New Diplomacy

Traditional diplomacy:

- Bilateral
- Representation
- Negotiation
- Information gathering and reporting
- Coordination of varied activities

New diplomacy:

- Multilateral
- Debate
- Voting and consensus
- Expanded agenda
- Segmentation by issue area

By its nature, diplomacy remains a technique of secret negotiations in which the participants attempt to reach agreement on a matter of shared interest or concern. Secrecy is essential to allow the parties to accommodate their differences and compromise in order to reach agreement. As a matter of logic in bilateral diplomacy, both parties must concur in an agreement, and those parties possess the means and the responsibility for carrying out agreements. These essential features of diplomacy tend to be obscured in multilateral conferences that operate either by votes or **consensus** and that are conducted in public.

In an immense gathering, such as the United Nations General Assembly, open debate occurs on an agenda that includes many diverse items, and voting on a resolution rather than unanimous agreement concludes the process. However, those voting may not have the responsibility for implementing a resolution. For example, over the course of many years, the General Assembly passed annual resolutions condemning the system of apartheid in South Africa, with the country that had the power and responsibility for bringing about change registering its opposition by voting against the resolutions. In contrast to traditional diplomacy, then, the actions of multilateral conferences separate votes from the means for implementation. Such conferences often provide the site for diplomacy, but that activity occurs off stage and includes no votes.

In addition, the disaggregation of subject matter into issue areas and the treatment of all activities on the same plane overlooks another important characteristic of diplomacy: its coordinating function. Modern embassies include specialists from many diverse areas of activity, but all of them are coordinated by the ambassador, who deals from the perspective of the interests of the state that he represents. Specialists in trade, agriculture, finance, intelligence gathering, military affairs, and other areas represent a growth in the complexity of the subject matter that states address, but they all need to be coordinated so as to serve the state's interest in maintaining its position in the international system.

In performing the coordinating role in the conduct of foreign policy, diplomats draw on various instruments to support their efforts to persuade other countries' representatives to accept their governments' views and proposals. These instruments may include economic and military assistance to support the object government's concerns. For example, American diplomacy's effectiveness in persuading Israel and Egypt to sign the Camp David Agreement in 1978 that led to their normalization of relations was undergirded by the promise of exceptionally large amounts of economic and military aid. Along a continuum lie a variety of instruments that support diplomacy. Quite distinct from providing assistance is the use of force or the threat of force to support diplomatic efforts in what is known as coercive diplomacy.[4] When tried against Iraq in 1990 and 1991, coercive diplomacy failed, and another instrument—war—was employed. Against a weaker adversary, Haiti, the United States in October 1994 successfully employed coercive diplomacy to gain the cooperation of the government it was determined to remove from office. The events of the Haiti case are detailed later in this chapter.

This **coordinating function of diplomacy** ensures a unity of purpose in the pursuit of foreign policy objectives. Nevertheless, **rationality** requires that objectives be obtained at the lowest possible cost, so persuasion with words and ideas, often based upon reputation, provides the least costly means of exercising influence. However, persuasion and reputation do not always accomplish the ends that are sought, and states, therefore, employ other instruments in the pursuit of their objectives.

Economics

Chapter 8 treated international political economy from the perspective of long-term processes and policy concerns. As explained there, each state strives to increase its wealth, thereby to maintain or enhance its position in the international system. In addition to such permanent concerns, states develop and pursue short-term goals that involve attempts to influence other states. Among the instruments that are employed in such attempts are economic tools, primarily involving the manipulation of trade, technology, and capital, either providing new benefits to recipients or depriving or disrupting established patterns of economic intercourse. These two aspects are referred to variously as **rewards and punishments,** carrots and sticks, or positive and negative sanctions. As with other categories of instruments and techniques used in foreign policy, the country subject to an influence attempt has options for responding to the use of economic tools. Thus, the success of such influence attempts depends not simply on the efficacy of the instruments but also on the reactions and the resourcefulness of the respondent as well as on the objectives to be served. In general, economic assistance in a context in which the countries agree on the objectives has greater efficacy and better chances of success than do economic sanctions and warfare that are used most often in an attempt to coerce the leaders of a country to comply with the policy demands of others with whom they do not share objectives.

• ECONOMIC ASSISTANCE

Ranking among the most successful uses of **economic assistance** in history, the United States' Marshall Plan aid to EUROPE in the aftermath of World War II clearly accomplished its objectives. With economic recovery in Europe lagging in a context of Soviet hostility to Western ideas and increasing Communist Party activity in France and Italy as well as Soviet domination of Eastern Europe, the United States extended major economic assistance to those European countries that agreed to cooperate in the planning and administration of the aid. Although turned down by the Soviet Union and the Eastern European countries, the Marshall Plan transferred some $12 billion to European recipients between 1948 and 1952. Not only was the goal of economic recovery achieved but so, too, was the implicit objective of promoting international cooperation to overcome the destructive nationalism that had led to World War II. Success in this case rested not only upon the economic instruments and their management by American foreign policy administrators but also upon the fundamental management and labor skill levels of the Europeans. Moreover, success was

also determined in part by the underpinning of military security and political stability that allowed economic determinants to flourish.

Similar results of economic assistance were shown in the case of Japan, for similar reasons. In this case, in addition, the Korean War which broke out in June 1950, also played an important part in determining the success of American economic assistance, for JAPAN became a major supplier of products and services to the American armed forces fighting in Korea. Building on its economic recovery after World War II and aided by the boost afforded by the Korean War, the Japanese have gone on to construct the world's second largest economy in the 1990s.

Another, quite disparate case of the successful achievement of foreign policy objectives by the employment of economic assistance has occurred since 1978. At that time, the United States decided to extend massive assistance to ISRAEL and EGYPT in support of their agreement to work toward peace and to establish normal diplomatic relations to replace the state of war that had characterized their relations until that time. That economic assistance, with Israel and Egypt being the two largest recipients, has been instrumental in establishing a measure of stability to the volatile Middle East region, thus serving to protect a variety of American interests there.

Not every use of economic assistance achieves all its objectives. Many aid programs from the advanced, industrial countries to less developed countries have failed to achieve the most far-reaching objective of industrialization, modernization, and advance to a self-sustaining stage of economic development.[5] In part, this may have been the result of holding unrealistic expectations. Additionally, the fundamental components for rapid economic development probably were not in place. Finally, the amounts of capital investment and technical assistance made available by the rich countries may simply not have been adequate for the achievement of ambitious goals. That such programs provided access for the donors to the recipients, along with a certain amount of diplomatic leverage that helped to shape policy in the recipient countries, can hardly be doubted. Moreover, both tangible achievements such as building bridges and intangible goals such as maintaining support for other diplomatic efforts have been met. No exact method is available for developing a balance sheet for the effectiveness of economic assistance, but governments continue to use the instrument as a productive means of exercising influence with other governments and groups.

During the 1980s, United States economic assistance to EL SALVADOR enabled the government of that country to maintain its economy while prosecuting a war against a formidable guerrilla movement, the Farabundo Marti National Liberation Movement (FMLN). In the end, the government was unable to defeat the FMLN, and the war came to a conclusion when the two sides signed a peace agreement that included provisions for integrating the FMLN into a democratic society. American economic assistance was essential to sustaining the Salvadoran economy, which underlay the ability of the government to avoid defeat. Thus, the economic instruments involved proved crucial to the success of United States policy. Moreover, the withdrawal of support by the Soviet Union for the FMLN was instrumental in inducing the rebels to enter into negotiations with the government.

Apart from such anecdotal evidence of the ongoing use and effectiveness of wealth as an instrument of power at the service of foreign policy, there is the pattern in which states that can afford it regularly use their wealth to achieve political purposes in their foreign relations. Wealthy Arab states extend subsidies to poorer Arab states. Venezuela and Mexico, petroleum exporting states, helped to sustain poor Central American states by subsidizing oil prices following the major price increases of 1973 and 1979. In the nineteenth century, Britain staved off threats to itself that might have emanated from continental Europe by regularly paying subsidies to rulers and their armies as a means of maintaining a balance of power in Europe. At the end of the Cold War, Germany—in effect, the West German government—agreed to pay subsidies to the Soviet Union for the removal of its troops from the eastern part of Germany after unification and for housing them in Russia itself. Examples are abundant, but enough have been cited to illustrate the point that every state that has sufficient wealth at its disposal is likely to employ its economic resources to support its objectives in other countries. The techniques, while diverse and complicated, are straightforward, and their use has never been limited merely to superpowers or particular eras.

Employment of economic means for the purchase of services and as inducements to support cooperative behavior by other countries combines ordinary economic activities and politics in a way that leads some analysts to treat such endeavors in a separate category from the exercise of power. On the other hand, no such confusion permeates the treatment of the employment of economic means as coercive instruments designed to compel others to behave in ways that they would not otherwise do.

• ECONOMIC SANCTIONS AND WARFARE

Economic instruments, like the other means of conducting foreign policy, apply in the context of interactions in which effectiveness of influence depends partly on the options and resourcefulness of respondents. Thus, it is more difficult successfully to wield economic instruments as weapons designed to coerce adversaries. A literature built on several "classic cases" argues that **economic sanctions** are not effective.[6] In his review of these as well as other cases, Baldwin argues that the cases do not support the argument that sanctions are ineffective or useless.[7] Part of his argument rests upon the usefulness of demonstrating commitment by the employment of economic sanctions. In this sense, the instrument belongs to a diplomatic repertoire in which various means are brought to bear in a bargaining situation.[8]

Sanctions are employed for different purposes, so it is important to consider the objectives sought. During the Cold War, the United States and its Western European allies, through a coordinating committee on export controls (COCOM), maintained a list of goods and technologies that were prohibited to the Soviet Union and its allies, and the alliance was able to sustain the effectiveness of this embargo for many years. Such actions resemble techniques used in wartime to deprive enemies of resources that they might use against those employing the sanctions. These techniques include preemptive buying of the production of former trading partners of the enemy state in order to deprive the enemy of the goods while alleviating any harm that might occur in the selling country because of the loss of trade. Even before the COCOM list, the Soviet Union had sought through espionage to acquire Western industrial and defense technologies, and it continued to do so throughout the Cold War. However, the COCOM mechanism made it much more costly and difficult to acquire these goods and knowledge and probably deprived the Soviets of some of them. In this case, alternative sources for the most advanced technologies did not exist.

Often, a country that faces economic sanctions can find alternative sources of the products denied to it. In the case of the United States embargo against CUBA that began in 1960, Western European allies were persuaded not to supply goods, but the Soviet Union did buy Cuban sugar and supply the island country with oil and subsidies. Thus, it is possible to argue that American sanctions were not effective. On the other hand, the flight of many Cubans to Florida indicated the effect of the sanctions at least on some classes of Cubans. Moreover, as the Soviets recognized the weaknesses of their own economy and thus reduced subsidies to Cuba and even more so after the collapse of the Soviet Union in 1991, the effects of the U.S. sanctions were shown to be devastating. Although the goal of driving Castro's regime from office was not attained, the sanctions did prove to weaken severely his government's ability to provide basic economic welfare for its people.

This case as well as other contemporary cases such as the sanctions against Iraq, HAITI, and Yugoslavia in the post-Cold War period illustrate their painful consequences on the weaker and poorer members of the population. To illustrate, although Haitians responded in 1994 to an oil embargo by smuggling petroleum in small containers across the Dominican Republic border, the Haitian economy was brought to a virtual standstill. Results of the economic hardship imposed by the sanctions included the spectacle of thousands of poor Haitians fleeing their country in hastily made boats. The military government of Haiti engaged in elaborate diplomatic maneuvers to maintain itself in power and was finally persuaded to leave only when faced with an imminent invasion by a force vastly superior to its own defense forces.

Essential to understanding the operation of economic sanctions are the **political dynamics** of the country subject to them. The argument will lay out four categories of political dynamics: 1) situations in which the population supports the government in the policies that brought on the sanctions; 2) situations in which the population has no effect on the dominant, usually repressive leadership but also in which no realistic opportunities for organized opposition exist or in which the organized opposition has been defeated; 3) situations in which a struggle for domination of the domestic polity is occurring but no established links with foreign countries operate to affect the situation; and 4) situations in which an organized opposition not only exists but is sustained in part by outside support, establishing links between the foreign countries that apply economic sanctions and the organized, internal opposition.

The first category may be illustrated in the case of sanctions against ITALY in 1935–1936 and partly illustrated in the Rhodesia case from 1966 to 1979. In part, the sanctions against Italy, which were designed to require it to desist from its invasion and conquest of Ethiopia, failed to achieve their objective because they were incomplete. They failed to deprive Italy of petroleum and coal, and many countries, including the United States, did not participate in the economic sanctions. On the other hand, Italians freely turned over their privately held gold to the government to offset the monetary losses because of sanctions. In a larger sense, the policy to stop Italian conquest remained ambiguous, for Britain and France held on to the hope that Italy would join them in a coalition to balance against Nazi Germany, a hope that obviously was not fulfilled, as Italy associated with Germany in the campaign of conquest in World War II.

When the government of RHODESIA, a British dependency in East Africa, issued a unilateral declaration of independence in 1965, the British government under warrant of its responsibility for arranging an orderly movement to independence, enlisted other countries under auspices of the United Nations to apply economic sanctions to Rhodesia. Galtung[9] has described the way in which the white minority population, on whose behalf the government declared independence, adjusted to the sanctions and actually increased their cohesiveness to support the government. In this sense, the sanctions appeared to prove to be only a minor inconvenience and, thus, were ineffective. On the other hand, the majority black population supported an opposition movement that, in 1979, came to power as the result of negotiations mediated by Britain and the United States that resulted in the state of Zimbabwe.

The second category may be illustrated in the cases of IRAQ and YUGOSLAVIA in the early to mid-1990s. The United Nations Security Council applied extraordinarily severe economic sanctions against Iraq in the wake of the Gulf War of 1990–91. These were designed to compel the Iraqi government to adhere to Security Council resolutions—and with the added hope of the United States that President Saddam Hussein would be overthrown. Despite the sanctions, the government remained securely in power and alternately defied and complied with the resolutions. Sanctions against the Serbian-led government of rump Yugoslavia had uneven effects, in part because in a December 1992 election, Serbian President Slobodan Milosevic handily defeated the opposition candidate. In both these cases, as in others to be discussed below, the hardships imposed by economic sanctions fall largely on the poorer and weaker members of society, not on the elite that dominates the politics of the country.

IRAN after the 1979 revolution provides an exemplar for the third category in which a struggle for power is occurring in a country against which economic sanctions are imposed but without any established links between any of the contending groups and other countries. American hostages were taken and held for over a year in this context. Despite severe economic sanctions against Iran as well as varied attempts by the United States to obtain release of the hostages, an impasse continued until a credible threat of force by a new American president, Ronald Reagan, added a new component that led to completion of negotiations and an agreement in January 1981 between the United States and Iran that included release of the hostages.

The fourth category, in which an organized internal opposition has links with foreign countries, is illustrated by the case of SOUTH AFRICA. A very powerful internal opposition led by the African National Congress (ANC) received economic assistance from the Soviet Union as well as from private sources in other countries, and the ANC conducted very effective informational activities throughout the world. Therefore, even when economic sanctions caused immense hardship for poor and oppressed black people in South Africa, the leaders of the ANC and others argued that the sanctions should be continued. Thus, foreign economic sanctions acted as a tool of influence to support the ANC within the South African internal political context. When ANC leader Nelson Mandela was released from prison in February 1990 and led in negotiations for new political arrangements with President Frederik W. DeKlerk, it was he, rather than major foreign powers, who actually chose the moment for sanctions to be lifted.

There may be variations on these categories, for they are not mutually exclusive. For example, the case of President Jean-Bertrand Aristide and Haiti in the early 1990s illustrates category 3—in which the population has no effective means of organizing internal resistance to the government because of repression—and category 4, in which there is a leadership, albeit in exile, that is connected politically with another power, in this case, the United States.

It also needs to be pointed out that in some of the cases cited, influence attempts using economic sanctions aimed to affect foreign policy behavior—in the cases of Italy, Rhodesia, Iran, Iraq, and rump Yugoslavia—whereas in other cases, the objective pertained to internal political arrangements—as in Haiti and South Africa. Regardless of the aspect of the country's political life that is subject to an influence attempt, the relationship of the government to the population affects the success or failure of that attempt. Nevertheless, it is probably correct to say that an influence attempt involving change in the structure of internal political arrangements has a greater chance of success than one that strives to affect foreign policy.

Sanctions in U.S.-Soviet Detente

In the Nixon administration (1969–1974), under the intellectual leadership of Henry Kissinger, the United States undertook an ambitious **detente policy** that included an economic dimension. Conceptually, the policy aimed to enmesh the Soviet Union in a web of economic relationships that would induce it to behave in conformity with American norms of behavior—particularly refraining from support for radical movements in the Third World—but holding the prospect that these relationships could be withdrawn or severed unilaterally by the United States to punish the Soviets, should they deviate. This carrot-and-stick policy ran into both logical and practical problems. Logical inconsistency arose from the promise of involvement of the Soviet Union in complex relations of interdependence that would result in long-term benefits on the one hand, and the belief, on the other hand, that the United States could cut off these benefits. This logical contradiction emerged in practice during the Carter administration in the late 1970s and the Reagan administration in the 1980s.

One of the economic components of the detente policy had been United States grain sales to the Soviet Union. Basically commercial transactions had led to contracts for the sale of American grain surpluses to the Soviet Union, which had been plagued for decades with an unproductive agricultural system and, thus, became dependent upon the reliable supply of American cereals. During the mid-1970s, Soviet activity in Africa fed American popular distrust of the Soviet Union and American official displeasure with its inability to control Soviet behavior. Tension peaked in 1979, when the Soviet Union invaded Afghanistan and the United States responded with economic sanctions that included a grain embargo as well as other actions, such as a boycott of the Moscow Olympic Games in 1980. Although American and others' displeasure was effectively conveyed to the Soviets, their response to the grain embargo included the accusation that the United States was not a reliable supplier, that it had violated its contracts to deliver grain.

Natural Gas Pipeline Sanctions

This issue of long-term contracts as a means of political influence came to the fore with greater and more significant impact in the early 1980s, following the imposition of martial law in Poland in December 1981. In the 1970s, American allies in Europe—particularly West Germany and France—had engaged the Soviet Union in long-term contracts to extend credits and technology to build a natural gas pipeline from the Soviet Union to the West, the credits to be repaid with earnings from the sale of natural gas when the pipeline was completed. Angry at events in Poland and elsewhere, the Reagan administration sought to stop the building of the pipeline by ordering European subsidiaries of American firms to cease the transfer of pipeline-building technology to the Soviet Union. In this case, however, the European governments resisted the United States and ordered the firms to fulfill their contracts, which they did. European leaders argued that fulfillment of the long-term contracts was needed in the pursuit of their own interests to obtain natural gas as well as to abide by commitments they had made. Thus, the pipeline sanctions policy of the American government failed because the government did not have control over the economic means. In addition, the reasoning underlying the policy was flawed. On the one hand, it promised long-term commitments under sacred contracts while, at the same time, holding that those contracts could be broken unilaterally for short-term political reasons.

Arms Transfers

A somewhat different and specialized segment of economic relations involves the sale and transfer of weapons and related technology, with an important subsegment involving nuclear arms. **Arms transfers** combine aspects of ordinary commerce with concerns for dangers and security as well as with an underworld dimension of high risks and high profits. The great dangers of nuclear arms are sometimes associated with nuclear-fission-generated energy.

During the Cold War, the Soviet Union relied heavily on weapons transfers as a result of the nature of its economy, which stressed heavy industry and military goods. In its first step in what political scientist Hans Morgenthau called a "policy of maneuver," the Soviet Union in 1955 arranged for the transfer of weapons produced in Czechoslovakia to Egypt in exchange for Egyptian cotton. This transaction occurred through a commercial arrangement but also included security overtones, for Soviet influence reached for the first time into the Middle East and Egypt acquired weaponry that enabled it more effectively to engage in hostilities with Israel.

Although the United States possessed a broader repertory of economic instruments, because of both its much greater wealth and the diversity of its economy, it too transferred large amounts of weapons to other countries during the Cold War. Where recipients were in a position to pay for the weapons, the transactions occurred on a commercial basis, even though they had been driven by security considerations. Often in relations with allies, demands for payment emanated from the United States in a vocabulary of "burden-sharing" in which rich allies were enjoined to pay a larger share of the burden of shared defense. Nevertheless, the fundamental impetus remained that of security.

On occasion, economic considerations seemed to override those of security. For example, during the Nixon administration in the early 1970s, IRAN was regarded as an anchor in regional security in the Persian Gulf region. Thus, the United States sold arms to the Shah of Iran to provide his armed forces with the means for defending Iran and maintaining stability in the region. However, for commercial reasons, the American government authorized the sale to Iran of its most advanced aircraft, far surpassing Iran's needs for defense. To maintain its own security position, the United States would logically depend on the superiority of its advanced technology. In addition, no other power in the region held weapons that required the most advanced aircraft to counteract. Nevertheless, Iran under the shah had the means to pay very high prices to acquire weapons for its own arsenal at the same time that they entered the American arsenal.

Another example of the subordination of security concerns to economic considerations occurred during the 1992 presidential election campaign when President George Bush, in an obvious bid for votes, authorized the sale of 150 advanced F-16 fighter aircraft to Taiwan. Furthermore, Defense Secretary Dick Cheney announced that the United States would sell 72 F-15s to Saudi Arabia. Both of these sales relied on the justification of saving jobs for American aircraft workers. In this case, the inextricability of politics, economics, and security demonstrates that these categories do not amount to discrete issue areas that are easily separable.

Even when transfers of military goods occur purely for security reasons, the purposes served may not be straightforward. For example, the United States supplied PAKISTAN with military hardware and training over the course of several decades as part of its strategy of containing the Communist countries. From Pakistan's perspective, however, the main adversary was India, with which it had a dispute over the territory of Jammu and Kashmir. Whereas for the United States China was an enemy to be resisted partly by weapons in the hands of Pakistanis, for Pakistan China provided a bulwark and friend against larger, better-armed India.

All of the examples used thus far involve open government transactions, but major powers also employ clandestine channels, often through private arms merchants, to transfer weapons to governments or movements that they support. In virtually every civil war situation, a clandestine flow of arms assists one side or another. During the civil war in El Salvador from 1979 to 1992, arms flowed to the FMLN. Before the triumph of Nicaraguans who overthrew the dictatorship in 1979, the traffic in arms supported by several neighboring countries helped to ensure victory for the Sandinista-led opposition front. Following that revolutionary victory and the ultimate monopolization of the Nicaraguan government by the Sandinista National Liberation Front, there arose an armed opposition that received a flow of arms supplied by the United States using both government and private channels. Arms transfers gave France for many years an effective tool for continuing to play an important role in several African countries after its imperial access ended as its colonies became independent.

Small or poorer countries as well use arms transfers as a foreign policy instrument. Czechoslovakia has traditionally been a manufacturer and supplier of arms to other countries, and Israel, Brazil, and India more recently entered the lists of those whose arms manufacturing prowess and ability to supply arms expand their repertory of foreign policy instruments.

Regardless of the economic dimensions of arms transfers, they always carry security implications, and these lead some countries to interfere with both the development of manufacturing capacity and the commerce of transfer. IRAQ provides dramatic evidence of a country that has tried to increase its military capabilities, including nuclear arms and other weapons of mass destruction, but has encountered exceptionally serious disruptions of its efforts. In 1981, Israel bombed Iraq's Osirak nuclear installation to stop the development of nuclear weapons. Despite Iraq's renewed efforts to acquire technology and weapons, it has met with setback after setback, first by the military actions of the allied coalition that inflicted heavy damage on Iraq's military installations during the Gulf War in early 1991 and then through United Nations mechanisms that sought to stop Iraq's advance toward the acquisition of major weapons systems.

Nonproliferation of Nuclear Weapons in the Post-Cold War Period

More broadly, the United States has led an effort to stop the spread of nuclear weapons to states that do not possess them. The formation of the nuclear non-proliferation regime, with the Non-proliferation Treaty, demonstrates the success of this effort. Under the NPT, states that possess nuclear weapons undertake not to transfer either weapons or the technology to produce them to nonnuclear states, and the latter undertake not to develop nuclear weapons nor to receive the transfer of weapons from nuclear states. In addition, the treaty provides that the nuclear states will work toward the elimination of nuclear weapons, and there are provisions for assistance in developing peaceful uses of nuclear energy. In some sense, then, the inducement to nonnuclear powers to refrain from the development of weapons is assistance in the promotion of nuclear power, medicine, and so on in their countries.

The dangers of nuclear weapons in the post-Cold War period have led the United States to use its wealth in two particular ways to reduce those dangers. First, the United States has undertaken to extend both economic and technical assistance to RUSSIA AND THE OTHER SUCCESSOR REPUBLICS of the Soviet Union possessing nuclear weapons to gain control of and dismantle the weapons. Thus, the major economic assistance program from the United States to Russia in the post-Cold War era involves the dismantling of nuclear weapons. Additionally, American diplomacy—backed by economic assistance—has successfully induced the other successor republics that had nuclear weapons on their soil— Ukraine, Belarus, and Kazakhstan—to transfer those weapons to Russia for dismantling. Apart from the dangers of losing control of these weapons within the territory of the former adversary state itself, there has been a fear that the weapons might be transferred to other countries through a clandestine commerce. Certainly, the traffic in conventional weapons from the former Soviet Union and other Eastern European countries has gained some prominence as other countries find opportunities to acquire arms at reasonable prices from merchants who have acquired access to Soviet weapons.

The second way that the United States has sought to reduce the dangers arising from proliferation of nuclear weapons in the post-Cold War time centers on smaller states, NORTH KOREA and IRAN in particular, that have vigorous nuclear programs with seeming intentions to produce nuclear weapons. With respect to North Korea, the United States negotiated an agreement in late 1994 to provide assistance for North Korean nuclear energy production in exchange for monitoring under NPT to ensure that weapons will not be produced. In the case of Iran, there are no diplomatic relations between the two countries, so the main instrument employed is an informational one that seeks to inform the world that Iran may be an incipient nuclear power. This instrument has been supplemented by diplomatic pressure on allies to refrain from transferring nuclear-related technology to Iran.

When one considers the alternative instruments that can be brought to bear on the problem of nonproliferation, one might contrast the Israeli policy in 1981 and the United States-led coalition policy against Iraq in 1990 and following years with the United States use of economic instruments in gaining the cooperation of Russia and the other Soviet successor republics as well that of North Korea. Both categories of instruments—military force and economic inducement—have achieved results. Had military force been brought to bear against North Korea, it was possible that the Kim Il Sung regime might have carried out its threat to attack South Korea with its formidable arsenal and military forces.

* * *

To conclude this section on economic instruments of foreign policy, then, economics can be employed as power. Like other instruments, however, their efficacy depends importantly on the responses of those to whom the tools are applied and on other countries affected by their use. While it is true that not every recipient of economic pressure caves in to the will of the wielder, neither does every person subject to bombing and other armed attacks capitulate to the country using force. In this sense, every instrument used in a power relationship shares the same dependence on the will and capacities of those to whom it is directed. As with diplomacy and economics, discussed so far, so it is with information, to which we now turn.

Information

A cliché has it that we live in a world of rapid communications. Television brings into living rooms throughout the world scenes of war and disaster as they occur, and computers put millions of people in touch with one another electronically. Computers also move data and money around the world every day to suit the needs of firms, banks, and individuals. These connections provide part of the context in which governments seek to protect and pursue their interests, but national environments also shape that context.

• INFORMATION MANAGEMENT AND PROPAGANDA

Although some contexts exist in which **propaganda** comprises a tool of foreign policy aimed at a specific, short-term objective, for the most part, the **management of information** aims more at creating a climate or at influencing attitudes, beliefs, and perceptions as a daily chore that also affects the longer term. Management may consist of providing accurate information, presenting interpretations and glosses on facts, and disseminating disinformation, that is, deliberate falsehood designed to mislead recipients on the facts of a situation. Unlike diplomacy, which is directed at officials, propaganda and cultural activities aim to affect the views of larger audiences.

Governments provide information directly through news releases, meetings of public officials with representatives of the mass media, official speeches, the activities of public relations officers, official radio broadcasts, and electronic messages. In addition, governments maintain relations with interest groups and the mass media to influence the information that they, in turn, disseminate to their members, readers, and viewers. Governments also sometimes pay private individuals to provide information and interpretation to promote their respective foreign policies.

For the most part, attitudes, beliefs, and perceptions are molded by national environments, and transnational ideas are at work regardless of informational activities directed by governments. Literature and science crossed national boundaries before the twentieth century, but because most people were illiterate, the interchange did not reach them. As literacy grew and communications technology increased the numbers of people reached by transnational information, governments set up barriers to control movements of people and to hinder and channel the flow of ideas: passports, radio jamming, censorship of news, travel restrictions, and so forth. At the same time, governments engaged in providing information to ensure that their respective views were heard.

Although the origins of the term *propaganda* lie in the distant past when it was first used by the Roman Catholic Church in referring to the dissemination of the faith, major governments in the twentieth century, especially but not exclusively totalitarian governments, have engaged in major attempts aimed at influencing attitudes, beliefs, and perceptions. Moreover, groups aiming at the overthrow or replacement of governments also have engaged in extensive informational activities to gain adherents to their respective causes.

In the late twentieth century, when informational policies have become routine, certain specific cases illustrate important ways in which such policies are able to achieve foreign policy aims. For example, the main instrument in the hands of the Ayatollah Ruhollah Khomeini, during his years in exile in Paris when he promoted the overthrow of the shah of Iran, became the tape cassette that conveyed his sermons and political messages to tens of thousands of his compatriots in Iran. Eventually in February 1979, he returned to his country at the head of a triumphant revolutionary movement that had been inspired by his words.

Not only revolutionaries but also political leaders employ words to mobilize their citizens on behalf of foreign policy goals. German Chancellor Adolf Hitler's rhetorical skills in arousing Germans to join his ambitious domestic and foreign policy agenda were impressive in the 1930s and 1940s, and resistance to those ambitions was strengthened by the equally impressive eloquence of British Prime Minister Winston Churchill. When France fell to the Germans in World War II and the collaborative Vichy regime was created, it was General Charles DeGaulle's brave appeals for resistance that kept alive a sense of French honor that allowed that country to resume its place after the war as a respected state.

American information policy aimed at Eastern Europeans during the Cold War exhibited its limitations in 1956 when, partly in response to rhetoric

about "liberation" and "rollback of Communism," Hungarians revolted against Soviet domination but were then crushed by Russian tanks on the streets of Budapest when the propaganda policy went unsupported by other instruments. Later in the Cold War, United States information policy directed to Eastern Europeans bolstered the aspirations of those protesting against oppression in their own countries. Events in Eastern Europe in 1989, the year in which the Cold War ended, were shaped primarily by people in those countries and by President Mikhail Gorbachev's "Sinatra doctrine." That precept—so named because of the singer's trademark song, "My Way"—allowed each country to determine its own "way" without further Soviet military support to maintain the rule of Communist parties. The resolve of those individuals who aspired to freedom had been bolstered by propaganda promoting Western ideas.

In whatever context, information policies face three tests of consistency. First, both domestic and foreign audiences receive the messages sent by governments. Governments work for political support, but they also seek foreign policy aims. Second, officials maintain ongoing confidential links with the governments of other countries through diplomatic channels while they simultaneously expound public information activities. Third, consistency gets tested in the realms of rhetoric and policy, for policy actions can only too easily undermine the words that leaders use to discuss their policies. In the United States, several presidents have found themselves in what is called a credibility gap when they have uttered brave words while discussing weak or contradictory policies.

Governments add to their specific informational repertories cultural relations in which an exchange occurs using people, books, films, music, and other media. Such exchanges of cultural things probably lead in attentive parts of populations to more complex views of other countries. Presumably, broader and more accurate perceptions should lead to more rational policies, but one remains skeptical about the impact of popular perceptions on governmental policies.

As is true with regard to other foreign policy instruments, propaganda relies for its effectiveness partly on the options available to and the responses of recipients. Responses, in turn, tend to be shaped importantly not just by life experiences and existential contexts but also by perceptions of successful models. For example, during the Cold War, many people in poor countries responded positively to

Soviet and Chinese propaganda, but with the collapse of the Soviet Union and China's embrace of market principles, the successes of market economies provided an important boost to the receptivity in poor countries to the ideas of democracy and capitalism.

In the Soviet Union and Eastern Europe, dissidents may have been heartened by Western propaganda, but their existential conditions made it very difficult to respond effectively to Western ideas. During the period of detente in the 1970s, however, the Western—especially United States—propaganda attached to the Helsinki review process gave groups such as Charter 77—a dissident group in Czechoslovakia—greater scope for protest against their own governments, in effect giving voice to democratic ideas. With Gorbachev's policy of refraining from military intervention to suppress democratic aspirations in the Eastern European countries, those groups were joined by tens of thousands of citizens, and events such as the "Velvet Revolution"—the peaceful transition from communism to democratic rule in Czechoslovakia—and the mass exodus of East Germans to the Federal Republic occurred. Events like these illustrate not just the operation of propaganda but also the power of words and ideas in foreign policy.

Public discourse comprises only one side of information; another side involves intelligence.

• INTELLIGENCE

Clandestine intelligence activities comprise governmental ventures that are extensions of traditional, open undertakings. The gathering of information about foreign countries makes up one of the basic tasks of the traditional diplomat, and the use of force against other military aggregates has always comprised the essential job of the soldier. In this sense, the gathering of intelligence and the conduct of operations by clandestine services such as the Soviet Union's KGB (Committee of State Security), the United States CIA, and equivalent agencies in other countries have a base in traditional foreign relations, except that they represent the institutionalization of covert, or underground, activities. Until the modern period, spying and other covert means of gathering information and the conduct of irregular warfare activities tended to be smaller and conducted by ad hoc arrangements rather than by specialized bureaucratic organizations, although traditionally armies used spies, special operations, disinformation activities, and the other paraphernalia involved in modern intelligence projects.

Intelligence and Operations

In the United States in the post-World War II period, intelligence has been divided into **intelligence,** and **operations.** Under the first rubric, library and documentary research forms the most important component, but clandestine observations, photography, cryptography, spying, and electronics also contribute to the gathering of information about other countries. Among the noted contributions to the provision of important information for American policy makers were the breaking of the Japanese code during World War II by American cryptographers, learning of Nikita Khrushchev's "secret speech" to a Communist Party Congress in 1956 denouncing Stalin, the precise aerial photography that enabled the United States government to learn of the clandestine Soviet deployment of nuclear missiles in Cuba in 1962, and the satellite photography and other technical means of learning of Soviet military deployments, nuclear testing, and so forth. By these various means, the Cold War adversaries were able to learn about the moves and capabilities of each other, and the better knowledge added importantly to the basis for making informed, rational decisions.

On the other side of intelligence work, operations include the conduct of clandestine actions, knowledge of which can plausibly be denied by top-level authorities. Such actions encompass attempts to undermine other governments by providing funds and various kinds of assistance to opposition groups, direct actions to overthrow foreign governments, and extending assistance to governments to help them remain in power through such means as providing secret electoral assistance to political parties and bribing newspaper reporters to write favorable stories. Sometimes, as in the mining of Nicaraguan harbors by the CIA in 1984, operatives of the agencies themselves conduct paramilitary operations against other governments.

Several problems arise in connection with intelligence activities that do not pertain to other foreign policy instruments. Although certain of these apply to authoritarian as well as to democratic governments, they have particular force for the latter.

The first of these arises from the separation of intelligence and operations. Viewed in the starkest terms, these two aspects of intelligence work appear easily separable and morally distinct: gathering information on the one side, and on the other, conducting paramilitary and other clandestine operations to weaken, undermine, or overthrow governments with whom one's own country has diplomatic relations. The first conveys an image of a scholar poring over documents to learn more about a foreign country, while the second projects a view of a cloaked figure with a dagger in his hand acting in a sinister fashion to overthrow a legitimate government. Learning is the task of the one; action is the business of the other. To examine the matter more closely, however, is to see that in reality the distinctions appear less sharp.

Although activity resembling scholarship forms an important part of intelligence gathering, it has other parts, and intelligence research, quite unlike academic work, remains secret and not subject to peer review. Stealing secret documentation, bribing officials for information, spying by individuals or mechanical and electronic means, and recruiting traitors comprise other activities of intelligence gathering. Such clandestine means of gathering intelligence do not appear easily distinguishable from establishing links with subversive individuals and groups in a country with the purpose of destabilizing their government. Moreover, when governments are overthrown, a substantial amount of documentation often becomes available to the victors that can be used for learning about not just that government but also its allies and their methods of operation.

Operations always involve interference in the domestic politics of a foreign country and thus violate norms of international law, but some rest on stronger justifications than others. In 1948, the UNITED STATES intervened in French and Italian elections to support liberal democrats against communists whose loyalty to Stalin and to the Soviet Union overrode their commitment to their own respective countries and to liberal values. In Guatemala in 1954 and in Chile in 1972–1973, on the other hand, the United States intervened on behalf of authoritarian groups against governments that had been freely elected. The SOVIET UNION frequently supported assassination and terror by groups devoted to various radical causes opposed to Western ideas and institutions. Clandestine operations by the Soviet Union contributed to the seizure of power in Czechoslovakia in 1948 by communists' overthrowing a democratically elected government. In neighboring Poland in the early 1980s, the United States provided clandestine aid to Solidarity, the massively strong labor movement opposed to the ruling party.

Other countries similarly intervene clandestinely to achieve various purposes. Shortly after the triumph of its revolution in 1959, Cuba began dispatching agents to lead armed insurrections against several legitimate Latin American governments. During the popular insurgency in Nicaragua against the dictator Somoza in 1978 and 1979, several neighboring Central American countries, including Costa Rica and Panama, participated in the clandestine supply of arms to the antigovernment fighters.

Although clandestine activities comprise regular techniques used by many governments, they remain inconsistent with the norms of international law and with the standards of democratic practice. By their nature, they are conspiratorial and sinister, in opposition to the **transparency** and **accountability** that characterize both honest practice and democratic values. On occasion when faced with evil, honest people find themselves obliged to take extraordinary actions to establish conditions that impose or restore safe, open, and democratic life. As the Cold War demonstrated, however, extraordinary actions can easily become routine, secrecy can easily reduce openness, and denial can replace responsibility.

Secrecy and Democracy

Among the issues raised for a democracy that conducts clandestine operations lies the problem of **responsibility** and **plausible deniability.** Despite an occasional claim that intelligence agencies undertake "rogue" operations not under the control of chief executives, the normal procedure provides that important operations have to be authorized by the responsible head of government. At the same time, when such activities become publicly known, they are an embarrassment to the chief executive who authorized them, for he must continue to represent his state in ordinary diplomatic intercourse. Thus, such activities tend to be conducted in such a way that the responsible executive can plausibly deny that he knew about them. Although such practices do save high officials from embarrassment, they also undermine the notion that democratically elected officials must be responsible and accountable for what they do.

These problems and others, such as the inconsistency between secrecy and democracy in general, will probably continue, for governments contend with challenges requiring information that may not always be publicly available. Additionally, they seek objectives whose achievement may be facilitated by clandestine actions. It may be possible for democratic polities to construct norms against such egregious practices as political assassinations and the overthrow of democratically elected governments. On the other hand, it is difficult to imagine that prohibitions against other kinds of clandestine activities would be erected even by democratic citizens who, after all, rely on the discretion of elected executives to make judgments about what may be necessary to protect the interests of the state in a hostile and dangerous world. Those concerned with such issues may derive some solace from the less hostile conditions in the wake of the Cold War that promise a reduced use of clandestine activities.

Military Force

Instruments of military force underlie and support the other tools of foreign policy, and in cases where those fail, they may be invoked to settle issues arbitrarily. Stability and security result from military means, and in cases where security problems have been settled, the other instruments come to the fore. On the other hand, where insecurity prevails, the prominence of military force is assured, and threats to employ those instruments invoked. In worst cases, military force, despite its higher costs, may actually be exercised.

• WEAPONS AND FORCES

Military instruments consist of various types of weapons, personnel, and supporting services that are conventionally categorized in several different ways. This discussion treats them by the arenas in which they are deployed, by whether they are offensive or defensive, by the level of technology that they embody, by whether they are conventional or nuclear, and, if nuclear, by whether they are designed for uses against other military weapons (counterforce) or against other targets (countervalue).

Traditionally, weapons and fighting forces were deployed on land and at sea, but in the twentieth century, air and space have been added as environments in which weapons as well as command and control systems operate. Over the course of the last two centuries, weapons and forces have grown in scope and intensity because of technological developments as well as political and organizational changes. Napoleon, an artillery officer who effectively employed the cannon, was also able to introduce the mass army because of the nationalism generated by the French Revolution. Since that time,

land warfare's scope and intensity have been increased by such innovations as the machine gun, the tank, the telegraph and telephone, and the railroad as well as by modern organizational capacities and the professionalization of the military. The tendency has been to increase the speed and efficiency with which killing can occur, although the murder of some half-million Rwandans by machetes and small arms in a few months during the spring and summer 1994 testifies that large-scale killing does not rely exclusively on massively destructive weapons, modern technology, and sophisticated organizational and command structures alone. **Land forces** can be used for a variety of purposes, but they are essential for taking and holding ground against opposing forces and for administering territory. Thus, foreign policy encompassing such objectives requires ground forces for their accomplishment. For example, to seek regional stability, India decided to deploy ground forces in neighboring Sri Lanka from mid-1987 until March 1990 to assist the government in quelling an armed rebellion.

Ground forces provide a tangible symbol of determination to defend ground and they serve as hostages for greater forces that would come to their aid in case of attack. For example, NATO forces in West Germany helped to deter aggression by the Soviet Union, and American forces in South Korea help to deter an attack by North Korea. Such forces also reassure allies who, in turn, are able to focus more of their energies on their economic development, confident that their security is ensured.

Sea power gives support to land forces by commanding sea lanes of communication and by bombardment, but it can also be used to disrupt supplies in war and to maintain commerce in peacetime. Britain sustained its overseas empire by use of its seapower; and the United States Navy after World War II by its command of two oceans provided the fundamental conditions for the burgeoning commerce that increasingly characterized international relations in the last half of the twentieth century. Major innovations that have made military instruments at sea more devastating have been the rifled gun, steel ships, the submarine and the application of nuclear energy to it in both engines and missiles, and the aircraft carrier. Command of the seas allowed the United States to deploy forces exceeding half a million personnel both in Vietnam in the late 1960s and in the Persian Gulf area in 1990–91. Local domination of sea lanes in 1962 provided an essential ingredient in the American policy of partly blockading Soviet shipments to Cuba during the missile crisis.

The twentieth century has borne witness to the opening up of two new deployment arenas, **air and space.** With the invention and perfection of the airplane and associated guidance technology, the reach of military weapons grew extensively. A country at war can attack the enemy's territory without the need to defeat its army.[10] This principle was extended further with the invention of ballistic missiles, which carry an implicit threat to a civilian population that traditionally had required conquest and occupation. Moreover, as Bernard Brodie has pointed out, thermonuclear weapons eliminate the need to discriminate among targets, for it has become impossible, for example, to bomb industrial facilities without also destroying civilian housing.[11] Although modern technological developments promise the ability to deploy weapons of mass destruction in outer space, none has yet been so deployed. On the other hand, satellites orbiting in space provide communications for command and guidance functions as well as carry photographic and other types of equipment associated with military intelligence. Aircraft used in conjunction with sea power has already been noted, but domination of airspace over land battles has proven decisive repeatedly in Middle Eastern battles won by Israel and in the 1991 Gulf War by the associated states in their quick victory in ousting Iraqi troops from Kuwait.

Some analysts also classify military instruments as offensive or defensive, although this distinction rests more upon the strategy and tactics of use than upon the intrinsic characteristics of the forces themselves. Permanent fortifications appear to be defensive in comparison with mobile weapons and troops, which appear to be offensive. However, strategists have long noted that fortifications can provide a base from which to attack a neighbor, and this principle applies as well to contemporary nuclear strategy. A shelter system designed to protect civilian lives seems to be purely defensive, but it might allow a nuclear power to launch an attack against an enemy with greatly diminished fear of the costs of retaliation, thus encouraging an offensive posture.

In his classification of the uses of force, Robert Art includes in his concept of defense preventive and preemptive attacks on enemies that a state believes will attack it or when a state believes that a delay will injure its interests.[12] Moreover, defense of one's own territory has historically been used to justify the taking of additional territory, requiring an offense. Thus,

determining whether a particular set of forces constitutes offensive or defensive weapons remains complicated. Nevertheless, prudence requires the calculation of the intentions of hostile states; to do so, force characteristics, deployments, and plans for their use provide evidence of such intentions. In addition, a foreign policy that aims at creating a stable regional situation may rest upon an arrangement in which the weapons and forces deployed enhance defense without being unduly provocative to other states. Robert Jervis goes so far as to argue that if offensive and defensive weapons and policies are readily distinguishable and the defense has a clear advantage, the security dilemma can largely be overcome.[13]

Weapons vary by the level of technology that they embody. Like other aspects of industry in the modern age, weaponry has evolved rapidly. Allusion was made above to the increasing efficiency and destructive power of weapons. Here, let it be noted that an important aspect of evolving technology embodies distance between fighters and targets. Hand-to-hand combat remains an ingredient in some battles today, but artillery, airplanes, and missiles have increasingly lengthened the distance between the killer and the killed. With the technology of intercontinental missiles and thermonuclear weapons, a handful of personnel have the capacity to destroy several cities and millions of people over some six thousand miles from the launch site. Such distancing not only gives an important advantage to the countries possessing such weapons but also makes possible such social changes as the deployment of women in combat roles where killing requires not the brutality and strength of face-to-face fighting but instead the skills of flying an aircraft or directing computer-assisted bombs at far-off targets.

Conventional and Nuclear Weapons

Finally, weapons are classed as **conventional** and **nuclear.** Sometimes, chemical and biological weapons may be combined with nuclear ones as **weapons of mass destruction,** or CBN (chemical, biological, nuclear) weapons. Because chemical and biological weapons are not susceptible to control and do not have the deadly efficiency of nuclear weapons, however, the more important categorization for most purposes is that of nuclear and nonnuclear, although this distinction has not been accepted by everyone. Partly, the debate over the distinction grows out of the context in which nuclear weapons were first used, but technological developments associated with strategic nuclear defense and imagined space-based weaponry have contributed to claims that nuclear weapons are not distinct.

Despite the horror expressed by Pablo Picasso in his painting of the bombing of civilians in Guernica in 1937 during the Spanish civil war and the pleas of American President Franklin D. Roosevelt not to bomb civilians in the impending Second World War, bombing of cities had become routine by the end of the war. German planes and rockets introduced Londoners and other urban residents of Britain to city bombing, and the Japanese had bombed Chinese cities during their invasion that began in 1937. As the war progressed in Europe, the British Bomber Command and the American Army Air Force perfected the technique of creating **firestorms** in German cities, first Hamburg and then others. The most infamous—its infamy gained because many argued that there were no military targets there—was Dresden. During two nights of bombing that created a firestorm, approximately 135,000 people were killed. With the end of European war, the United States turned its concentration to the Pacific and to a determination to defeat Japan. Using incendiary bombs to start fires in Japanese cities, the most terrible firebombing occurred in Tokyo, where, over the course of a few days, about 90,000 people died from the terror falling from the sky. Thus, when the first atomic bomb dropped on Hiroshima in August 1945, the 75,000 lives that it claimed did not seem out of proportion to the tolls by bombing in other cities.[14] From this perspective, the atomic bomb appeared to be a more efficiently destructive weapon, but it marked a technological increment rather than a wholly different sort of weapon. Another perspective, of course, views the immense toll of a single bomb and, horrified, recognizes that a multiplicity of such weapons might wreak such unprecedented destruction as to destroy human civilization. Moreover, calculated use of such devices for slaughter would also be unprecedentedly immoral.

In the early years of the nuclear age, both the unique characteristics of nuclear weapons and the conception that they could be used in war affected the thinking of policy makers. After the invention of thermonuclear weapons—whose destructive power was measured in megatons rather than kilotons (millions of tons of TNT equivalent as opposed to thousands of tons equivalent)—and the intercontinental missile, the uniqueness of the new weapons was given greater emphasis. Essentially, the distinctiveness of nuclear weapons lies in their speed and destructive power. Anything that can be done with

nuclear weapons can be done without them, but it would take a great deal more effort and significantly longer periods of time.[15] Since politics primarily involves the exercise of power and influence, it tends to use the threat of latent force to win its objectives. Conventional forces can be applied over time, threatening ever greater damage if the enemy does not comply. Thus, these weapons allow room for bargaining and compromise. However, the immense destructive power of nuclear weapons implies that they would destroy the valuables that are sought by their wielder. Moreover, the weapons' speed makes bargaining almost impossible during a battle. Thus, nuclear weapons can be employed only to deter an attack.

In the 1980s, however, American strategic thinking came to be dominated by the notion that nuclear weapons might be used to prevail in a nuclear war and that defenses against nuclear weapons are possible. Such defenses might include a variety of devices such as electronic particle beams, lasers, and massive rails that, guided by computers, could be hurtled against nuclear missiles in a war. All of the devices mentioned are nonnuclear, and the conception that they would be employed in defenses against nuclear weapons gave renewed credence to the assumption that no clear distinction should be made between nuclear and nonnuclear weapons.

As implied in much of the description of the array of weapons and forces, all weapons kill but some are more efficient than others, and every weapon is not appropriate for every mission. Some weapons are readily available to individuals and groups, whereas others remain in the hands of states, and still others endure within the provenance and control of the most powerful states. Varied accessibility affects the uses of weapons and forces, as will be seen in the following analysis of how they are employed.

• USES OF MILITARY FORCE

Actual uses of military instruments will engage our attention in this section, but absence of use must not be overlooked, for the most effective function of force remains its latency, in which force undergirds an order. A police officer whose nightstick and gun stay holstered represents a stronger effect of force than one whose stick beats and whose gun shoots criminals. An American fleet that patrols the Pacific without firing a shot or engaging in any hostile action reflects a stability promoting commerce, whereas ships engaging in combat struggle to prevail in an armed contest. In both of these examples, the demonstrations of latent force structure and channel politics, whereas the use of force are revealed in struggles without known outcomes.

Uses of force vary widely, and the forms that they take change over time. Objectives also range extensively, so there can be no settled categorization of the uses of force. To examine uses in a reasonably systematic fashion, the following treatment discusses threats and terrorism, civil war and national liberation, conquest and defense, deterrence, and nonmilitary use.

Threats to use force most often emanate from stronger states, though they are not confined to them. Threats are used most frequently in coercive diplomacy and deterrence. Coercive diplomacy employs threats of force and sometimes demonstrations of the use of force in conjunction with specific demands by one government on another. By promising to apply force, the demanding government attempts to coerce the recipient to comply with its demands. Having failed in the use of negotiations and economic sanctions over the course of several years, the United States succeeded in its employment of coercive diplomacy against the Haitian military government in 1994.

Jean-Bertrand Aristide had been elected president of HAITI in 1990, only to be ousted by the military in September 1991. The United States negotiated the Governor's Island accord in July 1993 under which Lt. Gen. Raoul Cedras agreed to allow President Aristide to return to Haiti from his exile in Washington and resume office. When Cedras reneged on this agreement, however, the United States persuaded the United Nations Security Council to embargo the shipment of arms and petroleum to Haiti, and, over time, these sanctions were tightened to include airline flights. Finally, in October 1994, following a propaganda campaign telling of planning for an invasion, the United States mounted an invasion force. Before dispatching it, however, President Bill Clinton sent a quasi-official delegation headed by former President Jimmy Carter and including former Chairman of the Joint Chiefs of Staff Colin Powell and U.S. Senator Sam Nunn to Haiti to try to arrange a peaceful solution to the crisis. During the time that the negotiating team was conferring with Haitian governmental leaders, U.S. troops began to be airlifted from their bases. When apprised of this action, Cedras and his colleagues agreed to step aside and go into exile and to allow

Haitian forces to cooperate with American military troops, who would land in Haiti without resistance. In this case against an exceptionally weak adversary, the United States successfully employed threats to use force because of the imminence of its striking.

On the other hand, coercive diplomacy proved wholly futile in the case of the GULF OF TONKIN incident in August 1964, when it was employed against North Vietnam by the United States. Vietnam had been divided temporarily in 1954, pending talks to hold elections throughout the country in 1956. However, backed by the United States, South Vietnam's ruler Ngo Dinh Diem refused to engage in the necessary preparatory talks, thus preventing the proposed elections from taking place. Furthermore, Diem acted vigorously against his opposition in South Vietnam. As a result, former Vietminh soldiers in South Vietnam began a guerrilla war to undermine the Diem government. As this campaign began to succeed, the United States increased its military advice and assistance in the early 1960s. Part of this help included patrolling in and near North Vietnamese waters by United States Navy vessels. The Gulf of Tonkin incident involved an encounter between one or two of these ships and North Vietnamese torpedo boats in early August 1964.

Although the facts of the encounter were unclear, President Lyndon B. Johnson announced that the North Vietnamese boats had attacked the USS *Maddox* on August 4, and a few days later, the Department of Defense claimed that two destroyers had been fired on. Johnson ordered a retaliatory bombing attack against North Vietnamese targets by U.S. warplanes. Moreover, he sent a resolution to Congress authorizing him to "take all necessary measures to repel any armed attack against the forces of the United States and to prevent further aggression." This resolution passed on August 8 with only a few dissenting votes. The object of Johnson's actions in this case was to persuade the North Vietnamese to end their campaign of intervention in South Vietnam. He pursued that objective by using limited military action that promised more severe punishment and by engendering political support. As the long war and ultimate American defeat in Vietnam attests, however, this bid to employ coercive diplomacy failed. Despite its inferiority in weapons, North Vietnam and its allies in South Vietnam not only fought valiantly but also showed their willingness to absorb casualties at a phenomenal level. They received weapons assistance from the Soviet Union and China to compensate for their technological weakness, but the tenacity with which they fought and their determination to expel the foreign intruder, the United States, supplied the major reactions that proved victorious in the end.

States also employ military threats to deter undesired action by other states. Although some analysts conflate conventional and nuclear deterrence,[16] the differences between the weapons result in very different strategic problems. Particularly when only conventional weapons are employed in deterrence, many calculations—about targets, risks, and will—make it relatively difficult to manipulate incentives in bargaining to deter an action. In contrast, the speed and indiscriminate destructiveness of nuclear, particularly thermonuclear, weapons ensure an ease to deterrence. **Deterrence** is an attempt to persuade another state not to undertake an action by promising to inflict high costs on it if it does begin the undesired action. So long as the military capabilities are extant, the will to retaliate may be presumed. Deterrence will be considered extensively later in this chapter.

Both states and groups use military force in terrorism to influence others. **Terrorism** involves the use of force against third parties—often the citizens of enemy states—to achieve some goal. For guerrilla fighters, as in the Vietnam War, systematic killing of local government officials—mayors, judges, school teachers—is designed to undermine confidence in the national government and destroy the legitimacy of authorities. Similarly, though for different purposes, drug lords in Colombia used terror against judges to ensure that they would be immune from conviction and to persuade everyone of the futility of informing on them. In one of the most effective uses of terror in modern history, the Palestine Liberation Organization, founded in 1967, transformed the Palestinian issue from a question of refugees to that of a national liberation movement and the formation of a Palestinian state by such actions as hijacking civilian airliners. A Palestinian group, Hamas, has employed terror systematically and regularly in Israel to try to derail the negotiated handover of the West Bank and Gaza to a Palestinian authority. However, not just nongovernmental agents like these but also states employ terror to gain their objectives.

Iran promoted the use of terror in the Middle East, particularly Lebanon, by assisting groups in kidnapping hostages and bombing civilian targets. Other states, including the Soviet Union, Syria, and Libya, similarly provided clandestine aid to terrorists in attempts to expel Western influence from the Middle East, including actions against Israel, which is regarded by many as a Western outpost of imperialism. France has used terrorism against those it dislikes, including systematic application of it during its losing colonial war in Algeria in the late 1950s. The Guatemalan government used systematic terror against its citizens in the late 1970s and early 1980s, and Argentina's "dirty war" of the late 1970s that had its army systematically employing assassination and torture against its citizens became infamous. Israel uses terror against civilian targets in Lebanon and in the occupied West Bank and Gaza to deter terrorist attacks against its citizens. In 1986, President Ronald Reagan ordered a bombing raid against civilian targets in Libya to try to dissuade that country from supporting terrorists. By its nature, terrorism strikes in sporadic and surprising ways.

Military force is also employed in coups, civil wars, and national liberation movements, as well as in revolutions. A **civil war** pits a government against either a group that aims by force to displace it and rule the country or a group that seeks autonomy and/or independence for a part of the country's territory. A **national liberation movement** seeks independence from another country that has ruled the territory in question as a foreign power. In both kinds of contests, other countries and international institutions may intervene to support one side or the other, or, alternatively, to seek a negotiated solution.

Challenges to established governments in a civil war most frequently occur when those in power are losing their legitimacy and have been unable to meet the demands of groups within civil society. Generally, when a group strives to wrest control of the government with the aim of putting into place a wholly different political order, both the government and the revolutionaries draw support from outside the country because of the great issues involved. Each of the successful revolutions of history—the French, Russian, Chinese, Cuban, Nicaraguan—drew other countries to support the sides on the basis of fundamental values at stake. Monarchs came to the support of a counterrevolutionary movement in France, while the German government sent Lenin to Russia in a sealed train so that he could capture the Russian revolution and decide to withdraw from the war against Germany. Cuba became a symbol of Cold War hostilities when the United States tried to overthrow and pressure the Castro regime while the Soviet Union subsidized the Cuban economy. In all of these cases, arms proved crucial to the outcomes, but there were obviously other forces at work.

Less dramatic because they entail less fundamental change, civil wars and wars of independence from imperial rule may be determined more decisively by arms. In the nineteenth century, the greatest war was that in North America between the secessionist Confederate States and the United States of America. At the end of the century, European countries and the United States had spread their rule across the world largely by virtue of their superior arms. As a dialectical outcome to that spread of empire, nationalism grew to demand independence from foreign rule. Additionally, with Japan's triumphs over China in 1894–95 and over Russia in 1904–05, non-Europeans were encouraged to believe that European mastery did not promise to be unending. Partly as a result of the defeat in World War I of Germany and the Austro-Hungarian and Ottoman empires, national liberation movements grew in strength and, when the occasion demanded it, took up arms. That period of decolonization ended in the 1980s, to be followed by a different era. During that period of dismantling of European overseas empires, the main processes did not entail the widespread employment of force, but certain of the liberation movements did. The French fought vigorously in Indo-China (Vietnam, Cambodia, and Laos) and in Algeria to retain their overseas possessions, but, in the end, the costs of military force left the French population without the stomach to continue the battle. In throwing off the shackles of European rule, many in Asia and Africa gained support from the contending sides in the Cold War. Thus, for example, Vietnam found Soviet and Chinese support in its wars, first against France subsidized by the United States and then directly against the United States.

When Portuguese rule collapsed in Angola, China, the Soviet Union, the United States, South Africa, and Cuba, in turn, intervened to help the different sides. In this particular case, the combat continued even after the Cold War, thus revealing the essentially local roots of the conflict. For the most part, however, the post-Cold War period has seen a different expression of armed combat as multiethnic, multinational states broke apart in the absence of strong rule and ideological glue to hold them together. These phenomena occurred primarily in the former Soviet Union and former Yugoslavia.

Some twenty-one nationalities had been officially recognized in the Soviet Union under the Communist regime. When the SOVIET UNION collapsed into fifteen successor states, some of these nationalities found themselves in distinct states, such as Lithuania, Georgia, Belarus, and Ukraine. Others formed but part of new states and fought for their own autonomy, as did the people of Nagorno-Karabakh, who sought independence from Azerbijian and who were assisted in their fight by Armenia. That armed dispute ended in 1994 with an internationally brokered settlement. For the most part, major powers other than Russia did not demonstrate any interest in intervening in such disputes, and Russia claimed special interests in the "near abroad," the successor republics other than Russia. However, in the Islamic, Turkic Central Asian states of Kazakhstan, Kyrgystan, Uzbekistan, Tajikistan, and Turkmenistan, although the question of arms did not arise, other countries including Iran and Turkey showed an interest. In Georgia, outsiders did not intervene in the armed conflict. In addition to these states that had become independent in the wake of the Soviet Union's collapse, the main successor, Russia itself, encompassed many ethnic and nationality groups that made claims for autonomy. The most visible of these was the Chechen Republic, whose claims for autonomy prompted Russia to intervene with force in December 1994. Even though the obviously bumbling and partly insubordinate Russian army defeated the main Chechen forces, Moscow nonetheless found itself negotiating a settlement with Chechen leaders and continuing to fight sporadic but determined resistance.

Former Yugoslavia

Another post-Cold War example of state decay leading to the use of military force is provided by former Yugoslavia. After several years of negotiations among leaders of the various constituent parts of Yugoslavia, the country broke apart in 1991 when Croatia and Slovenia declared their independence. The Yugoslav army assumed control of Slovenian border posts but was ousted after brief battle, and fighting broke out in Croatia when Croats clashed with Serbs who did not wish to submit to Croatian rule. Despite warnings by Serbs that they would not live under a Muslim-dominated government, in 1992 Bosnia-Herzegovina also declared its independence. As Serbs claimed autonomy within Croatia and Bosnia, they were supported by the Serbian leader of rump Yugoslavia, Slobodan Milosevic. After several efforts by the European Community to help to bring about a negotiated settlement, international reaction to the breakup of Yugoslavia was conditioned by

Germany's recognition of Slovenia and Croatia in December 1991. The EC followed suit in January 1992. It then recognized Bosnia-Herzegovina in April 1992, and the United States recognized all three new states, which were then admitted as new members of the United Nations.

The course of events in Croatia and Bosnia has been mostly determined by military force, even in the face of international intervention to alleviate human suffering and earnest diplomacy aimed at bringing about solutions to the various disputes. Serbs in both Croatia and Bosnia, urged on and supplied by Milosevic until 1994, fought against government forces to establish control over territory. Particularly in Bosnia, the Bosnian Serbs used tactics referred to as "ethnic cleansing" to drive out non-Serb residents of the territories they conquered. By the end of 1992, the Bosnian Serbs controlled approximately 70 percent of the territory of Bosnia-Herzegovina. In Croatia, Croatian Serbs had gained mastery over a portion of that country when fighting ended; but they were driven out in a Croatian government offensive in August 1995 that produced over 100,000 Serbian refugees. Military conflict continued in Bosnia, interrupted only by temporary cease-fire arrangements. The United Nations agreed in 1992 to impose a "no-fly" order—the prohibition of flights by aircraft—in Bosnia to be enforced by NATO.

Other countries intervened to try to stop the fighting and alleviate hardship to civilians. Jointly, the EC and the UN established a diplomatic mission headed by EC Representative Lord David Owen and UN Representative Cyrus Vance, who was replaced by Thorvald Stoltenberg in 1994. This mission sought a settlement based upon the preservation of Bosnia-Herzegovina as a single state divided into semiautonomous regions and ruled by a weak central government. Its plan entailed the redistribution of territory in which the Serbian portion would be reduced from 70 percent to 49 percent. Later versions retained the territorial proportions but allowed the possibility that the Serbian regions could later choose to join in a federation with Yugoslavia, or, in nationalistic parlance, Greater Serbia. Nevertheless, the Serbs continued fighting to ensure that they controlled continuous territory, and the Muslim-led Bosnian government continued fighting to preserve the integrity of the country it headed.

Because of the violence used against civilians, other countries intervened in two other ways. First, under auspices of the United Nations, beginning in May 1993, Britain and France and other countries deployed forces to establish "safe havens" in Sarajevo and other cities. Basically, the mission of these forces was to protect corridors of supply so that food and medicine could be brought in. Another mission aimed to prevent military attacks against the populations of these enclaves. However, the latter mission proved unattainable until, with the threat of bombing by NATO warplanes, Serbian artillery was withdrawn or impounded within twenty kilometers of Sarajevo. Toward the end of 1994, however, the threat to use outside force was determined not to be feasible in the events in and around Bihac enclave.

There, Bosnian government forces fought their way out of the enclave but were repelled in a counterattack by Bosnian Serb, Croatian Serb, and Bosnian Muslim forces not loyal to the central government of President Alija Izetbegovic. As the counterattack penetrated the ill-defined boundaries of the enclave, NATO warplanes conducted a minor bombing raid against a Serbian airport but refrained from attacking aircraft sitting on the ground. Restraint came in response to the request of the UN forces that remained in Bosnia. At one point, it appeared that those forces might have to be withdrawn, but, eventually, it was determined that they could remain. However, no further use of NATO military attacks occurred, and none was threatened in the Bihac area.

The ostensible lesson learned was that peacekeeping and enforcement actions are incompatible and cannot be conducted simultaneously. Peacekeeping is the function of keeping forces apart and providing access for supplies to civilians in the midst of war, whereas enforcement action entails the employment of military force to coerce behavior. With respect to the question at hand concerning the uses of force, the experience shows that force prevails against other means and that the only way to prevail over an actor determined to use force is to employ greater force against it. To do so, however, is to give up the role of peacekeeper and neutral intermediary. Further, it means taking sides and promoting the cause one of the parties to the conflict.

*   *   *

As with other instruments, then, force and diplomacy have to be used in conjunction with purpose. If purposes are confused or unclear, then neither diplomacy nor force can be used effectively. Whereas interventions in civil wars and wars for independence may not have proper guidance because of confounded purposes, other uses of force tend to be more straightforward.

The most traditional uses of military force involve **conquest** and **defense** of territory. Conquest is the forceful taking of territory, and defense is resistance to conquest. Although such uses of military force may be driven by politics, straightforward war entails combat that is largely decided by the fight itself. Thus, strategy, tactics, labor, equipment, and training intrude themselves as essential prerequisites to successful politics when war becomes the main instrument to achieve state goals. Because no calculus exists to forecast the outcomes of wars, military fights often result in unexpected consequences. For example, the Vietminh fought successful wars against France, then the United States, then South Vietnam. Except for the last, a forecast based upon aggregate capabilities and military forces almost certainly would have predicted triumphs by France and the United States. On the other hand, rough calculations of aggregate capabilities often provide accurate predictions of how military contests will turn out. When the Japanese attacked the United States in December 1941, they knew that ultimately the enemy was stronger militarily but hoped for a failure of will and a negotiated solution.

Sometimes, states decide to expand to increase their aggregate capabilities or for an ideological reason such as spreading revolution or achieving a vision such as America's nineteenth-century "manifest destiny," the slogan used to rationalize continental expansion. On other occasions, states expand to defend themselves. For example, a significant portion of European imperialism amounted to military conquest for the purpose of securing trading outposts. However, such conquests then become the status quo to be defended. History, rather than scientific analysis, affords the appropriate method for determining which side of the two traditional uses of force—conquest or defense—particular episodes or sequences belong to.

Unlike these traditional uses of force, deterrence threatens use under certain conditions. Deterrence may employ either conventional or nuclear weapons, but clarity in conditions for use and the speed and high level of destructiveness of nuclear weapons make deterrence easy to achieve. On the other hand, uncertainties surrounding the effects of conventional weapons as well as a much greater difficulty in defining the conditions under which military action would be taken make conventional deterrence a less efficacious endeavor.

Nuclear Deterrence in the Cold War

In the very long standoff between the United States and the Soviet Union between 1947 and 1989, nuclear deterrence worked effectively to restrain those powers. Given the immense destructive power of thermonuclear weapons, very few of them were needed to ensure that the two superpowers each possessed enough to inflict unacceptable damage on the other should it come under nuclear attack. Moreover, the speed with which that damage could be visited upon the territory of the other ensured that a negotiated truce that might arrest the devastation remained impossible to achieve. Given their speed and destructive characteristics, no genuine use of the weapons could support political objectives; thus, a nuclear attack became the simple, well understood condition for use of the weapons. With such clarity of condition of use and certainty of cost, nuclear deterrence worked effectively.

Some controversy arose between those, like Albert Wohlstetter,[17] who believed that deterrence provided a delicate calculation requiring a clear and effective second-strike capability and some demonstration of will to fire the weapons to make deterrence credible, and others who thought that the very existence of nuclear weapons provided an effective deterrent to their use.

This controversy continues in a slightly different form in the post-Cold War world surrounding the issue of nuclear nonproliferation. Most analysts and policy makers follow Joseph S. Nye, who believes that it is important that nuclear weapons not fall into the possession of dictators and untrustworthy regimes, such as those in Iran, Iraq, and North Korea. This view holds that individual dictators hold the key to use. Arguing to the contrary, Kenneth N. Waltz believes that possession of nuclear weapons causes its own effects of moderating behavior. Thus, even meglomanaical dictators, feeling the security afforded by nuclear weapons but also the fear of retaliation, would forego their use for limited political ends.[18]

Deterrence with Conventional Weapons

Deterrence remains much less certain with respect to conventional weapons, for several reasons. First, conditions of use tend to be more difficult to define, for the range of behaviors that have been the targets of deterrence attempts is very wide. Second, it is fairly easy to calculate that the threats will not be carried out, and, if they are, they can be met by resistance and defense. Third, conventional actions need to be carried out over substantial periods of time, thus allowing for the possibility that diplomacy may kick in to bring an end to armed hostilities.

* * *

Military forces may also be put to nonmilitary uses. Personnel can be dispatched to either domestic or foreign disaster areas to bring relief supplies to victims. They can be deployed in peacekeeping operations designed as a tangible diplomatic tool to keep apart former belligerents who have agreed to their presence. They can be used to suppress rioting, looting, and other civil disturbances. Drug interdiction has become a recent occupation of armed forces. Military displays add to the prestige of a country and are a symbol of autonomy, and military training has been used in many countries as a socializing influence to build up a sense of nationalism. Road-building and other civilian construction projects have sometimes employed armed forces. In defeated countries, military forces act as police and governmental administrations.

In noting some of the activities of military forces, we are brought back to the beginning of this essay but noting that prestige may be the most effective use. When a country has the prestige that comes from former conquest or successful defense, its reputation may be enough to gain it deference and respect from other countries without the need to fight. Combined with a set of ideas that commands the respect of others, such a country may achieve a position of hegemony in which it can lead powerfully in the establishment of a secure international order that may last until it is successfully challenged by another state aspiring to implement a different vision for the realm in which the old order operates.

As all of the varied instruments and techniques of foreign policy are brought to bear in discrete situations, with responses from the recipients of initiatives, distinctive interactions of frequent occurrence and some less recurrent kinds occur. These patterns of interactions are treated in the next chapter.

• IMPORTANT TERMS

accountability
air and space
arms transfers
civil war
conquest
consensus
conventional weapons
coordinating function of diplomacy
defense
detente policy
deterrence
diplomacy
economic assistance
economic sanctions
firestorm
intelligence
intelligence gathering and reporting
land forces
management of information
multilateral conferences
national liberation movement
negotiations
nuclear weapons
operations
plausible deniability
political dynamics
propaganda
rationality
representation
responsibility
rewards and punishments
sea power
terrorism
transparency
weapons of mass destruction

• STUDY QUESTIONS

1. What is the logic implicit in traditional diplomacy that makes it more likely that agreements reached by diplomacy will be carried out, in contrast to resolutions passed by a majority vote in an international conference?

2. What are the many twentieth-century trends that have affected the conduct of diplomacy, and what sorts of effects on practices have they had?

3. Cite examples of success and failure in the use of foreign economic assistance, and explain what accounts for the difference between success and failure.

4. Are economic sanctions effective? On what elements does effectiveness or failure depend?

5. To what extent can the internal politics of a country be manipulated through the employment of economic sanctions by other countries? Which variable has more effect: the state of internal political solidarity or cleavage, or the purpose and unity of the states invoking the sanctions?

6. Examine the ways in which arms transfers combine elements of economics, such as supply and demand and commercial transactions, with elements of security. Does the linking of security and economics always entail the subordination of business to military concerns? Explain.

7. What are the tests of consistency for propaganda campaigns?

8. Explicate the distinctions between the gathering of intelligence and operations, as well as the ways in which they are related and overlap.

9. Of what does the problem of responsibility in a democracy and plausible deniability consist? How would you deal with it?

10. In which ways do nuclear and thermonuclear weapons differ from conventional weapons, and in which ways are they similar? What implications for practical policy do these differences and similarities have? Does the

answer to the second question depend on one's response to the first? Explain.

11. Describe the various uses of force in international politics, using examples to illustrate them.

12. Why has nuclear deterrence proven to be quite effective, whereas attempts at deterrence with conventional weapons have often failed?

• ENDNOTES

1. David A. Baldwin, in *Economic Statecraft* (Princeton, N.J.: Princeton University Press, 1985), pp. 13–14, categorizes techniques in a similar though distinct way. He uses propaganda, diplomacy, economic statecraft, and military statecraft. Baldwin draws on the classic study of Harold D. Lasswell, *Politics: Who Gets What, When, How* (New York: McGraw-Hill, 1936), pp. 204–5, where Lasswell gives as a categorization of techniques "information, diplomacy, economics, force (words, deals, goods, weapons)."

2. Harold G. Nicolson, *Diplomacy*, 3d ed. (London: Oxford University Press, 1963).

3. See, for example, Robert O. Keohane and Joseph S. Nye, *Power and Interdependence*, 2d ed. (Glenview, Ill.: Scott, Foresman, 1989).

4. See Alexander L. George, David K. Hall, and William E. Simons, *Limits of Coercive Diplomacy* (Boston: Little, Brown, 1971). Also see George, *Forceful Persuasion*.

5. See Rostow, *The Stages of Economic Growth*.

6. Based largely on his reading of the use of economic sanctions against Italy in 1935–36, E. H. Carr, in *The Twenty-Years' Crisis*, argues that economic sanctions work only if they are backed by a willingness to use force. The other classic cases include the United States embargo against Japan in 1940 and 1941, restrictions on trade with the Communist countries by the United States and Western Europe from 1948 to 1989, the United States embargo against Cuba from 1960 to date, and the United Nations sanctions against Rhodesia from 1966 to 1979.

7. Baldwin, *Economic Statecraft* (Princeton, N.J.: Princeton University Press, 1985).

8. See Thomas C. Schelling, *The Strategy of Conflict* (Cambridge: Harvard University Press, 1960).

9. Johan Galtung, "On the Effects of International Economic Sanctions, with Examples from the Case of Rhodesia," *World Politics* 19 (April 1967): 378–416.

10. John H. Herz, "The Rise and Demise of the Territorial State," *World Politics* 9 (July 1957): 473–93; and John H. Herz, "The Territorial State Revisited—Reflections on the Future of the Nation-State," *Polity* 1 (Fall 1968): 11–34. Also, Schelling, *The Strategy of Conflict*.

11. Bernard Brodie, *War and Politics* (New York: Macmillan, 1973).

12. Robert J. Art, "To What Ends Military Power?" *International Security* 4 (Spring 1980): 4–35.

13. Jervis, "Cooperation under the Security Dilemma."

14. These estimates are disputed by some authorities who give quite disparate numbers of fatalities. Additionally, certain estimates include casualties and deaths that occurred much later from the effects of radiation.

15. See Schelling, *The Strategy of Conflict*.

16. See Robert Jervis, Richard Ned Lebow, Janice Gross Stein, with contributions by Patrick M. Morgan and Jack L. Snyder, *Psychology and Deterrence* (Baltimore: Johns Hopkins University Press, 1985), and Richard Ned Lebow and Janice Gross Stein, *We All Lost the Cold War* (Princeton, N.J.: Princeton University Press, 1994).

17. See his "The Delicate Balance of Terror," *Foreign Affairs* 37 (January 1959): 211–34.

18. See Waltz, "The Spread of Nuclear Weapons."

CHAPTER 11

Patterns of Interaction among States

Can patterns of behavior be discerned from the foreign policy actions of the powers that fight wars, make peace, fall out, engage in trade, and sometimes help but often oppress the weak? The ability of the powers to work together in one period, such as the 1820s when the Concert of Europe functioned, and their failure to find common ground, as occurred in the late 1940s as the Cold War emerged, seem to suggest that each historical episode is unique. Even though historical epochs—for example, the explosion of imperialism in the late nineteenth century, the Great War, the Cold War—have unique characteristics, repeated behaviors do fit into patterns. As they discover such regularities, analytic observers not only describe them but also seek to explain why states engage in reiterated actions.

Introduction

Recurring patterns of interaction have engendered literatures treating such patterns with both descriptive and explanatory analysis. This chapter examines five categories of these patterns: alliance; integration; relations of equals, including balance of power, concert, and accommodation; crisis management and prevention; and relations of inequality, including domination, imperialism, clientelism, and compliance.

Alliance

An **alliance** brings together two or more states in a cooperative military relationship to face a **common enemy** that either threatens them or has increasing capabilities and appears to harbor ambitions that would threaten them in the future. Sometimes, alliances contain an overlay of ideology or economic and cultural cooperation, but the common threat provides the essential glue to hold the allies together.

Most often, members of an alliance share interests that bring them into alignment, but sometimes they may have parallel interests and enter the alliance for the sake of convenience. As the discussion will show, there are many complications.

As histories of ancient Greece and Rome, India and China, and other regions testify, the formation of alliances against common threats characterizes relations among autonomous units regardless of their attributes or the era in which they exist. In the modern era, one of the great coalitions was that engendered by Napoleon's military conquests. This alliance brought together such disparate states as Prussia, Russia, Austria, and Britain to resist and roll back France's territorial acquisitions.

In the twentieth century, the effect of a common enemy on forging an alliance is illustrated by the GRAND ALLIANCE of World War II. That war began in Europe in September 1939 when Germany invaded Poland and the Soviet Union followed shortly thereafter under color of their agreement made in August. Because they had previously promised to fight Germany if it attacked Poland, Britain and

France declared war on Germany. In examining this equation, it is also important to remember that Germany and the Soviet Union had been declared enemies and that the Soviet Union's ideological hostility to the Western democracies had been reciprocated by Britain's and the United States' intense opposition to communism in the Soviet Union. After France was defeated by Germany in 1940 and divided into an occupied part and a part governed by the collaborative Vichy regime, Germany invaded the Soviet Union in June 1941 and at the end of that year declared war on the United States. For the remainder of the war, Britain, the Soviet Union, and the United States, together with their weaker allies, formed a Grand Alliance that eventually defeated Germany. Following the war, that alliance deteriorated, and a long period of hostility developed between the United States and its allies, including Great Britain, and the Soviet Union. Thus, during World War II, when countries that had been fundamentally and extremely hostile to one another were threatened by a common enemy, they forged an alliance and fought together to defeat that enemy, overcoming very deep-seated animosities and diametrically opposed political, economic, and social systems. Once that enemy had been defeated, the strains that had been present even during the time of the alliance broke out into the open, and the United States and the Soviet Union, in particular because of their power, ended in a position of hostility once again.

• COLD WAR ALLIANCES

The mutual animosity between them led each to develop an alliance with other countries against the other. In this case, the allies did something other than contributing to the strength of the leader. Both the United States and the Soviet Union relied much more on the strengthening of their own respective capabilities than on those of allies. Indeed, they extended their protection to their weak allies. For both leaders, the incorporation of states into their respective alliances deprived the other of access to those states. For example, an important Soviet objective in Eastern Europe was to establish a security **buffer** that would prevent another invasion from Central Europe like those it had suffered in the two world wars. To accomplish this aim, however, the Soviets went much farther by controlling the Eastern European countries through Communist parties and prohibiting their participation in ordinary commerce with the West and in organized endeavors such as

the Marshall Plan, which provided assistance for recovery from the war. The United States, with its long-term commercial expansiveness, had sought access to the Eastern European countries. Moreover, by the Declaration on a Liberated Europe of the Yalta Conference, which was held in March 1945, shortly before the end of the war in Europe, the Soviet Union had acquiesced in the appeal of the United States for free elections in Poland but rejected American criteria for such elections. In the one Eastern European country, Czechoslovakia, that held free elections, Communists with the support of the Soviet Union in 1948 staged a forceful takeover of the government and imposed a dictatorship. Much later, in 1955, following the admission of West Germany to NATO, the alliance between the Soviet Union and its Eastern European allies took a formal, institutionalized shape as the Warsaw Pact.

Just as the Soviet Union did not allow the United States and its allies access to Eastern Europe, the Western countries resisted Soviet access to Western Europe. Fearing that Soviet leader Stalin's intentions included a takeover in some Western European countries by Soviet-supported Communist parties, the United States intervened clandestinely in the French and Italian elections of 1948 to counter Communist influence. In the following year, the North Atlantic Treaty Organization came into being in response to European requests for American membership in an alliance. Also in 1949, the victorious allies' failure to cooperate in defeated Germany culminated in the unification of the western zones of occupation as the Federal Republic Germany (FRG) and the establishment in the Soviet zone of the Democratic People's Republic of Germany. United States protection was extended to the Western European countries through NATO, and that security protection was extended further to Greece and Turkey in 1951 and to the FRG in 1955. By means of this alliance, Soviet expansion as well as access were deterred and denied.

One of the most interesting questions raised in the wake of the **Cold War** concerns how long and in what form NATO will last, for the common enemy no longer poses a threat or even exists. Europeans clearly desire an American presence on their continent, and even such former allies of the Soviet Union as Poland, Hungary, Czech Republic, and Slovak Republic aspire to membership in the alliance. Even Russia has shown some interest in joining, and this possibility has not been turned down. In view of the fact that NATO faces no military threat, something else obviously drives it. Two factors seem to be at work. First, even during the Cold War, the American presence in Europe, in addition to the military protection that it supplied, gave **reassurance** to the allies. Second, one of the main contributors to making the twentieth century the bloodiest in history was the two world wars, which came about largely as a result of European quarrels and ended as they did only because the United States intervened. Succeeding these devastating events came a period of some forty years of prosperity and tranquillity that were accompanied by an American presence and deep involvement in Europe. With such a profound effect wrought by the American involvement in European affairs, the Europeans want the peace and prosperity that have accompanied the good times and wish to avoid the quarrels and deadly wars of bad times. Similarly, Japan continues to aim to preserve its alliance with the United States.

Other countries may vary their alliance strategies. INDIA, for example, adopted a **nonaligned** posture when it gained independence in 1947 and pursued its interests without joining either of the major Cold War coalitions. India was able to pursue such a course partly because it maintained an important measure of power but also because no superpower conflicts extended to the Indian subcontinent. On the other hand, when faced with new challenges from China and its continuing face-off with Pakistan over Kashmir, India in 1971 signed a treaty with the Soviet Union. Similarly, China and the Soviet Union joined in an alliance in 1950, shortly after the communist triumph in the Chinese revolution. However, following the development of major tensions and animosities between these two allies, China did not renew the alliance in 1980, for it had by that time embarked on a distinctive policy course.

Alliances form on both bilateral and multilateral bases. In addition to the already mentioned American Cold War alliances—multilateral NATO and bilateral United States–Japan—the United States allied with forty-two countries between 1949 and 1955. Alliances also form subcoalitions within larger groups. For example, in 1963 France and West Germany forged an alliance that entailed military and other forms of cooperation, even though both remained members of NATO.

Often alliances become formalized through a written treaty, which has the advantage of specifying the exact conditions under which the parties will assist each other and in what ways. On the other hand, alliances sometimes exist more informally, based simply on a **community of interest**.[1] For example, the UNITED STATES AND ISRAEL have never signed a formal security treaty, yet their policies often coincide and their shared interests in the Middle East have remained so obvious that many observers treat their relationship as an alliance. Unspecified interests may demonstrate a closer, easier relationship than a formal commitment to paper. This is illustrated by the cooperation between the Soviet Union and Egypt from 1955 to 1971, when the two countries signed a formal document only after tensions had entered their relationship.[2]

Both powerful and weak states engage in alliances, for all states may suffer from threats emanating from other states. In general, weak states ally with powerful states for protection from nearby countries. Powerful states tend to be wary in such situations, for they need to avoid being drawn into quarrels of weak allies that do not redound to their benefit and in which they do not share interests. On the other hand, weak states need to be concerned that they actually gain the protection for which they entered the alliance.

Powerful states join alliances with weak partners because those allies possess some **asset** that the powerful states need for their own purposes. Following the oil crisis of 1973–74, for example, the United States allied first with Ethiopia and then with Somalia, both in the Horn of Africa, in order to gain military bases close to the Arabian peninsula. In this case, the strategic location of the Horn provided the asset leading the United States to commit to an alliance. In other circumstances, willingness of a weak ally to support a global strategy of the powerful state might lead to alliance links, as was the case with Honduras, which offered itself as a platform for American policies aimed toward neighbors Nicaragua and El Salvador in the 1980s. Another example is provided by Zaire in the same years, for that African country provided a haven for an Angolan group fighting against the Angola government and a conduit for the United States to supply arms to other groups in the same fight. In this case, even though local, the fight pitted major Cold War adversaries against each other, and they needed regional allies to pursue their combat. The Soviet Union and Cuba had access directly to Angola, for they supported the government.

Both the benefits and the burdens of an alliance may be symmetrical or asymmetrical. In the informal alliance between BRITAIN AND THE UNITED

Horn of Africa and Arabian Peninsula

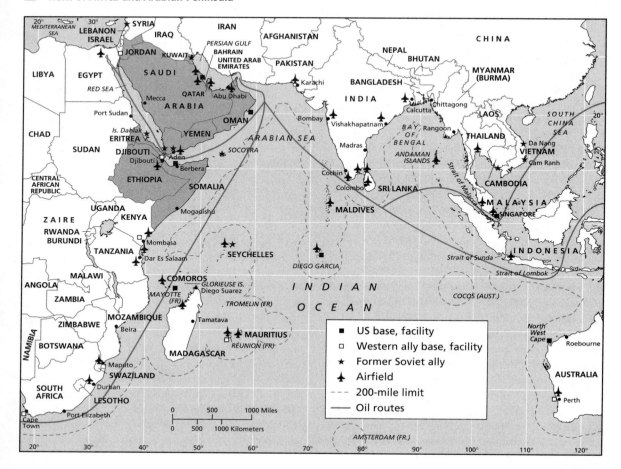

STATES, extending even to the periods of formal alliances from 1941 to 1945 and from 1949 to date, the benefits of avoiding any power's domination of the European continent have been shared equally by the two allies. Moreover, the security afforded by NATO redounded to the benefit of all the allies that shared in the stability and prosperity made possible by that security. On the other hand, by virtue of the uneven distribution of power and assets, more of the burden of the NATO alliance fell on some than on others. America's wealth and military force, particularly its possession of nuclear weapons, meant that the United States gave more to protect Western Europe than did the Europeans. Had a war occurred, however, West Germany was destined to bear the brunt of a Warsaw Pact invasion and would have endured much greater casualties and destruction than the other allies. As Europe recovered from World War II, the European allies assumed a greater

share of the costs of maintaining the alliance than they had earlier. In the Anglo-American alliance in the years 1914–18 and 1939–42, of course, Britain bore substantially greater burdens in fulfilling the purposes of the alliance than did the United States.

Because alliances rely on **common** or **parallel interests,** each ally necessarily has to be concerned about the **reliability of allies,** for circumstances may occur in which the interests that brought the alliance into being change. Such changes may result from the progress of events or from other altered circumstances. For example, in World War II Italy was allied with Germany, but, following its defeat by American and British forces, it switched sides and declared war on Germany and Japan.

Another, more subtle problem of reliability occurred within NATO during the Cold War. Until it became vulnerable to Soviet attack as a result of the invention of the intercontinental missile

(ICBM) in the late 1950s, the United States convincingly protected Western Europe by the threat of massive retaliation in case the Soviets should attempt to invade it. That threat was particularly credible because the United States itself was not easily subject to a counterattack. With the deployment of ICBMs in the early 1960s, however, Europeans began questioning whether the American nuclear deterrent could be relied on in all circumstances. After all, the reasoning went, why should the Americans risk the utter devastation of their own country for, say, a small piece of European real estate? President Charles DeGaulle of France, the most outspoken of those making such arguments, acknowledged that in the end, the Europeans did depend on the American deterrent and that, in most circumstances, he had confidence in it. Nevertheless, situations might occur in which Washington might have a view different from Europe and thus an unwillingness to risk its own destruction for a minor European cause. In such a situation, DeGaulle argued, it was imperative that the Europeans themselves—in this case, France—should have an independent nuclear deterrent to ensure that European interests were protected.

Although alliances show a pattern of behavior that occurs regularly in different international systems, they play different roles in bipolar and multipolar systems, and the choices available to weak countries in regions dominated by a single great power tend to be very limited. In bipolar systems, superpowers tend to rely for their security more on the buildup in their own respective capabilities than on the addition of the capabilities of allies. Countries allied to the superpower are considerably weaker than it is and thus depend on the superpower for their security. They certainly add some capabilities, but they primarily bring other **strategic assets** such as location, or they offer resources that their alliance leader wishes to deprive to its superpower adversary. Moreover, in bipolar systems, the range of choices available to weaker countries is limited to alliance with one of the superpowers or nonalignment. For an allied country that finds it in its interest to realign, its only choice is to join in a pact with the superpower adversary.

Multipolar systems hold more uncertainty and added flexibility. In many cases, an adversary may be unknown, and threats may stem from any of several different quarters rather than only from a second superpower. Possibilities for shifting alliances and participating in more than a single alliance open up in multipolar systems. Moreover, there tends to be much more reliance on adding the capabilities of allies together under multipolarity. Thus, a country may join an alliance to enhance its own capacity to secure itself in a multipolar system as opposed to protecting weaker states, in the case of a superpower, or being dependent on the protection of a superpower, in the case of weaker states. In a multipolar system, even great powers have traditionally relied on alliances, for, unlike superpowers in a bipolar system, they have not had sufficient capacity to build themselves up as the primary method of securing themselves.

Forms of alliances also tend to vary between multipolar and bipolar systems. Traditionally in a multipolar system, allies committed themselves to assisting other members of their alliance in case of war, but their troops were confined to their own national territories, sent abroad only in cases called for in the treaty of alliance. With the unfolding of the bipolar system after World War II, however, allies stationed their troops on the territories of alliance partners, and, though clearly dominated by the respective superpowers, they engaged in joint planning, maneuvers, training with similar equipment, and **integrated command structures** in which military commanders drawn from different countries served in the same chain of command.

Regional situations dominated by a single power comprise a special case of alliance constraints, with the WESTERN HEMISPHERE offering an outstanding case in which certain characteristics transcended bipolarity and multipolarity. In this region dominated by the United States, distant threats from France and Britain in the nineteenth century, Germany in the first half of the twentieth, and the Soviet Union after 1945 were opposed unilaterally or by an alliance led by the United States. The distant threats were effectively met. However, with some local exceptions, the main threat to the security of the Latin American countries, especially those in and around the Caribbean, came from the United States. Thus, the North American colossus intervened militarily in Cuba, Mexico, Nicaragua, Haiti, Dominican Republic, Panama, Grenada, and other countries, and it intervened diplomatically and clandestinely in Guatemala, Guyana, Brazil, Chile, and others. On occasion, one or the other of these countries sought some room for maneuver, to increase its autonomy and freedom of action, only to be met by American resistance, often forceful. Within these severe limits, Cuba suffered a U.S.–sponsored invasion in April

1961 and decades of economic sanctions in reaction to its shift of alliances, and Grenada, being weaker, suffered the fate of an invasion in 1983. However, by following a less drastic course, some other countries found it possible to gain increasing autonomy. One of these was Venezuela, which in the 1970s set a pattern of "globalization" of its diplomatic contacts that included relations with the Soviet Union and Cuba and gained for it both greater domestic security and more flexibility in its foreign policy.[3]

Until it withdrew from the Cold War in 1989, the Soviet Union maintained a similar dominance in EASTERN EUROPE, where it invaded Hungary in 1956 to suppress a move by the government to withdraw from the Warsaw Pact and, together with its allies, occupied Czechoslovakia in 1968 with a force of 500,000 troops to suppress a liberalization of the Communist regime. In such circumstances, the protection for weak allies against a distant threat comes at the price of vulnerability to threat and actual invasion by the protecting ally.

Countries cooperate not just for security purposes through alliances but also to achieve other goals, especially economic ones. Economic and political cooperation falls into another category that is treated under the rubric of integration.

Integration

After World War II, the United States determined to promote international cooperation, for its analysis of the prewar period included the conviction that excessive nationalism was one reason the war had occurred. As the recovery of Europe lagged, the United States in 1947 announced the Marshall Plan, a major program of capital transfers to Europe, to speed economic rejuvenation. However, the primary condition attached to the program required that the European countries themselves collaborate in planning and allocating the funds. This stipulation led the Soviet Union and—with its prompting—the Eastern European countries to reject participation, for they would have had to open up their governments, particularly planning agencies, to personnel from other countries, which the Soviets regarded as a form of spying. The Western European countries, on the other hand, embraced the plan along with its integrative features. Moreover, some of them went considerably further by developing their own institutional forms of integrated economic and political cooperation.

Meanwhile, another form of internationally promoted **integration** proceeded in the western occupation zones of GERMANY. Although efforts to cooperate on writing a peace treaty with defeated Germany broke on the rocks of great power interests and ideology, the United States and its two democratic occupying partners did combine to introduce in 1948 a currency reform, effectively uniting their zones of occupation. In reacting to this rebuff, the Soviet Union imposed a blockade around Berlin, and in response, the United States and Britain undertook an airlift, which was not challenged by the Soviet Union, that supplied the western sectors of Berlin. By the time that the Soviet Union entered negotiations and finally agreed in May 1949 to reopen land access to the embattled city, Germany had been effectively divided into two separate states, with Berlin remaining in an unresolved though occupied status and surrounded by East Germany. In 1949, the two German states officially gained diplomatic recognition as sovereign entities.

• WESTERN EUROPEAN INTEGRATION

At this point, French and West German policies dovetailed to produce an extraordinary level of integrative cooperation among a limited number of Western European states. France's aim was to ensure that Germany would not again rise to attack it as its Teutonic neighbor had in 1870, 1914, and 1940. To accomplish this, certain French visionaries developed the idea that Western European governments could join together in economic collaboration that would eventually lead to political cooperation. In conjunction with this goal, West Germany aspired to cooperate with its erstwhile enemies as a way of regaining normal state status, of rehabilitating its reputation after the horrors that Germany had wreaked on Europe and on Jews and other groups of its own population in World War II. Given the division of Europe between East and West that developed in the second half of the 1940s, even resulting in the form that Germany took, West German Chancellor Konrad Adenauer opted to demonstrate his country's promise by cooperating with the West.

The first institution in which these aspirations were embodied was the European Coal and Steel Community, which combined the efforts of six countries (in addition to West Germany and France, Italy and the Benelux countries—Belgium, the Netherlands, Luxembourg—comprised this group) in the entire supervision of coal and steel production in all of them. To accomplish this, they created a High Commission, a supranational body that regulated all aspects of these industries, including labor laws, production codes, marketing schemes, and so forth.

The success of the ECSC prompted the "six" to initiate other schemes to promote the integration of their countries. A first effort, the European Defense Community, failed, as the French parliament voted against it. By 1957, though, the Six signed the Treaty of Rome to create two new integrative institutions: the European Economic Community, which was a customs union, and the European Atomic Energy Community. Although attempts to widen the community faltered, with France's veto of Britain's application in 1963, cooperation among the Six proceeded apace. By 1967, the Six agreed on a common agricultural policy and brought the three extant communities under a single umbrella, the European Community. In 1973, together with Denmark and Ireland, Britain joined the EC, and the **widening** process continued when Portugal, Spain, and Greece were added in the 1980s. A further widening occurred in 1995, when Austria, Finland, and Sweden joined. In a referendum in late 1994, Norwegian voters advised their government not to join, and the government acted in conformity with that advice.

When the movement for regional integration in Western Europe got under way, there were supporters who aimed to build a federal European state that would unite its members, but they were opposed by others who thought that European organizations should reflect a conception of a "Europe of fatherlands." Institutional arrangements exhibit both these tendencies, though the Council of Ministers, composed of the member governments' foreign ministers, comprises the principal decision making body. Other institutions include a Commission that administers the affairs of the community and supervises the bureaucratic staff in Brussels. In addition, there is a Parliament with limited powers of consultation and the Court of Justice.

In 1985, the Europeans renewed their energy to deepen the community when they agreed to the Single European Act, which strengthened the institutions and set the goal of completing an internal market by the end of 1992. This completion entailed the free flow of trade, money, services, and workers among the members. Then, in 1991, the members agreed to the Maastricht Treaty that set Europe further along the road in its **deepening** process. In addition to the "pillar" of the European Community, the treaty added two additional "pillars": 1) Common Foreign and Security Policy and 2) Justice and Home Affairs. The treaty provided that the renamed European Union would create by 1999, for at least some of its members, a central bank with a common currency. In addition, the treaty undertook to begin to foster a common foreign and defense policy. Moreover, increased attention was brought to bear on an older organization dating from the Brussels Pact of 1948. This is a comprehensive alliance among Britain, France, and the Benelux countries that had been formed to defend its members against any attack. Germany and Italy were added in 1954. This entity, called the Western European Union, includes ten countries of the European Union as full members, with Iceland, Norway, and Turkey as associate members and Denmark and Ireland as observers. Discussions about this institution have gone forward, with some arguing for its integration within the EU and others advocating its use as a "bridge" between the EU and NATO. The association of three NATO members who are not also EU members indicates movement in the latter direction.

Several other attempts at economic integration have been tried in various parts of the world, but none has achieved the success of Western Europe. How can these contrasting experiences of failure in many areas and successful widening and deepening in Europe be explained? Two characteristics of the European situation—one international, the other domestic—may provide the explanation. Western Europe's fundamental security problem was solved by the bipolar system and the United States' commitment to provide for the defense of its allies. In the absence of a security threat, the Europeans did not have to concern themselves with the relative gains problem. Even though Germany—even truncated West Germany—may have retained its naturally dominant economic position in Europe, its partners in the EC had no need to be concerned that the Federal Republic would convert any of its relative gains into weapons that would confront them with a security threat. Neither did Germany have to worry about all or some of its partners turning their gains to its security disadvantage. This international structural explanation may have been reinforced by the high level of industrial skill and capacity that the Western Europeans had reached in their histories, offering them an extraordinary foundation upon which to build their economic advances. It was this latter factor that enabled the Europeans to benefit so handsomely from Marshall Plan capital assistance. No other region has embodied these same characteristics, and, of course, the bipolar structure that set the integration process in Western Europe on its way has disappeared.

At issue in the future will be the direction of further developments. One obvious possibility is that Europe's process of widening and deepening the association of member states will endure. In this case, the alternatives would consist of maintaining a Europe of fatherlands in which each state would persist in its control of its own destiny, and of merging into a great European state, the equal of other continental-size major powers such as the United States, China, and Russia. Another possibility, seldom reflected on, is the onset of a process of disintegration, in which the several European states would each go its own way. Such a breakup might occur over a long period of time in which mutual confidence would be eroded by the separate actions of one or more members. In contrast, disintegration could occur very rapidly if, faced with a major crisis, the individual states were to choose different sides and form into opposed alliances. Neither of these scenarios of decay appears ready to manifest itself, so the conclusion must be that the momentum of further integration seems more probable.

Integration has been able to proceed in Europe because, though unequal, the states that are members of the European Union have not been required to concern themselves with the security implications of economic activity. Prior to the emergence of the bipolar international structure, however, the major powers did have to address the security problems posed by the ambitions and anxieties of others. Moreover, the superpowers in the bipolar structure fixed their gazes each one upon the other, for the gains of the Soviet Union bore upon the security concerns of the United States, and those of the latter challenged the security of the USSR. Even while all states in an anarchic system need to help themselves, the problems of threat, domination, and security arise in most obvious form among the major powers within an international system, and typical patterns occur as the leading states compete with one another.

Relations of Equals

The primary pattern in the relations of equals, the balance of power, was described and analyzed in Chapter 4, for the balance of power concept provides the best general description of the way in which international politics operates when viewed from a systemic perspective. In this section, the operation of the balance of power resulting from the individual calculations of states is treated. As will be seen, that operation is marked by uncertainty and complexity. On occasion, effective application of balance of power requires a war of opposition to a state ambitious to dominate others. Unlike systemic treatment of this concept, the analysis of this section also includes attention to its operation on a regional basis. The role of the state in balancing the effects of the market will also be considered.

Relations of equal states are not exhausted by balance of power, for they sometimes form patterns of concerts of power, or "rule by a central coalition."[4] Although concerts have tended to last a very short time before disintegrating into more typical balancing behaviors, they comprise an important pattern during the periods in which they do exist. Another pattern making its appearance from time to time and tending to be short-lived is **accommodation** among equal powers. At various times and in particular circumstances, patterns of accommodation are called **detente, entente,** and **appeasement.** During the Cold War, a pattern of **crisis management** appeared, and the superpowers strove to build crisis prevention regimes.[5] These patterns occurred within a context of balancing, but they were the result of efforts to set limits on and rules for the underlying antagonistic contest.

• BALANCE OF POWER

Balance of power is a pattern arising out of the quest of a single state to dominate and the response of others in opposition to that quest. The great energy released by the French Revolution of 1789 led in the years following to its spread under the leadership of Napoleon. His was an attempt to dominate the entire continent of Europe. Although this venture attracted allies, it was eventually subdued in 1814 by the concerted actions of other powers to resist that domination and turn it back. This incarnation of the balance of power gave rise to many different wars and battles, ranging from the guerrilla war conducted by determined Spaniards against their French occupiers to the brilliant campaigns of the emperor at Austerlitz and finally to his ignominious retreat from Moscow, defeated not by confrontation with the Russian army but by the lack of food and the harsh winter. In retrospect, one may draw a sharp picture in black and white portraying Napoleonic France as the power that sought to dominate Europe brought down by a coalition resisting that force through the operation of a balance of power. At the time, however, people saw a multihued panorama of campaigns and battles, movements and mass armies, heroic deeds and starving, ragtag armies. From that panoply, however, emerges the tendency to maintain position in the international system in times of ambition by dynamic powers by resisting that quest for domination. On a temporary basis, not every state proved successful at holding its place. Nevertheless, in the end, many states were restored and an arrangement was made that sought to avoid a recurrence of conquest. In Germany, many smaller principalities were consolidated into larger units.

World War I Alliances

Because of the difficulty of recognizing a quest to dominate, states sometimes try to anticipate action by forming defensive alliances to protect themselves against any challenge that might arise. Following unification in the latter part of the nineteenth century and its war with France, Germany formed the Triple Alliance with Austria-Hungary and Italy in 1882. This alliance was countered at the turn of the century by the Triple Entente between France, Russia, and England. A variety of cross-cutting issues set the members of these groups against one another, but overall, the alliances were designed in anticipation of actions by adversaries that would have led to such strengthening that a single power—France or Germany—might rise to a position of dominance. Events did not proceed in a direct fashion, even though operation of a pattern of balance may be discerned in the construction of these alliances and the outcome of World War I, which they fought.

In the summer of 1914, uncertain of England's reliability, France and Russia mobilized against German and Austrian mobilization plans put into effect following the assassination of Archduke Ferdinand in Sarajevo by a Serbian nationalist. Italy declared its neutrality and later joined the coalition fighting against its former partners. The horrible war was not brought to a conclusion until the Bolshevik revolution in Russia led to that country's withdrawal from the war and previously neutral United States entered on the side of Britain and France. Some analysts have argued that, had England's determination to go to war been transparent, the war would never have started. Whether that counterfactual interpretation seems compelling or not, the fact remains that each state acted in the context in which it found itself for its own interests, yet the broad pattern of interactions can be read as a balance of power one.

World War II Alliances

World War II demonstrates quite a different configuration in how a balance of power may express itself, for alliances did not form in anticipation of a need for them. Instead, the powers did not recognize threats as they presented themselves, and they responded so tardily that they were compelled to fight a war to defeat the aspiring hegemon. In Europe in the late 1930s, as Germany sought to expand, Britain and France in a policy of appeasement placated the ambitions by actually condoning in 1938 Germany's takeover and dismemberment of Czechoslovakia. In anticipation that Hitler would next go after Poland, the democracies pledged to go to war in the event that Germany attacked its eastern neighbor. Meanwhile, unable to come to an agreement with the democracies jointly to oppose further German conquest, the Soviet Union joined in the partition of Poland in 1939. Britain and France proved ineffective as Germany swept over most of Europe, including France, by 1940 and then invaded the Soviet Union in mid-1941. Neither did any major power oppose the Japanese conquest of Manchuria in 1931 or its invasion of China in 1937. The United States applied economic sanctions to Japan as a method of signaling its resistance to further Japanese conquests. Only the direct attack by the Japanese on American bases in Hawaii and the Philippines, followed by Germany's declaration of war against the United States, brought the North American power into the conflict in alliance with Britain and the Soviet Union.

* * *

Shortly after the defeat of those who sought to dominate, a new and different pattern of balance arose in the late 1940s, a bipolar pattern in which only two superpowers vied for influence and acted to prepare themselves against the possibility that one or the other would undertake to become dominant in the world as a whole.

Because resistance is a response to the intention to dominate, states sometimes may miscalculate by going to war to oppose an action that had not been intended as a pursuit of domination. There is reason to believe that the United States' decision to intervene in KOREA in 1950 and its choice to escalate its intervention in VIETNAM in 1965 may illustrate this type of miscalculation. In the first case, President Truman's decision to defend South Korea against North Korea's invasion rested on the presumption that the Soviet Union was expanding. The opening of Soviet archives after the Cold War, however, tend to show that Stalin was most reluctant to endorse Kim Il Son's ambition to unite Korea by force, although in the end he did give the signal to proceed.[6] American determination in Vietnam was fueled by the view that China sought to dominate Southeast Asia, whereas the consensus of observers holds that Vietnamese unification was an entirely national endeavor, and both distant and recent history testify to the animosity between China and Vietnam.

Thus far, the illustrations apply to major powers, but REGIONAL BALANCES also tend to recur. For example, as global politics was dominated after World War II by the contest between the United States and the Soviet Union, India and Pakistan faced off in South Asia, both arming and maneuvering in relations with other countries to offset any tendencies to domination that either of the powers might develop. Another example during the same period is offered in the Middle East, where several elements of balance occurred between Israel and the Arab states and between Iran and Iraq. A subset of balancing behavior occurred in the competition between Syria and Israel over Lebanon to ensure that one of them did not gain sufficiently complete control of that state to threaten the other. To this end, Syria intervened in Lebanon with 15,000 troops in 1976, and Israel intervened to create a "security zone" in the southern part of the country; then, Israel launched an invasion in 1982.

These cases illustrate the uncertainty and lack of clarity in the operation of the balance of power while it is occurring, even though hindsight enables analysts to perceive a recurring pattern. They also depict anticipatory behaviors by leaders responding to impending or potential undertakings in pursuit of dominance. As mentioned, balancing patterns recur regularly in international politics, but they do not comprise an exclusive pattern of state behavior.

• CONCERT OF POWER

Another pattern that occurs with less frequency is a concert of power, that is, a collaborative undertaking by leading powers to put into place a system of domination to which they agree. Concerts tend to be constructed in the aftermath of wars, and they tend to be short-lived.

Upheld as a model of this type of major power collaboration, the CONCERT OF EUROPE was formed after the end of the Napoleonic Wars and the Congress of Vienna in 1814–15. Its institutional embodiment included Britain, Russia, Prussia, and Austria-Hungary comprising the Quadruple Alliance, which included France in consultations. The powers agreed that legitimacy—the divine right of kings—should be upheld against democratic revolutions and that contentious problems should be resolved through conferences among them. This concert faltered on several shoals, as democratic revolutions proceeded in 1830 and 1848, and the powers failed to find a solution to the crisis that led to the Crimean War in 1854.[7] Although the mechanism of multilateral conferences continued to be used late in the century—specifically the 1884 Congress of Berlin—the Concert of Europe as a normal arrangement for managing the problems arising from anarchy had long before failed.

In the twentieth century, the powers have turned to the more systematic methods of international organizations, in particular the League of Nations and the United Nations, which will be treated fully in Chapter 13. However, following the end of the Cold War, a renewal of interest in a concert became demonstrable.[8] The main ingredients for a consensus on a principle around which powers could collaborate consisted of the widespread adoption of market economics and of liberal democracy. Uncertainty about the structure of the international system and the dynamics underlying the changes taking place in the 1990s, however, made it difficult to foresee how established any concert might become and, if established, how long it might last.

• ACCOMMODATION

Equal powers often also engage in patterns of accommodation in which they attempt to make arrangements under which they can compete without going to war with one another. One of the major recent efforts in this pattern occurred between the United States and the Soviet Union as they engaged in various attempts to reach accords that would, if not settle their differences, set rules of engagement that would reduce the chances of direct clashes. These efforts began right after World War II and continued into the 1950s with little success. However, following the Cuban missile crisis of 1962, the superpowers succeeded in their policies of detente and coexistence, and they were able to make accommodations in arms control arrange-

.ments, trade, and the establishment of limited **crisis prevention regimes.**

United States–Soviet Union Detente

Accommodation between the United States and the Soviet Union was expressed in 1963 in several forms. A Partial Nuclear Test Ban Treaty that was negotiated by the superpowers plus Britain and open to others for signature prohibited nuclear tests in all environments except underground. Within a few years, the Cold War antagonists and other states had agreed to the Nuclear Non-proliferation Treaty, with the nuclear signatories undertaking not to transfer nuclear weapons or engineering and manufacturing technology to nonnuclear states, and nonnuclear signatories agreeing neither to develop nor acquire nuclear weapons. In addition to arms control measures, the United States and the Soviet Union signed bilateral trade and cultural agreements, as well as the so-called "hot line" accord. This arrangement established a direct telecommunications link between the White House in Washington and the Kremlin in Moscow, the absence of which made more difficult than necessary communication between Kennedy and Khrushchev during the Cuban missile crisis.

Despite what President Lyndon B. Johnson called a "bridge building" effort, further accommodation between the Cold War adversaries was slowed by the American war in Vietnam and the August 1968 Warsaw Pact invasion and occupation of Czechoslovakia to crush the liberalization movement called the "Prague Spring" that was designed to move toward "Communism with a human face."

In 1969, at the beginning of his administration, President Richard M. Nixon undertook a deliberate policy of detente toward the Soviet Union, and his dedication was matched by that of Secretary Leonid Brezhnev, who was guided by a concept of **peaceful coexistence.** Both leaders were steered by analyses of a changing distribution of power in the world, but their differing conceptions of the tasks rendered the terms of their agreements less than precise and ensured that difficulties would accompany implementation.

Central to their efforts were arms control measures that resulted in the Strategic Arms Limitation Treaty (SALT I), an agreement to cap temporarily the number of missiles that each would deploy while they negotiated a permanent limitation, and the Antiballistic Missile System Treaty (ABM Treaty), which provided that no continental defense against missiles would be deployed and that limited defenses

would be severely restricted in number. The ABM Treaty remained the centerpiece of arms control efforts that lasted through the end of the Cold War and beyond, even though technological change created pressures to modify it. Technological innovation—specifically the invention of the MIRV, which allowed the placing of multiple independently targeted nuclear warheads on a single launcher—had a deeper impact on the offensive missile pacts, for it allowed an intensification of the arms competition despite the treaties that presumably limited arms.

Superpower accommodation in the early 1970s also included the Basic Principles Agreement (BPA), which outlined codes of behavior for the parties. Shortly after its signature in 1972, events in the 1973 war in the Middle East demonstrated the limits of such crisis prevention arrangements. The BPA included a provision that each party would inform the other of any plans of their respective allies in the Middle East to go to war. From the Soviets' perspective, they fulfilled this obligation by passing on to the United States their observation that Egypt was planning an attack on Israel. In contrast, American officials felt that the Soviets had not completed the bargain because they had not given a precise warning of the Egyptian attack that included times, places, numbers of troops, and so forth.

Another aspect of the accommodation stemmed from weaknesses in Soviet agriculture and a need to import grain, together with an American desire to entice the Soviet Union into a web of commercial interdependence. This angle of detente was discombobulated by American congressional action that attached an amendment to the 1974 Trade Act, the Jackson-Vanik Amendment, that tied the granting of **most-favored nation (MFN)** treatment of Soviet commerce to revisions in that country's emigration law. Rejecting the condition as an unwarranted interference in their internal affairs, the Soviets also made known that they regarded the United States as an unreliable trading partner.

The detente between the superpowers in the 1970s failed for deeper conceptual and practical reasons than any of those surveyed so far, however. In their analysis of the changed **correlation of forces** in the world, the Soviets interpreted their rough equality in nuclear weapons as the achievement of equality with the United States in general terms. Even though American officials were aware of the nuclear balance and of their own country's relative decline since 1945, their analysis also showed that the American economy remained double that of the

Soviet Union and that their diplomatic skills and prestige far outpaced those of the adversary. Thus, from the American point of view, some accommodation was warranted, but the superiority of its analysis was proved in the successful United States policy of enticing Egypt to reverse alliances.

Another difference in conceptualization governed their policies with respect to the Third World. Soviet leaders wanted accommodation to ensure that war did not break out at the strategic level with the United States, but they wished to compartmentalize that relationship. They sought freedom to support wars of national liberation and Marxist revolutions in Africa, Asia, and Latin America. Following the logic of **compartmentalization,** the Soviet Union became very active in Africa, especially in Angola, Mozambique, and Somalia, in the mid-1970s; it invaded Afghanistan, an Asian neighbor, in 1979; and it extended assistance to revolutionary groups, including the triumphant one in Nicaragua, in Central America after 1979.

In contrast to compartmentalization, the United States sought **linkage.** Particularly as articulated by Henry A. Kissinger, Nixon's national security advisor and later secretary of state, the United States hoped to manage the Soviet Union's behavior in the Third World by manipulating "carrots and sticks" in the bilateral relationship. Thus, it was thought that the Soviets would be rewarded with trade in exchange for their refraining from belligerent activity in, say, Africa. Similarly, should they—in American eyes—misbehave in Africa, they could be deprived of commercial concessions.

With the collapse of communism in the Soviet Union and the disintegration of that empire into its constituent republics in 1991, such gulfs in thinking shrunk in the absence of ideological cleavage. Instead, it was possible for accommodation to proceed between various Western countries and Russia in a more pragmatic fashion. Important reductions in nuclear weapons inventories were achieved through negotiations, and the three other successor republics possessing nuclear weapons—Belarus, Kazakhstan, and Ukraine—agreed to transfer theirs to Russia. In former Yugoslavia, despite differing historical affinities and approaches, Russia and the Western European countries as well as the United States found a minimal basis on which to coordinate policies. Expansion of NATO by admitting Eastern European countries such as Poland and the Czech Republic remained in the mid-1990s a contentious matter, but both the United States and Russia handled it without rancor, despite their inability to accommodate the issue.

Comparing the Cold War and post-Cold War periods, one concludes that accommodation remains available to decision makers regardless of ideological differences and chasms in their definitions of national interest. Nevertheless, ideology and the conviction that one is facing an enemy put up obstacles to accommodation, which is more readily achieved when states face one another only over rational calculations of interest.

Crisis Management and Prevention

Particularly in the antagonistic relationships between the United States and the Soviet Union during the Cold War but also in other international relations, short-term conditions took on dangerous overtones, including the threat of war. Such crises occurred in 1948 with the Berlin blockade, in 1955 and 1958 in the Taiwan Straits, in 1962 when the Soviet Union proceeded to build nuclear missile installations in Cuba, in 1973 in the Middle East, and in various other circumstances. Lesser crises happened between ships at sea, in several American penetrations of Soviet air space, and in the Tonkin Gulf incident in 1964.

The paramount challenge for a protagonist in a **crisis** is to achieve goals without resort to force, and the antagonist aims to prevent injury to its values while avoiding war. Thus, even though the adversaries in a crisis strive for conflicting ends, they share an interest in not paying the high costs of war. Building on that shared interest, antagonists often try to manage crises, to manipulate their relationship in the short-term episode without the rupture that would be caused by the outbreak of war. Furthermore, based upon the expectation that an adversarial relationship will produce crises under given circumstances, the contenders sometimes try to construct an arrangement designed to avoid crises altogether.

Although a great deal of attention focused on the Cold War adversarial relationship between the United States and the Soviet Union, both of those countries faced crises in relations with allies and with other states. For example, late 1956 saw a major crisis between the United States and its NATO allies Britain and France when those European countries joined with Israel in attacking Egypt and the United States effectively opposed the action by both diplomacy and economic coercion. Simultaneously, the

Soviet Union and Hungary opposed each other over the issue of Hungarian alliance and internal policies, and the crisis ended with the Soviet military's crushing a Hungarian popular uprising in support of its government and replacement of that government with one ready to comply with Soviet commands. Additionally, the Soviet Union faced crises with allies Czechoslovakia and China, and the United States found itself embroiled in crises with allied states such as France and Japan and with revolutionary Iran, neutral Lebanon, and divided Angola. Other states as well—China and India, India and Pakistan, Israel and Syria, Iraq and Kuwait, Kenya and Tanzania, South Africa and Mozambique, Argentina and Chile, Brazil and Venezuela, Colombia and Peru, Nicaragua and Honduras, Honduras and El Salvador, China and the Philippines, Indonesia and Malaysia, to mention a few examples—have faced crises in their relationships.

Crises involve threats usually including the possibility of violence, which imply a shortened span of time for making decisions to deal with the situation. Because a crisis occurs publicly, the prestige of the states involved comes into play. From time to time, surprise may provide an additional element of a crisis. The nature of a crisis tends to impose the requirement that high-level policy makers focus on the situation, and such a focus often brings clarity to the analysis of stakes and interests by isolating a particular set of circumstances from the myriad issues pressing on these authorities. Crises that end in a resolution without war may be said to have been successfully managed. When crises end in war, one of two broad causes may be said to have been at work. Lack of skill or incompetence in managing a crisis might cause the situation to deteriorate into violence. On the other hand, the crisis might have been an alerting mechanism to reveal a deeper, more complex issue involving irreconcilable interests not susceptible to solution through management. In such a case, war may provide the only effective means for deciding the issue. These different outcomes may be illustrated by contrasting cases.

A crisis arose in 1948 in occupied Germany that focused on BERLIN and was resolved peacefully in 1949. For three years following the end of World War II, the occupying powers—Britain, France, Soviet Union, and United States—attempted to concert policies governing Germany, but the Soviet-capitalist cleavage made itself felt in their inability to find common ground. With inflation and other economic instability in Germany, there was an obvious need for a currency reform, but the occupying powers failed to agree on putting it into effect. To confront the economic problem, the United States, joined by Britain and France, jointly implemented currency reform in their zones of occupation, effectively uniting those zones into a single political unit. In response, the Soviet Union imposed a surface blockade around Berlin, the former capital city located deep within the Soviet zone of occupation, by denying access to Berlin by road, rail, and canal.

The United States and Britain perceived the blockade as an attempt to erode their right, earned by conquest, to have access to Berlin. Their response to the blockade took the form of an airlift of food, fuel, and supplies to Berlin that continued until, through diplomatic negotiations, the Soviets lifted the blockade. From the point of view of crisis analysis, the outcome that avoided war was quite successful. Skillful management had included a firm but not violent response by the United States to what was a belligerent act by the Soviet Union against the western zones of occupation in Germany. Seen from a larger perspective, this crisis provided the occasion for the division of Germany that lasted until 1990, for two German states were created in 1949 at the resolution of the crisis. Although Berlin found itself once again supplied by economical surface transport, the city remained an anomaly 110 miles inside East Germany, cut off from West Germany, which claimed residual jurisdiction over the city. Thus, the crisis did not end in war, but it did signal and consolidate the very profound divide of the Cold War between the Soviet Union and its allies and the United States and its allies that lasted for four decades. Moreover, the anomaly of Berlin allowed Soviet Premier Khrushchev to create and maintain a sense of crisis for several years beginning in 1958 with a threat to turn over control of access to Berlin to the East German government. Then, with East Germans escaping into West Berlin at the rate of one thousand per day in July 1961, the East German government, backed by the Soviets, closed off the two parts of Berlin by building a wall, which became a symbol of the East–West divide during the remaining years of the Cold War.

WORLD WAR I was a calamity, the bloodiest and most costly war in history to that time. Partly because of its enormity and its profound consequences, much effort has gone into the analysis of its causes. However, the immediate situation in 1914 leading to the outbreak of war was a crisis set off when a Serbian nationalist assassinated the archduke

Berlin During the Cold War

West Berlin, situated in the middle of the German Democratic Republic, 110 miles from West Germany, was for a long time (1947–1961) an unsettled situation in the Cold War.

Chronology:

1948–1949—blockade of Berlin by the USSR; American airlift

1961—construction of the wall cutting off West Berlin and preventing the exodus of East Germans

1989—dismantling of the wall, a symbol of the end of the Cold War and the division of Germany

of the Austro–Hungarian Empire. Other crises in the Balkans in preceding years had ended without violence, testimony to successful management. With all of the underlying causes at work that one can bring to bear in an explanation of the origins of the war, the immediate situation was one of crisis that was not managed effectively.

Bungled management took place, of course, in a context of rigid alliances arrayed against each other, shifting balances of power in which the major countries gained strength unevenly, such bureaucratic elements as fixed mobilization schedules, and attitudes of militarism. At the center, moreover, stood "imperial Germany . . . eager to disrupt the status quo . . . by war if necessary" and the strategically unprepared British who were "led . . . to pursue an indecisive middle course" that made it impossible for them to deter the Germans.[9] Nevertheless, those developments formed a background for the immediate crisis episode that ended with the guns of August thundering their announcement of the outbreak of war.

• INVASION OF KUWAIT CRISIS

Three-quarters of a century later, Iraq invaded Kuwait, setting off a crisis that culminated in the brief Gulf War of January–February 1991. Despite aspects of imperfect management, the violent outcome to the crisis fits more nearly the third scenario outlined above in which the crisis reveals an unforeseen but deep-seated divergence of interests that can only be resolved by war. Iraq had long pressed its view that the rich Rumailia oil fields lying along its border with Kuwait should be conceded to it, and in 1990, Iraq expressed its displeasure over Kuwait's selling oil at a rate that drove prices down. Even as Iraq mobilized troops along the Kuwaiti border in mid-July 1990 to signal its determination to press its claims, the United States made an official statement to President Saddam Hussein that it took no position in territorial disputes between Arab states, thus disavowing any intention of defending one party or another, although its position may have emboldened the Kuwaitis in their refusal seriously to negotiate differences with Iraq. Several Arab leaders had sought a diplomatic solution to the impasse but without success when the Iraqi army marched into Kuwait on August 2. President George Bush declared that Iraq should be forced to withdraw. Iraq offered to withdraw on the condition that the for-

mer government would not be restored to power in Kuwait, but Bush's belligerent determination on unconditional withdrawal and his demonizing of Iraq's leader made a diplomatic solution unlikely. Added to that, Hussein proved himself to be a stubborn and uncompromising leader when faced with coercion.

Over the course of months, the United States skillfully built a coalition of countries that supported the deployment of a half-million person expeditionary force in Saudi Arabia and the waters off Kuwait, and the United Nations Security Council conferred legitimacy on the undertaking by passing a series of resolutions requiring the complete withdrawal of Iraq from Kuwait. In the face of Iraq's refusal to capitulate, the United States and its allies launched a massive air attack against both the troops deployed in Kuwait and a variety of military and command and control facilities as well as infrastructure in Iraq proper. Following some forty days of air assault, the allied forces launched a ground attack that drove the Iraqi forces from Kuwait within several days. Altogether, the war lasted forty-three days, but sanctions applied against Iraq for a variety of activities not related to the invasion remained in place six years after the war ended.

Iraq's implacability, the United States's continued military presence in the Persian Gulf area, and the maintenance of sanctions designed to stifle Iraq's ambitions to become a military power testify to the **deep conflict** over power, prestige, territory, international norms, and control of oil production that underlay the Iraq–Kuwait crisis. That deep conflict appeared in shadows and hints before 1990, but the crisis brought clarity to a longer-term struggle among states that may not be resolved definitively for some time. Given the seriousness reflected by the crisis, it is difficult to imagine that the crisis could have been managed successfully had greater skill been present. Despite our ability to spot failures of management, misjudgments, and mistakes, the aftermath of deep hatred and unyielding animosity surely lead us to conclude that this conflict is one whose most likely solution will be by force. Because Iraq continues to show determination to struggle for its cause and the United States remains adamant in its dedication to supervising Iraq, one must expect that other crises will occur in the future. The conditions for creating a crisis prevention regime do not exist in the Gulf area.

Persian Gulf Region

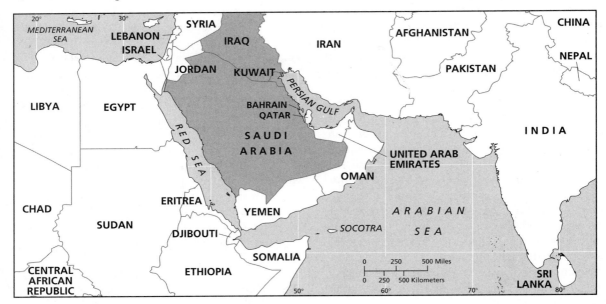

• CRISIS PREVENTION

Crisis prevention is a term that covers a variety of traditional diplomatic practices aimed at treating disputes that might arise among states in a manageable way to avoid the use of force.[10] During the Cold War, the United States and the Soviet Union employed techniques such as diplomatic consultations, territorial settlements, agreed-upon rules of conduct, arrangements for verifying adherence to agreements, and **confidence-building measures.** Such practices can occur only when parties with ongoing relations share an interest in avoiding war. Moreover, the disputes in question must be secondary in their hierarchy of interests, for **vital interests** are preserved even by war. Thus, during the detente phase of the Cold War, the Soviet Union found little difficulty in agreeing to consult with the United States with regard to dealing with allies in the Middle East, but the Soviets rejected American efforts to pressure them to modify their own emigration policies.

Thus, to construct a successful crisis prevention regime, it is necessary that the states involved have ongoing, complex relationships in which they can distinguish between primary and secondary interests. The interests involved in arrangements to prevent crises must lie in the second category, and the parties must give higher priority to avoiding violent engagement than to insisting on a particular outcome should a dispute arise. The difficulties of making such arrangements appear evident when one considers that crisis prevention often applies to areas of conflict outside the direct bilateral relations of two powers, thus involving allies. A crisis prevention regime may involve sacrificing the interests of an ally to the maintenance of a satisfactory relationship with an adversary power. An obvious example of this phenomenon is provided by territorial concessions by a small country that are imposed by major power agreements to create buffer zones between them.

In addition to the wide variety of patterns of interaction among equal powers in international politics, there are several clear patterns in the relations of unequal states.

Relations of Inequality

Not every unit in an international system can always be successful in maintaining its autonomy. Weaker units, in particular, sometimes suffer from the imposition of stronger units' wills or find themselves in a protective relationship whose advantages are bought at the cost of deferring to their protectors. **Relations of inequality** vary by the permanence of the relationship and by whether goals are shared or are opposed. Mentioned in the discussion of balance of power was domination of smaller states by a major power within its **sphere of influence,** as exemplified by the United States in the Western Hemisphere. A second form of friendly unequal relationship is a **patron-client** one, in which the greater power offers protection to a client, for example, the United States–Israel connection. Opposed unequal relations may be categorized as long-term and called **imperialism** and as short-term in which the stronger power gains the **compliance** of the weaker state through a variety of means. Britain in India from the end of the eighteenth century until the middle of the twentieth provides one of many possible examples of imperialism, and a case of compliance is supplied by the United States' coercion to gain the compliance of Iraq with a variety of demands in the wake of the 1991 Gulf War.

• DOMINATION

In noting above the vulnerability of a weaker state within a regional alliance to military intervention by the dominant partner, the discussion treated only the most extreme action in a relationship of domination: military invasion. However, falling far short of such violent measures, many alternatives for **domination** of regional allies remain available to the dominant state to ensure perpetuation of its preferences. In the Western Hemisphere for over a century, particularly in Central American and the Caribbean weak states, the United States has shaped events and institutions through diplomatic, economic, cultural, informational, clandestine, and institutional means.

In Central American countries, the American ambassador at times has ranked second only to the country's president in influence over government policies. Backed by both the economic resources and military power of his or her country, such an ambassador can effectively ensure that no substantial threat to United States interests is able to gain any powerful influence. In addition, much of the economic development in the nineteenth century in Central America was promoted by American entrepreneurs who built railroads, cultivated banana plantations, and founded the companies for processing and marketing the fruit, among similar activities. Until 1940, the national bank of Nicaragua was an American bank with headquarters in Connecticut. During World War II and in its aftermath, the United States conducted an informational (propaganda) campaign throughout Latin America to engender support for its policies. When the Central American countries decided in the late 1950s to form a common market, the United States ensured through its diplomacy that their arrangements did

not include any provisions that Washington thought might be inimical to its interests. Furthermore, the United States conducted military training missions in most of the Central American countries, working to provide forces that would counter armed subversion. Economic and technical assistance also added to the armamentarium of domination. When the debt crisis broke out in the 1980s and Latin American countries required assistance to overcome the depression of the "lost" decade, the United States joined with the international financial institutions in laying down conditions for aid. In part through these institutions and others such as the Organization of American States, the United States worked to ensure that its preferences prevailed in the hemisphere. On occasion, when immense threats occurred as in World War II or were perceived as in the crisis following the revolutionary Sandinista triumph in Nicaragua in 1979, the United States poured more resources into the area to maintain its domination.

In such patterns of domination, the weaker states strive to increase their autonomy, often with some success, but the process of achieving greater freedom of action is impeded in two respects. The first is the attention of the dominant power and its resources employed to channel the direction of weaker states' policies. Autonomy gets resisted. Secondly, however, the weakness of the smaller countries can, to some extent, be addressed by drawing on the help and resources of the dominant state, but these are made available only to compliant partners. Over the long run, Honduras, for example, has been able to achieve a position that is more autonomous in 1995 than it had been in 1895, but it still followed a subservient policy toward the United States in the 1980s.

In the post-Cold War era, it may be possible for the dependent states around the rim of or within the Caribbean to increase their autonomy with measures short of the kind of defiance of the goliath that was exhibited by General Manuel Noriega of Panama and General Raoul Cedras of Haiti. For the first time since independence, no power from outside the hemisphere poses any serious challenge to American domination. Despite the seeming anomaly, Latin American and Caribbean countries may be able to concentrate on their own state formation and economic development without very much concern by the United States. The reason lies in the absence of **security externalities** arising from relative gains. None of the countries in question by itself poses any threat to the United States. Over the course of most of the twentieth century, Americans feared that European states would gain a foothold in the hemisphere that would threaten them. During the Cold War, ideological affinity with the Soviet Union was regarded as a potential increment to Soviet power and, as such, had to be resisted. Without any potential allying adversary, any relative gains made by Latin American or Caribbean states can safely be disregarded by the United States. In this context, some Latin countries may be able to enhance their autonomy through their growing economic strength, political institutionalization, and effective government.

Another form of unequal relationship is imperialism, in which more powerful countries aim for and persist in the domination of weaker territories and peoples.

• IMPERIALISM

The wide-ranging literature of international politics presents many thoughts about imperialism, but the term has two essential meanings. First, it characterizes a *policy* aimed at expanding the direct and permanent control of a state to additional territories. Second, the word denotes a *condition* in which a state dominates by administering territories that retain their previous identification. Not every successful expansionist policy leads to an empire. For example, the United States' war with Mexico in 1846–48 led to the incorporation into the United States of nearly half of that country. Rather than retaining a separate identity, that territory was divided and the components incorporated in the American union as California and the states of the Southwest. In contrast, British conquest of India comprised part of the building of the British empire, for India retained its separate identity. Falling in between these two clear-cut examples was the French conquest of Algeria, with the North African territory incorporated as *departmentes* in metropolitan France, proven through war and a near-revolution in the home country not to be a viable permanent solution. More recently, the breakup of the Soviet Union into its constituent republics has demonstrated the impermanence of imperial arrangements. With fifteen successor republics, the Soviet Union left even some of these units as diverse ethnic and economic entities, though each remains an integral political unit. Nevertheless, continued tensions plague some of these units, as evidenced by the war in Chechnya in 1995 in which the Russian government clumsily employed brutal methods to try to bring secessionist

aspirations to heel before finding a negotiated solution to the conflict. Moreover, even that "solution" did not prove able to end the fighting, which continued sporadically in 1996.

Imperialism is the "domination or control of one nation or people by another."[11] Although occasionally a dominated territory may be nominally independent, as was Kuwait under the British empire, imperialism ordinarily involves military conquest and often includes colonies at least sufficiently large to administer the conquered land and people. Some writers include "economic imperialism" and "cultural imperialism" in their treatments of the subject, but the phenomena they include make *imperialism* such an elastic term that it loses any analytical quality.

Although examples of imperialism—both the foreign policy of expansion and the condition of empire—may be found throughout history, the phenomenon does not flourish continuously. Over the past couple of centuries, European countries expanded both on the continent and overseas and then contracted their imperial ambitions and practices, their empires collapsing. Britain won in its competition with France for domination of North America in the eighteenth century only to lose the United States and then go on to take India as the jewel in its imperial crown. Yet even India, as well as the rest of the British empire, was lost shortly after mid-twentieth century. Even smaller European countries such as the Netherlands and Portugal acquired overseas empires, but these too were lost after the mid-twentieth century. Older empires—Austria–Hungary and the Ottoman—collapsed at the end of World War I. By the late twentieth century, virtually the entire world was organized into territorial states, clearly unequal but largely without imperial orders. Doubtlessly, some large forces have been at work. Both internal dynamics and international circumstances affect imperialism, and many explanations have been offered. These fall into three categories: economic, political, and historical.

Economic Explanations

Most economic explanations for imperialism stem from the work of John A. Hobson, who thought that the overseas expansion of the European countries in the late nineteenth century emanated from imbalances in the capitalist economic system.[12] Hobson believed that more goods were produced by the industrial countries than were consumed and that surplus profits were not invested at home because workers did not gain an appropriate share of production. As a result of this **underconsumption,** entrepreneurs and their governments sought overseas markets in which to sell goods and invest savings. This Hobsonian analysis offered a relatively simple, straightforward solution: pay workers higher wages, enabling them to consume that surplus production, and invest surplus savings, and there would be no need to exploit overseas markets or to seek foreign investment opportunities.

Building on Hobson's analysis, Vladimir I. Lenin wrote that imperialism was a higher stage of capitalism in which the search for raw materials, markets in which to dispose of goods, and investment opportunities occurred when capitalist countries reached a point at which monopoly had grown such that financial and industrial capital merged, producing **surplus capital.** At this point, when capitalist countries were distinguished by the **export of capital,** they sought overseas territories to maintain monopoly control of resources involved in their economic activities.[13] Lenin went farther. He argued that similar developments had occurred in many capitalist countries, leading them to divide up the world. Extending the argument even more, Lenin concluded that, faced with the division of the whole world, the capitalist countries then went to war as the only method of gaining new territories for investment.

There are many refutations of the Hobson–Lenin thesis. Waltz points out not only that imperialism was known throughout history but also that even in the capitalist era, not all capitalist countries engaged in the scramble for overseas empires. For example, capitalist Sweden and Norway did not seek any imperial domains. Primarily, the more powerful states were the ones that sought expansion. Because powerful states have always proven to be expansive, the only thing different about the capitalist period is that the prevailing economic system proved to be an efficient way of gaining power for the major countries.[14]

D. K. Fieldhouse points out that most of the international commerce and investment of the capitalist countries did not occur in their overseas territories but rather in the other capitalist countries themselves. The continuing logic of this argument has been sustained by the evidence all the way up to the present period. Anyone tracing investments and the patterns of trade will note that the flows are mainly among the leading capitalist countries themselves. After 1870 when the scramble among Europeans to divide up Africa occurred, Fieldhouse argues, concerns for security and prestige were the driving forces of imperial expansion, and this period

was followed by one of "mystical nationalism."[15] Similarly, when George F. Kennan sought an explanation for the United States' overseas expansion to Puerto Rico and the Philippines after 1898, he was unable to uncover any rational calculation. He thus concluded that the United States had expanded because in that historical period, the American people "simply liked the smell of empire and felt an urge to range themselves among the colonial powers of the time."[16]

Joseph A. Schumpeter countered the Hobson–Lenin thesis by pointing out that capitalist activity flourishes under conditions of peace and security, leading most classes in capitalist societies to strive for stability and tranquility. Certain classes within capitalist—as well as many other—societies form a "warrior class" and may support or advocate imperial activities, but these tend not to be the predominant groups in capitalist societies.[17] Richard A. Barnet argued along the same lines during the Cold War by claiming that American foreign policy was directed by a class of "national security managers."[18]

Historical Analysis

With no satisfactory general explanation for imperialism, it is perhaps wiser to turn to a historical analysis that reviews the course of European imperialism in a panoramic but somewhat differentiated fashion. Out of the diversity of experience, then, certain causes or factors may be seen to have been at work. Moreover, such a historical view also provides a look at the breakdown of imperialism and the causes at work in that process. With this broader view, it is worthwhile to assess the effects of imperialism. The following narrative relies in major part on William Langer's treatment of the topic.[19]

In modern imperialism, there were complex motivations for European expansionism. During the age of discovery, adventure, a search for gold, and missionary activity all provided impetuses for imperialism. New technologies such as the compass, accumulating knowledge of currents and wind patterns, and political pressures such as the Ottoman Empire's restricting access to Asia through the Eastern Mediterranean and Asia Minor steered voyages of discovery of Columbus and others. All of these forces led to conquest and settlement of the Western Hemisphere. Many of the colonies, particularly those in the Western Hemisphere, became independent in the late eighteenth and early nineteenth centuries.

Different impulses governed continued imperial expansion in the early nineteenth century. In many places in Africa and Asia, expansion was designed to protect local territories that had been established for trading. On the other hand, predatory expansion characterized the British acquisition of India, Russia's conquest of Transcaucasia, and the United States' war of attainment against Mexico. After 1870, Africa and Asia became the foci for concerted expansion by the European powers. Many factors that ranged from a humanitarian impulse to do away with the remnants of the slave trade to the deliberate search for increased national power as well as outright aggressiveness and acquisitiveness and the ideology of social Darwinism drove the great European thrust at the end of the century. By the 1880s and 1890s, the Europeans were engaged in "preclusive imperialism," designed not so much to expand their own respective spans of control but to make impossible conquest of given territorial expanses by a competitor.

Hans Morgenthau has pointed to the opportunities for expansion provided by victory in war that led the Soviet Union to acquire substantial territories in Eastern Europe and Asia and the United States to acquire control over "strategic trust territories" in the Western Pacific.[20] Moreover, political vacuums and fundamentally empty spaces provided sufficient temptations for continental expansion by the United States and Russia. An expansionary ideology drove Mussolini to move into Ethiopia in 1936.

If we date the beginning of modern imperialism from Columbus' first voyage in 1492 and the end with the collapse of the Soviet Union and the disintegration of Yugoslavia in 1991, the five hundred-year cycle obviously reflects broad forces of expansion, resistance, and contraction. Great dynamism emanating from the Renaissance and the Enlightenment fueled European expansion, and the Industrial Revolution conferred technological superiority on the conquering forces. So many local differences resulted in a variety of patterns of resistance that it remains difficult to generalize. In the Western Hemisphere, first encounters with Indians were friendly, but the Spanish, British, and French met fierce resistance to their determined conquests in many places. In contrast, the great Monctezuman city of Tenochtitlan fell easily to Cortes without a fight because the conqueror was considered a god. Later, disease became a greater enemy of the Indians than the military power of the *conquistadores*.

So it was with the contraction of imperialism. Faced with its own weakness and a determined Indian national leadership possessing great moral authority, Britain withdrew peacefully from India. In contradistinction, the French clung to their imperial possessions in Indochina until militarily defeated, and the continuation of the effort at domination by the United States in Vietnam faced an extraordinarily competent and determined army that finally drove the United States from that country. Despite the difficulty in generalizing about the process, it may be said that if the strength and dynamism of Europe and its ideas and industrial base promoted imperialism, the subsequent weakening of Europe's economic base and the undermining of its moral claims assisted the demise of modern imperialism. Such obstinacy as that displayed by the Boers in the South African War of 1899–1902 showed the cost of victory over those who did not want to be ruled by foreigners. The utter determination by the Vietminh in Indochina in 1946–54 and by the Algerians in 1954–62 caused dissension and despair in France as a result of the drain of treasure and lives. Moreover, the triumph of the Japanese in their war against Russia in 1904–05 undermined the late-nineteenth century claims to rule other peoples based upon superiority of white European civilization.

Clearly, the imperial states of Western Europe suffered great weakening in World Wars I and II, and the exhaustion of the Soviet Union's political and economic order in the early 1990s led to that empire's dissolution. In the context of such weaknesses, imperial countries lost their moral claims, although these were quite distinct in the cases of the democracies and the Soviet Union. Moral claims of the democracies drew the allegiance of fighters from their overseas colonies in the great wars of this century. And the experiences of African and Asian soldiers infused them with confidence to claim the same freedom and self-determination that they had helped their imperial masters to protect against the predations of imperial powers in Europe and totalitarians who claimed superiority on the basis of race.

Moreover, the spread of imperialism, accompanied by certain levels of education and social mobilization, generated **anticolonialist** and nationalist movements throughout the dominated lands. Arising at the end of the nineteenth century, anticolonialism grew to become by the post-World War II period so forceful that it swept away virtually all of the democratic empires.

Collapse of Russian/Soviet Imperialism

As the Soviet economy reached a declining state in the 1970s and the end of a weakened leadership era, a new leader, Mikhail Gorbachev, in 1985 launched a program of reforms designed to reinvigorate social-ism and to rebuild the industrial base. To gain the focus needed for reform within the Soviet Union, Gorbachev consolidated his efforts by withdrawing from overseas commitments and imperial domina-tion in Afghanistan and Eastern Europe. This con-solidation was completed in 1989, symbolized by the opening of the Berlin Wall in November of that year. Never conceding that a shift from a command to a market economy was desirable, his political reforms undermined his and his Communist Party's legiti-macy, and the new basis for **legitimacy** that he inau-gurated affected the breakup of the country.

Gorbachev's reforms of *glasnost'* and *perestroika* aimed to achieve greater efficiency, but electoral restructuring contributed importantly to the Soviet Union's demise. Throughout its history, the Com-munist Party claimed a monopoly of political power on the basis of its superior knowledge of and insight into the unfolding of history. Under Gorbachev, however, the Soviet constitution was amended to allow other parties to field candidates in elections. Moreover, the restructuring devolved some author-ity to the country's constituent republics, and elec-tions were held. Thus, democratic election rather than Communist Party membership provided a new basis for legitimacy. Leaders, such as Boris Yeltsin, who was elected president of Russia, based their claims to govern on this new foundation for legiti-macy. At the same time, the man who had initiated the reforms had never been elected: his sole claim to legitimacy rested upon the discredited platform of communism.

Carrying forward his plans for restructuring, Gorbachev and the republic's leaders devised a new arrangement for sharing powers between the central government and the constituent republics. At that point, in August 1991, some old Communist leaders staged a *coup d'etat* that was ultimately defeated by Yeltsin and others. Meanwhile, the coup leaders held Gorbachev incommunicado, so that he had no influ-ence on the events as they unfolded. The failed attempt at reversing the course of reform then has-tened the dissolution of the Soviet state, which occurred in December 1991. Without a state to gov-ern, Gorbachev then had no official position and went into journalism. Armed with their electoral basis for legitimacy, Yeltsin and other political lead-ers continued to govern their respective republics. Thus ended the Russian/Soviet empire.

As the end of the twentieth century approached, the cycle of European imperial expansion that had begun with the Industrial Revolution and the Enlightenment several centuries earlier seemed to be nearing the end of its contraction, the world seem-ingly embarked on a different course whose direction cannot be discerned at the time of this writing.

• CLIENTELISM

Another form that relations of inequality take is that in which a major power and a weaker ally form a partnership that serves their respective but clearly distinctive interests. Israel's close pattern of cooperation with the United States since 1967 illustrates a patron-client relationship. Although dependent in some respects on the United States, Israel nevertheless pursues its national objectives even when they diverge from patronal preferences. The United States provides more foreign assis-tance, including major military matériel, to Israel than to any other state. Observers often remark that such aid gives the United States **leverage** over Israeli policies. In the Gulf War in 1991 when Israel was under attack by Iraqi rockets, American leverage enabled it to persuade the Israeli govern-ment, despite the provocation it was suffering, not to join in the coalition fighting against Iraq. In contrast, Israel launched a full-scale invasion of Lebanon in 1982, flouting United States protesta-tions against the policy. For many years, the Soviet Union acted as patron to Cuba, and their policies often coincided. On the other hand, Cuba pursued quite independent policies, as it did in dispatching forces to Angola in the 1970s and in maintaining a close relationship with Grenada in the early 1980s while the Soviet Union kept the Grenada govern-ment at a cool distance.

Other cases demonstrate that leverage ranges from nothing more than access for the patron to the ability virtually to impose the patron's policies on the client. Wherever the United States maintains an Agency for International Development (USAID) presence that dispenses economic assistance, it joins in a dialogue with the government of the host coun-try with regard to that government's economic poli-cies. However, host countries as often as not make their own independent decisions that do not entail acceptance of USAID's advice. In contrast, during the 1980s, the United States treated Honduras almost as an afterthought in using that country's ter-ritory as the base for ongoing military maneuvers to intimidate neighboring Nicaragua and for base camps for Nicaraguan rebels and their dependents.

In exchange for substantial assistance, the Honduran government acted as an abject client without a will of its own.

These patterns of patron-client relations vary with the determination of the patron, the importance of its independent objectives to the client, and the international context of their interactions. All of these ingredients may vary over time, so it becomes difficult to make generalizations even about fairly stable bilateral relations.

• COMPLIANCE

As patron-client relations tend to continue over extended periods of time, there are also short-term episodes in which a major power insists on the compliance of a smaller state or a group of such entities. For example, in 1983 when the United States decided to launch an invasion of Grenada, it gained the compliance of several small Caribbean countries that either simply gave their consent or issued formal requests for the United States to do what it wished to do. One or two actually contributed police forces to the operation.

Very powerful states sometimes even invoke forceful instruments to gain compliance with their demands. Such instruments range from paying bribes to government officials to vote in a directed way at a conference to actual intervention by clandestine subversion or with military force. When smaller states defy the major power, the imposition of sanctions and the use of force may or may not gain compliance.

• IMPORTANT TERMS

accommodation
alliance
anticolonialism
appeasement
asset
buffer
Cold War
common enemy
common interests
community of interest
compartmentalization
compliance
confidence-building
    measures
correlation of forces
crisis

crisis management
crisis prevention
    regime
deep conflict
deepening
detente
domination
entente
export of capital
imperialism
integrated command
    structure
integration
legitimacy
leverage
linkage

most-favored nation
    (MFN)
nonaligned
parallel interests
patron-client
    relationship
peaceful coexistence
reassurance
relations of inequality

reliability of allies
security externality
sphere of influence
strategic assets
surplus capital
underconsumption
vital interests
widening

• STUDY QUESTIONS

1. What are the different bases upon which alliances form? Do the same considerations account for the dissolution of alliances?

2. Why do questions of an ally's reliability arise from time to time? Illustrate your answer with specific examples.

3. How did major power alliances in the bipolar structure differ from those in multipolar structures?

4. What does the concept of integration mean? How has integration expressed itself institutionally in Western Europe in the post-World War II period?

5. Explain the meaning of uncertainty as it pertains to the operation of the balance of power in a multipolar international system structure.

6. How would you account for success in international concerts and arrangements of accommodation, such as the detente period in United States–Soviet Union relations?

7. Do you think that the type of crisis determines whether it can be successfully managed? Explain.

8. How successful have the powers been in constructing crisis prevention regimes? Give examples.

9. Why might it be possible for smaller states to escape the worst effects of great power domination in the post-Cold War era? What are those effects, and what would be the advantages of escaping them? What would be the costs of such escape?

10. Compare and contrast the various explanations for imperialism. Which do you believe is best?

11. How would you account for the end of imperialism?

12. Discuss the ins and outs of the concept of leverage.

• ENDNOTES

1. See Morgenthau, *Politics Among Nations*, 6th ed., pp. 203–6, for a discussion of the Anglo-American alliance.
2. See Walt, *The Origins of Alliances*, p. 12.
3. See Carlos E. Nones Sucre, *The Globalization of Venezuela's Foreign Policy, 1969–1979* (Ph.D. diss., City University of New York, 1995). A briefer version of this thesis was published as *The Worldwide Expansion of Venezuela's Foreign Policy*

in the 1970s, Bildner Center for Western Hemisphere Studies Working Paper No. 12 (New York: City University of New York Graduate School and University Center, September 1995).

4. Richard Rosecrance, "The New Concert of Powers," *Foreign Affairs* 71 (Spring 1992): 64–82.

5. See Charles F. Hermann, *International Crises: Insights from Behavioral Research* (New York: Free Press, 1972); Alexander L. George, *Managing U.S.–Soviet Rivalry: Problems of Crisis Prevention* (Boulder, Colo.: Westview Press, 1983); and Alexander L. George, Philip J. Farley, and Alexander Dallin, ed., *U.S.–Soviet Security Cooperation: Achievements, Failures, Lessons* (New York: Oxford University Press, 1988).

6. See Kathryn Weathersby, trans. and commentary, "From the Russian Archives: New Findings on the Korean War," *Cold War International History Project Bulletin* (Fall 1993): 1, 14–18.

7. See Henry Kissinger, *Diplomacy* (New York: Simon and Schuster, 1994), chapter 4.

8. See Robert Jervis, "From Balance to Concert: A Study of International Security Cooperation," *World Politics* 38 (October 1985): 58–79; and Charles A. Kupchan and Clifford A. Kupchan, "Concerts, Collective Security, and the Future of Europe," *International Security* 16 (Summer 1991): 114–61.

9. Donald Kagan, *On the Origins of War and the Preservation of Peace* (New York: Doubleday, 1995), pp. 209, 214.

10. See Paul Gordon Lauren, "Crisis Prevention in Nineteenth-Century Disputes," in Alexander L. George, *Managing U.S.–Soviet Rivalry: Problems of Crisis Prevention* (Boulder, Colo.: Westview Press, 1983).

11. William L. Langer, "Farewell to Empire," *Foreign Affairs* 41 (October 1962): 115–30, reprinted in *World Politics*, 2d ed., ed. by Arend Lijphart (Boston: Allyn and Bacon, 1971).

12. John A. Hobson, *Imperialism: A Study* (London: Allen and Unwin, 1938 [1902]).

13. V. I. Lenin, *Imperialism: The Highest Stage of Capitalism* (New York: International Publishers, 1939 [1916]).

14. Waltz, *Theory of International Politics.*

15. D. K. Fieldhouse, *Colonialism, 1870–1945: An Introduction* (London: Weidenfeld and Nicolson, 1981).

16. George F. Kennan, *American Diplomacy, 1990–1950* (Chicago: University of Chicago Press, 1951), p. 17.

17. Joseph A. Schumpeter, "The Sociology of Imperialism," in Joseph A. Schumpeter, *Imperialism and the Social Classes,* trans. by Heinz Norden (New York: Meridian Books, 1955 [1919]).

18. Richard A. Barnet, *Roots of War* (New York: Penguin Books, 1973).

19. Langer, "Farewell to Empire."

20. Morgenthau, *Politics among Nations*, 6th ed., p. 67.

PART 5

Fundamental Processes in International Politics

CHAPTER 12

Conflict among States

Conflict is so universal that some people fight with themselves. The Reverend Dr. Martin Luther King, Jr., highlighted the inventive side of conflict when he talked about the "creative tension" engendered by confrontation through marches for civil rights. On the other hand, conflict sometimes degenerates into brutal violence that proves very destructive. In international politics, conflict can lead to war. Thus, it remains important to understand basic notions involved in planning and conducting wars.

This chapter begins by placing conflict in the context of bargaining. It discusses how the tactics of pursuing conflict may involve not just a contest, as in a game with rules and umpires, but also an extended struggle over the nature of the game.

Each country thinks strategically, shaping its overall goals in the context of its geopolitical and economic situation. We explore strategy and strategic thinking both abstractly and through case studies of two countries that face dramatically different strategic situations and have very distinct histories: the United States and Germany.

We then take up many aspects of war and its processes, and we end with a treatment of positional conflicts—maintenance of the state's position in the international system—and structural conflicts, which involve principles and radical disputes.

Introduction

Three C's—conflict, cooperation, and change—comprise the fundamental processes of international politics to which this and the two following chapters are devoted. Virtually every international situation encompasses all three of these processes, but we achieve analytical utility by treating each discretely.

In this chapter on **conflict,** stress will be given to those processes in which states pursue incompatible objectives, design strategies to achieve them, and employ a variety of means in attempts to impose their wills on others or to gain enough control to fashion their own principles of conduct for international behavior. The next chapter on **cooperation** will emphasize the efforts at and obstacles to reaching objectives through collaboration with others. Such efforts often include institutional and normative arrangements that provide frameworks within which states make their respective choices of goals. The following chapter on **change** addresses the subtle and dramatic, hidden and apparent sources and forms of change in international politics.

Crude analyses sometimes force these broad processes into narrow schools of thought. Such analyses claim, for example, that realists cling to conflict while liberals retain a monopoly on cooperation, with critical theorists having the only profound sense of change. In the following analysis, these stereotypes will be avoided, for the real life of international politics is suffused with all of these activities. Scholarly factions do contribute their particular insights to the processes, but none retains the keys to the kingdom of knowledge.

Bargaining

If conflict means incompatibility, opposition, and hostility, the concept of **bargaining** draws attention to the fact that neither conflict nor cooperation exists in a pure state. Even as the United States imposed its will on Japan by using atomic bombs that killed over a hundred thousand Japanese people, it needed the cooperation of a defeated government to bring the deadly struggle of World War II to an end through an orderly surrender process. The alternative would have been the chaos and brutality of an anarchic battle for every square inch of Japanese home territory. Even in the almost wholly cooperative partnership of the United States and Britain during and after World War II, conflicts over many issues intruded themselves.[1]

Nevertheless, bargaining endures as the tactics of conflict. Essentially, it entails the process of seeking to impose one's will on another, while that other either seeks actively to engage in reciprocal bargaining or to resist that will. In international politics, the reliance of each state on itself extends not simply to making choices of objectives but to deciding on the means of attaining those objectives and on its own understanding of the nature of any given conflict.

• COMPLEX UNCERTAINTY: BOSNIA

Thus, the world as a whole looked on the savage war raging in Bosnia from 1992 to 1995 and regarded the United Nations "safe havens" as minimal humanitarian enclaves for alleviating the suffering of battered civilians. Time after time, Bosnian Serbs humiliated UNPROFOR (United Nations Protection Force) troops, violated understandings regarding safe passage for supplies, and sometimes reclaimed artillery pieces that had been placed, under duress of NATO air bombings, in the custody of UN peace-enforcement troops. To outside observers, the use of NATO air strikes in May 1995 to stop the increasing artillery bombardment of Sarajevo was a late, weak attempt to regain some modicum of prestige for the discredited international operation and to provide a bit of relief for the besieged civilian population that died slowly from sniper fire and starvation.

But the view of the BOSNIAN SERBS stood in stark contrast to this outlook. These warriors fought for territory, dignity, and independence. NATO air strikes were acts of war against them. Not having access to American and other bases from which the aircraft were launched, the Bosnian Serbs retaliated against UNPROFOR and six of the enclaves the force was designed to protect. They took United Nations troops hostage to deter further air attacks against themselves. In summer 1995, the Bosnian Serbs overran some of the safe havens, and the powers sought to coordinate an effective response to preserve their honor and the futures of NATO and the UN.

On any given day of the sordid war in the former Yugoslav territory, it was hard to perceive issues in any agreed-upon terms. Diplomats sought peace, though the powers simultaneously strived for the contradictory value of justice. They established a war-crimes tribunal that aimed to punish leaders whose collaboration was required if peace were to be achieved, and they also rejected either an imposed settlement or a territorial partition because those alternatives were considered unjust. In 1992, the world had been horrified at "ethnic cleansing," the practice of expelling people from their homes, murdering some of them, and using torture and incarceration to achieve territorial settlements based upon ethnicity. The rallying cry of **ethnic nationalism** offended the democratic world's sense of toleration as well as the principles, espoused by the Bosnian government, of multiculturalism and ethnic diversity.

Thus, the bargaining possessed a complex character. Conflict occurred over not just clear objectives such as territory but over methods to be employed, fundamental principles, and norms to be observed in the conduct of hostilities. Moreover, this conflict included the decay of the state of Yugoslavia and the formation of successor states. In the cases of Slovenia and even Croatia, hostilities were brief. Territorial boundaries, although not completely settled in the latter case, had a definition characterized at least by aspects of straightforwardness and clarity. But the agony of Bosnia-Herzegovina lingered in part because the claimants of the new state were a minority clinging to a founding principle of multiethnic toleration that did not appear viable in the face of a determined minority who rejected the state and its principle. That agony has also been prolonged by the contradictions between peace and justice that are simultaneously valued by the powers. Additionally, in the name of humanitarian relief, the powers sought to create new rules of engagement in warfare through the creation of safe havens. In trying to put those rules into effect, however, some of those powers placed forces in a position in which they were hostage to the belligerents. Not enough force was committed to impress those rules on the belligerents, but occasional bombing provoked a retaliation that worsened the condition of those whom UNPROFOR was designed to protect.

This sort of bargaining situation in which it is difficult to understand what is at stake, the boundaries of the contest, and the means for contending has a name: **complex uncertainty.** Sometimes, authorities and analysts employ a cybernetic approach to decision making as a means of coping with the immense uncertainty. A **cybernetic approach** means that there is a very limited set of responses to a very constrained set of stimuli. A classic example of cybernetics relates to a thermostat in which a switch is turned on or off—a very limited set of responses—to established changes in temperature—a very constrained set of stimuli. Steinbruner[2] has shown how, in international politics where complexity prevails, authorities achieve a very constrained set of stimuli by the cognitive mechanisms of simplification and then adopt quite simple response sets. Thus, different observers adopt simplified images of international events and then champion equally simplified policies. For example, in the former Yugoslav case, some advocates point out that Bosnia is a country recognized by the powers and the United Nations, that it is at war, and, therefore, that the international community should indulge in a collective security action to put things right. Once having gained such a cybernetic understanding, no further thought, analysis, or debate is required.

In contrast to a cybernetic angle, one may take an **analytical approach** to an episode or set of events in international politics. Such a means of grappling with a problem requires difficult thought about the complexities and confrontation with the goals, means, constraints, alternatives, and choices involved. Without going into a lengthy analysis of the situation in Bosnia, however, one notes that any comprehensive analysis would need to include both the civil war and international dimensions, the strategies and battlefield tactics of the belligerents, the interests and involvement of five major powers, structural conflicts over principles of how to order a polity, humanitarian concerns and principles of minority rights, errors of recognition and diplomatic bungling, considerations of prestige and historical memories, dimensions of peace and justice, institutional factors, and processes of state formation that involve both internal and international features.[3]

Many bargaining situations in international politics do not involve such complexity as that in the former Yugoslavia in which nearly every facet of the conflict came into contention. Nevertheless, the potential for opposing positions to emerge in all aspects endures in every conflict in the self-help system. It is partly to overcome this profoundly hostile possibility that rules and institutions to promote cooperation have been devised.

• FUNDAMENTALS OF GAME THEORY

Game theory, which will provide an interesting conceptual apparatus for analyzing cooperation—to be treated in the next chapter—illustrates in its fundamentals some of the essentials of bargaining. A mathematics based on advanced algebra, game theory was invented in the 1940s by two Princeton University mathematicians, John Von Neumann and Oscar Morgenstern. Its essential concepts are **two-person** and **n-person games, zero-sum** and **nonzero-sum** games, **utilities,** and **rationality.** Mathematicians have calculated a solution to a two-person, zero-sum game with assigned utilities. This so-called "minimax" solution, however, hardly applies to social and political problems. Otherwise, game theory can be used as a model by analogy with the real world.[4] Riker provided an insightful analysis using **coalition theory,** in which an n-person, zero-sum game is transformed through the formation of a coalition of minimum winning size into a two-person encounter.[5] A zero-sum game is one in which the winner's gain equals the loser's loss, for example a presidential election. A nonzero-sum game does not conform to this definition and may be either a positive-sum or negative-sum game. Multilateral trade negotiations that result in increased global wealth give an example of the former, while a thermonuclear war in which adversaries destroy each others' societies would illustrate a negative-sum game. These basic concepts seem straightforward enough, but utility and rationality remain more problematical, though more interesting as well.

The Bosnian war furnishes insight into the difficulties with the concept of utility. To achieve a mathematical or even an ordinary rationality, utilities must be assigned exogenously, that is, by an outsider not involved in the game itself. However, as illustrated in the Bosnian case, the values assigned to outcomes vary not just among the participants but also by a single participant over time and in different circumstances as the game unfolds. For example, BOSNIAN SERBS may value the goodwill of the powers when they seek a concession on territorial arrangements during diplomatic negotiations. On the other hand, bombing unarmed civilians and humiliating United Nations peacekeepers show an utter disregard for the good opinion of the powers. It is, of course, possible to find relatively stable situations in which an observer can gain an accurate understanding of the utility functions of participants in a restricted international circumstance. In such studies, the insights garnered can prove valuable. However, the generalization must remain that the nature of international politics allows the potential for rapidly changing and inconsistent utility functions. Lest the reader believe that only people as crazy as the Bosnian Serbs change the values of their utility functions, consider the UNITED STATES with regard to Iraq and Kuwait in 1990–91. The American position shifted from no intrusion in Arab territorial disputes to the conduct of a war to oust Iraq from Kuwait and the imposition of a regime in northern Iraq that effectively denied the Baghdad government access to its own territory.

Rationality in game theory contains the same sort of ambiguity. In its ordinary meaning, rationality is the application of a reasoning process that may be contrasted with an emotional approach to problem solving. Game theoretic rationality, contrariwise, means that a player follows the most efficient series of moves through the bargaining game to achieve his goal. These extremely different meanings of rationality are captured in an anecdote.

John and Mary are a couple discussing what to do on Saturday night. John states that he would prefer to go dancing, whereas Mary proposes that they attend a movie. To bolster her choice, Mary points out that their favorite reviewer acclaimed the movie in question and that both the star and the director are people whom John has admired. In response, John whines that if Mary loves him, she would go dancing, and then he begins to cry. In this context, the couple quickly makes the decision to go dancing. Although Mary's employment of logic and appeal to reason seemed rational in the ordinary sense, John's invocation of emotion proved an efficient way to obtain his goal and was, thus, rational in a game theory sense.

If two men armed with knives are locked in a room and one of them can convince the other that he is insane and has no fear of being killed or wounded, he would have an advantage that might be more effective than the one using rational restraint in his behavior. It was in this pattern that President Richard Nixon engaged in the "Christmas bombing" of Hanoi and the Port of Haiphong in North Vietnam in 1972. Nixon acted on the presumption that if he could convince the North Vietnamese that

he was crazy, he would be able to extract greater concessions from them in the negotiations to end the war that were to resume in Paris in January.

Such violence sometimes forms a crucial component in a bargaining situation, but in other cases, the mere threat of violence may achieve results. In the CUBAN MISSILE CRISIS of 1962, for example, American President John Kennedy sought the removal of intermediate-range missiles that the Soviet Union had clandestinely installed in Cuba. To convince Soviet Premier Nikita Khrushchev to comply, Kennedy ordered a naval blockade to intercept Soviet vessels carrying missile-related equipment to Cuba, and he repositioned aircraft in Florida to convey the threat that the United States would bomb the missile sites if Khrushchev failed to submit. In this case, Kennedy also made a secret offer to remove American missiles from Turkey, and he gave assurances that the United States did not intend to invade Cuba should the Soviets remove the missiles. With a successful conclusion, from the point of view of the United States, this case was widely interpreted to offer a successful bargaining model of modulated restraint in the context of measured threats. The efficacy of those threats in achieving the desired outcome, however, should not be underestimated.

Similarly, in the bargaining that occurred in the case of restoring President Jean Bertrand Aristide of HAITI to the office from which he had been deposed, the United States prevailed only when invasion forces had already left their bases in the United States and were on their way to Haiti. Previously, the military junta in Haiti had been able to remain in power through shifting positions, failing to carry out agreements, and other devious tactics that endured in the face of the overwhelming power of the United States.

Many of these illustrations point to the observation that stronger powers in a bargaining situation have the luxury of invoking standard rules of behavior and widely accepted norms as levers to assist their cause. In contrast, weaker parties fall back on deviousness, breaking of agreements, and other behaviors that shock the civilized world, for they surely lose when they accept the rules of the strong. Only by inventing tactics and changing rules can weaker parties find advantages in the bargaining situation against stronger powers. When stronger powers are determined to win or develop commitments that they highly value, they too invoke surprise, deceit, force, and ruthless intimidation to achieve their goals. Thus, anarchy drives each state to act in brutish ways when it places a higher value on the objective than on the means for achieving it.

Force and other less savory tactics do not always emerge into the forefront of bargaining. Instead, they may linger unobtrusively in the background of diplomatic negotiations, not noticed or only dimly seen as in shadows. Bargaining involves persuasion, after all, and logical argument—the presentation of features of a bargain that stress the advantages—and appeals to mutually held values also comprise part of the repertoire that may sometimes prove sufficient. Such tactics, when invoked against the backdrop of powerful economic and military incentives, gain even greater persuasive power.

However, even the most forceful means does not guarantee that one can determine the outcome of a bargaining situation. In surveying the history of attempts to prevail by the infliction of pain, Schelling has demonstrated the limits to intimidation even with the sustained use of force.[6] Neither the German siege of Leningrad for nine hundred days in World War II in which the inhabitants who had not starved to death were reduced to eating rats nor the dropping on Vietnam from 1965 to 1973 of a greater tonnage of bombs than used in World War II induced the target populations to capitulate. Indeed, in both cases, their political units went on to win wars against attackers who sought their decimation.

Schelling's main point is that, to be effective, the use of force to inflict pain can be used convincingly only in bargaining situations in which the adversary can be induced to cooperate in future behavior. Should the bargaining partner endure the infliction of pain without giving in, the power to destroy and hurt remains limited to, at most, the ability to conquer and overwhelm. At the least, that power gives the capacity to wreak only destruction without any compensating gain.

The notion of bargaining gives a flavor of the essential condition in which conflict occurs, but it deals with tactics, the details of interaction in which one party attempts to gain the assent of an opposed party to its objectives. Conflict tends to be treated in a larger conception by strategy.

Strategy

Essentially a military concept, **strategy** treats the achievement of political purpose through armed force and its threat.[7] Although in the liberal tradition of civilian control of the military, strategic decision making adheres to an elected leadership while concerns about the deployment and use of weapons and personnel on the battlefield are exclusively the domain of generals, the distinction is not a sustainable one. Military planners must think strategically, for their essential role requires them to achieve the broad purpose set by the civilian leadership. Similarly, the achievement of state objectives sometimes lies in the means employed, so civilian leaders necessarily concern themselves with tactical issues. To put the matter another way, civilian leaders need to understand enough about weapons and personnel deployment to ensure their control of the military, and military leaders must have a grasp of broad political aims to fulfill their mission of accomplishing those goals. Both are responsible for protecting the security of the state.

Each country faces different circumstances that affect its security, and some confront military challenges daily, whereas others enjoy the luxury of living without any substantial threat. Because each state necessarily develops its own strategic objectives, alliances endure problems of coordinating those aims or fashioning overarching strategies that bring the allies into coordinated activities.

• UNITED STATES STRATEGIC CONTINUITY

A deep logic that is grounded in geographical position, the size and character of neighbors, and historical experience affects strategy. This logic may be illustrated in a narrative of the United States' strategic continuity. Formed as an independent country near the end of the eighteenth century, the United States benefited from European quarrels that it early on decided to stand clear of. While profiting from British mastery of the Atlantic, the United States expanded across the North American continent in the space between Canada, the largest remaining British possession, and that portion of Mexico that had not been conquered in the 1840s. In the Monroe administration in 1823, the United States drew a clear distinction between Europe and the Western Hemisphere, giving a promise of noninterference in Europe—at a time of peace there—and demanding that Europeans refrain from intervening in the Western Hemisphere. By the beginning of the twentieth century, the United States found itself not only able to enforce its preclusion of outsiders but also capable of working its own will upon its hemispheric neighbors. Moreover, American security gained when the U.S. Navy projected its power into the Pacific during the last half of the nineteenth century. Thus, over the course of a century, the new country developed a strategy that provided it with exclusive domination of a hemisphere that was also insulated by two oceans in friendly hands. When ambition led in 1898 to annexation of the Philippines and in 1903 to acquisition of the Panama Canal Zone, the strategy gained a new forward configuration. To protect its Atlantic flank, the United States entered World War I after German submarines began attacking American neutral shipping. Germany and Japan forced the United States to fight in World War II, and the upshot was that America's **forward strategy** placed it militarily in Europe and on the eastern side of Asia. From the end of the war until 1989, the United States protected itself and its allies by a policy of containment aimed at the Soviet Union and its allies. A new aspect of the forward strategy developed in Korea in 1950, where an American military presence remains in the mid-1990s, and in Vietnam in the mid-1950s to the early 1970s, ending in a tactical defeat for the superpower. Later, in the late 1970s, the American military presence was extended to the Persian Gulf and Indian Ocean areas as President Jimmy Carter declared that the Persian Gulf formed an arena in which the American national interest was engaged. Despite the end of the Cold War, the strategy of the United States remains one that seeks abundant security through involvement in European and Pacific affairs as well as the Arabian peninsula with its oil riches. Since the end of the Cold War, the United States has added the extension of democracy and liberal economics as an additional layer of security protection on the grounds that liberal states do not go to war against one another.

Consistency marks the overall strategic thrust of the United States: continental expansion and protection; maintaining a clear distinction between the Western Hemisphere and the rest of the world, clearing that hemisphere of external powers and insisting on domination there; forward strategy to secure the ocean flanks; resistance to any power in Europe that would dominate that continent and use it as a launching pad more directly to threaten American security; and using broad security as a basis upon which to pursue commercial interests. Nevertheless, variations in strategy have occurred by such departures from practice as intervening in European wars, joining permanent alliances, and extending commitments to the Middle East. Additionally, technological change, particularly the advent of nuclear and thermonuclear weapons, has driven United States

strategy to new directions such as the face-off of nuclear deterrence during a time that one scholar has called "the long peace."[8]

The overall consistency combined with adaptation to new circumstances and technologies mean that the United States has followed a successful strategic pattern. Never invaded and seldom subjected to direct attack, the United States enjoys unparalleled security, and its strategy has gained not just safety but also prosperity, imitation, and allies. Few countries have benefited from the advantageous location, wealth, and profitable choices that have characterized the United States' strategy.

• GERMANY'S STRATEGIC POSITION

A remarkably different lot has befallen Germany, for example. After military triumphs that led to unification under Prussian leadership in 1871, Germany under Chancellor Bismarck was a dynamic, powerful country in central Europe that sought peace through a strategy of alliances intended to reassure neighbors. However, after 1890, Germany sought increased power and expansion that led, through a series of crises early in the twentieth century, to World War I. Following its exhaustion in that war and the imposition of a punitive peace settlement, Germany entered a period in which it suffered pariah status until 1933, when a new chancellor, Adolf Hitler, consolidated a totalitarian regime and embarked on a policy of building up German power at home and then launching a war of conquest abroad. Its conquests were reversed and Germany itself was thoroughly defeated, occupied, and divided at the end of the war. To regain its place in the world, the larger part of Germany, the Federal Republic, embarked on an economic plan of recovery and a strategy that tied both its economic and political destiny to its allies, the United States and others in NATO, and France and others in the European Community, and that insisted on its legitimacy to speak for all of Germany. After the end of the Cold War, the two parts of Germany unified, and the whole country remained in those allied enterprises. And the force of the Federal Republic's legitimacy was recognized by the victorious powers of World War II that had retained residual rights of conquest. Still a powerful, dynamic country in central Europe at the end of the century, Germany sought to strengthen its European ties and to assist in the liberal development of states to its east. The inconsistencies and discontinuities of German strategy demonstrate its success for twenty years, followed by failures over the course of

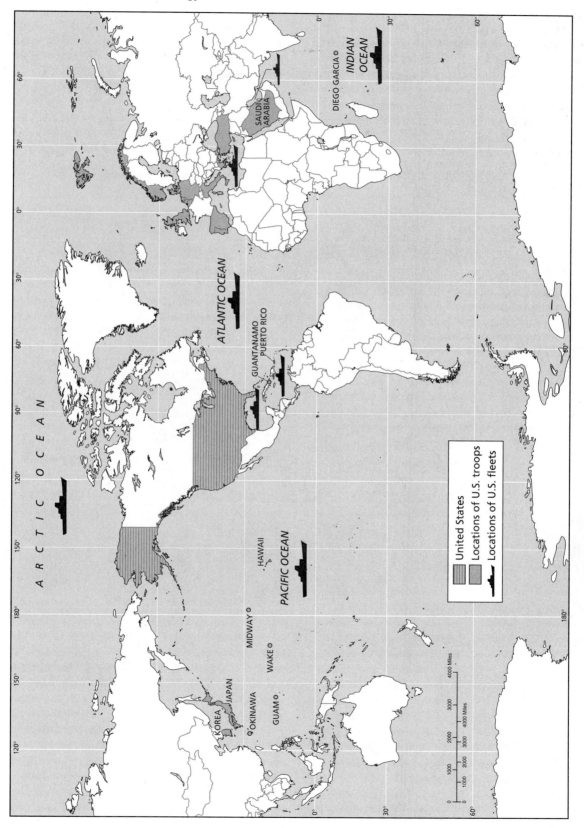

ARCTIC OCEAN

ATLANTIC OCEAN

PACIFIC OCEAN

INDIAN OCEAN

SAUDI ARABIA

DIEGO GARCIA ○

GUANTANAMO
PUERTO RICO

HAWAII

MIDWAY ○

WAKE ○

KOREA

JAPAN

OKINAWA ○

GUAM ○

United States

Locations of U.S. troops

Locations of U.S. fleets

4000 Miles

3000

2000

1000

0

4000 Miles

the next sixty years. In the past fifty years, nevertheless, a continuous strategy has paid large dividends, and that success may promise more of the same. Whether new circumstances will emerge that lead Germany to adopt more clearly military means to secure its objectives remains to be seen, but the country certainly does not enjoy the scope for strategic activity that the United States does. Instead of being flanked by oceans, it lies adjacent to neighbors who have suffered from a dynamic Germany in the past and would, thus, have good reason to fear a central European power with renewed expansive inclinations.

• STRATEGIES DRIVE PROCESSES

The strategies of states drive the processes of international politics: bargaining, war, crises, trade, and structural conflict. When states divine strategies that

■ Germany's Strategic Position

seek only their own security and wealth, those international processes tend to proceed peacefully. However, confidence in its security and the accretion of wealth very likely tempt a state to become dynamic and expansive. In the case of the United States discussed above, North American Indians and small states of the Caribbean and Central America were easily defeated or dominated, and the Europeans drew down one another's energies. America's forward strategy succeeded in the face of the weakening of Europe, but its success in the Pacific also required the military defeat of Japan. Prospects of European infringement on the Atlantic and the Western Hemisphere in the two world wars required mounting major military efforts to turn back those challenges. American strength prevailed in the Cold War and triumphed in the face of Soviet weakness and disintegration.

On the other hand, the case of Germany shows a very different pattern, for Germany's dynamism placed demands on other states that resisted the central European power's military thrusts. Few countries have the space and the capacity to extend their sway over so much of the globe as has the United States. More likely, a dynamic country runs into the sort of opposition that Germany did. Thus, state dynamics leads to conflict in international politics. That conflict occurs in war, crisis, trade, and broader structural conflict. Each has characteristic patterns in which conflict is conducted.

War

Because it incurs such steep costs and is attended by inordinate risks, war tends to occur infrequently in any given place. On the other hand, war entails some of the most essential and common processes in international politics. Very few years in history can be counted as peaceful if one takes the globe as the unit of consideration, for wars are almost always going on somewhere. Certain goals, such as territorial conquest, can be achieved only by war, and defense against another state's belligerent activity necessitates warfare.

War is the use of organized violence to break an enemy's will for the achievement of political objectives. Whether designed to accomplish circumscribed or unlimited aims, or conceived as an effort to compel an enemy to desist from a limited activity or to surrender unconditionally, war employs violence to overcome opposed force and to wreak sufficient destruction and terror to break an enemy's will.

War includes the inflicting of immense pain; it kills human beings and it destroys property; and its conduct involves cruelty and brutality and, often, baseness. Through both destruction and the expenditures on the means of inflicting havoc, war incurs very high costs. The toll in lives and maiming, in the suffering of the families of those killed and wounded, and in the ancillary travails of those in combat and of civilians brushed by wartime activities mounts to incalculable dimensions even in small wars. With modern weapons, the price of war extracted from those involved has reached horrendous proportions.

Wars may last a short or long time. In 1967, Israel defeated the Arab alliance against it quickly, in six days. In contrast, after fighting against Japan in World War II, Vietnam began its war of independence against the French in 1946 and, after defeating that European power in 1954, found it necessary to fight the United States and a U.S.-backed regional government until victory was finally achieved in 1975.

With modern airborne weapons, immense destruction can be wreaked in a brief period, as witnessed by the devastation of Iraq's infrastructure in just over a month in 1991. But primitive weapons in RWANDA were sufficient to kill some half-million people in the massacre of members of the Tutsi tribe by Hutus over the course of four months from April to July 1994. Factional ground forces without heavy weapons in the civil war that racked LIBERIA from 1989 to 1991 drove some 70 percent of the population from their homes to become displaced persons.

Involvement of civilians in war characterizes the total wars in the twentieth century. But also it has become common for civilians to be caught up in combat situations in the post–World War II period with the adoption on a broad scale of **guerrilla warfare.** With its origins in the American war of independence against Britain and the Spanish resistance to Napoleon's occupation, guerrilla war is a tool of the weak. Guerrillas rely for their protection on their ability to melt into the civilian population. Subject to some variation over time, the strategy of guerrillas is directed at undermining the government while building power. Terror against governmental authorities aims for the first goal, and a combination of providing service, spreading propaganda, and intimidating the civilian population is directed at the second. Successful guerrilla movements transform their operations to regular warfare in which their armies can defeat the governing army. That government can be an occupying force, as Napoleon's was, a colonial power such as France in Indochina, or an indigenous government as those in El Salvador in the 1980s or in Algeria during the 1990s.

Modern total war has had a deep impact on attitudes toward war, which generally tend to view it with revulsion. Nevertheless, that general tendency does not encompass all viewpoints on war in the modern world. If it did, one could hardly imagine that the extraordinary violence that has marked the twentieth century would not have diminished since the end of World War II. However, wars and their attendant deaths continue to occur with great frequency and intensity.[9] Shortly after the end of the First World War, Mussolini wrote in the Italian encyclopedia an article embodying the opinion that mankind's nobility was revealed only in war, when courage, dedication, and selflessness demonstrated themselves in the brave deeds of soldiers. Frantz Fanon wrote in the post-World War II period that in political violence, those who had lived under European colonialism would find freedom and even mental health as well as their national destinies.[10]

Apart from those broad philosophical attitudes toward war, however, opinions tend to vary by the historical and political condition in which one finds oneself. In the post-Cold War era, many are comfortable and are inclined to fight only for such grand goals as human rights, whereas others are filled with ethnic hatreds that drive them to enthusiasm for war against those they regard as ancient enemies. In the age of nuclear weapons, leaders and populations have been restrained by the projected high costs of fighting a nuclear war. Still, the major efforts at preventing the spread of nuclear weaponry testify to fears that some country or even a group might someday be willing to undertake nuclear warfare or at least employ it as a serious threat.

Thus, despite claims that war has become obsolescent[11] or less efficacious,[12] the overwhelming evidence leads to a conclusion that war remains a normal process in international politics and state formation. No war presents a typical case, so the best method of learning about the processes of war is to read histories of many wars. Nevertheless, there are identifiable aspects to the processes of war and examples that illustrate those different processes that work themselves out through armed conflict.

• PLANNING, STRATEGY, TACTICS, AND LOGISTICS

Planning involves the conceptualization of objectives and the means for accomplishing them.

Thinking through ends and means may seem obvious; yet, one finds no difficulty in citing examples of failures of planning at the most basic level. In 1982, the United States stationed forces in Beirut, LEBANON, without having any clear objective to accomplish. These forces were vulnerable to attack by armed factions in the civil war in whose midst U.S. marines were based. On October 23, 1983, a suicide bomber drove a truck laden with explosives into an American compound, blowing up a barracks and killing 241 marines. The absence of an objective for those forces is evidenced by the withdrawal of remaining U.S. forces. These actions appear to demonstrate careless military activity, devoid of serious thought or planning.

In sharp contrast, the INVASION OF EUROPE across the English Channel in 1944 by American, British, and allied forces constituted the largest amphibious military operation in history, and its success depended on several years of planning and preparation. That undertaking included not just developing a clear overall objective and many subordinate goals but also amassing an invasion force together with its equipment as well as coordinating land, sea, and air forces that involved personnel from several countries. As in any military operation, success depended on many factors, but planning gave foundation to the operation.

Both planning and the execution of war and battle encompass strategy, tactics, and logistics. Although it has several meanings, **strategy** fundamentally deals with the overall direction of war and sets priorities among activities. Generally, strategy lies within the purview of general staffs and even political leadership who determine the military goals that give substance to the political aims striven for in any war endeavor. Thus, a broad plan such as the Schlieffen Plan that governed German strategy at the outset of World War I links military undertakings to state goals. The Schlieffen Plan provided for an attack on France through Belgium to achieve a quick victory, which, in turn, would allow Germany to turn east to confront Russia. Aiming at the state goal of broader European domination, the plan took into account Germany's geographical position requiring it to strike out on two fronts, but it handled this problem by sequencing the actions.[13]

Although not always sharply distinguished in practice from strategy, **tactics** pertains to the conduct of military operations on the battlefield. Tactics involves the moving of personnel and weapons in ways designed to prevail in particular battles that form components of a war. Thus, General Sherman's march through Georgia during the American Civil War, destroying property as his forces swept across the state, may be regarded as a tactical action that proved an important part in the overall victory of the Union over the Confederacy. Similarly, the use of free-fire zones by the United States in Vietnam, in which civilians were removed from broad tracts of land to afford the military the scope to use firepower indiscriminately because they could assume that only Vietcong fighters were present in those zones, formed a tactic.

Another critical process in war is **logistics:** the procurement, maintenance, and transportation of military personnel, equipment, and supplies. One of history's military masters, Napoleon regarded logistics as central to warfare; his aphorism is often quoted: "An army marches on its stomach." Nevertheless, his defeat in the Russian winter of 1812, requiring his bedraggled army ignominiously to retreat across the frozen plains of western Russia and Poland, may be attributed to the failure of his logistics to match the overextended lines of his infantry and artillery. Distance has historically comprised a formidable barrier to extended operations because of the logistical nightmares involved, but the impressive ability of the United States to send expeditionary forces of over a half-million well-equipped and supplied troops to both Vietnam and Saudi Arabia during the Gulf War gives powerful evidence that modern transportation has breached the barrier of distance.[14]

• COMMAND, CONTROL, COMMUNICATIONS, AND INTELLIGENCE

Strategy, tactics, and logistics comprise the science of the military, but command, its attendant features, and fighting form the art. **Command** entails not simply the issuing of orders but also, training disciplined soldiers, inspiring them, and requiring that they fight; effectively managing and coordinating the layers of leadership necessary to a complex organization; and retaining aplomb under the most gruelling and distracting of circumstances. Command runs through a military organization, for even the isolated, frontline soldier must retain command of himself and his equipment. As one moves up a military hierarchy, each layer of command takes responsibility for those under its charge.

Command is frequently joined with the other components of C^3I (**command, control, communications, intelligence**). In the exercise of command, it is necessary to exert control over those forces arrayed under that command. Communications form an important link in that control, for orders must be conveyed to dispersed and often far-flung forces. Infantry in positions forward of headquarters, tanks rolling across plains or deserts, submarines and aircraft carriers at sea, and bombers in the air, not to mention crews in missile silos, all need to receive instructions. Some of them are in a position to observe enemy action as well as report their own conditions, thus providing feedback to their commanders. Such information as well as details from more remote observations and spies comprise important aspects of the intelligence upon which tactics are adjusted and directions given. In World War II, the British and Americans derived great intelligence advantage from having broken the secret codes of the Germans and Japanese, thus learning in advance of many of the plans and movements of the enemy.

Clausewitz discussed how C^3I can be disrupted in the **fog of combat,** the confusion and seeming chaos of intense battle in which it is not clear to anyone exactly how the battle is being decided and what the effects of one's own actions are. During the fog of battle, the command of the self and the training and discipline of soldiers and sailors rise perhaps to their zenith, for the continued actions of individuals may then turn the tide in a way that, while not readily apparent, may shape the outcome of the battle and, perhaps, even the war.

• OTHER ACTIONS AND PROCESSES OF WAR

Military commanders use a variety of techniques in the conduct of war, and wars take on characteristics according to the way in which they are fought. A **war of maneuver** seeks to defeat an enemy army by moving and directing actions at vulnerable spots. Often maneuvers involve deception and surprise and sometimes daring. For example, in September 1950, when North Korean forces had driven South Korean and allied forces nearly off the Korean Peninsula, U.S. General Douglas MacArthur engaged in a risky landing at Inchon on the western coast, placing his forces in a position to drive the enemy army out of South Korea.

In a different mode, a **war of attrition** seeks to wear down the enemy to the point of exhaustion until it surrenders. Both the American Civil War and the European campaign in World War II were wars of attrition. During World War II, even before the allied expeditionary force landed at Normandy in June 1944, the British and American air forces sustained a massive bombing campaign against German cities that was designed to break morale and sap German will. Those aims were no more accomplished than were the identical aims of the Germans when they bombed England from August to October 1940 in the Battle of Britain. Following the allied land invasion, the fighting included both maneuver and attrition, but the course of the war largely wore down the German forces.

World War I took on a different cast from either of these types, for, instead of ending quickly, it fell into a pattern of stalemate, with the opposing armies dug into trenches from which attacks were launched against opposing trenches. An immense slaughter occurred over very small patches of ground, but no tactic or weapon was available for decisively changing the balance of forces. In the confines of trench warfare are illustrated the actions of attack from a defended position and counterattack designed not simply to defend but also to push back and break through the attacking lines.

A very different pattern occurred at the outbreak of World War II when the German army employed *blitzkrieg*, a lightning strike with massed mechanized forces, against Poland. The tactics accomplished a quick victory of offensive forces over surprised defending troops using inferior equipment. In the 1973 war between Egypt and Israel, the initial attack by Egypt employed a similarly lightening-like mechanized attack, but the Israeli counterattack overwhelmed and then surrounded the Egyptian forces.

The 1973 case illustrated what has become an important characteristic of American and allied warfare in the late twentieth century, **air superiority.** Actually, by 1945 in Europe, the United States and Britain so completely controlled the skies that their aircraft could fly almost with impunity. But it was in the Middle East that the effectiveness of air superiority in battle was demonstrated time after time, most recently in the Gulf War. Far from making ground warfare obsolete, though, air power combines with ground forces to gain control of the battleground.

This combination of forces has been extended in modern warfare to include naval forces. Above all else, naval warfare aims at gaining control of the sea lanes, thus engaging enemy vessels to sink them in order to dominate the seas. With such domination, then, a power can transport troops and supplies to distant theaters as well as protect the homeland from invasion. The aircraft carrier, which has become the central weapons system in modern sea battle, adds to the arsenal for attacking ground forces and dominating the air above the battleground. Submarines have also proven effective weapons for destroying enemy shipping, and they have gained a new role in nuclear deterrence, which will be treated below.

Although not yet used in a major way, space-based weapons are also thought by some to have the potential for contributing to control of battlefields. Already very practical and used to great effect in battle as well as in other activities are **surveillance satellites,** which provide significant intelligence that was not available before the space age.

A basic principle of military operations is the **control of positions** that dominate the battleground, and this principle extends throughout these various means of fighting. Taking the high ground impels the infantry. Similarly, naval forces aim to control sea lanes, and, as we have seen, air superiority serves effectively in the late twentieth century as the analogue. Whether space-based weapons will embody the same principle remains to be seen.

Another principle guiding fighting units is **concentration of force.** The ability of an army to concentrate its power at a point remains the essential component to achieve a breakthrough, whether in an infantry line, the advance of a tank battalion, an aggregation of ships confronting an enemy naval force, or the invasion of a country. Air and artillery bombardment may precede an attack by land forces to "soften up" defending troops.

Two sorts of warfare pose great challenges to this principle of concentrating force, but the difficulties in the two are quite distinct. **Two-front wars** pose one sort of challenge, but **counterguerrilla wars** test leaders in different ways. Germany faced a two-front war in both world wars, meeting it in both cases by attacking first in the west and then turning its forces in a concentrated way against Russia and the Soviet Union, respectively. In the Second World War, the Soviet Union avoided a two-front war until the last few days by negotiating a nonaggression pact with Japan. The United States, forced to fight a two-front war, concentrated its forces in Europe against Germany while managing a significant second front in the Pacific against Japan. Only with the defeat of the Nazi war machine in May 1945 could the United States concentrate its forces in the Pacific.

Counterguerrilla wars make it extraordinarily difficult to concentrate forces against an enemy because guerrillas employ tactics of attack and withdrawal, dispersal and melding into the general population. Successes against guerrillas were achieved in the Philippines and Malaysia, where guerrillas were isolated from the general population. Moving people out of their homes into strategic hamlets in Vietnam did not achieve the intended effect. Only when guerrilla warfare shifts to conventional battle can the principle of concentration of force be used, but even then, it does not promise victory for counterguerrilla forces. The final great battle of the French in Indochina was at the fortress of Dien Bien Phu, where the Vietnamese also concentrated their forces for battle and won.

• WEAPONS OF MASS DESTRUCTION

Chemical, biological, and nuclear weapons have been little used in battle, but they tend to be regarded with particular horror because of their devastating and indiscriminate effects. Mustard gas was used extensively in World War I; Egypt used gas in Yemen during its intervention in the civil war there from 1962–67; and the Iraqi government employed gas against its own Kurdish people. Although the powers have developed and stockpiled biological agents—primarily disease-bearing organisms—they have not been applied in battle. The United States dropped two nuclear weapons on Japan in August 1945 to hasten the end of World War II and avoid an invasion of the enemy's homeland. Despite the production of tens of thousands of nuclear and thermonuclear weapons, however, they have not been used in battle since. These weapons have in common that characteristic of so much of the war apparatus in the twentieth century: they do not discriminate effectively between soldiers and civilians. They also hold immense destructive power and are, thus, not easily employable for the rational attainment of political goals. That is to say, their costs outweigh the benefits that might be gained from their use. They retain some utility for deterrence but not for effectiveness in war.

With all of the dismaying potential for destructiveness in the modern world and powerful negative attitudes about weapons and war, martial and belligerent activities remain an important part of international politics. Sometimes, even very important questions are settled by war. For example, the virtual disappearance for fifty years of respect for the ideas of fascism may be attributed to the effectiveness of the military defeat of the countries that were led in World War II by regimes espousing the doctrines now so despised. Lesser issues—such as who rules Vietnam, the continued existence of Israel, and who

controls the flow and price of Arabian Peninsula oil—have also been settled by war.

Many questions, of course, are settled in different ways. Moreover, some questions do not get settled, but when they are raised in important clashes, crises occur that sometimes end in war but sometimes not. War, however, does not comprise the only form in which conflict occurs. In addition to military instruments, economic means also are employed in the international conflict.

Economic Conflict

States and coalitions of states contend using economic instruments in two broad dimensions, **positional conflict** and **structural conflict.** The first encompasses the struggle of each state to maintain its position in the international system, a competition that includes the pursuit of wealth as the foundation of state power. Furthermore, a special case of positional economic conflict involves the leading power in the international system fighting to maintain its domination through cooperation, coercion, and denial. The rise and fall of the major powers constitutes a third manifestation of positional conflict, but this will be treated in Chapter 14.

Structural conflict entails friction over the principles upon which the international political economy should be based.[15] Such contention formed part of the struggle during the Cold War between the liberal principles of the United States and the socialist principles of the Soviet Union. At a less strategic level, such principles as import substitution industrialization followed by Latin American countries and state-coordinated development strategies employed by Japan clashed as variants of liberal market principles with the United States' version of market economics. As the group of less developed states became dissatisfied in the 1960s and 1970s with the pace of their own economic growth, they adopted a program called the New International Economic Order that they presented to the rich countries as a set of demands to change the principles on which international commerce was ordered.

• POSITIONAL CONFLICT

Most commonly, states engage in competition as they strive to develop, produce, and trade as means to maintain their respective positions in the international system. Although, as Krugman argues,[16] states do not have a bottom line and do not engage directly in economic competition as firms do, they must strengthen their own economies and increase their own productivity at the same rate as others to remain in position. What one country accomplishes relies primarily on its own efforts, with little dependent on its trade with other countries. As discussed in Chapter 8, selection of development strategies and uneven development processes affect relative positions mightily, and each state conflicts with the others. Even in liberal states in which multinational firms spearhead efforts to grow economically through investments, repatriated profits and diversified investments in the home market assist in the accumulation of wealth and power, even when their foreign activities may also assist other countries in their own accumulation. To the extent that they fail to serve the conflictful interests of their home states, their activities tend to be restricted by their home governments.

In addition to these ordinary manifestations of conflict through economic means, the special case of a leading power's maintenance of its domination can be illustrated by the United States in the post-World War II period. Perhaps the most effective manner in which the United States ensured its predominance was by cooperating with allies and other countries, and perhaps the most effective means was its soft power. Before discussing specific cases in which this domination was ensured, a comment is warranted on the paradox of regarding **cooperation as conflict.**

The leader of a cooperative effort engages in conflict on two fronts: with its allies and with its adversaries. Within the alliance, the leader gains not only the prestige attached to heading an aggregate of states, but its ideas tend to be followed both because of their compelling nature and the benefits that cooperation brings to the followers. Within the North Atlantic partnership between the United States and its North American and Western European associates, there were occasions when Britain, France, Germany, Canada, and others came into conflict over either a policy or a larger issue. Though not always, the United States usually prevailed, both because of its power and because the cost of breaking the alliance overwhelmed the benefit of winning the issue at stake.

On the adversarial front, an alliance leader, of course, gains strength from cooperating with allies in facing its opponents. Moreover, as noted in a previous chapter, domination within an alliance also deprives an adversary of access to the assets of the grouping. To a large extent, the international system

position of a superpower stems from its position as alliance leader. Certainly, loss of that position would diminish the state's international standing. Thus, during the Cold War, both the United States and the Soviet Union gained strength from heading their respective alliances, even though each dominated and provided security to their respective followers. Cooperation within NATO formed part of the United States' conflict with the Soviet Union and its allies. When China defected from the Soviet alliance system, a new conflict developed in place of the cooperative effort that helped to shape the conflict with the United States and its allies. Finally, the collapse of the Soviet position in Eastern Europe and the defection of the Eastern European countries— not only from the alliance but also from the ideological and governing system that had helped to unify the coalition—immensely weakened the Soviet Union. Obviously, it was the prior weakness of the superpower that allowed those allies to defect.

Several episodes in the history of the Atlantic alliance in the post-World War II period serve to illustrate the argument that domination is preserved by cooperation and that cooperation in turn suppresses or defeats alternative policy preferences and structural arrangements. An early episode involved the NETHERLANDS' wish to persevere in its war against Indonesian nationalists fighting for independence. Faced with an American threat to stop the flow of Marshall Plan aid, the small, northern European country desisted from its imperial preservation policy and entered into negotiations that led to the independence of Indonesia in 1949.

Fearing the recklessness of its superpower leader, CANADA sought during the Korean War to restrain the United States, even while it remained the most faithful of allies.[17] Another faithful but less obeisant ally, France developed an independent nuclear weapons program in the face of opposition from the United States. Furthermore, France required in 1966 that the headquarters of NATO to be removed from French soil as the country refused further participation in joint planning and command within the alliance. France under President DeGaulle even developed ambitions of becoming leader of the Third World, an alternative to the conflicting alliances of the Cold War.

Perhaps the greatest crisis in NATO history occurred in 1956 when Britain and France, together with Israel, explicitly rejected American preferences for a peaceful solution of the SUEZ CANAL CRISIS and launched an invasion of Egypt. The United

States coerced the withdrawal of its two NATO allies by refusing to extend them credits for the purchase of the oil needed to fuel their undertaking.

Other conflicts within the alliance cropped up over the years. In the early 1960s, France and the United States exerted opposing pressures on West Germany for military cooperation. France signed agreements for limited cooperation with Germany in the military as well as other sectors, while the United States pressed upon the West Germans a multilateral force in which they would seemingly share in nuclear decision making.[18] With the advent of detente during the Nixon administration in 1969, WEST GERMANY advanced its own conceptions of relaxing tensions and changing the terms of its relations with the East; this had a substantial impact on the course of breaking down what was known as the iron curtain, the division between East and West in Europe that ran through Germany and Berlin. Germany essentially sought to make East Germany more accessible and to provide some means for giving East Germans access to West Germany.

By means of COCOM throughout the Cold War and in the natural gas pipeline dispute of the 1980s (both treated in Chapter 10), the United States pressed allies to deprive their adversaries of strategic and related goods. Similarly, in the post-Cold War period, the United States pressed Russia not to export nuclear energy technology to Iran for fear that that country had embarked on a nuclear weapons program. Moreover, the United States in 1995 required that a subsidiary of an American oil company, CONOCO, rescind a contract that the company had signed for the exploration of oil in Iran. In this case, European companies gained a market for their services that had first been won by a U.S. company.

IRAN has also been the subject of economic coercion by the United States as a means of maintaining its position of domination in the international system. Deprivation of access to nuclear weapons has been a policy of the United States since 1945, and a coalition of other countries joined that endeavor with the Nuclear Non-proliferation Treaty, which took effect in 1970 and was indefinitely extended in 1995. Challengers to that policy have included Iran, Iraq, and North Korea, and the United States has made major efforts to coerce those countries to agree not to acquire nuclear weapons, which would affect their relative positions.

All such discrete conflicts discussed in this section occurred within an established international economic structure. However, on occasion, countries try to change the international structure by promoting alternative principles of economic organization.

• STRUCTURAL CONFLICT

The fundamental structural conflict involving economic principles over the course of the last century and a half pitted capitalism against its profound critics who embraced socialism. That difference of principle became a contest in international politics mainly as one of the dimensions of the COLD WAR confrontation between the Soviet Union and its adherents on the one hand and the capitalist countries on the other. As expressed in conventional terms, the Soviet Union embodied and advocated a command economy in which a central planning agency guided all economic activities, including savings, investment, production, labor, marketing, and so forth. Both the success of the Soviet Union in its industrialization and the promise of an egalitarian future appealed to many in the world, giving the leading socialist state a measure of soft power in its contention during the Cold War with the United States. Particularly for very poor states newly independent after a period of colonialism, socialism held the appeal of more rapid as well as more egalitarian development than did capitalism, with its structural inequalities.

Counterpoised to the command economy stood the market economy, which provided productivity, a supply of consumer goods, and prosperity. In contrast to the egalitarian distribution promised by socialist economics, capitalism held out both freedom and the opportunity for enrichment. Ultimately triumphant at the end of the Cold War, this aspect of the American program of leadership held appeal during the struggle as well, though often attraction to market principles was offset by resentment and criticism of the rich countries.

Part of that struggle entailed intellectual debates over terms of development and analysis of conditions. As noted in Chapter 8 on political economy, analysts contended over whether every country would pass through essentially the same stages or whether the less developed countries were stuck in a permanent condition of dependency. Such encounters occurred not just in classrooms and academic meetings, think tanks and governmental conferences, but also at the international level when dependency theory formed the intellectual basis for the demands made by the poor countries in the United Nations for a NEW INTERNATIONAL

ECONOMIC ORDER. The passage of a resolution in the UN General Assembly in 1974, in turn, gave impetus for negotiations in many forums over subsequent years in attempts to replace liberal principles of trade and investment with the new, statist principles embodied in that resolution.

International clashes did not monopolize the structural conflict between capitalism and socialism. Part of the struggle occurred within states as different governments adopted variations on the two systems. One finds examples of the success and the failure of each economic system. SWEDEN elected a socialist government in 1936 that adopted aspects of central planning, public ownership of the means of production, and egalitarian distribution that were to produce a prosperous, healthy, and satisfied society over the course of the next half century and beyond. Somewhat less success may be found in INDIA, which created a modern industrial sector through the application of socialist principles but which faces near the end of the century the need to adopt market principles to overcome many of the inefficiencies of its economy. Further along the continuum from success to failure is the collapse of the Soviet and EASTERN EUROPEAN ECONOMIES, along with their admission of their failures by a wholesale adoption of market principles.

In the era of triumph of liberal market ideology, it is easy to forget an equally mixed capitalist record. For all of the immense success of the United States, Germany, Japan, South Korea, and others, matching failures may be found to lie along a continuum similar to the socialist one. Like India, the PHILIPPINES may be marked as a partial failure on the capitalist side of the ledger. Although having made significant strides in development in the post-World War II period, the Philippines fell under a corrupt regime, and its capitalist economy is riddled with failure, unable to achieve a level of production to employ and provide for its people. For greater failures, Latin America has produced the capitalism of GUATEMALA that favors a very small elite but denies freedom and consumption to the vast majority of its population, some 85 percent of whom live below the poverty level. Furthermore, other economies have not met the test of maintaining their respective positions in the international system.

Thus, the economic structural conflict process works through intellectual debate, the embodiment of principles in states that provide models imitated by other states, the successes and failures of those models and their varied embodiments, and diplomatic negotiations. Phrased this way, that conflict appears to exist largely in the realm of ideas and practice, of soft power and the persuasiveness of success. However, model imitation is moved along by the provision of security, funds, and ideological support by the major powers. Additionally, adoption of principles of economic organization has been strongly encouraged or discouraged by diplomacy, propaganda, economic sanctions, and military intervention.

For example, without distracting from the hard work, savings, investment in education, wise decisions, and entrepreneurship of South Koreans, one acknowledges that American-provided security, diplomatic and military support, investment, and transfer of technology have contributed much to SOUTH KOREA's success as a capitalist economy. Similarly, the long-term trade embargo and many other hostile United States actions against CUBA after its adoption of socialist principles have done serious injury to that country and made it very difficult to succeed. With the collapse of Soviet support for its economy, Cuba has fallen into the direst of straits. Unrelenting American pressure in the mid-1990s may ultimately promote the demise of socialist principles in Cuba, and much of that collapse will be attributable to international pressures, making it difficult to assess the extent to which the principles of socialism themselves can be blamed for the failure. Clearly, the process of structural conflict embodies several facets.

In addition to the variety of experiences under capitalism and socialism that affected the structural conflict during the Cold War, there were contentions within those systems of economic organization that also expressed aspects of structural conflict. Most prominently, China confronted the Soviet Union in the late 1950s and early 1960s with an alternative path to communism, the end goal of the socialist endeavor. After the Cold War, some liberal countries have engaged in struggle over appropriate models of market economics, the most visible being Japan and the United States.

The dispute between CHINA AND THE SOVIET UNION manifested itself in a number of ways, but the economic aspect involved a shortcut to socialism labeled the Great Leap Forward that the Chinese adopted in contrast to the Soviet model of extensive development that Stalin had spearheaded in the 1930s and 1940s. Mao Zedong's model consolidated rural peasants into communes and involved such innovations as backyard furnaces to produce steel. In practice, the scheme proved disastrous: it not only failed as a method of economic development, but it also caused the death of some 20 to 30 million people.[19]

Even preceding the end of the Cold War, in an attempt to resolve its trade deficit, the UNITED STATES ENGAGED JAPAN to reform its domestic economic system to benefit American commerce. American demands have included the imposition of quotas on exports to the United States, devaluation of the yen against the dollar, the reduction of inspections and other restrictions on imports, reform of the Japanese wholesale and retail distribution systems, and the imposition on Japanese firms of import quotas for certain commodities such as auto parts.

In addition to conflicts like these that can be encapsulated within the terms of socialism and capitalism, IRAN after 1979 exerted its will in the structural conflict between these worldwide models and its own economy organized in conformity with Islamic principles. These principles, for example, reject the concept of interest on loans, which constitutes the main mechanism in liberal economics for efficiently allocating savings to investments. Although these principles are practiced only in Iran and that country's theocracy has little appeal in other states, the broad movement of what is referred to in the West as Islamic fundamentalism does pose in the realms of both economics and politics a structural alternative to other ways of organizing states and societies.[20]

Deep differences over how to organize economies cannot be divorced from questions of how to organize politics. Thus, structural conflict extends to the political realm.

Structural Conflict in Politics

Perhaps the most profound structural conflict occurs in situations in which wholly different civilizations confront each other, as in the European conquest of North and South America. The various Indian civilizations in the Western Hemisphere organized their societies on such a different basis from those of the conquerors that they evoked no understanding or insight. Naked Caribbean Indians met elegantly dressed Columbus, and men who kept themselves warm in winter by smearing their bodies with bear grease hailed the buttoned-up Pilgrims who landed in Massachusetts. Cortes' successors destroyed what is now known as *Templo Mayor*, the great temple of the Aztecs in Tenochtitlan, and built a Christian cathedral nearby in renamed Mexico. This deep structural conflict continues to the end of the twentieth century in southern Mexico and Guatemala, where Mayans maintain many cultural traditions and languages outside the main currents of national life of the countries.

The modern era in international politics began in 1648 with the conclusion of the Thirty Years' War by the Treaty of Westphalia, which recognized the authority of the sovereign of each state to choose the religion to which his subjects would adhere. This termination of religious wars with the establishment of the sensible principle of exclusive jurisdiction within a territory did not end structural conflict over political principles. Though ameliorated by a recognition of sovereignty, international politics has continued to display structural conflict between states that contend for principles.

Napoleon's wars of conquest spread the principles of the French Revolution, and his armies were resisted in good measure in opposition to those postulates. The Congress of Vienna designed a post-Napoleonic order that aimed to protect legitimacy against democratic revolution. In the greatest war of the nineteenth century, the American Union fought against the Confederate States on behalf the principles of unity and freedom against those of states' rights and slavery. Although World War I cannot be described as a structural conflict, it acted as midwife to the Russian revolution and its Bolshevist successor, which battled for some seventy years on behalf of the world socialist revolution. Moreover, the United States burst forth on the world stage in World War I in a much more prominent role than it had played before, its president articulating Wilsonian principles that his successors have promoted to the present day.

Taking a broader perspective, one might conceive the twentieth century as a long period of struggle between **democracy** and **totalitarianism,** between forms of government in which authorities are limited and subject to periodic elections and those in which powerful leaders, unchecked, may strive for total solutions to their respective societies' problems that allow the brutalization and killing of citizens on behalf of abstractions. From this perspective, the victory at the end of the twentieth century appears to have gone to democracy and those conceptions of freedom that allow individuals and firms to pursue their interests.

Still, structural conflict persists in the politics of the post-Cold War world, with two manifestations especially outstanding. The first entails the issue of

■ The Arab World

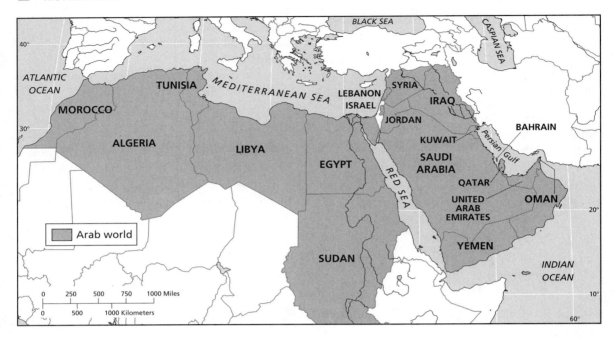

HUMAN RIGHTS, which the United States and some of its allies, as well as groups from civil society, promote by advocacy, informational policies, and sometimes economic measures. Furthermore, the process of conflict has been extended to another realm in which proponents of human rights from one society find refuge and sustenance in another. For example, since the Tiananmen Square massacre of demonstrating students in June 1989 by the Chinese government, many young Chinese have pursued their educations in the United States. They remain in touch with relatives and friends in China for information and the maintenance of morale. These men and women will be in a position to return to China should conditions allow them scope for political activity. On the other hand, like some other political refugees, they may not enjoy such opportunities and may remain within the confines of the state that is more sympathetic to their political aspirations.

Struggles between secular but often corrupt regimes in the ARAB WORLD and political activists who seek to construct Muslim states, either theocracies or participant polities characterized by a strong religious orientation, comprise the other major structural conflict in international politics at the close of the twentieth century. Apart from the internal strife noted, the contention is observed with great interest

by the main powers of Western Europe and North America, for Islamic states are very likely to remain hostile to the leading powers. On the whole, the status quo in the Arab world—including the Mahgreb, the Fertile Crescent, and the Arabian peninsula— favors the interests of the powers, for most of the states are headed by allied or at least friendly regimes that Islamists will have to defeat in elections or overthrow to come to power. One needs to be very skeptical about the potential for a transition by elections in light of the experience of ALGERIA, where in 1992 the government canceled a second round of elections in which Islamic parties appeared destined to triumph. Without the channel of the ballot box, the more militant of those parties launched a guerrilla war against the government that has continued inconclusively to the date of this writing.

Contention remains fundamental to politics, including international politics, with an extensive array of processes for conducting conflict. Few conflicts, however, are unrelieved by elements of cooperation. Moreover, though harmony seldom characterizes the interactions of humans, cooperative endeavors comprise an important part of political experience. Cooperative undertakings often seek merely to overcome conflict, but they also hold out the possibilities for joint achievements that would be impossible in solitary quests.

• IMPORTANT TERMS

air superiority
analytical approach
bargaining
C³I (command, control,
   communications,
   intelligence)
change
coalition theory
command
complex uncertainty
concentration of force
conflict
control of position
cooperation
cooperation as conflict
counterguerrilla warfare
cybernetic approach
democracy
ethnic nationalism
fog of combat

forward strategy
guerrilla warfare
logistics
nonzero-sum
n-person game
planning
positional conflict
rationality
strategy
structural conflict
surveillance satellite
tactics
totalitarianism
two-front war
two-person game
utilities
war
war of attrition
war of maneuver
zero-sum

• STUDY QUESTIONS

1. What does it mean to engage in bargaining under conditions of complex uncertainty? Illustrate your answer with examples.

2. Define and explain the fundamental concepts of game theory: two-person and n-person games, zero-sum and nonzero-sum games, utilities, and rationality. How does the game theory conception of rationality differ from the ordinary meaning of that term?

3. Compare and contrast the long-term strategies of the United States and Germany. How do you account for the differences?

4. What are the roles in war played by the components of military planning, strategy, tactics, and logistics?

5. Where are the components of command, control, communications, and intelligence located in fighting wars? How do they operate, and how are they connected?

6. What are the obstacles to concentrating forces in modern military operations? Illustrate your answer.

7. What are the differences between structural conflict and positional conflict? Give examples.

8. How can a leading power contribute to the maintenance of its position in the international system through means of economic and political cooperation? Are components of conflict implicit in its relations with its allies? Explain.

9. Which contentious issues during the Cold War period illustrated structural conflict in international poli-

tics? Illustrate your answer with examples from the central Cold War conflict and other disputes.

10. Does it make sense to conceive of the twentieth century as a time of struggle over the structures of liberal democracy and capitalism versus those of totalitarianism and command economies? Explain.

• ENDNOTES

1. This fundamental idea and the illustrations are drawn from Schelling, *The Strategy of Conflict*.
2. Steinbruner, *The Cybernetic Theory of Decision*.
3. For extended treatments, see David Owen, *Balkan Odyssey* (New York: Harcourt Brace, 1996); Laura Silber and Allan Little, *Yugoslavia: Death of a Nation* (New York: TV Books/Penguin USA, 1996); and Susan L. Woodward, *Balkan Tragedy: Chaos and Dissolution after the Cold War* (Washington, D.C.: Brookings Institution, 1995).
4. See Duncan Snidal, "The Game Theory of International Politics," in *Cooperation under Anarchy*, ed. by Kenneth A. Oye (Princeton, N.J.: Princeton University Press, 1986).
5. William H. Riker, *The Theory of Political Coalitions* (New Haven: Yale University Press, 1962).
6. Schelling, *Arms and Influence* (New Haven: Yale University Press, 1966).
7. For classic statements of strategy, see Edward Earle Mead, ed., *Makers of Modern Strategy* (Princeton, N.J.: Princeton University Press, 1943), and Peter Paret, ed., *Makers of Modern Strategy from Machiavelli to the Nuclear Age* (Princeton, N.J.: Princeton University Press, 1986). See also Edward Luttwak, *Strategy* (Cambridge: Belknap Press of Harvard University Press, 1987).
8. See John Lewis Gaddis, "The Long Peace: Elements of Stability in the Postwar International System," *International Security* 10 (Spring 1986): 92–142.
9. For example, the Lentz Peace Research Laboratory, an institute that tracks such matters, reported that more wars occurred in 1987 than in any year in recorded history. Moreover, the death toll from wars in that year was recorded as 507,000. Laina Farhat, "Computer Analysis Tells Grim Tale of War," *San Francisco Chronicle*, 23 October 1990, p. A21. The figures are particularly impressive when considered in the context of the superpower accommodation that was occurring in the late 1980s.
10. Frantz Fanon, *The Wretched of the Earth*, trans. by Constance Farrington (New York: Grove Press, 1963).
11. Mueller, *Retreat from Doomsday*.
12. Richard Rosecrance, *The Rise of the Trading State: Commerce and Conquest in the Modern World* (New York: Basic Books, 1986).
13. This account relies upon Kagan's judgment about German state goals. See Kagan, *On the Origins of War*.
14. See Albert Wohlstetter, "Illusions of Distance," *Foreign Affairs* 46 (January 1968): 242–55.
15. The term is Stephen D. Krasner's. See his *Structural Conflict*.
16. Paul Krugman, "Competitiveness: A Dangerous Obsession," *Foreign Affairs* 73 (March/April 1994): 28–44.
17. Stairs, *The Diplomacy of Constraint*.

18. The best case study of the MLF is Steinbruner, *The Cybernetic Theory of Decision*.

19. This is the estimate given by John King Fairbank in his *China: A New History* (Cambridge: Belknap Press of Harvard University Press, 1992), p. 368.

20. See Huntington, "The Clash of Civilizations?" in which he argues that the post-Cold War fault lines will occur between such broad aggregates as Western secularism and Moslem fundamentalism.

CHAPTER 13

Cooperation among States and Groups

With millions of transactions every day and thousands of organizations that transcend borders, international cooperation in today's world is rife. Moreover, that cooperation suffuses not just economic activities but also matters involving security. In the midst of the conflict and potential for war that were treated in the last chapter, the challenge to analysts is to explain why cooperation occurs and under what conditions it emerges.

Aspects of game theory beyond those considered in the preceding chapter help to elucidate responses to those questions. This chapter discusses the dimensions of incentive structures, shadow of the future, and number of players. In addition, the complex interdependence model, the concept of regimes, and the role of international organizations add to the analyst's tools for understanding cooperation. One of the central mechanisms during the Cold War for promoting cooperation between the superpowers involved arms control, and in the post-Cold War period, security cooperation in Europe exemplifies a critical aspect of the contemporary world. Not only states but also nongovernmental organizations remain deeply involved in the processes of cooperation. All of these topics together comprise the subject matter of this chapter.

Introduction

Just as elements of cooperation ordinarily remain in conflict situations, traces of conflict linger in cooperative arrangements. By emphasizing cooperation, nevertheless, analysts have devised some interesting ideas for examining the actions and patterns of states acting together to achieve common or mutual goals. Central to a theoretical or conceptual understanding, game theory provides a set of analytical notions for grasping the components of cooperation and for guiding policy that aims to enhance cooperation. In addition, functionalism and its variant, neofunctionalism, offer through cooperation a solution to the problem of war. More recently, the idea of regime has contributed new insights into cooperation, and the concept of complex interdependence gives an additional way of thinking about cooperation. Institutions—particularly organizations—remain closely associated with cooperation, for, by embodying the principle of hierarchy, they seek to overcome the anarchy of the international system and provide assets that facilitate and promote cooperation.

Game Theory

Cooperation rests upon an optimistic outlook: that in the appropriate circumstances, states are likely to collaborate to achieve gains that they would not be able to accomplish alone. Thus, analysis aspires to specify those circumstances and to understand the means to achieve them. Optimism suffuses such an approach in an even deeper way by assuming that states are predisposed to cooperate, that the main problem does not lie in the realm of inducing cooperation but merely in avoiding defection. **Game theory** offers an analytical description of the circumstances under which cooperation is more likely to succeed. The description includes three components: **incentive structures, iteration,** and **number of players.**

• INCENTIVE STRUCTURES

Although variations in the arrangement of incentives are endless, a limited number of arrangements point to the way in which structures make cooperation more or less likely. Because they regard **defection** as the main problem, analysts using game theory express incentive structures in terms of assigned preferences to cooperate (C) or defect (D), and they assign names to specific preference orderings. These names signify anecdotes that encapsulate those orderings.

Cooperation is unnecessary in **Harmony** (CD > DC), for player A prefers to cooperate rather than defect, even if player B defects. Thus, a lover remains steadfast even if her partner acts unfaithfully. Similarly, the possibility of cooperation does not arise in **Deadlock** (DD > CC), inasmuch as both players prefer to compete rather than to cooperate, as might occur in a situation in which two firms favor trying to win over one another's customers rather than colluding to divide up market shares. In international politics, a faithful ally that fights even when a partner defects, says France in World War I after the Russian withdrawal from the war, exemplifies an incentive structure like that in Harmony. Similarly, West German Chancellor Konrad Adenauer's refusal to discuss the Soviet Union's offer in 1952 of settling the German question by trading unification for neutrality gives an instance of Deadlock, as does the Soviet Union's rejection of Marshall Plan participation.

The classic story from Rousseau of the stag hunt conveys an incentive structure conducive to cooperation. Several hunters take their posts collaboratively to catch a stag in order to be well fed, but any hunter may be tempted to abandon her post to snag a hare, gaining a single meal for herself but leaving the others hungry. **Stag Hunt** (CC > DC > DD > CD) sets up an incentive structure that has a higher payoff for cooperation, inasmuch as it leads to everyone's eating well, but there is an incentive to defect to catch the hare. Thirdly, should every hunter defect to ensnare a hare, that would be preferable to the situation in which the first hunter remained at her post while the others defected. Generally, an international trade pact that lowers tariffs or other barriers to free trade resembles Stag Hunt, for everyone benefits from increased trade. Although there may be some temptation to cheat while others cooperate, even universal defection is preferred to circumstances in which one country maintains free trade while its trading partners employ discriminatory practices.

Prisoner's Dilemma comprises the incentive structure most often invoked by international politics analysts, for it illustrates how a structural arrangement can lead to most unfortunate consequences even when both players act rationally. A sheriff arrests two drug dealers but has enough evidence in hand to indict them for only a small-time infraction of possession. However, if she could extract a confession from one of them, it would be possible to put the other away in prison for a long time on a drug-dealing charge. Separating the prisoners, the sheriff offers release to one should she confess while the other remains silent and faces a ten-year sentence. Should both remain silent, the evidence will allow a conviction carrying only a one-year sentence. On the other hand, should both confess, it would be possible to obtain a three-year term for each. Finally, should the first prisoner remain silent while her comrade confesses, she would face a ten-year term. This incentive structure (DC > CC > DD > CD) leads rationally to defecting confessions and a three-year term for both, even though cooperative silence would have resulted in a better result for both prisoners. Resembling the normal state of affairs in much of international politics, Prisoner's Dilemma captures the difficulties of cooperation.

In an illustration of Prisoner's Dilemma applied to international politics, the United States preferred to maintain its monopoly of nuclear weapons (DC) but offered to give up its weapons if every country would agree to place its nuclear industry under United Nations authority (CC). However, the country clearly prefers to remain one of several possessing nuclear weapons (DD) rather than find itself at the disadvantage of being without them while others arm themselves with such arsenals (CD).

Finally, analysts regularly invoke **Chicken** as an incentive structure that captures honor or prestige as a stake in human relations as well as international politics. Two teenagers drive at high speeds in cars headed toward each other straddling the center line of a highway. Cooperation requires swerving to avoid a disastrous collision, but defection gains prestige, a reputation for nerve and risk-taking. The Chicken incentive structure (DC > CC > CD > DD) possesses no intrinsically rational solution, for the player who cooperates loses reputation, and mutual defection leads to destruction and death. When Hitler ordered his army to reoccupy the Rhineland in March 1936 in violation of the Versailles and Locarno treaties (D), France did not resist, though it was strong enough to do so (C). In 1938, Britain and France acquiesced in the German annexation of Austria and collaborated with Hitler in dividing Czechoslovakia (CC). A year later, France and Britain's declaration of war against Germany upon its invasion of Poland meant six years of destruction and death (DD). Not once during this sequence of events did Hitler cooperate, though many observers conclude that he would have done so in 1936 had France taken action against the Rhineland occupation (CD).[1]

■———————————————————

• • • • • • **Incentive Structures in Game Theory**

GAME	INCENTIVE STRUCTURE	EXAMPLE
Harmony	CD > DC	France continued to fight in World War I after Russia withdrew from the war.
Deadlock	DD > CC	Soviet Union rejected Marshall Plan aid.
Stag Hunt	CC > DC > DD > CD	International trade agreement
Prisoner's Dilemma	DC > CC > DD > CD	United States policy on nuclear weapons
Chicken	DC > CC > CD > DD	Sequence leading to World War II (Germany —France)

The payoff structures of Stag Hunt and Chicken make cooperation more likely than Prisoner's Dilemma, whose rational solution leads to mutual defection. Recall, however, from the last chapter that in game theory, values are exogenously set; that is, they are assigned by someone other than the players themselves. In real life, where such analysis is often applied, though, there are means for changing the values attached to the payoffs. For example, in Prisoner's Dilemma, the differences between the punishments can be changed, so that the penalties for defection are lessened and the rewards to cooperate are increased.[2] Moreover, there is no reason in real life for the parties not to communicate, even though isolation of the prisoners forms an essential component of the game structure. Oye has noted that the multilateral means of regimes and **disaggregation of play** can be employed to shift the values attached to outcomes.[3] For example, if a million dollar agreement were broken into four quarter-million

dollar segments, the incentive to cheat on any single transaction would be considerably diminished.

• **SHADOW OF THE FUTURE**

The model game of Prisoner's Dilemma occurs only once, and it is a single play that produces the logic of a costly outcome. By introducing iterated play, one gains a **shadow of the future** that encourages cooperative behavior in the expectation that it will be reciprocated. Moreover, as Oye explains, the shadow of the future can be extended by disaggregation, breaking a cooperative relationship into many segments, as an annually renewable trading partnership illustrates. Furthermore, **reciprocity** works better when choices are clear, usually involving only a yes or no response, such as whether a country will employ tariffs of 5 percent or no tariffs at all. In addition, **transparency** and **surveillance** make reciprocity work better than reliance on secrecy and trust.

To make cooperation more likely, Axelrod devised a **tit-for-tat strategy** that seems to promote cooperation.[4] Tit-for-tat simply means that a country wishing to cooperate with another initiates cooperation by acting cooperatively. If the second state responds with a cooperative act, the first reacts in kind. Should the second state respond by defecting, however, the first also defects. At some point, the first may reinitiate with a cooperative step, again responding in kind according to the type of action taken by the second country. Nuclear weapons testing activities during the Cold War illustrated tit-for-tat, as the United States and the Soviet Union at different times initiated moratoria on nuclear testing, but when one defected, the other reciprocated. Similarly, so long as one refrained from testing, so did the other.

• **NUMBER OF PLAYERS**

Essentially, the problem of this dimension, two-person and n-person games, resembles that of bipolarity and multipolarity. Difficulties encountered in n-person arrays include barriers to obtaining information and anticipating behavior, the likelihood of "autonomous defection and of recognition and control," and a decrease in the "feasibility of sanctioning defectors."[5] As discussed in sections dealing with multipolarity, increased uncertainty and greater flexibility characterize the involvement of many states in a system. To increase the potential for cooperation, bilateral arrangements obviously assist, and regional arrangements such as NAFTA bolster cooperation. Within multipolarity, regimes such as the GATT help to gain cooperation among large numbers of states.

These three dimensions of game theory offer insight into the processes of cooperation and even guidance on how to manipulate the arrangements to encourage and sustain cooperation in international politics. Nevertheless, other conceptual notions place cooperation in longer-term, more explicitly institutionalized ways. With its grounding in mathematics, game theory tends not to be historical, and its stylized definitions and concepts seem more of an overlay on international politics than do conceptual apparatuses evolving from traditional concerns. Ideas of integration, functionalism, and neofunctionalism grow out of the search for solutions to the problem of war.

Complex Interdependence

In the ideal type set forth by Keohane and Nye, **complex interdependence** has three main characteristics.[6] First, **multiple channels** provide complex opportunities for contact. Interstate channels engage governments in diplomacy and other traditional forms of intercourse. Second, official agencies not centrally directed establish **transgovernmental channels,** as illustrated, for example, by links between assistant secretaries at the U.S. Department of Commerce in Washington who talk by telephone regularly with their counterparts at the Canadian Ministry for Industry, Trade, and Commerce in Ottawa. Third, **transnational channels** exist in which corporations and other nongovernmental entities engage in activities across international boundaries.

The second main characteristic of complex interdependence is the **absence of hierarchy** among issues. Rather than being dominated by high politics, the activities of governments and others extend across a wide range of matters that include economic and other concerns, that is, low politics. Complex interdependence, finally, is marked by the characteristic of a **minor role for military force** in international affairs.

These characteristics lead to certain processes that do not attend international politics under the conditions associated with realism in which coherent states dominate, force remains effective, and high politics overrides low politics. Keohane and Nye do not contend that conditions of complex interdependence have entirely replaced those of realism. They hold simply that sometimes conditions

approximating the one ideal type prevail and that at other times those close to the other ideal type characterize the circumstances.

Included in the processes associated with complex interdependence are the disaggregation of goals and resources by **issue area.** Thus, without hierarchy, it is difficult or costly to bring force to bear on economic issues, which must be processed by economic means alone. Of course, even under interdependence, powerful states may link issues, as the United States on occasion has placed human rights demands on trade matters. Complex interdependence also makes **agenda formation** a more important process in international relations. This implies that domestic groups may agitate to bring such issues as trade and investment to the forefront of the agenda of their state's central decision makers. Moreover, such activities combine with the characteristic of multiple channels to reduce the distinctions between domestic and international politics. In addition, complex interdependence implies that international organizations assume a more prominent place in international politics.

• SENSITIVITY AND VULNERABILITY

States are sensitive to one another and to private transactions in international relations in that they incur costs in response to events and phenomena outside their borders. For example, increases in interest rates in the United States draw savings from other countries, and those savings are not then available for investment in, say, Canada or France. Poverty and war in Central America and Mexico tend to drive the most desperate people to flee to the United States, and similar phenomena in Algeria have the same effect on migration to France. Speculators all over the world can impose great pressure on weak currencies, and increases in commodity prices by producers can hurt consumers. Such **sensitivity** interdependence characterizes the modern world, making it a more interesting place than otherwise.

For the most part, though, states, at least the more powerful ones, adjust to changes so that whatever costs may be incurred do not last long. In the case of a rise in United States interest rates, for example, Canadian banks may match the increase within a day or so. A major power may offset an adversary's introduction of a new weapons system by deploying its own parallel one. When producer prices go up, consumers can often conserve such difficult-to-replace commodities as oil or find substitutes such as natural gas or coal. Although sensitivity requires adjustment and the ability to adapt as conditions change and does carry short-term costs, it holds little theoretical interest.

In contrast, **vulnerability** holds great interest, for it embodies the opposite side of the autonomy coin. Within the context of thinking about interdependence, vulnerability means that a country incurs costs as a result of events or phenomena abroad and does not have the capacity to adjust to those events to lower the costs. For example, JAPAN imports nearly all of its oil and does not possess resources such as coal and natural gas that could substitute for oil. Some possibilities exist for conservation, but the Japanese are so dependent on petroleum that they must absorb increased costs generated in the Middle East or elsewhere. This case illustrates also that vulnerability is a matter of dependence, the petroleum exporting countries are not mutually dependent on Japan. Indeed, when considering vulnerability, the term **interdependence** proves to be somewhat misleading. While there are cross-cutting dependencies in which various states rely on others, as the example of raw materials exporters and exporters of manufactured goods who depend on each other's products illustrates, **dependency** rather than interdependence provides a better conception on which to focus analysis.

Furthermore, dependency varies from one country to another, with relative vulnerability providing a meaningful concept for comparing the positions of states. In the case of petroleum, for example, the United States remains much less vulnerable than Japan. As a producer of petroleum, natural gas, and coal, the United States possesses the resources to substitute one for the other. Moreover, the extraordinary level of waste in its high-consumption society affords scope for conservation of petroleum that renders the country quite autonomous. There as been no political acceptance of the proposal first made in 1973 to encourage conservation through the imposition of a sales tax on gasoline. In a world in which nearly everyone else pays some $3 or more for a gallon of gasoline, Americans paid on the average in 1995 less than $1.50 per gallon, a comparison that speaks volumes about the relative vulnerability of states.

Although writers on interdependence invoke asymmetries that enable some countries to manipulate ties binding different countries to exercise influence, Waltz stresses that the world remains one characterized by inequality in which some countries can take care of themselves while most cannot and that, therefore, the international system as a whole could not accurately be described when he wrote in 1979 as an interdependent one.[7] In part, however, Waltz's argument rests upon the number of major powers in the system, two at the time of his writing. With the disintegration of the Soviet Union and the impending emergence of a multipolar system, it may be worthwhile to explore further the possibilities for growing interdependence in the future.

Even in a world in which the powers might become more dependent on, say, international trade than the superpowers were in the bipolar structure of the Cold War, inequalities of condition and relative levels of autonomy and vulnerability will remain. The puzzle presented is whether increasing sensitivity and higher levels of vulnerability will promote greater cooperation in international politics, with mixed agendas, little use of military force, and multiple channels.

No definite solution can be given to that puzzle, for the future cannot be foretold. One's expectations undoubtedly depend to a large extent on one's premises. Those of realism maintain that states will remain the dominant actors, that those states strive for autonomy, and that the great uncertainties implicit in a multipolar structure of the international system will make cooperation very difficult. Liberalism's premises hold that growing institutionalism in international politics draws states closer together and that regimes and international organizations are likely to play more significant roles in an increasingly interdependent world. Furthermore, the spread of the liberal ideas of markets and democracy to increasing numbers of states gives further credence to expectations of enhanced cooperation, for liberal states do not go to war with one another and they allow their civil societies to engage in extended contact and commerce promoting competition within cooperative constitutional and normative frameworks. Beyond considering premises, one needs to examine the growth of both the concept and the reality of regimes as well as the state of international organizations at the end of the century.

Regimes

The post-World War II era has witnessed the burgeoning of international cooperative arrangements. In the economic sphere, the World Bank and the International Monetary Fund as well as several regional development banks have pooled the resources of member states and applied them to solving problems. In addition, these agencies act as catalysts for the generation of private-sector loans and direct investments, which give further impetus to growth and development. Through the General Agreement on Tariffs and Trade (GATT), the European Union (EC, now EU), the Central American Common Market (CACM), the Association of Southeast Asian Nations (ASEAN), and other institutions, states have collaborated to achieve unprecedented levels of economic prosperity. The Organization of Petroleum Exporting Countries (OPEC) succeeded in redesigning patterns of investment, taxation, pricing, and marketing of oil by means of coordinated activities of its member states.

Nor has organized cooperation been restricted to economic matters. The United States developed an elaborate alliance system involving over forty countries. Arab states built an apparatus and repertoire for handling disputes and issues of common interest. Patterns of cooperation impressed themselves on the Western Hemisphere and in African politics. As the Cold War moved along, even the superpower adversaries constructed arrangements for managing their relations, with special reference to arms control. Moreover, in the post-Cold War period, European officials have been giving increased attention to problems of constructing new security arrangements on the continent, which now faces an entirely different set of circumstances than it had during the Cold War, when it was divided.

Some political scientists have devised the notion of **regime** in an attempt to conceptualize these patterns of cooperation, and consensus centers on a standard definition. "International regimes are . . . principles, norms, rules, and decision-making procedures around which actor expectations converge in a given issue-area."[8] Although this delineation allows a wide range for interpretation, and some analysts reject the notion as being useless,[9] the concept regime affords a way to examine international cooperative arrangements. Krasner's definition directs attention to the existence of shared principles and norms that form a basis for cooperation, for each state can anticipate that other participants in a collaborative endeavor will act in conformity with such principles and norms. Perhaps the clearest example of the first of these is the **most favored nation** principle that governs the international trade regime. Despite its somewhat awkward terminology, the principle is one of equality, for it requires that a state will grant to each of its trading partners the identical terms of trade that it extends to the most favored nation with which it trades. A second honored principle in international trade is reciprocity: the precept that a state will extend to each of its trading partners the identical terms that each of them provides to it. Norms includes such rules as the long-term reduction of tariffs and other barriers to trade.

Regimes come into existence through the initiation of a country or countries that seek to stabilize relations within some subject area, such as trade or arms control. Regimes then persist because they facilitate cooperation by providing information to all participants and greater predictability concerning one another's behavior. Often, regimes also provide standardized means for punishing defection from the rules established. Thus, the concept regime proves useful in describing certain cooperative arrangements in international politics.

Nevertheless, the concept's limitations spring clearly into view at times of defection and recalcitrance by states that find themselves in circumstances that make it impossible or undesirable to adhere to a regime's established patterns. Britain's opting out of the European Community's monetary agreement under pressure of speculation against the pound demonstrates that unilateral action by an autonomous state remains a viable option. North Korea's nuclear programs within the nuclear nonproliferation regime illustrate that effective management of defection may rely on traditional diplomacy and adept employment of the foreign policy instruments at the disposal of that diplomacy, rather than on any rules or procedures inherent in the regime.

• BRITISH DEFECTION ON MONEY

In their quest for deepened integration, the EC members had established in the late 1970s a mechanism for linking the various currencies, and this arrangement formed a critical consideration in the plans developed by the Single European Act and the Maastricht Treaty. The alignment of national currencies and monetary practices was to lay the groundwork for the creation of a European Monetary Union and a single currency. However, in September 1992, the British pound came under severe attack by speculators, and the British government opted out of the European monetary regime. Although remaining members sustained the regime for themselves, the British action revealed that each country ultimately retains its prerogative to withdraw. At the same time, continuation of the regime preserves an arrangement that Britain is free to reenter under more fortuitous circumstances. Thus, while Britain asserted its freedom of action to protect its own economy, the maintenance of the regime by the other states continues to hold out an option for British policy that would not otherwise exist and that British action could not create by itself.

• NORTH KOREAN DEFECTION ON NUCLEAR ARMS

The North Korean nuclear program illustrates another type of limitation of the regime concept. Despite North Korea's endorsement of the Nuclear Non-proliferation Treaty, the United States claimed in 1994 that it held evidence that the country was engaged in a nuclear weapons program. Although the NPT regime provides for inspections by an International Atomic Energy Agency (IAEA), North Korea President Kim Il Sung refused to give IAEA personnel access to his country's nuclear facilities. Members of the United Nations Security Council considered imposing economic sanctions. Within the United States, voices expressed an inclination to attack North Korean nuclear facilities militarily, but these were countered by President Clinton and his administration, which preferred a diplomatic approach. A complicated course of events ensued. Former President Jimmy Carter traveled to North Korea; then, long-time North Korean dictator Kim Il Sung died. These events were followed by a period of uncertainty before the dictator's son was confirmed as successor. In the following months, extensive negotiations required the mobilization of broad international support to supply North Korea with light-water nuclear reactors to replace the more dangerous ones that they agreed to dismantle. Additionally, the complex deal became snagged when North Korea attempted to isolate South Korea, even though the latter was to supply most of the technology and funds to its northern neighbor. South Koreans sought to link the nuclear deal to a broader context of relations between the two parts of the divided country, whereas North Koreans sought recognition from the United States and other countries at the expense of the south. In the end, the arrangement that finally brought a respite if not an end to what had been a crisis emanated from ad hoc diplomacy rather than from regime procedures and decision making rules. Once again, however, the regime principles had supplied guidelines to be enforced or at least approximated in the extraregime determination.

* * *

In addition to demonstrating both the limitations and advantages of regimes, these cases reveal the important role that leading powers can play in enforcing a regime, as in the case of the United States in the North Korean situation, or in sustaining it, as Germany and France have done with respect to the European monetary agreement. One must expect, should leading powers fail to enforce and sustain regimes, that the institutionalized arrangements would collapse, be severely weakened, or become irrelevant.

One concludes, therefore, that regimes provide helpful mechanisms to facilitate cooperation, provide principles and norms as guidelines, and offer opportunities to foreign policy makers. Nevertheless, those regimes are built on the conscious choices of states, particularly leading powers. They rely for continuation as well as enforcement on the commitment of those powers, which sometimes must invoke sanctions or instruments that may lie quite outside the terms of the regime. Consequently, as a concept, regime proves descriptively useful, but explanatory analysis resides in states and in the distribution of power across them.

In this discussion, the overlapping of regimes and international organizations remains apparent, for organizations, too, comprise instruments for cooperation. Most often founded on principles and norms, organizations routinely operate according to standardized procedures and decision rules. With few exceptions, however, international organizations gear themselves more broadly than regimes, covering a variety of issue areas. Organizations are not essential to regimes, but, of course, they often comprise the information centers and coordinating mechanisms of regimes. Still, they require separate analysis.

International Organizations

As treated in Chapter 5, basic classifications of **international organizations** represent them as global or regional and general purpose or limited purpose. The United Nations stands as the most prominent of global, general purpose organizations, and such agencies as the World Health Organization and the Universal Postal Union may be invoked as examples of global, limited purpose ones. The Organization of

American States and the Organization of African Unity exemplify regional, general purpose associations, while NATO and the Asian Development Bank provide exemplars of regional, limited purpose organizations The contemporary world has hundreds of intergovernmental organizations.

Regardless of its class, each intergovernmental organization results from the signing of a treaty among the states that comprise its membership. Ordinarily, member states make basic organizational decisions, though most international organizations include secretariats whose officials necessarily make implementing and more detailed decisions. Some organizations create divisions of labor, in which organs or decision making bodies with limited membership act for the organization as a whole, as does the United Nations Security Council in matters of international peace and security.

• THE UNITED NATIONS

Created at the end of World War II to replace the failed League of Nations, the United Nations perpetuated some of the core ideas institutionalized earlier but also added innovative approaches to address the problems of war that it was designed to confront. Both the principles and the structure are expressed in the United Nations Charter, the treaty that each member state has signed. The organization has a structure that, as Claude has understood, reflects a variety of theories about the causes of war and conditions of peace.[10] In addition to a broad-based organ—the General Assembly—the other main organs are assigned specific functions that their names reflect: Security Council, Economic and Social Council (ECOSOC), Trusteeship Council, Secretariat, and International Court of Justice. In addition, a series of specialized agencies, each based upon its own treaty, is associated with the United Nations, and ECOSOC monitors their work. Originally an organization of 51 members, the United Nations has grown to include 185 members at the opening of the General Assembly in September 1995.

General Assembly

Underlying the operation of the General Assembly is the notion that open debate, to which every country may bring its concerns and grievances, contributes to peace. Instead of nursing grievances and dealing secretly with contentious issues, states can present demands and offer solutions in a forum that gives them a hearing and that may contribute support or offer alternatives. As a technique for taking up problems, the "grand debate" approach to peace characterizes many other organizations as well. In addition to meeting in a plenary session each year, the General Assembly also organizes itself into seven main committees and a number of important special committees, each with representation from every member state.

Although precluded from considering an issue that is actively before the Security Council, the General Assembly may place on its agenda any issue, and that agenda has grown to include virtually every item that concerns any state. Following debates, the General Assembly passes resolutions, but these possess no binding quality and remain recommendations only. Ordinarily, resolutions require a vote, a majority for most issues but an exceptional two-thirds on a few. In recent years, though, the General Assembly as well as other multilateral international forums have employed a decision-making technique of **consensus.** Without taking a formal vote, the participants consider that a resolution has been adopted so long as no party makes a formal dissent. Thus, bargaining occurs between the majority and intense minorities to word resolutions in such a way as to avoid provocation of a formal objection. Not inconsistent with this technique, delegates may still offer glosses or objecting remarks in qualifying their association with such resolutions.

Economic and Social Council

ECOSOC consists of fifty-four members and has responsibility for supervising the activities of the specialized agencies and directing United Nations activities in the economic and social realms, where some 80 percent of budgets and administrative personnel operate. ECOSOC's reputation persists as the least effective of the UN's main organs, for the range and variety of the programs it supervises defy rationalization. Priorities conflict, and demands remain endless. Some critics believe the council is too large and unwieldy.[11] Clearly, the goals of attaining economic and social development, adequate food supplies, education, and all of the other goods that come under ECOSOC's purview are worthy. However, no clear principle enables the organ to allocate priorities, and no clarity marks the relationship between its activities and world peace. The underlying notion that people who are well-fed, well-housed, well-educated, and so forth contribute to the maintenance of peace appears problematical at best and probably false. An examination of the wars of the last several hundred years belies any theory that poverty, hunger, and ignorance have caused them. Causes of war lie in quite different realms.

Trusteeship Council and Decolonization

Another main organ, the Trusteeship Council, specialized in supervising the process of bringing certain dependent territories to independence. Although left without any role at the end of the century, the Trusteeship Council earlier performed important functions. The body assumed, with modifications, the work of the League of Nations mandates system and discharged it over the years. After World War I, the tradition of transferring the overseas colonial territories of the losers—particularly Germany—to the victors as spoils was rendered complicated by requiring that the victors assume an obligation to bring the dependent territories to a condition of readiness to govern themselves. Thus, for example, Tanganyika was transferred from Germany to Britain, and the latter reported to a Permanent Mandates Commission the steps it was taking to help the East African territory move toward self-rule. Under the League of Nations, the supervisory mechanism remained quite weak, but the founders of the United Nations strengthened the Trusteeship Council by balancing the number of trustees with other states and increasing the reporting requirements. This trusteeship arrangement, however, formed only a part of a broader decolonization process that had been engendered by the deep forces of nationalism and the weakening of the European powers in the two great wars of the twentieth century. In the United Nations, the historical movement gained momentum as new states joined the organization. In 1960, the General Assembly passed a Declaration on the Granting of Independence to Colonial Countries and Peoples, and in the following year, it created a special Committee on Decolonization to monitor the implementation of that declaration.

Altogether, the decolonization process represented a most profound prototype of peaceful change. It began with the founding of nationalist movements in the colonial areas at the end of the nineteenth century, was pushed along by collapse of the Austro-Hungarian and Ottoman empires in World War I, and then accelerated in the post–World War II period. Roughly one-half the world's population moved from a condition of imperial rule to that of political independence. Despite certain bloody exceptions, such as Indochina and Algeria, this sea change occurred in a largely nonviolent manner. An increase of United Nations membership from 51 in 1945 to 185 in 1995 indicates how widespread the phenomenon was. In addition to facilitating decolonization, the United Nations also conferred status on the new states and provided an arena in which they were able to pursue foreign policies, an activity, given their weakness, that many could not otherwise have done.

Security Council

Central to the work of the UN, the Security Council exercises special functions in the area of international peace and security. Its composition includes five permanent members—Britain, China, France, the Soviet Union (now Russia), and the United States—and ten others elected by the General Assembly for two-year terms, five each year. Except on procedural issues, passage of resolutions requires nine votes, including those of the permanent members. In practice, however, an abstention or absence of a permanent member does not constitute a veto, though the council cannot pass a resolution if any of them votes no. Unlike the other organs, the Security Council has authority, under certain circumstances, to pass binding resolutions. According to charter provisions, the Security Council may take peaceful measures to deal with matters affecting international peace and security, and it may also take forceful action. In the latter case, a coherent theory of collective security underlies the approach to maintaining or restoring international peace and security. The theory predates the UN, for it also shaped the League of Nations' conceptual approach to security.

Collective Security

Fundamentally, **collective security** seeks to deter war by threatening to bring overwhelming force to bear against an aggressor state and, should such an aggressor not be deterred, actually to bring the collective force of all other states to the aid of the victim of aggression to restore the status quo ante. This appealingly simple formula for ensuring peace and security holds an array of assumptions within it, and these help to explain why collective security has not worked very well. A few analysts claim that the United Nations employed collective security in the Korean War, and more view the Gulf War as an instance in which the concept proved practicable.

First, the approach treats war as a legal issue in which an aggressor and a victim are easily distinguishable. Although some altercations lend themselves to such an easy classification of the belligerents, many do not. By assigning responsibility to the Security Council for authoritatively designating fault against which action should be taken, the UN arrangement gives effect to the need to make a decision. Second, a relatively equal distribution of power should prevail in order that the international community might act against any state that commits an act of aggression. Obviously, no array of overwhelming force could be brought to bear against the Soviet Union when it invaded Afghanistan, and it would be unthinkable for the international community to stand overwhelmingly against any of several powers. To meet the assumption that all countries would put assistance to the victim before their own interests, collective security requires that no alliances take form and that each country has no internal restraints that deny its freedom to act, such as Germany's Basic Law or the United States' requirement that Congress declare war. In the Korean War, two major powers, the Soviet Union and China, sided with North Korea, which had been condemned as an aggressor. In point of fact, when threatened by American forces near its border, China introduced troops to fight against what some called a collective security action. Although conditions at the time of the Iraq's invasion of Kuwait proved propitious for an international coalition to drive Iraqi forces out, the action was an entirely ad hoc one. Before Iraq's action, no collective security arrangement had existed to offer even a threat of deterrence, and the coalition put together by the United States was entirely that country's instrument, legitimized by UN Security Council resolutions drafted by the superpower.

Peacekeeping Operations

In the mid-1950s, with the Korean War having emphasized the world's ideological divide and shown the severe limits on the UN's capacity to employ collective security, Secretary-General Dag Hammarskjöld and Canadian Ambassador Lester B. Pearson created a new approach to making the United Nations germane to conflict reduction. They called the new techniques **preventive diplomacy** or **peacekeeping.** Quite in contrast to collective security, peacekeeping operations occurred only with the permission of the country on whose soil the action took place and only as a visible presence to implement an agreement between belligerents that had been concluded before the introduction of the UN forces. Additionally, the UN troops exercised only surveillance powers. They did not fight and were not equipped to fight, carrying only side arms for personal protection. The peacekeeping forces refrained

meticulously from interfering in the domestic affairs of the country to which they were dispatched. They constituted diplomatic instruments rather than military tools. When the first peacekeeping operation—United Nations Emergency Force—was told to leave Egyptian soil where it was stationed, it did so immediately in 1967.

The United Nations mounted various peacekeeping operations during the Cold War, but in the mid-1980s as that period of hostility wound down, it began to undertake many more activities, some of a new type. These included monitoring elections in Nicaragua, Namibia, Mozambique, Angola, and Cambodia, as well as overseeing the implementation of a peace agreement in El Salvador. So long as the parties had agreed to the appropriate functions of the operations, several of which included civilian contingents as well as military personnel, performance matched the tasks assigned, and one may assess the operations as successful.

However, the United Nations also engaged in some operations that proved disastrous not just for the organization but also for many of the nationals caught in the fighting. Three actions in particular demonstrate the failures of effectiveness, loss of moral authority, and conceptual confusion. These are the operations in Somalia, Rwanda, and Bosnia. The Rwandan situation drew less United Nations intervention but proved more deadly for the people involved than either of the others.

In the early 1990s, SOMALIA was racked by civil war in its southern part. The conflict was occurring among armies headed by factional leaders who derived part of their authority from their clan affiliations. A good deal of hunger resulting from the effects of the war led to a humanitarian intervention by the United Nations and later by the United States and other countries. However, the humanitarian operation immediately got embroiled in politics. To ensure that food deliveries could be made to those in need, some of the international agencies paid fighting forces with portions of their supplies, and these, in turn, were sold to earn cash to buy weapons. Thus, inadvertently, humanitarian aid fueled the violence of the war. Matters became even worse when the United States and the United Nations fundamentally altered the terms of the intervention by deciding to arrest one of the factional leaders, General Muhammad Farrah Aidid. This action transformed the international intervention from a humanitarian mission to a forceful military intrusion into the civil war, making the United States and the United

Nations partial to one side against the other. It did not take long for the powers to recognize their mistake, seek to arrange a cease-fire, and finally withdraw completely from Somalia. Afterwards, it became common for those analyzing United Nations interventions to call for avoiding a repetition of the mistakes made in Somalia in the patois of the day, referring to Somalia's capital city: "Avoid crossing the 'Mogadishu line.'"

UNPROFOR in Former Yugoslavia

Such caution affected policies in Bosnia, where the United Nations mounted an effort to provide food and supplies for certain enclaves that were under siege by Bosnian Serb forces. In one sense, the United Nations Protective Force was charged with a humanitarian mission of assisting besieged civilians in a civil war. However, the Bosnian government retained its soldiers and weapons within the enclaves. Although seriously outgunned by the Bosnian Serbs, these forces nevertheless occasionally launched mortar attacks from within the enclaves, and in 1994, they broke out from the Bihac area and in 1995 mounted an offensive to break the siege of Sarajevo. Meanwhile, with NATO airpower backing, the United Nations in 1994 acquired possession of Bosnian Serb artillery surrounding Sarajevo. In the following year, however, when subjected to NATO bombing, the Bosnian Serbs took some three-hundred UN soldiers hostage until assured that NATO airpower would not be used against them. This led to reinforcement of British and French units and to the consolidation of the UNPROFOR for better security. However, the reinforcements served only to protect UNPROFOR troops and not to deliver food, supplies, and medicine to Bosnian government enclaves. In mid-1995, there was a general expectation that all the United Nations forces would be withdrawn, perhaps by the end of the year, although that expectation was modified following a Croatian offensive in August that expelled all ethnic Serbs from the Krajina area of Croatia.

Taking advantage of the changed military circumstances, the United States undertook a campaign that included both NATO bombing of Bosnian Serb positions and a diplomatic initiative that led to a peace conference among the warring parties—although President Slobodan Milosevic of Serbia negotiated on behalf of the Bosnian Serbs whose leaders were excluded. Those negotiations concluded with the Dayton Agreement, which provided for the allocation of authority to Bosnian Serbs

over about half of the country's territory and to a Bosnia-Croatian federation over the other half. To enforce the separation of the fighting contingents, the agreement provided for a sixty-thousand troop NATO and allied Implementation Force (IFOR) to remain in Bosnia for a year. Meanwhile, the agreement also provided for a civilian force to remain in the country to assist in rebuilding the economy and resettling refugees. UNPROFOR was withdrawn from Bosnia, though UN troops continued to play a minor role in Slavonia, a region of Croatia.

Assessments about the success or failure of the UN activity in Bosnia varied considerably. Defenders argued that the operations should be measured by the delivery of food and lives saved. One account claimed that in contrast to the 100,000 who had died in the year prior to creation of the enclaves, 3,000 and 1,500 lives were lost in the war in the following two years, respectively.[12] In contrast, critics pointed to the humiliation of the United Nations by the Bosnia Serbs and the effectiveness of those belligerents in obtaining a promise that NATO air strikes against them would no longer occur.

In response to the UNPROFOR hostage crisis in June 1995, Britain and France began introducing heavier weapons and additional fighting forces to protect their UNPROFOR contingents, which they regrouped into more defensible positions. These new troops and weapons, comprising a so-called rapid reaction force, provided a new technique that some in the United Nations thought might give leverage to the United Nations in redefining the terms of UNPROFOR's presence in Bosnia.[13] Had this interpretation prevailed, the United Nations would have found itself in the position of bargaining over the terms of conflict, mocking its claim to legality. On the other hand, without the turn of events that led to the Dayton Agreement, the rapid reaction force might have turned out to be simply a mechanism preparatory to full UNPROFOR withdrawal.

Conceptual confusion reigned in the approach of the powers through the United Nations to former Yugoslavia. The center of that confusion lay in believing that neutral peacekeeping and humanitarian service could be combined with what was called **peace enforcement,** that is, the employment of military power to enforce temporary arrangements. A second level of confusion occurred in believing that United Nations forces could be placed in enclaves in which troops and weapons of one party to the conflict—the weaker side, to be sure, but still a belligerent—without becoming hostages and remaining perceived as neutrals in the conflict. To the extent that United Nations forces were neutral, they became pawns to be manipulated by one side or the other. These two levels of confusion combined when NATO aircraft were employed to bomb Bosnian Serb gun emplacements used to bombard Sarajevo but could not be employed against Bosnian government mortar positions within the city, for that would have subjected both civilians and UNPROFOR troops to bombing. An even more fundamental confusion provided a foundation for the mess. The powers conceded to the Bosnian government the right to self-determination and secession from Yugoslavia and further encouraged that government to form a federation with Croatia. Simultaneously, those powers refused the right of self-determination to the Bosnian Serbs and denied their potential for forming a federation with Serbia. Thus, the powers intervened on the basis of a fundamentally confused set of premises, interfered with the fighting that might have brought the war to an end, and rejected the logical diplomatic solution—partition on the basis of ethnic self-determination. At the same time, the powers refused to commit sufficient forces to bring about an enforced solution to the problem or even enough forces to give adequate protection to the so-called safe areas. IFOR may prove more efficacious, but that could not be determined at the time of writing.

* * *

Perhaps even more than in Somalia, then, the United Nations saw its moral authority eroded. Because of their prolonged duration, these undertakings corroded the organization's moral authority, but the situation in RWANDA proved a greater disaster for the inhabitants of that country. Despite many people's proclivity to bandy about the term **genocide,** the deliberate killing—urged by the Hutu-led government—of some 500,000 persons in Rwanda in the late spring and early summer of 1994 because of their Tutsi ethnicity amounted to the world's first act of genocide since the Holocaust of the early 1940s. While this immense tragedy was occurring, the powers and the United Nations did virtually nothing except to reduce the UN presence in the country. To compound the enormity, in the aftermath relief supplies were often channeled through the authorities representing the wicked government who used the leverage gained to bolster their plans for an armed return invasion of their country to reinstall the murderous regime. To serve that end, they also blocked return of the refugees from camps in Zaire to their country, thus extending the misery of those poor people. Thus, the powers and other countries followed initial inaction with supplying relief based upon a humanitarian impulse. However, in the absence of any political focus, the humanitarian undertaking came to serve a particularly sordid enterprise. Meanwhile, the new government of Rwanda begged for but failed to obtain the resources that would enable it to govern and work effectively toward rebuilding the country.

* * *

These three failed cases of cooperative intervention represent not just conceptual confusion in the midst of the post-Cold War disorder in the world. They also indicate that, in the absence of direct interest, egoistic states do not feel compelled to act with any decisiveness. No power has any direct interest in either Somalia or Rwanda. In former Yugoslavia, the powers hold distinct interests, but none of them is compelling enough to warrant the payment of any great costs. Fears of the spread of the Balkan war and of the potential for many more fleeing refugees, combined with a sense of concern about a war in Europe after nearly a half-century of peace, drive the powers to cooperate at a minimum level. Lacking substantial interests, however, the powers remained until late 1995 disinclined to commit important resources or clear thought to the situation in former Yugoslavia. The conflicts in Southeastern Europe continue to present extraordinary complexity and intractability.

Secretariat

Although states make the decisions to undertake such operations and supply the troops and civilian personnel to implement those decisions, they rely for coordination of peacekeeping activities on the Secretariat, another main organ of the United Nations. Some 80 percent of the work of the Secretariat consists of economic, social, and technical activities. Personnel representative of all the states of the world comprise the international civil service that provides secretarial and other support for the organization. The Security Council and General Assembly together appoint the secretary-general who heads the Secretariat. His position enables him to remain in close contact with governments, and his functions allow him to make presentations to the main deliberative organs of the UN. The Security Council and General Assembly often call on him to prepare reports on various matters, and they have directed secretary-generals over the years to establish and supervise the peacekeeping operations that were discussed above. Although in some ways the secretary-general serves as a symbol of the United Nations, his effectiveness relies importantly on the support of the powers and other states that supply the means for him to do his job.

International Court of Justice

The last of the major organs associated with the United Nations is the International Court of Justice, which sits in The Hague, Netherlands. Consisting of fifteen judges, each elected for a nine-year term by the Security Council and General Assembly, the court hears cases brought by states that wish to appear before the court. Few cases are brought, but the court also may render advisory opinions to one of the other main organs of the UN.

* * *

Running through all of the organs of the United Nations is, the idea that disputes should be settled peacefully. Additionally, the concept that cooperation can occur among autonomous states using the resources and mechanisms of the organization permeates the charter and the thinking that underlies it. Despite failures and setbacks, the United Nations and other international organizations remain dedicated to the tasks of collective problem solving.

As game theory makes clear, though, large numbers often impede cooperation. Sometimes, bilateral ventures without any formal organization serve cooperation better than do multilateral enterprises equipped with support systems and ancillary services. Arms control represents an important area of endeavor in this regard.

Arms Control, Limitation, and Disarmament

Although the general term **arms control** covers quite a lot of ground, some distinctions need to be made among the related concepts in this area. Control has two meanings captured by accounting and governance. An accountant controls books in the sense of organizing entries into meaningful categories, such as costs, income, expenditures, profits, losses, and so forth. Thus, an accurate accounting of numbers and types of weapons, troops, deployments, maneuvers, and so forth can be thought of as arms control. Even monitoring to acquire accurate information falls within this meaning of control. In the sense of gov-

ernance, one controls a car by steering, accelerating, braking, and so on. The meaning can be applied to armaments by maintaining careful command over orders to employ, using locks that prevent a single person from firing a missile, maintaining a hierarchy and discipline within the forces that control weapons, ensuring that a crisis does not escalate into military combat, and preventing the transfer of weapons to additional states.

Arms limitation is another term used in treating the matters under consideration. *Limitation* means putting limits on weapons. One sort of limitation is a geographical one; for example, the Treaty of Tlatelolco provides that no nuclear weapons shall be tested or deployed in Latin America. However, limits need not mean prohibition or reduction. The Vladivostok agreement concluded by President Gerald Ford of the United States and Premier Leonid Brezhnev of the Soviet Union in November 1974, for example, provided that neither country's MIRV missiles would exceed twelve hundred. At the time of the agreement, the United States possessed 750 such missiles and the Soviet Union had none. Although each had plans to manufacture and deploy more than the agreed-upon numbers, the deal nevertheless gave such great scope for introducing many more weapons than existed at the time while also imposing limitations.

A third important term, **disarmament,** means that existing arms are actually reduced by taking them away. Weapons are retired and dismantled or destroyed and troops are demobilized. Toward the end of the Cold War, U.S.–Soviet agreements actually achieved disarmament, but, for the most part, cooperation in the area of arms control simply helped to manage the Cold War conflict. Even as arms control arrangements were concluded, growth rather than reduction continued to characterize arms production and deployment.

• ARMS CONTROL DURING THE COLD WAR

Although they had engaged in arms control negotiations, the United States and the Soviet Union failed to conclude formal bilateral agreements until they had experienced the Cuban missile crisis. In the late 1950s, with the invention of rockets and their potential combination with nuclear and thermonuclear weapons, public concerns about health and official fears about the dangers of global war led to unilateral moratoria on the testing of nuclear weapons, and a single multilateral treaty that declared Antarctica as a nuclear-free continent was signed in 1959. Following the 1962 crisis, however, the superpowers concluded several agreements designed to reduce the dangers associated with nuclear weapons.

Recognizing that no direct communications link connected the White House and the Kremlin, United States President Kennedy and Soviet Premier Khrushchev agreed in 1963 to establish a teletype "hot line" that allowed such communication. During the 1970s, President Nixon and Secretary Brezhnev agreed to modernize the connection using satellite communications. Although not involving arms in any exact sense, the hot line accords permitted greater control in crises by the top political leaders of the superpowers.

Joined by Britain, the two superpowers also concluded in 1963 the Partial Nuclear Test Ban Treaty, which precluded all but underground nuclear testing, and they invited the other nuclear powers to adhere to the treaty. The superpowers also took the lead in agreements to ban weapons of mass destruction from outer space and the seabed. To slow the spread of nuclear weapons, in 1967 they also concluded the Nuclear Non-proliferation Treaty, which went into effect in 1970 and was extended indefinitely in 1995.

By 1970, the Soviet Union had achieved parity with the United States in nuclear arms, and such new technologies as accurate guidance systems for intercontinental missiles and the development of antiballistic missile defenses affected attempts to reach agreements. In 1972, the superpowers concluded two important treaties, The first, a permanent pact that formed the centerpiece of what came to be known as the arms control regime, was the Antiballistic Missile (ABM) Treaty, which provided for a permanent ban on countrywide ABM systems and allowed each superpower to deploy just two local systems, one to protect the national capital and the other to guard one intercontinental missile base. This treaty was later modified to reduce permitted systems to one apiece, and by the end of the Cold War, the United States had none, for it had dismantled its single system protecting the intercontinental missile base at Grand Forks, North Dakota.

The second 1972 agreement, a temporary pact signed during President Nixon's visit to Moscow that was to be succeeded by subsequent conventions, was SALT I. It imposed numerical limits on missile launchers, but it did not restrict the number of warheads that could be mounted on a single launcher. Taking advantage of a new technology, the United States began to deploy the multiple independently targeted reentry vehicle, placing up to twelve warheads on a single launcher. In this manner, the number of warheads in the U.S. arsenal grew rapidly, and that growth was duplicated by the Soviet Union. Thus, not only did the SALT I agreement fail to hold back the increase in numbers of nuclear weapons, but it also provided a mechanism for accelerating the superpower arms race.

Although the negotiating partners did agree on a more complicated SALT II, President Jimmy Carter withdrew the treaty from Senate consideration following the Soviet invasion of Afghanistan. Nevertheless, both states adhered to its terms until President Ronald Reagan allowed a violation in 1986 when he authorized the deployment of B-52 bombers armed with cruise missiles. Despite their faults, these agreements did help to stabilize U.S.–Soviet relations. Conducive to the stabilization was the confidence gained through **satellite surveillance** of each other's territory, which allowed each superpower to obtain accurate information about the deployments of the other. Such knowledge reassured each that the other was complying with the agreements. When questions arose about compliance, the treaties allowed for consultative mechanisms in which to thrash out interpretations of ambiguous data.

Nevertheless, the period of superpower detente that had begun in the late 1960s came to an end, and a new Cold War ensued in the early 1980s. Specifically, Reagan used newly belligerent rhetoric and authorized a research program called the Strategic Defense Initiative (SDI). Although it produced research but no actual weapons, the SDI conceptually aimed at the deployment of space-based weapons and other technologies that would, if operational, violate the terms of the ABM agreement. The program frightened both the Soviets and citizens of the allied countries and the United States.

• ARMS REDUCTIONS AT THE END OF THE COLD WAR

With Mikhail Gorbachev's ascension to power in the Soviet Union in 1985, a new era of cooperation began that produced significant arms control and arms reduction measures. Indeed, the superpower relationship in this area was actually transformed from one of very limited cooperative bargaining to a genuinely cooperative one. Summit meetings in Geneva in 1986 and Reykjavik in 1987 enabled the two superpower heads of state to move arms control negotiations along, and in 1989, Gorbachev's renunciation of the use of force to support Communist governments in Eastern Europe allowed for immense progress in arms control matters. Moreover, the collapse of the Soviet Union in 1991, while presenting certain new dangers, also led to greater breakthroughs in nuclear weapons reductions.

In their first agreement to reduce inventories of weapons, the United States and the Soviet Union signed the Intermediate Nuclear Forces (INF) treaty in December 1987. Implementation of this pact eliminated all so-called theater nuclear weapons in Europe—those with a range of approximately three hundred to thirty-four hundred miles. Furthermore, the INF treaty innovated in another way, by providing for **intrusive inspections** to verify that the accord was being implemented, and this breakthrough in verification techniques paved the way for similar provisions in the Strategic Arms Reduction Talks (START) treaties.

A set of negotiations held in Helsinki and Vienna between representatives of NATO and the Warsaw Pact led to the Conventional Forces in Europe (CFE) agreement in 1990. Under this accord, the concepts of transparency and **confidence-building measures** took hold. Transparency signifies that actions are subject to observation, and confidence-building includes arrangements to ensure that activities are well-known, unsurprising, and open. Thus, the CFE pact provided that both alliances would make public the numbers, composition, and locations of their forces. They would announce maneuvers and training exercises at least six months in advance, and they would invite observers from the opposing alliance to watch those operations.

Meanwhile, negotiations within the START between the Soviet Union and the United States led to an agreement in July 1991 that provided for significantly lower limits on the numbers of strategic weapons deployed by the two superpowers. Over time, the START I convention yielded the dismantling of thousands of nuclear weapons until each of the signatories would retain only six thousand strategic warheads apiece, in contrast to the more than seventy-five hundred each held at the time of signing. Implementation of this accord become complicated with the disintegration of the Soviet Union at the end of 1991, for strategic weapons remained in the territories of four successor states: Russia, Belarus, Kazakhstan, and Ukraine. President George Bush pursued a diplomatic campaign to gain the agreement of the three other Soviet successor states to transfer their strategic weapons to Russia, and President Bill Clinton followed up in subsequent negotiations to realize full compliance with this concordance. Additionally, before he left office, Bush reached agreement with President Boris Yeltsin of Russia to reduce the two countries' strategic nuclear arsenals to three thousand each.

Another endeavor to slow down the spread of weaponry was undertaken by the United States, Japan, and Western Europe in 1987, when they created a Missile Technology Control Regime (MTCR) designed to prohibit the transfer of the means to carry nuclear warheads by missile. In the wake of the Cold War, both Russia and China have signed on to the MTCR, although China has on occasion defected from this cooperative undertaking by selling missile technology to Pakistan and Iran.

Post-Cold War Security Cooperation in Europe

With the Cold War standoff in Europe at an end, the powers sought new security arrangements. These included the Commonwealth of Independent States, a loose and not well-defined aggregate of Soviet successor states. Others, however, reached across the old fault line in Central Europe. Russia began to promote the Conference on Security and Cooperation in Europe (CSCE, redesignated OSCE), but the more successful institutional mechanism has proved to be NATO. OSCE remains essentially a broad forum of some fifty states that has only minimal institutional shape and is primarily a mechanism for consultation, not an instrument for extensive action, though it has a role in implementing the Dayton Agreement in Bosnia.

On the other hand, NATO possesses full institutional form and broad working experience in cooperative action. Additionally, several of the Eastern European states—specifically Poland, the Czech Republic, Slovakia, and Hungary—have actively been seeking membership in NATO. To accommodate these aspirations, the United States devised the Partnership for Peace, which allows for association with NATO in anticipation of eventual membership when appropriate conditions are met. These conditions include such internal arrangements in candidate states as effective democracy and a working market economy as well as militaries that are trained and equipped in ways compatible with NATO standards and procedures. Meanwhile, members of the

■ Post-Cold War Security in Europe

Members of NATO

Members of Partnership for Peace

Members of Partnership for Peace (PfP) as of November 1995:

- Albania
- Armenia
- Austria
- Azerbaijan
- Belarus
- Bulgaria
- Czech Republic
- Estonia
- Finland
- Georgia
- Hungary
- Kazakhstan
- Kyrgystan
- Latvia
- Lithuania
- Malta
- Moldova
- Poland
- Romania
- Russia
- Slovakia
- Slovenia
- Sweden
- Turkmenistan
- Ukraine
- Uzbekistan

Partnership for Peace have access through the North Atlantic Cooperation Council, established in December 1991, to NATO planning and ministerial meetings, and their armed forces conduct joint exercises with NATO units. The earliest prospective dates for the admission of new members from Eastern Europe into NATO are 1999 and 2000.

One major difficulty that faces NATO expansion lies in the fact that military alliances traditionally aim to defend their members against a predetermined adversary. Originally, that adversary was the Soviet Union, so its main successor, Russia, expresses not entirely surprising concern about what direction an expanded NATO might take. Such a concern seems particularly sound in view of Poland's rationale for joining the alliance, which is protection against Russia. How this sensitive issue will be resolved cannot be predicted, but the eventual relationship between NATO and Russia is likely to prove to be the key to the success or failure of NATO expansion.

Central to the argument for the retention of NATO, whether with an expanded or a stable membership, is the continued presence of the United States in Europe. It is generally understood that Western Europe's stability and burgeoning prosperity have been founded on the American security guarantee and the presence of U.S. forces in Europe. Even though in the aftermath of the Cold War, Europeans would be perfectly capable of providing their own security without relying on the United States, no other institutional connection remains between the North American superpower and Europe. If that centrality of the United States to European security—which has been evidenced by the two world wars as well as the Cold War—is to persist, then, NATO may provide the only practical means for keeping a U.S. presence in Europe.

Nongovernmental Organizations

Although international cooperation occurs most significantly among states, private nongovernmental organizations also participate. They do so in two ways: first, by agitating within their own societies to advocate the sorts of international activities they are respectively concerned with; and second, by acting as contractors to carry out the cooperative activities agreed to by governments. Business firms and university contractors remain prominent in both of these functions, but many other organizations exist primarily for purposes of promoting and carrying out international cooperative activities rather than engaging in them in a way ancillary to their main purposes. Many of these organizations have recognized standing at the United Nations, with access to the headquarters and often invitations to present their views to the ECOSOC. Certain of these organizations, such as Doctors Without Borders, Catholic Charities, and the International Rescue Committee, have gained substantial prominence for their humanitarian relief work. Others, such as Amnesty International, are prominent in their advocacy for human rights.

* * *

Processes of conflict and cooperation are geared largely to the shorter term in which states pursue explicit, short-term aims within a settled order. Sometimes, however, these processes include a dimension of change in that order, leading us to give consideration to another fundamental process in international politics.

• IMPORTANT TERMS

absence of hierarchy	iteration
agenda formation	military force, minor
arms control	role for
arms limitation	most favored nation
Chicken	multiple channels
collective security	number of players
complex	peace enforcement
interdependence	peacekeeping
confidence-building	preventive diplomacy
measures	(see *peacekeeping*)
consensus	Prisoner's Dilemma
cooperation	reciprocity
Deadlock	regime
defection	satellite surveillance
dependency	sensitivity
disaggregation of play	shadow of the future
disarmament	Stag Hunt
game theory	surveillance
genocide	tit-for-tat strategy
Harmony	transgovernmental
incentive structures	channels
international	transnational channels
organization	transparency
intrusive inspection	vulnerability
issue area	

• STUDY QUESTIONS

1. Review the various incentive structures employed in game theory analysis, and explain how each facilitates or hinders international cooperation. Cite examples.

2. How does communication assist in changing the effects of incentive structures?

3. How does iteration of interaction enhance the possibilities for cooperation?

4. Explain how the number of players in an international arrangement affects the potential for cooperation.

5. What do regimes and international organizations have to do with international cooperation?

6. Compare and contrast the complex interdependence and realist models of international cooperation.

7. Why do realists emphasize vulnerability rather than sensitivity when treating interdependence?

8. Discuss the relationship between regimes and traditional diplomacy.

9. Describe and explain the main organs of the United Nations and their functions. Evaluate the strengths and weaknesses of the United Nations as a set of instruments for maintaining international peace and security.

10. Compare and contrast collective security and peacekeeping. Using historical examples, assess the efficacy of the two forms of United Nations activity.

11. Compare and contrast peacekeeping and peace enforcement. What problems have resulted from their confusion?

12. Why do you think that the United Nations has succeeded in some post-Cold War interventions and failed in others? Discuss specific cases.

13. Reviewing the history of arms control, limitation, and disarmament since 1945, evaluate this area of cooperative endeavors by the superpowers.

14. Analyze the problems, dilemmas, and opportunities of security cooperation in Europe in the post-Cold War period. How do you think things are going? How do you think they should go?

• ENDNOTES

1. See, for example, Kagan, *On the Origins of War*, p. 363.
2. Jervis, "Cooperation under the Security Dilemma," demonstrates how payoff structures can be manipulated even in the area of military competition.
3. Kenneth Oye, "Explaining Cooperation under Anarchy: Hypotheses and Strategies," in *Cooperation under Anarchy*, ed. by Kenneth Oye (Princeton, N.J.: Princeton University Press, 1986). This section on game theory concepts draws heavily on Oye's work.
4. Robert Axelrod, *The Evolution of Cooperation* (New York: Basic Books, 1984).
5. Oye, *Cooperation under Anarchy*, p. 19.
6. Keohane and Nye, *Power and Interdependence*.
7. Waltz, *Theory of International Politics*, chapter 7.
8. Stephen D. Krasner, "Structural Causes and Regime Consequences: Regimes as Intervening Variables," in *International Regimes*, ed. by Stephen D. Krasner (Ithaca, N.Y.: Cornell University Press, 1983), p.1.
9. See Susan Strange, "*Cave! Hic Dragones:* A Critique of Regime Analysis," in *International Regimes*, ed. by Stephen D. Krasner (Ithaca, N.Y.: Cornell University Press, 1983).
10. See Inis L. Claude, Jr., *Swords into Plowshares*, 3d ed. (New York: Random House, 1964).
11. See, for example, *The United Nations in Its Second Half-Century, A Report of the Independent Working Group on the Future of the United Nations* (New York: Ford Foundation, 1995).
12. Background source who cited figures given to 1995 NATO defense ministers' meeting by United States Secretary of Defense William Perry.
13. Background interview, June 20, 1995.

CHAPTER 14

Change in Politics and the International System

The French have a saying: *Plus ça change, plus c'est la même chose* (The more that changes, the more it's the same thing). While acknowledging change, the quotation stresses continuity. This view is reflected in Robert Gilpin's statement about international politics:

> One must suspect that if somehow Thucydides (the fifth-century B.C. Greek historian) were placed in our midst, he would (following the appropriate short course in geography, economics, and modern technology) have little trouble in understanding the power struggle of our age.— *War and Change in World Politics,* p. 211

Others, however, challenge that view by emphasizing the reach and pervasiveness of change in the modern world. James N. Rosenau voices it in the following way:

> The seemingly daily occurrence of unexpected developments and the numerous uncertainties that prevail in every region, if not every country, of the world are so pervasive as to cast doubt on the viability of the long-established ways in which international affairs have been conducted. It almost seems as if the anomalous event has replaced the recurrent pattern as the central tendency in world politics.—*The United Nations in a Turbulent World,* p. 11

This chapter is dedicated to working through the puzzle of how much change and how much continuity the world faces as we approach a new millennium.

Introduction

Change persists in human affairs, occurring at an unpredictable pace, sometimes quite slow and at other times very quick. Slow, accumulative changes appear much less dramatic than revolutionary upheavals and swift transformations, but they may over time have as great an impact. The fifty-year rise of Japan from the ashes of World War II to its prominence as the world's second largest economy in the mid-1990s contrasts with the sudden dissolution of the Soviet Union in 1991 but may rank as nearly as important. Through a process of flowing and ebbing, European imperialism spread across the world beginning in the sixteenth century. It then contracted to the point of disappearance by the end of the twentieth century. Over the course of centuries, feudalism gave way to capitalism and the modern system of states, but the structure of the modern system was transformed from one of multipolarity to a bipolar array in the few years of World War II. With modern weapons, computers, and democratic polities, humanity lives in a profoundly changed world from that our ancestors inhabited a few centuries ago, with its autocratic empires and primitive technology.

Given the ubiquity and timelessness of change, one faces the analytic problems of defining change, identifying sources and dynamics, and understanding its consequences. Underlying forces and secular trends remain hidden, so the analyst has greater difficulty in identifying them and the mechanisms of change. Often, the empirical fact of change has to be recognized, but even deep transformation does not carry with it an analytical logic. Thus, the analyst of international change faces hurdles of understanding. Confrontation of these difficulties forms the main task of this chapter as it examines change. First, it is important to recognize the wide variety of phenomena that the concept change entails. Some examples illustrate varieties of change.

Varieties of Change

Within states, **regimes** and **leaders** change in ways that may have important consequences for international politics and foreign policy. In 1959, for example, FIDEL CASTRO came to power in Cuba and led his country to reverse alliances in the Cold War and transform Cuban society in a way that satisfied the deprived classes but drove the middle and privileged classes to Miami. Castro also promoted the spread of revolution to Latin America and carved out for Cuba an important role in international politics. Although he was not directly responsible for the most severe superpower crisis of the Cold War, that crisis could not have occurred without Castro's revolution and policies. More directly, Hitler's rise to power in Germany in 1933 led to World War II and its profound effects around the world.

Not only do leaders and regimes within established states shift but also **territorial units** themselves become constructed, acquire and lose expanse, disintegrate and disappear, and change form. GERMANY, the greatest disruptive state in the international system in the twentieth century, did not exist before Prussia united many smaller political units into an empire in 1871. Driven by the principle of self-determination, the peacemakers after World War I created the new multiethnic states of CZECHOSLOVAKIA and YUGOSLAVIA, the first of which divided itself peacefully on January 1, 1993, while the second tore itself apart after 1991 in a prolonged, brutal, and tragic war. Empires collapse, to be succeeded by constituent states, as occurred at the end of World War I with the Austro–Hungarian and Ottoman empires and at the end of the Cold War with the Soviet Union. Great territorial transfers significantly change the shape and expanse of countries, such as the growth to continental size of the United States during the nineteenth century, partly at the expense of others, including Mexico.

Shifts in power comprise another sort of change in international politics. Every country strives to maintain its position, and some are more successful than others. As a result, countries such as South Korea greatly increase their power positions relative to other states, while others such as Argentina fall back, if we consider the period between 1955 and 1995. Although such shifts remain interesting, the more significant expression continues to be the **rise and decline of major powers,** for these shifts have broader implications as these states contend for domination and cooperate to manage the international system.

• • • • • • Shifting Power Positions over Time

COUNTRY	1820	RANK IN 1914	1937	1978	1992
Austria	7	7			
Brazil				10	10
Britain	4	3(*)	2	6	8
Canada				9	
China	1			8	2
France	3	5	5	5	6
Germany	10(+)	4	4	4(++)	4
Italy		6	6	7	7
Japan	6	8	7	3	3
Russia	5	4	3(^)	2(^)	9
Spain	8				
United States	9	1	1	1	1

Notes: * in 1914 figure for British Empire
+ in 1829 figure for Prussia
++ in 1978 figure for Federal Republic Germany
^ in 1937 and 1978 figures for USSR

Sources: 1820 and 1992 data from Angus Maddison, *Monitoring the World Economy, 1829–1991* (Paris: Development Centre of the Organisation for Economic Cooperation and Development, 1995), Table 1–8; 1914 and 1937 data from Paul Kennedy, *The Rise and Fall of the Great Powers: Economic Change and Military Conflict from 1500 to 2000* (New York: Random House, 1987), Tables 21 and 31 (Kennedy derived his figures from Quincy Wright, *A Study of War.* Chicago, 1942); 1978 data from Charles Lewis Taylor and David A. Jodice, *World Handbook of Political and Social Indicators, Vol. 1: Cross-National Attributes and Rates of Change,* 3d ed. (New Haven and London: Yale University Press, 1983). All figures rounded from original.

Over the past two centuries, the states occupying the leading positions have changed dramatically; new challengers for domination have arisen, and still others may be discerned on the horizon; and the techniques and styles of management have changed to reflect the trends of the era and the internal arrangements of the leading powers. Consider that after defeat of Napoleonic France's quest for domination, the leading powers putting into place the Concert of Europe were Britain, Austria, and Russia, joined by Prussia and France. In the interval, Germany and Italy constituted themselves, and the former, together with the United States and Japan, rose to prominence in the industrialization process of the late nineteenth and twentieth centuries, first to battle over domination in the two world wars of the century and to emerge after the Cold War as partners in system management, joined by Russia and China. During the Cold War, the United States and the Soviet Union gingerly sparred to manage their own relationship, but the latter exerted dominance within its sphere of influence and the former exercised hegemonic leadership over much of the remainder of the world. As the end of the century approaches, the challengers such as Iran and Iraq lack the power to overturn prevailing patterns of system management and dominant powers, but China, with its extraordinary economic growth working to increase its many assets, is thought by some to bear watching as a potential challenger that would put into place different management arrangements should it reach a hegemonic position.

Meanwhile, challenges to some of the prevailing management principles and rules arise from lesser states. For some decades, voices within the United States and other countries have opposed the principle of free trade that governs the world's commerce. Broad movements of religiously based political organizations in the Arab world aim to topple secular governments that align themselves with the West. Hostage taking and terrorist activities against civilians have become more common in recent decades, challenging the norms of the dominant powers. States occasionally pursue avenues other than those provided by current institutional arrangements, thus challenging those provisions of world order. Without the power to dominate, however, these challenges may be regarded as more interesting than significant.

Even more important than great power shifts, which provide much of the dynamic for international politics, are changes in **systemic structure** and **principles of jurisdiction.** Recall that international systemic structure consists of an ordering principle and a distribution of power across the units comprising the system. Clearly, a transfer from an anarchical to a hierarchical ordering principle would constitute change of the most profound kind. Certain utopian writers imagine that such a **transformation** might be accomplished, and others think that the world may be headed in the direction of a hierarchical global political system. A somewhat less fundamental but still significant change is a redistribution of power from a multipolar to a bipolar pattern.

Finally, some writers believe that deeper change lies at the level of the principles of jurisdiction governing the units. Ruggie, for example, argues that the shift from the principle of **heteronomy**—overlapping jurisdictions and variable obligations—of the medieval period to that of sovereignty in the modern era represents profound change in international politics.[1] Some have claimed that nongovernmental entities such as multinational firms form another kind of unit that has gained significance in international politics. Other critical theorists set forth propositions concerning transformations that either recognize or envision different sorts of units.[2] In reply to those critical thinkers who believe that sovereignty is eroding in the current era, Thomson argues that sovereignty remains firm.[3] She concludes that **sovereignty**—defined as territorially based legitimate violence dispersed among juridically equal states—remains empirically under attack on some fronts, as it always has been, but on the rise on others. Moreover, no evidence presents itself to support the notion that another principle of jurisdiction is replacing sovereignty.

In addition to his views on the change from medieval to modern, Ruggie claims that an increase in dynamic density—"the quantity, velocity, and diversity of transactions"[4]—generates deep change, and this leads him to conclude that the contemporary international system is undergoing fundamental change as a result of the growth of international trade, multilateral institutions, and other global transactions.

Given its continuousness and variety, change needs to be differentiated by type to sort out the deeper and more important shifts from transitory and relatively superficial alterations that occur.

Types of Change

Gilpin categorizes change as interactional, systems, and systemic.[5] **Interactional change** occurs within ongoing systemic arrangements. Alliance formation and decay, the rise and fall of regimes, agenda formation, and so forth, all fall within this type. **Systemic change** involves a shift in control or governance of the system. When a new empire or state supplants a previously dominant power and puts into place different rules, that comprises a systemic change involving a redistribution of power and its implications. **System**

change involves alteration in the nature of the actors, for example, movement from medieval units to the modern state system. Should multinational firms and international organizations join states as coequal actors, that would also constitute a systems change.

■
・・・・・・ **Types of International Changes**

TYPE	FACTORS THAT CHANGE
Systems change	Nature of actors (empires, nation-states, etc.)
Systemic change	Governance of system
Interaction change	Interstate processes

Source: Robert Gilpin, *War and Change in World Politics* (Cambridge: Cambridge University Press, 1981), Table 2.

The most interesting questions involve systemic and systems changes that can be regarded as transformational. Is the world changing in ways that have a superficial impact but are not profound? Or are the changes so deep that entirely new units and rules are coming into effect? Can we expect a new **world order** or the endurance of old and recognizable units and patterns of behavior?

Should a new challenger such as China become dominant and assume a role as **hegemon,** employing different principles of governance of the international system than those adhered to by the United States and its partners, the systemic change would be apparent. As this is being written, such a consequential shift in the distribution of power seems improbable in the foreseeable future. On the other hand, the emergence of a multipolar arrangement that lacked the coordinative aspects of the American-led postwar and post-Cold War coalitions would also make a significant impact on the ways in which international politics is conducted.

A systems change with an entirely different basis of authority and with new units as the main locus for political activity makes its appearance primarily through the speculations of analysts. In examining sources of change, we can weigh these speculations in light of whatever evidence may be afforded.

To avoid unnecessarily narrowing consideration of change, let us invoke the problematic outlined in the first chapter of this book. Any changes that bear upon the problematic need to be examined. Thus, changes affecting power, justice, causes of war, conditions of peace, anarchy, and state formation will be treated. As sources and effects are examined, they will also be evaluated in terms of whether they

appear transformative, either systemically or from one system to another.

Sources and Effects of Change

Ordinary things like the **cycle of life** provide a source of change. Three deaths of old Soviet leaders in the course of a few years preceded Mikhail Gorbachev's ascent to power. His policies aiming at reconstruction and revitalization of the Soviet system led to both the end of the Cold War and the unintended result of the Soviet empire's disintegration. Surely, Gorbachev's leadership sought to gain control over deeper forces at work in his country and the world that engendered change, but the banal mattered as well. At the base of the fundamental change occurring lay the inability of the Soviet regime to adapt its economic and political system to information-based phase of industrialization, what some call postindustrial society. By failing to compete effectively with the leading capitalist states that had adapted to new technologies, the Communist regime lost its claim to legitimacy as the possessor of the historical mantle to surpass capitalism. Meanwhile, Gorbachev introduced political reforms that disowned the Communist Party's claim to a monopoly on political power and provided a new basis of legitimacy through democratic elections, though only at the constituent unit level, not at the central state or imperial plane. That is to say, Gorbachev himself never faced a democratic electorate, even though he had introduced the new foundation for legitimacy.

Beyond the banal, then, this discussion has pointed to several other factors responsible for engendering change: **technological innovation,** loss of **regime legitimacy** through an inability to match its claims with performance, the substitution of a new basis of legitimacy that supported regional leaders against the center, and the failure of the political system to maintain the position of the state in the international system as a result of its **inflexibility.**

This case includes many of the varieties of change surveyed in the first section: regime, leadership, state disintegration and the founding of new states, degrading of power, and shift in the power distribution in the systemic structure. Furthermore, a metamorphosis in Russia's and other Soviet successor states' conceptions of justice—substituting liberal democracy and market economics for authoritarian dictatorship and command economies—ended an era of hostility against the leading powers of the world, removing a cause of war and shifting the conditions of peace.

Because this vast transmutation occurred without war, it raises the fundamental question of **deep sources of change.** In the realist tradition, war has been seen as the fundamental source of change in international politics. For example, Waltz characterizes World War II as a system-transforming war, for it eliminated rival powers and produced a bipolar distribution in place of the multipolar order that had prevailed before the war.[6] Inasmuch as this systemic change has been equaled only by the end of bipolarity, one is left with the puzzle: Is war, or is something else, the agent of fundamental change in the international system?

• WAR

It seems obvious that **war** causes great change. With some exceptions, war causes the losing side to change regimes. Saddam Hussein remained in power after his defeat in the Gulf War, but Napoleon lost his position as the French republic was replaced by a restoration of the monarchy, and Kaiser Wilhelm's German empire gave way to the Weimar Republic after its World War I defeat.

Wars sometimes also weaken the winning side to the extent that states can no longer bear previous responsibilities. For example, the costs of the two world wars to Britain were immense. In the first, Britain raised money to prosecute the war by selling most of its Latin American investments to investors in the United States, and the second war so severely weakened the country that it was required over following years to withdraw from its overseas empire and to be reduced to a second-rate power. Simultaneously, the United States profited from both wars, becoming a net creditor in the first and growing economically in the second to become the world's leading producer.

War in the modern age speeds up technological innovation. It would be foolhardy to argue that inventions would never have been made, but the rapidity with which radar, sonar, jet engines, rockets, and the atomic bomb entered the world's repertory during the six years of World War II is impressive. Only when juxtaposed to the introduction of the calculator, the computer, MIRVs, space exploration, and other more recent technologies does technology, rather than war, appear to be a generator of change. However, the calculator, the computer, MIRVs,

space exploration, and other technologies were introduced in peacetime. Thus, it appears that technology rather than war is the generator of change. Clearly, war creates a sense of immediacy that compels discovery, but other pressures in the world obviously also promote invention, and the introduction of new technologies by definition brings about change in the instruments of competition.

Among the results of war one must count the triumph of philosophies and modes of thought that are applied by the victors in managing the international system. As a corollary, war erases the political effectiveness of defeated outlooks and values, such as fascism and nazism associated with the losers in the Second World War. Clearly, the institutional arrangements and orderly rules of international society in the postwar period have reflected the views of the victors, primarily the United States but others, including the Soviet Union, as well. Had Germany and Japan won the war, they would have put into place very different principles of trade, relations with allies, treatment of defeated countries, and so forth.

Looked at from a slightly different perspective, however, the triumph of the victors, not war itself, accounts for systemic governing arrangements. That observation, in turn, leads one to try to account for why the victors triumphed. Kennedy argues that in the modern period, superior **productive capacity** constitutes the essential cause of victory in major-power wars.[7] War tends to be so unpredictable that one does not expect to discover any single factor that will explain the outcomes of war in general. Defeat of both the French and the Americans by Vietnam over the course of the twenty-three years following the end of the Second World War should give pause to anyone who wishes to place absolute confidence in Kennedy's formula.

In both world wars of the twentieth century in which the major powers were pitted against one another, outcomes appear to have been shaped importantly by the reserve productive capacity of the United States. That capacity allowed the allies to bring unprecedented firepower against their adversaries until, particularly in the 1939–45 war, they were utterly defeated. The stakes in the war—principles of international order—generated the commitment and broad popular support that allowed the mobilization of productive capacity on behalf of the war effort. That condition was not present during the Vietnam War. Although the United States dropped a tonnage of bombs on Vietnam greater than all the bombing of World War II, its citizenry was cleaved, and it was constrained not to invade North Vietnam to inflict defeat. Thus, political will and the mobilization of productive capacity appear to operate very differently in systemic wars and lesser conflicts.

■

• • • • • • Arms Production Capacity of the Powers in World War II

	1940		1941	
	Aircraft	Arms Production (billion 1944$)	Aircraft	Arms Production (billion 1944$)
Allies				
Britain	15,049	3.5	20,094	6.5
United States	12,804	(1.5)	26,277	4.5
Soviet Union	10,565	(5.0)	15,735	8.5
Axis				
Germany	10,247	6.0	11,776	6.0
Italy	1,800	0.75	2,400	1.0
Japan	4,768	(1.0)	5,088	2.0

	1943		1944	
	Aircraft	Arms Production (billion 1944$)	Aircraft	Tanks
Allies				
Britain	26,263	11.1	26,461	5,000
United States	85,898	37.5	96,318	17,500*
Soviet Union	34,900	13.9	40,300	29,000
Axis				
Germany	24,807	13.8	39,807	17,800
Italy	1,600			
Japan	16,693	4.5	28,180	

* The United States produced 29,500 tanks in 1943.

Source: Paul Kennedy, *The Rise and Fall of the Great Powers: Economic Change and Military Conflict from 1500 to 2000* (New York: Random House, 1987), Tables 33, 34, and 35.

These observations lead to the conclusion that war itself plays a crucial part in systemic change but that its role is an instrumental or enabling one, whereas more fundamental economic and political forces actually drive the processes affecting systemic change. War does appear elemental to many other types of change, such as territorial shifts and undermining the legitimacy of defeated regimes. War also forms the essential mechanism for resisting ambitious powers seeking domination. Finally, war accelerates technological change. Through all, however, it seems clear that an explanation for profound change in international politics requires an examination of economic and political dynamics.

• ECONOMIC DEVELOPMENT AND DECAY

Economic growth stimulates change, for it occurs at different rates over time, in different states, and within different sectors of the economy.[8] Both within national economies and the world at large, a business cycle produces both upward trends in production and income and downward contractions of economic activity. Moreover, longer-term movements occur as states choose development strategies that produce rapid growth but then deteriorate. For example, the Mexican economy grew at an annual rate of 7 percent or so for forty years but then faced a severe crisis when, in 1982, Mexico could no longer service its debt, and the country suffered a deep depression during the so-called lost decade. Similarly, the world as a whole grew rapidly in the decade after World War I, only to face a precipitate decline during the Great Depression after 1929. Then, after World War II, the world economy grew to achieve widespread and unprecedented prosperity. In addition to unevenness over time, economic growth varies from state to state and sometimes regionally, and it occurs unevenly within specific states. Growth rates within Western Europe, for example, vary among West Germany and France, Britain and Italy, Netherlands and Spain, even though all are banded together in the European Union. Japan's much more rapid rate of economic growth between 1950 and 1995, compared with that of the United States, accounts for the former's rise from defeated power to the state with the world's second largest economy. Very slow rates of economic growth in Africa account for that continent's slide to greater weakness than before, just as very rapid rates of growth in East Asia explain that region's rise to prominence. The Soviet Union offers a clear example of differing rates of growth over time within the same country, for the Soviet economy expanded until the early 1970s, only to decline so far that Russia and the other successor republics depend on foreign assistance in seeking recovery and rebuilding, and many people endure hardship through the adjustment process.

Economic growth also varies within sectors of the economy. Certain industries flourish while others fade from prominence. During the period of industrialization in the leading powers, chemical and steel industries occupied notable positions, whereas more recently they have faded in comparison with computer and related information industries. Both innovative technologies and competition affect particular industries, whose fortunes increase or diminish.

The market tends to diffuse technology and investment, so leading states constantly have to innovate and build advanced technology industries as older techniques and whole industries move to countries with lower wage costs and other competitive advantages. Failing that, those leading powers are likely to decline, losing position in the international system. Weaker states that succeed in acquiring wealth-producing activities most likely will rise in position. Such processes of economic activity, thus, engender changes in the relative position of states.

None of these economic processes functions automatically, for **choices** always remain available to policy makers and citizens. In his book tracing the rise and decline of great powers, Kennedy stressed that a balance among consumption, investment, and security expenditures endures as a prerequisite to a leading power's maintaining its predominant position in the system.[9] Choices made to husband and nurture the economic base by innovation, savings, and investment or to dissipate it through excess consumption or reckless military expenditures and unsustainable foreign commitments cannot be entirely autonomous, but they do count a great deal.

In arguing that choices always remain accessible, one does not posit that those choices are easy. Such choices pose immense difficulties for political leaders who attempt to manage the politics of their own countries and those involving the maneuvering of the powers in the international system. Despite the fact that this discussion has been about economics as a source of fundamental change, the problems of choice fall into the realm of politics, for economic change rewards some groups and states while it punishes others. Those punished, or who fear punishment as a penalty for change, seek to protect their positions in the status quo and so resist choice on behalf of change. To the contrary, those rewarded not only favor change but also seek to gain a political voice as a result of their new wealth and status. Thus, the imminence of economic change and the change itself generate political conflict.

Similarly, the major powers engage in political conflict as they vie for position through economic and other forms of contention. In addition to the concerns that disadvantaged firms and workers in domestic society may exhibit, each of the contending powers has to worry about the security aspects of the relative gains of the others.

From the point of view of international politics analysis, there are no purely economic matters. Insofar as it relates to international relations, economics always involves politics and societies.

• POLITICS AND SOCIETY

By achieving positions of dominance and putting into place their conceptions of justice, certain groups build states. If successful in placating the aspirations of other groups in society or repressing them, sustaining regime legitimacy, and maintaining the position of their state in the international system, such groups may endure in power. On the other hand, political demands and competition arise from many sides, and some regimes find themselves unable to endure. One important source of failure to survive stems from **rigidity,** the absence of sufficient flexibility to cope with changing circumstances. As discussed above, the disintegration of the Soviet Union can be traced in part to this root of failure.

Olson has noted that such rigidities occur not just among governing groups but also in other segments of dominant coalitions.[10] For example, he attributes to labor unions in advanced industrial societies a tendency to cling to entrenched privilege. Olson's theory of decline provides a basis for grasping how less developed societies are able to achieve economic growth at faster rates, thus shifting relative positions in the international system, for rigidities in advanced countries contribute to their decline. One would expect such rigidities affecting political, social, and economic competition to enter the political process on a regular and sustained basis. In this routine sense, they affect transactional changes. At rare times, nevertheless, societal and political regime rigidities in the face of profound pressures lead to revolutionary changes. In the twentieth century, the Russian and Chinese **revolutions** induced quite profound effects in international politics. Moreover, similar revolutions in Egypt, Libya, Cuba, Nicaragua, and Iran engendered effects that had less than tsunami-like repercussions only because the states embodying the deep changes possessed lower levels of power than did Russia or China.

Political and social developments that fall short of revolutionary can induce significant change. Hitler came to power in 1933 under terms of the democratic Weimar constitution but shaped a regime that overturned Germany's political order, conducted war against a large portion of its own people, and conquered most of Europe. Similarly, Mikhail Gorbachev's ascension to power in the Soviet Union fell far short of a revolutionary event, yet his leadership engendered the series of events that resulted in the end of the Cold War and the disintegration of the country. China launched a vast economic reform in the late 1970s that led to immense economic growth that promises to shift the country's international system position significantly. Whether the ruling groups will manage to survive the stresses engendered by the profound changes occurring in the society remains to be seen. Whatever the outcome—stability and increased prominence of position in the international system or disorder and economic stress—developments in China are likely to have important effects in international politics, though they need not provide causes of systemic change.

A phenomenon old but newly prominent in the post-Cold War period, **ethnic conflict,** gives rise to political and social divisions that sometimes engender war, the breakup of states to create new entities, and severe stresses on neighboring states as well as difficulties for management and intervention by the powers. For the people involved in a situation like that in former Yugoslavia, life and death can be painful and devastating. Given the suffering and scars of political and social division and warfare, there may be long-term repercussions that are impossible to fathom. For the international community in the first half of the 1990s, however, little real effect has been rendered, and no profound change has occurred.

Perhaps, a new standard of tolerance by the liberal community for human suffering has emerged: for the specter of virtual silence over the world's first case of genocide since the Holocaust that happened in Rwanda in 1994 may portend some shift in sentiment, though one living at the time does not possess the perspective necessary for making a definitive evaluation. Attitudinal shifts, nonetheless, do not qualify as systemic changes. Except when linked with a policy of expansion by a major power, ethnic nationalism holds implications for changes only within states or narrow regions, for the aim of such movements appears to be confined to establishing a state based upon ethnic identity. It is always possible that an ethnic group dominating a major state might, like Nazi Germany, employ the conviction of its own superiority as a justification to engage in conquest of other peoples whom it regards as inferior, but such an expression of ethnic nationalism remains quite

uncertain and unpredictable, and it has not arisen in the 1990s.

• TECHNOLOGY

Technology causes change in two ways. As a form of knowledge, technology increases the efficiency of factor inputs to production. For example, the output of a welding machine and its operator can be increased by the introduction of robotic technology that allows a single operator to oversee four machines, and metallurgical technology might produce alloys that can be welded more rapidly with fewer points of contact. Then, plastics may be substituted for some of the metal, diminishing the amount of welding that needs to be done. Aside from such mechanical production processes, communications technology by satellite and other wireless methods has increased exponentially the output of such inputs as telephone equipment, and digital computer technology has vastly expanded the production of information. As productivity from such efficiencies grows, those states making most effective use gain an advantage in maintaining or increasing their positions in the international system because their economies continue to be augmented. Those states failing to apply knowledge to increase productivity fall behind. Thus, technology contributes to the rise and decline of powers.

The second way in which technology causes change in international politics occurs through the introduction of new products, particularly weapons, that prove decisive or at least partly determining for the outcomes of leading power contests. In the 1991 Gulf War, the technological superiority held by the allied coalition dramatized the difference that weaponry can make. Even during the more evenly matched conflict of World War II, such products as radar and jet aircraft contributed partly to the determination of the outcome, and the atomic bomb proved decisive in bringing the war with Japan to a rapid end.[11] Moreover, nuclear and thermonuclear weapons and their related technologies created a deterrence system during the Cold War that sustained a dangerous but restrained *modus operandi* in the relationship of the superpowers that was quite different from that of earlier times. So stable was the period of superpower rivalry in the bipolar era that a prominent historian of the period has referred to it as "the long peace."[12] Those weapons are likely to continue to modulate the behavior of powers even in a multipolar world of the future by changing the nature of their security problem, thus rendering relative gains considerations less portentous.[13] By making the acquisition of security easier and less costly than it would otherwise have been, therefore, nuclear weapons have modified a consequential dimension of international politics.

Countering an emphasis on the positive and beneficial effects of technology, some observers point to the costs that modern industrial society imposes on nature by depleting nonrenewable resources and causing deterioration of the natural environment.

• RESOURCE SCARCITY AND ENVIRONMENTAL DETERIORATION

In the early 1970s, a group called the Club of Rome published The Limits to Growth.[14] This study concluded that there are limits to growth, that the earth's capacity is finite, and that those limits will be reached within one hundred years. The authors also claimed that the situation could be altered, and they warned that the sooner altered behaviors occur, the better. Their recommendations entailed placing limits on economic growth and accepting reduced standards of living. Inasmuch as the world's wealth has tended to increase since that time and no resource scarcities have been detected, the response of Julian Simon to the Club of Rome's argument seems persuasive.[15]

That argument posits that, by definition, there can be no **finite resources**, for it remains impossible to know what quantity of any given resource exists. Moreover, shortages of any resource fuel both technological innovation and a search for substitute resources. For example, a scarcity of iron ore would have the economic effect of stimulating research to find a more efficient extractive process that retrieves a greater proportion of iron from existing ore. Similarly, an inventor might seek effective means of recycling old iron. Simultaneously, an entrepreneur might begin producing nonferrous products that can be substituted for iron in some manufacturing applications. Moreover, when one considers not the resource itself but instead the service that it provides, then identical services may be conveyed by substitute products. For instance, a modern automobile composed of much plastic substituting for the steel used in cars of yore provides more reliable service, more comfort, greater fuel economy, and so forth than did its predecessors. This economic process historically has led to a decline in price of natural

resources. Moreover, Simon concludes, there is no reason not to expect that in the future resources will continue to be available at lower prices than today's.

Given the force of this counterargument, it becomes difficult to perceive an exhaustion of natural resources as a fountain of change in international politics. Nevertheless, the distribution of natural resources contributes to the innate inequality of the international system, and competition for control can become an issue among states, as petroleum did in 1990–91. Moreover, a commodity's price and supply can provide a wrench for political and economic leverage, as happened with oil in 1973–74. These matters enter international politics as routine affairs, however, and do not count as elements causing systemic change.

The other aspect of modern technology and its associated consumption patterns that concerns many observers is **environmental damage** exerted by expanding industrialization and increased populations. In particular, analysts and political leaders direct attention to the **depletion of renewable resources,** such as forests, and the decline of genetic diversity. More specifically, concern has mounted with regard to **global warming** through a greenhouse effect that might raise the world's average temperatures, which, in turn, would exert climatic changes, raise sea levels, induce migration from inundated areas, and deeply affect agricultural production. Increased heat globally would impose costs on tropical regions but grant benefits to colder areas. For example, flood plains in Bangladesh might have to be abandoned, with loss of arable land. In contrast, the great steppes of Russia might become magnificent producers of grains. Such problems enter the agenda for global management, and they may lead to some reallocation of favorable conditions for production, but they do not portend fundamental changes in international politics. One does not in any sense wish to treat environmental degradation and climate change as trivial, but assessing properly the place for such phenomena in our problematic remains important. Our conclusion must be that these phenomena, while serious, do not appear to be causes of systemic change in international politics.

In discussions of such global problems, some analysts treat them as forces that lead inevitably to systems change, that is, transformation from a state-based and -driven international system to a globally based world system. Such analysts often argue that it is incumbent upon right-thinking people to think globally rather than nationally, and they invoke such metaphors as global commons, spaceship earth, and others that treat the world as a unit rather than as a system of competing units. Underlying the logic of a position embodying such concepts is another notion: that ideas are a source of change.

• IDEAS

In his masterful comparison of realism and utopianism, E. H. Carr noted that, in contrast to realists' belief in determinism, utopians recognize that **ideas** form a basis of social causation.[16] By emphasizing the scope available for human will in political affairs, utopians—later called idealists and more recently labeled liberals—offer imaginative ideas as possible futures. That is to say, one can imagine a world in which sovereign states are superseded by a universal government based on liberal principles, and it may be possible to construct such an order by working toward the idea of it. Recently, critical theory poses arguments along this causal path.[17] Instead of assuming the persistence of states, one postulates that new forms of social organization can be constructed by redefining identities and giving new meanings to such concepts as sovereignty. Critical theorists credit human beings with substantial power to manipulate words and concepts, and they reject realists' emphasis on power and given arrays of forces that can be managed but not changed.[18] Indeed, some argue that the "realities" that mainstream international politics theorists expound are but arbitrary concepts that are used to bolster the power of dominant groups. Thus, a concept such as sovereignty has no intrinsic meaning. Instead, human beings have attributed meaning to it, and other people have the ability to redefine its connotations, eventually even to reject the concept and substitute some other term.

Such a constructivist approach to politics treats language and human discourse, rather than the things that they signify, as meaningful. Although one would not wish to denigrate the importance of language and talk for political affairs, they do not substitute for the institutions, political processes, structures, and power relationships that those things reflect. Ideas can have consequences, and discourse can be persuasive to those who act, but, as the old saying goes, actions speak louder than words. Nevertheless, ideas have inspired many actions. The phenomenon is perhaps best illustrated by revolutionary activity.

In the early 1960s, six NICARAGUANS met and devised a conception of a political regime and society favoring peasants and workers. That conception drew on the ideas of Marxism and Augusto Sandino, a national guerrilla leader who had been killed nearly thirty years earlier. The six created a revolutionary organization called the Sandinista National Liberation Front consisting only of themselves. At the time, Nicaragua remained under sway of a United States-backed dictator and his family, the Somozas, which had persisted in power since 1936. An objective analyst at any time during the 1960s and early 1970s would have regarded the arrangements of power in Nicaragua as wholly favoring the Somoza regime. After his soldiers in 1969 killed several leaders of the FSLN, the dictator declared the movement finished. Yet, in 1979, that same organization, now bolstered by broad support throughout Nicaraguan society, came to power as the leading faction in a coalition government. Within two years, it held authority by itself. One needs to count as causation those ideas held by a tiny band of men whose will and dedication over the years led them to accumulate power to achieve their goals.

More revolutionary enterprises have failed than succeeded, but the fact that a few have won their battles and put their inspirational ideas into place indicates that, at least sometimes, ideas cause actions that cause change. Other examples come to mind: the conception of a theocracy germinated in the mind of Ayatollah Ruhalloh Khomeini to become a reality in Iran, and Slobodan Milosevic inspired his fellow Serbs with the idea of ethnic purity to support a vision of a Greater Serbia, a conception that helped to sustain a long war in Bosnia-Herzegovina.

These nonliberal examples have been offered quite deliberately to support the critical and liberal argument that ideas cause change. The reason for doing so lies in the unspoken assumption of those advocating the power of ideas that liberal ideas are the ones that will triumph in the world. Although it is impossible to predict which, if any, ideas might gain ascendancy, what continues to be clear is that liberals do not have a monopoly on ideas. Furthermore, it also remains true that ideas cannot be disembodied, cut off from the power to support them. Dedication and will, moreover, may lead to such personal investments in attaining power that those willful individuals might be quite unwilling to submit to such liberal indignities as free criticism from their opponents and electoral defeat in open, popular contests. Just as certainly, some people persevere dedicated to liberal norms and work mightily to put them into practice, but liberals clearly do not monopolize ideas or the will to give them effect.

In all of these examples, ideas that cause change do so within the context of the state. Left hanging is the question of whether ideas are likely to form causes of international systemic or systems change.

Developments in international organization, treated in the last chapter, provide something of a test of the proposition that ideas amount to sources of change. The idea of collective security was linked to institutional arrangements in the League of Nations and the United Nations. If that idea promoted altered norms of behavior in international politics, as its originator Woodrow Wilson advocated, then one could conclude that the idea provided a source of systemic change. However, as we saw in the previous chapter, states have continued to adhere to norms and rules of behavior in keeping with a self-help international system. Some modification of rules occurred because the United States committed its resources and leadership to acting in a way, in the Korean and Gulf wars, that allowed for an interpretation that collective security norms prevailed. Nevertheless, the United States acted in both cases in conformity with its own interpretation of its interests, and it does so consistently. For the most part, collective security ideas have no relevance except as justification to support major power interests. Thus, the power and interests of the superpower endure, and, when convenient, that entity invokes ideas that support its interests. The United States government summoned quite different ideas to justify its war against Vietnam, for the idea of collective security would have carried no conviction. Furthermore, the most prominent invocation of the idea of collective security involved the American summons of the symbol to support its commitment to NATO, an alliance directed against the Soviet Union. Yet, collective security means a universal deterrent and collective action against any aggressor, not an alliance directed against a predetermined adversary.

Some critical theorists and liberals call for increased attention to such low politics problems as environmental deterioration, population increase, drug trafficking, and human rights violations, with arguments that changed conditions in the international environment require new norms of international behavior. Should states shift their attention away from security and economic matters, then one might make an argument that a systemic change had occurred. However, powerful groups and states have not made such a shift. They have attended to these other concerns, but they also give singular and devoted attention to high politics and economics.

Despite the lack of evidence of systemic changes resulting from ideas, the critical theorists' views need further consideration, for they most commonly claim that the most profound change occurring is a system change. New units and new power centers assert their authority, and novel networks of people and organizations relating across state boundaries without state supervision form a process of change that is transforming the world.[19] After World War II, broad coalitions were thought to have become the new territorial units,[20] and new forms of political and economic organization seemed to be emerging in Europe. At the end of the century, one of the enduring themes embraced by European leaders is that the European Union consists of states. Midway in the Cold War, some writers argued that the multinational corporation was moving forward to compete with, undermine, and replace the state. Since then, it has become clear that the multinational corporation and the state coexist, with the former dependent on the latter.

States have continued to form, and the world has been organized by states as one composed of states. As empires have broken up, they have been replaced by states. The newly conspicuous force of ethnic nationalism aims always at creating states to give institutional means for achieving the aspirations of nationalists.

None of this experience, however, should dampen the enthusiasm of liberals and critical thinkers for systemic and system change. If ideas can be imagined, they can perhaps be brought to life. Realists who stress power may remain skeptical of the force of ideas, but adherents of a belief in the efficacy of human will and imagination may cling to their optimism that the world can be made a better place. Surely, reform cannot come without struggle, but neither can it take shape without ideas to inspire those who do battle.

For a political analyst, nevertheless, speculation about the future may provide an escape from attempting to explain contemporary and past events. An excitement attends the extrapolation of futures from present realities, and that emotion would only be dampened by recognizing one's inability to know what the future portends.

• LIBERAL PEACE

In recent years, a different claim regarding transformation in international politics avers that history has already demonstrated that liberal states do not go to war with one another. Sometimes called the **democratic peace,** this thesis holds that states with liberal democratic regimes have never gone to war with another. Originally formulated by the German philosopher Immanuel Kant, the argument holds that world peace can come about through a league of republics that establish peaceful relations among themselves.[21] Kant's thesis was taken up in the mid-1980s first by Michael Doyle, who claimed not just that such an arrangement would be possible to construct but that no liberal state had ever gone to war against another liberal state.[22] This is a separate peace, for liberal states do conduct war just as much as does any other kind of state. Doyle goes on to explain why this separate peace has been established. Liberal states induce **caution** both because citizens are reluctant to pay the costs and their leaders are subject to rotation in office. Furthermore, **international law** promotes respect as well as publicity and accommodation among liberal cultures. Finally, **cosmopolitan law** adds material incentives, for liberal states provide hospitality and a spirit of commerce derived from the division of labor, and the market removes production and distribution from state policy, thus deflecting conflict into private activities. Other writers attribute democratic peace to institutional constraints and democratic norms and culture.[23]

Neorealists have been quick to criticize liberal peace theory by emphasizing that the structure of the international system constrains all states, including liberal ones. Part of the problem arises from the fact that liberal or democratic regimes can be transformed into dictatorial ones. Hitler, after all, came to power through democratic elections and constitutional means under the liberal Weimar constitution. Moreover, realists point out that the United States and Britain fought against each other in the War of 1812, that the liberal peace thesis requires that Wilhelmine Germany was not liberal whereas its regime differed little from Britain's, and that the greatest war fought during the century between 1815 and 1914 was the American Civil War between a liberal state and a secessionist segment of that same country. Furthermore, there have been too few liberal states in a position to go to war to give confidence to the generalization.[24] In a trenchant criticism based upon a careful examination of several cases in which liberal states almost went to war, Layne found that the reasons for not entering a state of belligerence are provided by realist theory. In his view, the evidence leads one to reject the liberal explanation.[25]

Two other facets of the issue also warrant comment. First, most of the history of liberal states' not warring with one another occurred during the Cold War in which its supremacy enabled the United States to extend security protection to its liberal allies, thus relieving them of any need to protect against neighbors' security threats. Should American power recede, the concerns might be different. Additionally, the United States used its power to intervene in other democratic countries by means other than military force, such as bribery, propaganda, and other techniques designed to destabilize regimes. Although such interventions were not infrequent, the most notorious illustration was the United States' interference in Chilean politics from 1964 forward and especially in the 1970 election and its aftermath, when this intervention helped to create the conditions leading to the military overthrow of the democratically elected Allende regime in 1973. Moreover, in 1954 the United States fomented, assisted, and participated in the overthrow of Guatemala's President Jacobo Arbenz, who had been chosen in a democratic election. These examples suggest that liberal states use force, and are likely to do so in the future, against other liberal states that they believe pose threats to them.

Meanwhile, in the era suffused with liberal ideology and dominance by a liberal superpower, the conception of a liberal or democratic peace has many adherents. One can treat the assertion at a minimum as a hypothesis that may be further tested in the future.

Put into practice by a major power such as the UNITED STATES, which in the Clinton administration had a declared policy of enlarging the number of democratic states in order to widen the separate liberal peace, the advocacy of liberal peace perpetuates a **moralism** in international affairs that the realist tradition has found not useful. A clear line is drawn by liberals between liberal and other states, and leaders attempt to coerce nonliberal regimes to introduce reforms. For example, President Clinton threatened China with economic sanctions to promote a shift in that state's domestic human rights policies. In the end, he backed off because American liberal economic interests would have been injured. This case reveals the tension between market economics and democratic politics that affects **liberal peace theory.** Regardless of such a tension, however, the moralist impulse that sometimes even leads to the use of force persists.

This impulse to reform other polities extends even to other liberal states. For example, a major thrust of American foreign policy in the 1980s and

1990s has aimed to make the Japanese internal market more like that in North America. Despite the deep cultural differences between the United States and Japan, American leaders and people exert great pressures on Japan to give greater access to American firms and products. In 1995, President Clinton threatened to impose 100 percent tariffs on imported Japanese luxury cars, in violation of international trade law, as a means to press Japan to accept more American automobile parts. Although this threat was lifted because the two countries reached a negotiated settlement of the dispute, one wonders how much threat and hostility might drive the two democracies to take separate paths that might one day lead to war. The 1995 bilateral trade dispute, of course, did not come close to war, but neither did it reflect important elements of liberal peace theory. Commerce became the focus of state-to-state conflict rather than being left to individual firms. The United States issued a clear threat to impose sanctions that would have violated international law, and it showed little respect to its second-largest trading partner.

Self-righteousness tends to be exhibited even more blatantly in relations with nonliberal states. During the Cold War, United States policy aimed to change the internal arrangements within the Soviet Union, and in the post-Cold War period, similar postures have been adopted toward other states. Generally, democratic publics do not support the crusading spirit to change other states' regimes if doing so entails war and those regimes pose no serious threat.

Still, the issue uncovers the deep fissure in thinking between realists and liberals. The former urge toleration of states and diplomatic accommodation on the basis of power. In contrast, the latter wish to tolerate only democratic regimes and prefer accommodation on the basis of liberal principles, regardless of power. Liberals have faith in improvement and expect transformation to occur to bring about that better world. Counterpoised, realists believe that little change has occurred in international politics and that we should be prepared to cope with power and threats in the future as we have in the past.

Peaceful Change

Within a system of states whose ordering principle is anarchy, **peaceful change** remains a persistent quest because forceful change entails such high costs. Some recent history provides encouragement, for immense changes have occurred without resort to international violence. For the most part, the decolonization process occurred peacefully, and the head of the largest empire gracefully accepted reduction to second-class status. On the other hand, France's strong fight to cling to empire in Indochina and Algeria shows the difficulty of achieving change peacefully. Similarly, the Soviet Union disintegrated in a peaceful manner, and Czechoslovakia broke into two parts without a war. Still, Nigeria fought a bitter war in 1967–70 to stay intact, and Yugoslavia has suffered scalding violence as it has broken up.

Examples of both violent and peaceful change abound, but the analytical and theoretical difficulty endures. No one understands why Czechs and Slovaks can part amicably while Serbs and Bosnians must kill one another.

Some analysts offer international institutions as the means for implementing peaceful change, but the obvious failures of international organizations and processes to manage violent change attest to the difficulties if not the impossibility of resolving this challenge. Moreover, no sound theory of change has ever been offered to explain why anyone should expect that peaceful change can be institutionalized.[26]

It remains, then, that the powers have to manage global change as well as they can through such mechanisms as balance of power and diplomacy. Inadequate as these mechanisms continue to be, they offer the best means within a system of anarchy. In thinking of alternatives, however, some writers have turned their imaginations to the possibilities for transformation of the international system into a hierarchical one governed by the rule of law. Presumably, it would be a democratic system as well.

Transformation

For idealists, a transformed world is a dream. For realists, it is a nightmare. Despite the absence of likelihood that a transformation to hierarchy will occur, some consideration of these alternative visions might prove worthwhile.

The absence of war gives the most promising prospect to a transformed world, but such a universe would also be governed by law passed by a democratically elected legislature, and an impartial court system would enforce justice. Such a system undoubtedly would also provide for a redistribution of resources, so poverty and disease would be alleviated. For those imagining such a world, North American and Western European states provide a model, with liberal polities, market economics, and welfare systems contributing norms.

For realists lacking the imagination to foresee such benevolent outcomes, a hierarchical world might very well be headed by a totalitarian government ready to repress its citizens. Immense force would have to be placed in the hands of such a government to suppress rebellions by constituent units that had been sovereign states. In the event that democracy were to prevail, the majority would be made up of the people of China, India, Russia, and Japan. Or, perhaps, coalitions of Latin Americans and Africans might form a legislative bloc to enact laws greatly to the disadvantage of the privileged of Europe and North America. No guarantee would protect liberal economics, which might very well be replaced by a command economy or some other arrangement not envisaged by utopians. To such a world, or even to the risk of it, a realist stands opposed and points to the advantages of the pluralistic world that anarchy allows. He also notes that in whatever kind of political arrangement, power endures as the necessity for accomplishing goals. Groups continue to organize to protect themselves and to achieve their aims. Such realities persist in any kind of system, and they would do so in a hierarchical world order.

Some schemes explicitly envisage that alternative principles would be embodied in an alternative world order. For the most part, these plans aim to provide equality and social justice on a global scale. These values would not be sought within the framework of a pluralistic world of states that also provide security and protect cultural values of different peoples. Instead, a global authority would ensure that every person received his just due. Such an authority, of course, would require a hierarchical ordering principle, and international politics as it has been understood would come to an end.

It is impossible to know whether any scheme aimed at transforming the basic way of organizing world politics will succeed in replacing the Westphalian system. Thus far, such blueprints as Clark and Sohn's world peace through world law have remained ideas rather than practice.[27] More recent academic schemes put forward by Richard Falk have not commanded the attention of groups with the power to implement them.[28]

Thus, the question of transformation of the international system is by no means closed, but advocacy of transformation clearly remains in the realm of idealism. At the end, the conclusion has to be that transformation of international politics is not on the horizon. Thus, we are left to cope in a world of states.

That is not a terrible condition, for states provide a basis for identity, protect their people, and yield welfare. These are things that people desire, and utopian dreams do not offer more. A transformed world could only provide the same things by different means, and it is not clear that it could establish a basis for identity.

With unprecedented prosperity, a long peace, and widespread group satisfaction, one wonders from whence can come any broad demand for transformation. Until such a broad call for a new world order is heard, people and officials must cope as best they can in an uncertain and anarchic world.

• IMPORTANT TERMS

caution	limits to growth
choices	moralism
cosmopolitan law	peaceful change
cycle of life	principles of jurisdiction
deep sources of change	productive capacity
democratic peace (see	regime legitimacy
liberal peace theory)	regimes
depletion of renewable	revolution
resources	rigidity
economic growth	rise and decline of
environmental damage	major powers
ethnic conflict	shifts in power
finite resources	sovereignty
global warming	system change
hegemon	systemic change
heteronomy	systemic structure
ideas	technological
inflexibility	innovation
interactional change	territorial units
international law	transformation
leaders	war
liberal peace theory	world order

• STUDY QUESTIONS

1. What is change?

2. How useful do you find the categorization of change into three types: interactional, systems, and systemic?

3. Do you believe that war is a source of fundamental change in international politics?

4. How do economic factors shape important change in international politics?

5. Compare the effects of the market, politics, and society on significant change in international politics.

6. What effects on deep change does technology have? How does it exert these effects?

7. Compare and contrast the views of those who believe that there are limits to growth and those who think that resources will continue to be available in the future at a lower cost than today's prices. Which views do you think are more nearly right? Why do you think so?

8. How important are ideas in bringing about serious change in international politics? What ideas do you believe are powerful?

9. Give the case for a liberal peace, and then consider the views of its detractors. What is your position on the issues?

10. What do you think about the idea of a world government? Would you favor or oppose it? Explain your position.

• ENDNOTES

1. Ruggie, "Continuity and Transformation."
2. See, for example, Alexander Wendt, "Collective Identity Formation and the International State," *American Political Science Review* 88 (June 1994): 384–96.
3. See Janice E. Thomson, "State Sovereignty in International Relations: Bridging the Gap between Theory and Empirical Research," *International Studies Quarterly* 39 (June 1995): 213–233. Also see her *Mercenaries, Pirates, and Sovereigns: State-Building and Extraterritorial Violence in Early Modern Europe* (Princeton, N.J.: Princeton University Press, 1994).
4. Ruggie, "Continuity and Transformation," in *Neorealism and Its Critics*, p. 148. The concept and definition are drawn from Emile Durkheim, *The Rules of Sociological Method* (New York: Free Press, 1964/1895), p. 115.
5. Robert Gilpin, *War and Change in World Politics* (Cambridge: Cambridge University Press, 1981), p. 40.
6. Waltz, *Theory of International Politics*, p. 191.
7. Kennedy, *The Rise and Fall of the Great Powers.*
8. Robert Gilpin in *The Political Economy of International Relations*, p. 93, notes three tendencies of uneven growth: regions, sectors, and time.
9. Kennedy, *The Rise and Fall of the Great Powers.*
10. Olson, *The Rise and Decline of Nations.*
11. For a dissent from this view, see Murray Sayle, "Letter from Hiroshima: Did the Bomb End the War? *New Yorker*, 31 (July 1995), pp. 40–64.
12. John Lewis Gaddis, *The Long Peace: Inquiries into the History of the Cold War* (New York: Oxford University Press, 1987), and "The Long Peace." See also Charles W. Kegley, Jr., *The Long Postwar Peace: Contending Explanations and Projections* (New York: HarperCollins, 1991).

13. See Waltz, "Nuclear Myths and Political Realities," and "The Emerging Structure of International Politics."
14. Donella H. Meadows and others, *The Limits to Growth: A Report for the Club of Rome's Project on the Predicament of Mankind*, 2d ed. (New York: Universe Books, 1974).
15. Julian L. Simon, "The Infinite Supply of Natural Resources," in *The Ultimate Resource* (Princeton, N.J.: Princeton University Press, 1981).
16. Carr, *The Twenty Years' Crisis.*
17. For example, see Wendt, "Collective Identity Formation."
18. See, for example, R. B. J. Walker, *Inside/Outside: International Relations as Political Theory* (Cambridge: Cambridge University Press, 1993).
19. See, for example, James N. Rosenau, *Turbulence in World Politics: A Theory of Change and Continuity* (Princeton, N.J.: Princeton University Press, 1990). Also see John G. Ruggie, "Territoriality and Beyond: Problematizing Modernity in International Relations," *International Organization* 47 (Winter 1993): 139–74.
20. See Herz, "The Rise and Demise of the Territorial State."
21. Immanuel Kant, *Perpetual Peace*, ed. by Lewis White Beck (New York: Liberal Arts Press, 1957 [1795]).
22. Michael W. Doyle, "Kant, Liberal Legacies and Foreign Affairs," *Philosophy and Public Affairs* 12, Part 1 (Summer 1983) and Part 2 (Fall 1983); and idem, "Liberalism and World Politics," *American Political Science Review* 80 (December 1986): 1151–69.
23. For example, Russett, *Grasping the Democratic Peace.* Also see John M. Owen, "How Liberalism Produces Democratic Peace," *International Security* 19 (Fall 1994): 87–125.
24. See David E. Spiro, "The Insignificance of the Liberal Peace," *International Security* 19 (Fall 1994): 50–86.
25. Christopher Layne, "Kant or Cant: The Myth of the Democratic Peace," *International Security* 19 (Fall 1994): 5–49.
26. See John J. Mearsheimer, "The False Promise of International Institutions," *International Security* 19 (Winter 1994/95): 5–49. See also replies in *International Security* 20 (Summer 1995). These include Robert O. Keohane and Lisa L. Martin, "The Promise of Institutionalist Theory," pp. 39–51; Charles A. Kupchan and Clifford A. Kupchan, "The Promise of Collective Security," pp. 52–61; John Gerard Ruggie, "The False Premise of Realism," pp. 62–70; and Alexander Wendt, "Constructing International Politics," pp. 71–81. These are followed by Mearsheimer's "A Realist Reply," pp. 82–93.
27. Clark and Sohn, *World Peace through World Law.*
28. See, for example, Richard A. Falk, *On Humane Governance: Toward a New Global Politics* (University Park, Pennsylvania State University Press, 1995); idem, *The Constitutional Foundations of World Peace* (Albany: State University of New York Press, 1993); and idem, *Economic Aspects of Global Civilization: The Unmet Challenges of World Poverty* (Princeton, N.J.: Center of International Studies, Princeton University, 1992).

PART 6
Conclusion

CHAPTER FIFTEEN
The Accommodating Discipline

CHAPTER 15
The Accommodating Discipline

A view presented in Chapter 1 claimed that international politics is "a dividing discipline." In the interval between that statement and this place, we have considered many different aspects of the subject and a variety of viewpoints and approaches to studying it. Although not every slant has withstood careful examination, many different analytical ideas have contributed to understanding the complexities of international relations. In this chapter, rather than agreeing that the discipline is a divisive one, we review the main line of argument and conclude that the discipline is an accommodating one, enriched by many different perspectives.

As an academic discipline, international politics manifests paradoxical qualities. The central empirical and normative concerns about causes of war and conditions of peace unify scholars, but they are divided by disagreements on disciplinary boundaries and on questions of whether the international realm wholly differs from or partly resembles domestic politics. Deep philosophical divisions persist between realists and liberals, and reflective or critical theorists take potshots at both. All three, nevertheless, debate questions that each recognizes as important. The state, nationalism, war and peace, the role of international organizations, the efficacy of force, political economy, the impact of technology on modern life, international interdependence, and related matters concern all of them. Still, differences persist over interpretations and emphases as well as over fundamental matters.

Some think that the field should focus on politics, with concerns like economics and psychology brought to bear as needed by political analysis. Others believe that the field should be called international relations and defined as an interdisciplinary one. Whereas the former contingent stresses the high politics of security and diplomacy, the latter wishes to broaden the definition of security to include such matters as the physical environment, drug trafficking, human rights, and migration. Discontinuity characterizes the latter group, while the former stresses continuity with the past.

These divisions and others have led to the characterization of the discipline as a dividing one. Yet, an observer might just as well characterize international politics as an accommodating discipline. Despite recurrent attacks on its ideas, realism remains the main guideline to analysis, provides the most enduring concepts and modes of analysis, and has generated better theory than other ways of addressing the central problems of international politics. Within problem-solving theory, however, liberalism has acted as persistent critic and advances analyses supplementary to those offered by realists. Liberalism draws attention to matters downplayed or overlooked by realism, and it holds out alternatives to action in the future. Both of these broad schools of thought work within the assumption that actors in international politics continue as rational egoists: states pursuing their calculated interests after weighing the costs and benefits of various courses of action. That central assumption and other matters shared by realists and liberals constitute targets for reflective theory, which acts as a deeper antagonist to realism than does liberalism. The reflective approach offers both radical criticism and radical alternatives to the world as realists understand it. Going to the roots of matters, reflective theorists provoke the thoughtful analyst of whatever stripe profoundly to rethink assumptions and other ideas taken for granted.

In examining many views draw from these varied schools of thought, the discussion in this book has adopted those that provide insight into the problematic of international politics or add useful ways of analyzing the puzzles offered by the complexities of international politics. At some points, the perspectives offered have not appeared helpful to our project and the reasons for leaving those positions aside have been stated. Despite the fact that what is left aside may be quite important, it often belongs to a different area of study from that pursued by international politics scholars.

International politics grew traditionally out of history and philosophy, the two related disciplines that continue to offer the greatest rewards for those interested in our problematic. International law provided an ancillary viewpoint traditionally important to international politics. The discipline has been greatly enriched by the attention given to economics and sociology—the study of wealth and of groups, respectively—and psychology has contributed as well.

Contention and cooperation in international politics involve many values, but the core ones identified in this project include at the center power and justice, the pith of politics. In addition, wealth, security, order, peace, and community give focus to cooperative aspirations and conflictful interchanges.

There would be no such thing as international politics without states and the systemic structure that results from their coaction. Thus, great emphasis in research and thinking has been put on these units and that structure. Because states embody the mechanisms by which groups give shape to their aspirations, it is important to understand groups, particularly nations. States are constituted by groups, families, and individuals, all of which comprise civil society. Other units such as international organizations also deserve the attention of international politics analysts, but all of these units make analytic theoretical sense only when focused on or filtered through the fundamental concepts of state and system of states.

Inasmuch as states come and go, great attention needs to be given to the processes of state formation and decay and to the problem of maintenance of position in the international system. Many of the views offered in this book would not be accepted by some scholars. This approach offers much more emphasis on and a more thorough examination of the basic unit of the state than international politics analysts have traditionally given it. As the discussion throughout has shown, though, the state suffuses virtually every aspect that enters the field of vision of an analyst of international politics. Like other matters, it can be taken for granted, but the discussion has shown how useful it can be to give explicit and extended attention to the state.

Other major divisions such as force, political economy, and foreign policy would be addressed by almost every instructor in an introductory course in international politics. Despite extensively varied assessments of these subjects and widely divergent attitudes toward them, most would agree that they form important parts of the study of international politics. As we have seen, force does not remain constantly in use, but its presence underlies all of political life, and the instruments of force lie at the ready to be employed when necessary. Force often proves to be decisive in important disputes. Political economy forms an important part of the life within states and, increasingly, among them. Moreover, the process of uneven development endures as the fundamental cause of the rise and fall of the powers as well as of the changing fortunes of other states. Although this process occurs as a very long-term one, states tend to be much more highly focused on shorter-term interactions. Even those interactions, however, are often shaped by longer-term strategies and consistent patterns, as was demonstrated by the cases of American and German foreign policy.

Broadly speaking, international politics involves three processes: conflict, cooperation, and change. Treatment of these subjects employed the concepts and modes of analysis that scholars have contributed to them. Over the years, the discipline of international politics has produced a great many studies that have contributed not just empirical knowledge but also conceptual and analytical enrichment. Knowledge of all of these processes has benefited from that enhanced scholarship, and much of the work has been driven by world events and developments.

The literature on conflict burgeoned during the Cold War, when the animosity between the superpowers and their allies seemed to provide the basic dynamic of international politics. Memories of economic nationalism before and totalitarian aggression during World War II added credence to this outlook. It was in the early 1970s—when the United States pursued detente and the Soviet Union followed a course of peaceful coexistence, when the 1973–74 oil crisis emerged, and when economic matters appeared more urgent—that a great amount of scholarly attention was drawn to cooperation and political economy. In the age of space and increasing environmental consciousness, many analysts turned their attention to matters that affect and seem to promise greater effects on the natural environment, such as global warming, loss of species, and environmental deterioration. Important strides in superpower cooperation in the late 1980s, the end of the Cold War, and the disintegration of the Soviet Union led to an expanded interest in change. If the bipolar structure made the world seem stable, the shift away from it appeared to promise fundamental change.

In the analysis of the last three chapters, this book has attempted to put those basic processes of conflict, cooperation, and change into context by arguing that all three processes endure in international politics all of the time. Because of events, more attention may be given to one or the other, but in reality, they proceed universally at all times. Their paces may vary, and their composition may shape events more greatly at one time or another in one part of the world or another.

Nevertheless, the prudent analyst of international politics should remain conscious of the persistent, unending matters of which politics among states is constituted. The universe in which states interact does not consist of either conflict or cooperation: it includes both. It is not shaped by either stability or change: both elements endure.

Moreover, a flicker of renewed nationalism or tranquillity does not necessarily mean that the world has been transformed. It probably signifies that some constraints may have been lifted or some decisions have been made. The panorama of international politics continues to unfold in fascinating diversity and complexity.

Clearly, international politics is not simple. Nevertheless, it is hoped that, keeping in mind the problematic and applying the concepts and analytical tools set out, the reader of this book will have in hand the means to make greater sense of that complex world than he or she had before.

Historical Glossary

Acheson, Dean G., 1893–1971. United States lawyer, statesman, author, and political adviser. As undersecretary, 1945–47, and secretary of state, 1949–53, he led in the formulation of the policy of containment of the Soviet Union, including the promotion of economic and military assistance to allies. He also led in the policy of defending South Korea against the invasion in 1950 by North Korea. His most important book is *Present at the Creation* (1969).

Adenauer, Konrad, 1876–1967. German statesman and political leader. A respected political leader in the Weimar Republic, he was dismissed by the Nazis in 1933 from his post as mayor of Cologne and later imprisoned by them. One of the founders of the Christian Democratic Union in 1945, he was elected chancellor of the newly formed Federal Republic Germany (FRG) in 1949 and reelected several times. Under his leadership, the FRG grew economically and gained the restoration of its sovereignty in 1955.

African National Congress (ANC). Founded in 1912 as a political organization to protect the rights of blacks against the white Afrikaaner-dominated government that gained power at the end of British imperial rule, the ANC became the leading opposition group against the Nationalist government of South Africa during the period 1948–94 and winner of the elections in the latter year. In the post-1948 period, the government had promoted a system of **apartheid,** or strict racial separation. Under the leadership of **Nelson Mandela,** the ANC forms the largest party in the government of South Africa under its new, nonracial constitution.

Agincourt, battle of, October 25, 1415. A battle in the Hundred Years' War (1337–1453) in which a smaller force of English, under Henry V, defeated a much larger French force by inflicting about ten thousand casualties on the French while suffering none themselves, largely because of the massed use of the longbow; the victory enabled the English to conquer much of France.

Aidid, Muhammad Farrah. Clan and military leader in Somalia. During the United Nations and United States intervention in Somalia in 1993, the intervening forces undertook an action to capture General Aidid but failed to do so. Later, he was one of several leaders with whom the United Nations negotiated to calm the situation in Somalia.

American Civil War, 1861–65. The war between the United States of America and the Confederate States of America, fought primarily over maintaining the unity of the country and slavery.

Amnesty International. An international nongovernmental group that monitors and reports on human rights violations in countries throughout the world. Advocates on behalf of increasing human rights, including abolition of the death penalty.

Angola civil war. Civil war that began in Angola shortly after Portugal ended its colonial rule in 1975 among the Popular Movement for the Liberation of Angola (MPLA), the National Front for the Liberation of Angola (FNLA), and the National Union for the Total Independence of Angola (UNITA). Although elections and a peaceful progression to independence had been planned for Angola, fighting erupted among the MPLA, FNLA, and UNITA. Angola also became a battleground in the Cold War. The FNLA dissolved as a viable political force in the late 1970s, but the MPLA garnered the support of the Soviet Union and Cuba, while UNITA received backing from the United States, South Africa, and Zaire. A peace agreement was signed in 1991, and elections were held in 1992, with the MPLA gaining the most votes. However, UNITA refused to accept the outcome and resumed its guerrilla warfare.

Antarctica Treaty, 1959. Multilateral treaty to preclude nuclear weapons from the continent of Antarctica.

Antiballistic Missile (ABM) Treaty, 1972. Formal permanent agreement between the United States and the Soviet Union that provided that each country would be prohibited from deploying a comprehensive antiballistic missile defense but would be allowed to deploy two ABM systems, one to protect the capital city and the other to defend a single intercontinental ballistic missile site. Later modified to allow the deployment of only a single ABM site.

Apartheid. Policy of racial separation in South Africa from 1948 to 1992 that included domination of majority black population by white minority through the operation of a series of repressive laws.

Arab League. An alliance founded in 1945 to enhance the level of cooperation among Arab states. The original treaty was initiated by Egypt, Iraq, Syria, Lebanon, Transjordan, Saudi Arabia, and Yemen; membership has increased to twenty-two. Egypt was suspended from the League in 1979 for signing a peace treaty with Israel but readmitted in 1989. Egypt broke ranks again in 1990 when it joined with Saudi Arabia in condemning Iraq's occupation of Kuwait and authorized Arab League troops to participate in the Gulf War operation. This action created a permanent rift in the league, and a majority of the Arab states joined Iraq in condemning Egypt for abandoning the principle of Arab solidarity.

Arafat, Yasir, 1924–. Palestinian political leader. Chairman of the Palestinian Authority and leader of the Fatah movement, which holds a majority of seats in the Palestinian Council. Chairman of the Palestine Liberation Organization, 1969–.

Archduke Francis Ferdinand. Heir to Austro-Hungarian throne whose assassination on July 28, 1914, in Sarajevo led to the outbreak of **World War I.**

ARENA (National Republican Alliance), 1980–. El Salvadoran conservative political party. With election of Alfredo Cristiani to the presidency of the country in 1989, ARENA as ruling party implemented an economic structural adjustment program and ended civil war by supporting an agreement with the FMLN.

Arias Sanchez, Oscar, 1941–. Costa Rican statesman. Served as president of Costa Rica, 1986–90. Author of Esquipulas II peace plan in August 1987, for which he won the 1987 Nobel Peace Prize.

Aristide, Jean-Bertrand, 1953–. Roman Catholic priest and political leader in Haiti. He was elected president of Haiti in December 1990 but was deposed by a military coup the following September. He was restored to office in October 1994 by diplomacy backed by threat of United States invasion and completed the term in December 1995. In 1995, he resigned from the priesthood.

Asia Pacific Economic Cooperation (APEC). A regional forum founded in 1989 to enhance economic cooperation among the countries of the Pacific Rim. Some envision a free trade zone that would include East Asia, Australia, and parts of the Western Hemisphere. Others view it as a vehicle for integrating the U.S. market with the rapidly expanding economies of East Asia.

Asian Development Bank. Established in 1966, one of several regional banks dedicated to extending loans for purposes of development. Favors projects that engender supplementary private capital.

Association of Southeast Asian Nations (ASEAN). A regional association of Southeast Asian countries founded in 1967. The original member countries were Indonesia, Malaysia, the Philippines, Singapore, and Thailand; Brunei joined in 1984 and Vietnam, in 1995. The primary objectives of ASEAN were to encourage the economic and social development of the region through cooperation, act as a buffer during the Cold War against great power competition, and create an arena in which member states could resolve differences.

Austro-Hungarian Empire, 1867–1918. Multinational state united under a dual monarchy. Part of Triple Alliance in World War I, suffered military defeat. Following the principle of self-determination, the empire was divided in the peace settlement into many national states.

Axis, 1936–45. A coalition of countries headed by Germany, Italy, and Japan that fought and lost World War II.

Basic Principles Agreement. Agreement reached in 1972 between United States President Richard M. Nixon and Soviet First Secretary Leonid Brezhnev that attempted to codify the principles upon which the detente that they had embraced would develop further. It provided for periodic meetings, promises to continue to try to reach agreements, to exercise restraint in their relations, and not to seek unilateral advantages at the expense of the other.

Battle of Britain. Air battle from August to October 1940 in which a small British air force defeated a German air attack that had been launched as a prelude to invasion. It was the first German defeat of **World War II.**

Benjedid, Chadli. Algerian military officer and statesman. President of Algeria in 1979–92. Forced in 1992 by the military to resign after Islamic fundamentalist parties made electoral gains.

Berlin blockade, 1948–49. In response to moves to create a common currency that was a step toward consolidating a West German state that would include the western sectors of Berlin, an enclave well inside the Soviet occupation zone of Germany, the Soviet Union closed off all ground and water transportation routes between West Germany and Berlin. To uphold their rights of occupation and access to Berlin, the United States and Britain mounted an airlift that brought supplies to the besieged city until the blockade was lifted.

Berlin crisis, 1958–62. Extended crisis arising from Soviet Premier Nikita Khrushchev's threat to turn over control of access routes from West Germany to Berlin to East Germany if the United States, Britain, and France would not negotiate the "normalization of the situation in Berlin." Khrushchev set various "deadlines" but did not carry out his threats. However, in the face of an immense flow of East German refugees to West Berlin, he ordered the sealing of the border, first with barbed wire and then with the Berlin Wall in 1961. Although this action diminished the crisis, all tension did not abate until after the Cuban missile crisis in 1962.

Berlin wall. Wall built in 1961 to prevent East Germans leaving for West Berlin. Although constructed near the end of the more tense phase of the Cold War, the wall came to symbolize the East-West divide and the Cold War. It was breached in November 1989 and subsequently torn down.

Biafra. Name of a state proclaimed by leaders of a region in eastern Nigeria that seceded from the Nigerian state in 1967 and fought a civil war before surrendering in 1970.

Bismarck, Prince Otto Von, 1815–98. German statesman who was instrumental in the creation of the German Empire in 1871 and became its first and most influential chancellor. He devised conservative social policies in response to the conditions created by the Industrial Revolution. In a move that foreshadowed the modern welfare state, Bismarck introduced state insurance for sickness in 1883, accident insurance in 1884, and old-age pensions in 1889 in a deliberate attempt to undermine the socialists in his country and defuse any revolutionary tendencies of the workers.

Boland Amendment. United States laws passed in 1983 and 1984 that, respectively, prohibited the Department of Defense and the Central Intelligence Agency from overthrowing the government of Nicaragua and denied any military or paramilitary assistance to the Nicaraguan contras.

Bolshevik. A radical, revolutionary faction, led by V. I. Lenin, that split off from the Russian Social-Democratic Labor Party. Lenin and the Bolsheviks led the revolution of November 1917. After Lenin assumed leadership in Russia, the Bolshevik Party formed the government and later became the core of the Communist Party in the newly established Union of Soviet Socialist Republics.

Bolshevik revolution, November 1917. Takeover of the revolutionary government of Russia headed by Aleksandr Kerensky that had ruled since the February 1917 revolution that had overthrown the czar. The Bolsheviks were led by **Vladimir Lenin,** who was carried to Russia from Switzerland in a sealed train provided by the German government. Following the takeover, the new government withdrew Russia from World War I and dedicated itself to fighting a civil war, building an authoritarian socialist regime, and addressing economic problems.

Bretton Woods Conference A conference held at the end of World War II in Bretton Woods, New Hampshire, to devise an international monetary system providing mechanisms to manage the international economy and prevent the desperate conditions that led to the Great Depression and the Second World War. The International Monetary Fund (IMF) and the International Bank for Reconstruction and Development, also known as the World Bank, were founded at this conference.

Brezhnev, Leonid, 1906–82. Soviet political leader. General secretary of the Communist Party of the Soviet Union from 1968 until his death. Helped to oust **Nikita Khrushchev** from power in 1964. He ordered the Warsaw Pact invasion of Czechoslovakia in 1968, and his name is attached to the Brezhnev Doctrine, which held that the Soviet Union had the right to intervene militarily in Eastern European countries to uphold socialist regimes. Promoted a policy of peaceful coexistence with the United States and signed several important agreements as part of the detente between the two countries, including the Antiballistic Missile Treaty, the **Strategic Arms Limitation Treaty I,** and the **Basic Principles Agreement** in 1972, as well as the **Vladivostok Agreement** in 1974 and the **Strategic Arms Limitation Agreement** in 1979. His policies also led to active Soviet intervention in Africa in the 1970s, and he ordered the invasion of Afghanistan in 1979.

Brussels Pact. Defensive alliance of Western European countries established in 1948. Predecessor of the **North Atlantic Treaty Organization.**

Bush, George, 1924–. American statesman. President, 1989–93; vice-president, 1981–89. In the 1970s, served as director of the Central Intelligence Agency and as ambassador to China. Led broad coalition of countries in the Gulf War (1990–91), which ousted Iraq's occupying army from Kuwait. Oversaw the orderly ending of the Cold War.

Camp David Agreement, September 1978. Interim agreement between Israel and Egypt that prepared the way for the peace treaty between the two countries, negotiated by Egyptian President Anwar Sadat, Israeli Prime Minister Menachem Begin, and United States President Jimmy Carter.

Carter, James Earl (Jimmy), 1924–. American businessman and statesman. President, 1977–81; governor of Georgia, 1971–74. He negotiated the Panama Canal Treaties, which provided for the transfer of control over the canal to Panama by 1999; assisted in the negotiations for the independence of Zambia; brokered the Camp David Agreement; and completed the negotiations for the SALT II agreement. He extended full diplomatic recognition to China and abrogated the 1954 defense treaty with Taiwan, and he organized sanctions against the Soviet Union to protest its intervention in Afghanistan. He was ineffective in dealing with Iran after the revolutionary regime supported the taking of American diplomatic personnel hostages, but he began the third major American military buildup of the Cold War that culminated in the first term of the Reagan administration (1981–85). After his retirement from the presidency, Carter remained active in international diplomacy, leading an international team to observe the 1990 Nicaraguan elections, diplomatically intervening with North Korea in the 1994 crisis between that country and the United States concerning North Korean nuclear policy, and negotiating the departure of the military junta from Haiti in 1994.

Castro, Fidel, 1926–. Cuban revolutionary and political leader. Premier, 1959–. After leading a revolutionary force that succeeded in taking power in 1959, Castro established an authoritarian socialist regime that collectivized agriculture and promoted education and health care for all. He reversed alliances during the Cold War from the United States to the Soviet Union. Until the late 1960s, he promoted the spread of revolutionary activity in other Latin American countries. Later, he pursued an exceptionally active foreign policy that took Cuban troops and personnel to Africa. Although faced with great hostility from the United States, he persisted in power even after the collapse of the Soviet Union. He wrote *Ten Years of Revolution* (1964) and *History Will Absolve Me* (1968).

Catholic Charities. Nongovernmental organization active in providing relief and emergency assistance internationally.

Cedras, Lt. Gen. Raoul. Haitian military leader who led overthrow of President **Jean-Bertrand Aristide** in September 1991. He ruled Haiti until Aristide's restoration in October 1994, at which time he went into exile in Panama.

Central America. Isthmus region south of Mexico and north of Colombia, including the five states of the Central American Federation (1825–38) and the Central American Common Market (1960–)—Costa Rica, El

Salvador, Guatemala, Honduras, and Nicaragua—and Belize and Panama.

Central American Common Market (CACM). A collaborative effort undertaken by Costa Rica, El Salvador, Guatemala, Honduras, and Nicaragua in an attempt to coordinate economic policies and enhance import substitution industrialization strategies. It was created as a result of the 1960 General Treaty of Common Customs Tariffs.

Central Europe. Region of Europe centered on Germany and including Czechoslovakia and Austria and, sometimes, Poland and Hungary.

Central Intelligence Agency (CIA). United States government agency established in 1947 to conduct intelligence-gathering activities and clandestine operations and to coordinate all intelligence activities of the national government.

Cerezo, Marco Vinicio, 1942–. Guatemalan political leader. President, 1987–91. He initiated the Esquipulas meeting of August 1987 that led to the Central American peace initiative known as Esquipulas II.

Chamberlain, Neville, 1869–1940. British statesman. Prime minister, 1937–40. Pursued policy of appeasement until March 1939, when he promised support to Poland if Germany invaded it. Led Britain at opening of World War II in September 1939 but resigned in May 1940.

Chamorro, Violeta Barrios de, 1929–. Nicaraguan political leader. President, 1990–96. She is the widow of Pedro Joaquin Chamorro, publisher of the daily *La Prensa*, which opposed the Somoza regime, who was killed in 1978. She joined the first Sandinista-led government following the 1979 revolution but resigned in 1981. In 1990, she was elected president of Nicaragua at the head of multiparty coalition opposed to the Sandinista government.

Charter 77. A human rights manifesto signed by seven hundred Czech former government leaders and intellectuals in 1977. Subsequently, a Czechoslovak nongovernment civil rights organization, Civic Forum, agitated for greater civil and political rights. One of its founders, the playwright Vaclav Havel, became president of the country in 1989 following the end of the Communist regime.

Chinese civil war. Struggle between Communists and Nationalists in China that lasted from 1927 to 1949. From the time of the Japanese invasion of China in 1937 until the end of World War II, the two foes fought against the Japanese. From 1946 to 1949, however, the struggle between the two groups gained in intensity, with the Communists winning in October 1949 and the Kuomintang retiring to the island of Formosa (Taiwan). With the establishment of two governments, one in Beijing (Peking) and the other in Taipei, both claimed jurisdiction over all of China. During the Korean War (1950–53), the Chinese Communists fought against the United States. Later in the 1950s, the Nationalists and

Communists shelled each other's territory. Not until 1971 did the Beijing government gain the right to represent China at the United Nations and the Kuomintang government lost its seat.

Chinese revolution. See **Chinese civil war.**

Christmas bombing, 1972. Intensive aerial bombardment by the United States of North Vietnam, particularly the capital city of Hanoi and the port city Haiphong, during the latter part of December 1972. Its declared purpose was to extract further concessions from North Vietnam from the peace talks that were being simultaneously conducted in Paris to bring about an end to the United States intervention in Vietnam.

Churchill, Winston, 1874–1965. British statesman, author, and soldier. He served in India, Sudan, and in World War I as a soldier. His reporting on the South African War won his reputation as a journalist. From before World War I to 1940, he served in a number of cabinet posts in both the Liberal and the Conservative parties. With the forced resignation of Neville Chamberlain in 1940, Churchill assumed the position of prime minister and led the British through World War II. His government lost the 1945 elections, but he returned as prime minister from 1951 to 1955. His wartime speeches inspired his countrymen, as well as others in the world. The collected speeches and his later writing, especially his six-volume *The Second World War* and his four-volume *History of the English-Speaking Peoples* gained him the Nobel Prize in Literature in 1953. Acknowledged as one of the most renowned political leaders of the twentieth century.

Clinton, William Jefferson (Bill), 1946–. American political leader. President, 1993– ; governor of Arkansas, 1979–81 and 1983–92. In the first post-Cold War presidential election, Clinton stressed economic over security concerns. Nevertheless, he faced crises in former Yugoslavia and Haiti; promoted a peace negotiating process in the Middle East; supported the building of democracy in Russia and Eastern Europe; devised and fostered the Partnership for Peace, a scheme for admitting former Warsaw Pact countries as members of NATO; and promoted increased trade with East Asia.

Cominform, 1947–56. Acronym for Communist Information Bureau, an association of the Communist parties of Bulgaria, Czechoslovakia, France, Hungary, Italy, Poland, Rumania, Soviet Union, and Yugoslavia, established for the purpose of exchanging information and maintaining ideological conformity. In 1948, Yugoslavia was expelled. A reconciliation between the Soviet Union and Yugoslavia was accompanied by dissolution of the Cominform.

Common Agricultural Policy. See **European Union.**

Commonwealth of Independent States. An organization of independent states established in December 1991 as a successor body to the Soviet Union. Eleven of the fifteen former Soviet Republics chose to join, including: Armenia, Azerbaijan, Belarus, Kazakhstan,

Kyrgystan, Moldova, Russia, Tajikistan, Turkmenistan, Ukraine, and Uzbekistan. The primary function of the CIS is to provide a forum that enables the states to deliberate over issues of common concern.

Communism. A system of social organization in which property is held in common by the members of society. In the twentieth century, the term has referred to the political movement embodied in Communist parties and to the theories expressed by Marx and Engels in *The Communist Manifesto* (1848) as well as by others that attempt to explain history on the basis of historical materialism that leads to a utopian society.

Communist Party of the Soviet Union (CPSU). The political party that ruled the Union of Soviet Socialist Republics from 1922 until 1991. The CPSU grew out the Bolshevik Party that was founded by Lenin and led the November 1917 takeover of the Russian revolution. Until 1990, the CPSU was the only legal political party in the Soviet Union. In 1991, following the attempted coup in August, the general secretary of the CPSU, Mikhail Gorbachev, resigned and terminated the governing powers of the party leadership.

Concert of Europe. Established at the Congress of Vienna in 1815, a system designed to manage the relations among the great powers of Europe, which at that time consisted of Austria, Great Britain, France, Prussia, and Russia. The concert system was an attempt to maintain the balance of power by facilitating through periodic conferences cooperation in foreign policy and restraint in the use of force.

Conference of Berlin, 1884–85. An international meeting to deal with the problems involved in the European countries' imperial division of Africa.

Conference on Security and Cooperation in Europe (CSCE), 1975. Conference of thirty-five states from Europe and North America that produced the Helsinki Final Act. With the dissolution of the Soviet Union, membership increased to fifty with the addition of the successor republics, and the name was changed to Organization of Security and Cooperation in Europe. Provides a forum for countries of both Eastern and Western Europe.

Congress of Vienna, 1814–15. Conference convened by the victors of Napoleonic Wars. The purpose of the meeting was to reconfigure the national boundaries in Europe and reestablish the balance of power. The congress also served to codify the rules of modern diplomacy and establish the ranking system for the diplomatic corps.

Contadora Group. Named after a Panamanian island where they first met, a diplomatic effort by the leaders of several Latin American countries—notably Mexico, Colombia, Venezuela, and Panama, but supported by others—that attempted to find a solution to the crisis in Central America precipitated by the Nicaraguan revolution of 1979 and the civil war in El Salvador that drew in the United States to oppose the Nicaraguan government

and support the regime in El Salvador. Ultimately, the Contadora effort failed, but its cause was taken up by Esquipulas II.

Containment. Overall strategy of United States foreign and security policy from 1947 to the end of the Cold War based on the principle of opposition to Soviet and Communist expansion and the maintenance of the United States and its allies as confident, prosperous societies. As originally articulated, containment envisioned a flexible policy that would cause the "mellowing" of the Soviet state, but its institutionalization included the formation of NATO and other alliances.

Conventional Forces in Europe (CFE) Treaty, 1990. Agreement between the members of the **North Atlantic Treaty Organization** and the **Warsaw Treaty Organization** establishing limits on the numbers of nonnuclear weapons and troops deployed in Eastern and Central Europe.

Coordinating Committee for Multilateral Export Controls (COCOM). North Atlantic Treaty Organization committee that during the Cold War devised plans and drew up schedules of strategic goods that were not to be traded with the Soviet Union and its allies.

Crimean War, 1853–56. War of Russia against Turkey, England, France, and Sardinia. Although Austria remained neutral, its threats prompted Russian withdrawal from Moldovia and Wallachia, which were then occupied by Austria. The war reduced Russian influence in Southeastern Europe, and Russian-Austrian relations remained strained.

Cristiani, Alfredo, 1947– . El Salvadoran landowner and statesman. President, 1989–94. Put into effect economic structural adjustment program and other reforms. Negotiated and signed peace agreement with FMLN, ending twelve-year civil war.

Crusades. A succession of European military campaigns into the holy land usually numbered at eight. The Crusades occurred over the period 1095 to 1270 a.d. During the Middle Ages, Europe underwent a resurgence of religious fervor and commercial expansion, which both led to a heightened interest in Jerusalem and other holy places in the East. The Crusades were initiated to overthrow Muslim control of Jerusalem and the Christian shrine of the Holy Sepulchre.

Cuban missile crisis, 1962. Most severe confrontation of the superpowers during the Cold War. In the face of denials that it was doing so, the Soviet Union began building medium- and intermediate-range missile sites in Cuba in the summer of 1962. Through aerial photography, the United States gathered convincing evidence of this deployment, and President John F. Kennedy demanded that the missiles be removed and the sites dismantled. The United States deployed a naval blockade around Cuba to intercept Soviet shipping, and it stationed a bomber force in southern Florida to back up its demands. After nearly two weeks of tense bargaining, the Soviet

Union agreed to withdraw its missile deployment, and the United States tacitly promised not to invade Cuba.

Cuban revolution, 1959– . Armed seizure of power in Cuba by Fidel Castro, who marched into Havana on January 1, 1959, following several years of fighting against the dictator Fulgencio Batista, who fled the capital. The revolution introduced many reforms, particularly in the areas of education and health, that favored the working classes. Policies of nationalization but especially the alignment of Cuba with the Soviet Union and Castro's declaration of his allegiance to communism, drove much of the middle class into exile, primarily in Miami.

Czechoslovakia coup, 1948. Communists in Czechoslovakia, who controlled the police and other ministries of government, agitated against the government beginning in 1947 and, with the moral support of the Soviet Union, staged a *coup d'etat* in February 1948. This action made a profound impression on the West and marked an important event in the development of the Cold War as the Western countries, in response, formed the North Atlantic Treaty Organization.

Czechoslovakia, Warsaw Pact invasion, 1968. Following a period of liberalization under the leadership of Alexander Dubchek in what was called the "Prague Spring," which aimed to build "Communism with a human face," a disapproving Soviet Union and its Warsaw Treaty allies placed approximately 500,000 troops in Czechoslovakia and installed an orthodox Communist government that repressed liberal tendencies.

Daladier, Edouard, 1884–1970. French statesman. Premier, April 1938 to March 1940. Signed Munich Agreement in September 1938. Interned by Germans from 1942 until 1945. Member of National Assembly, 1946–58.

Dayton Agreement, 1995. Agreement negotiated under auspices of United States diplomacy at an isolated air base near Dayton, Ohio, among the warring parties in Bosnia-Herzegovina: the Bosnian government, Croatia, and the Bosnian Serbs, who were represented by the president of Serbia. The agreement provided for a separation of the armed forces and a loose confederation between the Bosnian Serbs, who would control approximately half of Bosnia, and a Bosnian government-Croat federation, which would control the other half. Provision was also made for the deployment of an **Implementation Force** of sixty thousand troops to enforce the agreement to separate forces and for the dispatch of a civilian contingent to assist in economic rebuilding and refugee resettlement.

Death squads. Clandestine organizations formed from military and police personnel or civilians supported by governments in several Latin American countries that operated from the 1960s to the 1980s. Standard procedures included kidnapping, torturing, and killing citizens whose activities governments did not tolerate. Often victims were labor union organizers and citizens who spoke critically of their governments.

Declaration on a Liberated Europe. Declaration that formed part of the agreement at the Yalta summit meeting in March 1945 among United States President **Franklin D. Roosevelt,** Soviet Generalissimo **Josef Stalin,** and British Prime Minister **Winston Churchill.** The parties promised to hold free and fair elections in all of the liberated countries of Europe after the end of **World War II.**

Declaration on Granting Independence to Colonial Countries and Peoples. Resolution passed by the United Nations General Assembly in 1960 calling for rapid decolonization.

De Gaulle, Charles, 1890–1970. French general and statesman. His ideas on mechanized warfare were rejected by the interwar government, but he joined the government as undersecretary of war in 1940. In the defeat by Germany, he rejected the armistice and went into exile, organizing the Free French forces, which included fighters from overseas colonies. Following the liberation of France in 1944, he became head of the provisional government but resigned in 1946. After some partisan activity, De Gaulle dissolved his party and went into retirement in 1953. During the crisis in Algeria, he was called back to government in 1958 and created the Fifth Republic, under which he was elected president. He opposed British entry into the European Community, and he required the withdrawal of all NATO allied forces from French soil by 1967. Following the defeat of a referendum on constitutional reform in 1969, De Gaulle resigned and returned to private life.

DeKlerk, Frederik W., 1936– . South African statesman. President, 1989–94. DeKlerk provided the white leadership to dismantle the system of **apartheid** in the country. He released **African National Congress** leader **Nelson Mandela** from his long imprisonment and entered into negotiations with him to bring the country a new constitution, free elections with a universal franchise, the end to white-dominated rule, and an interim government.

De la Madrid, Miguel, 1934–. President of Mexico, 1982–88. During his six-year term, Mexico began moving away from an autonomous foreign policy and self-sufficient economic system toward economic interdependence and cooperation with the United States.

Development and the Environment, International Conference on. See **Earth Summit.**

Diem, Ngo Dinh, 1901–63. Political leader of South Vietnam. After the Geneva Accords brought an end to the French-Indochina War in 1954, he became the leader of South Vietnam. With United States backing, he canceled the elections that were to have been held in 1956 to unify Vietnam, and he repressed his opposition as it became more intense. In 1963, he was overthrown by a military coup and killed.

Doctors Without Borders. French-based nongovernmental international organization that dispatches medical personnel to ravaged areas.

Dresden Bombing,   1945. Near the end of World War II, over the course of two nights in February 1945, the British Bomber Command and the United States Army Air Force bombed Dresden, creating a firestorm and killing an estimated 135,000 people. The bombing drew criticism not only because of the large number of deaths but also because many of those residing in the city were civilian refugees and because the city did not rank as an important military target. Furthermore, the bombing was a tragedy because Dresden had been regarded before then to have been one of the most beautiful cities in the world and a center of the arts and architecture.

Duarte, José Napoleón,   1926–90. El Salvador statesman. President, 1984–88; member of civilian-military junta, 1980–84. In collaboration with and with support of United States, pursued war against FMLN.

Earth Summit,   June 1992. International conference of heads of state and government concerned with protection of the environment and economic development, held in Rio de Janeiro, Brazil.

Eastern Europe.   Region of Europe during the Cold War that encompassed the Warsaw Treaty allies of the Soviet Union: East Germany, Poland, Czechoslovakia, Hungary, Rumania, and Bulgaria.

East Germany (People's Democratic Republic), 1949–90. One of two successor states to the Germany defeated in World War II. Created out of Soviet zone of occupation. In the wake of Soviet President Gorbachev's abjuring the use of force to maintain communism in eastern Europe, East Germans demonstrated and emigrated. Government eventually agreed to absorption of successor states (provinces) by West Germany to create a unified Germany.

Economic Commission for Latin America (ECLA). This organization was founded in 1948 by the UN (the Caribbean was added in 1984 to create the Economic Commission for Latin America and the Caribbean or ECLAC). Its primary function is to formulate development plans to address the economic problems that confront Latin America, and it has had a considerable influence on public policy in the region.

Economic Community of West African States (ECOWAS).   A regional organization composed of fifteen African states that was founded in 1975 with the signing of the Treaty of Lagos. The agreement was intended to contribute to the leveling of disparities in the development among the member countries through the elimination of restrictions on trade; the free movement of people, capital, and services within the region; and collaboration on defense, communications, and transportation systems.

Ejido.   In Mexico and Latin America, communal agricultural land.

Enlightenment.   Term applied to thought that emerged in the eighteenth century promoting rationalism and secularism and that was characterized by a belief in progress.

Ethiopia, Italian Conquest of.   Italy had possessed colonies in the surrounding region in Africa and had designs upon Ethiopia (then known as Abyssinia) after an Italian invasion was repulsed in 1896. Italian dictator Benito Mussolini decided to invade Ethiopia in 1935. Ethiopia appealed to the League of Nations in 1936, but the League's condemnation and actions proved ineffective. Ethiopia regained its independence with Italy's defeat in World War II.

Ethnic cleansing.   Policy that attempts to render an area ethnically homogeneous by killing and/or expelling all those inhabitants who do not belong to the dominant ethnic group. Promoted mainly by Bosnian Serbs in the war that developed in Bosnia following its independence in 1992, but similar policies were also followed on a smaller scale by the other parties. The largest expulsion occurred in 1995, when the Croatian army drove out approximately 100,000 Serbs from the Krajina region of Croatia.

European Coal and Steel Community (ECSC). See **European Union.**

European Defense Community (EDC).   See **European Union.**

European Economic Community (EEC).   See **European Union.**

European Free Trade Association (EFTA).   A regional organization established under British leadership in 1960 as an alternative to the nascent European Economic Community. The original members were Austria, Denmark, Great Britain, Norway, Portugal, Sweden, and Switzerland. Unlike the Common Market, EFTA did not include a common external tariff or a common agricultural policy. After Great Britain, Denmark, and Portugal joined the European Community and Iceland, Finland, and Liechtenstein joined EFTA, a combined EC-EFTA European Economic Area (EEA) came into effect in 1993, creating the world's largest trading area.

European Monetary Union.   See **European Union.**

European Union.   Organized arrangements based on reconciliation of Germany and France after World War II to gain economic, and possibly political, cooperation among Western Europeans. The European Coal and Steel Community (ECSC) was created in 1952. The Treaty of Rome (1957) created the European Economic Community and the European Atomic Energy Community. These were merged in 1967 in a single European Community (EC), with headquarters in Brussels, whose main institutions are the Commission, an executive bureaucracy; the Council of Ministers, the executive representing member states; a parliament with limited powers; and a Court of Justice. Original members were France, West Germany, Italy, Belgium, the Netherlands, and Luxembourg. In 1973, Britain, Denmark, and Ireland were added, and Spain, Portugal, and Greece joined in the 1980s. Further widening occurred in 1995 when Austria, Finland, and Sweden joined. The EC achieved a common agricultural policy, a common tariff, and coordination of exchange rate policies. The Single European Act (1985) provided for a common internal market for goods and labor by 1992. At the beginning of 1993, it achieved a common market in goods and services and eliminated passport controls on citizens traveling among the member countries. The Maastricht Treaty, signed in December 1991, changed the name to European Union and aims to create a common currency and a single central bank. Moreover, the treaty projects the possibility of creating common foreign and defense policies. Long-term plans entail the admission of additional members, including Eastern European countries of the former Soviet bloc.

Farabundo Marti National Liberation Front (FMLN), 1980–92. An organization formed to coordinate the activities of five guerrilla groups in El Salvador in fighting to seize power from the government. With the election of a new president in 1989, the government entered into peace talks with the FMLN that culminated in an agreement to end the civil war, disarm the guerrillas, and integrate the opposition groups into a democratic political process.

Fascist Italy, 1922–43. Italy under the Fascist Party regime of Benito Mussolini. Ruled by intimidation and secret police. Glorified state and war. Conquered Ethiopia in 1936. Joined the Axis and was defeated in World War II.

Ferdinand II, 1452–1516. King of Aragon who married Isabel of Castile, effectively uniting Spain, except for Granada, which they conquered in 1492. The rulers expelled the Jews from Spain (1492) and established the Inquisition. They also patronized Christopher Columbus' voyages of discovery.

Food and Agricultural Organization (FAO). A specialized agency affiliated with the United Nations that was founded on October 16, 1945. The FAO endeavors to eliminate hunger throughout the world, by implementing programs that address all aspects of agriculture and development.

Ford, Gerald R., 1913– . American statesman. President, 1974–77; vice-president, 1973–74; member of the House of Representatives, 1949–73. He was appointed by President **Richard M. Nixon** as vice-president upon the resignation of his predecessor, and he acceded to the presidency upon Nixon's resignation. Shortly thereafter, he pardoned Nixon for crimes committed during his tenure as president. Ford continued Nixon's foreign policy of detente with the Soviet Union.

Fourth French Republic, 1946–58. Constitutional arrangement in France from the end of the provisional government after World War II. Joined NATO and led development of institutions of the European Community. Withdrew from Indochina after defeat in 1954 and

extended independence to Morocco and Tunisia but fought to maintain Algeria as part of France. Republic ended when an army revolt in Algeria threatened to spread to metropolitan France and Charles De Gaulle returned to power to create the Fifth Republic.

French Indochina, 1887–1954. Group of territories in Southeast Asia acquired by France in nineteenth century and united as Indochina, including Laos, which was added in 1893. Occupied by Japan during World War II. Reassertion of French control was resisted by the Vietnamese, who defeated the French in 1954. Vietnam was divided until 1975. Successor modern states are Cambodia, Laos, and Vietnam.

French Revolution. A democratic revolution in 1789 that overthrew the French feudal state structure. Influenced by Enlightenment thought, progressive aristocrats and the liberal element in France allied with the working masses in a successful attempt to usurp the Bourbon monarchy. Based on the values of liberty, fraternity, and equality, the revolution aspired to create more equitable forms of political and social organization.

Freud, Sigmund, 1856–1939. Austrian psychiatrist, author, founder of psychoanalysis. He viewed human behavior as shaped by two impulses: a sexually driven wish for life (eros) and a wish for death (thanatos). He thought that patterns were set in the first five years of life and that problems (neuroses and psychoses) that emerged in later periods resulted from the repression in the individual's unconscious of early experience. Through the technique of free association, the unconscious could be brought to a state of consciousness and treated rationally. Freud's thought has affected other disciplines, such as anthropology and political science as well as art and literature, by emphasizing the role that the irrational (the emotional) plays in human behavior. His major books are *Studies of Hysteria, The Interpretation of Dreams, Three Contributions to the Sexual Theory, The Ego and the Id, Totem and Taboo, Moses and Monotheism, A General Introduction to Psychoanalysis, New Introductory Lectures on Psycho-Analysis, Basic Writings, and Civilization and Its Discontents.*

General Agreement on Tariffs and Trade (GATT). A 1947 multilateral trading agreement based on principles of free trade, reciprocity, and equal treatment of trading partners. Under auspices of the GATT, several multilateral negotiations have succeeded in reducing tariffs and nontariff barriers to trade. In the Uruguay Round (1987–94), agreement was reached to create a new mechanism called the World Trade Organization to carry forward the work of the GATT in applying rules and providing procedures for adjusting trade disputes.

Geneva Summit, 1985. First meeting of American President Ronald Reagan and Soviet General Secretary Mikhail Gorbachev. Although no specific agreements were reached, the United States and the Soviet Union restored cultural relations that had been broken in 1979 after the Soviet invasion of Afghanistan, and the two leaders committed themselves to meeting again.

Germany, unification of, 1866–71. Loosely federated under Austrian domination following the Napoleonic Wars and the Congress of Vienna (1815), Germany experienced nationalism and liberalism, which were linked in the unsuccessful 1848 revolutions. Prussia gained dominance in the Zollverein, a customs union from which Austria was excluded. Germany was united under Prussian domination by the Austro-Prussian War of 1866 and the Franco-Prussian War of 1870–71.

Gorbachev, Mikhail, 1931– . Soviet statesman. General secretary and president, 1985–91. His reforms—*glasnost'* (openness), *perestroika* (restructuring), and "new thinking"—led to the Soviet Union's withdrawal from foreign commitments and to fundamental political reform and important economic reform. Initiated end of Cold War by abjuring use of force in eastern European countries in 1989. Signed important arms reduction agreements with United States. After surviving a coup in August 1991, he lost his official positions when the Soviet Union ceased to exist in December 1991.

Governors' Island Accord. Agreement reached between the governments of the United States and Haiti to restore deposed President **Jean-Bertrand Aristide** to office.

Gramsci, Antonio, 1891–1937. Italian journalist, thinker, and Communist organizer. His thirty-four *Prison Notebooks* contain most of his ideas about politics. He emphasized the role of ideas and intellectuals in society, and viewed the state as a system of domination in which force was combined with an ideology that convinced citizens freely to accept authority.

Granada. Part of Spain that had been ruled by the Moors, who were defeated in 1492. Granada was then added to Castile and Aragon, completing the unification of Spain.

Grand Alliance, 1941–45. A coalition of countries headed by Britain, Soviet Union, and United States that fought and won World War II.

Great Leap Forward, 1958–60. A program undertaken in China by Mao Zedong that aimed to industrialize rapidly and mobilize the population into agricultural communes. The program ended in economic disaster resulting from the production of inferior goods, bad weather that contributed to three consecutive crop failures, and the ending of Soviet economic assistance.

Great Proletarian Cultural Revolution, 1966–69. A campaign initiated by Chinese Communist Party leader Mao Zedong in 1966 that pitted the party against the government. With more than 20 million high school and college students enlisted in the Red Guard, education in China was effectively shut down for two years. The Red Guard persecuted millions of officials and intellectuals who were required to work at menial jobs and to suffer "reeducation" regimens.

Great War. See **World War I.**

Gromyko, Andrei Andreevich, 1909–89. Soviet foreign minister from 1957 to 1985, including periods of crisis with the United States as well as the detente of the 1970s. He helped Mikhail Gorbachev attain the post of general secretary of the Communist Party of the Soviet Union in 1985 and became the chairman of the Presidium of the Supreme Soviet that same year; he retained the post until his retirement in 1988.

Grotius, Hugo, 1583–1645. Dutch jurist. Wrote on international law and argued that relations among states were governed by natural law just as relations among individuals are.

Group of 77. A caucusing group of developing countries founded in 1964 at the first United Nations Conference on Trade and Development. Initiated the New International Economic Order (NIEO) resolution passed by the General Assembly in 1974.

Group of Seven (G-7). Informal group of the leading industrialized countries—Britain, Canada, France, Germany, Italy, Japan, and the United States—whose representatives have met annually since 1975 to confer on international economic policy.

Guernica. See **Picasso, Pablo.**

Gulf of Tonkin Resolution, 1964–70. United States congressional resolution authorizing the president to use force in Southeast Asia. In response to reports of North Vietnamese attacks on American destroyers in the Gulf of Tonkin, the Johnson administration authorized air attacks against several targets in North Vietnam, and the president asked for congressional authorization to defend against attacks and to protect allies in Southeast Asia. The ensuing resolution was used to justify the intensified war in Vietnam, but it was repealed in 1970.

Gulf War, 1990–91. War in which a large Western- and Arab-state coalition, headed by the United States and operating from Saudi Arabian territory, defeated and drove from Kuwait Iraq's forces that had occupied that country in early August 1990. A bombing campaign, begun in mid-January and lasting forty-three days, was carried to Iraq and followed by a one hundred-hour ground assault that drove all of the occupying forces out of Kuwait. As they were leaving, Iraqis set fire to over five hundred oil wells; these fires were put out over the course of the next year. United Nations sanctions continued to be applied to Iraq for its failure to comply with a number of resolutions passed in connection with the war.

Haig, Alexander M., Jr., 1924– . United States secretary of state in Reagan administration, 1981–82. Emphasized opposition to communism in El Salvador.

Hallstein Doctrine. Named after West German Foreign Minister Hallstein, the policy of the Federal

Republic Germany government followed from 1955 to 1966 not to recognize any government, except the Soviet Union, that had diplomatic relations with any Eastern European regime.

Hamas.   Opposition group that uses terror in opposition to the Palestinian Authority on the West Bank and in Israel.

Hammarskjöld, Dag,   1905–61. A Swedish diplomat and economist who was the secretary general of the United Nations from 1951 to 1961. He was an extremely effective secretary general and was instrumental in expanding the competencies of the position. Among his accomplishments were helping to alleviate the 1956 Suez Crisis, in which he established the first UN peacekeeping force, and negotiating the Congo's transition to independence, for which he was awarded the Nobel Peace Prize posthumously.

Haymarket riot.   A demonstration in Chicago on May 4, 1886, organized by a small group of anarchists but attended by about fifteen hundred people, that turned into a riot when police began to disperse the crowd and a bomb exploded. Although it was never proved that the anarchists threw the bomb, several were convicted of inciting a riot. Four were hanged, but three others who had been sentenced to prison were pardoned in 1893.

Hegel, Georg W. F.,   1770–1831. German philosopher. Taught idealism that is developed from and understood through a dialectical logic in which an idea (thesis) engenders its opposite (antithesis), with the conflict between them generating a new idea (synthesis). His view was that in world history, the state is the culmination of the ethical ideal in which reason prevails.

Helsinki Final Act,   1975. A diplomatic agreement signed by thirty-three European countries and the United States and Canada in Helsinki, Finland on August 1, 1975, the final act of the Conference on Security and Cooperation in Europe, providing for 1) recognition of existing state boundaries in Europe, 2) increased trade and exchanges between western and eastern Europe, and 3) undertaking by governments to respect the human rights of their citizens. To monitor implementation of the agreement, periodic meetings of the CSCE followed, and these put pressure on communist governments in Eastern Europe to comply with the human rights standards they had agreed to.

Heng Samrin,   1934– . Cambodian statesman. Served as puppet head of state during Vietnamese occupation of country, 1979–92.

Hezbollah.   The "Party of God" or "Party of Allah" is a radical Shi'ite Muslim organization committed to the creation of a fundamentalist Islamic state in Lebanon. Founded in 1982, it has carried out a program of terrorist activities primarily directed against Israel and the United States.

Hitler, Adolf,   1889–1945. German dictator. Chancellor and führer (leader) January 1933 to April 1945. Led National Socialist German Workers Party (Nazis). Began World War II by invading Poland in September 1939, led mass assassination of Jews, and ruled through secret police. Wrote *Mein Kampf*, trans. 1940.

Ho Chi Minh,   1890–1969. Vietnamese political leader. President of North Vietnam, 1954–69. Founded a Vietnamese independence movement, Vietminh, and led a guerrilla fight against Japanese occupation in World War II. After the war, he led the struggle against the French and, later, the United States.

Hobbes, Thomas,   1588–1645. English philosopher. His contract theory of government derived from his conception of a state of nature in which people are selfish and acquisitive. Out of a fear of death, people accept rule by government. He thought that states in international politics exist in a similar state of nature.

Holocaust.   Attempt by German Nazis during World War II to eliminate all Jews in which an estimated 5 to 6 million people, primarily Jews but also others, were killed.

Hot line agreement,   1963. Accord between the United States and the Soviet Union to establish a teletype for direct communication between the White House and the Kremlin.

Hussein, Saddam,   1937– . Iraqi political leader and dictator. President and prime minister, 1979– ; joined Ba'ath (Renaissance) Socialist Party, 1956. Initiated war with Iran in 1980, which lasted eight years but ended indecisively. Has pursued active policy of modernization, including acquisition of sophisticated weapons, and expansion of influence in Arab world. Has maintained national unity by suppression of autonomy movements of Kurds in northern part of country and Shi'ite Moslems in south. Ordered invasion of Kuwait in 1990, but troops were expelled by coalition force in 1991.

Implementation Force (IFOR).   A sixty thousand-person armed force established by the Dayton Agreement to enforce the provisions of that pact that provide for the separation of factional armed forces and the establishment of security in Bosnia-Herzegovina.

Industrial Revolution.   Term used to characterize the period since 1750 in which large-scale economic and social changes occurred as a result of the transformation from agriculture and artisanal production to factory production. Sometimes confined to the period 1750–1850.

Inter-American Court of Human Rights.   An international intergovernmental organization, part of the Organization of American states, that rules on cases brought by individuals against their own governments.

Intermediate-range Nuclear Forces (INF) Agreement,   December 1987. Treaty between the Soviet Union and the United States to eliminate all nuclear weapons of an intermediate range (approximately three hundred to three thousand miles) from Europe.

International Atomic Energy Agency (IAEA).   An international body, established by Nuclear Nonproliferation Treaty, to administer safeguards to ensure that no nuclear products are diverted from peaceful to weapons uses.

International Civil Aviation Organization (ICAO). One of the specialized agencies of the United Nations established in 1947 to promote the development and regulation of all aspects of civil aviation around the world. It sets international safety standards and promulgates recommended practices of performance in the air transport and civil aviation fields.

International Court of Justice, 1945– . Principal judicial organ of the United Nations; successor to the Permanent Court of International Justice, 1921–45.

International Monetary Fund (IMF), 1945– . Specialized agency affiliated with United Nations. Works closely with World Bank. It lends funds provided by member states to other countries to stabilize exchange rates. Also provides technical assistance to countries that have difficulty in maintaining conditions conducive to monetary stability.

International Rescue Committee. Nongovernmental international organization, created in 1945, dedicated to relief and refugee work.

Iran-Contra Affairs, 1983–86. Secret policies of American government during the Reagan administration in which arms were sold to Iranian government in exchange for American hostages in Lebanon, despite declarative policy that denied it, and use of the profits to support Nicaraguan contras, despite congressional prohibition of such aid. Also involved arrangements through private arms dealers as well as the government of Israel. Solicitation of funds from private citizens and third governments also took place. Direction of policy undertaken by president's national security adviser and a member of the National Security Council staff seconded from the Marine Corps. Policies ended upon their discovery in late 1986.

Iran-Iraq War, 1980–88. War initiated by Iraq to take over disputed territory, the Shatt-el Arab at the mouth of the Tigris River, and to destroy the Iranian revolution. Although both countries suffered enormous casualties, neither won the war.

Iron curtain. Term employed to describe the division of Europe between East and West after World War II.

Isabel of Castile, 1451–1504. Spanish queen. Her marriage to Ferdinand II of Aragon effectively began the unification of Spain. In their reign, the Spanish expelled the Jews from Spain (1492), conquered Granada (1492), established the Inquisition, and patronized Christopher Columbus' voyages of discovery.

Islam. The youngest of the "world religions," Islam is a faith based on the teachings and the writings of the seventh-century prophet Muhammad, which are contained in the Koran. People who follow Islam are called Muslims and comprise about one-fifth of the world's population. The origins of Islam are Arabic, but the community of Muslims or *umma* is very historically, politically, and socially diverse, for large concentrations of Muslims can be found in North Africa, the Middle East, and South Asia.

Islamic fundamentalism. Term used to characterize a variety of nongovernmental opposition groups in the Arab and Islamic worlds that endorse Muslim principles and oppose secular governments.

Israeli-Arab War, 1948. The first major war, in series of four major military confrontations that constitute a history of Arab-Israeli conflict. The 1948–49 conflict was the Israeli war of independence. Violence broke out almost immediately after Israel proclaimed its independence in May 1948. The fighting ended with an Arab defeat in 1949, and Israel was able to occupy 50 percent more territory than it had actually been granted under the 1947 UN Partition Plan.

Israeli-Egyptian War, October 1973. In an attempt to recover territory lost in the 1967 war against Israel, Egyptian President Anwar Sadat ordered an attack across the Suez Canal. After initial advances in the Sinai Peninsula, Egyptian forces were turned back and surrounded by the Israeli army. However, the United States intervened diplomatically to gain a separation of the two armies, and this led to a series of withdrawals of the Israeli forces. Eventually the step-by-step diplomatic process led to reconciliation between Israel and Egypt. See **Camp David Agreement.**

Jackson-Vanik Amendment. Controversial amendment to the United States Trade Reform Act of 1974, sponsored by Senator Henry Jackson (D-Washington) and Representative Charles Vanik (D-Ohio). It required that the president certify to Congress that free emigration is permitted from the Soviet Union before extending most favored nation status to that country. The Soviet Union rejected its terms on the grounds that the provision amounted to unwarranted interference in Soviet internal affairs. Inasmuch as enhanced trade relations had been intended as a component of the detente between the United States and the Soviet Union, the amendment made relations more difficult.

Japanese-Russian War, 1904–5. Imperial conflict over Manchuria and Korea in which Japan defeated Russia and established its potential as a major power. Russia's defeat was one of the causes of the Russian revolution of 1905.

Johnson, Lyndon B., 1908–73. American political leader and statesman. President, 1963–69; vice-president, 1961–63; senator (D-Texas), 1949–61; majority leader in the Senate, 1955–61; member of the House of Representatives, 1937–46. Johnson supported the New Deal and led in the enactment of the first civil rights in the United States since Reconstruction. As president, he prodded Congress to enact the 1964 Civil Rights Act, the 1965 Voting Act, and a series of antipoverty and welfare programs—including Medicare—which he dubbed the Great Society. However, his domestic achievements were overshadowed by the war that he conducted in Vietnam. Opposition to that war grew until, in 1968, Johnson reversed his escalation policy in Vietnam, which had increased American troops in that country to over 500,000 and which had entailed a massive bombing campaign, and he announced his decision not to run for reelection. His memoirs are entitled *The Vantage Point* (1971).

Just war. A medieval Christian doctrine defining standards under which a war may be considered just: 1) its cause is just; 2) the means used are proportionate to the ends sought; and 3) a distinction is maintained between combatants and noncombatants.

Kant, Immanuel, 1724–1804. German philosopher. Wrote on metaphysics and reason as well as universal morality. With regard to international politics, his *Perpetual Peace* envisioned a commonwealth of republics that would promote international cooperation and ensure peace.

Kennedy, John Fitzgerald, 1917–63. United States statesman and author. President, 1961–63; senator (D-Massachusetts), 1953–60; member of the U.S. House of Representatives, 1947–53. Following World War II in which he served, Kennedy was briefly a journalist. His honors thesis from Harvard was published in 1940 as *Why England Slept,* and he published another book, *Profiles in Courage,* in 1956. As president, his program aimed at economic stimulus and a vigorous pursuit of containment. He built up American armed forces in response to the Berlin crisis and building of the Berlin Wall in 1961. Kennedy authorized an invasion of Cuba in April 1961 by American-trained and -equipped Cuban exiles that failed, and he reinforced the American advisory contingent in Vietnam. Both the Peace Corps, a program that sent Americans to foreign countries to provide low-level assistance, and the Alliance for Progress, a program of economic assistance to Latin America combined with counterinsurgency aid, were Kennedy initiatives. He required the removal of Soviet missiles from Cuba, where installations had been clandestinely built in 1962. In 1963, he promoted a relaxation of tensions with the Soviet Union and accepted limited agreements. He was assassinated in November 1963.

Keynes, John Maynard, 1883–1946. British economist and governmental advisor. His reputation was first gained with his resignation from the British delegation to the Versailles peace conference and publication of *Economic Consequences of the Peace* (1919). His main ideas are expressed in *General Theory of Employment, Interest, and Money* (1936), in which he advocated government intervention in the market, including deficit spending to increase employment and aggregate demand.

KGB (Committee of State Security). Soviet secret police agency; successor to other agencies (GPU, OGPU, NKVD, MVD) that used terror to assist in governing in the Soviet Union.

Khadaffi, Muammar (Gaddafi, Mu'ammar Muhammad al-), 1942– . Libyan military and revolutionary and political leader. President of Libya, 1977– ;

Chairman of Revolutionary Command Council, 1969–77; Commander-in-chief of armed forces, 1969– . Author of three-volume *The Green Book.* Has pursued active foreign policy of intervention in several African states, including Uganda and Chad.

Khmer Rouge. Radical Communist Organization of Cambodia (Kampuchea). Under its leader, Pol Pot, took control of Cambodian government in 1975. Imposed severe program of emptying cities and applying austerity measures to countryside, killing an estimated 1 million Cambodians out of a total population of 7 million. Overthrown by Vietnamese forces in 1979, though continued to be recognized as legitimate Cambodian government at the United Nations. Remained as fighting force and one of three factions contending for power following 1991 agreement for Vietnamese withdrawal and a United Nations-supervised election in 1993.

Khomeini, Ayatollah Ruhollah, 1900–89. Islamic clerical leader and Iranian statesman. A very learned man, Ayatollah Khomeini from exile led the 1979 Iranian revolution that overthrew the shah. As the most prominent clerical leader, he gave spiritual and political guidance to Iranian affairs after the revolution until his death. Engendered hostility of rest of world for endorsing the capture and holding of American hostages for over a year.

Khrushchev, Nikita S., 1894–1971. General secretary of the Communist Party of the Soviet Union, 1954–64. During Stalin's rule, he was an avid and committed Stalinist; however, after Stalin's death in 1953, he became one of the main forces in dismantling and discrediting Stalin's legacy. Khrushchev, in the now famous "Secret Speech" delivered at the Twentieth Congress of the Communist Party in 1956, was the first Soviet leader to denounce Stalin's reign of mass terror, totalitarianism, and the "cult of personality." During Khrushchev's term, the Soviets entered the space race, engaged in bilateral agreements with the United States, and promoted a vision of the USSR as an equal partner in world affairs.

Kim Il-Sung, 1912–94. Reclusive dictator of North Korea from 1945 to 1994. A dedicated communist, Kim Il-Sung maintained close relations with both the Soviet Union and China, but domestically, he was an old-fashioned oriental despot. Over the years, he shunned contact with other countries. He decided on and led the invasion of South Korea in June 1950, and in subsequent years, he pursued hostile policies toward South Korea that included assassinations.

Kissinger, Henry A., 1923– . United States scholar, author, and statesman. Political scientist at Harvard University and consultant before appointment as National Security Council advisor to President Richard M. Nixon in 1969. Secretary of State, 1973–77. Helped plan and negotiate Strategic Arms Limitation Talks; negotiated detente arrangements with the Soviet Union and American opening to China; negotiated the end of the Vietnam War, for which he won the Nobel Peace Prize; and negotiated disengagement of Israeli and Egyptian military forces after the

1973 war. His major books are *A World Restored: Castelreagh, Metternich and the Restoration of Peace, 1812–1822, Nuclear Weapons and Foreign Policy, The Necessity for Choice, White House Years, Years of Upheaval,* and *Diplomacy.*

Kohl, Helmut, 1930– . German statesman and political leader. Chancellor of the Federal Republic Germany since 1982. Since his decisive maneuvering after the fall of the Berlin Wall in 1989, he has achieved successful unification of East and West Germany and has attained the status of chancellor of a united Germany, which he still held in 1996. Kohl has also been a strong advocate of European integration through the mechanisms of the European Union and has been instrumental in strengthening economic and political ties with France.

Koran.   Holy book of Islam and second most popular book in world after the Bible. Provides guidance to Moslems and is a unifying force of Islam.

Korean War, 1950–53. Conflict between North and South Korea and their allies that began with the invasion of South Korea by North Korea. The United States and other countries, acting under auspices of the United Nations, came to the assistance of South Korea to repel the attack. However, in late 1950, the allied armies drove into North Korea, precipitating China's intervention in aid of North Korea. After the opposing forces reached a stalemate near the 38th parallel, which had been the dividing line between the two parts of Korea, a truce was signed in July 1953.

Kremlin.   Walled central section of Moscow that serves as the government and administrative center of Russia and formerly of the Soviet Union.

Kuomintang.   Chinese political party and armed force. Founded in 1912 by Sun Yat-sen, it was dedicated to parliamentary democracy and socialism. After its suppression, it was reorganized in 1922 with Soviet assistance, and after 1928, General Chiang Kai-shek assumed leadership. He purged communists from the party and fought against them even during the war against the Japanese invasion of 1937–45. Following World War II, an all-out civil war led to the success of the Communist revolution, and the Kuomintang fled to Taiwan, where it dominated the government, operating until an emergency decree was lifted in 1991.

Latin America.   Region composed of those countries of the Western Hemisphere in which the dominant language is Spanish or Portuguese. Includes most of South America (except Guyana and Dutch Guiana), most of Central America (except Belize), and Mexico.

League of Nations.   An international organization founded in 1919 by the Treaty of Versailles. It was the direct predecessor of the United Nations and the first permanent association of its kind vested with the responsibility for preserving international peace and security. The U.S. Senate failed to approve the Treaty of Versailles, the agreement in which the League Covenant was imbedded;

and, therefore, the United States never became a member. As outlined in the League Covenant, the organization was supposed to provide for collective security, an arrangement in which each member is protected against foreign aggression by the collective action and combined strength of all the members. However, when the League was confronted with Japanese and Italian aggression in the 1930s, it failed to commit to military intervention or take decisive action. And in the ultimate test, it was unable to prevent the Second World War. The League ceased to function in any sort of security capacity in 1941 and officially disbanded in 1946.

League of Nations Covenant.   The founding document of the League of Nations that was drafted at the Paris Peace Conference in 1919. The main intellectual forces behind the framing were Robert Cecil of Great Britain, Leon Bourgeois of France, and especially President Woodrow Wilson, who first called for a League of Nations in his famous "Fourteen Points" address to Congress. The articles of the covenant outlined such issues as collective security and procedures for resolving international disputes, and introduced the punitive use of economic sanctions as a tool of foreign policy.

Lebanon, invasion by Israel, 1982. Following a civil war that began in 1975, control over territory was lost by the Lebanese government to various armed groups. Israel invaded the southern part of the country to establish a "security zone" to stop attacks against its territory.

Lenin, Vladimir Ilyich, 1870–1924. Russian revolutionary leader of the 1917 Bolshevik takeover of the Russian revolution and ruler of the Soviet Union until his death. He withdrew Russia from participation in the First World War and instituted a communist dictatorship, including the establishment of a secret police, in Russia and founded the Third International to promote revolution throughout the world. Although his regime abolished private property, Lenin adopted a New Economic Policy in 1921 that allowed some private ownership. Before assuming power, Lenin wrote, among other pamphlets, *What Is to Be Done?* (1902), *Imperialism: The Highest Stage of Capitalism* (1916), and *The State and Revolution* (1917).

Liberian civil war, 1989– . Intensive war among several armed factions. The war rendered approximately 70 percent of Liberia's population refugees within the country. An intervention by armed forces sponsored by the Economic Community of West African States failed to bring an end to the fighting until 1995.

List, Friedrich, 1789–1846. A German economist whose most influential work is *The National System of Political Economy* (1841). Stressing productive wealth rather than trade, he advocated protection of industry for lagging countries but free trade in agricultural products.

Locarno Pact, 1925. Conclusion of a conference held by Belgium, Britain, Czechoslovakia, France, Germany, Italy, and Poland that involved a series of treaties of mutual guarantee to uphold the provisions of the 1919 Treaty of Versailles. Germany was promised admission to the League of Nations. When Hitler remilitarized the Rhineland, he denounced the Locarno Pact.

Lomé Convention.   A succession of agreements—the first of which was signed at Lomé, Togo in 1975—reached between the nine members (fifteen in 1995) of the European Community (EC) and the forty-six (sixty-nine in 1995) African, Caribbean, and Pacific (ACP) states, most of which were former colonies of France and Britain. Under the provisions of the Lomé Convention, the EC provides financial and technical assistance and extends preference to ACP products for entry into European markets.

Lon Nol,   1913–1985. Cambodian military officer and statesman. Led overthrow of Prince Norodom Sihanouk during latter's absence from country in 1970. Allowed United States military aerial bombing and ground invasion ancillary to war in Vietnam. Displaced in 1975 by forces of the Khmer Rouge.

Lumumba, Patrice,   1925–61. Political activist and statesman in the Congo (now Zaire). In 1958, Lumumba co-founded and chaired the nationalist party Mouvement National Congolais (MNC). After the Congo achieved independence from Belgium in 1960, Lumumba's MNC party won the national elections, and he was named prime minister. Shortly after the elections, the army mutinied, political order deteriorated, and one province tried to secede from the Congo nation-state. After a struggle among government leaders, Lumumba was imprisoned by Col. Joseph Mobutu and executed on January 17, 1961.

Maastricht Treaty.   See **European Union.**

MacArthur, Douglas,   1880–1964. A United States general who had pivotal roles in World War I, World War II, and the Korean War. In World War I, he commanded the 42nd Division in France, and was subsequently named U.S. Army chief of staff. He retired from active service in 1937 but was recalled in 1941 to serve as commander of the U.S. and allied forces in the Pacific. In this capacity, he accepted the Japanese surrender in 1945. As supreme commander of allied powers, he spent the following five years directing the occupation of Japan. In 1950, when war erupted between North and South Korea, MacArthur was charged with leading the United Nations forces. After openly criticizing U.S. policies regarding China's involvement in the war, he was relieved of his command by President Harry S. Truman in April 1951.

Machiavelli, Niccolò   1469–1527. Italian author and statesman. His *The Prince* and *Discourses* present a modern conception of politics and government.

Maginot Line.   System of fortifications in eastern France designed to protect against a German invasion and named for Andre Maginot, defense minister from 1929 to 1931. The line was not complete in 1940 when Germany attacked France with a flanking movement.

Malvinas/Falklands War,   1982. Conflict between Great Britain and Argentina, precipitated by Argentina's invasion of the Malvinas Islas/Falkland Islands, a dependency of Britain claimed by Argentina. A British expeditionary force recovered control of the islands after a brief naval and ground encounter.

Manchuria crisis.   On September 18, 1931, the Japanese occupied the Manchurian city of Mukden. This incident was only the first of many Japanese offensives in its drive to control all of Manchuria. In 1932, Japan created a puppet government in so-called Manchukuo. The Japanese invasion was one of the League of Nations' first tests of whether it would be able to manage international conflicts. A special commission of the League handed down the decision that Manchuria was still rightfully Chinese territory; Japan withdrew from the League in protest. Japan continued its occupation of Manchuria until its defeat in World War II.

Mandates system.   Arrangement under League of Nations, 1919–46, providing for the temporary transfer to respective victors in World War I of dependent territories taken from losers, with the obligation, under international supervision, to prepare the territories for independence. Succeeded by trusteeship system under United Nations.

Mandela, Nelson,   1918– . South African political leader and statesman. A prominent leader of the **African National Congress (ANC),** Mandela was imprisoned from 1964 to 1990. At the time of his release, the government ban on the ANC was lifted, and Mandela entered into negotiations with South African President **DeKlerk** to dismantle the **apartheid** system and to write a new constitution. In the first election in South Africa with universal suffrage in 1994, Mandela was elected president.

Manhattan Project,   1942–45. The United States program, under the direction of Army Gen. Leslie R. Groves and involving large numbers of American and expatriate European scientists, to develop an atomic bomb.

Mao Zedong (Mao Tse-tung),   1893–1976. Chinese Communist ideological and military leader and dictator. He was a founder of the Chinese Communist Party in 1921 and after 1927 led a long guerrilla war against the Kuomintang (Nationalist) government that continued even while both fought against the Japanese invasion, 1937–45, and afterwards. With the Communist triumph in 1949, Mao became the head of the new government. In 1958, he launched the Great Leap Forward, a disastrous economic reform program, and from 1966 to 1969 promoted the Cultural Revolution, a period of great social agitation in which universities were closed and ideological conformity was induced by requiring professionals to work at farm labor and attend "reeducation" sessions that required their confessions of wrongdoing. Under Mao's leadership, China broke with the Soviet Union in the late 1950s and early 1960s. Domestic moderation and detente with the United States were introduced after 1971.

Marshall Plan,   1948–52. Officially called the European Recovery Program, an undertaking by the United States to promote economic growth in Europe after World War II. The program provided that the European countries would determine their needs and the United States would transfer funds to the participating states. With its rejection by the Soviet Union and the Eastern European countries, the Marshall Plan provided assistance only to the Western European countries and Austria.

Marx, Karl, 1818–83. German intellectual and revolutionary. One of the most influential political philosophers and social theorists of the nineteenth and twentieth centuries, around whose work a doctrine was created and an entire movement and worldview was born. His most important work is *Capital*, a thorough critical analysis of capitalism.

McKinley, William, 1843–1901. American president, 1896–1901. During his presidency, the United States acquired Cuba, Puerto Rico, Guam, and the Philippines after the Spanish-American War in 1898. He also was responsible for annexing Hawaii in 1898 and acquiring Wake Island and Samoa in 1899. He was assassinated in 1901.

McNamara, Robert S. 1916–. Secretary of defense in the Kennedy and Johnson administrations and active in decision making during the Cuban missile crisis in 1962 and in the Vietnam War. As president of the World Bank (1968–81), he undertook to reassess the institution's development strategy and make the reduction of poverty and inequality its chief objectives.

Mexican-American War, 1846–48. War between the United States and Mexico following annexation of Texas by the former. By its victory, the United States acquired 40 percent of Mexican territory, including California, which had been an object of policy.

Middle Ages. The period of European history from the fall of the western Roman Empire in about 395 a.d. to the period marked as the Renaissance, which is traced to the beginning of the thirteenth, fourteenth or even fifteenth century, depending on what part of Europe is being looked at.

Milosevic, Slobodan, 1941– . Yugoslav and Serbian political leader. As president of Serbia when Yugoslavia began disintegrating in the late 1980s and early 1990s, Milosevic advocated a program of ethnic nationalism. He backed Bosnian Serbs in their war against the Bosnian government; and he negotiated the **Dayton Agreement** on their behalf.

Missile Technology Control Regime (MTCR), 1987. Agreement by Britain, Canada, France, Germany, Italy, Japan, and United States not to transfer technology associated with missiles used to carry weapons of mass destruction to other countries. Later expanded to twenty-five countries; China, Israel, Romania, and Russia have agreed to follow MTCR rules but not join.

Mobutu Sese Seko, 1930– . African political and military leader. President of Zaire, 1967– . Led a military coup against the central government of the Congo in 1960; staged another coup in 1965 and assumed office of prime minister in 1966. In 1967, changed government to presidential type and renamed country. A repressive and self-enriching ruler, Mobutu allied with the United States in helping UNITA in the Angolan civil war.

MPLA (Popular Movement for the Liberation of Angola). A Marxist party that formed the government of Angola during the long civil war between 1974 and 1991.

Muhammad (the Prophet), d. 632 C.E. The prophet whose direct message from God is contained in the Koran, the holy book of the Islamic faith.

Multilateral force (MLF). A scheme proposed in the early 1960s in which crews drawn from several NATO countries would serve together on ships armed with nuclear weapons. It was designed to satisfy a presumed German longing for access to nuclear weapons. Dropped in 1964.

Munich Agreement, September 1938. A summit meeting among Prime Minister Neville Chamberlain of Great Britain, Prime Minister Edouard Daladier of France, and Chancellor Adolf Hitler of Germany, in which the first two acceded to Hitler's demand to annex the Sudetenland, a portion of Czechoslovakia inhabited mostly by German speakers.

Napoleon Bonaparte, 1769–1821. French general and emperor of France from 1804 to 1815. He was an autocratic ruler who ascended to power in a military coup in 1799 due to the political confusion and ideological disarray that reigned in France after the French Revolution. He proclaimed himself emperor of France in 1804 and undertook a military campaign to conquer all of Europe. He ruled until a coalition of conservative European powers overthrew him in 1814. In 1815, he returned to battle but was defeated and exiled to St. Helena Island, where he died.

Napoleonic Wars. A series of military campaigns that Napoleon Bonaparte launched in the early 1800s in his attempt to conquer all of Europe. He defeated the Austrians in 1800 and declared war on Britain in 1803. His most famous victory was the Battle of Austerlitz in 1805 against Austria and Russia. From that time on, he was able to consolidate most of Europe into his empire by 1810. The beginning of the end for Napoleon was his invasion of Russia in 1812, which ended in disaster. This defeat heartened the rest of the European powers and caused them to join forces. Consequently, he was forced into exile in 1814. However, in 1815, he returned to France only to engage in the Battle of Waterloo, which marked his conclusive defeat.

National Endowment for Democracy. A United States government agency established in the Reagan administration to administer funds and technical assistance to groups in other countries who were working on behalf of democratic elections.

National Security Council (NSC). United States government institution created in 1947 to advise the president on national security affairs. Members include the president, the vice-president, the secretary of state, and the secretary of defense. The chairman of the Joint Chiefs of Staff is an advisor, and the NSC is served by a staff headed by a national security advisor.

Nazi Germany, 1933–45. Germany under the National Socialist Workers Party (Nazi) regime of Adolf Hitler. The Nazis achieved economic recovery from the Great Depression but ruled by repression and secret police. They promoted an extremely radical nationalist and racist ideology that led to the Holocaust, in which were killed up to 6 million Jews as well as other people considered by the Nazis to be undesirable.

New Economic Policy (NEP), 1921–29. A program initiated by Lenin at the Tenth Russian Communist Party Congress in 1921 in response to civil war. State control over many aspects of the economy was relaxed and private activity was tolerated temporarily, although socialism as a goal was never abandoned.

New International Economic Order (NIEO). A package of political and economic demands adopted at a special session of the United Nations General Assembly on May 1, 1974. It was devised by the Group of 77 in an attempt to counter what it viewed as the negative impact of the prosperity of the industrialized nations on the developing world.

Nicaraguan contras. Armed opposition to the Sandinista government (1979–90) in Nicaragua. The contras fought primarily in northern Nicaragua, but one component was based for a time in Costa Rica, operating in the south. Supplied and trained by the United States, contra forces and their dependents resided mostly in Honduras. Leaders and fighters were drawn from two sources: former National Guard members who had fled the revolution and peasants and farmers who opposed Sandinista policies. According to terms of the Esquipulas II agreements, the contras were to have been resettled in their country, and some were. However, tensions continued even after the end of the war between the Sandinistas and the contras.

Nietzsche, Friedrich, 1844–1900. German political philosopher and social critic. Nietzsche rejected any notion of a universal moral law and celebrated egoism and man's responsibility to himself as master of his own existence.

Nixon, Richard M., 1913–94. American statesman and author. President, 1969–74; vice-president, 1953–61; senator (R-California), 1951–52; member of the U.S. House of Representatives, 1947–51. As president, Nixon reduced American involvement in the Vietnam War and negotiated a peace agreement that was concluded in January 1973; he also pursued a policy of **detente** with the Soviet Union, concluding the **Salt I** treaty and the **ABM treaty,** and opened relations with China, which had been severed at the time of the **Korean War.** In 1971, Nixon took the United States off the gold standard, ending the **Bretton Woods** monetary arrangements that had

governed post-World War II international trading relations. After a series of revelations of corruption and misuse of power that led to the House of Representatives passing articles of impeachment, Nixon resigned from office in August 1974, the only president to do so. Shortly after his resignation, his successor, **Gerald Ford,** issued a pardon for any crimes Nixon may have committed while serving as president. Although he faced immediate disgrace, Nixon engaged in a long-term rehabilitation of his reputation through writing. At the time of his death, he was regarded as a highly intelligent and insightful thinker concerning international affairs. His books include *Six Crises* (1962), *The Memoirs of Richard Nixon* (1978), *Real War* (1980), *Real Peace* (1984), *No More Vietnams* (1985), *1999: Victory Without War* (1988), *In the Arena: A Memoir of Victory, Defeat, and Renewal* (1990), and *Seize the Moment: America's Challenge in a One-Superpower World* (1992).

Nonproliferation Treaty, 1967. Taking effect in 1970, a twenty-five-year, multilateral agreement designed to control the spread of nuclear weapons. Signatories fell into two classes: nuclear powers, which agreed not to transfer their weapons or technology to nonnuclear states; and nonnuclear states, which agreed neither to develop nuclear weapons nor to accept their transfer from other countries. In 1995, the treaty was renewed for an indefinite period.

Noriega, Manuel Antonio, 1938– . Military leader and dictator of Panama. As commander of the Panamanian Defense Forces, Noriega governed Panama from 1983 to 1989, when the United States invaded to arrest him on drug trafficking charges. In 1992, he was convicted and began to serve a sentence in a U.S. prison.

North American Free Trade Association (NAFTA). A treaty creating a common market among Canada, Mexico, and the United States that came into effect in 1994. Negotiations with Chile that began in May 1995 embodied the envisioned possibility of expanding membership.

North Atlantic Cooperation Council. See **North Atlantic Treaty Organization.**

North Atlantic Treaty Organization (NATO) 1949– . An alliance that grew out of earlier European defense alliances, particularly the Brussels Pact. It brought together into a defense alliance two North American countries—the United States and Canada; a North Atlantic country—Iceland; and nine European states—Britain, France, Italy, Belgium, Netherlands, Luxembourg, Denmark, Norway, and Portugal. In 1952, Greece and Turkey joined, and in 1955, West Germany was admitted. In addition to its conventional alliance characteristics, NATO included an integrated command structure in which military leaders from various countries served together and in which troops were deployed in allied countries during peacetime. In the post-Cold-War period, NATO initiated a program called Partnership for Peace, which was designed to allow former Warsaw Pact members limited affiliation with the alliance but with a view that they would eventually be eligible for full membership. In the interim, the Eastern European countries observed NATO meetings and gained access to some NATO operations through an arrangement called the North Atlantic Cooperation Council.

Nunn, Sam, 1938– . United States senator (D-Georgia), 1973–97. Specialist in military affairs.

Operation Mongoose. A covert operation during the Kennedy administration by the Central Intelligence Agency to assassinate Cuban dictator Fidel Castro.

Organization of American States (OAS). A regional organization created in 1948 to promote multilateral cooperation among most Western Hemisphere states. Canada refrained from joining until the end of the Cold War. The primary aims of the OAS have been to encourage cooperation in economic and security concerns, as well as the promotion of democracy and the protection of human rights.

Organization of African Unity (OAU). A regional organization founded in 1963, designed to promote solidarity and cooperation among the fifty-one independent African countries it represents. One of the original intentions of the OAU was to help maintain and defend the territorial integrity and sovereignty of the postcolonial African state system and to find African solutions to the continent's problems, excluding former colonial countries.

Organization of Petroleum Exporting Countries (OPEC). An association of countries from the Middle East (Iran, Iraq, Kuwait, Qatar, Saudi Arabia, United Arab Emirates), Africa (Algeria, Gabon, Libya, Nigeria), Latin America (Ecuador, Venezuela), and Asia (Indonesia) formed in 1960 that became very influential in the early 1970s when members raised oil prices fivefold and nationalized production facilities. The price increases resulted in the transfer of dollars to the member countries and contributed to the ensuing debt crisis of the 1980s as oil importers borrowed to finance purchases of oil. With new petroleum supplies brought into production, OPEC's influence over the supply and price of oil declined in the late 1980s.

Organization of Security and Cooperation in Europe (OSCE) Intergovernmental organization of fifty European countries as well as Canada and the United States; successor after the Cold War to the Conference on Security and Cooperation in Europe, which had been established as a mechanism for NATO and Warsaw Treaty countries to discuss the matters that eventuated in the **Helsinki Final Act** of 1975. The OSCE continued to provide a means for communicating among the Western European countries, the Eastern European countries, and the successor republics of the Soviet Union.

Ottoman Empire, thirteenth century to 1918. Extensive realm founded by the Ottoman Turks. Based upon Turkey, it extended to Hungary, parts of modern Romania and Iran, and Arabia, Greece, Bosnia, Herzegovina, and northern Africa.

Owen, Lord David, 1938– . British statesman. Leader of the Social Democratic Party, 1983–87; foreign minister, 1977–79. Representative of the European Union to the joint EU-UN negotiating team that attempted to bring an end to the war in Bosnia after 1992.

Oxfam. An international nongovernmental relief organization, the Oxford Committee for Famine Relief (Oxfam) was founded in 1942 and is committed to alleviating poverty, particularly in the developing world.

Palestine Liberation Organization (PLO). Coordinating organization of Palestinian guerrilla groups, founded at first Arab summit meeting in 1964. Dominated by Al Fatah, the largest group, it has been led since 1968 by Yasir Arafat. Following a period of decline after its expulsion from Lebanon in 1982, the PLO assumed, first, the position of negotiating partner with Israel and, second, the authority to administer the Israel-occupied West Bank. The negotiations between the Israeli government and the Palestinian Authority were expected to lead eventually to a Palestinian state.

Panama Canal Treaties, 1979. Treaties between the United States and Panama providing for the assumption of control of the Panama Canal by Panama at the end of 1999 and for the complete withdrawal of American military forces from the Panama Canal Zone.

Panama Canal Zone. An area within Panama extending five miles on either side of the Panama Canal, established by a 1903 treaty between Panama and the United States, and administered by the United States. Following the 1979 treaties between the two countries, jurisdiction over the zone reverted to Panama, and a separate zone has ceased to exist.

Parti Quebecois (PQ). A Canadian political party that was founded in 1968 by René Levesque and other French-Canadians supporting the separation of Quebec from Canada. The PQ won the 1976 Quebec election and initiated but lost a 1980 referendum on whether the province should negotiate a new federal relationship with the rest of Canada. On October 30, 1995, another referendum, calling for Quebec to form an independent French-speaking country, was defeated by a little more than 1 percent of the vote.

Partial Nuclear Test Ban Treaty, 1963. Treaty entered into by Britain, the United States, and the Soviet Union, open to other signatories, that prohibited the testing of nuclear weapons in all environments except underground.

Partnership for Peace. See **North Atlantic Treaty Organization.**

Pearson, Lester B., 1897–1972. Canadian diplomat, statesman, and author. Prime minister, 1963–68. After serving as Canada's senior advisor at the founding of the United Nations, he was Canadian delegate to the United Nations. From 1947 to 1958, he served as minister of External Affairs and won the 1957 Nobel Peace Prize for his contribution to the establishment of the United Nations peacekeeping operations. His most important books are *Democracy in World Politics, Diplomacy in the Nuclear Age,* and *Memoirs* (three volumes).

Permanent Mandates Commission.   Agency established by the League of Nations Covenant to oversee the administration of nonself-governing territories by states given responsibility for preparing them for independence. The territories in question had been taken from the losers in World War I, and the administering powers were the victors. Although the Permanent Mandates Commission had only minimal powers, its establishment marked an important departure from historical practice in which at the end of wars dependent territories were simply transferred from the losers to the victors.

Philippines, annexation of.   Despite having fought a war of independence against Spain and declared a republic, the Philippines was transferred from Spain to the United States by the 1898 Treaty of Paris ending the Spanish-American War. Beginning in February 1899, the Filipinos, under the leadership of Emilio Aguinaldo, revolted against United States rule, but the United States fought a counterguerrilla war until it conquered the Philippines in 1901.

Picasso, Pablo,   1881–1973. Spanish painter, sculptor, and graphic artist. Following the aerial bombing of the town of Guernica in 1937 by fascist forces, he made *Guernica,* an allegorical, antifascist, antiwar painting. He ordered that it should hang in New York in the Museum of Modern Art until democracy was restored in Spain. It now resides in Madrid in the Prado Museum.

Plato,   427?–347 b.c. Greek philosopher. He developed a comprehensive philosophy based on an idea of the good. His quest for justice included his concept of an ideal state, presented in the *Republic.*

Pol Pot (born Saloth Sar),   1925– . Dictator and leader of the Khmer Rouge guerrilla forces in Cambodia, which he re-named Kampuchea. During Pol Pot's period as prime minister from 1976 to 1979, an estimated 1 to 3 million people died as a result of forced labor, starvation, disease, torture, or execution resulting from his policies, which included mass evacuations of cities. He was deposed in 1979 by a Vietnamese invasion but continued to lead the Khmer Rouge.

Population Conference,   1994. Intergovernmental conference held under auspices of the United Nations in Cairo, Egypt.

Powell, Colin,   1937– . American soldier. Chairman of the Joint Chiefs of Staff during the 1990–91 Gulf War.

Prague Spring.   Brief period in Czechoslovakia under the leadership of Alexander Dubchek in 1968 when the Communist Party and others sought to liberalize the regime and present "Communism with a human face." The period was brought to an end in August when

Warsaw Pact troops occupied the country and installed a government willing to comply with communist orthodoxy as stipulated by the Soviet Union.

Prebisch, Raúl,   1901–86. Argentinean economist and diplomat who was the executive secretary for the Economic Commission for Latin America (ECLA) from 1950 to 1962 and the first director of the United Nations Conference on Trade and Development (UNCTAD) from 1964 to 1969. Prebisch essentially founded the school of structural development economics and was the first to apply a non-Marxist variant of dependency theory to explain the relationship between the industrialized and developing nations.

Quadruple Alliance,   1814. Alliance of Austria, Britain, Prussia, and Russia against Napoleon; renewed in 1815 to enforce the terms of the 1815 Treaty of Paris.

Reagan, Ronald,   1911– . American film actor and political leader. President, 1981–89; governor of California, 1967–74. Promoted a large arms buildup, including the Strategic Defense Initiative (or Star Wars), which was financed by foreign borrowing. Signed important arms reduction agreements with the Soviet Union.

Reagan Doctrine.   Policy followed during the administration of United States President Ronald Reagan (1981–89) that aimed at the overthrow of Marxist governments; applied particularly to Nicaragua and Afghanistan.

Red Army Faction.   A German leftist terrorist group that emerged during the student protest movement in the late 1960s and claimed to be agitating for a world revolution to overthrow the capitalist state. In 1990, after the fall of the Berlin Wall, it was uncovered that the group was under the command of the East German communist government.

Renaissance,   fourteenth to seventeenth centuries. Rich development of Western civilization in the transition in Europe from the Middle Ages to the modern era in which the classical traditions of art and learning were renewed.

Renan, Ernest,   1823–92. French philosopher and historian. He was one of the leading minds in the school of critical philosophy in France. His most famous works were contained in a series entitled *Histoire des origines du christianisme* (*History of the Origins of Christianity*). Provided a widely used definition of nationalism.

Reykjavik Summit,   1987. Second meeting between Soviet leader Mikhail Gorbachev and United States President Ronald Reagan, held in Iceland. Although no agreements were reached, the meeting moved forward Gorbachev's "peace agenda," with both sides offering deep reductions in nuclear weapons.

Rhineland occupation,   1936. Militarization of the Rhineland region of Germany by Nazi Germany in violation of the Versailles Treaty and the Locarno Pact. The region had been occupied by French forces until 1930.

Ricardo, David, 1772–1823. British economist and statesman whose main contribution to the discipline of international political economy was his theory of comparative advantage, which lays the groundwork for the liberal market model of the international system.

Roman Catholic Church. A religious and political institution that has taken an active role in the world affairs for two thousand years. The headquarters of the Roman Catholic Church are in Vatican City, which is situated in Rome, Italy, but became an independent city-state in 1929. The temporal leader of the Vatican City and the Roman Catholic Church is the pope. As moral leaders of the considerable number of Catholics that live mainly in the Western Hemisphere and Europe, popes have been aggressive in addressing major social issues. A pope exerts influence by direct communication with church members and clergy and by diplomatic contacts with governments.

Roosevelt, Franklin Delano, 1882–1945. Statesman and political leader during the United States' two greatest crises of the twentieth century: the Great Depression and World War II. After serving as assistant secretary of the Navy from 1913 to 1920, he ran unsuccessfully as the Democratic vice-presidential candidate in the 1920 election. Although stricken and crippled by polio in 1921, he remained active in politics and was elected governor of New York State in 1928. Elected president in 1933, he vigorously promoted measures to combat the Depression and later pushed through social welfare legislation known as the New Deal. As war broke out in Europe, he won an unprecedented third term and went on to forge an alliance with Great Britain. After the United States entered the war in 1941, Roosevelt, together with Prime Minister Winston Churchill of Great Britain and Generalissimo Josef Stalin of the Soviet Union, led the Grand Alliance to victory. Roosevelt died in 1945, shortly before the end of the war in Europe.

Rousseau, Jean-Jacques, 1712–78. Swiss-French philosopher. Premised on a belief in the innate goodness of human beings, advocated education and freedom but the submission of the individual to the general will, which is what rational citizens would select for the common good.

Russian revolution, 1917. Violent upheaval, following decades of unrest, that overthrew the Czar in Russia in February and established a provisional government. In October, the provisional government headed by Kerensky was overthrown by the Bolsheviks under Lenin. From 1918 to 1920, the Whites, a coalition of anticommunist forces, fought a civil war against the Reds, the Bolshevik, or Communist, regime. Foreign intervention complicated the task of the government, which eventually won and formed the Soviet regime.

Rwanda genocide, 1994. In a rampage urged on by the government through radio broadcasts, between April and July 1994, an estimated 500,000 people were killed by Hutu soldiers and others, while some 2 million others fled to neighboring countries. Those designated to be killed were primarily identified as members of the Tutsi, although some Hutu who had collaborated with a previous Tutsi government also were slain.

Safe haven. Designation given to several urban enclaves in Bosnia in 1992 when the United Nations introduced UNPROFOR troops into the country to deliver food and humanitarian assistance during the civil war that raged from 1992 to 1995. The towns and cities were Gorazde, Mostar, Sarajevo, Srebrenica, Tuzla, and the Bihac enclave.

Sadat, Anwar al-, 1918–81. Egyptian statesman. After serving in various governmental positions, he was named vice-president in 1969 and then succeeded Gamal Nasser as president of Egypt from 1970 to 1981. He led the war against Israel in 1973, but he also took the initiative to make peace with that country and negotiated and signed the Camp David Accords of 1979. Sadat shared the Nobel Peace Prize with Israeli Prime Minister Menachem Begin in 1978 as a result of the negotiation and signing in 1978 of the Camp David Agreement. Because of his decision to make peace with Israel, he was accused by Muslims of betraying the Palestinians and the entire Arab world. This factor, in addition to continued economic difficulties at home, prepared the way for his assassination by an Islamic fundamentalist in 1981.

Salinas de Gortari, Carlos, 1948– . Mexican economist and statesman. President, 1988–94. Continued economic liberalization policies of President de la Madrid and negotiated the North American Free Trade Agreement with the United States and Canada.

Sandinista National Liberation Front (FSLN). Nicaraguan political and military organization that fought against the Somoza dictatorship, leading the effort to overthrow it in 1979. Formed a coalition government but remained in power after other groups left the coalition in 1981. Promoted a program of literacy, extensive land reform including collectivization, and a mixed socialist-capitalist economy. Organized society through neighborhood associations and labor unions affiliated with the FSLN. Fought war against United States-sponsored contras and withstood economic sanctions and intimidation by the United States. After its defeat in the 1990 elections, the FSLN formed the major opposition party in the legislature and retained leadership of the armed forces.

Sandino, Augusto, 1895–1934. Nicaragua political leader. Actively resisted United States intervention in Nicaragua through guerrilla action. Never captured, he returned to Managua after the American withdrawal of its Marines in 1933 but was executed on the orders of National Guard leader Anastasio Somoza. The Sandinista National Liberation Front, founded in 1960 and ruling the country from 1979 to 1990, was named after him.

Schlieffen Plan. Plan developed by Field Marshall Alfred Graf von Schlieffen when he was chief of the German general staff (1893–1905), which aimed at solving the problem of fighting a war on two fronts by attacking France and then turning toward Russia. Partly implemented in World War I; a modified plan was used in World War II to defeat France.

Second (Socialist) International. International coalition of socialist parties formed in the 1870s. With the attainment of better working conditions in many countries, the socialists divided on whether to engage in revolution or seek to reform capitalist societies. They also divided on whether to fight wars as part of national armies or to give precedence to class solidarity across nation-state boundaries and refuse to fight, an issue settled in 1914 when the working classes of each state participated in World War I as fighters in their respective armies.

Shah of Iran. Ruler of Pahlevi dynasty, 1925–79. By a coup in 1921, an army officer established a military dictatorship but was elected in 1925 as hereditary shah. He abdicated in 1941 in favor of his son, Muhammad Reza Shah Pahlevi. After fleeing Iran in a crisis in 1953, the shah was restored to his throne with the help of the American Central Intelligence Agency. Using his country's oil wealth, he attempted to modernize Iran, including acquiring modern arms from the United States. As a result of a revolution led by the exiled Ayatollah Ruhollah Khomeini, the shah was forced again to leave his country, this time permanently, in January 1979.

Shi'ite. A sect of Islam that split from the main Sunni branch in the seventh century. Militancy, righteous rebellion, and martyrdom for the purity of Islam are central to the Shi'ite faith. Shi'ites constitute only a tenth of the world's Muslim population, and because of their minority status and theological divergence, they have been persecuted in many predominantly Sunni states such as Iraq and Saudi Arabia. Iran is the only country in which Shi'ites comprise the majority, which has enabled them to control the government and create a religious state that conforms to their interpretation of Islam.

Sihanouk, Prince Norodom, 1922– . Cambodian statesman. Has served in capacities ranging from king to prime minister, but has also spent years in exile. After breaking relations with the United States in 1965 over Cambodian casualties resulting from United States and North Vietnamese incursions, he was overthrown by a military coup led by Lon Nol. After spending some years in exile in China, he returned to Cambodia during the rule of the Khmer Rouge, although during part of that time he was under arrest. In 1990, a peace was negotiated among warring factions, and Sihanouk returned to Cambodia in 1991 as president of a transitional Supreme National Council and head of a tenuous coalition government of previously warring Cambodian factions.

Sinai. Peninsula in Egypt linking Asia and Africa. Scene of fighting in Egyptian-Israeli wars in 1956, 1967, and 1973. Israel captured and withdrew from the Sinai in the 1956 war but occupied it in the 1967 war. Egypt gained then lost territory there in the 1973 war and recovered only part through negotiations in 1974. The entire peninsula was restored to Egypt in 1982 under terms of the peace treaty with Israel.

Single European Act. See **European Union.**

Six-Day War, June 5–10, 1967. War between Israel and several Arab states—Egypt, Syria, and Jordan. Egypt required the withdrawal of UNEF forces from its frontier with Israel, mobilized its army, and closed the Gulf of Aqaba to Israeli shipping. Israel serially attacked Egypt and gained control of the Sinai Peninsula, then Jordan from whom it gained control of East Jerusalem and the West Bank, and Syria from whom it captured the Golan Heights. East Jerusalem was annexed by Israel, but the Sinai Peninsula was returned to Egypt in 1982 under terms of an Egyptian-Israeli peace treaty. Steps toward the establishment of a Palestinian state on the West Bank were taken in 1994 and 1995 with the establishment of an agreement for turning over administration of the territory to the Palestinian Authority. Eventual return of the Golan Heights to Syria was expected by all parties, though negotiations between Syria and Israel proved painstaking and slow.

Skybolt affair, 1962. Cancellation of an airplane-launched missile project by the United States and reaction of the British government, which had planned to obtain and install the missiles on its aircraft fleet. One of the consequences of the affair was French President Charles De Gaulle's veto of the British application to the European Common Market.

Smith, Adam, 1723–90. Scottish philosopher and economist whose most influential work, entitled *The Wealth of Nations* (1776), challenged the mercantilist conception of the international economy that was dominant prior to the Industrial Revolution. Smith advanced a theory that contended that optimal and efficient allocation of resources could only occur under conditions of free competition with minimal government interference.

Smith, Ian, 1919– . Prime minister of Rhodesia (now Zimbabwe) who unilaterally declared independence from British colonial rule in 1965. Smith was the leader of the primarily white government, which refused to concede to an eventual black majority rule.

Social Darwinism. Popular ideology in the late nineteenth century derived from the theories of Herbert Spencer that held that the superiority of the white race gave sanction to European and American imperialism in Africa and Asia.

Socialism in one country. Policy under Josef Stalin in which the building of a strong socialist state in the Soviet Union was given preference over the fomenting of revolutionary activity abroad. Differences over these preferences formed part of the contest for leadership as Lenin's successor between Stalin and Leon Trotsky.

Solidarity. A broadly based union in Poland that grew out of negotiations between the government and striking shipyard workers in Gdansk in 1980. Under the leadership of Lech Walesa, the union grew to a membership of 10 million and had the support of the majority of Poland's 35 million people. Gaining the right to strike, the movement effectively challenged the legitimacy of the Communist regime, which ruled in the name of the workers. Finally, in December 1981, the government headed by Gen. Wojciech Jaruzelski arrested the leaders of Solidarity and declared martial law. With the decline of Communist rule in Eastern Europe in 1989, however, Solidarity was legalized, and elections were held in which the union was allowed to hold only a limited number of seats. To assuage opinion, a new upper house of the legislature was created, with open, democratic elections in which Solidarity gained ninety-nine of one hundred seats.

Somoza Debayle, Anastasio, 1925–80. Younger son of Nicaraguan dictator Anastasio Somoza, he became head of the National Guard in 1966 and served in that capacity until his overthrow in 1979. Served as president from 1967 to 1972 and after 1974 but continued to rule through his military position. Responded ineffectively to the 1972 Managua earthquake and dealt with both demands for reform and revolution only by repression.

South African War, 1899–1902. War between the South African Republic and the Orange Free State against Britain that included both conventional battles and guerrilla warfare. The war ended, after intense fighting and heavy losses, by a negotiation in which the South Africans accepted British sovereignty in exchange for self-government.

Southeast Asia Treaty Organization (SEATO), 1954–77. Alliance of Australia, France, Great Britain, New Zealand, Pakistan, the Philippines, Thailand, and United States to oppose spread of communism following the French defeat in Indochina in 1954. Under a protocol to the Defense Treaty, Cambodia, Laos, and South Vietnam were eligible, after consultations, for protection by the parties. The United States partly justified its war in Vietnam from 1961 to 1973 on this instrument.

Southwest Africa. Former German colony entrusted to South Africa under the League of Nations mandates system. After long resistance by South Africa, achieved independence as state of Namibia in 1991.

Southwest Africa People's Organization (SWAPO). Political and military organization that fought a guerrilla war for independence of Southwest Africa (Namibia) from South Africa. Under a negotiated settlement, UN-supervised elections were held in 1989, with SWAPO forming the largest party in the government of the newly independent state.

Soviet Union, 1922–91. Union of Soviet Socialist Republics (USSR), successor of the Russian empire, which ended in 1917. A federal state of many nationalities that united Russia, Ukraine, Byelorussia, Kazakhstan, and eleven other republics. Following an industrialization program that began in 1928 and grew in World War II (1940–45), the Soviet Union rose to become one of the world's two superpowers. A long period of economic decline and a shorter period of political and economic reform, with an unsuccessful coup d'etat in August 1991, led to its disintegration into fifteen successor states in December 1991.

Stalin, Josef, 1879–1953. The leader of the Soviet Union from the time of Lenin's death in 1924 to his own death in 1953. His reign included a period of forced industrialization and the Second World War. Stalin was a proponent of **socialism in one country,** as opposed to Trotsky's vision of internationalism. Stalin pursued a course of rapid industrialization with a series of five-year plans. To support industrialization, Stalin forcibly collectivized individual farms. As a brutal dictator, Stalin purged other leaders in the party and the military. An estimated 60 million people died in Stalin purges and collectivization programs.

Star Wars. See **Strategic Defense Initiative (SDI).**

Stockholm Conference, 1972. United Nations Conference on the Human Environment. As a result of Third World pressures, the conference gave as much emphasis to development as to environment. The conference recommended the establishment of a United Nations Environment Program, which was created by the UN General Assembly in 1973, with headquarters in Nairobi, Kenya, the first UN agency headquarters to be located in a developing country.

Stoltenberg, Thorvald, 1931– . Norwegian political leader and diplomat. United Nations High Commissioner for Refugees, 1989–90; minister of foreign affairs, 1987–89; minister of defense, 1979–81. United Nations representative involved in negotiations concerning the Bosnian crisis.

Strategic Arms Limitation (SALT) Treaty I, 1972. Treaty between the United States and the Soviet Union that imposed temporary limits on the number of missiles that each deployed.

Strategic Arms Reduction Treaty (START). Result of talks between the United States and the Soviet Union, begun in 1982, to reduce strategic nuclear arsenals. In 1991, START I was signed, providing for reduction in the total number of strategic warheads from over twenty-three thousand to about fifteen thousand by 1999. A second treaty, START II, was signed in 1993 by the United States and Russia to reduce warheads further by 2003 to approximately sixty-five hundred.

Strategic Defense Initiative (SDI). A research undertaking begun in 1983 by the United States to develop a partly space-based means to protect the country against intercontinental missile attack. The program was sometimes referred to as Star Wars.

Sudetenland. German-speaking region of Czechoslovakia, which was annexed by Germany under terms of Munich Agreement.

Suez Canal. A canal built by the British and the French in the nineteenth century on Egyptian territory.

The canal provided an extremely important trade route for Britain. In July 1956, President Gamal Nasser of Egypt nationalized the Suez Canal, prompting the **Suez crisis.**

Suez crisis, 1956. Invasion of Egypt in October 1956 by Israel, Britain, and France, which ended in their withdrawal by early 1957 under auspices of the United Nations, which created it first peacekeeping force to monitor the separation of Egyptian and Israeli forces. Following the withdrawal in July by the United States of promised support for building the Aswan dam, an irrigation project necessary to Egypt's economic development, President Gamal Nasser nationalized the Suez Canal, which had been owned by a British-French consortium. The invaders sought to regain control of the canal and overthrow Nasser, but their action was opposed by the United States and other countries.

Sunni. The orthodox Islamic majority sect. Most Arab states have a majority Sunni population.

Super 301. A provision of the United States 1988 Trade Act that empowers the trade representative to identify the countries that have the most prohibitive trade practices and to initiate retaliatory measures in an effort to eliminate the barriers. Super 301 requires an executive order. Although the original provision lapsed in 1990, President Bill Clinton revived the law in April 1993. The law has been directed primarily at Japan, which maintains a substantial trade surplus with the United States.

Taiwan Straits crises, 1955, 1958. Episodes in which China bombarded the offshore islands of Quemoy and Matsu, which were defended by the Chinese Nationalists controlling Taiwan. The crises presented challenges to the United States, which had pledged in a 1954 treaty to defend Taiwan. President Dwight D. Eisenhower indicated that he would defend the islands if an attack on them formed part of an assault on Taiwan itself. The 1958 crisis presented a challenge also to the Soviet Union, which declined to be drawn into the Chinese-American quarrel when China asked it for help against the United States.

Tenochtitlan. Aztec city that existed on the site of present-day Mexico City at time of Spanish conqueror Hernan Cortes' arrival in 1519.

Thatcher, Margaret, 1925– . British political leader and stateswoman. Prime minister of Britain 1979 to 1990, she led a major conservative retrenchment, selling off government enterprises that had been nationalized by previous Labor governments and using tough policies to weaken labor unions. She led Britain in its war against Argentina over the Falkland Islands/Malvinas Islas, and her tough advice to United States President George Bush in 1990 encouraged him to adopt his staunch policy against Iraq's invasion of Kuwait.

Thirty Years' War, 1618–48. Complex and extraordinarily devastating war fought mainly on German territory for many reasons, including religious ones that pitted Protestant German princes against a number of foreign powers, including France, Sweden, Denmark, and the Netherlands. Ended with Treaty of Westphalia, which included the principle that the religion of the ruler would prevail in any given territory.

Thorez, Maurice, 1900–64. French political leader. He was a member of the French Communist party and served as its secretary general from 1930 until his death. He helped to form the Popular Front of leftist groups in 1934, was minister of state in France in 1945–46, and became deputy premier in 1947.

Thucydides, 455–400 B.C. Athenian historian. His *The Peloponnesian War* remains one of the seminal texts on international politics. Many realists invoke his analysis as the beginning of their approach to international affairs.

Tiananmen Square massacre, June 1989. Incident in Beijing, China, in which government military forces attacked a prodemocracy demonstration in the large public square. Several hundred demonstrators were killed.

Tito, Josip Broz, 1892–1980. Yugoslav Communist leader and statesman. He led Croatian forces in defeating the occupying Axis powers in World War II and maintained the unity of his country in a federation after the war by appealing to non-Serbian components of the population and through the use of secret police and political repression. Yugoslavia was ousted from the **Cominform** in 1948 but defied Stalin and accepted Western financial assistance. Together with President Gamal Nasser of Egypt and Prime Minister Jawaharlal Nehru of India, he founded the non- aligned movement during the Cold War. In later years, Yugoslavia was reconciled with the Soviet Union, and the internal regime in the country was liberalized.

Tlatelolco, Treaty of, 1967. International agreement to prohibit nuclear weapons from Latin America.

Tolstoy, Leo Nikolayevich, 1828–1910. Russian novelist and social theorist whose most famous works include *War and Peace* and *Anna Karenina*. Tolstoy has been classified as a communitarian anarchist in that he believed in the fundamental illegitimacy of the state, but rather than ascribing to self-interested libertarianism, he held that cooperative communities based on a mutual understanding of the collective good was the most sensible and humane way of organizing social life.

Torrijos Herrera, Omar, 1929–81. Panamanian general and politician. The leader of the military coup that overthrew the government of President Arnulfo Arias in 1968. In 1977, he concluded the negotiations on the Panama Canal Treaties with the United States that provide for the transfer of control of the Canal Zone to Panama by the year 2000. One of the architects of the Contadora process.

Trade Act, 1988. Originally entitled the Omnibus Trade and Competitiveness Act passed in September 1988, it is a piece of United States legislation designed to regulate and monitor foreign trade. The most controversial aspect of the act is the **Super 301** provision.

Trade Reform Act, 1974. United States legislation that became controversial because of the Jackson-Vanik Amendment, which required that the president should not extend trade privileges to the Soviet Union and other countries until satisfied that they allowed free emigration.

Treaty of Rome. See **European Union.**

Triple Alliance. An agreement created in 1882 among Austria- Hungary, Germany, and Italy to provide mutual aid in case of attack. The pact was renewed every five years until World War I, when Italy rescinded its pledge of support and joined the opposition group, the Triple Entente.

Triple Entente. A military alliance between France, Great Britain, and Russia that was formed in 1894. Each agreed to come to the other's defense if attacked by either Austria or Germany. The pact among the three countries, with successive agreements in 1904 and 1907, created the foundation for the alliance that was able to counter the Central Powers of Germany and Austria-Hungary in the First World War.

Trusteeship system. Arrangement under the United Nations to supervise the administration of colonial territories that had been taken from the losers of the two world wars; successor to the mandates system under the League of Nations. The trusteeship system included more rigorous supervision than its predecessor.

Truman, Harry S, 1884–1972. American political leader and statesman. President 1945–53, succeeding Roosevelt upon the latter's death; vice-president 1944–45; senator, 1934–44. After attending the Potsdam conference with Stalin, and Churchill (and Clement Atlee), he ordered the atomic bombing of Japan in 1945 as a way of quickly ending the war. Truman formulated the policy of containment of the Soviet Union, initiated the Marshall Plan, and led in the formation of the North Atlantic Treaty Organization (NATO). Elected to the presidency in 1948. His domestic program carried forward the New Deal. He initiated a loyalty and security program, and he authorized the building of the hydrogen bomb. In response to North Korea's invasion of South Korea, Truman ordered United States forces to defend South Korea, and he sought the endorsement of the United Nations for that policy. He concluded a peace treaty with Japan in 1951.

Union of Soviet Socialist Republics (USSR). See **Soviet Union.**

UNITA (National Union for the Total Independence of Angola). A conservative guerrilla movement in the Angolan civil war that opposed the Marxist government.

United Nations. Organization established in 1945 by the victors in World War II through a charter to provide for international peace and security and other purposes.

United Nations Charter. Founding treaty of the United Nations that was signed by fifty states at the San Francisco Conference on June 25, 1945.

United Nations Economic and Social Council (ECOSOC). A principal organ of the United Nations, operating under the authority of the General Assembly, which considers matters relating to economic and social activities and is supposed to supervise the work of the specialized agencies. Composed of fifty-four members elected by the General Assembly for staggered three-year terms.

United Nations Emergency Force (UNEF), 1956–67. First peacekeeping force created by United Nations, composed of forces from small and medium-sized states. Used as a tangible diplomatic presence between Egyptian and Israeli armies as Israeli invading forces withdrew from Egypt in 1957. Stationed on Egyptian territory at frontier with Israel. Forces were lightly armed only for self-protection. They were compelled to withdraw in 1967 at the request of President Gamal Nasser.

United Nations General Assembly. Principal organ and main deliberative body of the United Nations. All member states are represented, and each has a single vote, although deliberations aim at consensus. Important decisions on peace and security matters, budget concerns, and the admission of new members, require a two-thirds majority, but other decisions can be reached with a simple majority. Detailed deliberation on most issues is carried out by one of the seven main committees, which then submits a draft resolution to the General Assembly for adoption. Decisions of the General Assembly are recommendations.

United Nations Operation in the Congo (ONUC), 1960–63. Large civilian and military undertaking, with over twenty thousand personnel, to restore order after a military rebellion, administer the government, and end a provincial secession. Although authorized by the Security Council, the operation came under increasing criticism by the Soviet Union and became a cause of crisis in the United Nations. The Soviet Union recommended a constitutional reform of the Secretary General's office and refused to contribute to the ONUC budget. In response, the United States attempted to coerce payment from the Soviet Union and other countries but failed.

United Nations Protection Forces (UNPROFOR). Military forces created in 1992 to protect United Nations High Commissioner for Refugees' delivery of supplies to refugees. In 1993, "safe areas" were created in six cities of Bosnia, and UNPROFOR was assigned the mission of delivering aid them.

United Nations Secretariat. Principal organ of the United Nations that provides support services to members. Headed by a secretary-general.

United Nations Security Council. Principal organ of the United Nations with primary responsibility for maintaining international peace and security. Has authority to invoke collective security measures as well as peaceful settlement practices. Consists of five permanent members with veto power—China, France, Russia, Great

Britain, and the United States—and ten others elected by the General Assembly for staggered two-year terms.

United Nations Trusteeship Council.   Successor to the Permanent Mandates Commission, principal organ of United Nations charged with supervision of the administration of trust territories. All of those territories have become independent.

United States Agency for International Development (AID).   U.S. government agency with primary responsibility for foreign assistance programs to less developed countries.

United States-Canada Free Trade Agreement (FTA). A bilateral treaty creating a free trade area between the United States and Canada. It came into force in 1989 and was intended to remove all tariffs and nontariff barriers to trade between the two countries by 1998. Based upon cooperation, the two countries entered into negotiations with Mexico to create the **North American Free Trade Agreement** (NAFTA), which took effect in 1995.

United States Intervention in Chile,   1964–73. Beginning in the early 1960s as part of its anticommunist campaign in Latin America, the United States gave financial assistance to the Christian Democratic Party. Then, after the election in 1970 of Marxist Salvador Allende of the Popular Unity Party, the United States engaged in a campaign of support for opposition groups, with the intention of "destabilizing" the government. Those activities ended with a *coup d'etat* led by Gen. Augusto Pinochet, who then headed an authoritarian government.

United States Intervention in France and Italy, 1948. Through the newly instituted Central Intelligence Agency (CIA), the United Statees gave clandestine support to democratic parties in the elections of 1948, fearing gains by the Communist parties.

United States Intervention in Guatemala,   1954. Concerned about growing Communist influence on the government of Jacobo Arbenz, which had been democratically elected in 1951, the United States clandestinely supported an armed forces uprising that placed Col. Carlos Castillo Armas in power.

Universal Postal Union (UPU).   International administrative agency founded in 1874 to coordinate the delivery of mail throughout the world.

UNRG (National Guatemalan Revolutionary Unity).   Coalition of the four most prominent Guatemalan guerrilla groups.

Uruguay Round.   Most recent of a series of multilateral trade negotiations held under auspices of the General Agreement on Tariffs and Trade (GATT). The Uruguay Round, so named because it was first convened in Punta del Este, Uruguay in 1986, extended free trading principles for the first time to agricultural products and intellectual property, and it created the World Trade Organization as the successor to the GATT.

Vance, Cyrus R.,   1917– . American lawyer and government official. Served as secretary of state in the Carter administration from 1977 until he resigned in 1980. Later, in 1992–93, he served as the representative of the United Nations in a joint EU-UN project to negotiate a settlement of the Bosnian War that resulted in the Vance-Owen Plan.

Velvet Revolution.   Peaceful transition in 1989 from Communism to a democratic regime in Czechoslovakia.

Versailles Treaty,   1919. Main treaty ending World War I. It provided for self-determination for the former territories of the Austro-Hungarian and Ottoman empires and formed the League of Nations. The instrument also imposed reparations payments, territorial concessions, and restrictions on the size and deployment of military forces on Germany. Although active in negotiating its terms, the United States did not ratify the treaty because of the Senate's refusal to give its consent.

Vichy regime.   Government of Marshall Henri Petain, established in 1940 following the French army's defeat by German forces, to administer unoccupied France. In 1942, Hitler annulled the agreement allowing the independence of rump France and occupied the entire country. During the occupation, the Vichy regime remained in office under German supervision but collapsed as World War II came to an end.

Vietminh (League for the Independence of Vietnam).   Coalition of nationalist and Communist forces that fought against Japanese occupation during World War II and led the war against the French (1946–54).

Vietnam War,   1957–73. War to unite Vietnam, which had been temporarily partitioned in 1954. Began as guerrilla war against the South Vietnamese government whose president, Ngo Dinh Diem, had canceled elections scheduled for 1956 to reunite the country. The guerrillas, organized as the National Liberation Front in 1960, were supported by North Vietnam, led by Ho Chi Minh. United States military support of the South Vietnamese government began in 1961 under President John F. Kennedy and increased dramatically after 1965 under President Lyndon B. Johnson, when a bombing campaign against North Vietnam began and a large number of U.S. ground troops were dispatched to South Vietnam. A peace agreement was signed in Paris in January 1973. The country was unified in 1975 when North Vietnamese troops entered Saigon (now Ho Chi Minh City) and all Americans fled.

Vladivostok agreement,   1974. Agreement between United States President Gerald Ford and Soviet Premier Leonid Brezhnev to limit the number of nuclear warheads that could be placed on MIRV missiles. The agreement formed part of **SALT II.**

War of 1812.   War between the United States and Britain from 1812 to 1815 over the issue of neutral shipping rights.

Warsaw Pact.   See **Warsaw Treaty Organization.**

Warsaw Treaty Organization, 1955–91. Alliance of Eastern European states—Soviet Union, East Germany, Czechoslovakia, Poland, Hungary, Romania, Bulgaria, and Albania—formed in response to the remilitarization of West Germany. Under the pact, Soviet troops were stationed in several countries.

Waterloo. Battle that marked Napoleon Bonaparte's decisive defeat. After his defeat on June 18, 1815, Napoleon was forced to abdicate as emperor of France for the second time and went into exile.

Weber, Max, 1864–1920. German sociologist. Contributed ideas about social science methodology, political economy, and government. His definition of government (the state) included the stipulation that it had a claim to a monopoly of legitimate violence. His work includes an analysis of the sources of legitimacy.

Weimar Republic, 1919–33. Governing system of Germany established after the abdication of Kaiser Wilhelm at the end of World War I. Ended with the establishment of dictatorial powers in the hands of Nazi Adolf Hitler.

Western Europe. Portion of Europe during the Cold War not under the control of the Soviet Union.

Western European Union. See **European Union.**

West Germany (Federal Republic Germany), 1949–90. One of two successor republics to the Germany defeated in World War II. Formed by the consolidation of the three western (American, British, and French) zones of occupation, the FRG demonstrated exceptional economic growth and provided leadership in the formation of the European Coal and Steel Community and of the European Community (Union). Member of North Atlantic Treaty Organization (NATO), and host to American and other allied forces and arms. Following the end of the Cold War, the FRG absorbed the five successor states (provinces) of East Germany to become a unified Germany.

Westphalia, Treaty of, 1648. Agreement ending the Thirty-Years' War in Europe that included the first legal recognition of sovereignty as a principle of exclusive jurisdiction within a territorial state. Generally recognized as the beginning point of modern international politics.

White House. Residence and offices of the president of the United States in Washington, D.C.

Wilhelmine Germany, 1890–1918. German empire under Wilhelm II, which engaged in commercial rivalry with Britain that included a naval arms race and expanded German interests throughout the world. Defeated in World War I.

Wilson, Woodrow, 1856–1924. United States scholar and statesman. President, 1913–21; governor of New Jersey, 1910–12; president of Princeton University, 1902–10. Wilson endorsed a policy of neutrality for the United States during World War I; however, when Germany renewed unrestricted submarine warfare, Wilson asked Congress for a declaration of war in April 1917. He formulated the Fourteen Points plan for peace and was an active participant in the Versailles Peace Conference, which approved his project, the League of Nations. However, the U.S. Senate did not consent to the peace treaty, and the United States did not join the League of Nations. Despite this defeat, Wilson is regarded as a pivotal figure in twentieth-century history. His writings include: *Division and Reunion, 1829–1889* (1893); *George Washington* (1893); *A History of the American People* (five volumes, 1902); and *Constitutional Government in the United States* (1908).

Women, Conference on, 1995. International conference sponsored by the United Nations, held in Beijing, China.

World Bank (International Bank for Reconstruction and Development). An international economic institution created at the Bretton Woods conference in 1944, it was designed to assist in postwar reconstruction and development projects. The bank has expanded beyond its founding mission of lending to countries for development projects at commercial interest rates. What is now called the World Bank Group includes the International Finance Corporation, which encourages private investments and includes the International Securities Group to advise and encourage investments in emerging markets; the International Development Association, which includes a "soft loan" feature (long-term, exceptionally low interest); and the Multilateral Investment Guarantee Agency, which promotes private equity investment in developing countries by insuring against losses from political risks.

World Health Organization (WHO). Specialized agency, established in 1948 and based in Geneva, that is dedicated to promoting health and is affiliated with the United Nations.

World War I, 1914–18. War fought primarily in Europe between two alliances. Germany and Austria-Hungary, the Central Powers, were joined by the Ottoman Empire, and these fought the Triple Entente, made up of France, Great Britain, and Russia. Following a stalemate in the fighting, the United States entered the war in April 1917. Later that year, the new Bolshevik revolutionary government of Russia withdrew from the war under terms of the Brest-Litovsk Treaty. After a revolution broke out in Germany, an armistice was signed, and German troops were withdrawn from all foreign territory.

World War II, 1939–45. General war fought between the Axis powers—Germany, Italy, Japan, and others—and the Grand Alliance—France (1939–40), Soviet Union (1941–45), United Kingdom (1939–45), United States (1941–45), and others, including China—on several fronts in Europe, Africa, Asia, and the Pacific. The first war fought in all parts of the globe and the most destructive war in history.

Wright, James, 1922– . United States political leader. Member of the House of Representatives, 1954–89, and speaker, 1987–89. Instrumental in gaining American support for the Esquipulas II process that helped to bring peace to Central America in the late 1980s and early 1990s.

Yalta Conference, March 1945. Wartime conference among the heads of the leading states of the Grand Alliance: United States President Franklin D. Roosevelt, British Prime Minister Winston Churchill, and Soviet Generalissimo Josef Stalin. The main agreements concerned the terms for Soviet entry into the war against Japan; the disposition of forces in central Europe at the end of the war, including occupation zones in Germany; certain provisions regarding the United Nations; and the Declaration on a Liberated Europe.

Yeltsin, Boris, 1931– . Russian political leader. President of Russia, 1991– . In 1990, Yeltsin resigned from the Communist Party and led a movement to bring down Mikhail Gorbachev and dismantle the Soviet Union. At the time of the August 1991 coup against the Soviet state, Yeltsin appeared on the streets of Moscow to demonstrate against the coup. With the demise of the Soviet Union in December 1991, Yeltsin remained head of what became the most important successor republic and presided over the transition from a command economy to a market economy.

Yom Kippur War   See **Israeli-Egyptian War.**

Yugoslav civil war. A conflict that exploded in 1992 in the formerly communist country of Yugoslavia. The six republics that until 1991 comprised Yugoslavia are: Bosnia-Herzegovina, Croatia, Macedonia, Montenegro, Serbia, and Slovenia. Following a period of failed negotiations, in 1991 Slovenia and Croatia declared independence, followed by Bosnia-Herzegovina in 1992. After these defections, Slobodan Milosevic, the Serbian nationalist leader, unleashed a civil war ostensibly to protect the Serb minorities in Bosnia. The war continued in Bosnia, with Croatian and Serbian involvement until the signing of the Dayton Agreement in 1995.

Index